Date Due

D1716035

Microcomputer-Based Expert Systems

OTHER IEEE PRESS BOOKS

Principles of Expert Systems, *Edited by A. Gupta and B. E. Prasad*
High Voltage Integrated Circuits, *Edited by B. J. Baliga*
Microwave Digital Radio, *Edited by L. J. Greenstein and M. Shafi*
Oliver Heaviside: Sage in Solitude, *By P. J. Nahin*
Radar Applications, *Edited by M. I. Skolnik*
Principles of Computerized Tomographic Imaging, *By A. C. Kak and M. Slaney*
Selected Papers on Noise in Circuits and Systems, *Edited by M. S. Gupta*
Spaceborne Radar Remote Sensing: Applications and Techniques, *By C. Elachi*
Engineering Excellence, *Edited by D. Christiansen*
Selected Papers on Logic Synthesis for Integrated Circuit Design, *Edited by A. R. Newton*
Planar Transmission Line Structures, *Edited by T. Itoh*
Introduction to the Theory of Random Signals and Noise, *By W. B. Davenport, Jr. and W. L. Root*
Teaching Engineering, *Edited by M. S. Gupta*
Selected Papers on Computer-Aided Design of Very Large Scale Integrated Circuits, *Edited by A. L. Sangiovanni-Vincentelli*
Robust Control, *Edited by P. Dorato*
Writing Reports to Get Results: Guidelines for the Computer Age, *By R. S. Blicq*
Multi-Microprocessors, *Edited by A. Gupta*
Advanced Microprocessors, II, *Edited by A. Gupta*
Adaptive Signal Processing, *Edited by L. H. Sibul*
Selected Papers on Statistical Design of Integrated Circuits, *Edited by A. J. Strojwas*
System Design for Human Interaction, *Edited by A. P. Sage*
Microcomputer Control of Power Electronics and Drives, *Edited by B. K. Bose*
Selected Papers on Analog Fault Diagnosis, *Edited by R. Liu*
Advances in Local Area Networks, *Edited by K. Kümmerle, J. O. Limb, and F. A. Tobagi*
Load Management, *Edited by S. Talukdar and C. W. Gellings*
Computers and Manufacturing Productivity, *Edited by R. K. Jurgen*
Selected Papers on Computer-Aided Design of Analog Networks, *Edited by J. Vlach and K. Singhal*
Being the Boss, *By L. K. Lineback*
Effective Meetings for Busy People, *By W. T. Carnes*
Selected Papers on Integrated Analog Filters, *Edited by G. C. Temes*
Electrical Engineering: The Second Century Begins, *Edited by H. Freitag*
VLSI Signal Processing, II, *Edited by S. Y. Kung, R. E. Owen, and J. G. Nash*
Modern Acoustical Imaging, *Edited by H. Lee and G. Wade*
Low-Temperature Electronics, *Edited by R. K. Kirschman*
Undersea Lightwave Communications, *Edited by P. K. Runge and P. R. Trischitta*
Multidimensional Digital Signal Processing, *Edited by the IEEE Multidimensional Signal Processing Committee*
Adaptive Methods for Control System Design, *Edited by M. M. Gupta*
Residue Number System Arithmetic, *Edited by M. A. Soderstrand, W. K. Jenkins, G. A. Jullien, and F. J. Taylor*
Singular Perturbations in Systems and Control, *Edited by P. V. Kokotovic and H. K. Khalil*
Getting the Picture, *By S. B. Weinstein*
Space Science and Applications, *Edited by J. H. McElroy*
Medical Applications of Microwave Imaging, *Edited by L. Larsen and J. H. Jacobi*
Modern Spectrum Analysis, II, *Edited by S. B. Kesler*
The Calculus Tutoring Book, *By C. Ash and R. Ash*
Imaging Technology, *Edited by H. Lee and G. Wade*
Phase-Locked Loops, *Edited by W. C. Lindsey and C. M. Chie*
VLSI Circuit Layout: Theory and Design, *Edited by T. C. Hu and E. S. Kuh*
Monolithic Microwave Integrated Circuits, *Edited by R. A. Pucel*
Next-Generation Computers, *Edited by E. A. Torrero*
Kalman Filtering: Theory and Application, *Edited by H. W. Sorenson*
Spectrum Management and Engineering, *Edited by F. Matos*
Digital VLSI Systems, *Edited by M. I. Elmasry*
Introduction to Magnetic Recording, *Edited by R. M. White*
Insights into Personal Computers, *Edited by A. Gupta and H. D. Toong*
Television Technology Today, *Edited by T. S. Rzeszewski*
The Space Station: An Idea Whose Time Has Come, *Edited by T. R. Simpson*
Advanced Microprocessors, *Edited by A. Gupta and H. D. Toong*

ii

Microcomputer-Based Expert Systems

Edited by
Amar Gupta
Bandreddi E. Prasad
Sloan School of Management
Massachusetts Institute of Technology

A volume in the IEEE PRESS Selected Reprint Series,
prepared under the sponsorship of the IEEE Computer Society.

IEEE PRESS

The Institute of Electrical and Electronics Engineers, Inc., New York

Library of Congress Cataloging-in-Publication Data

Microcomputer-based expert systems.

(IEEE Press selected reprint series)
Includes indexes.
1. Expert systems (Computer science) 2. Microcomputers—Programming.
I. Gupta, Amar. II. Prasad, Bandreddi E. (Bandreddi Eswara) III. Series.
QA76.76.E95M53 1988 006.3'3 87-31059
ISBN 0-87942-221-1

Contents

DEDICATED TO

Beena
and
Ramesh

Amar Gupta

Ramarao
and
Nagabhushanam

Bandreddi E. Prasad

Preface

PROGRESS in the field of computer science has occurred, and continues to occur, at a faster pace than that in virtually all other fields. Within computer science, the subfield of expert systems (in particular, microcomputer-based expert systems) is the area witnessing the fastest rate of growth.

Expert systems technology is a product of the eighties. When this technology first emerged, many observers felt that computer-based expert systems would never be able to come up to the standards of human experts. The feeling was that computer-based systems might be able to provide coarse solutions at best, but real solutions would have to be provided by humans. However, reality has turned out to be different. Already, there are a number of diverse applications, ranging from chess playing to mineral exploration, in which computer-based expert systems outperform their creators.

In spite of being the result of a nascent technology, expert systems are beginning to make their impact felt in practically all disciplines. There is a growing interest to find out what they can and cannot do. But, as is the case with all fast-evolving fields, while there is a large number of research papers, there are very few sources that offer a consolidated picture of all dimensions to the issue.

This book, together with its companion volume *Principles of Expert Systems,* is intended to fill this void. It focuses on implementation of prototype systems in a microcomputer environment. Various developmental languages, off-the-shelf shells and tools, and customized options are considered along with a variety of example systems operating within widely different scenarios. The companion volume concentrates on general principles and the anatomy of expert systems, and includes a detailed discussion of each of the major components.

This book was made possible through the support and encouragement provided by Reed Crone, Hans Leander, Laura Kelly, Randi Scholnick, and many other IEEE PRESS staff members. We also acknowledge the assistance provided by Stuart E. Madnick, Hoo-min D. Toong, Mei Hsu, D. Sriram, and Rich Wang. Finally, we would like to thank Barbara Grzincic and Graham Ramsay for taking our scribbled notes and turning them into a professional piece of work. We would appreciate receiving feedback from the readers of this book.

AMAR GUPTA AND BANDREDDI E. PRASAD
Massachusetts Institute of Technology
Cambridge, Massachusetts

Part I
Introduction

THE area of microcomputer-based expert systems is one of the fastest evolving components of the computer industry. Currently, the growth rate for this area, in terms of percentage increase per year, far exceeds the rate for microcomputers in general, as well as the rate of increase for the overall artificial intelligence industry. At the beginning of this decade, microcomputer-based expert systems were virtually nonexistent; by the end of the eighties, expert system tools will be in common use both in the office and at home.

The rapid evolution of this area has been catalyzed by three factors: (i) advances in expert systems technology; (ii) advances in microprocessor technology; and (iii) proliferation of microcomputers. The role of each of these factors is examined in the following.

ADVANCES IN EXPERT SYSTEMS TECHNOLOGY

The honor of being known as the first expert system is usually given to the DENDRAL system developed at Stanford University in the early seventies [6]. Around the same time, researchers at the Massachusetts Institute of Technology were developing the MACSYMA system [7]. These systems permitted inferences to be drawn in specific areas—the DENDRAL system focused on molecular structures and the MACSYMA system concentrated on algebraic areas.

An important component of all expert systems is their corpus of knowledge. This knowledge is frequently expressed in terms of facts and rules. For example:

FACT: PROFESSIONAL SOCIETIES PUBLISH EDUCATIONAL BOOKS.

RULE: IF A BOOK HAS BEEN PUBLISHED BY A PROFESSIONAL SOCIETY, AND THE PROFESSIONAL SOCIETY IS IEEE, THEN THE BOOK HAS BEEN PUBLISHED IN NEW YORK.

Contemporary expert systems are organized to hold problem-domain knowledge separate from problem-solution knowledge. The former is termed the "knowledge base," while the latter is called the "inference engine." In both MACSYMA and DENDRAL, the focus was primarily on the inference engine. Such systems are usually classified as first-generation systems. Second-generation systems distinguish between the knowledge base and the inference engine. Most currently available expert systems fall under this category. Research continues on the development of a third generation of systems with more sophisticated knowledge-restructuring and inference-drawing capabilities than their predecessors [1].

Among the different methods available today to structure a knowledge base, the rule-based approach and the frame-based approach are most commonly used. In a rule-based representation, knowledge is organized in the form of IF–THEN rules, while a frame-based system uses a hierarchical organization based on frames. At the top level of the hierarchy, the object represents a "class" or a "parent"; below it, there are "slots" representing attributes that describe the main object. These slots in turn contain additional slots or frames.

The inference engine is responsible for deciding which rules should be executed, using either a forward-chaining approach or a backward-chaining approach, and when. In the forward-chaining approach, one starts with a given set of evidence and invokes all the production rules in a sequence until all conclusions have been drawn. In the backward-chaining approach, one starts by making an assumption about the goal, and then works backward to see if any known fact or rule has been violated. If so, the assumption is incorrect. If not, the assumption can indeed be true. Additional information may be needed to select one definite conclusion.

Concepts in the areas of knowledge acquisition, knowledge representation, inference mechanisms, and heuristic programming have been studied and refined by researchers during the last three decades. In the mid-fifties, there was a utopian dream of using nascent computer technology to develop systems that would mimic human intelligence. During the next three decades, it became clear that since the computer functions very differently from the human mind, the latter is not the best paradigm for designing new generations of computers. The current thought is that while computer systems are far inferior to human beings in dealing with unforeseen problems, these systems can be infused with extensive expertise in narrow domains to match, and even outperform, human experts. Examples include programs for playing chess and software for locating hidden materials.

The harbingers of today's expert systems served two major functions. First, they helped to develop new techniques and methodologies for dealing with knowledge, as opposed to simple data. Second, the early systems helped to reduce expectations. Gradually, a consensus emerged in favor of dealing effectively with small areas of expertise rather than coming up with superficial solutions for larger scenarios. This emphasis on smaller domains and the advent of better tools and techniques led to increased popularity of expert systems.

So far, we have focused on the field of expert systems. (This field is discussed in greater depth in [1].) However, even with all the advances in expert systems, the field of low-cost systems would have remained a distant reality had the microprocessor not been invented in the early seventies. We now turn our attention to advances in the field of microprocessors.

ADVANCES IN MICROPROCESSOR TECHNOLOGY

The term "microprocessor" was first used in 1972. However, the distinction of being the first "computer on a chip'' goes to the Intel 4004, introduced in 1971. Since then, microprocessors have improved both in terms of power and functionality.

The computational power of a microprocessor is determined primarily by two factors—its word size, which governs the width of the computer's data path, and the frequency of its electronic clock, which synchronizes the computer's operations. The trend in microprocessors is toward a larger word size and a higher frequency. As the word size increases, an operation can be completed in fewer machine cycles; as the frequency increases, there are more cycles per second [2]. The Intel 4004 used a 4-bit word. Subsequently 8-bit, 16-bit, and 32-bit microprocessors were introduced in 1972, 1976, and 1981, respectively [3]. During the last 15 years, the clock frequency has increased by a factor of 50, and the overall throughput by three orders of magnitude [4].

Apart from the two determinants described above, the power of a microprocessor is a function of the complexity, or the density, of the microprocessor chip. In early microprocessors, the limited number of devices that could be implanted on the chip restricted its capabilities. Additional chips were required to generate timing signals, to provide primary memory for program and data storage, and to interface with peripheral units. During the last 15 years, the upper limit on the number of devices per chip has increased by a factor of 500 [3]. This has allowed complex functions to be performed in fewer iterations than ever before. Also, since a very small number of chips are now needed to put together a fully operational computer, such machines can be designed, developed, and marketed within a few months of the introduction of a new microprocessor. This lag time is much less than that in the case of mainframe computers (typically 3–5 years) of the sixties and minicomputers (1–2 years) of the seventies.

The growing power of microprocessors makes it possible to use them for hosting expert systems of increasing levels of sophistication. Conversely, the same expert system can be hosted on ''older'' and relatively less expensive microprocessors, as time passes. In 1986, one expert observed that expert systems which then ran only on AI machines, could be hosted on top-of-the-line personal computers in 3 years, and on ubiquitous home computers in 6 years [5]. His concept of systems in three categories (for 1986) was as follows: (i) Top Category—Symbolics 3675 with all options; (ii) Medium Category—IBM PC/AT with a Turbo card and Intel 80386 processor; and (iii) Lowest Category—Apple IIe. As predicted, expert systems are being increasingly hosted on less expensive and more commonly available hardware.

PROLIFERATION OF MICROCOMPUTERS

In the previous section, it was mentioned that the microprocessor era is less than two decades old. Before the turn of this century, the population of microprocessors in use will exceed the population of people living on this planet [4]. Many of these microprocessors will be used in common gadgets and appliances ranging from door closers to automobiles; however, a very significant number of microprocessors will be used for general-purpose computing applications.

Twenty years ago, the cost of a computer could be justified only if the machine served the needs of a large organization.

Today, a microcomputer is acquired if it meets the needs of a single individual. Already, the total global investments in microcomputers exceed the total investments in mainframe computers. It is therefore appropriate that most companies are concentrating on developing expert systems for the microcomputer environment rather than for larger computers.

EXPERT SYSTEMS DEVELOPMENT

Expert systems are most relevant in areas where:

(i)   the domain of application is narrow,
(ii)   there are few experts in the domain,
(iii)   the experts can perform significantly better than amateurs,
(iv)   the expertise can be stated in a form that permits knowledge to be represented and inferences to be drawn,
(v)   the expertise can be formulated on an incremental basis,
(vi)   there is agreement among the specialists about the knowledge,
(vii)   there is a need to disseminate the expertise for cost or performance reasons,
(viii) adequate time and resources can be committed, and
(ix)   the potential benefits are high.

Also, it is helpful to know if any expert systems have been developed for a closely related domain.

Once it has been determined that the development of an expert system is justified and practical, the expert must be requested to provide as much knowledge as possible. The system builder uses this information and converts it into a structured form. In order to do so, it becomes necessary, at a very early stage, to make a fundamental decision about the implementation process.

For very simple scenarios, it is feasible to develop the expert system from scratch using a language such as Lisp or Prolog. For more complex systems, it is usually advantageous to use an off-the-shelf expert system building tool. These building tools provide a predefined structure for storing information about the application domain. The development time and effort can be significantly reduced by using these tools.

It is extremely important to choose the right expert system building tool. Tools are now available that make use of the different approaches to knowledge representation; some of these approaches have been described in [1]. Depending on the application environment, some approaches may offer faster response times than others. Having selected the approach and the tool, the system builder is in a better position to deal with the knowledge acquisition and knowledge representation aspects. Many of the new expert system development tools are designed to permit the specialist to enter information directly without the assistance of the system builder.

ORGANIZATION OF THIS BOOK

This book is divided into four parts as follows:

Part I: Introduction

An overview of the field of expert systems is presented in this part.

2

Part II: Languages

The most popular languages for implementing expert systems are described. The relative merits and demerits of each language are also covered.

Part III: Tools

This part covers tools for developing expert systems. Both off-the-shelf and experimental tools are considered.

Part IV: Case Studies

A number of expert system developmental efforts, pertaining to many different sectors and applications, are described.

It should be mentioned here that this book is not intended to serve as a directory of all expert system tools and languages. Given the explosive rate of growth of this field, such a directory would become obsolete in a very short span of time. Instead, the aim here is to present a broad discussion covering all the important alternatives.

This part (Part I) presents the views of three people. In the first paper, Hayes-Roth discusses the importance of knowledge-based expert systems. He highlights the fact that technology is evolving at an annual pace of between 50 and 200% in many areas of knowledge systems and argues that future needs should increase, especially since human work is comprised primarily of knowledge-based reasoning.

The second paper, by Kinnucan, contrasts the anatomy of expert systems of today and that of expert systems of tomorrow. The author describes many areas that could potentially benefit from expert systems technology in the near future. The discussion covers all types of expert systems, large and small.

The third paper is by Shafer, who concentrates on the microcomputer arena. After analyzing several examples, he comes to the conclusion that microcomputer implementations of expert system development tools appear no less capable than their minicomputer and mainframe counterparts at producing useful expert systems. He feels that the advent of super-micros and optical memories for microcomputers will catalyze progress in this area.

In the next part, various languages for implementing expert systems will be considered.

REFERENCES

1. Gupta, A. and B. E. Prasad (Eds.), *Principles of Expert Systems.* New York, NY: IEEE Press, 1988.
2. Toong, H. D. and A. Gupta, "Personal computers," *Sci. Amer.,* pp. 89–99, Dec. 1982.
3. Gupta, A. and H. D. Toong (Eds.), *Advanced Microprocessors.* New York, NY: IEEE Press, 1983.
4. Gupta, A. (Ed.), *Advanced Microprocessors, II.* New York, NY: IEEE Press, 1987.
5. Wiig, K. M., "Expert systems: Impacts and potentials," in *Proc. of KBS '86.* Pinner, United Kingdom: Online Publications, 1986.
6. Buchanan, B. G. and E. A. Feigenbaum, "DENDRAL and Meta-DENDRAL: Their application dimension," *Artificial Intelligence,* vol. 11, pp. 5–24, 1978.
7. Martin, W. A. and R. J. Fateman, "The MACSYMA system," in *Proc. of the Second Symp. on Symbolic and Algebraic Manipulation,* Mar. 1971, pp. 59–75.

BIBLIOGRAPHY

Ernst, M. and H. Ojha, "Business applications of expert systems," *Future Generations Computer Systems,* vol. 2, pp. 173–185, 1986.

Gupta, A. (Ed.), *Multi-Microprocessors.* New York, NY: IEEE Press, 1987.

Gupta, A. and H. D. Toong (Eds.), *Insights into Personal Computers.* New York, NY: IEEE Press, 1985.

Kline, P. J. and S. B. Dolins, "Problem features that influence the design of expert systems," in *Proc. of AAAI-86,* Philadelphia, PA, 1986, pp. 956–962.

Schwartz, T. J., "Artificial intelligence in the personal computer environment: A panel session," in *Proc. of the ACM SIGSMALL Symp. on Small Systems,* Danvers, MA, May 1985, pp. 484–491.

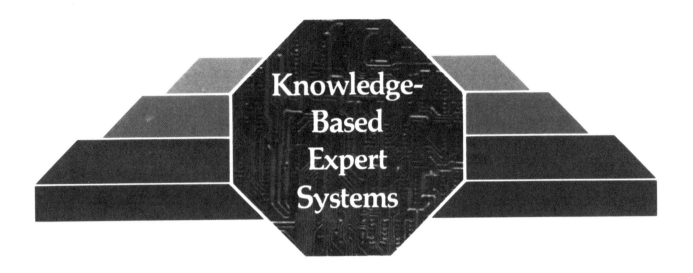

Knowledge-Based Expert Systems

Frederick Hayes-Roth
Teknowledge, Inc.

**More than techno-
logical wonders,
knowledge systems are
valuable human
assistants, equalling or
surpassing experts in
reasoning and judg-
ment. Since human
work consists mostly
of knowledge-based
reasoning, future needs
should increase.**

For years it remained little more than a bold experiment, an avantgarde technology with matchless capabilities but with painfully restricted applications.

Since 1981, however, the emerging field of expert and knowledge-based systems has changed dramatically. No longer the exclusive property of diagnosticians and a few other medical specialists, the systems are finally starting to broaden their user base and wriggle their way into mainstream, commercial applications. Like infants taking their first halting steps, expert and knowledge-based systems are slowly toddling out of basic research laboratories and making places for themselves in big business.

—*Computerworld,* May 7, 1984. [1]

Something extraordinary is happening. Knowledge-based expert systems, or "knowledge systems" for short, have evolved over a 15-year period from laboratory curiosities of applied artificial intelligence into targets of significant technological and commercial development efforts.[2] These systems employ computers in ways that differ markedly from conventional data processing applications, and they open up many new opportunities. The people who build these new systems have adopted the title of "knowledge engineer" and call their work "knowledge engineering." Recently, many commercial and governmental organizations have committed themselves to exploiting this technology, attempting to advance it in dramatic ways and beginning to adapt their missions and activities to it. A staggering number of events occurred during the last five years:

- Schlumberger, a leading oil services firm, determined that its future growth depended on knowledge engineering and formed two groups to build expert data interpretation systems.
- Japan's Ministry of International Trade and Industry determined that the country's future economic viability required leadership in knowledge system technology and launched a $500 million, 10-year program in fifth-generation computing.[3]
- Responding to a perceived technological and competitive threat, UK's Alvey Commission retracted that country's long-standing disapproval of AI and urged a major push forward in knowledge systems technology, a recommendation that the Thatcher government implemented.

Reprinted from *IEEE Computer,* vol. 17, no. 10, pp. 263–273, Oct. 1984.

- The European Economic Community set up the Esprit program to fund the development of a strong European infrastructure in this technology.
- The US Department of Defense claimed that knowledge systems would become the front line of US defense in the 1990's and initiated a $500 million, five-year strategic computing program.
- IBM licensed and sold its first AI software program (Intellect) and publicly endorsed the AI field as relevant and applicable.
- IBM's principal competitors teamed to form MCC and identified knowledge systems as an area of primary concern.
- General Motors took an equity position in a knowledge-engineering firm to hasten the introduction of knowledge systems into its business.[4]

Introducing knowledge systems

To describe the current state of knowledge systems technology and its commercialization, we must first try to define knowledge systems and place them in an historical context and then review major ideas. Unfortunately, we cannot give a precise definition of "ex-

pert systems" any more than we can list all the attributes of an "expert." Therefore, rather than seek an elusive precision, I'll just say what an expert system is and what it isn't and tell how to recognize one.

What is an expert system? An expert system is a knowledge-intensive program that solves problems normally requiring human expertise. It performs many of the secondary functions that an expert does, such as asking relevant questions and explaining its reasoning. Characteristics common to expert systems are best seen by examining what they do:

- They solve very difficult problems as well as or better than human experts.
- They reason heuristically, using what experts consider effective rules of thumb.
- They interact with humans in appropriate ways, including the use of natural language.
- They manipulate and reason about symbolic descriptions.
- They function with erroneous data and uncertain judgmental rules.
- They contemplate multiple competing hypotheses simultaneously.

- They explain why they're asking a question.
- They justify their conclusions.

What isn't it? When compared with a human expert, today's expert system appears narrow, shallow, and brittle, lacking a human expert's breadth of knowledge and understanding of fundamental principles. It apparently does not think as a human does: perceiving significance, jumping to conclusions intuitively (albeit hastily), and examining a single issue from diverse perspectives. Rather, the expert system of today simulates an expert's thinking rather grossly. It makes major decisions by elucidating many of the relevant criteria and by making many of the educated guesses that experts would if they were forced to verbalize the thought process. Unlike humans, however, expert systems don't resort to reasoning from first principles, drawing analogies, or relying on common sense. Also, today's expert systems do not learn from experience (but then, neither do some experts).

In contrast to advanced data processing systems, expert systems seem specialized and unusual. While conventional DP systems automate time-consuming clerical functions by amassing and processing large volumes of data algorithmically, expert systems ordinarily address small tasks typically performed by professionals in a few minutes or hours: interpreting, diagnosing, planning, scheduling, and so forth. To accomplish these tasks, an expert system makes judicious use of data and reasons with it. In contrast to what happens in the algorithmic data processing approach, the expert system generally examines a large number of possibilities or constructs a solution dynamically.

How do you recognize one? Simply remember that expert systems generally relieve a human professional of some difficult task. Find a computer that performs a function previously done by an expert. Locate the expert or team of experts who now maintain the program's knowledge base. Determine if the knowledge in the system is ac-

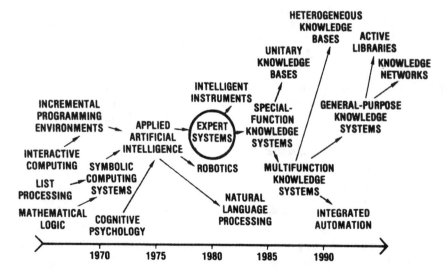

Figure 1. Expert systems in the evolution of computing.

cessible: can you read it—ask for explanations requiring it and justifications validating it—and modify it? Confirm that the system stores a substantial body of knowledge and reasons with that knowledge in flexible ways. Although any good programmer can implement a procedure by integrating a few heuristics, incorporating hundreds or thousands of heuristics into a computer system requires knowledge engineering. Systems employing this magnitude of judgmental knowledge are expert systems.

Long ago and far, far away...
Now that we have the subject more or less defined, let's consider where it fits in the field of computing. To understand where knowledge engineering came from, we have to go back some 30 years.

Figure 1 positions expert systems around 1980-1981, when efforts were begun to commercialize the technology. The first company formed exclusively to promote expert systems—in the field of genetic engineering—was Intelli Genetics. Shortly thereafter, Teknowledge was formed as the first knowledge-engineering company. These companies spun off from Stanford University's Heuristic Programming Project, which had led the development of knowledge engineering during the seventies.

In the 1950's, researchers were developing the foundation of AI, including mathematical logic and recursive function theory, which led to the formulation of list processing and the Lisp language itself. Lisp provided a very simple syntax for data and programs and an interpreter for evaluating recursive symbolic expressions. These capabilities supported the development of practical symbolic computing systems. At the same time, interactive computing emerged and made it possible to develop programming environments for incremental program development and debugging. At about the same time, cognitive psychologists—students of human thinking—developed standard ways of investigating thought processes. These included recording an expert's "thinking-out-loud protocol" and modeling the apparent decision-making process in terms of conditional production rules.

The field of applied artificial intelligence merged the techniques from these areas,[5] focusing on what were labeled "real-world" problems, as opposed to the artificial, small but tough "toy" problems that theoreticians were contemplating. From a decade of work emerged three primary subfields: expert systems; natural language; and robotics, including vision, speech, and locomotion. Today, only a few small commercial companies occupy positions in each of these subfields.

Developments in expert-system technology are expected to lead over time to the construction of high-value knowledge bases.

To date, researchers in knowledge engineering have focused primarily on creating artificial experts to solve real-world problems. The Stanford group pioneered in this orientation, developing the first truly expert system, Dendral; the first successful learning system, Meta-Dendral; and a variety of applications in medicine. This group's recipe for success had two key ingredients: (1) attack problems amenable to the techniques of applied AI, and (2) consider only important, difficult, high-value problems. Specifically,

- Seek problems that experts can solve via telephone.
- Choose a problem that experts can solve in three minutes to three hours.
- Choose a problem the solution of which requires primarily symbolic reasoning.
- Select high-value problems if possible.
- Rule out problems in which experts disagree about solution correctness.
- Rule out areas in which you cannot solve initial problems with a limited subset of the expert's total knowledge.

- Select an initial class of problems for solving that requires only a subset of a given knowledge area.
- Identify training problems and collect the expert's problem-solving protocol.
- Build a knowledge base that contains explicit and declarative representations of the expert's concepts and heuristic reasoning rules.
- Develop an initial expert system to solve the training problems as the expert does.
- Ask the expert to review the system's solutions and its lines of reasoning.
- Augment the system to accommodate the expert's critique.
- Apply the system to more training cases and augment its knowledge base incrementally.
- Evaluate the system's performance on test cases.

Developments in expert-system technology should follow a somewhat predictable course. In the near future, we can anticipate an emphasis on (1) intelligent instruments that couple data collection with expert data interpretation, and (2) numerous high-value, specialized systems. Over time, these systems will lead to the construction of high-value knowledge bases. Initially, these knowledge bases will have a unitary, self-contained character. Each will employ its own conventions for knowledge representation and will address a specialized problem from one perspective. Examples of such knowledge bases now under development include the entire body of information stored in the Caduceus system, which includes 100,000 disease symptom associations.[6] Those desiring the knowledge in Caduceus can gain it only by using the system, which is limited to performing a single function—diagnosis.

Other potential uses of Caduceus's knowledge, such as instruction, question answering, and experimental design, would require new architectures and related reorganizations of the knowledge base.

Within a few years, multifunction knowledge systems will emerge. That is, a single system will contain knowledge of benefit to many applications. As diverse bodies of knowledge cooperate to solve a single problem, more heterogeneous knowledge bases and general-purpose knowledge systems will develop. At the same time, these systems will join other technologies, producing integrated automation systems for manufacturing and other commercial activities.

In the distant future, we can expect knowledge systems with broad and general-purpose knowledge bases to utilize other computer and communications developments. A new medium will be formed, comprising active libraries that will provide know-how and help for persons in need, and knowledge networks for the exchange and marketing of new commodities. Buyers and sellers of knowledge will be able to exchange know-how completely electronically.

What's happening now?

In surveying the state of the art and the state of commercialization of expert systems, we need to understand a few key points:

- Knowledge systems transform book knowledge and private knowledge into an active inspectable form capable of performing high-value work.

- Knowledge today takes many different forms, necessitating a variety of tools or instruments for knowledge engineering.

- Knowledge systems must integrate with data processing systems, but knowledge-engineering work differs greatly from conventional software work.

- A number of companies make money today from knowledge-engineering products and services.

- One cannot predict accurately the direction of commercialization.

- Both the technology and commercial applications should grow steadily and rapidly through the turn of the century.

This section describes the key ingredients of knowledge systems technology, the forces affecting its development, and the current state of that development. Figure 2 depicts the technology as consisting of two basic ingredients: symbolic programming and knowledge engineering. Symbolic programming technology includes the fundamental science of symbolic computation, practical techniques for constructing symbolic programming systems, and techniques for building incremental programming environments. Knowledge engineering adds its own three key ingredients: problem-solving engines, knowledge bases, and aids for knowledge acquisition and knowledge-base maintenance.

Knowledge-engineering technology. Problem-solving engines organize the activity of knowledge systems to solve problems. To understand these engines, we need to relate their implementation to their design and intended purpose. Today's knowledge systems aim to solve specific problems. A knowledge engineer analyzes the problem to be solved and then adopts an overall approach generally consisting of (1) a problem-solution paradigm, such as top-down refinement or multidirectional opportunistic search; (2) a general knowledge-system architecture that reflects specific choices about system design, including what kinds of knowledge to represent, in what formalism, for what kinds of inference, and to allow what kind of flexibility; and (3) a specific problem-solving strategy that determines which knowledge to apply in what order. Today's problem-solving engines provide specific devices for implementing the knowledge engineer's choices.

These engines provide a specific knowledge-representation formalism and a related interpreter, a high-level control architecture and executive, and an inference procedure and related inference engine. The knowledge-representation formalism may include handy ways to describe conceptual taxonomies and conditional heuristic rules. A conceptual taxonomy includes relationships among types of objects, classes, and individuals and determines how properties of one apply to another. For example, many problem-solving engines can accommodate and exploit these kinds of facts:

The Warsaw Pact includes the USSR, Poland, Hungary. . . .
The USSR is a country.
Cuba is a client state of the USSR.
All Warsaw Pact countries are client states of the USSR.
Every client state of any country will do whatever that country does regarding participation in the Olympics.

Heuristic rules represent judgmental knowledge. In fact, the last statement actually represents such a heuristic. Most current problem-solving engines provide a stylized "IF-THEN" formalism for representing such heuristic

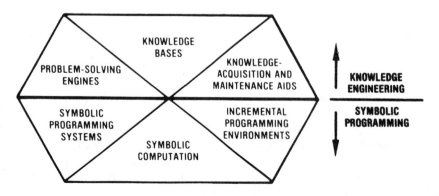

Figure 2. Key components of knowledge system technology.

knowledge. By using the above example, several kinds of heuristics and formalisms can be supported by current engines:

```
IF there is a client state (CS) of some
country
    (C) and the behavior of C regarding the
    Olympics = =B
THEN the behavior of CS regarding the
Olympics = B (cf = .9).

IF client-state(C,CS) and country (C) and
olympics-behavior (C,B)
THEN olympics-behavior (CS,B) (cf = .9).

(client-state C CS (cf X1))
(country C (cf X2))
(olympics-behavior C B (cf X3))
-->
(olympics-behavior CS B (cf (eval(times .9
(min (X1 X2 X3)))))).

(forall C (country C X2)
    (forall CS (client-state C CS X1)
        (forall B (olympics-behavior C B
        X3)
            (implies-with-uncertainty .9
            (X1 X2 X3)
                (olympics-behavior
                CS B CF)))))

olympics-behavior(CS,B,CF) :-
    client-state (C,CS,X1),
    country (C, X2),
    olympics-behavior(C,B.X3),
    .9 * (min(X1,X2,X3)) = CF.
```

All these expressions represent the same intended inference, reflecting differences in syntax, implicit semantics, and implicit control architectures in the various tools available. In these examples, the variable CF stands for the "certainty factor" associated with any conclusion produced by applying this rule.[7]

The following examples of other kinds of heuristics that various problem-solving engines can exploit should illustrate their uncertain nature:

- If you see an oily sheen on the surface of the water, hypothesize oil has been spilled.
- If you hypothesize an oil spill but cannot smell petroleum or feel slime, rule out that hypothesis.
- If you have competing hypotheses, you can identify the correct one by trying to rule them all out.
- If all hypotheses but one have been ruled out, accept that one.
- If you need to schedule N events, schedule the most constrained one first.

- If you need to determine how constrained an event is, rate any event whose time and date are already committed as "highly constrained"; rate any event that is a weekly date with a friend as "weakly constrained," etc.

In addition to the knowledge-representation formalism and related interpreter, the problem-solving engine provides a high-level architecture; executive; inference procedure; and related inference engine. These components structure the knowledge system's problem-solving work and carry it out, generally using a goal-directed backward-chaining mech-

---

A knowledge system's problem-solving work is generally carried out using a goal-directed backward-chaining mechanism to determine a solution.

---

anism (most frequently used architecture today) to determine a solution. In this approach, the system initially possesses a set of candidate general solutions, each of which it considers in turn. For each candidate solution, it seeks knowledge base rules that can achieve that solution and attempts to find data for each that satisfy the antecedent condition of the rule. If that doesn't work, it will attempt to find other rules that can infer or achieve the necessary conditions. Failing that, it may query the end user to establish the prerequisites. Each rule and intermediate conclusion in such systems usually possesses a measure of certainty (the certainty factor). As the system draws new inferences, it calculates their certainty factors according to some heuristic method. This architecture has worked well for selection, diagnosis, and consultation applications.

Several architectures other than the goal-directed backchaining approach have proved useful, the two most significant being the data-driven or forward-chaining systems[8] and the Hearsay-like or "blackboard" systems.[9] In

forward chaining, the problem-solving engine operates by selecting one satisfiable rule to execute at a time. At any time, the input data and previous conclusions determine which rules can be satisfied, namely those whose conditions appear true or "certain" enough. Usually, the systems opt for executing the one rule that has most recently become satisfiable or the one satisfiable rule that is most specific. Once executed, the rule produces new intermediate conclusions that may make additional rules satisfiable. The select-execute cycle then repeat. This architecture has proved useful for modeling cognitive processes and for solving diverse problems requiring very broad, but shallow knowledge.

The Hearsay-like systems emphasize the use of multiple cooperating subexpert systems, or "specialists." Each of these examines a global problem-solution database, called the "blackboard," for intermediate relevant results. Generally, these systems segment the blackboard into distinct levels of abstraction and impose on it spatial or temporal dimensions as dictated by the problem domain. Each independent specialist then volunteers to make a contribution, and the potential actions of each are prioritized by a scheduling specialist, which maintains an agenda. This architecture has proved attractive for complex problems in speech, vision, design, and planning.

Once knowledge engineers adopt a particular problem-solving engine, they must fill out the knowledge base before starting the application. Knowledge bases generally consist of conceptual taxonomic relations and rules. Some generally valid heuristic rules about knowledge bases are

- An interesting demonstration of the technology requires only 50 rules.
- A convincing demonstration of a knowledge system's power requires about 250 rules.
- A commercially practical system may require as few as 50 rules.

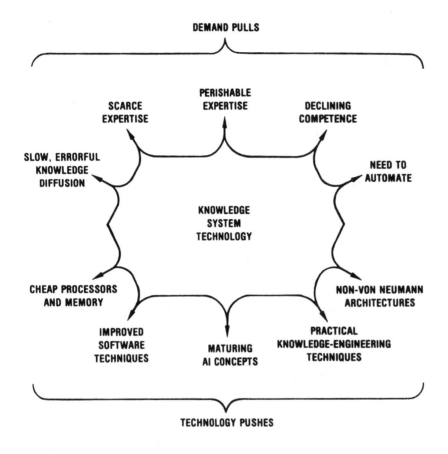

Figure 3. Forces of "pull and push" that are expanding the technology.

Table 1. Estimated measures of current technology capacities.

ITEM	1984 LEVEL	1984-1985 CHANGE (%)
Knowledge system prototypes under development	100	50
Knowledge systems being deployed	20	100
Knowledge systems being maintained	10	200
Knowledge-engineering departments established	20	150
Senior knowledge engineers	50	50
Knowledge engineers	200	50
Knowledge engineer trainees	400	100
Applied AI graduate students	300	20
Undergraduate students in AI	1500	50
Lisp or Prolog programmers	2500	50
Lisp or Prolog installations	500	100

- An expert level of competence in a narrow area requires about 500 to 1000 rules.
- Expertise in a profession requires about 10,000 rules.
- The limit of human expertise is about 100,000 rules.

To help amass and maintain these rule bases, most research and commercial knowledge-engineering tools provide various automated aids. These generally include a range of supports from token completion and spelling correction to line-of-reasoning traces, knowledge-base browsing, and automated facilities for system testing and validation.

Knowledge system technology. Figure 3 shows ways we can see technology expanding. In the upward direction, user needs drive advances in knowledge systems technology and determine the economic and functional niches the technology will occupy. Specifically, knowledge systems address problems that arise from difficulties in retaining, transmitting, and applying know-how. For example, knowledge systems can preserve fragrance-blending knowledge after a perfume manufacturing expert retires, or can disseminate the diagnostic methods of a master mechanic in Dayton, Ohio, to worldwide service facilities. Knowledge systems provide a means to employ know-how where it is needed, when it is needed, and at great speed. These are the qualities that attract those in factory automation, process control, safety systems, military intelligence, and weapons systems.

In the downward direction (as shown in Figure 3), the field will expand in response to technology pushes. These include improved forms of conventional hardware and software for symbolic computing, less expensive memory and processors, standardized and increasingly reliable knowledge-engineering techniques, and possibly novel non-von Neumann architectures, such as those that the US Defense Advanced Research Projects Agency's and Japan's fifth generation programs now pursue. However, I do not anticipate any near-term break-throughs that will affect technology development. Rather, steady improvements in these directions should reduce cost, expand capability, and increase reliability, making an already practical technology much more so.

Assessing technological capacities. To assess the state of technology, we need better measures than we have now. Table 1 estimates the levels and rates of change of some key technology measures.

To assess the rate of progress, we need a way to measure the productivity of the knowledge-engineering team. Although systems built thus far differ greatly, they can reasonably be treated as collections of heuristic rules. Typically, a knowledge engineer and an expert collaborate to create the rules that enter a system. By fixing 500 to 1000 rules as the typical size of an interesting application, I have estimated the rate of system development over numerous applications.

Figure 4 displays development times in terms of engineering person-hours per rule. The graph shows an approximate doubling of productivity every two years over the last 15 years, which I attribute to two factors: first, technological changes in the best available methods for doing knowledge engineering; and second, improvements typically made when learning by using a given method. The figure identifies five successive periods in the technology for knowledge system construction: programming languages, such as Lisp; programming environments, such as Interlisp; research tools, such as Emycin; commercial tools, such as S.1; and anticipated generic knowledge systems that incorporate a user's own knowledge into a prefab heuristic problem-solving package like a personal financial planner. With the emergence of commercial knowledge-engineering tools, many useful systems will be able to go public in a year or sooner.

In summary, the knowledge-engineering field has developed from a laboratory activity 15 years ago into an emerging technology. Knowledge systems convert the inactive knowl-

edge in books and manuals and the private, practical know-how of experts into inspectable, electronic, active forms. Knowledge systems address the need to preserve, distribute, and reason about knowledge electronically, and because knowledge is varied and resists efforts to represent or apply it in a standard way, we have numerous representation schemes and application architectures and can look forward to additional varieties in the future.

In spite of its immaturity and broad scope, the knowledge-engineering field has developed numerous practical aids, some of which have recently been commercialized. In terms of the number of people and rates of productivity, the field has reached "critical mass." The fulfillment of its potential lies in the integration of its tools and systems into the industrial and com-

mercial world—and many challenges still face us before that can happen.

Weaknesses in current technology. While many applications today seem straightforward, many others present difficulties that tax or go beyond current technology. The barriers most frequently encountered include a need for flexible and general natural language understanding, which may arise when users need to exercise initiative in directing the activities of a knowledge system; a need to incorporate knowledge that is hard to represent, which often arises in situations requiring spatial or temporal reasoning; a need to combine and unify the knowledge of multiple experts without benefit of established standards; and a need to apply broad bodies of knowledge quickly, a need that may arise in solving real-time command-and-control

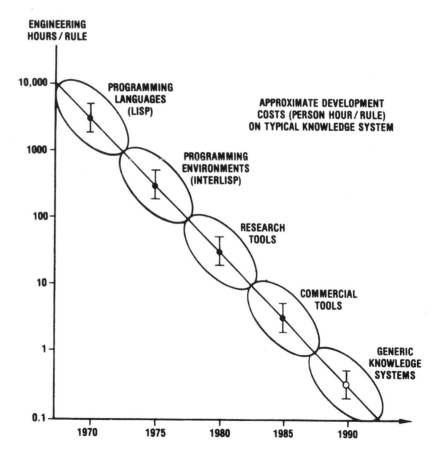

Figure 4. Technology efficiency in knowledge engineering. As the figure shows, efficiency is doubling every two years.

problems. Applications today generally work around these technological shortcomings or force advances in the state of the art.

Commercialization

Knowledge systems, and tools for creating them, have begun to enter the commercial world. The first systems to find regular use grew from long-term academic research. Dendral, which determines molecular structure from mass spectroscopic and NMR data, was under development for over 15 years at Stanford.[10] Numerous pharmaceutical companies now access it on the national Sumex-Aim medical computing network. Stanford was recently granted an exclusive commercial license on Dendral. Similarly, Macsyma evolved over many years of MIT

research.[11] Eventually, it became a superhuman expert in its specialty, the evaluation of mathematical expressions, and it too was commercialized (see Table 2).

Within the last five years, many companies have applied knowledge engineering to their internal problems. DEC reports a $10 million annual savings from an expert system for configuring Vax orders;[12] Schlumberger claims its knowledge-based Dipmeter adviser will increase its revenues from interpretation services significantly; Elf-Aquitaine expects to field a drilling adviser system that it says should reduce total drilling costs by more than one percent; and numerous other companies have undertaken confidential and proprietary applications. Very recently, three types of commercial applications have emerged, the first being tools for the construction of knowledge systems; the second, spe-

cialized hardware and systems software for general AI programming; and the last, the commercial expert system, a problem-specific artificial adviser. These applications have arisen in a variety of areas, including CAD, data interpretation, computer selection, and mathematical problem solving.

Figure 5 illustrates the current and projected state of commercialization. The kernel hexagon represents the major ingredients of knowledge system technology, and the three rings represent increasing commercialization. The first ring shows the types of commercial products now available: supporting hardware and software, knowledge-engineering tools and equipment, and knowledge system applications. The next ring portrays the primary areas of new product focus anticipated in the next three years. In the outermost ring are the key midterm

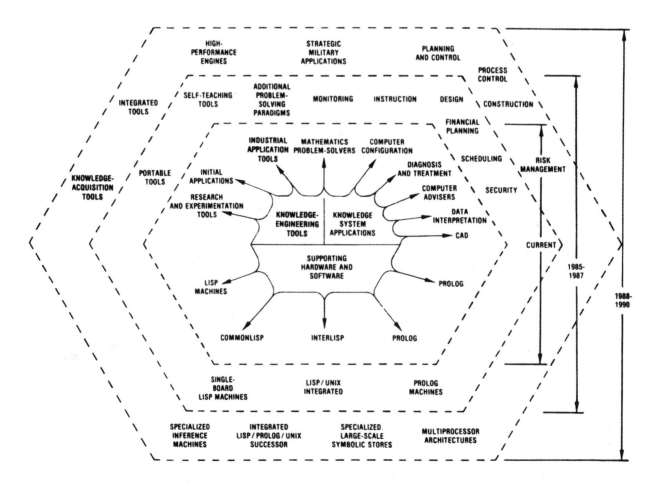

Figure 5. The commercialization of knowledge system technology.

commercial targets I expect companies to hit by 1990.

Table 2 lists a representative set of available products, which are categorized according to end-user applications, commercial application tools, research and experimentation tools, and supporting systems. End-user applications today address problems in which people have trouble assessing products (selecting microcomputer hardware and software, for example), find it difficult or tedious to solve ordinary problems like simultaneous equations, or can no longer do their jobs reasonably well without assistance from knowledge systems, such as in electronic design and plasma physics. As knowledge engineering moves into commercial applications, many companies will begin to offer artificial experts in lieu of or in addition to human ones. Vendors of end-user applications emphasize their problem-solving capabilities, accessibility, and cost competitiveness.

Commercial applications tools address the need for quality software to support the knowledge-engineering enterprise. Several large companies have formed knowledge-engineering centers, and they desire reliable, well-documented, and well-maintained software to support their people. Generally, to use these software tools, we need some knowledge of programming and even some general understanding of AI concepts. Vendors of commercial tools emphasize software reliability, learnability, documentation, maintenance, and portability.

Tools for research and experimentation address the needs of AI researchers, offering a diversity of functions within the structure of a programming environment, usually an extension of the Maclisp or Interlisp environments. These tools help the experienced AI programmer address knowledge-engineering problems more quickly than would be possible starting from Lisp. Vendors of research tools emphasize knowledge-engineering concepts at the frontiers of the technology.

The supporting systems consist primarily of Lisp and Prolog and their variations. To date, the vast majority of applications work has employed Lisp, and nearly 20 years of work in Lisp by AI and knowledge-engineering professionals has yielded elaborate programming environments. However, while these environments offer many productivity aids, they do require considerable computing resources—a requirement that has motivated the development of specialized, personal Lisp workstations. In Europe and Japan, Prolog captures

Table 2. Products representative of knowledge system technology.

AREA	NAME	VENDOR	FUNCTIONS
End-user Applications	Questware	Dynaquest	Personal computer HW/SW selection
	Logician	Daisy	Electronic design
	TK! Solver	Software Arts	Equation solver
	SMP/Macsyma	Inference, Symbolics	Mathematical simplification and problem solving
Commercial Applications Tools	S.1	Teknowledge	Industrial diagnostic and structured selection problems
	M.1	Teknowledge	Microcomputer tool for small expert system applications
	OPS8	DEC	Vax AI programming language used in-house
Research and Experimentation	KEE	Intellicorp	Extended programming environment; frames
	Loops	Xerox	Extended programming environment; objects
	Art	Inference	Varied representations and inference techniques
	Rosie[13]	Rand Corp.	Legible, intelligible symbolic programming language
	KL-Two	BBN, ISI	Knowledge representation schemes
Supporting Systems	Commonlisp	DEC, LMI, Symbolics	New attempt to standardize Lisp
	Interlisp	Xerox, ISI	Mature programming environments
	Franzlisp	Berkeley	Unix-based Lisp
	Lisp Machines	LMI, Xerox, Symbolics	Integrated graphics, personal workstation
	Prolog	Expert Systems, LMI	Formal semantics, logic-based programming language
	Poplog	Systems Designers, Ltd.	Integrated procedural language (Pop-2) with Prolog

13

as much interest as Lisp does in the US. Although it does not yet afford a mature programming environment, Prolog offers a simple and powerful knowledge programming system based on logic. Vendors of supporting systems emphasize performance, price, and compatibility with existing and planned computing systems and standards.

The current commercial situation reflects a wide diversity of products and a relatively immature market. A number of companies have profitable lines of business based on knowledge system technology, and independent forecasts of market growth suggest that demand should increase rapidly for at least a decade. Although I have sketched the current state of commercial activity and predicted what seem to be the most likely near-term growth paths, no one can predict accurately how a new industry will develop. Because the technology addresses a fundamental problem—that of retaining, distributing, and applying know-how electronically—it should continue to prosper. On the other hand, we can expect this technology to combine with other emerging technologies in surprising ways.

The future

For nearly 500 years, books have been the primary means of retaining knowledge and transmitting it to humans. To achieve excellence in a profession, humans have studied, interpreted, and memorized these books; apprenticed and trained with someone who could clarify and illustrate the book's principles; then practiced for years and learned practical rules from experience. The development of printing made an enormous impact on human culture by providing a means to distribute records of human expertise to large numbers of potential practitioners. However, because it could not explain or apply its knowledge directly, the passive book left much of the work to the reader.

As technology progressed and economies advanced, knowledge transfer

became a bottleneck in cultural development. In highly advanced fields, such as medicine and electronics, knowledge creation outpaced knowledge dissemination and use. In information-processing fields, such as military intelligence and earth resources, data was acquired faster than it could be analyzed and interpreted. In highly capitalized fields, such as automotive and electronics manufacturing, global competition based on price and quality has highlighted the need to integrate and coordinate knowledge about all phases of product development. This challenge is exacerbated by the significant acceleration of new technologies and rapid shortening of product lifetimes. In all these areas, the same point is evident: the computer has created both the need and the opportunity to enhance knowledge distribution. Knowledge systems address that need.

What will the future bring? Three basic trends seem certain. First, this technology will spawn many new and speculative products. Some will succeed wildly, even becoming fads. The big success may be an expert system that advises users about wardrobe colors, or job searching, or improving personal finances. Perhaps the big success will be a nonexpert, broad knowledge system: for example, one that could be a computerized pen pal or tell all about the Bible or everything you always wanted to know about whatever. One cannot predict which consumer-oriented knowledge systems will succeed, but unfortunately most systems in this category will probably fail.

The second fairly certain trend is the broad penetration of knowledge engineering into industrial and commercial organizations. Unlike many information-processing applications, knowledge system applications often present substantial near-term payback potential. Most large organizations will find many high-value applications of this technology. For example, the typical expert system may raise the average level of performance on a task by a factor of two to 10 over current practices. If the organization processes

thousands of transactions per year, and the benefit of such performance improvement exceeds $100 per transaction, the company may realize an annual payback of more than a million dollars for each application. Since these numbers appear to be quite typical, more and more people will perceive the attractiveness of this technology in years to come.

The third trend is toward closer integration of knowledge systems and data processing. In many knowledge-engineering applications, there is a need to access and analyze the computer-readable data in conventional databases. In addition, many knowledge systems formulate plans for controlling other electronic systems. Both types of applications will push the two technologies closer together.

What industrial and commercial application areas will the technology emphasize? I can point out several areas that arise repeatedly in studies of likely ways to exploit the technology: expert systems for automotive and equipment repair; heuristic control systems for military functions and industrial automation; knowledge-aided design systems; knowledge-based planning aids; and automated interpretation systems for sensors and instruments. However, the flow of technology into all sectors of the economy will be unpredictable because it is an alternative means of supplying an essential input —namely knowledge. In the long run, industry will use knowledge systems technology wisely, and it will become standard in most industries.

We can also expect knowledge systems to bring about significant changes in existing economic and social institutions. Knowledge transfer, a long-standing problem, has given rise to service professions and institutions such as accounting, law, consulting, and teaching; book publishing and libraries; schools and universities; and numerous specialized vocational fields. As new knowledge was developed, people looked for new ways to distribute and exploit it. Because the new technologies of knowledge engineering, personal computing, and telecommunications combine to provide a fundamentally new basis for addressing these needs, we can anticipate that many individuals and companies will attempt to meet old needs with new products. Many new products will create, in turn, opportunities for new professions, new institutions—and new needs. We can expect to see widespread home banking and financial planning; a centralized electronic university; the replacement of the library-as-archive by the library-as-information-network-access-node; electronic accountants and consultants; and expert-to-expert and company-to-company knowledge exchanges.

Knowledge system technology offers a basically new way to address the age-old problem of transferring know-how from the experienced to the inexperienced person. In the past, this function required a trained human and led to the development of university training programs, professions, accreditations, and service industries. When some of these transfer needs started to be met electronically, the initial applications of knowledge engineering justified the high costs and risks usually associated with a new technology, since the benefits of solving the particular problems it addressed were so great. As the technology matures and its costs decline, we can expect it to spread widely. In the long run, knowledge systems will increase individual and social potential by preserving know-how, distributing knowledge more effectively, and improving performance of tasks that require expertise. □

References

1. J. Beeler, "Expert Systems Inching into Business," *Computerworld*, May 7, 1984.

2. F. Hayes-Roth, D. A. Waterman, and D. B. Lenat, *Building Expert Systems*, Addison-Wesley, Reading, Mass., 1983.

3. E. A. Feigenbaum and P. McCorduck, *The Fifth Generation: Artificial Intelligence and Japan's Computer Challenge to the World*, Addison-Wesley, Reading, Mass., 1983.

4. J. Holusha, "GM's Silicon Valley Stake," *The New York Times*, Apr. 24, 1984, p.1, "Business" section.

5. A. Barr and E. A. Feigenbaum, *The Handbook of Artificial Intelligence*, Vols. I and II, William Kaufman, Menlo Park, Calif., 1981, 1982.

6. H. E. Pople, J. D. Myers, and R. A. Miller, "Dialog Internist: A Model of Diagnostic Logic for Internal Medicine," *Proc. Int'l Joint Conf. Artificial Intelligence*, Vol.4, 1975, pp. 849-855.

7. E. H. Shortliffe, *Computer-Based Medical Consultation: MYCIN*, American Elsevier, New York, 1976.

8. C. L. Forgy, "The OPS4 Users Manual Technical Report," tech. report CMU-CS-79-132, Carnegie-Mellon University, Pittsburgh, Penn., 1979.

9. L. D. Erman et al., "Hearsay-II Speech-Understanding System: Integrating Knowledge To Resolve Uncertainty," *Computing Surveys*, Vol. 12, No. 2, Feb. 1980, pp. 213-253.

10. R. K. Lindsay et al., *Applications of Artificial Intelligence for Organic Chemistry: The Dendral Project*, McGraw-Hill, New York, 1980.

11. W. A. Martin and R. J. Fateman, "The Macsyma System," *Proc. Second Symp. Symbolic and Algebraic Manipulation*, 1971, pp. 59-75.

12. J. McDermott, "R1: An Expert in the Computer Systems Domain," *Proc. First Annual Nat'l Conf. Artificial Intelligence*, 1980, pp. 269-271.

13. F. Hayes-Roth et al., "Rationale and Motivation for Rosie," tech. report N-1648-ARPA, The Rand Corporation, Santa Monica, Calif., 1981.

Hayes-Roth's address is Teknowledge, Inc., 525 University Ave., Palo Alto, CA 94301.

COMPUTERS THAT THINK LIKE EXPERTS

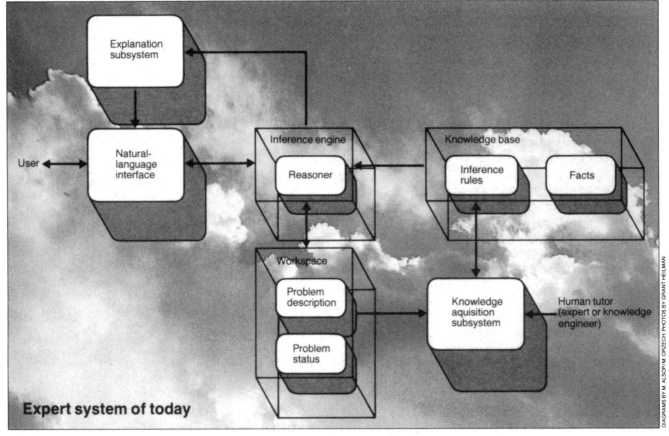

Expert system of today

A bold new breed of supersmart computers is taking shape in artificial intelligence laboratories. Modeled on human experts, these systems will use sophisticated problem-solving techniques and vast stores of knowledge to solve problems beyond the reach of conventionally programmed computers. Already a first generation of systems that reason from rules of experience (surface knowledge) has begun to move from the laboratory into practical applications. Meanwhile researchers are beginning development of a far more powerful second generation that will reason from "first principles" (structural and behavioral models and basic laws of nature). These so-called "deep knowledge" systems could be ready for practical applications by the late 80's.

In the last decade, laboratory prototypes of expert systems demonstrated an ability to solve complex problems in a broad assortment of scientific, medical, business, military, and educational applications. But high development and hardware costs confined them to the laboratory. Now hardware costs have dropped to the point where expert systems appear to be economically feasible.

As a result, interest in expert systems has exploded in industry and government. The Defense Department and other government agencies, such as the National Institutes of Health, have put high priority on development of these systems. Foreign countries, notably Japan, have also launched development

by Paul Kinnucan

efforts. Japan's fifth-generation computer project, for example, is focused on providing high-power inference engines for expert systems.

The number of organizations developing knowledge-based systems has multiplied sharply. Many aerospace, electronics, and oil exploration companies have created in-house research programs. A good deal of the research consists of building prototype systems—a necessary first step to proving feasibility in a particular application. Other companies are turning for expertise to knowledge engineering firms that specialize in developing expert systems. A slew of such firms has emerged in the last two years, many founded by prominent AI researchers. In the venture-capital community, the frenzy to invest in knowledge engineering firms

Reprinted with permission from *High Technol. Mag.,* vol. 71, pp. 30–42, Jan. 1984.

16

Knowledge-based systems are tackling problems that once required human expertise

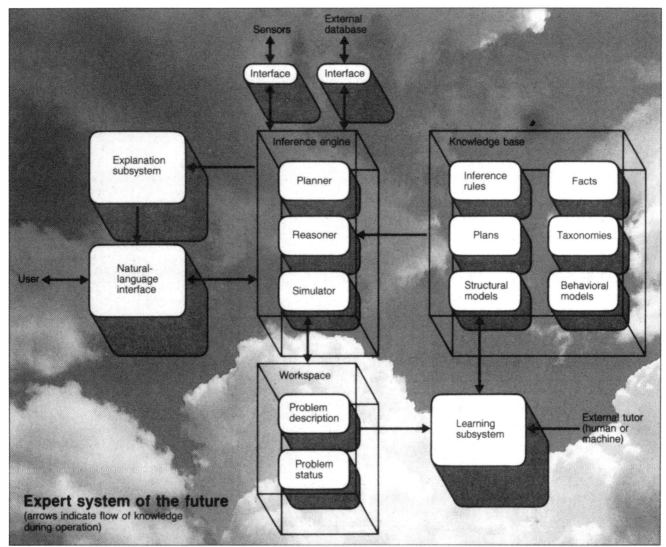

Sensors

External database

Interface

Interface

Inference engine

Planner

Reasoner

Simulator

Knowledge base

Inference rules

Facts

Plans

Taxonomies

Structural models

Behavioral models

Explanation subsystem

User

Natural-language interface

Workspace

Problem description

Problem status

Learning subsystem

External tutor (human or machine)

Expert system of the future
(arrows indicate flow of knowledge during operation)

Inference engine of a current expert system uses rules and facts about a problem domain stored in its knowledge base to solve a particular problem described in the system workspace. The system may request more information from a user and explain its reasoning through a natural-language interface. A knowledge acquisition subsystem enables the automated expert to acquire additional rules and facts directly from a human authority. In future systems, conceptual networks (taxonomies) stored in the knowledge base will allow the system to make decisions based on the meanings of words. Structural and functional models will enable the use of simulations to predict the behavior of the human body, electronic gear, and other systems. Expert systems will be able to acquire information directly from sensors or other systems instead of relying exclusively on a user. Perhaps most significant, automated experts may be able to learn from experience and thereby surpass their human creators in wisdom.

is being compared to the genetic engineering craze of the late 70's. Research has spread and intensified in academia, spurred by an influx of industry and government funds.

Why this sudden surge? Because these systems, if they can be made cost-effective, could reduce reliance on human experts, who are expensive and in short supply. Immortal machines serving as "clones" of human experts could perpetuate and spread expertise throughout an organization. The race to find practical applications is fierce. The only one implemented thus far is fairly mundane: creating and checking computer configurations. But other uses are expected to emerge soon.

Indeed, someday expert systems are expected to find widespread application as advisers on subjects ranging from medicine to finance. As embedded systems, they will also serve as the super-intelligent brains of robots, automatic weapons, photocopiers, and many other industrial, business, military, and consumer machines.

How soon other practical applications will emerge is anybody's guess. Optimists believe that there are many practical applications within the reach of the present state of the art. Pessimists believe that most practical uses may turn out to require more knowledge than can be economically stored and processed by present computers, and more sophisticated programming techniques than those presently used to create expert systems. In any case, a shortage of knowledge engineers—the specialists who build expert systems—will certainly slow development initially.

But one thing seems certain: Expert systems have a brilliant future. The state of the art in programming these systems is progressing rapidly. The next generation may include systems that will learn by experience. Researchers are going for deep-knowledge machines that will be able to examine their own reasoning processes and tune them to improve performance. The cost of computer hardware continues to drop sharply while processing power rises. Such trends will make possible the creation of expert systems capable of handling an ever broadening range of practical applications.

Expert systems derive their problem-solving power from a new approach to computer programming developed by artificial intelligence researchers. Instead of being programmed to follow step-by-step procedures, a computer is programmed to follow a few general procedures for finding solutions to problems. Facts, rules of thumb, models, and other general knowledge about solving a particular class of problems (a "problem domain") are encoded and stored in the computer's memory. To solve a particular problem, the computer uses facts about the problem supplied by a user plus its domain knowledge and general problem-solving procedures to find and apply a specific solution.

A typical knowledge-based system consists of an inference engine, a knowledge base, and a workspace (see diagram). The inference engine solves a problem by interpreting the domain knowledge contained in the knowledge base. The workspace is an area of memory set aside for storing a description of the problem constructed by the system from facts supplied by the user, or inferred from the knowledge base during a consultation. A system may also include a natural-language interface for communicating with a user, a reasoning explanation subsystem, and a knowledge acquisition subsystem for expanding the knowledge base.

An inference engine is essentially a computer programmed to process symbols that represent objects. Actually all computers are symbol processors. In traditional computer applications, however, symbols primarily represent numbers and mathematical operations. In expert systems, symbols may represent virtually any type of object: a person, a concept, a process, a class of objects. Objects considered elementary by the

system ("atoms") are represented by strings of alphanumeric characters ("atomic symbols"). For example, the character string BIRD might stand for the atomic concept *bird*, IS-A (is a) for the atomic relationship of membership in a class, and MAMMAL for the atomic class of animals. Complex objects are represented in memory by connected lists of atomic symbols. For example, the fact that all birds are mammals might be represented by the list BIRD IS-A MAMMAL.

The computer reasons by processing such symbols. The most important symbol-processing operations are matching two character strings, joining or separating two strings, and substituting one string for another. Such operations allow automatic reasoning. For example, to find all assertions relevant to birds, the computer would search its memory for all lists containing the character string BIRD. A matching operation followed by a substitution operation and deletion operation would allow a system to conclude that BIRD IS-A ANIMAL from the facts BIRD IS-A MAMMAL and MAMMAL IS-A ANIMAL.

Representing knowledge. Expert systems use an assortment of techniques for representing knowledge, including:

Production rules. These are two-part rules whose antecedent represents some pattern and a consequent that specifies an action to be taken when the data matches the pattern. The antecedent typically contains several clauses linked by the logical connectives AND and OR. The consequent consists of one or more verb phrases that specify the action to be taken. A typical rule might be "IF the patient has a fever AND the patient has a runny nose THEN conclude that the patient has a cold." When its condition is met, this rule causes the system to add the assertion "the patient has a cold" to its knowledge base.

Semantic networks. This is a scheme for representing abstract relations among objects in the system's knowledge domain, such as membership in a class. A typical representation might be ROBIN IS-A BIRD, SPARROW IS-A BIRD, BIRD IS-A ANIMAL. Such relations may be represented graphically by a network of nodes and links where nodes represent objects and links represent the relations among the objects. In this case the nodes would represent the objects ROBIN, SPARROW, BIRD, and ANIMAL. The links would represent the relation IS-A, and the network as a whole forms a taxonomy.

Frames. These are prototypes that represent objects by certain standard properties and relations to other ob-

This frame-based semantic network (only a small fragment is shown) represents knowledge needed to identify berries that grow in California. The directed graph shows relationships among the objects related to berry identification. Each object is represented by a frame (inset). The frames' slots correspond to variable attributes. Each slot specifies a value or range of values that an attribute may have. Conditions for inheriting attribute values from other frames are shown in parentheses. (Source: Intelligenetics)

jects. For example, a sparrow frame might represent sparrows as belonging to the class of BIRDS and having such attributes as PARTS, COLOR, HABITAT, and so on. A framework system is essentially a semantic network in which objects are represented by frames instead of atomic symbols. To save memory space, most framework systems define inheritance relations, in which objects can inherit the attributes of more abstract objects. Frames may also contain "default" values for variable attributes. These values define the system's expectations about objects. For example, an elephant frame might list "grey" as the default value for the color attribute (albino elephants exist).

First-order logic (FOL). This is a formal way of representing logical propositions and relations between propositions. For example, a system could represent the facts that all men are mortal and that Socrates is a man by these FOL representations, where x is a variable: ALL x MORTAL(x) IF MAN(x) and MAN(Socrates). The rules of logic can be applied to these representations to derive any fact that follows logically from the propositions they represent. For example, a system could automatically infer that Socrates is mortal from the facts above.

Each of these schemes has advantages. For example, production rules are especially useful for representing procedural knowledge—methods for accomplishing goals. Semantic networks are good for representing relations among objects. Frame-based semantic networks can concisely store an immense amount of knowledge about object properties and relations. FOL supplies a means for explicitly expressing virtually any type of knowledge. Early expert systems tended to use one scheme or another exclusively. More recently the tendency has been to combine representations, with each scheme being used for the knowledge it represents best. A system might use production rules to define procedures for discovering attributes of objects, semantic networks to define the relationships among the objects referenced in the rules, and frames to describe the objects' typical attributes.

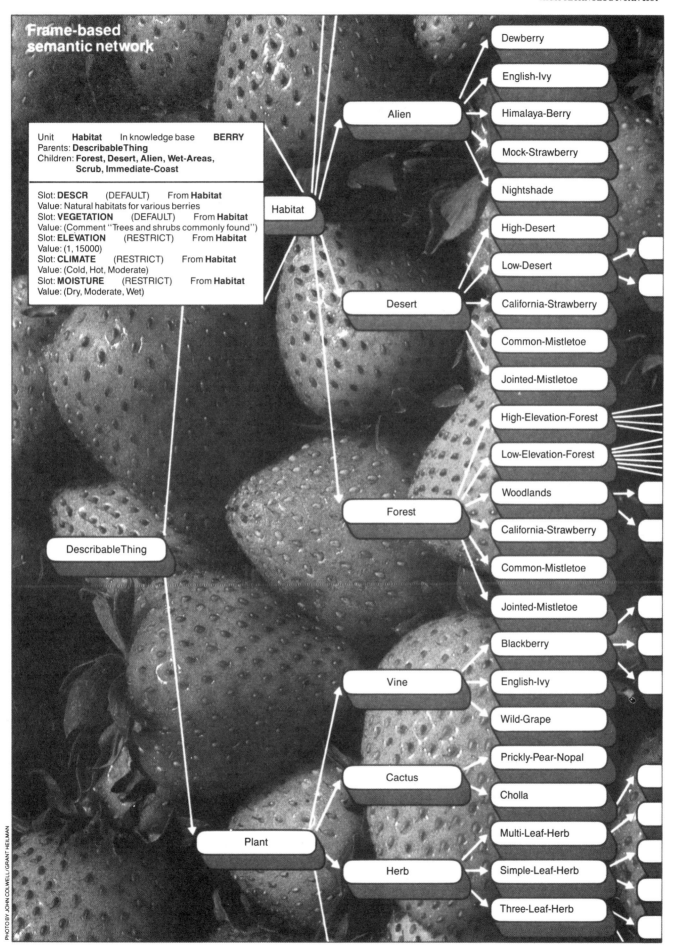

Frame-based semantic network

Unit **Habitat** In knowledge base **BERRY**
Parents: **DescribableThing**
Children: **Forest, Desert, Alien, Wet-Areas, Scrub, Immediate-Coast**

Slot: **DESCR** (DEFAULT) From **Habitat**
Value: Natural habitats for various berries
Slot: **VEGETATION** (DEFAULT) From **Habitat**
Value: (Comment "Trees and shrubs commonly found")
Slot: **ELEVATION** (RESTRICT) From **Habitat**
Value: (1, 15000)
Slot: **CLIMATE** (RESTRICT) From **Habitat**
Value: (Cold, Hot, Moderate)
Slot: **MOISTURE** (RESTRICT) From **Habitat**
Value: (Dry, Moderate, Wet)

Dewberry

English-Ivy

Himalaya-Berry

Mock-Strawberry

Nightshade

Alien

High-Desert

Low-Desert

California-Strawberry

Desert

Common-Mistletoe

Jointed-Mistletoe

High-Elevation-Forest

Low-Elevation-Forest

Habitat

Woodlands

California-Strawberry

Forest

Common-Mistletoe

Jointed-Mistletoe

DescribableThing

Blackberry

English-Ivy

Vine

Wild-Grape

Prickly-Pear-Nopal

Cactus

Cholla

Multi-Leaf-Herb

Plant

Simple-Leaf-Herb

Herb

Three-Leaf-Herb

PHOTO BY JOHN COLWELL/GRANT HEILMAN

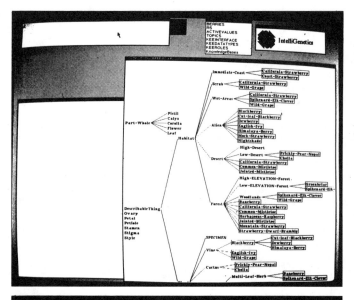
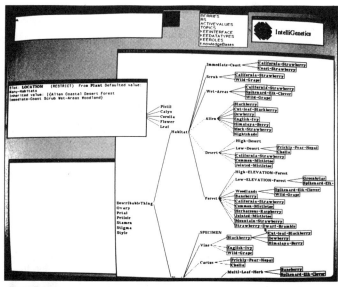
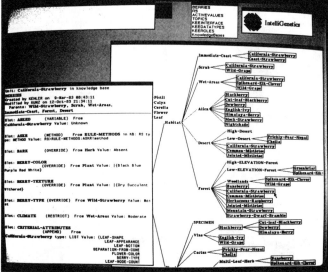
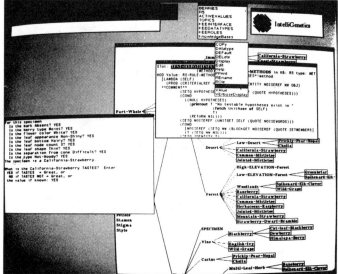

The multiwindowed graphics displays of LISP machines can substantially speed inspection and modification of large knowledge bases, thus speeding development. In this sequence, knowledge engineer first displays a graphical representation of a taxonomy of California berries. Next a frame describing an individual element—a California strawberry—is displayed in an adjacent window. An attribute of the strawberry is then displayed. Next, the engineer activates the frame (which is also an object in programming terminology) by sending it a message. This causes the frame to lead him through a series of questions that would determine whether an unknown plant is a California strawberry.

Two reasoning mechanisms are commonly used in inference engines, either alone or in combination. In forward (data-driven) inferencing, the system attempts to reason forward from the facts to a solution. In backward (goal-driven) inferencing, the system works backward from a hypothetical solution (the goal) to find evidence supporting the solution. Often this entails formulating and testing intermediate hypotheses (subgoals).

The specific implementation of a reasoning mechanism depends on the representation of the knowledge it manipulates. For example, backward inferencing is achieved with production rules by a process called backward chaining. A system begins by searching the knowledge base for a rule (or rules) whose firing would give the desired conclusion. It then attempts to match the antecedent part of the rule against the initial problem description stored in the working memory. If the antecedent matches, the search is finished. Typically, however, the match fails. The system then searches the knowledge base for another rule whose firing would satisfy the first rule. This process continues until either a rule is found that has an antecedent matching the initial problem description or the system asks for information from the user.

Often human experts reach conclusions from partial or uncertain evidence by following plausible lines of reasoning. Some expert systems mimic this process by applying numeric certainty factors (CFs) to facts and rules. The CF for a rule states the reliability of its conclusion, assuming that the conditions in its antecedent are met. If the conditions are uncertain, then the CF of the conclusion is reduced accordingly. For example, a car maintenance expert might discover in its memory the rule "IF the lights are dim THEN the battery is weak WITH CF 0.9" and the fact "Lights are dim with CF 0.5." It could then conclude "The battery is weak with CF 0.45" by multiplying the two CFs. In this manner, systems propagate CFs forward along a rule chain to produce a certainty factor for the final conclusion.

Expert systems employ various control strategies. The most common is to use backward inferencing to explore a series of hypotheses in the order of their prior likelihood. Each hypothesis is explored in turn, until all hypotheses have been exhausted. The system then ranks the hypotheses by the degree to which they are supported by the evidence. A simple data-driven control strategy is to gather some initial evidence. The system then considers each item of evidence in turn, attempting to work forward to a goal. Data-driven reasoning will never terminate if the initial evidence does not lead to a conclusion. For this reason, most expert systems are primarily goal-driven.

Another commonly used strategy combines goal- and data-driven inferencing. First, data-driven inferencing is used to suggest a set of hypotheses based on initial data. The system then begins to consider each hypothesis in turn, as in a pure goal-driven system.

However, whenever a new item of evidence is discovered during backward inferencing, the system switches to forward inferencing to see if the new evidence would suggest another goal or a short-cut to achieving the current goal.

A recent development in control strategies is to make the inference engine itself an expert on its own operations. The inference engine uses meta-knowledge (knowledge about the contents of the knowledge base and about reasoning strategies) to choose an appropriate approach to solving the current problem. Such introspective systems promise to be more flexible—and hence more powerful—than their unreflective predecessors.

Another fairly recent innovation is to allow multiple knowledge sources to pursue various aspects of a problem independently, periodically combining their results. In such systems the knowledge sources communicate by posting notices in a highly structured workspace called a blackboard.

Interacting with a system. Most expert systems are intended to be used interactively in a consultation mode. The system prompts the user for information relating to the problem, and it may ask for a numeric certainty factory expressing the user's confidence in an answer. Most systems operate in a so-called mixed-initiative mode. This

This graph represents a portion of the knowledge base of a system designed by AI&DS to search a database of news stories. It shows the result of applying inference rules for identifying stories on the 1982 World Series. The top node of the graph represents the concept: 1982 World Series. Lower nodes represent related concepts. The terminal nodes represent keywords whose presence in a text indicates that it is about a corresponding low-level concept. The numbers in parentheses indicate the degree of user confidence in the suggestive value of the keywords on a scale of 0 to 1. By searching the text for the keywords and combining the resulting certainty factors, the system can determine the likelihood that a story is about the 1982 World Series.

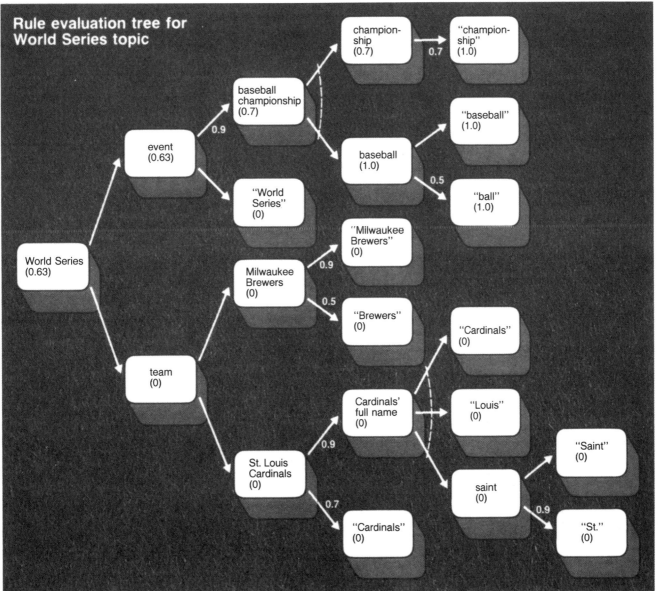

means the user may interrupt the system (i.e., seize the initiative) at any time to seek explanations for why a question is being asked or how the system reached a particular conclusion.

An advantage of production rules is that they simplify the generation of prompts. To prompt the user for information, a rule-based system need merely turn the rule's condition into a question. For example, the rule "IF the patient has a temperature greater than 100 degrees THEN the patient has a fever" might prompt the question "Is the patient's fever greater than 100 degrees?" by a simple rearrangement and expansion of the words in the condition.

Production rules also simplify the generation of explanations. For example, when a rule-based system asks a user for more information (e.g., "What is the patient's temperature?"), it is trying to establish the conclusion of a rule (e.g., "The patient has a fever."). A slight recasting of the rule gives the user an explanation of the request (e.g., "A temperature greater than 100 degrees indicates a fever.").

Expert systems are built iteratively. Initially a knowledge engineer looks for an expert to serve as a source of knowledge on the problem domain. (The term knowledge engineer was coined in 1977 by Edward Feigenbaum, chairman of the Stanford computer science department.) Based on initial interviews, the knowledge engineer selects knowledge-representation schemes and reasoning strategies. A prototype is built and tested on a few cases suggested by the expert. Usually the system does not match the expert's performance at first. The knowledge base is expanded or modified until the system reaches expert performance on the initial test cases. New cases are tested, and the debugging process is repeated until the system reaches a consistently high level of performance on new test cases. Even then the system may not be ready for operational use. In most applications it is impossible for an expert to foresee all the possible cases that might come up in actual operation so that all the necessary rules are included. As a result, extensive field testing is often required.

Some expert systems include primitive knowledge acquisition subsystems that acquire knowledge directly from a domain expert. Typically such systems prompt the expert for new rules when a system fails to reach a correct conclusion. This reduces the need for a knowledge engineer during the debugging phase of development.

The current generation of expert systems has many advantages. They are tireless and immortal, and can be improved and reproduced indefinitely.

Their problem-solving capability is far superior to that of conventionally programmed machines. They can use knowledge about a problem to find short-cut solutions—a technique known as heuristic problem solving. There are many problems for which an efficient algorithm does not exist or the data required to solve the problem by an algorithmic method is missing or unobtainable.

Ease of maintenance and expansion is another potential advantage. In an expert system, knowledge about a problem is segregated from control information and is explicitly represented in small modular chunks. This makes knowledge-based systems relatively easy to modify. In a conventional program, knowledge about a problem is often implicit in the code and is interspersed with control knowledge. A change in one fact may require an exhaustive modification of the program.

Expert systems also have significant drawbacks. Development and production costs are much higher than for conventionally programmed systems. Building one from scratch is a lengthy process. Often the expert's knowledge is not well formulated. If the problem domain is new, there may be no expert. The system builder must then become the expert. Still, experience and new, sophisticated programming tools have drastically cut the time and cost to build such systems. A full-scale prototype can be built now in about 5 person-years, instead of 20 person-years for early systems. However, this is still significantly longer than for most conventional systems. The cost of fielding the systems has dropped dramatically—from more than $1 million to less than $100,000 per system in many cases. It will soon be possible to run knowledge-based systems on personal computers.

In intellectual capacity these systems are no match as yet for human experts. The high cost of computer memory and the serial style of computer processors put practical limits on the amount of knowledge they can store and manipulate. The amount is far less than for a small child, let alone an adult expert.

When debriefing an expert, knowledge engineers search for rules that associate facts, such as a cause with an effect or an object with its property. Cognitive scientists call such knowledge "surface" or "compiled" knowledge, in the theory that it is distilled by experts from deeper knowledge about the world—knowledge embodied in physical and structural models. Relying on surface knowledge presents two problems. First, systems tend to offer shallow explanations for their reasoning. For example, a diagnostic system when asked to explain an attempt to verify the existence of a certain symptom will simply tell a user that the symptom is typically associated with the disease it is trying to diagnose. It can't tell the user why the symptom is associated with that disease.

A more serious problem is that these systems are unable to handle novel situations. A diagnostic system confronted with a new disease or symptom will fail, because its knowledge base will lack an association between the disease and the symptom. This means that in designing a system based on shallow knowledge the knowledge engineer must program rules for every possible association between disease and symptom. The system's ability to interact with human consultants is extremely primitive compared to that of a human expert. It is limited to prompting a user for information and explaining lines of reasoning. This is because expert systems, unlike human experts, have no conception of the need, wants, limitations, and behavior of their interlocutors. This severely limits the ability of knowledge-based systems to interact intelligently with a user. In interacting, it often becomes important for the system to reason not about what is true but about what the user knows or believes is true (which may in fact be false).

Problem domains. These technical limitations restrict present systems to narrow problem domains where the problems are stereotyped and the payoff is large enough to warrant high development costs. Researchers believe they have identified such domains in a broad assortment of applications. They include:

Science. A rule-based program (Dendral) for identifying chemical compounds from laboratory data performs this task better than chemists because it tirelessly considers all possible candidates—even those that a human expert might initially rule out as unlikely. Developed by Stanford University in the late 60s, Dendral is now widely used by industrial and academic researchers. Another Stanford program (MOLGEN) plans experiments for determining the coding sequences of DNA molecules and for synthesizing such molecules. Its knowledge base encodes the DNA synthesis and analysis procedures of some of the world's leading genetic engineers.

Medicine. A Stanford-developed medical consultant program called MYCIN matches the performance of human specialists in diagnosing meningitis and other blood-borne bacterial infections. The system also recommends therapy. Another Stanford consultant program (ONCOSYN) recommends drug treatments for cancer patients based on treatment protocols developed by human experts. It is regularly consulted by doctors in a cancer outpatient clinic associated with Stanford. The University of Pittsburgh is developing a general diagnostic consultant (Caduceus) whose knowledge base will span the whole of internal medicine. Judging by the performance of an initial prototype, its developers expect it to meet a target operational date of 1990. Research in medical applications is being sponsored primarily by the National Institutes of Health under the aegis of the SUMEX-AIM program.

Computer configuration. A knowledge-based program developed by Digital Equipment Corp. (Maynard, Mass.) uses procedural rules derived from human experts to determine a computer system's configuration from a skeletal specification—a task that previously required tedious searching through the company's voluminous catalogs. ("Configuration" refers to the components of a computer system and their interconnections.) The system, called XCON, is used by DEC salesmen while taking orders and by DEC order processing clerks to check and flesh out incoming orders. In operation since 1981, the program reportedly has saved the company millions of dollars in labor costs. NCR (Dayton) is developing a similar program.

Trouble-shooting and repair. An experimental knowledge-based program for diagnosing faults in disk drive controllers compared favorably in diagnostic ability with field service engineers in a recent field trial at an IBM service support center. A prototype system for diagnosing telecommunications network failures, developed for Shell, matched the performance of intermediate-level technicians in recent tests. After successful laboratory testing, General Electric Co. has sent a prototype for an automated locomotive repair system to a customer for field testing. ELF, the French national oil company, is pursuing further development of a drill-rig troubleshooting system after successful laboratory testing of a prototype. Developed for ELF by Teknowledge, a Palo Alto–based knowledge engineering firm, the system recommends procedures for releasing stuck drill bits.

Oil and mineral exploration. An automated adviser developed by Schlumberger infers the existence of geological formations from dipmeter data, using knowledge derived from the company's best dipmeter expert. (A dipmeter is an instrument lowered into exploratory holes to measure angles of strata.) An experimental geological consultant system developed by SRI In-

General Electric Co.'s CATS-1 expert system for diagnosing diesel locomotive malfunctions can display locomotive components on a graphics screen (right) and demonstrate repair procedures on a video monitor (left). A prototype is now being tested at selected repair shops. CATS-1 is a typical first-generation system that combines forward and backward inferencing on a knowledge base of diagnostic rules and facts derived from David I. Smith, GE's top locomotive repair expert (standing). The system's developer, Francis S. Lynch, is shown seated at the keyboard.

ternational in Menlo Park, Cal., reportedly has discovered a multi-million-dollar copper deposit in British Columbia.

Military. A target classification system developed for the Navy by Advanced Information and Decision Systems has demonstrated an ability to classify naval ships from side-looking radar images. (The system has been turned over to Hughes Aircraft, the radar's maker, for further development.) The company has also developed an expert system that selects news stories from a database, using concepts rather than keywords.

Computer-aided education. Bolt Beranek and Newman (BBN—Cambridge, Mass.) has developed a computer-based tutor for training steamship operators that is able to explain and demonstrate the operation of the steamship's powerplant.

The growth of research in knowledge-based systems has created a severe shortage of experienced knowledge engineers. There are probably less than 200 in the country. Virtually all are from academia, think tanks, or industrial labs like Xerox PARC, and virtually all are researchers.

Universities are doing very little to train knowledge engineers. "Universities are more interested in research," says Peter Hirsch, director of the

knowledge engineering group at IBM's Science Center in Palo Alto, Cal. Conventional computer science courses do not provide adequate preparation for the task. Knowledge engineering is a black art, demanding different types of skills and knowledge. Interviewing experts is one such skill. This requires the ability to find an automatic reasoning procedure that best matches the expert's thought processes. Practitioners learn the art by doing.

Companies are training knowledge engineers through in-house apprenticeship programs and by sending novices to courses offered by Teknowledge and other knowledge engineering companies. The list of companies that have sent people to Teknowledge's courses reads like a who's who of American industry.

The shortage has been a bonanza for experienced knowledge engineers. A postdoctoral student in artificial intelligence with no previous experience in industry can command a starting salary of $70,000 or more. Most prefer to go into entrepreneurial companies, where they can get a piece of the action rather than be a cog in a big company.

Because of the shortage of knowledge engineers, the lack of development tools is becoming a major source of frustration for companies interested in expert systems. "There is a huge demand for knowledge-based systems but very little software to support development," complains IBM's Hirsch.

LISP is the most widely used language for building expert systems. Indeed, it was developed by AI researchers to simplify creation of expert systems and other symbol-processing programs. A LISP datum is a list of symbols. The symbols may represent any object, including list-processing functions. LISP assumes the existence of a specialized computer capable of performing the basic set of list-processing operations: match, join, substitute, link, and so on. Since some of these functions are not available on general-purpose computers, to use them it is necessary to have a LISP interpreter, a program that performs the list-processing functions.

Even in LISP, expert system development is time-consuming. This is because the LISP interpreter supplies only a few basic symbol-processing functions. LISP has other drawbacks. It tends to be inefficient on general-purpose computers because they do not perform list-processing functions directly. These functions have to be interpreted by software before they can be executed by hardware. LISP is also little known outside the AI community—a drawback for companies eager to tap the existing pool of systems engineers for expert system development. LISP programs are notoriously unreadable.

There is another issue: program portability. An expert system written in a particular language can run only on computers for which there exist translators for that language. Unfortunately, LISP interpreters are available on relatively few computers. There is also a bewildering array of LISP dialects, with very little standardization. A program written in one dialect will not run on a machine that supports another dialect. All this means that a company may have to invest in a new computer to begin development of expert systems. More seriously, the finished systems will run on only the few types of computers that handle LISP. Or else the user may have to rewrite the LISP program in a more common language. Computer makers are beginning to offer LISP translators on a broader range of their products.

LISP machines mitigate some of these drawbacks. They are personal computers that perform the basic set of list-processing functions assumed by LISP programs. Consequently they can run LISP programs, including expert systems, as efficiently as general-purpose mainframe computers costing two or three times as much. They come with sophisticated text editors, data inspectors, and other program development

tools that considerably ease the problems of creating and debugging LISP programs. Multiwindowed graphics displays make it easy for a user to inspect the contents of knowledge bases. For example, a graphical representation of a semantic network can be displayed on the screen next to a display of a frame that represents one of its nodes. This allows a user both to inspect the contents of a node and to see its relationship to other objects. Such features can significantly lower the cost of developing and reproducing knowledge-based systems, which are large and which in the past have generally required mainframe computers. These machines are available from Xerox Corp. (Pasadena, Cal.), Symbolics (Cambridge, Mass.), and Lisp Machine (Culver City, Cal.). Their prices range from $50,000 to $100,000.

> *Deep-knowledge systems will be able to function in domains where novel problems are frequent.*

For expert system development many companies are turning to general-purpose programming languages, such as FORTRAN, PL/1 and Pascal. The advantage is portability; translators for these languages exist for a wide variety of computers. This means that an expert system developed in these languages can be duplicated on many different computers.

Building a system in these languages is time-consuming compared to LISP; yet any programming language can be used, points out Ira Goldstein, a computer scientist at Hewlett-Packard's Computer Reseach Center in Palo Alto. "The issue is how much you sweat." Many companies feel that the extra development effort may be offset by significant savings in program distribution costs. Even Goldstein, a staunch LISP advocate, concedes: "If I were building an expert system today, it would probably be in a general-purpose language, such as Pascal."

Framework systems are another system-building tool. These are essentially skeletal expert systems that come with

knowledge representation and reasoning mechanisms, but without a knowledge base. In addition, many include debuggers, editors, and translators for rendering English-like knowledge representations in computerese. A knowledge engineer customizes this software to a specific application by creating a knowledge base for that domain. With framework systems, it is possible to build a working prototype of an expert system in a few days. Many of these systems are written in LISP; others, in general-purpose languages.

Framework systems were first developed in the 70s by AI researchers. They are available for nominal fees from leading research centers, notably Stanford University (EMYCIN, AGE, UNITS), Rand Corp. (ROSIE), and Carnegie-Mellon University (OPS 5).

But nonacademic users have not been happy with these systems. "System-building tools developed by AI researchers are hard to understand, which makes them difficult to modify or develop," explains Walt Perkins, head of the knowledge engineering group in the signal processing laboratory at Lockheed Research Center in Palo Alto. They also are poorly supported and so do not keep pace with advances in the field.

As a result, many companies have developed their own framework systems, either from scratch or by rewriting the academic systems. Most knowledge engineering firms have developed or are developing such systems, both for in-house use and for possible licensing to other firms. Big companies have also developed them for internal use.

One such company is Lockheed, which has developed an in-house system called the Lockheed Expert System (LES). "We wanted to develop a system that we really understood, using the current state of the art," explains Perkins. It took 18 months to develop the system. However, it took only four months, using LES, to develop a working prototype of an expert system for diagnosing faults in a baseband distribution switching network. LES is now being used to develop an expert photo-interpretation system. LES is written in PL/1 rather than LISP, Perkins says, because the former is more efficient and is available on a wider range of machines, including microcomputers.

IBM is developing a framework system that will support both frames and inference rules as well as mechanisms for interrogating a user and for explaining the system's reasoning process. In addition, the system will include a mechanism for retrieving data from other systems, such as the output from sensors or information from databases. This will cut down on the number of questions asked of a user. For example, an expert system for diagnosing computer hardware failures could obtain diagnostic data directly from the ailing computer, saving the technician the laborious task of entering the information. The system will have a high-level control language so that different inferencing techniques can be specified. The system will support both statements and rules. IBM is readying it for demonstration in April.

Licensing systems. Some private firms are beginning to offer in-house-developed systems for licensing. Companies that offer or plan to offer such systems include IntelliGenetics (KEE, available now for $30,000), Inference Corp. (ART, available later this year), Software Architecture and Engineering (KES, available now for $16,000), Teknowledge (System 1, available later this year), Prologica (Prolog, $3500), and Xerox (LOOPS, available now on a nonsupported basis for a nominal duplication fee). The commercial systems command stiff fees, but their vendors claim that they will be better supported and easier to use than the academic systems.

Already, competitive claims about these systems are beginning to fly. Inference Corp., for example, claims that ART will support the most powerful set of inference mechanisms on the market when it becomes available next year. Teknowledge says that its system will be easy to use, though at the cost of generality. It is basically a goal-directed production system. SAE claims that its KES system can be used by domain experts, because rules and frames are expressed in English syntax. IntelliGenetics touts the object orientation of its KEE system—a feature that facilitates modular design. (Objects are program units consisting of instructions and data. The units are activated by the interchange of messages.) Xerox boasts of the versatility of its system, which supports object-, data-, and procedural-programming paradigms and both rules and frames for knowledge representation.

The acid test of these commercial systems will be successful implementations. None of the commercially available framework systems has been used to build a successful application system.

The shortage of knowledge engineers is spurring development of knowledge acquisition subsystems that can acquire knowledge directly from an expert. "We would like to minimize the need for knowledge engineers," says IBM's Hirsch. IBM is developing a system that is expert in eliciting knowledge about a domain from the user. It is also exploring another approach, proposed by Michie, of the University of Edinburgh, where the system would analyze case studies entered by an expert. "Most experts learn by example, so why shouldn't an expert system?" says IBM's Hirsch.

Eventually expert systems may imitate their human tutors by learning directly from experience, further lessening their demand on human time and opening the possibility of acquiring expertise beyond that of their tutors. There have been some encouraging laboratory successes, notably at Stanford, the leading academic center for knowledge-based system research. Stanford's MetaDendral, for example, has developed instrument-data analysis rules that have been used in Dendral, an expert system developed by Stanford for analyzing mass-spectrogram data. MIT is developing systems that would learn by analogy.

Deep-knowledge systems. The limitations imposed on expert systems by exclusive reliance on shallow knowledge are spurring development of systems that reason from deep knowledge—knowledge of the structure, function, and behavior of objects. Already such systems are being developed at MIT, Stanford, and other leading AI research centers for such applications as medical and equipment diagnosis and computer-aided design (see "A deep-knowledge system").

Deep-knowledge systems will be more robust than current systems because they will be able to function in domains where novel problems are frequent. With a knowledge of pathways of interaction between components and the normal behavior of the components, for example, the systems can infer correct behavior by running simulations. The systems can then compare the actual behavior with the expected behavior and thereby detect discrepancies that indicate malfunctions—even discrepancies never before encountered.

Deep-knowledge tutorial systems will be able to explain the operation and structure of a device and its behavior and demonstrate that behavior by simulating the device. When combined with computer graphics, simulations can be dramatic, as in the Steamer system being developed by BBN.

Some researchers dislike the terms "shallow" and "deep" knowledge because of the value judgments implied by the terms, as though the latter were better because it is more profound. Actually, associational knowledge is quite useful, since there are many instances where deep explanations are unavailable. Doctors, for example, are not quite certain why a fever is often associated with bacterial infections. Moreover, associational knowledge allows quick solutions to a problem. For example, the knowledge that a nonstarting car is often associated with a dead battery gives a quick solution and recommendation for action. Reasoning from first principals in this case would be wasteful. Cognitive scientists believe that much deep knowledge is "compiled" by human experts into associational rules

A deep-knowledge system

A group headed by Randy Davis at MIT is developing an expert system for diagnosing electronic equipment, a system based on knowledge of the structure, function, and behavior of circuits. This system will represent both the physical and functional structure of the system as defined by a schematic.

These systems work by pathways of causation. Representation of both physical and functional structure of the system is necessary because functionally adjacent components may be physically separated. For example, the circuits that make up a single subsystem may be physically separated on a printed circuit board. Yet two physically adjacent circuits may belong to quite different functional units. Physical representation allows the system to detect faults such as a solder bridge between two pins of an integrated circuit, as well as those that can be logically traced through functional linkages.

The system models devices by treating them as black boxes with input and output ports that are in turn connected to other devices. The normal function of the device is represented by simulation rules that specify an output for a given input, and inference rules that state what can be inferred about the inputs of the device from the values of its outputs, assuming the device is functioning normally. This representation is hierarchical. Each of the major components of a system can be broken down into smaller parts. This allows the expert system to deal with the enormous complexity of computers and other electronics systems.

It makes diagnoses by a procedure Davis calls "discrepancy detection." The system simulates the behavior of a suspect device to establish its normal outputs. It then compares the device's actual output with the simulated output. If there is a discrepancy, the component is known to be faulty.

for quick problem solving.

Future systems will probably combine shallow knowledge with deep knowledge, with the former being used for routine problem solving for efficiency's sake and the latter being used as a fallback for difficult or unusual problems. They will also employ logic schemes that can cope with subjective knowledge—knowledge about the needs, beliefs, wants, and knowledge of

people and other agents. Development of deep-knowledge systems is in the very early stages. Their implementation will probably demand more powerful computers than are available today.

However, research is already beginning in Europe, America, and Japan on a new generation of supercomputers that would be designed especially to run knowledge-based programs. With very large-scale circuit integration and

the use of parallel processing, these fifth-generation computers will be both cheap and enormously powerful, further broadening the range of applications for automated expertise. They will undoubtedly supply the processing power needed for the deep-knowledge systems of the future. □

Paul Kinnucan is a senior editor of HIGH TECHNOLOGY.

Microcomputer-based expert systems: where we are, where we are headed

Abstract: *While the idea of developing 'true' expert systems in the current microcomputer environment continues to be a subject of derision among serious AI researchers, undaunted developers and designers of microcomputer-based systems continue to make progress on the personal computer front. This article presents an overview of the current state of expert systems in a microcomputer environment and then offers some prognostications about the near-term future of expert systems on desktop and personal computers. It is suggested that the history of software developments on the small computers indicates that a pattern of growth exists. If this same pattern is applied to expert systems, the author contends, the near-term future of micro-based knowledge-based systems is at least forecastable if not predictable.*

DANIEL G. SHAFER

*President,
Strategy Consulting
220 Edgewood Road
Redwood City
CA 94062, USA*

1. Introduction

If one wishes to stimulate laughter in an expert systems research group, about all one would have to do would be to suggest, in seeming seriousness, that one could develop a 'real' expert system on an IBM PC or Apple Macintosh desktop computer. The reaction in virtually all circles of expert systems development to such a proposal would be derision bordering on hysteria. In fact, the author, at various seminars, conferences and discussions with expert systems professionals, has had exactly that effect by suggesting the possibility of such development. The general feeling seems to be that 'microcomputer-based expert systems' is a mutually exclusive phrase.

As a rule, the skepticism of expert systems professionals regarding the development of meaningful tools and, ultimately, products on a microcomputer seem to focus on hardware issues: the lack of memory, the lack of processing speed and the lack of adequate mass storage are at the heart of such concerns.

Nonetheless, despite such feelings on the part of most expert systems professionals that micro-based systems are at best useful 'toys' and at worst part of the problem of unrealistic expectations encountered by the entire AI community in recent years, a not-inconsiderable number of developers continue to develop and market expert system development tools, traditionally AI and expert systems languages and even expert or advisory systems themselves on microcomputers. The phenomenon, far from yielding to those skeptics who doubt its viability, continues to grow and to increase its rate of growth with each passing month.

The purpose of this article is to examine the current state of affairs *vis a vis* expert systems on microcomputers and to extrapolate from that examination to an assessment of where the near-term future will lead in this often-ignored segment of the exploding field of expert systems. Far from being exhaustive, this article will attempt to look only briefly at a relative handful of the increasing number of development tools, languages and expert systems which are now or soon will be available on personal computers.

At the outset, it should be noted that current developments in the general arena of microcomputer software would not give one a great deal of confidence in the near-term future of expert systems and AI concepts in the microcomputer environment. Programmers and systems designers have, by and large, ignored the valuable lessons they could have taken from their AI and expert systems colleagues and have failed to apply these ideas to their own, 'unintelligent' programs. As a concomitant point, an increase in dialogue among microcomputer software developers and expert systems professionals, whether the latter are involved in the microcomputer world or in the larger mini and mainframe environments, is needed if progress is going to be anything but halting and hesitant in bringing AI and expert systems concepts to bear on the kinds of traditional computing problems being addressed by microcomputer-based software. Dr. Roger Schank of Yale University points out, for example, that, "you don't need a learning, thinking, AI-type machine to have someone at the side of a businessman who is up-to-date on all the details of his business. But you do need AI's techniques to process English commands and to define this businessman's fuzzy questions." [1]

Today, the microcomputer-based expert systems 'industry', if indeed one can be said to exist in any cohesive or identifiable sense of the word, is at the stage of developing, implementing and marketing relatively primitive development tools. Although, as we will see, there is no dearth of such tools or of languages suitable to one degree or another to the development and implementation of expert systems, the tools themselves as yet lack the sophistication expert systems professionals have long since come to expect in their minicomputer, mainframe and dedicated microcomputer programming environments.

2. The microcomputer software 'cycle'

The current state of microcomputer-based expert systems will not surprise anyone familiar with the broad history of software development on microcomputers. When microcomputers first began to appear on the commercial scene in the early 1970s, software for their use was quite primitive.

Reprinted with permission from *Expert Syst.*, vol. 2, no. 4, pp. 188–195, Oct. 1985.

Development tools did not exist. As a result, the little machines tended to be seen, quite properly, as mere toys and gimmicks for hobbyists. Then the programming language known as Basic became available on the early microcomputers and suddenly there was as explosion of programs on the market for the small systems. First games and then business software and finally more sophisticated tools of various kinds became available.

Interestingly, the microcomputer industry's early product developers did not follow the mainframe world's approach to software design and development. Whereas languages like Cobol and Fortran had been well-entrenched as the primary languages on the larger systems, Basic quickly took over the microcomputer as the language of choice. This was due at least partly to Basic's ability to fit into a small memory space and run in interpreted, rather than compiled, form. Basic took over despite the fact that Cobol is arguably easier to learn, consisting of far more English-like constructs and statements than many other languages.

But Cobol was not an interactive language; it was always compiled and always used in a batch processing mode. Clearly, if the newly emerging microcomputers were going to be single-user machines, interactivity was of a far higher value than batch processing. Basic was available, it was interactive, being interpreted rather than compiled, and (perhaps most important) it could be forced into the rather tight memory constraints of the day's microcomputers, which typically had less than 16K of memory capacity available.

As applications programs began to be developed on microcomputers, a pattern of software growth on at least the smaller computers began to emerge. It is a pattern which can be observed in many aspects of the microcomputer industry.

First, development tools are produced, though they are often fairly primitive ones, with which other products and tools can be made and developed. In the case of microcomputer software, this would be the Basic language, assemblers, debuggers, editors and the like which facilitated the early program development. In the world of expert systems, these tools such as Lisp and Prolog, are now emerging on the marketplace (see Section 4).

Next, custom or semi-custom applications emerge. The first accounting programming done on microcomputers, for example, tended to be customized for a particular user's needs. Issues like account number format, output format, and data stored tended to be resolved on the basis of what the specific customers paying for the program needed or felt they needed. These programs were not general-purpose; the program developed for the pharmacist on the corner could not be used by the architect up the block. In expert systems, this will correspond to the early availability of in-house and extremely domain-specific knowledge-based expert systems.

At some point, some microcomputer developer took a look at all of the general ledger programs he and others had developed for specific clients and concluded, quite correctly of course, that they seemed to have much more in common than they had as points of differentiation. That realization led to the development of more general-purpose microcomputer software. A general ledger could be and was designed which would accommodate the needs of most types of businesses which were likely to use microcomputers as business tools. There were at least two positive tangible results of this change in the industry. First, more people could and did adopt microcomputers as solutions because it was now possible to buy an off-the-shelf solution to one's financial management problems without spending relatively large sums on custom programming. Second, it forced programmers and systems designers to come up with other creative tasks which the microcomputer could legitimately be 'asked' (i.e., programmed) to solve or assist users in solving. There was some limit to the number of individuals and companies who could devise and market general ledger programs without finding it difficult to explain the advantages of one's own package against the features of a competitive product. In the world of expert systems, this phase will probably correspond to the emergence of systems which are capable of automatic or at least semi-automatic knowledge acquisition and extension. Arguably, this phase could be considered the phase of the expert system 'shell' — i.e., a more general-purpose tool for expert system development.

Soon, relatively general-purpose packages for all phases of accounting, word-processing, database management and other tasks has appeared on the microcomputer software market. Very little customized programming work was being done by the mid-1970s, simply because off-the-shelf programs were accessible and affordable, even if they were sometimes difficult to learn to install and use. Then a smart designer-programmer named Dan Fylstra got the idea of generalizing microcomputer software one step farther with something we now refer to as the 'electronic spreadsheet'. Spreadsheets could now be used to develop custom and semi-custom general ledgers, accounts receivable, payroll management and other packages. The precursor of the general purpose problem solver had arrived. In the world of expert systems, this phase will correspond to the emergence of the general-purpose problem solver, a product which has so far eluded AI researchers and quite probably will for some years to come.

3. The role of microcomputers in expert systems work today

One of the interesting observations which emerges from any reasonable analysis of the history and growth of the microcomputer software industry is that people developing software for micros have traditionally found ways to do things that their mainframe and minicomputer counterparts have argued would be unattainable.

They have done so by being willing to 'think outside the box', to find new ways of solving the admitted problems of microcomputers when compared to their more powerful, larger predecessors. They have developed ways of taking better advantage of the more limited internal memory and mass storage available on microcomputers. They have often been willing to settle for less information being stored by the computer itself so that ultimately more topics could be covered in somewhat less depth. They have invented or adapted ideas from mainframes such as virtual storage, 'swapping', cache memory and a host of other 'tricks' which make the microcomputer act as if it were a larger system with greater capacity than it actually had.

In the field of expert systems, this has led, for example, to the idea of the compiled knowledge base found in such products as Expert-Ease [2]. On a mainframe computer with several megabytes of main memory and hundreds of megabytes of disk storage capacity, compiling the knowledge base for an expert system, while often done for other reasons, would probably not be seen as essential to the success or usefulness of the program. In a micro, one way to achieve sufficient size capacity for a 'meaningful' expert system implementation is to compile the knowledge base so that it occupies less space. It turns out that this also leads to faster access and usage, but that is a useful fringe benefit of the original compilation and compression work, rather than its primary goal.

Despite the usefulness of microcomputer-based expert systems, it is clear that the desktop computers are less powerful, have less capacity and process information more slowly than their larger counterparts. Perhaps more importantly for the purposes of this discussion, it is *perceived* to be true that microcomputers are less capable of performing certain kinds of processing tasks involved in AI and expert systems design than are the minicomputers and mainframes on which such work has traditionally been carried out. As a result, even some tasks which might be *feasible* on a microcomputer are not *attempted* by expert systems professionals because of their belief that such an effort would be doomed to failure. In spite of these limitations and perceptions, microcomputers are today playing an arguably significant, if not pivotal role, in shaping the near-term future of expert systems development.

They do so primarily by becoming tools for experimentation, exploration, learning and assessment. Because some relatively capable expert systems tools are already available on microcomputers (see Section 4), it is possible for a company to experiment with expert systems ideas and potentialities without making a sizable investment in resources and, perhaps equally importantly, without alerting too many people at too many levels of the firm to the existence of the experimental work itself.

Another interesting observation about AI and Expert Systems in the world of microcomputers has to do with the emergence in the last few years of the so-called 'Lisp Machines' from a number of manufacturers. Lisp machines tend to be dedicated programming environments for single users or small groups of such users. It is difficult to categorize such systems as minicomputers or microcomputers because they have some of the features of both kinds of systems. This tendency of computer categories to blur has, of course, been observed by many industry watchers and participants. It is difficult, for example, to argue that IBM's PC-AT is somehow 'less' a real computer than a small minicomputer. Coupled with the news that Digital Equipment Corporation has developed a one-chip version of its highly regarded and widely used Vax machines, the emergence of such systems as the PC-AT of necessity gives us pause in our efforts to define sharply the differences among the minicomputer and the microcomputer. Perhaps, in the final analysis, the distinction will simply disappear of its own accord.

Yet another aspect of the current state of microcomputer-based expert systems work focuses on the fact that some serious development has in fact already begun. The author, in researching a forthcoming book [3], for example, encountered a true story involving a Westinghouse engineer who used an IBM PC and Expert-Ease to analyze and solve an elusive and sticky manufacturing problem which he estimated saved his company a substantial amount of money annually when it was implemented. In a recent industry magazine article [4], a product developer indicated she had produced two reasonably sophisticated expert systems using Expert-Ease. The first, called Chest Pains, helps to diagnose potential heart problems with accuracy she says "makes the correct decision, snap, snap". Her second product is as yet unnamed but helps to predict the likelihood of a clot in the left ventricle of the heart [5]. Such clots can lead to embolisms, which can be fatal. The developer described the process of learning Expert-Ease as somewhat painful but now says, "the system is incredibly simple".

A final point in taking an overview look at expert systems on microcomputers should perhaps be made. Marketing experts in the microcomputer industry are unabashed in their eagerness to move expert systems work onto the small desktop machines in the form of real, useful products. The key target machines today are clearly the IBM PC and the Apple Macintosh. Where marketing people see potential sources of revenue, developers will inevitably see potential places to implement expert systems. There is thus a certain inevitability about the development of micro-based expert systems. It may seem somewhat Pollyannish to suggest that merely because the marketing people want something, the technologists will find a way to invent it, but such has been the short history of microcomputers. The pathway to the success of Apple and IBM in the microcomputer marketplace is strewn with the bodies of scoffers who felt that their own domain of expertise was somehow safe from the penetration of microcomputers because it was simply too complex or too unusual or too unprofitable.

4. Software for microcomputers in expert systems today

Let us now turn our attention to a brief examination of the software tools available to expert systems workers who wish to operate in the scaled-down world of microcomputers. As there are dozens of such products on the market, with more emerging every month, this article can do no more than survey a portion of the field.

4.1 AI programming languages

The traditional AI programming languages have become available on microcomputers in recent months. The number of Lisp implementations available for the PC is probably approaching a dozen, with three presently dominant in the market. Those three are: Golden Common Lisp from Gold Hill Computers of Cambridge, MA [6]; MULISP/83 from the microcomputer software giant Microsoft of Bellevue, WA [6]; and TLC Lisp from AI pioneer John Allen's The Lisp Company in Redwood Estates, CA [7]. The prices for these micro-based, commercially supported Lisps ranges from as little as $49.95 to a top of just $495, putting the US language of choice for AI development within easy reach of anyone with a serious interest in the subject. Furthermore, there is a public-domain version of the language called XLisp which can be obtained for only $7 (or free if one has a modem and access to a bulletin board system which contains it).

Nor is Prolog, the seeming choice of the rest of the world in AI research, left out. At least seven versions of Prolog are now available for the PC, with several more rumored to be in development and ready for imminent release. Those which are already available include: Arity/Prolog [8] from Arity Corp. of Concord, MA; Ada Prolog [8] from Automata Design Associates of Dresher, PA; Prolog V [8], produced by Chalcedony Software of LaJolla, CA; Prolog-1 [8] from Expert Systems International of King of Prussia, PA; Prolog-86 [8], marketed by Solution Systems in Norwell, MA; LPA Micro-Prolog [8], a product of Logic Programming Associates, Milford, CT; and Logicware's MProlog [8], produced in Newport Beach, CA.

These are the PC tools. The Macintosh, having been on the market substantially less time, has not yet attracted so many implementations as has the PC. But ExperTelligence, an up-and-coming company in the expert systems world which has decided to focus heavily (but not exclusively) on the Macintosh, has released its ExperLisp [9] along with two other products which will be discussed later in this article. ExperTelligence is also reported to be examining the possibility of acting as the focal point for the development of a public-domain design for Prolog for the Mac, perhaps written in Lisp.

4.2 Conventional languages

Another interesting development in expert systems and AI research on micros has been the willingness of developers and students to create such products using more traditional languages. A reasonably complete expert system development tool has been written and made available commercially in Forth [10], a threaded interpretive language which seems at first blush only marginally suited to such work. Pascal has been used in some university programs to teach AI and expert systems concepts.

Basic — the microcomputer's 'native language' historically — has even been used for expert system development, though confined for the most part to programs whose purpose is educational rather than commercial. For example, a recent book on building expert systems on microcomputers [11] presents a functional expert system written entirely in Basic for the Apple II and Sinclair Spectrum computers.

The book includes an expert system development tool which permits the construction and examination of small knowledge bases (where the size of the knowledge base is limited by the memory capacity of the computer as well as inherent software limitations in the program). It also presents an expert system which focuses on weather forecasting. The 'knowledge base' consists of a collection of data statements, rather than a disk file (consistent with the Sinclair Spectrum's hardware limitations), so there is a practical limit to how much information a user is willing to type into the program and then be able to edit only with some difficulty. One of the main programs in the book is a multi-node, menu-driven Bayesian inference engine in just over 100 lines of Basic code.

Another language which has gained some limited popularity as a possible language with which to experiment with AI and expert systems is Logo [12]. In many ways, Logo resembles Lisp. This is evident not only in Logo's ability to manipulate lists and deal with properties but also internally in the way it represents data. In early 1985, ExperTelligence introduced ExperLogo as its first product. This was the first compiled Logo language available on a microcomputer and it also incorporated access to the disk for data files and to the Macintosh's not-inconsiderable graphic capability. The author's book, *AI Experiments for Your Macintosh* [13], presents several full-length listings of AI-like programs in ExperLogo.

4.3 Expert system development tools

In addition to languages for programming activity, expert system development tools which require little or no programming knowledge on the part of the user are also becoming available. In fact, there is a virtual spate of such products emerging so quickly that simply keeping track of the market would require a full-time effort.

Perhaps the best-known expert system development tool for the micro world in Expert-Ease [2], originally a product of Dr. Donald Michie and now marketed in the United States by Human Edge Software of Palo Alto, CA. This is an example-driven apprentice model expert system development tool which has an electronic spreadsheet-like appearance that appears to make it relatively easy for knowledge workers unfamiliar with programming techniques to use.

Expert-Ease produces rules by inference from examples provided by the user. Each problem file can describe a problem with up to thirty-one attributes, each of which can contain up to thirty-two variable values. Between 200 and 300 rules can usually be contained in a model given a 256K memory capacity, though the theoretical limit is 30,000 examples per problem file.

These limitations are mitigated somewhat by the fact that problem files may chain to one another using forward-chaining techniques. There is no apparent limit to the number of such forward-chaining steps a single problem set can be required to take. Information is not, however, carried forward from one file to the next, each new file presenting a new decision tree in the process. Expert-Ease will point out clashes in examples, and permits the use of a 'wild card' feature to mean 'don't care' in any given attribute field(s). The user can then expand any such wild cards so that all possible values for that attribute are produced in the spreadsheet-like layout into which examples are entered.

Perhaps the next most widely used and discussed PC-based expert system development tool is EXSYS [14] from the software company of the same name in Albuquerque, NM. It is one of the relatively few microcomputer-based expert system development tools which permits the developer to specify the probability of a conclusion being correct. Probability can be rated on a scale of 0 to 10 or using the full range of 0% to 100%. If full percentages are chosen, the user has the additional option of treating the total of percentages as a simple average calculation or of calculating them as dependent or independent variables.

If a person using an expert system developed and running in EXSYS responds in such a way that multiple answers are feasible, EXSYS continues to ask questions until it either resolves the ambiguity or concludes that it is unable to do so. In the latter event, the program will evaluate the alternative solutions and recommend the course of action to which a higher degree of certainty has been assigned by the designer/expert.

EXSYS has one other significant feature: it is one of the few micro-based expert system development tools with a specific run-time module, permitting developers to sell products built using EXSYS without their customers being required to buy or use the full power of the development module.

Recently introduced in the United States and already in somewhat wide use in Europe is another strong contender, ES/P Advisor [15] from Expert Systems International. Early reviews in the United States trade press have pointed to the power, flexibility and Prolog interface of ES/P Advisor as being particularly strong characteristics. The product seems particularly well suited to the more sophisticated user with some programming experience who wishes to have maximum flexibility in constructing knowledge bases and their access systems.

One of the most intriguing characteristics of ES/P Advisor is what the developer calls 'text animation'. This is a process which permits the developer to make available to the user at each stage of interaction with the system all of the information he needs to answer questions. In essence, this feature allows the designer to set up a 'script' through which the user can interact with the system.

When a design using ES/P Advisor has been completed, the designer compiles the resulting knowledge base into optimized Prolog. This Prolog code is then passed through a consultation shell, which then handles the interaction with the user and the management of the system's activities under user control.

The newest such product of which we are aware is a full implementation of Carnegie Mellon University's widely used OPS5 expert system development tool which has just been released by ExperTelligence under the commercial name ExperOPS5 [16]. It runs under ExperLisp, which the user must also own. In numerous experiments, the author has not found an OPS5 application published in the literature which would not run under ExperOPS5 because of any implementation differences (though many will obviously not fit into the available memory space of the Macintosh.)

ExperOPS5 is a microcomputer implementation of the expert system language made popular by Carnegie Mellon University. A program in ExperOPS5 consists of a series of if_then rules and knowledge descriptions. In this sense, it resembles Prolog. Although rule-oriented, OPS5 more closely resembles a goal-based system in which the rules are merely guides for attaining pre-defined objectives.

The only known implementation difference between ExperOPS5 and the traditionally minicomputer version is in the use of the '^' character, which must be separated from its arguments by a space in ExperOPS5.

Micro Data Base Systems of Lafayette, IN, has announced a new expert system development tool called 'Guru', built around their somewhat successful KnowledgeMan database management system. Since the product is being introduced as this is being written, very little is known about the product. KnowledgeMan used a quasi-natural language interface and it seems likely that Guru will expand on this interface and provide some additional power.

The author has explored a very inexpensive (under $100) production rule generation program from Level 5 Research of Melbourne, FL, called 'Insight' [17] which can accommodate up to 2,047 rules and several thousand facts in a PC with 256K of memory available. This program consists of two modules: Production Rule Language and associated compiler called PRGEN; and Insight, the inference system which executes the knowledge base.

Ordinary text files are used as the source input for Insight. Files are produced using any word- or text-processor, following a small number of rules regarding format and syntax. This knowledge base is then passed to PRGEN, which compiles the knowledge base into a form which is usable by Insight. The end user of the expert system then runs Insight, which prompts him for information and draws conclusions as any inference-engine driven system would.

Even though the product is low-end, both in terms of cost and in terms of such features as documentation and built-in editing and checking, its power encompasses confidence levels and a global value called 'threshold' which determines the minimum confidence level the system should permit to be used in drawing a conclusion.

One of the most recently released products in this field is Autologic from KDS Corporation, Wilmette, IL [18]. Autologic, which operates on IBM PC and compatible systems, uses examples to produce rules. As many as 4,096 examples may be entered into a knowledge base, each or which can consist of up to 512 attributes. Values for attributes may be true, false or 'don't care'. Forward-chaining of files is supported. Each conclusion reached may carry with it an associated confidence value.

Autologic incorporates a number of editing functions, including the ability to back-up during development and during execution of the expert system to correct errors.

Although Autologic does not implement fuzzy logic as such, it permits the user, at run-time, to enter as many 'don't know' responses as he wishes, consistent with limitations imposed by the system designer, and then attempts to resolve these unknown values. Where it cannot with confidence reach a single conclusion because of the number of unknown data, Autologic will present the user with the three most probable choices, ranked in decreasing order of likelihood, and inform the user if other possible outcomes exist. Autologic also permits the system developer to see a value called 'Figure of Merit' for each rule in the system. This value permits the developer to examine the number of rules generated by each rule and inference and also the usefulness of each such rule. This permits the pruning of examples and rules by the developer. Autologic also explains to the user how it reached its conclusions.

The common thread which seems to run through all of the products of this kind is their inherent limitation on the number of rules which can comprise the knowledge base to be managed. Beyond that single limitation — and one could debate whether even that limitation is a true commercial hindrance given these products' abilities to handle several thousand rules — microcomputer implementations of expert system development tools seem no less capable than their mini- and mainframe counterparts of producing useful expert systems.

To be sure, there are inherent differences in today's microcomputer-based development tools for expert systems and those which exist on larger computers. Some of these differences involve uncertainty handling, knowledge acquisition and, in some cases, limitations on representation techniques. There is also arguably a decrease in the degree of user-exercised control available to the user of a microcomputer where trade-offs between control and capability are often necessary and most frequently made in the direction of capability. But these limitations tend to have more impact on the expert system *developer* than on the user or the commercial viability of the system under development.

4.4 'Real' microcomputer products

We are now poised at the beginning of what promises to be a spate of real expert systems being developed, implemented and sold on microcomputers.

Besides medicine, the fields which seem most susceptible to expert systems implementation include banking, insurance and the legal profession. Many companies have already announced products in some of these arenas.

Dr. Donald Waterman of Rand Corporation and his colleagues have been working for several years on the application of expert systems to certain aspects of civil litigation [19–21]. There are dozens of smaller-scale, individually developed and designed legal assistance packages in one stage or another of development. Dean Schlobohm, a San Francisco attorney and a partner in Micro-AI, the company which developed Prolog-86 [13], recently won first prize in the artificial intelligence programming contest conducted by the esoteric *Dr. Dobb's Journal* for a Prolog-based system which assists attorneys in dealing with one of the most complex issues in United States tax law [22]. Others have developed prototypical systems dealing with assault and battery analysis, offer and acceptance problems in contract litigation, corporate reorganizations under bankruptcy laws and analysis of secured transactions in sales law.

5. The near-term future: a possible scenario

As we can see from even this very partial and somewhat cursory examination of the state-of-the-art in microcomputer-based expert systems, there is definitely a future for such products and such research. It does not require an expert system crystal ball to predict that the next year will see explosive growth in this arena, primarily in two areas of interest: hardware developments and software implementations.

5.1 Hardware advances: here come the super-micros

There can be very little doubt that the day of the super-microcomputer is here. IBM's PC-AT is the first highly visible such product, but it is only one of a number of multi-user, multi-tasking systems with large-capacity hard disks and multi-megabyte memory capacities which challenge, in performance and capacity, the minicomputers and mainframes at all but the very high end. These systems feature thirty-two-bit architectures which are capable of great expansion (thirty-two bits is the same size as the DEC minis and Vax systems). They can effectively and efficiently support multiple megabytes of 'core' storage and fifty or more megabytes of disk capacity.

As more of these systems emerge and their price/performance becomes competitive with minicomputers, it will be truly possible to attain the desired processing speeds, knowledge base sizes and operational efficiencies which will make large-scale expert systems a reality on such microcomputers.

Another hardware advance which will be of significance to the expert systems developer interested in cultivating microcomputer-based markets will be the emergence in the second half of 1985 of optical mass memories for desktop systems. The first such systems for the IBM PC have already been announced and prototypes have been shown. These disks will enable us to store tens of megabytes of retrievable information where it cannot be altered accidentally and where its retrieval is very fast. Knowledge bases of respectable size can certainly be stored on such media.

5.2 Software steps

In the software arena, we can expect software developers who are involved in traditional programming tasks to make increasing use of the techniques and ideas of expert systems and AI development. They will apply this knowledge in the design of operating system interfaces, database structures and other, similar places where the usefulness of AI's products can be felt immediately by a broad base of users.

In addition, the rudimentary beginnings of the broader-purpose expert systems development tool will emerge. This will fit the script outlined earlier of the trend toward generalization once a few domain-specific knowledge bases are on the market.

However, expect to see the sales of expert system 'shell' programs on microcomputers in the foreseeable future confined to developers rather than to end users. The reason has little or nothing to do with technology but everything to do with marketability. Most people who use

microcomputers — with the exception of that small group which has come to be referred to as 'power users' — are not comfortable trying to design database management applications. General purpose and (arguably) easy-to-use database managers have been on the market for micros for years. But aside from serious business users, they have not met with great success in terms of the numbers of people who use them for problem resolution. Similarly, electronic spreadsheets have sold very well but primarily to people who use them in conjunction with other peoples' products called 'templates' or 'overlays'. In other words, end users of such products are not using them to *design* solutions but only to *adopt* solutions programmed by others. They buy the database manager or the spreadsheet only because they can't run the templates or overlay without it.

The author expects that in the world of expert systems, a similar process may well emerge, with one important difference: compiled knowledge bases requiring little or no expert system 'shell' software to drive them will become the order of the day. General-purpose 'shell' development tools will become available but will be bought almost exclusively by researchers, students, hobbyists and developers. They, in turn, will generate products which are domain-specific knowledge bases which require perhaps only a word-processor-created overlay to use. The intelligence will, for once and finally, reside where the user doesn't have to understand it to use it.

5.3 Beyond the near-term

Once we have reached the point in micro-based expert systems products where significant numbers of vertical markets have been penetrated with templates, overlays and specific products, the next logical step will be the emergence of the general-purpose problem-solver which absorbs and encompasses all of the previously emergent products. There are, of course, hundreds of thorny problems between where we are today and the creation of such a product on a mainframe computer. Its translation to the microcomputer environment will of necessity take considerable time beyond that step.

6. References

[1] Roger Schank with Peter G. Childers, *The Cognitive Computer: On Language, Learning, and Artificial Intelligence*, Reading, MA, Addison-Wesley, 1984, p. 195.

[2] Scott Mace, 'Expert-Ease Creates Expert Systems on the IBM PC,' *InfoWorld*, 19 March 1984, p. 11.

[3] Daniel G. Shafer, *Silicon Visions*, Brady Communications, in press.

[4] Kevin Strehlo, 'Of Butterflies, Pretenders, and Dumb Luck,' *Infoworld*, 15 July 1985, p. 8.

[5] Evlin Kinney, Untitled article, *American Heart Association Journal*, in press.

[6] Ernie Tello, 'The Language of AI Research,' *PC Magazine*, 16 April 1985, p. 173.

[7] Jonathan Sachs, TLC-Lisp from the Lisp Company,' *InfoWorld*, 19 January 1981, p. 14.

[8] Namir Clement Shammas, 'PC Prologs,' *Computer Languages*, July 1985, p. 95.

[9] ExperTelligence, *An ExperLisp Reference Guide*, Santa Barbara, CA, 1985.

[10] Jack Park, *Expert-2*, Mountain View, CA: Mountain View Press, 1983.

[11] Chris Naylor, *Build Your Own Expert System*, Wilmslow, Cheshire, England: Sigma Technical Press, 1983.

[12] A. Bundy (ed), *Artificial Intelligence: An Introductory Course*, Edinburgh, Edinburgh University Press, Scotland, 1978.
[13] Daniel G. Shafer, *Artificial Intelligence Experiments for Your Macintosh*, in press.
[14] Frank J. Derfler Jnr., 'An Affordable Advisor,' *PC Magazine*, 16 April 1985, p. 113.
[15] Ernie Tello, 'Raw Power for Problem Solving,' *PC Magazine*, 16 April 1985, p. 131.
[16] ExperTelligence and Science Applications International Corporation, *ExperOPS5 User's Manual*, Santa Barbara, CA, 1985.
[17] Level 5 Research, *Insight Knowledge System User's Guide*, Rev. 1.1, Melbourne Beach, FL, 1984.
[18] Anon., 'KDS-Autologic Expert Systems Software Program Released,' *Applied Artificial Intelligence Reporter*, May 1985, p. 7.
[19] D.A Waterman and M.A. Peterson, 'Models of Legal Decisionmaking, Report R-2717-ICJ, The Rand Corporation, 1981.
[20] D.A. Waterman and M.A. Peterson, 'Evaluating civil claims: an expert systems approach,' *Expert Systems*, **1**, 1, July 1984, pp. 65–76.
[21] M.A. Peterson and D.A. Waterman, 'An Expert Systems Approach to Evaluating Product Liability Cases,' *Proceedings of the First Annual Conference on Law and Technology*, West Publishing, 1985.
[22] Dean A. Schlobohm, 'Tax Advisor: A Prolog Program Analyzing Income Tax Issues,' *Dr. Dobb's Journal*, March 1985, p. 64.

Part II
Languages

THERE are two distinct approaches to implementing expert systems. The first approach involves development of the expert system from scratch using a programming language. The second approach involves the use of an expert system development tool. In the latter case, other individuals have invested time and effort to develop the tool using some programming language. In either case, the choice of the language plays a role in determining the performance of the final expert system.

The most popular languages for implementing expert systems are Prolog and Lisp. It is therefore appropriate to begin this part with two papers that examine why Prolog is popular for this work. In the first paper, Subrahmanyam assesses the viability of Prolog in the face of competition from Lisp. His contention is that, although Prolog offers many important advantages over other languages, it is still necessary to modify and to enhance Prolog in order to retain its competitive edge.

In the second paper, Helm *et al.* evaluate Prolog as a medium for writing expert system shells as well as a language for knowledge representation. The authors use two case studies: (i) the Tertiary Education Assistance Scheme (TEAS) which uses exact inference; and (ii) the MARLOWE system, in which both the domain and the expert's knowledge may be imprecise. They conclude that, while representation of knowledge with Prolog is simple and natural, slight drawbacks can be overcome through careful implementation.

As is the case with all popular languages, Prolog has matured to a level where several different interpreters and compilers have become available on the market. Weeks and Berghel evaluate various versions that can be hosted in a microcomputer environment. The authors begin their paper with a brief description of each product followed by a functional characterization of all products using several criteria.

The fourth paper, by Winston, attempts to answer why Lisp is so popular. The author points out that although Lisp is almost as old as Fortran [1], it has continued to evolve vigorously [2] whereas Fortran has remained virtually unaltered. He feels that today's Lisp is ideally suited for simple rule-based paradigms and for more sophisticated expert systems.

In the fifth paper, by Kahane and Johannes, three Lisp interpreters for microcomputers are evaluated. The authors begin with a description of the more commonly used dialects of Lisp, and then introduce three products that they have selected for comparison purposes. An important highlight of this paper is a set of benchmark statistics.

After having seen the major characteristics of both Prolog and Lisp, and a number of products in both categories, it is appropriate to compare the two languages. In the next paper,

Warren *et al.* conclude that Prolog offers significant advantages over Lisp. Their reasons are as follows:

(i) Prolog allows a program to be specified in smaller units, each having a natural, declarative reading;
(ii) Prolog provides generalized record structures with an elegant mechanism for manipulating them;
(iii) Prolog is comparatively less machine and implementation dependent; and
(iv) Prolog avoids the "unfortunate syntax and variable binding mechanism" employed by Lisp.

It should be emphasized here that, because of the multiple dialects and implementations of both languages, comparisons cannot be made in global terms. Some versions offer superior results and mitigate language weaknesses better than others.

The seventh paper, written by members of the Xerox Learning Research Group, describes the Smalltalk-80 programming environment. This system consists of objects which interact solely by sending and receiving messages. Extending ideas from ALGOL, SIMULA, and earlier versions of this system, Smalltalk-80 offers basic data-structure classes as well as class descriptions to support interactive graphics, networking, and hard-copy printing.

In the last paper of this part, Glasgow *et al.* describe the Nested Interactive Array Language (Nial). This is an interactive, general-purpose programming language that captures the notion of parallelism. Using data structures similar to those of APL and Lisp, Nial is based on a theory of nested rectangular arrays originally introduced by T. More in 1979. Nial is considered to be an ideal language for fifth-generation systems [3].

This part describes the characteristics of the major languages along with some of their advantages and disadvantages. In the next part, expert system development tools will be examined.

REFERENCES

1. McCarthy, J., "History of LISP," *ACM SIGPLAN Notices,* vol. 13, no. 8, pp. 217–233, Aug. 1978.
2. Steele, G. L., "An overview of common LISP," in *Proc. of the 1982 ACM Symp. on LISP and Functional Programming,* Aug. 1982, pp. 98–107.
3. McCrosky, C. D., J. I. Glasgow, and M. A. Jenkins, "NIAL: A candidate language for fifth generation systems," in *Proc. of ACM Annual Conf.,* Oct. 1984, pp. 157–165.

BIBLIOGRAPHY

Bortz, J. and J. Diamont, "LISP for the IBM personal computer," *BYTE,* pp. 281–291, July 1984.
Colmerauer, A., "PROLOG in 10 figures," in *Proc. of IJCAI,* Aug. 1983, pp. 487–499.
Stabler, E. P., Jr., "Object-oriented programming in Prolog," *AI Expert,* pp. 46–57, Oct. 1986.
Weiner, J. L., "The logical record keeper: Prolog on the IBM," *BYTE,* vol. 9, no. 9, pp. 125–131, 1984.

The "Software Engineering" of Expert Systems: Is Prolog Appropriate?

P. A. SUBRAHMANYAM

Abstract—This paper is a preliminary assessment of the viability of Prolog as a basis for the design of expert systems, where the major competition is assumed to be from Lisp and Lisp-based systems. We critically examine the basic features of Prolog from various perspectives to see to what extent they support (or hinder) expert system development. Our conclusion is that while Prolog has significant assets along several dimensions, Prolog as it exists today needs to be modified and appropriately enhanced to make it competitive to extant Lisp-based systems; we suggest the nature of some of these modifications.

Index Terms—Expert systems, Lisp, logic programming, programming environments, Prolog.

I. INTRODUCTION

THE advent of the Japanese fifth generation project [7], the associated reassessments, and the almost concomitant (albeit independent) recognition of the commercial ramifications of expert systems [14], has generated considerable debate centered around various aspects of logic programming in general, and Prolog in particular.[1]

This paper is a preliminary assessment of the viability of Prolog as a basis for the design of expert systems, based upon argument and experience. The major competition for Prolog is assumed to be from Lisp—various Lisp dialects (e.g., Common Lisp [8], Interlisp [48], Zetalisp [43]), as well as Lisp-based systems (e.g., LOOPS [40], KEE [19], ART [16], OPS [5]). We examine the relative advantages and disadvantages of various features of Prolog from several perspectives that are of relevance in the design of expert systems. These include: features of the basic language and the underlying computational model, appropriateness of the programming paradigm for different problem subclasses, facilities for incremental development of programs (and the incremental modifiability of such programs), amenability to verification, support programming environments, efficiency of available implementations and hardware support for such implementations, and expert systems support environments.

Our conclusion is that while Prolog has some significant assets that aid the development of expert systems, Prolog

Manuscript received June 3, 1985; revised July 2, 1985.
The author is with AT&T Bell Laboratories, Holmdel, NJ 07733.

[1]Prolog is not, and does not claim to be, the definitive logic programming language. However, it is the prototypical representative of logic programming languages, and is the most widely implemented. In this paper, we use the word "Prolog" in two senses: 1) to represent the specifics of the language Prolog as it exists (along with its dialects); 2) to be representative of a class of logic programming languages, stripped of some of the idiosyncratic features of Prolog as it exists today. We also discuss various enhancements to Prolog as it is currently defined and understood; while it is obvious that any such modifications to Prolog will result in a different language, we sometimes also use "Prolog" to connote the resulting language(s). For the most part, the particular mode of our usage will be disambiguated by the context of use.

as it exists today needs to be modified and enhanced to make it competitive to extant Lisp-based systems; we suggest the nature of some of these modifications. When these modifications are in place, and competitive in cost, we argue that resulting paradigm might have some advantages. Despite its current drawbacks, the existing facilities of Prolog and its easy availability make it very suitable for the rapid prototyping of certain kinds of small-to-medium scale systems.

Many of the individual observations in this paper are not new, and we do not claim any radical contributions to the disciplines of expert systems or logic programming. Rather, in view of the growing interest in these areas, we have attempted to highlight, for the readers of this journal who are not familiar with logic programming, some of the salient features of the *currently widely available* Prolog systems. It is important to underline the fact that while we believe the conclusions of this paper apply now, we expect them to change soon, as work on Prolog-based programming environments progresses.

In the next section, we briefly review expert systems, focus on some of their characteristic features, and indicate the nature of available support for their development. In subsequent sections, we critically examine Prolog from various perspectives to see to what extent it supports (or hinders) expert system development. Some concluding remarks are contained in Section IV.

We assume that the reader is familiar with Lisp and the flavor of Lisp-based programming environments. While the essentials of Prolog are reviewed in Section III, a more leisurely treatment may be found in [27].

II. EXPERT SYSTEMS, PROLOG, AND THE COMPETITION

A. Expert Systems

Expert systems are computer programs intended to solve problems normally requiring human expertise, or to augment the decision making processes of human experts. They typically consist of a knowledge base and an "inference engine" that provides mechanisms for symbolic reasoning, search, and explanation [14].

The knowledge in an expert system is usually represented as production rules having the form **if** *condition* **do** *action*. The inference mechanism governs how these production rules are used to infer conclusions from the input data. The most common mode of inference is goal directed or backward chained: the input is viewed as a goal to be satisfied, and the production rules are used to generate subgoals that must in turn be satisfied. The process terminates when it is asserted—either by facts in the knowledge base or by the inference mechanism—that the

Reprinted from *IEEE Trans. Software Eng.*, vol. SE-11, no. 11, pp. 1391–1400, Nov. 1985.

goal is satisfied (or unsatisfiable). An alternative mode of inference is forward chained: the system repeatedly applies satisfied rules, inferring new data from existing data; the new data are used in subsequent inferences. More complex inference mechanisms may be built up by using a combination of these two basic modes, e.g., the goals may be generated on the basis of having several possible perspectives (or models) of the problem domain, and by evaluating which perspective is best suited to the available information in the knowledge base; PROSPECTOR [13] is an expert system that uses such a mechanism.

The design of expert systems requires support for knowledge acquisition, knowledge representation, knowledge-based inference, and search-based computation, along with facilities for explanation, probabilistic reasoning, and the development of expert system shells. Furthermore, since an expert system is, after all, a program, expert system development also benefits from facilities that support the development of good software: a rich programming environment (and associated support for editing, graphics, debugging, program maintenance, etc.), simplicity of semantics and verifiability, support for incremental program development and incremental modifiability of the resulting programs, rapid prototyping facilities, etc. [50].

B. The Competition and Prolog

The early expert systems were written in specialized language interfaces built upon languages such as Fortran and Lisp. The experience gained from the first generation of expert systems led to the evolution of a set of languages, e.g., KRL [46], FRL [15], HPRL [54], and ROSIE [51] incorporating features that attempted to support prototypical paradigms for the development of expert systems, e.g., frames for knowledge representation, etc. While these languages have had successes in some local sense, they are best described as research efforts. More recently, a number of commercially available systems for expert system development have been spawned, e.g., KEE [19], S1 [49], LOOPS [40], and OPS [5].

Concomitantly, but independently, efficient implementations for representatives of logic programming languages, Prolog in particular, matured and became competitive in efficiency to Lisp [32]. Prolog is a general purpose language based on first-order predicate logic [22]. Its semantics are simple, and provide for backward chained inference mechanisms. Prolog has been used to develop a variety of expert systems, e.g., for representing aspects of British legislation [3], [35], for drug design and architectural design [24], [45], [55], VLSI design and modeling [41], and graphics [21], [28]. Some offshoots of Prolog have also been used for systems programming [25], [37]. There has been reluctant acceptance of Prolog in the United States, in part due to the dearth of powerful programming environments. In the rest of this paper, we critically examine the pros and cons of various aspects of Prolog, and indicate how some of its deficiencies can be addressed.

III. SUITABILITY OF PROLOG FOR EXPERT SYSTEMS

In this section, we explore some of the basic features of Prolog, and Prolog-based systems, and comment on their appropriateness for expert system development. For the sake of completeness, we first briefly summarize the basic syntax of Prolog programs and its underlying computational model. We then discuss how these attributes influence the representation of knowledge, knowledge-based inference, and search-based computations. It is emphasized that inadequate control over the search involved in the execution of a Prolog program is a source of drawbacks, as is the dearth of true logical operators for representing knowledge bases that evolve over time. In this context, we elaborate upon a few of the suggestions aimed at improving the flexibility of control in Prolog; the thrust of many of these efforts is to explore computational models that integrate the functional and logic programming paradigms. We then examine the extent to which Prolog offers support for other facets of expert systems programming: inexact or probabilistic reasoning, the construction of expert system shells, facilities for user interaction, domain dependent explanations of program behavior, and knowledge acquisition. Finally, we comment upon how the features of the language and available (or planned) programming environments support or hinder the software engineering of large systems.

A. Language Features/Computational Model

A Prolog program comprises a set of *procedures*, each of which constitutes the definition of a certain *predicate*. A procedure consists of a sequence of *clauses* which have the general form

$$A:-B_1, B_2, \cdots, B_n$$

to be interpreted as

"A (is true) if B_1 and B_2 and $\cdots$ and B_n (are true)."

A is said to be the *head* of this clause, and $B_1, B_2, \cdots, B_n$ its *body*. If n is zero, then the clause simply asserts a fact, and is written as

$$A.$$

The clauses A and B_i are examples of *goals* or *procedure calls*, consisting of a predicate applied to some arguments, e.g., $R(x, y)$.

A Prolog program has a primarily *declarative syntax*: the clauses can be read as implications, universally quantified by the variables occurring in the clause. This facilitates declarative statement of knowledge in an expert system. It also enables declarative statements about program function, which is an important asset from a software engineering perspective: a Prolog program can be viewed as a high level specification of the task to be performed. Since the semantics of Prolog programs are consistent with logic, this enables such specifications (programs) to be manipulated in a formal fashion.

B. Procedural Semantics. Inference Mechanisms

Given a query (viz. a goal to be satisfied), Prolog tries to determine its truth in two ways. First, since facts are always true, a goal is successful (i.e., is concluded to be true) if it matches an existing fact; the match yields a set of bindings for the variables in the goal, and these bindings are available as part of the result [34].[2] Second, a goal is concluded to be true if it matches the head A of a rule "A if $B_1, \cdots, B_n$", and if the subgoals $B_1, \cdots, B_n$ can be concluded to be true. A goal consisting of a conjunction of atoms $B_1 \& B_2 \cdots \& B_n$ is satisfied by first attempting to satisfy B_1, resulting in a substitution instance $[B_1]$ σ_1, where σ_1 is a set of variable bindings. This is followed by an evaluation of the query $[B_2 \& \cdots \& B_n] \sigma_1$, i.e., the variable bindings are passed on to the remaining subgoals. If all of the subgoals are eventually satisfied, then so is the initial goal. If the attempt to match a (sub)goal to facts in the knowledge base fails, and there remain alternative (untried) rules or facts, Prolog will backtrack and try these alternatives. If all alternatives fail, the initial goal is declared to be unsatisfiable.

We now examine the ramifications of the clausal syntax and procedural semantics of Prolog programs.

C. Knowledge Representation in Prolog

The declarative syntax of Prolog programs, in conjunction with their procedural operational semantics, allows for a combination of declarative and procedural representation of knowledge in a cohesive logical framework. However, the basic mechanism that Prolog provides for knowledge representation is somewhat bare, and allows only a flat collection of rules or facts. It lacks facilities to modularize knowledge, to construct hierarchies of concepts, and to deal with incomplete knowledge, features that are essential to knowledge representation. Techniques for knowledge representation that have been proposed on top of Prolog include hierarchical frame based representations, [29], [30], [47], actor formalisms [23], schema-based techniques [52], is-a hierarchies [53], etc. Some of these variants allow for multiple perspectives on data, and inheritance of properties from superclasses. Others supplant extant extralogical operators. A potentially useful extension is one that supports the dynamic creation of logical theories as first class objects, and inference in the context of such theories. This enables a logical characterization of frames, default hierarchies, semantic nets, and generalized control strategies. Most of these proposals have not yet matured to the same extent as comparable Lisp systems. We will here examine only the basic means of representing knowledge in Prolog via rules and facts.

As previously stated, assertions about known facts in a knowledge base can be made using clauses that do not have a body, e.g.,

is-possible-cause(artificial-heart, internal-bleeding).

Rules of the form *if B then A*—naturally read as *A if B* in the Prolog context—may be represented directly using the clause form

$$A :- B.$$

An occasional inconvenience is that Prolog rules do not allow the explicit statement of negative information. Thus, a statement of the form (*not A*) *if B* cannot be made, i.e., it is not possible to assert that a statement A is false if some conditions B hold. Oftentimes, when the need for asserting negative statements arises, it becomes necessary to "reword" the facts relating to the statement such that the need to assert negative facts is obviated.

Several suggestions directed at dealing with the representation of negative assertions have appeared in the literature, e.g., [1], [22]; most of these are unsatisfactory in one sense or another. Consider, for example, the problem of trying to formulate "Alice likes whatever Queen dislikes, and dislikes whatever Queen likes." A naive translation of this into Prolog results in rules of the form[3]

not likes(alice, X) :- likes(queen, X).

which are illegal in Prolog. However, it is possible to circumvent this problem by using a modified predicate such as "likes", and expressing the above statement as

likes(alice, X, true) if likes(queen, X, false)
likes(alice, X, false) if likes(queen, X, true)

However, this representation then involves extra assertions about the connection between likes(Y, Z, false) and likes(Y, Z, true), which is beyond the intrinsic support provided by Prolog.

The experience of Prolog programmers seems to suggest that while this problem does arise occasionally, it can usually be circumvented by using a combination of tricks and knowledge about the intricacies of Prolog.

D. Inference Mechanisms and Control of Search

1) Inference Mechanisms: We now examine how the operational semantics of Prolog supports various forms of inference.

Recall that a goal $B_1 \& \cdots \& B_n$ is evaluated by attempting to unify B_1 with the head of a rule, and, if the unification is successful, then attempting to satisfy the subgoals in the body of this rule. Thus, pattern matching (in particular, syntactic unification) and resolution provide the basic computational model for the execution of Prolog programs [22]. Logically, a statement is true only if it is (logically) implied by the rules and facts in the program (knowledge base). Note that the initial set of rules and assertions is typically modified during the course of execution in an expert system (by virtue of "newly discovered facts" being added to the knowledge base).

The underlying computational model for Prolog thus *directly* supports pattern matching (unification in particular), and backward chained inference—both of which are

---

[2]In Prolog, two terms are said to match if and only if they are *unifiable*, i.e., if they have a common instance. The process of unification, if successful, yields a substitution for the variables in the given terms; this substitution produces the most general common instance. For example, if f and g are function symbols, x, y, and z are variables, and a is a constant, the terms $t_1 = f(x, g(a, z))$ and $t_2 = f(g(y, z) x)$ are unifiable; the substitution $\{x \leftarrow g(a, z), y \leftarrow a\}$ yields the common term $f(g(a, z)(g(a, z))$, and is said to be a *unifier* for t_1 and t_2.

[3]In DEC-10 Prolog, variable names are distinguished by having their first letter capitalized, whereas constants have a lower case first letter. We will adhere to this convention in the program fragments presented in the rest of this paper.

key features of most expert systems. Furthermore, with appropriate modifications, these basic mechanisms can also be used to support *constraint based programming* [33]—a common paradigm advocated in the context of expert systems. Thus, for example, it is possible to express a constraint such as

centigrade(X)
$\quad$ = plus(32, times(9, divide(fahrenheit (X),5)))

which embodies the desired relationship between quantities of the form centigrade(X) and fahrenheit(Y). The easiest way to think of this is to note that a constraint is nothing but a relation (between program variables) that must always hold; a relation is synonymous with a logical predicate in Prolog.

In comparison to Prolog, the basic formalization of most imperative and functional programming languages (e.g., Pascal, C, Ada, Lisp, ML) lacks knowledge-based inference abilities to cope with computations involving search. In addition, there are several well-known problems for which functional solutions are either very complex or somewhat inscrutable. In comparison, the solutions to several of these problems expressed in Prolog are relatively elegant. This is mainly because Prolog can save intermediate computational results for subsequent use by sibling computations. The primary mechanism that facilitates this is the notion of a "logical variable" that enables suspended variable bindings to be dealt with in a very natural manner [9].

2) Controlling Search: In contrast with the above mentioned advantages, current Prolog systems lack 1) the concept of "evaluation" of "function invocations," leading to the relational formulations of some problems being unnecessarily opaque, and 2) a means to describe terminating computations on conceptually infinite data structures.

Both these problems are indirectly related to the (inadequacy of) mechanisms for user control on the flow of "execution" in a Prolog program. In Prolog, the order of evaluation of goals within a clause is from left to right, while the search of the knowledge base (the entire set of clauses in a program) is done in sequential order. This ordering on the search is chosen purely for reasons of efficiency, and yields a depth-first search strategy. To provide additional programmer control over the search, i.e., to override these default modes of search, Prolog provides a "cut" operator (denoted "!" in DEC-10 Prolog [32]). Both these decisions—the implicit (i.e., default) order of clause selection and the explicit provision of the cut operator—sometimes lead to subtleties in the execution of Prolog programs that are not easy to discern by a superficial inspection of its code. In particular, it is no longer necessarily the case that a goal will be successful if it is logically implied by the facts and rules available in the knowledge base. The following example from [27] illustrates this fact.

Suppose that we wish to compute the number of parents somebody has. The rules below state that Adam and Eve have 0 parents, and that everybody else has 2 parents.

number-of-parents(adam,0) : − !.
number-of-parents(eve,0) : − !.
number-of-parents(X,2).

The cut operator "!" is intended to prohibit the resatisfaction of a goal once it has been successfully satisfied, i.e., to freeze points at which backtracking can occur. Here, it is intended to prevent backtracking from ever reaching the third rule in the case the first or second rules succeed, i.e., if the person under consideration is Adam or Eve. The use of the above rules to find the number-of-parents for various people will yield the expected answer, as shown below.

number-of-parents(eve,X).

X=0;
no /* no more alternatives */

number-of-parents(fred, X).

X=2;
no /* no more alternatives */

number-of-parents(eve,2).

yes /* surprise ! */

Note that when we tried to ascertain whether Eve has 2 parents, we obtained an affirmative answer. While this is obviously unexpected, it is explained by the fact that since the first two rules do not match the assertion that Eve has 2 parents, the third rule is tested for applicability, and succeeds! The specific rules given above may of course be modified to deal with this problem, but the point here was merely to highlight the subtleties associated with the use of the cut operator. A general rule of thumb is that the cut operator can be used reliably only if there is an established manner in which queries (goals) will be presented to the system.

Other occasions on which one is forced to exercise caution occur when programs contain either recursive rules or negation. The relative ordering of the rules and facts is very often critical in such a case. Typically, facts must be placed before rules, and the rules must be ordered from the most specific to the most general. If this is not done, the program may enter an infinite loop, since repeated attempts are made to satisfy a rule without ever getting to the point in the program where relevant facts are asserted.

As a consequence, the "clean" control of program execution becomes a challenging problem in the Prolog context—one which is significantly alleviated when using a functional (applicative) style. Furthermore, while functional behavior can certainly be simulated by using relations (using cuts to prevent unnecessary backtracking), it is somewhat artificial to view what is naturally thought of as a one-way function as being a two-way relation. Several ongoing efforts to address these issues are directed at the development of suitable combinations of the functional and logical programming environments [10], [20]. Some of these proposals allow an underlying functional model whose reduction mechanism is "lazy" in that expressions are evaluated only when their value is *needed* during the course of a computation (cf. [31]).

The notion of "semantic unification" allows executable functions to be used in Horn clauses and to be "reduced by need", i.e., the underlying resolution is based upon semantic unification. As a simple example, assume that factorial is a function defined by the equations

factorial(1) = 1.
factorial(x) = x * factorial ($x-1$).

When an attempt is made to match $p(x, x)$ with p(factorial(1), 1), and normal unification fails, factorial(1) is "reduced" (i.e., simplified) to yield the value 1; at this point $p(x, x)$ can be unified with $p(1, 1)$ to yield the unifier $\{x \leftarrow 1\}$. On the other hand, if one attempts match $p(x, x)$ with p(factorial(1), factorial(1)), conventional "syntactic" unification succeeds immediately with the unifier $\{x \leftarrow$ factorial(1)$\}$; in this case, the expression factorial(1) is not reduced, since this reduction is not needed in order to obtain a successful match. Consistent with one's expectations, an attempt to match $p(x, x)$ with p(factorial(1), 0) will fail, but only after factorial(1) is reduced to 1 and a subsequent attempt to unify $p(x, x)$ with $p(1, 0)$ fails.

A computation model based on semantic unification can be viewed as a restricted version of first order logic with equality. If the full flavor of first order logic with equality is desired, more general unification algorithms that "reason" about equality in a broader sense can be used.[4] Such frameworks significantly alleviate the degree of "control" difficulties typically encountered in Prolog programs for solving certain classes of problems. This is achieved 1) by providing the ability to write program segments where the underlying computational mechanism is function reduction without any backtracking; and 2) by explicitly embodying the concept of "evaluation" (of function invocations) in the programs. Furthermore, it is sometimes convenient to have the ability to compute with conceptually infinite data structures. By "computing with infinite data structures," we mean that the program can manipulate as a whole data objects that are conceptually infinite, even though the user may, in any given computation, only wish to obtain a finite portion of the potentially infinite objects. This ability provides a programming style in which one can separate the data processing aspect from possibly complex boundary conditions, thus enabling elegant solutions to certain classes of problems, e.g., [31]. While there are certain inherent difficulties that arise in Prolog when attempting to terminate computations on such structures, some of the newer formalisms we have mentioned here naturally support such computations.

As an example, consider the evaluation of a polynomial of order n at a series of x-values in a given range—such evaluations are used in plotting curves. A polynomial of order n may be represented by a list of n coefficients. For example, $2*x^2 + 4*x - 5$ is represented by the list $[-5,$

4, 2]. The program below uses

1) a function poly(X, L) to evaluate a polynomial represented by the list L at a point X;
2) a function curve (X, Inc, L) that generates a (potentially infinite) stream of points on the curve L at the points X, $X +$ Inc, $X + 2*$Inc, $\cdots$; and
3) a clause curve__in__range which actually plots the curve within a finite interval.

We use A L to denote a list whose head is A and whose tail is L. We also use the construct $[x1, \cdots, xn]$ to denote a list consisting of the elements $x1, \cdots, xn$. The parameters used in the clauses defining curve__in__range and range are briefly explained below.

Start: Starting point for the plot on the X-axis.
End: End point for the plot on the X-axis.
Inc: Intervals on the X-axis at which the curve is to be plotted.
Coeffs: Coefficients of a polynomial.
Y__values: Values on Y-axis (i.e., the points defining the plot).
Current: Current x value being used for plotting.

```
/* poly(X, L) defines the evaluation of a polynomial at
the point X. */
/* The polynomial is represented by the list L. */
poly(X, [ ]) = 0
poly(X, An ^ L) = X*poly(X, L) + An

/* The function curve defines an infinite series of
points */
/* defining the curve represented by the list L */
curve(X, Inc, L) = poly(X, L) ^ curve(X + Inc, Inc,
L)

curve__in__range(Start, End, Inc, Coeffs, Y__values)
   :- range(Start, End, Inc, curve(Start, Inc,Coeffs),
   Y__values).
range(Current, End, Inc, L, [ ]) :- Current > End.
range(Current, End, Inc, A ^ L1, A ^ L2)
```

In defining the function *curve*, one does not have to worry about boundary conditions, that is, the engineering of how the function terminates. This makes it easier to program and yields improved flexibility.

In the context of expert systems, this facility allows a very modular implementation of the "generate and test" paradigm: the "generator" can generate a (potentially infinite) stream of candidate answers, while the decision as to which of these answers are satisfactory and when the computation should be terminated can be made independently.

E. Inexact Reasoning

Some expert systems, e.g., MYCIN [4] and PROSPECTOR [13], use inexact or probabilistic reasoning. This involves associating probabilities or "certainty factors" (typically a numerical value between 0 and 1) with assertions and rules; the derivation of a conclusion also yields an associated probability or certainty factor of the conclusion being valid. This can be done in Prolog in several ways. A fairly naive approach is to add an extra argument to all of the predicates which are associated with probabilities. Thus, $R(x, y, z, \cdots)$ can be augmented to be $R(x, y, z, \cdots, p)$ which may be interpreted as $R(x, y, z, \cdots)$ is true with probability p. Each rule that deals with probabilities (certainty factors) must be modified to compute the probability (certainty) of the conclusion, given the probability (certainty) of its antecedents. Another approach which is more modular is elaborated upon in the next subsection, and does not require the knowledge base to be modified. Instead, a "shell" or meta-interpreter can be written that accounts for certainty factors.

F. Expert System Shells

The experience gained from developing large expert systems has led to the notion of an expert system "shell" which may be visualized as an expert system without its expert knowledge i.e., a collection of inference mechanisms, and the support facilities for providing explana-

factors, for example:

```
solve(true,1).
solve([Goal1, Goal2], Certainty) : −
    solve(Goal1, Certainty1), solve(Goal2, Certainty2),
    min(Certainty1,Certainty2,Certainty).
solve(Goal, Certainty) : −
    rule(Goal, Body, Certainty1), solve(Body, Certainty2),
    times(Certainty1,Certainty2,Certainty).
```

Accounting for (un)certainties in this fashion, i.e., via a shell, is somewhat more modular than the technique of the preceding section which involved modifying the knowledge base itself. It is also important to note that the choice of the "min" function in the above example is merely illustrative; in general, any appropriate function can be used to propagate certainties or probabilities in an inference net.

A forward chaining interpreter can have the form

```
forward-chain : − Termination-condition. /* done ? */
forward-chain : − rule(Action, Condition), /* pick a rule */
    Condition, /* if its preconditions hold */
    Action,      /* evaluate its body */
    forward-chain. /* and repeat the process */
```

tions, development and debugging of the system, etc. The precise dividing line between an expert system and its shell is often elusive. As a consequence, while the concept of an expert system shell aids the development of a specific system, the usefulness of a "general expert system shell" is unproven.

The application-specific features of an expert system shell often include domain dependent computation rules, incorporate of modes of inexact reasoning, domain specific explanation rules, etc. Prolog supports the development of expert system shells rather well. This owes to two facts. First, its pattern matching, rule-based knowledge representation, backward chaining, and backtracking mechanisms are directly inherited by a shell. This frees the programmer from having to explicitly provide these features, and allows him to focus upon the application's specific control and/or more sophisticated knowledge representation schemes. Second, any extra tailoring involved is supported by the fact that Prolog is a general purpose language with associated facilities.

As an illustration of the ease of contruction of shells, we first consider a (naive) shell that provides for straightforward backward chaining, pattern matching and backtracking. This is essentially an interpreter for Prolog written in Prolog.

```
solve(true).
solve([Goal1, Goal2]) : − solve(Goal1), solve(Goal2).
solve(Goal) : − rule(Goal, Body), solve(Body).
solve(Goal) : − system(Goal).
```

where rule(Goal, Body) matches rules with facts in a program, i.e., finds a rule in the knowledge (rule) base that has the form *Goal if Body*.

Inexact reasoning abilities can be added to this shell by adding an extra argument that keeps track of the certainty

The first rule evaluates a termination condition, i.e., forward chaining is terminated if these conditions are satisfied; the second rule performs *repeated* evaluation and application of rules, thus yielding a forward chaining effect. Such a kernel is appropriate for implementing some learning techniques.

As a final example, we indicate how it possible to keep track of proofs. This can be done very simply by adding an extra argument which "remembers" the proofs of goals.

```
solve(true,true) : − !.
solve([Goal1, Goal2], [Proof1, Proof2]) : −
    !, solve(Goal1, Proof1), solve(Goal2, Proof2).
solve(Goal, implies(Proof, Goal, Body)) : −
    rule(Goal, Body), solve(Body, Proof).
solve(Goal,system) : − system(Goal), !, Goal.
```

Once such proofs are available, appropriate explanation facilities can easily be written. This is discussed in the next section.

G. Knowledge Acquisition, User Interaction, and Explanation Capabilities

The first commercially available Prolog expert system shell was APES [12]. It augments micro-Prolog [26], and is a backward chained expert system shell which inherits Prolog's computation rule. The key features of APES (the likes of which are now appearing in the newer commercial systems, cf. Section III-H) include the following.

• *User Interfaces:* Templates enable queries, rules and facts to be displayed in natural language. For example, a predicate such as surface-appearance(oil-spills, silvery) may be paraphrased as

The surface appearance of oil-spills is silvery.

- *Interaction:* Query-the-User [36] is a facility implemented by APES that provides interaction by determining which questions are to be asked of the user. Validity and consistency checks are performed before recording the user's answers. For instance, if a goal human(spock) is encountered, but has not been asserted as a fact, the query generated is of the form

Is spock a human?

The user can then provide an appropriate response, e.g., **no.**

- *Explanation:* Explanations are provided in APES by displaying an edited form of the execution trace; this basically describes how rules and facts were used to evaluate a query (satisfy a goal).

Query-the-User views the user as an extension of the program, and elicits from him missing facts that are necessary for the evaluation of a goal. While the "explanation" obtained from the edited display of the execution trace is certainly useful, it is less flexible than providing for domain specific explanation in the expert system shell, e.g., in the manner of XPLAIN [42]. Some of the other problems in APES arise because it inherits the same shell as Prolog. Thus, regardless of the original query, questions arising from a given Prolog rule are always asked in exactly the same sequence. If a rule is applicable in different contexts, then this tends to give rise to APES-generated queries that are somewhat mysterious.

Consider, for example, the following set of clauses.

```
on-board(X, enterprise) : —
      friendly(X,kirk),
      member-of-the-starship-fleet(X,enterprise).
friendly(X, kirk) : — human(X).
friendly(X, kirk) : — not klingon(X).
```

Now consider a Prolog query (i.e., goal) of the form

on-board(spock,enterprise)?

If the answer to the query *Is spock a human?* is **no,** and if the answer to a subsequent query *Is spock a member-of-the-starship-fleet of enterprise?* is also **no,** then no amount of backtracking on the sub-goal "friendly (spock,kirk)?" is going to satisfy the goal "on-board(spock,enterprise)." However, blind backtracking will give rise to the query: *Is spock a klingon?* which is uncalled for in this context. Intelligent backtracking e.g., [6], is liable to improve the quality of such interactions, in addition to yielding improved efficiency.

H. Software Engineering Perspectives

We now comment briefly on some of the factors that bear upon the development of any large program: the availability of rich programming environments, incremental modifiability, reusability, modularity, verifiability, and the availability of cost-efficient implementations.

1) Programming Environments: The development of large software systems benefits from paradigms and tools that support their conceptualization, creation, prototyping, refinement, and maintenance.

As was elaborated upon in Section III-D, while the logic programming paradigm supports the conceptualization of certain classes of problems, it can benefit from integration with other programming paradigms without losing its semantic elegance. In particular, some of the current efforts directed at the integration of the functional and logic-based programming paradigms, will, we believe, naturally support an object-based programming paradigm.

The initial creation and subsequent modification of programs is facilitated by tools for interactive editing, tracing, breaking, debugging, and incrementally (re)compiling programs. This in turn spawns the need for programs that enable the inspection of the state of a system during execution, the ability to "backup" this state to suitable points in the execution history of a program, and to continue execution from such intermediate states after making modifications to a program segment. Furthermore, it is very important to preserve an appropriate level of abstraction at the interfaces of such tools.[5] The interactive "proof editors" provided in some of the newer Prolog implementations are a step in this direction.

Once a program has been developed, its fine-tuning is aided by mechanisms for monitoring system performance along various dimensions. Finally, maintenance is aided by tools that aid in "book-keeping" (e.g., Masterscope [48]), and tools that support consistency checking in programs. The latter is an aspect in which we believe that the current Lisp-based systems are deficient. This is because the complicated nature of the underlying "Lisp base" makes it very difficult to formally analyze large Lisp programs, let alone provide automated tools for supporting this task. Prolog, on the other hand, has the potential to support the future development of tools in this direction, although much research needs to be done before this is brought to fruition.

2) Incremental Modification/Development of Expert Systems: One positive ramification of the rule-based programming paradigm is that Prolog facilitates incremental modification of its knowledge base. However, the support for modification in the *structure* of its programs (or data) is somewhat less evident. Adding fields to structures in a *post facto* manner is often inconvenient. Often, the need for such modifiability forces one to simulate list structures; this has the effect of diminishing the direct use of Prolog's pattern matching capabilities. This drawback in Prolog is analogous to the rigidity of, say, the record structures in Pascal (or any language of its ilk) contrasted with the flexibility provided by Lisp's property lists.

3) Modularity, Reusability, and Verifiability: Besides offering a rule-based paradigm, Prolog does very little to support the development of modular programs. This owes primarily to the flat structure of the clauses (the rules and facts) in a Prolog program. The use of a global name space complicates the development of large programs, although this drawback is not intrinsic to any aspect of logic programming.

In several imperative and functional languages, various forms of type checking are used to detect certain kinds of

---

[5]The sentiment here is avoid error messages that read "addressing interrupt at address 0997" and produce a core dump, rather than trying to offer a more intelligent perspective on the cause of program failure.

syntactic and semantic errors at compile time. In addition, the notion of abstract data types is useful in improving the modularity of programs, and parameterizable abstract types can arguably aid the reusability of software modules [11]. In this context, there is ongoing research on providing typing facilities that are consistent with the paradigm of programming in Prolog. While much of this research is in its early stages, it is safe to say that the simple semantics of logic programs (particularly those that do not need or use the cut operator) are an immense aid to formally reasoning about the behavior of programs, and in proving program correctness.

4) Prolog Implementations, Hardware Support: Prolog implementations are currently available on a wide variety of machines, including "personal computers" such as the Macintosh and the IBM-PC, 68000 and VAX (VMS and UNIX) based systems, mainframes such as the DEC-10, DEC-20, and IBM 3081, and personal Lisp machines. While many of the earlier implementations provided only an interpreter and perhaps a compiler for basic Prolog, the newer implementations offer interactive editors, incremental compilers, and other features that increasingly resemble those available in current Lisp implementations. The ability to interface newly written programs to existing software, databases, and hardware is an important concern that is involved in the development of any nontrivial software system. To address this concern, the more recent implementations are attempting to provide varied interfaces to other languages (most typically Lisp and C).

We list below a few of the currently available Prolog implementations and Prolog-based systems. Our intent is merely to convey the flavor of the systems available today, not to be exhaustive.[6]

• Arity/Prolog [2] runs on the IBM-Personal Computers and compatible machines. It supports UNIX-style systems functions and file I/O.

• The "Logic WorkBench" Prolog [38] is available on 68000-based UNIX systems. It supports an interface to C, and to an external database. It also offers the ability to store large Prolog databases on disk and use them without first downloading them into main memory.

• POPLOG [39], developed at the University of Sussex, is implemented on a wide variety of intermediate sized machines (including VAX and 68000-based systems), and features a combination of the languages POP-II, Lisp and Prolog. It supports incremental compilation and provides interfaces to routines written in C, Fortran, and Ada.

• MProlog [18], which is available on a wide spectrum of machines, features a program development environment that includes an interactive program editor, a proof editor, and trace facilities. It also supports user-defined error handling and interfaces to external routines.

• Quintus Prolog [44], available on the VAX and SUN workstations, features an incremental optimizing compiler and a C interface.

• LM-Prolog [17] (which stands for Lisp Machine Prolog) runs on the LMI and Symbolics Lisp machines. It features a compiler which can unfold predicates, microcoded hardware support, multiple worlds (or contexts), and some constraint mechanisms. In addition, it supports a Concurrent Prolog interpreter with graphics facilities. In common with the emerging Lisp-based Prolog systems, LM-Prolog offers an interface to Lisp and access to a full Lisp machine environment. A DEC-10 Prolog compatibility package is available.

In general, the extant support for developing large Prolog systems is poor, particularly when compared to the various Lisp environments that are commercially available. However, the sophistication of programming environments for Prolog is rapidly improving, and some of the newer implementations on personal machines incorporate several of the recent developments in the research community. They also provide improvements in efficiency by using specialized hardware support and microcoding. It is very likely that the richness of these environments will begin to match those of Lisp-based systems within a few years.

IV. Summary and Conclusions

The basic features of Prolog that aid the design of expert systems are

• support for search-based computation via backward chaining,

• use of (syntactic) unification as a basic pattern matching technique to support a clause-based style of programming,

• the ability to have suspended variable bindings via the logical variables, and

• simple and elegant semantics that offer a cohesive framework for rule-based systems, and which allow the formal manipulation of logic programs.

The current drawbacks of Prolog are

• inadequate flexibility in controlling the search involved in program execution,

• inadequate means for cleanly and efficiently replacing the notion of "destructive assignment" used in imperative languages and database implementations,

• inappropriate means for supplanting extralogical features such as the operators for dynamic addition and deletion of clauses, and evaluable input–output predicates

• the inappropriateness of the backward chaining mode of inference for some problem classes,

• the inappropriateness of the clause-based programming paradigm for certain problem classes,

• the absence of advanced programming environments for supporting the development and debugging of large programs, and

• the absence of suitable means to partition the name

[6]The references to most of these implementations are mainly in the form of (unpublished) manuals that are obtainable from the implementers. Much of the information here has been obtained through informal sources; while we believe it is fairly accurate, we make no guarantees to this effect. The cost of these systems ranges between $100 and $15 000, although many of the systems are priced at the lower end of this scale. The performance of Prolog implementations is typically quoted in terms of the average number of logical inferences performed per second, measured in multiples of 1000 and called KLIPS. The performance of these implementations varies between <1 KLIP to over 100 KLIPS on the higher end machines.

space of Prolog clauses to improve the modularity of programs developed.

Some of these drawbacks are not really connected in any basic way to either logic programming or Prolog, e.g., the presence of a global name space and the absence of sophisticated programming support environments. It is reasonable to envision that these drawbacks can be overcome if sufficient interest in the development of logic programming/Prolog persists. Other drawbacks (or idiosyncracies) are more tightly intertwined with the language as it exists: e.g., the lack of control features, inability to handle conceptually infinite data structures, and negation. There are several ongoing research efforts directed towards alleviating some of these drawbacks [10]. Another area of work aims at providing means of concurrent programming in the logic programming paradigm to support systems programming [37]. Other attempts at language enhancement are directed towards providing features explicitly catering to the development of expert systems (and less to general programming per se), e.g., knowledge representation capabilities that enable multiple views, and inheritance from multiple superclasses. A third category of drawbacks relates to efficiency issues: a number of proposals for hardware microcode support, and parallel architectures and execution models for Prolog are evolving in an attempt to address this facet.

It is obvious that whatever the eventual outcome of this combination of research efforts is, the resultant language will be quite different along several dimensions from the specifics of Prolog as it exists today. However, it can be argued that if the semantics of the future generation languages are kept simple and consistent with (equational) logic, then the formal symbolic manipulations of the programs and the verification of the consistency of the resulting systems will be facilitated to a much greater extent than is the case in the existing Lisp-based programming systems. From this (we believe, important,) perspective, the outcome will be superior to the extant richer Lisp-based systems. If, on the other hand, the new systems offer similar functionality but succeed in destroying the underlying elegance and clean semantics of the logic programming paradigm (as is the case with some of the emerging systems that merge Prolog with Lisp) then the advantage of the resulting product will be, in our opinion, far less pronounced. In this eventuality, the choice between the available options when both paradigms are appropriate, will become mainly a subjective one, and perhaps more theological than technical. It is open to speculation as to whether *any* language can become successful in the sense of Lisp and still remain pristine: there is strong temptation to draw a parallel here between the (relative simplicity of) early versions of Lisp (e.g., LISP 1.5) and Prolog.

Currently, despite the strong competition from the available Lisp-based environments for expert systems development (which are available primarily only on the more expensive machines) the existing advantages of Prolog and the fact that it is readily available on several of the lower

priced machines make it very suitable for prototyping a variety of small to medium scale expert systems.

ACKNOWLEDGMENT

I wish to thank B. Ensor, J. Gabbe, T. London, and an anonymous referee for helpful comments on an earlier draft of this paper.

REFERENCES

[1] K. L. Clark, "Negation as failure," in *Logic and Databases*, H. Gallaire and J. Minker, Eds. New York: Plenum, 1978.

[2] *Arity Prolog User Manual*, Arity Corp., Concord, MA, 1985.

[3] H. T. Cory, P. Hammond, R. A. Kowalski, F. R. Kriwaczek, F. Sadri, and M. Sergot, "The British nationality act as a logic program," Dep. Comput., Imperial College, London, England, 1984.

[4] E. H. Shortliffe, *Computer Based Medical Consultations: MYCIN*. New York: American Elsevier, 1976.

[5] C. Forgy, "The OPS5 user's manual," Carnegie-Mellon Univ., Pittsburgh, PA, Rep. CMU CS-81-135, 1981.

[6] P. T. Fox, "Finding backtrack points for intelligent backtracking," in *Implementations of Prolog*, J. A. Campbell, Ed. Chichester, England: Ellis Horwood, 1984, pp. 216–233.

[7] K. Fuchi, "The direction of FGCS project will take," *New Generation Comput.*, vol. 1, pp. 3–9, 1983.

[8] G. L. Steele, Jr., *Common Lisp Reference Manual*. Digital Press, 1984.

[9] G. Lindstrom, "Functional programming and the logical variable," in *Proc. 11th ACM Symp. Principles of Program. Lang.*, Jan. 1985, pp. 266–281.

[10] D. DeGroot and G. Lindstrom, *Logic Programming: Relations, Functions and Equations*. Englewood Cliffs, NJ: Prentice-Hall, 1985.

[11] J. A. Goguen, "Parameterized programming," *IEEE Trans. Software Eng.*, vol. SE-10, pp. 528–552, Sept. 1984.

[12] P. Hammond, "APES (a prolog expert system shell): A user manual," Dep. Comput., Imperial College, London, England, Doc Report 82/9, 1982.

[13] R. Duda, J. Gashnig, and P. Hart, "Model design in the PROSPECTOR consultant system for mineral exploration," in *Expert Systems in the Micro-Electronic Age*, D. Michie, Ed. London, England: Edinburgh University Press, 1979.

[14] F. Hayes-Roth, "Knowledge based expert systems," *Computer*, Oct. 1984.

[15] R. B. Roberts and I. P. Goldstein, "The FRL manual," Massachusetts Inst. Technol. Cambridge, AI-Memo 409, 1977.

[16] *ART User's Manual*, Inference Systems Inc., 1984.

[17] *LM-Prolog*, LMI Inc, Los Angeles, CA, Dec. 1983.

[18] *MProlog*, Logicware Inc., Newport Beach, CA, 1984.

[19] *KEE Software Development System User's Manual*, IntelliCorp, Inc., Jan. 1985.

[20] P. A. Subrahmanyam and J. H. You, "FUNLOG: A computational model integrating functional and logic programming," in *Logic Programming: Relations, Functions and Equations*, D. DeGroot and G. Lindstrom, Eds. Englewood Cliffs, NJ: Prentice-Hall, 1985.

[21] S. Julien, "Graphics in micro-Prolog," Dep. Comput. Sci., Imperial College, London, England, Tech. Rep. 82-17, 1982.

[22] R. A. Kowalski, *Logic for Problem Solving*. New York: Elsevier North-Holland, 1979.

[23] K. Furukawa, A. Takeuchi, H. Yasukawa, and S. Kunifuji, "Mandala: A logic based knowledge programming," in *Proc. Int. Conf. 5th Generation Comput. Syst.*, Nov. 1984.

[24] Z. S. Markusz, "Logic based programming method and its applications for architectural design problems," (in Hungarion), Ph.D. dissertation, Eotvos Lorand Univ., Budapest, Hungary, 1980.

[25] K. L. Clark and F. G. McCabe, "Prolog: A language for implementing expert systems," in *Machine Intelligence 10*, J. E. Hayes, D. Michie, and Y. Pao, 1982.

[26] —, *Micro-Prolog: Programming in Logic*. Englewood Cliffs, NJ: Prentice-Hall, 1984.

[27] W. F. Clocksin and C. S. Mellish, *Programming in Prolog*, 2nd ed. New York: Springer-Verlag, 1984.

[28] H. Gallaire and J. Minker, Eds., *Logic and Database*. New York: Plenum, 1978.

[29] H. Nakashima, "Knowledge representation in Prolog/KR," in *Proc.*

45

1984 Int. Symp. Logic Program., IEEE Press, Feb. 1984, pp. 126–131.

[30] F. Mizoguchi, Y. Katayama, and H. Owada, "LOOKS: Knowledge representation system for designing expert system in the framework of logic programming," in *Proc. Int. Conf. 5th Generation Comput. Syst.*, Nov. 1984.

[31] P. Henderson, *Functional Programming.* Englewood Cliffs, NJ: Prentice-Hall, 1980.

[32] D. H. D. Warren, L. M. Pereira, and F. C. N. Pereira, "Prolog: The language and its implementation compared with LISP," in *Proc. Symp. Artificial Intell. and Program. Lang.* (SIGPLAN Notices/SIGART Notices, vol. 12, no. 8), Aug. 1977, pp. 109–115.

[33] R. G. Bandes, "Constraining unification and the programming language unicorn," in *Proc. 11th Annu. ACM Symp. Principles of Program. Lang.*, ACM, Jan. 1984.

[34] J. A. Robinson, "A machine-oriented logic based on the resolution principle," *J. ACM*, vol. 12, no. 1, pp. 23–41, Jan. 1965.

[35] M. J. Sergot, "Prospects for Representing the Law as Logic Programs," *Logic Programming*, Academic Press, (1982). A.P.I.C. Studies in Data Processing No. 16.

[36] ——, "A query-the-user facility for logic programs," in *Integrated Interactive Computer Systems*, P. Degano and E. Sandwell, Eds. 1983.

[37] E. Y. Shapiro, "Systems programming in concurrent Prolog," in *Proc. ACM Symp. Principles of Program. Lang.*, Jan. 1984.

[38] *The Logic WorkBench*, Silogic, Inc., Los Angeles, CA, 1985.

[39] *POPLOG*, Systems Designers Software, Inc., Falls Church, VA, Mar. 1985.

[40] D. G. Bobrow and M. Stefik, "The LOOPS manual," Memo KB-VLSI-81-13, Aug. 1981.

[41] N. Suzuki, "Concurrent Prolog as an efficient VLSI design language," *Computer*, pp. 33–40, Feb. 1985.

[42] W. R. Swartout, "XPLAIN: A system for creating and explaining expert consulting programs," *Artificial Intell.*, vol. 21, pp. 285–325, 1983.

[43] *Zetalisp Reference Manual*, Symbolics, Cambridge, MA, 1984.

[44] *Quintus Prolog*, Quintus Computer Systems, Inc., Palo Alto, CA, 1985.

[45] F. Darvas, I. Futo, and P. Szeredi, "A logic based program system for predicting drug interactions," *Int. J. Biomed. Comput.*, vol. 9, no. 4, 1977.

[46] D. G. Bobrow and T. Winograd, "An overview of KRL-0, a knowledge representation language," *Cogn. Sci.*, 1977.

[47] Y. Ogawa, K. Shima, T. Sugawara, and S. Takagi, "KRINE—An approach to integration of frame, prolog and graphics," in *Proc. Int. Conf. 5th Generation Comput. Syst.*, Nov. 1984, p. 643.

[48] W. Teitelman, *The Interlisp Reference Manual*, Xerox Palo Alto Research Center, Palo Alto, CA, Aug. 1979.

[49] *SI User's Manual*, Teknowledge Inc., CA, 1984.

[50] W. Teitelman, "A tour through Cedar," *IEEE Trans. Software Eng.*, vol. SE-11, pp. 285–301, Mar. 1985.

[51] J. Fain, D. Gorlin, F. Hayes-Roth, S. Rosenschein, H. Sowizral, and D. Waterman, "The ROSIE Language Reference Manual," Rand Corp., Rep. N-1647-ARPA, 1981.

[52] B. P. Allen and J. M. Wright, "Integrating logic programs and schemata," *IJCAI*, pp. 340–342, 1983.

[53] C. Zaniolo, "Object oriented logic programming," in *Proc. 1st Int. Conf. Logic Program.*, 1984, pp. 265–270.

[54] I. P. Goldstein *et al.*, "HPRL reference manual," Hewlett Packard Res. Lab., 1984.

[55] F. Darvas *et al.*, "A Prolog-based drug design system," (in Hungarian), in *Proc. Conf. Program.Syst.*, 1978.

PROLOG FOR EXPERT SYSTEMS: AN EVALUATION

A. Richard Helm, Kimbal Marriott

Catherine Lassez

Department of Computer Science
University of Melbourne
Parkville, 3052, Australia

IBM Thomas J. Watson Research Center
Yorktown Heights
New York, 10598, USA

Abstract

Through two case studies, TEAS and MARLOWE, Prolog is evaluated both as a language for writing expert systems shells and as a language for knowledge representation. These systems were chosen because they represent two different classes of expert system. TEAS uses exact inference and is concerned with representing government legislation. MARLOWE is used for white collar crime risk analysis and is an example of systems that reason with uncertain data or knowledge where both the domain and the expert's knowledge may be imprecise.

Introduction - Expert Systems and Prolog

Expert systems are computer programs that model an expert's problem solving skills in a domain of expertise. They are usually composed of a knowledge base, and mechanisms for symbolic reasoning, intelligent search and explanation[28].

The expert's knowledge is often represented in the knowledge base as production rules of the form

if condition do action

The expert system's inference mechanism controls how these rules are used to infer conclusions from the input data. Most commonly the inference is goal directed or backward chained, the rules are used to repeatedly generate sub-goals that must in turn be satisfied. Alternatively, the inference may be forward chained, the system repeatedly applies satisfied rules, inferring new data from old to be used in subsequent inferences. Combinations of these two approaches may be used to implement more complex inference mechanisms such as PROSPECTOR's[18] model driven inference which uses models best fitting the "current state of the world" to generate goals.

The first expert systems such as MYCIN[4], EXPERT[52] and PROSPECTOR were written in specialized languages implemented on top of an existing language such as Fortran or Lisp. The effort required to construct these early expert systems has led to the development of expert system shells. An expert system shell is best described as an expert system with the expert's knowledge removed. Usually it contains an inference mechanism (or number of inference mechanisms), explanation facilities, and tools to aid the construction and debugging of an expert system. For example EMYCIN is MYCIN without its medical knowledge. Although such shells may simplify the construction of expert systems, several studies[15,20] have suggested that shells are not general purpose construction aids. An alternative is to use a general purpose

expert systems programming language such as ROSIE[21], RLL[26], OPS[22,23] or recent commercially developed environments such as IntelliCorp's KEE, Teknowledge's S.1 or LOOPS[2].

The programming language Prolog has also been used for constructing expert systems. This language has received recent world wide attention through the Japanese Fifth Generation Project[24]. In Europe, Prolog has been used to implement a variety of expert systems, for instance in Hungary, systems for drug design[17], drug interaction[16] and architectural design[36]. Recently, a large project has been undertaken at Imperial College in London for representing legislation[13,44,43].

Prolog is a general purpose rule based language with a backward chaining inference mechanism[9,10]. Prolog is easy to learn and its versatility has been demonstrated by its use in VLSI design and modeling[49], graphics[31], deductive databases[39] and even systems programming[48,8].

The United States reluctant acceptance of Prolog, compared with Lisp's, is partly attributable to Prolog's poor programming environment, inefficient implementation and lack of hardware support. However, compiled Prolog is as (in)efficient as Lisp[51] and forthcoming commercial versions will correct these shortcomings.

This paper critically examines Prolog's suitability for constructing expert systems. Through two case studies, TEAS and MARLOWE, Prolog is evaluated both as a language for writing expert system shells and as a language for knowledge representation. These systems were chosen because they represent two different classes of expert system. TEAS uses exact inference and is concerned with representing government legislation and is described in section 2 which also introduces Prolog. Section 3 presents MARLOWE which is used for white collar crime risk analysis and is an example of systems that reason with uncertain data or knowledge where both the domain and the expert's knowledge may be imprecise. Section 4 contains a further discussion of Prolog's properties and limitations for knowledge representation and expert system construction. Finally, section 5 discusses Prolog expert system shells and includes two examples that provide a basis for constructing forward and backward chaining shells. A list of commercially available Prolog systems is given in the appendix.

Case Study I - The Tertiary Education Assistance Scheme (TEAS).

The Tertiary Education Assistance Scheme (TEAS) is an Australian government scheme to provide financial assistance for students in tertiary education. This scheme is governed by

Reprinted from *Proc. IEEE Expert Systems in Government Symp.*, pp. 284–294, Oct. 1985.

the Student Assistance Act 1973 and its Regulations. The TEAS system was developed to assist students applying for tertiary assistance by determining a student's eligibility and calculating the entitled allowance.

TEAS regulations as Prolog clauses.

Government regulations are usually expressed as rules. For example, the TEAS document[12] states the general eligibility requirements to be:

> To be eligible for TEAS, in addition to undertaking an approved course you (the applicant) must meet requirements in relation to:
> - citizenship
> - obligation to an employer
> - other commonwealth assistance
> - full time study
> - satisfactory progress in previous year
> - previous study in another course.

and the definition of valid citizenship status as being

> You have a valid citizenship status if you are an Australian citizen, or a permanent resident of Australia, or if you have applied for and are likely to be granted permanent residency.

This can be translated into the Prolog rules

> X is_eligible if
>   X has_valid_citizenship_status and
>   not X has_obligation_to_employer and
>   not X receives_other_assistance and
>   X full_time_student_in_approved_course and
>   X has_made_satisfactory_prior_progress and
>   not X disqualified_by_previous_study
>
> X has_valid_citizenship_status if
>   X is_Australian_citizen or
>   X has_permanent_resident_permit or
>   X has_applied_for_and_is_likely_to_be_granted_residency

where X denotes the applicant.

A more complex example is the determination of the amount of allowance. The benefits are described as follows:

> TEAS provide four benefits:
> - living allowance
> - Incidentals allowance
> - Allowance for a dependent spouse and/or child
> - Fares allowance
>
> Living allowance is paid subject to an income test. A student must qualify for living allowance to receive the other allowances.

This is interpreted as:

> If the living allowance is greater than 0 then the benefits are the sum of the living allowance, the incidentals allowance, the dependents allowance and the fares allowance otherwise the benefit is 0.

and translated as:

> amount_of_benefits_is X if
>   living_allowance_is Y1 and
>   either
>   Y1 > 0 and
>   incidentals_allowance_is Y2 and
>   dependents_allowance_is Y3 and
>   fares_allowance_is Y4 and
>   X = Y1 + Y2 + Y3 + Y4
>   or
>   X = 0

The entire set of regulations can be expressed in this way.

The above rules may be used to determine a student's eligibility. Given the following facts about *Peter* and *John*:

> Peter is_Australian_citizen
> Peter full_time_student_in_approved_course
> Peter has_made_satisfactory_prior_progress
>
> John has_permanent_resident_permit
> John full_time_student_in_approved_course

the fact:

> Peter is_eligible

may be concluded from the program because each condition in the first rule can be proved. For example *Peter has_valid_citizenship_status* is true because it follows from the second rule and the fact *Peter is_Australian_citizen*. The condition *not Peter has_obligation_to_employer* is true because *Peter has_obligation_to_employer* cannot be proved from the facts. Hence Prolog will answer *yes* to the query *Peter is_eligible ?*. However Prolog will answer *no* to the query

> John is_eligible ?

The query fails because the condition *John has_made_satisfactory_prior_progress* cannot be proved.

Prolog assumes that all relevant facts and rules are in the program. Only facts which follow from the program are considered to be true. If something can be shown not to follow from the program it is assumed not to be true. This is described more fully in[32,6].

Although Prolog assumes that all information relevant to each applicant is present in the program, in this case *Peter* and *John*, it may not always be practical to include this information before asking a query. If information is missing, it would be better if the user was prompted to provide it, allowing the interactive evaluation of queries.

Not unnaturally, applicants would like an explanation of the reasoning used to evaluate their application. Prolog does not provide such explanation. However, the evaluation trace of a query can be used for that purpose.

As we shall see in the next section, Prolog expert system shells provide interaction and explanation.

TEAS implemented in APES

APES[27], the first commercially available Prolog expert system shell, augments micro-Prolog[9] by adding interaction and explanation. The major features of APES are:

- interaction: APES provides interaction by implementing Query-the-User[45]. Query-the-User determines which questions are to be asked and, before recording the user's answers, performs validity and consistency checks.

- explanation: Upon request, APES provides explanations by displaying an edited execution trace. This describes how rules and facts were used to evaluate a query.

- user interface: Templates enable queries, rules and facts to be displayed in a natural language.

Interaction Query-the-User treats the user as an extension of the program. Necessary facts not found in the program but required during a query's evaluation may be elicited from the user. In the previous example the query *John is_eligible* failed because the program contains insufficient information about John. However, with Query-the-User, Prolog will ask

Is John has_made_satisfactory_prior_progress true?

Replying *yes* will, in effect, add the fact

John has_made_satisfactory_prior_progress

to the program and enable the query to succeed. Replying *no* will cause the query to fail as before.

Facts provided by the user are checked for consistency with the knowledge already in the program. If consistent, they are recorded so previously asked questions will not be asked again.

Answers to questions may be validated against conditions contained in the program. For example, a student's age can be checked by

valid Age if
    Age > 0 and
    Age < 99

Invalid answers produce a warning message and the question is asked again.

Explanation After a query is evaluated, the user may request an explanation. For instance, the explanation of the answer to the query *Peter is_eligible ?* appears below. User's responses are in bold type.

To deduce that
    Peter is_eligible
I used the rule:
X is-eligible if
    X has_valid_citizenship_status and
    not X has_obligation_to_employer and
    not X receives_other_assistance and
    X full_time_student_in_an_approved_course and
    X has_made_satisfactory_prior_progress and
    not X disqualified_by_previous_study

I can also show that
  1 Peter has_valid_citizenship_status
  2 not Peter has_obligation_to_employer
  3 not Peter receives_other_assistance
  4 Peter full_time_student_in_an_approved_course
  5 Peter has_made_satisfactory_prior_progress
  6 not Peter disqualified_by_previous_study
Type a number: **1**

To deduce that
    Peter has_valid_citizenship_status
I used the rule:
X has_valid_citizenship_status if
    X is_Australian_citizen or
    X has_permanent_resident_permit or
    X has_applied_for_and_is_likely_to_be_granted_residency

I can also show that
  1 Peter is_Australian_citizen
Type a number: **1**

Peter is_Australian_citizen is a fact.

User Interface Natural language templates can be used for the display of rules during explanation and to replace the standard question formats. For instance the previous question:

Is John has_made_satisfactory_prior_progress true?

can be replaced by:

Has John's prior progress been satisfactory
(see Reference R12 for more information) ?

or

Est-ce que les progrès de John jusqu'ici ont été satisfaisants?

Summary of Case Study I

Most of the TEAS system was developed as a term project by students who had no prior knowledge of Prolog. The complete system contains approximately 60 rules plus the templates. It runs on an IBM-PC.

Our experience with TEAS and a system currently under development for Australian Social Security Legislation suggests that Prolog's rules provide a natural representation of legislation and regulations. In most instances Prolog's rules correspond to the actual wording of the regulations and Prolog's evaluation of queries is easily understood.

The TEAS regulations change from year to year. Implementing those changes is easily done because Prolog programs, in common with other production systems, are modular. Individual rules or sets of rules can be tested and modified independently from the rest of the program. Only those rules representing regulations that are changed need to be rewritten; the rest of the program is not altered. This simplifies program development and maintenance.

The case study suggests that APES is suitable for applications
- which require exact reasoning
- which have a straightforward correspondence between the expert system rules

and the domain knowledge
- for which Prolog's inference mechanism is appropriate.

However, some problems were encountered and these are explored in section 4.

Case Study II - MARLOWE

MARLOWE is a prototype expert system designed to evaluate the risk of white collar crimes, such as redirected cheques, unapproved requisitions or kickbacks, that may occur in management systems. MARLOWE can also be used as a management tool, suggesting additional controls and detection procedures that may reduce risks to acceptable levels. It also allows management to simulate changes in policy and then check for possibly introduced risks.

MARLOWE is being developed in collaboration with Kevin Fitzgerald from the Chisholm Institute of Technology's Computer Abuse Research Bureau (CIT-CARB). Kevin, our expert, is one of Australia's leading consultants in the analysis of an organization's risks arising from computer related crime which includes clerical, programming and telecommunication based crime.

MARLOWE's operation corresponds to the way our expert performs his risk analysis. Like our expert, MARLOWE uses a collection of "typical" white collar crime models to determine if a crime may occur. Each crime model is representative of a class of similar crimes. It consists of possible *modi operandi* that describe how the typical crime can be committed. A model includes necessary conditions for each *modus operandi* to occur. The conditions state tools, such as documents or bank accounts, that the perpetrator requires and specify the breaches of standard company practice that must occur for the crime to take place. To evaluate a risk, MARLOWE first evaluates the model's conditions to determine if a particular crime may occur. It then determines if management controls are present that will detect the occurrence of the crime. Finally, MARLOWE produces a summary of risks, possible *modi operandi* and whether or not the crime is likely to be detected.

The Kickback Crime Model

The kickback crime model is a typical crime model. This model's *modus operandi* is:

"A potential perpetrator, the Accounts Clerk or Purchasing Officer say, enters into a collusive agreement with a supplier to provide favoured treatment of a supplier. This may be unfair

selection of supplier, early payment of invoices or preferential allocation of payment terms. In return, the perpetrator(s) will receive a kickback of goods, services or funds."

Unfair supplier selection may occur if the potential perpetrator
- has social contact with supplier
- has job sovereignty in allocating supplier

The crime is more difficult to commit if
- there are written quotes
- single quotes are not allowed

These conditions may be translated into the Prolog rule:

opportunity_for kickback
through unfair_supplier_selection by Person if
    Person does supplier_selection and
    Person has_social_contact_with_supplier and
    Person has_job_sovereignty_in supplier_selection and
    not (written_quotes and not single_quotes_allowed)

The other conditions associated with MARLOWE's crime models are described using rules similar to the one above. The risk of kickback is determined using the rule:

risk kickback if
    any_of
    opportunity_for kickback
        through unfair_supplier_selection by Person
    opportunity_for kickback
        through early_invoice_payment by Person
    opportunity_for kickback
        through preferential_terms by Person
    are_true

Evaluating Crime Models

The evaluation of a crime model by MARLOWE and our expert is imprecise. This is because both MARLOWE and our expert

- *must deal with uncertain data*

For example it is difficult for the user to determine whether the condition

Person has_social_contact_with_supplier

is false. The user might know that they have social contact, but he cannot be sure that they do not.

- *use crime models that are necessarily incomplete*

Crime models are incomplete because describing every possible *modus operandi* precisely is impractical. Criminal ingenuity is seemingly boundless. For example, even though the condition

not (written_quotes and not single_quotes_allowed)

might be false, our expert, although unsure of what the precise *modus operandi* would be, still felt a sufficiently motivated criminal could commit the crime.

MARLOWE determines the risk of a crime being committed by evaluating the associated model's conditions. Like our expert, MARLOWE does not reject a model if some of the conditions are not met, rather, it just states that the crime is less likely to occur. To enable MARLOWE to perform and explain its risk analysis, MARLOWE's shell implements a mechanism that returns the truth value of any condition, regardless of whether or not it is satisfied.

MARLOWE's shell also provides APES-like explanations, interaction based on Query-the-User, templates and justifications for its rules and questions. MARLOWE's operation is illustrated in the following sample session:

MARLOWE can evaluate the risk of
1 Kickback
2 Illegitimate purchasing : Individual Scheme
3 Extra charges Approved
4 Unapproved Manual Cheques
5 Redirected Cheques
Other Options
6 abort
Select item: **1**

Does the Purchasing Officer have possibility of social contact with supplier ? **yes**

Does the Purchasing Officer have job sovereignty for the task supplier_selection ? **yes**

Do there exist written quotes ? **yes**

Are single quotes allowed ? **no**

There is some risk of:
kickback through
unfair_supplier_selection by the Purchasing Officer

This is because the following conditions suggest it can occur:
Purchasing Officer has_social_contact_with_supplier
Purchasing Officer has_job_sovereignty_in supplier_selection

While the following conditions suggest it cannot occur:
not(written_quotes and not single_quotes_allowed)

Do you require an explanation ? **no**

Note that MARLOWE considers there is some risk of kickback, even though the condition *not(written_quotes and not single_quotes_allowed)* was not satisfied.

In addition to APES-like explanations of how a risk was determined, MARLOWE also provides justification for its rules and questions. Justification is different to explanation[50]. Whereas an explanation describes how the program's rules are used by the program when making a decision, justification relates the rules and concepts in the program to the real world. Justifications contain the expert's implicit knowledge that was used to design the system's rules. MARLOWE, if asked to justify the question about job sovereignty, would produce:

Does the Purchasing Officer have job sovereignty in the task supplier_selection ? **justify**

The Purchasing Officer has job sovereignty if he has sole responsibility for the task supplier_selection. This means that breaches involving this task will remain undetected.

MARLOWE when asked to justify the previous rule pertaining to kickback through unfair supplier selection will generate:

The modus operandi for kickback
through unfair_supplier_selection is:
(1) Purchasing Officer meets the supplier socially
(2) Purchasing Officer enters into collusive agreement with supplier to bias selection in favour of the supplier
(3) Purchasing Officer performs biased selection of supplier, to do this Purchasing Officer requires sovereignty in the selection task
(4) Purchasing Officer receives kickback of goods, services or funds from the supplier

Biased selection of supplier may be detected if more than one written quote is required

Summary of Case Study II

This case study has described MARLOWE, a Prolog expert system for a domain requiring inexact reasoning. MARLOWE uses "typical" crime models that are inexactly matched against an organization's environment. In contrast, because of the vast number of different *modi operandi* for any given crime, an exact approach, in which every possible crime is explicitly enumerated, is not feasible.

Although MARLOWE uses inexact reasoning, a probabilistic approach like that of EMYCIN or PROSPECTOR was not used. Our expert felt this approach was not relevant as he did not use probabilities in his analysis; moreover little empirical data exists upon which to base the probabilities. If probabilistic reasoning had been required, a specific shell in Prolog could have been easily built[47].

We found that Prolog was easily understood by our expert. Initially unfamiliar with Prolog, within a short time he was reading and suggesting modifications to MARLOWE's rules.

MARLOWE is currently implemented for the sub-domain of Accounts Payable systems and contains the five crime models named in the example. MARLOWE's specially designed expert system shell was written in Prolog in less than a man week.

Some Limitations of Prolog for Expert Systems

Prolog for Knowledge Representation

Methods for knowledge representation in Prolog include hierarchical frame based representations[41,38], actor formalisms[25], schema-based techniques[1] and 'isa' hierarchies[53]. MARLOWE and TEAS represent their respective domain knowledge only as Prolog rules and facts. This section investigates the limitations of such a representation.

As we have seen, knowledge may be represented in Prolog using rules and facts. Rules are of the form:

A if B

which states that if the conditions in the body *B* hold then the head *A* may be concluded to be true. Facts are always true.

The major problem with Prolog rules for knowledge representation is that they cannot explicitly represent negative information. A Prolog rule cannot be of the form:

not A if B

It cannot state the head *A* is not true if the conditions in the body *B* hold.

The need to represent negative information does arise. For instance, the initial regulation from the TEAS case study:

> You have a valid citizenship status if you are an Australian citizen or a permanent resident of Australia or if you have applied for and are likely to be granted permanent residency.

governing a student's valid citizenship status was amended to be:

> You have a valid citizenship status if you are an Australian citizen or a permanent resident of Australia. If you have a temporary entry permit you are not eligible.

To affect this amendment, the rule for *has_valid_citizenship_status* was rewritten as:

> *X has_valid_citizenship_status if*
> *X is_Australian_citizen or*
> *X has_permanent_resident_permit*

Although the obvious rule

> *not X is_eligible if X has_temporary_entry_permit*

corresponds to

> If you have a temporary entry permit you are not eligible

it is not a valid Prolog rule. However, the new rule for *has_valid_citizenship_status* and the definition of *is_eligible* from case study I implicitly state:

> *X is_eligible if and only if*
> *X has_valid_citizenship_status and*
> *not X has_obligation_to_employer and*
> *not X receives_other_assistance and*
> *X full_time_student_in_approved_course and*
> *X has_made_satisfactory_prior_progress and*
> *not X disqualified_by_previous_study*

> *X has_valid_citizenship_status if and only if*
> *X is_Australian_citizen or*
> *X has_permanent_resident_permit*

This is because the program contains no other rules for *is_eligible* and *has_valid_citizenship_status*. Hence the additional rule is not necessary. But this is unsatisfactory because the program contains no mention of the second half of the amendment.

If the amendment needs to appear explicitly there are other solutions which are all unsatisfactory to varying degrees, but this is beyond the scope of this paper. The interested reader is referred to program completions [32,6].

Recently, these difficulties have been discussed in solutions to the "Alpine Club Problem"[35] which have appeared on the computer network[*]. The Alpine Club Problem requires the representation of negative information. Part of the problem is to formulate

> Mike likes whatever Tony dislikes and dislikes whatever Tony likes.

as Prolog rules. A naive translation results in illegal Prolog rules. One possible representation[**] is:

> *likes(Mike, X, true) if*
> *likes(Tony, X, false)*
> *likes(Mike, X, false) if*
> *likes(Tony, X, true)*

This representation is quite natural. However, rather than using Prolog's underlying mechanism, a program containing these rules must be able to reason about the logical connection between *likes(Y, Z, true)* and *likes(Y, Z, false)*.

Although it is difficult to represent negative information with Prolog rules, these examples have shown that solutions may be found through a better understanding of Prolog and some ingenuity. Furthermore, Hammond and Sergot's experience with the British Nationality Act Project[13] and our experience with TEAS and MARLOWE suggests that, at least for these expert systems, this problem is not common.

Prolog's Inference Mechanism

Like the majority of expert systems, Prolog uses a backward chained inference mechanism. This section discusses its inherent limitations and their impact on expert systems.

Prolog's inference mechanism is natural and easy to understand. Prolog tries to determine the truth of a query in two ways. First, since facts in a program are always true, a query is concluded to be true if it matches a fact. Second, a query is concluded to be true if it matches the head *A* of a rule *A if B* and the query *B* can be concluded to be true. Hence if all queries eventually match with facts, the initial query is evaluated to be true. If the matching of query to fact or rule fails and there exist untried alternative rules or facts, Prolog will backtrack and try these alternatives. If all alternatives fail, the initial query is assumed false.

Prolog considers rules in their textual order and queries are evaluated from left to right. This is Prolog's computation rule. A complete treatment may be found in [32,30].

Prolog's computation rule is simple, fast and easy to implement. However it may lead to problems with programs containing recursive rules or negation. These problems are also encountered in expert systems whose shells inherit Prolog's

---

[*] USENET's Prolog Digest and net.lang.prolog.

[**] Using a standard prefix notation for the rules.

computation rule. Such shells also have problems involving interaction and explanation.

Recursion The use of recursive rules may lead to infinite computations. For example, given the program

```
X is_a Y if
    X is_a Z and
    Z is_a Y

kangaroo is_a marsupial
marsupial is_a mammal
platypus is_a monotreme
echidna is_a monotreme
monotreme is_a mammal
```

and the query

```
kangaroo is_a mammal ?
```

Prolog will perform an infinite computation because the rule is repeatedly used; the facts are never considered. If the facts are placed before the rule the query succeeds.

However the query

```
mammal is_a kangaroo ?
```

will also cause Prolog to perform an infinite computation rather than failing as one would expect. To eliminate this problem, the program may be rewritten as

```
X is_a Y if
    X type_of Y
X is_a Y if
    X type_of Z and
    Z is_a Y

kangaroo type_of marsupial
marsupial type_of mammal
platypus type_of monotreme
echidna type_of monotreme
monotreme type_of mammal
```

This program behaves as expected for all queries.

It may also be necessary to consider the memory requirements of recursive programs. Memory usage may be significantly reduced by using a Prolog implementation with Tail Recursive Optimization(TRO) [9] and appropriately rewriting the program.

Negation Another problem arising from Prolog's fixed left to right query evaluation may occur when negation appears in the body of a rule or as part of a query. For example, consider the following fact

```
tony is_a_name
```

The query

```
X = fred and not X is_a_name
```

will succeed whereas the query

```
not X is_a_name and X = fred
```

will fail. Clearly this is inconsistent.

When evaluating a query containing *not*, if the argument to *not* still contains variables, inconsistent results may occur. Hence,

negation must be used cautiously. Fortunately, in some Prolog implementations, for example MU-Prolog[40], the evaluation of *not* delays until all variables are bound.

The problems associated with negation and recursion may be avoided, but this requires an understanding of Prolog's computation rule.

Interaction and Explanation

APES is a backward chained expert system shell which inherits Prolog's computation rule. Using this computation rule with interactive programs may lead to the following problems.

Regardless of the original query, questions arising from a given Prolog rule are always asked in exactly the same sequence. If APES uses a Prolog rule in different ways, it may ask questions that seem out of context resulting in an obscure sequence of questions to the user. This problem has also been noted in[45].

Another reason why APES may ask questions that seem out of context is because the computation rule does not implement intelligent backtracking. For example, the query *Peter is_eligible ?* leads to the following dialogue with TEAS

```
Is Peter an Australian citizen ? yes
Does Peter have an obligation to an employer ? yes
```

At this point, because the condition *not Peter has_obligation_to_employer* is not true, APES backtracks looking for alternative ways to satisfy the query. This leads to the question

```
Does Peter have a permanent resident permit ?
```

which should not be asked as any answer to this question will not change the reason for failure. Previously, intelligent backtracking for Prolog has been considered for reasons of efficiency[14,3,5]. We suggest intelligent backtracking is also necessary to obtain the desired behaviour of interactive programs.

Furthermore APES cannot explain why and where backtracking has occurred during the successful evaluation of a query. Given the rules

```
Student receives_an_allowance_of X if
    Student adjusted_income_is Y and
    X = 3870 - Y and
    X > 0
Student receives_an_allowance_of 0
```

and the query

```
Ann receives_an_allowance_of X ?
```

the following dialogue is generated:

```
What is Ann's gross income ? 6500
Ann receives_an_allowance_of 0 how
Ann receives_an_allowance_of 0 is a fact
```

APES simply states that the second rule was used without explaining that the first rule has failed. This is clearly inadequate.

Building Expert System Shells in Prolog

Our experience and that of other researchers[15,20] suggest that a general purpose expert system shell is not suitable for all applications.

An expert system shell may need to provide task specific features for inference and explanation. Inexact reasoning and an application dependent computation rule might be needed to emulate the expert's reasoning process and justification may need to be provided if there is not an obvious correspondence between the knowledge and its representation. As we have seen, a shell determines the expert system's inference mechanism and knowledge representation. It will be satisfactory only if its implicit expert system's domain is sufficiently similar to the application's domain. An unsuitable shell will result in an unsatisfactory system. In many circumstances, the expert system's shell must be designed specifically for the application; required domain specific features must be added to an existing shell or a new shell constructed.

Building a Prolog expert system shell enables the expert system designer to construct domain specific control and include either Prolog's rule base knowledge representation or more complex knowledge representation schemes. Since Prolog's pattern matching (unification[42]), rule based knowledge representation, backward chaining and backtracking mechanisms can be inherited directly from Prolog, they need not be explicitly implemented, greatly simplifying the shell's construction. This is illustrated by the following two interpreters which may be used as the basis for forward and backward chaining shells.

The following Prolog program is a backward chaining Prolog interpreter, inheriting unification, Prolog's rule based knowledge representation, backtracking and Prolog's computation rule. It may be used as the basis for backward chained shells such as APES and MARLOWE's and is concisely and elegantly written in just three rules.

```
interp (true)
interp (A and B) if
    interp (A) and
    interp (B)
interp (A) if
    rule (A if B) and
    interp (B)
```

where *rule(A if B)* matches rules and facts in the program. Facts are represented internally by Prolog as rules of the form *A if true*.

This interpreter may easily be extended to provide Query-the-User*. This is done by adding the following rules.

---

* This interpreter implements a version of Query-the-User for facts that contain no variables.

```
interp(A) if
    not A is_a_compound_query and
    not rule(A if B) and
    told(A).

told(A) if
    was_told(A,yes).
told(A) if
    not was_told(A,X) and
    writeln(['Is',A,' true ?']) and
    read(Ans) and
    assert( was_told(A,Ans)) and
    told(A).

C and D is_a_compound_query
```

where *assert(P)* adds the fact or rule *P* to the program.

This backward chained interpreter for Prolog can be also extended to keep execution traces for explanations as in APES, to implement probabilistic reasoning[47] for EMYCIN-like systems, to provide justifications like MARLOWE or even debugging features[46]. The construction of shells similar to APES is discussed further in [7].

It is just as easy to implement a forward chaining Prolog rule interpreter.

```
forw if
    termination
forw if
    rule (if Condition do Action) and
    Condition and
    Action and
    forw
```

The first rule evaluates a termination condition and the second performs the repeated evaluation and application of rules. This forward chaining inference mechanism's conflict resolution scheme and working memory structure[37] are determined by Prolog's computation rule.

Conclusion

Prolog can be used for knowledge representation, expert system shell construction, and as a general purpose programming language.

The representation of knowledge as Prolog rules is, in most cases, simple and natural. However the representation of negative knowledge as Prolog rules has difficulties which, with care, may be overcome. Our experience with TEAS and MARLOWE suggests this problem occurs rarely during the development of expert systems.

Prolog is particularly suited to the development of expert system shells because Prolog's pattern matching, rule based knowledge representation, backtracking and backward chaining are directly inherited. General purpose expert system shells are not suitable for all applications. But because Prolog is a versatile programming language, any required domain specific features may be implemented. MARLOWE's development has demonstrated how easily a backward chained expert system shell may be constructed. We have indicated how both forward chained and probability based expert system shells may be simply and elegantly implemented in Prolog.

Prolog was originally developed for natural language understanding[11]. Recent research in language understanding and graphics promises a natural user interface to expert systems developed in Prolog.

Prolog is easy to learn; a number of countries use Prolog to teach computer programming to children[33,34,19]. Hence an expert can rapidly learn to understand, without the mediation of the knowledge engineer, not only how knowledge is represented in Prolog but also how it is used within the expert system.

Since Prolog is available on micro-computers, it is easily accessible and does not require a large financial outlay for specialized hardware and software. And because a demonstrable expert system need only contain about 50-100 rules[15,29], Prolog allows the cheap and rapid prototyping of expert systems.

Acknowledgements

The authors wish to thank Jean-Louis Lassez for his continued support and many helpful discussions. Also they wish to thank Graeme Port and Rajeev Gore for their valuable comments on an earlier draft of this paper. Richard Helm and Kimbal Marriott especially wish to thank Kevin Fitzgerald, MARLOWE's expert, and also bbJ Computer Services for their assistance with the MARLOWE project. The authors also wish to thank Bruce Smith for his kind permission to use entries from his list of Prolog implementations and to thank Isaac Balbin for the use of the extensive logic programming bibliography from his and Conrad Leucot's forthcoming book.

References

[1] B.P. Allen and J.M. Wright, Integrating Logic Programs and Schemata, *International Joint Conference on Artificial Intelligence-83*, , 340-342.

[2] D. G. Bobrow and M. Stefik, The LOOPS Manual, Memo KB-VLSI-81-13, Xerox Palo Alto Research Center, California, Aug 1981, rev. 1982.

[3] M. Bruynooghe and L.M. Pereira, Deductive Revision by Intelligent Backtracking, in *Implementations of Prolog*, Artificial Intelligence, J.A. Campbell, (ed.), Ellis Horwood, 1984, 194-215.

[4] *Rule-Based Expert Systems: The MYCIN Experiments of the Stanford Heuristic Programming Project*, B.G. Buchanan and E.H. Shortliffe, eds., Addison-Wesley, 1984.

[5] T.Y. Chen, J.-L. Lassez and G.S. Port, Maximal Unifiable Subsets and Minimal Non-Unifiable Subsets, Technical Report 84/16, Dept. of Computer Science, University of Melbourne, 1984.

[6] K.L. Clark, Negation as Failure, in *Logic and Databases*, H. Gallaire and J. Minker, (eds.), Plenum Press, 1978.

[7] K.L. Clark and F.G. McCabe, PROLOG: A Language for Implementing Expert Systems, *Machine Intelligence 10*, 1982.

[8] K.L. Clark and S. Gregory, Notes on Systems Programming in PARLOG, *Proceedings of the International Conference on Fifth Generation Computer Systems 1984*, Tokyo, November 1984, 229-306.

[9] *Micro-Prolog: Programming in Logic*, K.L. Clark and F.G. McCabe, eds., Prentice Hall, 1984.

[10] W.F. Clocksin and C.S. Mellish, *Programming in Prolog*, Springer Verlag (2nd Edition), New York, 1984.

[11] A. Colmerauer, H. Kanoui, R. Pasero and P. Roussel, Un Systeme de Communication Homme-Machine en Francais, Rapport Technique, Groupe d'Intelligence Artificielle, Univ d'Aix Marseille, Luminy, 1973.

[12] *Tertiary Education Assistance Scheme 1985: Information for Applicants*, Commonwealth Department of Education and Youth Affairs, 1985.

[13] H.T. Cory, P. Hammond, R.A. Kowalski, F.R. Kriwaczek, F. Sadri and M.J. Sergot, The British Nationality Act As A Logic Program, Department of Computing, Imperial College, 1984.

[14] P.T. Cox, Finding Backtrack Points for Intelligent Backtracking, in *Implementations of Prolog*, Artificial Intelligence, J.A. Campbell, (ed.), Ellis Horwood, 1984, 216-233.

[15] A. d'Agapeyeff, Report to the Alvey Directorate on a Short Survey of Expert Systems in Business, *Alvey News. Supplement to Issue 4.*, London, April 1984.

[16] F. Darvas, I. Futo and P. Szeredi, A Logic Based Program System for Predicting Drug Interactions, *International Journal of Biomedical Computing 9*, 4 (1977).

[17] F. Darvas and Others, A Prolog-Based Drug Design System, *Proc. of Conf. on Programming Systems*, Zseged, Hungary, 1978. In Hungarian.

[18] Richard Duda, John Gashnig and Peter Hart, Model Design in the PROSPECTOR Consultant System for Mineral Exploration, in *Expert Systems in the Micro-electronic Age*, D. Michie, (ed.), Edinburgh University Press, 1979, 153-167.

[19] Richard Ennals, *Beginning micro-PROLOG*, Ellis Horwood Heinemann, London, 1983.

[20] S.P. Ennis, Expert Systems: A User's Perspective of Some Current Tools, *AAAI82* , Pittsburgh, Pennsylvania, August, 1982 , 319-321.

[21] J. Fain, D. Gorlin, F. Hayes-Roth, S. Rosenschein, H. Sowizral and D. Waterman, The ROSIE Language Reference Manual, N-1647-ARPA, Rand, Santa Monica, CA 90406, 1981.

[22] C. Forgy and J. McDermott, OPS: A Domain-Independent Production System Language, *International Joint Conference on Artificial Intelligence-77*, 1977, 933-939.

[23] C. Forgy, The OPS5 User's Manual, CMU CS-81-135, CMU, Pittsburgh, Pennsylvania, 1981.

[24] K. Fuchi, The Direction the FGCS Project Will Take, *New Generation Computing 1*, 1 (1983), 3-9.

[25] K. Furukawa, A. Takeuchi, H. Yasukawa and S. Kunifuji, Mandala: A Logic Based Knowledge Programming System, *International Conference On Fifth Generation Computer Systems*, November 1984.

[26] R. Greiner and D. Lenat, A Representation Language Language, *AAAI-1*, , 165-169.

[27] P. Hammond, APES (A Prolog Expert System Shell): A User Manual, Doc Report 82/9, Department of Computing, Imperial College, 1982.

[28] Frederick Hayes-Roth, Donald A. Waterman and Douglas B. Lenat, *Building Expert Systems*, Addison Wesley, 1983.

[29] Frederick Hayes-Roth, Knowledge Based Expert Systems, *Computer Magazine*, October 1984.

[30] Christopher J. Hogger, *Introduction to Logic Programming*, Academic Press Incorporated, London, 1984.

[31] S. Julien, Graphics in Micro-Prolog, Technical Report 82-17, Computer Science Department, Imperial College, London, 1982.

[32] R.A. Kowalski, *Logic for Problem Solving*, Elsevier North-Holland, New-York, 1979.

[33] R.A. Kowalski, Logic as a Computer Language for Children, Technical Report 82-23, Computer Science Department, Imperial College, London, 1982. Also Published in New Horizons in Educational Computing, M. Yazdani (ed), Ellis Horwood, 1984.

[34] Catherine Lassez, Problem Solving with the Computer: Logo versus Prolog, *Proc. of ACS Computers in Education Conference*, Sydney, 1984.

[35] Zohar Manna, *Mathematical Theory of Computation*, McGraw Hill, 1974.

[36] Z.S. Markusz, Logic Based Programming Method and Its Applications for Architectural Design Problems, Ph.D. Dissertation, Eotvos Lorand University, Budapest, Hungary, 1980. In Hungarian.

[37] J. McDermott and C. Forgy, Production System Conflict Resolution Strategies, in *Pattern Directed Inference Systems*, D. A. Waterman and Frederick Hayes-Roth, (eds.), Academic Press, New York, 1977, pp177.

[38] F. Mizoguchi, Y. Katayama and H. Owada, LOOKS: Knowledge Representation System For Designing Expert System in the Framework of Logic Programming, *International Conference On Fifth Generation Computer Systems*, November 1984.

[39] L. Naish and J.A. Thom, The MU-Prolog Deductive Database, Technical Report 83-10, Department of Computer Science, University of Melbourne,Australia, 1983.

[40] L. Naish, *MU-Prolog 3.1db Reference Manual*, Melbourne University, 1984.

[41] Yutaka Ogawa, Kenichi Shima, Toshiharu Sugawara and Shigeru Takagi, Knowledge Representation and INference Environment: KRINE — An Approach to Integration of Frame, Prolog and Graphics., *International Conference on Fifth Generation Computer Systems*, Tokyo, November 1984, 643.

[42] J.A. Robinson, A Machine-Oriented Logic Based on the Resolution Principle, *Journal of the ACM 12*, 1 (Jan. 1965), 23-41.

[43] M.J. Sergot, Programming Law: LEGOL as a Logic Programming Language, Technical Report, Imperial College, London, 1980.

[44] M.J. Sergot, Prospects for Representing the Law as Logic Programs, in *Logic Programming*, K.L. Clark and S.-A. Tarnlund, (eds.), Academic Press, New York, 1982. A.P.I.C. Studies in Data Processing No. 16.

[45] M.J. Sergot, A Query-The-User Facility for Logic Programs, in *Integrated Interactive Computer Systems*, P. Degano and E. Sandwell, (eds.), North-Holland, 1983. Also available as Technical Report 82-18 from Imperial College, London - Also Published in New Horizons in Educational Computing, M. Yazdani (ed), Ellis Horwood, 1984.

[46] E.Y. Shapiro, *Algorithmic Program Debugging*, MIT Press, 1983. Ph.D. thesis,Yale University,May 1982.

[47] E.Y. Shapiro, Logic Programs With Uncertainties: A Tool for Implementing Rule-Based Systems, *Proceedings of the International Joint Conference on Artificial Intelligence*, Karlsruhe, Germany, 1983.

[48] E.Y. Shapiro, Systems Programming in Concurrent Prolog, *ACM Symposium on Principles of Programming Languages*, Salt Lake City, Utah, January, 1984.

[49] Norihisa Suzuki, Concurrent Prolog as an Efficient VLSI Design Language, *Computer Magazine*, February 1985, 33-40.

[50] W.R Swartout, XPLAIN: a System for Creating and Explaining Expert Consulting Programs, *Artificial Intelligence 21*, (1983), 285-325, North-Holland.

[51] D.H.D. Warren, Luis M. Pereira and Fernando C.N. Pereira, Prolog: The Language and its Implementation Compared with LISP, *Proceedings of the Symposium on Artificial Intelligence and Programming Languages. SIGPLAN Notices/SIGART Notices 12*, 8 (August 1977), 109-115.

[52] S.M. Weiss and C.A. Kulikowski, EXPERT: A System for Developing Consultation Models, *International Joint Conference on Artificial Intelligence-79*, 1979, 942-947.

[53] Carlo Zaniolo, Object Oriented Logic Programming, *Proc. of First International Conference on Logic Programming*, 1984, pp 265-270.

Appendix - List of Some Commercially Available Prologs

This list is provided for information only and does not claim to be comprehensive.

NAME:	C-Prolog
SOURCE/OS:	C/UNIX 4.1/2 BSD, C/VMS
CONTACT:	EdCAAD
	Dept. of Architecture
	University of Edinburgh
	20 Chambers Street
	Edinburgh EH1 1GZ UK

NAME:	Quintus Prolog
SOURCE/OS:	4.2 UNIX, VMS
CONTACT:	Quintus Computer Systems Inc.
	2345 Yale Street
	Palo Alto, CA 94304
	(415)494-3612

NAME:	Horne
SOURCE/OS:	Franz Lisp
CONTACT:	James Allen
	University of Rochester

NAME:	LM-Prolog
SOURCE/OS:	ZetaLisp (LMI and Symbolics)
CONTACT:	Elaine S. Donley, LMI
	6033 West Century Blvd.
	Suite 900
	Los Angeles, CA 90045

NAME:	micro-PROLOG
SOURCE/OS:	MS-DOS/IBM-PC, Z80/CPM
CONTACT:	Logic Programming Associates
	36 Gorst Road
	London SW11 6JE UK

NAME:	MPROLOG
SOURCE/OS:	IBM VM/CMS, VAX-VMS,
	UNIX, M08000, IBM-PC
CONTACT:	Ian McLachlan
	Logicware Inc.
	581 Boylston Street
	Suite 300
	Boston, MA 02116
	(617) 547-2393

NAME:	PROLOG V
SOURCE/OS:	IBM-PC
CONTACT:	Chalcedony Software
	5580 La Jolla Blvd.
	Suite 126 B
	La Jolla, CA 92037
	(619) 483-8513

NAME:	UNH Prolog
SOURCE/OS:	C/UNIX, C/VMS
CONTACT:	James L. Weiner
	Dept. of Computer Science
	University of New Hampshire
	Durham
	New Hampshire 03824

NAME:	Unix Prolog
SOURCE/OS:	PDP-11 Assembly/V6
	V7 Unix
CONTACT:	Robert Rae
	Dept. of Artificial Intelligence
	University of Edinburgh
	Forrest Hill
	Edinburgh EH1 2QL
	Scotland, U.K.

NAME:	Waterloo Prolog
SOURCE/OS:	IBM 370 Assembler
CONTACT:	Sandra Ward
	Dept. of Computing Services
	University of Waterloo
	Waterloo, Ontario N2L 3G1
	CANADA

NAME:	VPI Prolog
SOURCE/OS:	Pascal/VMS.
CONTACT:	Prof. John Roach
	Dept. of Computer Science
	Virginia Polytechnic Inst.
	Blacksburg, Va.
	(703) 961 5368

A COMPARATIVE FEATURE-ANALYSIS OF MICROCOMPUTER PROLOG IMPLEMENTATIONS

John Weeks
Hal Berghel

Department of Computer Science
University of Nebraska
Lincoln, NE 68588

Abstract: In recent years, no programming language has received the international attention of PROLOG. Currently the Japanese Fifth Generation Computing Systems Project (ICOT) is attempting to build an entire series of computers around this language in order to implement a new generation of computers based on symbolic inferencing techniques. In the United States and Europe, PROLOG is being used in relational database applications, natural language processing, theorem proving and automated reasoning, and a variety of other artificial intelligence applications.

In this article, we compare several of the newer PROLOG interpreters and compilers with regard to their functionality. This information is useful to researchers in selecting the product which will be the most relevant to their applications.

I. INTRODUCTION:

PROLOG is a high level programming language which is based upon a subset of first order predicate logic (predicate logic which allows quantification over subject but not predicate variables). The particular restrictions imposed by PROLOG are that 1) all expressions must be in Skolem normal form, and 2) the truthfunctional structure of each expression must be restricted to Horn Clauses [12] (i.e., where each clause is an elementary disjunction with at most one unnegated atomic formula.) These restrictions impose only practical limitations on PROLOG, for a logic so defined is for all intents and purposes coextensive with the full First Order Logic (for further discussion, see [3]). From a procedural point of view, PROLOG combines a simple rule of inference (Robinson's resolution principle [27]) which is based upon the principle of Disjunctive Syllogism, with an appropriate method of instantiating variables (unification) and a standard control strategy, to provide a mechanism for theorem proving.

PROLOG was first suggested as a programming language by Colmerauer [8],[9], based upon the earlier work of Kowalski [13], [16],[18],[19] and others [11],[20]. The first working system was introduced in in 1972. A subsequent refinement, written in FORTRAN, was introduced the following year. This latter system was then exported to a wide audience, with the result that derivative implementations soon appeared in Hungary, Edinburgh and Waterloo. These, in turn, gave rise to newer offspring, culminating in the microcomputer-based products now under study.

Reprinted with permission from *SIGPLAN Notices*, vol. 21, no. 2, pp. 46–61, Feb. 1986.

II. PROLOG TERMINOLOGY AND THEORY

There is a fairly large variance in the terminology associated with PROLOG implementations. This is a reflection of the historical differences in the origin of the various PROLOGs. There appear to be three de facto standards on which implementations are modeled, however. These include the DECsystem-10 implementation [24] (as discussed in Clocksin/Mellish[7], hereafter, CM), micro-PROLOG[22], and MPROLOG[21], which appears to have its roots in the earlier Marseilles implementation. In the discussion to follow, we will employ the notation of Clocksin and Mellish.

The basic unit of a PROLOG program is the clause, which has the logical form 'P if Q'. 'P' is the head of the clause and 'Q' is the tail. They are joined by the neck which is written ':-'. Clauses which have no tail, or have 'true' for the tail, are called facts.

The head of a clause is an n-ary predicate with n arguments. The tail, if present, is a conjunction of 1 or more such predicates. The clause is satisfied if all of the predicates in its tail (antecedent) are satisfied. Clauses are are also called procedures and are grouped into sets of procedures with the same predicate name and arity.

Each argument of a predicate is a term. Terms are defined recursively. Simple terms include character constants ('man', 'tall', 'peggy'), numeric constants (12, 5.5), special/symbolic constants (':-', '?-') and variables. Structured terms consist of an n-ary functor symbol followed by n terms, e.g. older_than(tom,erik), is_between(cincinatti,chicago,new_york), and .(a1,.(a2,. (a3,[])))).

It is the structured term which provides facilities for data structures in PROLOG. Since structured terms can have other structured terms as arguments, we can define tree structures by embedding them. The main functor is the root, and each argument represents a branch with the node labeled by the functor symbol if the argument is a structured term, or a leaf labeled by the term otherwise.

This terminology is consistent with the "Edinburgh" DEC 10 implementation and that of Clocksin & Mellish. Arity/Prolog, A.D.A VML PROLOG, and PROLOG-86 follow this standard for the most part. The terminology (and syntax) for MPROLOG and micro-PROLOG differ greatly from this and from each other. For example, in MPROLOG an atom is called a name and a term is an expression. Micro-PROLOG uses 'atom' to refer to atomic formulae (a predicate with its arguments). What constitutes a PROLOG program varies in the literature from a procedure set to a module to the contents of a file.

III. METHODOLOGY

Many comparisons are possible between language implementations. These would include various types of benchmarks, discussions of implementation strategy, stack organization and usage, and so forth. However, in this paper we deal exclusively with a functional characterization, based upon an analysis of the features offered by the products. We feel that a functional characterization is of primary concern, for if a product will not support the range of features required by the application, questions of efficiency are irrelevant.

IV. IMPLEMENTATIONS COVERED IN THIS COMPARISON

Unfortunately, although PROLOG is rapidly becoming a de facto standard in such areas as Artificial Intelligence, Natural Language Processing, Computational Linguistics, Expert Systems Development and Automated Theorem Proving, many interested researchers have been denied access to the variety of PROLOG implementations because of the costs involved and the limited range of supportive hardware.

In recent years, this situation has changed. Now, there are over a half-dozen PROLOG implementations available for microcomputers (mostly, for MS-DOS). This opens up the world of PROLOG programming to virtually every laboratory. In this paper, we will compare six such packages: Arity/Prolog[2], micro-PROLOG[22], MPROLOG[21], PROLOG-2[25], PROLOG-86[26] and A.D.A VML PROLOG[1]. To provide a frame of reference, we have also included the mainframe package, CProlog[5], which is a descendant of the original Dec-10 implementation designed by Warren, et al, at Edinburgh. One newly released product, PROLOG-V, was not included at the request of the manufacturer.

V. GENERAL DESCRIPTION OF THE IMPLEMENTATIONS.

CProlog

We included one main-frame PROLOG for purposes of comparison. The CProlog implementation we reviewed runs on a VAX-780 under the Unix operating system. As indicated in the data, CProlog provides a full set of arithmetic functions. In addition there is support for an internal term database.

Arity/Prolog

Arity/Prolog was apparently designed partly as an in-house development tool. Because of this background, one would expect a professional environment and this is what we found.

Arity/Prolog seems to have been designed with the PC/MS-DOS environment in mind, and as a result close integration is apparent. An excellent set of facilities are provided for controlling and interacting with the DOS environment, and a shell facility is provided in the interpreter so that the user can either execute DOS commands directly from within the interpreter or exit the interpreter, work in the DOS environment, then re-enter the interpreter without rebooting from the keydisk.

Arity provides both an interpreter and a compiler to produce stand alone programs. There is no context editor. Notable features of the Arity implementation are its support of a string data type, an explicitly keyed term database, environment support features (e.g. text positioning and display attribute controls), clause grammar support, and C and assembly language routine interfaces.

LPA's micro-PROLOG

Micro-PROLOG was developed to run on Z-80 based micro-computers without sacrificing any of the capabilities of mini-computer implementations. It supports floating point math, modules, and comes with a variety of extensions. Two of these provide syntactic sugar for the basic syntax covered below.

Others provide an interactive trace facility and a context editor.

Micro-Prolog was one of the first PROLOGs available on microcomputers. It is available in both CP/M and MS/DOS versions and has been widely adapted in this environment, especially in England. Its popularity has prompted several texts (e.g., Clark & McCabe], [6]).

MPROLOG

MPROLOG provides a powerful application program development environment with a context editor facility. Versions of MPROLOG for larger computer systems have a sophisticated module support system. Although not available in the PC/DOS version reviewed for this article, module support is scheduled for later PC/DOS versions.

MPROLOG is apparently rooted in versions of PROLOG developed in Hungary, and thus employs a slightly different vocabulary from PROLOGS derived from DEC 10 PROLOG. As mentioned above, atoms are called 'names' and terms are called 'expressions'. In addition, most of the "standard" predicates are present but under different names and following slightly different syntactic convention. This makes source code less portable than that of some other implementations.

PROLOG-2

PROLOG-2 is the newest of the implementations, and is based on an earlier implementation, PROLOG-1. PROLOG-2 provides almost all of the desirable features for a production system, including a compiler, context editor, virtual memory and module support.

PROLOG-2 not only bases its syntax on DEC-10 Prolog but claims to be upwardly compatible with DEC-10 source code. Thus there are a variety of predicates that are recognized but are not recommended to be used in programs designed for PROLOG-2 programs.

PROLOG-86

PROLOG-86 is an inexpensive implementation intended for educational purposes. It closely approximates the set of predicates defined in Clocksin & Mellish, and the publishers provide an explicit list of variations from this theme.

Sample source programs are provided in the areas of games (Tower of Hanoi), list and set processing, symbolic differentiation, goal programming, expert systems and natural language processing.

VML PROLOG

This implementation supports a tree structured domain system of modules and virtual memory which places no limit on the size or number of modules used. Floating point math and Grammar Rule Notation are supported. VML PROLOG is intended to be used in the development of application programs.

The documentation supplied with the review copy was minimal. The intention was apparently to document only the points in which VML differed from Clocksin & Mellish. There are discrepancies which remain undocumented, and the reviewers had difficulty getting some features to work.

VI.   DISTINCTIVE FEATURES OF PROLOG IMPLEMENTATIONS

VI.a.   OVERVIEW

Product:	CP	AR	LPA	MP	P2	P86	VML
Version:	1.2	3.2	3.0	1.5	1.1	1.12	1.33
Virtual Memory	-	+	-	-	+	-	+
Modularization	-	-	+	-	+	-	+
Compiler Option	-	+	-	-	+	-	-
Shell Support	+	+	-	-	-	-	-
Context Editor	-	-	+	+	+	-	-
Clause Grammar	-	+	-	+	+	-	+
# b-i preds (approx.)	95	145	60	175	183	65	85

Discussion: Following common usage, the presence of virtual memory implies that the PROLOG workspace is restricted only by the limitations of secondary storage. Modularization provides some method for isolating predicate names, terms and functor symbols in a set of PROLOG procedures in order to avoid conflicts with other procedure sets. Since PROLOG has no built in facilities for modularization, these must be provided as extensions. PROLOG compilers provide stand alone executable modules. By shell support, we mean that the user has the ability to suspend PROLOG and execute independent object modules without altering the state of the interpreter. A context editor is one that is tightly linked to the PROLOG interpreter environment such that the memory image of the current program may be altered. Clause Grammar refers to the '-->' notation, a syntactic sugar for representing grammars as definite clauses, as defined by Colmerauer[10], Kowalski[17], Pereira and Warren[23] and extended to transformational grammar by Berghel and Weeks[4].

VI.b. BUILT-IN PREDICATES

VI.b.1 I/O PREDICATES

Product:	CP	AR	LPA	MP	P2	P86	VML
Program/Clause I/O	3	5	2	*	5	4	14
Character I/O	6	17	0	6	13	5	9
String I/O	8	4	0	0	0	0	0
Term I/O	6	12	11	28	16	7	14
Stream/File Control	11	5	6	7	31	8	9

(* performed by context editor functions.)

Discussion: The classification of I/O predicates is somewhat arbitrary. For example, we classify predicates that open or close files, set or reset streams, or report on their respective status as control predicates, rather than I/O predicates. However, we apply the same classification scheme to all products.

The Program/Clause I/O predicates include the domain management predicates for VML. Of the 14 Program/Clause I/O predicates for VML, 8 were for domain management. The Character I/O predicates include those for the output of special control characters for new lines, pages, and tabs.

The presence of such a large number of MPROLOG Term I/O predicates is due in part to the presence of a set of predicates that report on features of the I/O system (e.g. the number of lines read from a stream, the number of columns left on an output line, output line length, etc.).

VI.b.2 Program/Clause I/O Predicates

Product:	CP	AR	LPA	MP	P2	P86	VML
save ws by predicate(s)	-	-	+	-	-	-	-
delete ws by file	-	-	-	-	+	+	+
replace ws w/file	-	-	-	-	+	+	-
update file from ws	-	-	-	-	-	-	+
load/save binary image	-	+	-	-	+	-	-
load/save state	-	-	-	-	+	-	-

Discussion: For program/clause I/O predicates, the two basic operations are load file into workspace and save workspace to file. The load operations are initiated by variations of the CM consult and reconsult predicates . However, there are several useful enhancements to the basic load/save operations. Saving by predicates, for example, allows the user to save selected portion of the workspace and rearrange the contents of disk files.

In CM PROLOG, load file commands are always cumulative with regard to the workspace. PROLOG-86 supports a variation that first clears the entire workspace, then loads a file into it. VML allows workspace to be maintained on disk in a virtual memory mode, and there are load and save file commands that operate with this virtual workspace as well as with real memory. Arity/Prolog supports a buffered load command for greater speed. PROLOG-2 can load and save modules from and to files.

VI.b.3. Character I/O Predicates

Product:	CP	AR	LPA	MP	P2	P86	VML
get char from stream/file	+/-	+/+	-/-	-/-	+/-	+/-	+/-
get pr char (stream)	+	+	-	-	+	-	-
get w/o echo (stream)	-	+	-	-	-	-	+
skip to char (stream/file)	+/-	+/+	-/-	-/-	+/-	+/-	+/-
skip w/o echo (stream)	-	-	-	-	-	-	+
put char to stream/file	+/-	+/+	-/-	-/-	+	+/-	+/+
newline (stream/file)	+/-	+/+	-/-	+/-	+	+/-	+/+
newpage (stream)	-	-	-	+	-	-	-
tab (stream/file)	+/-	+/-	-/-	+/-	+	+/-	+/+
write spaces (stream)	-	-	-	+	-	-	-

Discussion: LPA and MPROLOG require each character to be read or written as a term. Several implementations support both stream and file oriented I/O, and have separate predicates to perform similar functions in each case. Special output characters for newline(s), pages, tabs etc. are provided by most implementations.

63

VI.b.4. String I/O Predicates

Product:	AR	CP	LPA	MP	P2	P86	VML
get string from stream/file	+/+	-/-	-/-	-/-	-/-	-/-	-/-
put string to stream	+	-	-	-	-	-	-

Discussion: Arity/Prolog and MPROLOG are the only implementations that use the string data type. MPROLOG doesn't use special I\O predicates for strings.

VI.b.5. Term I/O Predicates

Product:	CP	AR	LPA	MP	P2	P86	VML
read term from stream/file	+/-	+/+	+/+	+/-	+/-	+/-	+/+
read token from str/file	-/-	-/-	-/-	+/-	-/-	+/-	+/
read number from str/file	-/-	-/-	-/-	-/-	-/-	-/-	+/
write to stream/file	+/-	+/+	+/+	+/-	+/-	+/-	+/+
write quoted to str/file	+/-	+/+	-/-	+/-	+/-	-/-	-/-
write ops prefix str/file	+/-	+/+	-/-	-/-	+	-/-	+/+
read/write formatted	-	-	-	-	+	-	-
declare operator	+	+	-	+	-	+	+
remove operator	-	+	-	+	-	-	+
get info about operator	-	+	-	+	-	-	-
define a prompt for I/O	+	-	-	-	-	+	-
direct file access position	-	+	+	-	-	-	+
fixed length file access	-	-	+	-	-	-	-
report on output environment	-	-	-	+	-	-	-
direct access read/write	-	-	+	-	+	-	-

Discussion: All of the implementations of PROLOG have the capability of reading/writing a term from/to either the terminal or a file. In some cases all I/O is stream oriented, streams being associated with either files or devices. The Arity, LPA, and VML implementations allow term I/O with respect to named files as well. Similar considerations apply to I/O predicates for specific types of terms (tokens, numbers, etc).

Operator declaration predicates are included here because the operators used in PROLOG provide a syntactic sugar in the form of infix notation during I/O operations. All operators are uniquely declared by providing a name, precedence, and associativity declaration.

MPROLOG provides a set of 5 special predicates to report on the current status of the output environment. These can report on the current output column, the number of columns left in the current output line, the number of columns required to print a term, and the length of the output line and the number of lines read. MPROLOG also provides six special purpose input predicates for recognizing the end of file, line or expression, or for reading special terms like comments or line oriented records.

VI.b.6. CONTROL PREDICATES

Product:	CP	AR	LPA	MP	P2	P86	VML
Stream/File Control	11	5	6	7	31	8	9
Success/Failure	2	2	2	2	2	2	2
Backtracking	2	3	1	6	17	2	2
Complex Goal	6	9	8	12	13	4	7

VI.b.6.a. STREAM and FILE CONTROL PREDICATES

Product:	CP	AR	LPA	MP	P2	P86	VML
create a file	-	+	+	-	-	-	-
open a stream/file	+/-	+/-	-/+	+/-	+/+	+/-	+/+
close a stream/file	+/+	+/-	-/+	+/-	+/+	+/+	+/+
create/open/close modules	-	-	+	-	+	-	+
temporary redir stdin	-	+	-	-	-	+	-
temporary redir stdout	-	+	-	-	-	-	-
turn on/off error calls	+	-	-	-	+	-	-
report existence of a file	+	-	-	-	+	-	-
rename a file	+	-	-	-	+	-	-
erase a file	-	-	+	-	+	-	-
directory facility	-	-	+	-	-	-	+
link files	-	+	-	-	-	-	-
control default drive	-	-	-	-	+	-	-

Discussion: There are four different conventions for designating sources and destinations of I/O used in these PROLOG implementations. One is to designate a file by a file name derived from the operating system. The others involve the notions of streams, handles or file numbers, and channels. Arity uses the convention of a numeric handle assigned when a file or device is created or opened, and MPROLOG uses the notion of a channel in much the same manner. One of the three channels 'infile', 'outfile' or 'printer' is associated with either a disk file from the host system or the terminal designations 'input' and 'output'. The rest of the implementations use the notion of a stream. As far as we can tell there is no intended difference between these three, so we consider them all as a stream.

Both VML and Arity/Prolog provide predicates which allow files to be opened in specified modes for reading, writing, appending etc. Arity then associated the file with a file number. CProlog, PROLOG-86 and VML include the traditional 'see, seeing, seen, tell, telling, told' predicates. MPROLOG provides separate predicates for input and output channels for setting, closing, and reporting channels.

VI.b.6.b. SUCCESS/FAILURE PREDICATES

All implementations have two forcing predicates: one forces a goal to succeed, the other forces a goal to fail.

VI.b.6.c.   BACKTRACKING PREDICATES

Product:	CP	AR	LPA	MP	P2	P86	VML
cut	+	+	+	+	+	+	+
repeat	+	+	-	+	+	+	+
logical set	+	+	+	+	+	+	+
explicit procedure call	+	+	-	-	+	+	+
special termination	-	+	-	+	+	-	-
number of solutions	-	-	+	-	-	-	+

Discussion: In the spirit of PROLOG, this should be a skimpy section, since the job of the PROLOG interpreter is to make the major decisions with respect to control and search. But programs which relied wholly on the built-in control and search strategies would be impractical and inefficient when executed on sequential architectures. Hence, even though control mechanisms like the cut are regarded much like the 'goto' in procedural languages [28] the provision of standard and special control mechanisms is one place where designers can customize the environment. Consequently there is a large variety of special control predicates with little overlap.

All implementations have the cut predicate and the standard set of logical operators required to form PROLOG queries and rules: 'and', 'or' and 'not'. Both MPROLOG and LPA have an implementation of an 'if...then...' predicate. Almost every implementation has a 'repeat' predicate to force looping for predicates which do not backtrack.

In addition to the standard 'success' and 'failure' predicates, some implementations provide special ways in which goals can be terminated. MPROLOG provides one predicate to cause failure without backtracking, some predicates to decide whether terms are evaluable and sometimes evaluate them, and a means of finding the trail of ancestor predicates to the one currently being evaluated.

Both VML and LPA PROLOGs provide sets of predicates for controlling the number of solutions provided for a goal. The basic options are to return the first solution, or to automatically continue backtracking until all solutions are returned.

Arity/Prolog has a counter mechanism for iterative control. This consists of 32 counters with predicates to set, increment, decrement, and report the counter values.

VI.b.7.   TERM CLASSIFICATION AND CONVERSION PREDICATES

Product:	CP	AR	LPA	MP	P2	P86	VML
Total:	8	9	8	17	8	6	5
is a variable	+	+	+	+	+	+	+
is a non variable	+	+	-	+	+	+	+
is an atom	+	+	-	+	+	+	+
is a number	+	+	+	+	+	+	+
is either atom or number	+	+	+	+	+	+	+
is a list	-	-	+	-	-	-	-

Discussion: Variables, atoms and numbers are the simple terms found in all implementations of PROLOG. Implementations that have floating point routines provide separate predicates for integers and reals, as well as for any additional types (e.g. strings) supported by that implementation. Some predicates play a dual role for classification and conversion or instantiation, due to the mechanism of unification that is involved. Implementations which support special forms of internal representation usually provide predicates for converting between the internal and ordinary forms.

VI.b.8. TERM COMPARISON PREDICATES

Product:	CP	AR	LPA	MP	P2	P86	VML
Total:	8	8	4	12	7	8	6
matching plus unification	+	+	+	+	+	+	+
does not match	+	+	-	+	+	+	+
equivalence	+	+	-	+	+	+	+
not equivalent	+	+	-	+	+	+	+
relational inequalities	+	+	-	+	+	+	+

Discussion: All of the term comparisons can be performed in LPA PROLOG, but where separate predicates are provided for each comparison for the other implementations, one predicate does the job of several in LPA. For instance, instead of using both a 'less than' and a 'greater than' predicate, there is one predicate which does the work for both, depending on how the programmer uses it.

The set of relational inequalities includes predicates for 'less than', 'greater than', 'less than or equal to' and greater than or equal to'.

VI.b.9. ARITHMETIC EVALUATION PREDICATES

Product:	CP	AR	LPA	MP	P2	P86	VML
Total:	7	7	5	10	7	1	6
evaluate and unify	+	+	-	+	+	+	+
arithmetically equal	+	+	-	+	+	-	+
not arithmetically equal	+	+	-	+	+	-	-
full relational set	+	+	-	+	+	-	+
nearest integer	-	-	+	-	-	-	+

Discussion: The arithmetic evaluation predicates force the evaluation of their argument expressions before the comparisons take place. Unlike the term comparison predicates discussed above, it is the values of these argument expressions that are matched and unified. In turn, these expressions are generally formed using arithmetic operators, which are only evaluated when forced to be by one of these predicates.

LPA Prolog presents a unique situation in its basic syntax, where not arithmetic operators are provided. Instead predicates which both specify an operation and cause evaluation are provided for addition and multiplication. The same predicate is used for both addition and subtraction, the operation effected depends on which of its three arguments are instantiated. A similar situation holds for multiplication and division. One predicate, 'LESS', provides both the '<' and '>' tests, depending on how its arguments are ordered.

VML provides a predicate to convert integers to floating point, and MPROLOG provides predicates which convert a string to a number, and generate pseudo-random numbers.

(Note: the 'full relational set' is the set of operators that includes '<', '>', '<=', and '>=' or their notational equivalents.)

VI.b.10. ARITHMETIC OPERATORS

Product:	CP	AR	LPA	MP	P2	P86	VML
int(f or n)	-	-	-	-	-	-	+
float(f or n)	-	-	-	-	+	-	+
atoi(<ascii>,<int>)	-	-	-	-	-	-	+
stof(<ascii>,<flt>)	-	-	-	-	-	-	+
-X	+	+	-	+	+	-	+
exp(X)	+	+	-	-	-	-	+
log(X)	+	-	-	-	-	-	+
log10(X)	+	+	-	-	-	-	+
ln(X)	-	+	-	-	-	-	-
abs(X)	-	+	-	+	-	-	-
round(X,N)	-	+	-	-	-	-	-
sqrt(X)	+	+	-	-	-	-	-
sin(X)	+	+	-	-	-	-	+
cos(X)	+	+	-	-	-	-	+
tan(X)	+	+	-	-	-	-	+
asin(X)	+	+	-	-	-	-	+
acos(X)	+	+	-	-	-	-	+
atan(X)	+	+	-	-	-	-	+
floor(X)	+	-	-	-	-	-	-
X^Y	+	-	-	+	+	-	+
X/\Y	+	+	-	+	-	-	+
X\/Y	-	+	-	+	+	-	-
X && Y	-	-	-	-	-	-	+
X/Y	+	+	-	+	-	-	+
X ## Y	-	-	-	-	-	-	+
X ^ Y	-	-	-	-	-	-	+
X ^^ Y	-	-	-	-	-	-	+
\X	+	+	-	-	+	-	+
X<<Y	+	+	-	+	+	-	-
X>>Y	+	+	-	+	+	-	-
cputime	+	-	-	-	-	-	-
heapused	+	-	-	-	-	-	-
[X]	+	+	-	-	-	-	-
fix(X)	-	-	-	-	+	-	-
truncate(X)	-	-	-	-	+	-	-
read_round(X)	-	-	-	-	+	-	-

Discussion: Expressions formed from these operators, or from any operators specified using the 'op' predicate, are only evaluated when present as arguments of the arithmetic evaluable predicates discussed above.

All implementations except LPA include besides those operators and functions listed in the table the full arithmetic set (+, -, *, and /). In addition CProlog, MPROLOG and PROLOG-2 provide built in operators for integer division, and Arity, MPROLOG, PROLOG-2, PROLOG-86 and VML provide modulo operators.

VI.b.11. DATABASE OPERATION PREDICATES

Product:	CP	AR	LPA	MP	P2	P86	VML
Clause Control	15	12	7	25	16	6	8
Term Control	6	8	0	0	3	0	0
Structure Manipulation	5	7	0	9	5	8	4

VI.b.11.a. CLAUSE DATABASE CONTROL PREDICATES

Product:	CP	AR	LPA	MP	P2	P86	VML
list all clauses	+	+	+	+	-	-	+
list specified clauses	+	+	+	+	+	+	-
assemble/disassemble clause	+	+	+	+	+	+	+
add a clause to the database	+	+	+	+	+	+	+
remove:							
first clause for predicate	+	+	+	+	+	+	+
all clauses for predicate	+	+	+	+	-	-	-
report presence of predicate	+	+	-	+	-	-	-

Discussion: The basic function of this set of predicates is to control and report on what clauses are in the database at any time. It is surprising that PROLOG-86 appears unable to list all of the clauses in the database. Thus to get a listing of a particular clause, you have to know what clauses are there. The ability to assemble and disassemble clauses, along with the ability to add and delete clauses to and from the data base allows the construction of programs which dynamically modify themselves.

There are a wide range of variations on how implementations add and delete clauses, but the general techniques are to add a clause to the beginning of a predicate definition, the end of a predicate definition, or at a specified point in the predicate definition. Similar options are generally available for deleting clauses. MPROLOG allows the programmer to specify whether the clauses should be reinstated ore removed on backtracking. There are also usually predicates that confirm the existence of or locate a predicate in the data base.

VI.b.11.b. TERM DATABASE CONTROL PREDICATES

Product:	CP	AR	LPA	MP	P2	P86	VML
record term	+	+	-	-	+	-	-
erase term	+	+	-	-	-	-	-
report term	+	+	-	-	+	-	-
replace term	-	+	-	-	-	-	-
manipulate reference #	-	+	-	-	-	-	-

Discussion: Both Arity/Prolog and CProlog provide similar facilities for maintaining and manipulating internal databases of terms. The set of predicates provided by Arity is more extensive, with a sophisticated set of predicates for moving forward and backward in a linked list of terms stored under a key.

VI.b.12. STRUCTURE MANIPULATION PREDICATES

Product:	CP	AR	LPA	MP	P2	P86	VML
structure unification predicate	+	+	−	+	+	+	+
get the Nth argument	+	+	−	+	+	+	+
convert between list/structure	+	+	−	+	+	+	−
convert between list/atom	+	+	−	+	+	+	+
convert between list/string	−	−	−	+	+	−	−
length of a list	−	+	−	+	+	+	−
sort the elements in a list	+	+	−	+	−	−	−

Discussion: The structure in PROLOG consists of a functor followed by arguments in parentheses. A list corresponding to a structure has the functor name as the first element and all arguments contained in it or any of its arguments, added recursively in a depth first manner.

Several predicates which deal with atoms (and in one case strings) are included here because the atoms are being converted to structures (lists). The sort predicates for lists are included here again because lists are structures.

VI.b.13. SET PREDICATES

Product:	CP	AR	LPA	MP	P2	P86	VML
Total:	3	4	0	2	2	0	0
set unification predicate	+	+	−	+	+	−	−
bag unification predicate	+	+	−	+	+	−	−

Discussion: The difference between a set and a bag is that all duplicates are removed from a set but not from a bag. The set is provided as an ordered list, the bag as an unordered list.

VI.b.14. STRING PREDICATES

Product:	CP	AR	LPA	MP	P2	P86	VML
Total:	0	10	0	12	3	0	0
search for substring	−	+	−	−	−	−	−
get substring	−	+	−	+	−	−	−
get position of substring	−	+	−	+	−	−	−
get length of substring	−	+	−	+	−	−	−
get length of string	−	+	−	−	−	−	−
concatenate strings	−	+	−	+	−	−	−

Discussion: In Arity, a string is stored as an array, and a string will only unify with a copy of itself. Arity provides a variety of predicates for converting between strings and terms, atoms, integers and reals. MPROLOG provides predicates for converting cases, truncating trailing blanks, finding prefixes, and testing for character, letter or string status. PROLOG-2 has predicates for testing string status, and converting between terms and strings.

VI.b.15. DEBUGGING AND TRACE PREDICATES

Product:	CP	AR	LPA	MP	P2	P86	VML
Total:	10	5	6	16	18	3	5
trace program execution	+	+	+	+	+	+	+
trace goal execution	+	+	+	+	+	+	+
report goals to be traced	+	+	+	+	+	+	+

Discussion: trace facilities allow the programmer to walk through the execution of a program, displaying intermediate results. Goals can be skipped or traced at users option. A spy facility allows particular goals to be traced during the execution of other programs.

VI.b.16. MISCELLANEOUS PREDICATES

Arity/Prolog provides an extensive and sophisticated set of system control and error predicates. These include text display predicates which control screen attributes and text positioning, system predicates that allow escape to the operating system, garbage collection, and statistics on Arity system resources. There is a set of predicates to manipulate the tree structured directory system of PC/MS-DOS, and to perform usual file maintenance operations. Error predicates control turn on and off syntax and file error messages, and retrieve the most recently issued error code.

MPROLOG provides 16 different predicates for error control and handling. There are a 9 predicates to control system resources: stacks, evaluations, state indicators, and garbage collection.

Arity/Prolog, PROLOG-86, MPROLOG and VML provide Definite Clause Grammar support as defined in Clocksin and Mellish.

VII. SUMMARY

This analysis is a byproduct of our continuing efforts to select the most suitable implementations for a variety of our own research projects. We hope that the present work will be useful to other researchers in selecting the appropriate PROLOG products for their own applications.

Acknowledgments: We wish to thank Eric Traudt and Dale Finkelson for their assistance with this project. In addition, we thank the Arity Corporation, Automated Design Associates, Logicware, Inc., Expert Systems International, and Solution Systems for providing the latest versions of their products for review purposes.

REFERENCES:

[1] "A.D.A. VML Prolog Documentation", Automata Design Associates, Dresher, Pa. (1985).

[2] "Arity/Prolog: The Programming Language", Arity Corporation, Concord, MA (1984).

[3] Berghel, H. and J. Weeks, "The Logic of Prolog", (forthcoming).

[4] Berghel, H., and J. Weeks, "On Implementing Elementary Movement Transformations with Definite Clause Grammars", Proceedings of the Fifth Phoenix Conference on Computers and Communication, IEEE Computer Society, [in press].

[5] "CProlog User's Manual- version 1.2", on-line documentation.

[6] Clark, K. and F. McCabe, micro-PROLOG Programming in Logic, Prentice-Hall, Englewood Cliffs (1984).

[7] Clocksin, W. and C. Mellish, Programming in Prolog, Springer-Verlag, New York (1981).

[8] Colmerauer, A., "Les systemes-Q ou un Formalisme pour Analyzer et Synthesizer des Phrases sur Ordinateur", Publication Interne No. 43, Dept. d'Informatique, Universite de Montreal (1973).

[9] Colmerauer, A., H. Kanoui, R. Pasero and P. Roussel, "Un Systeme de Communication Homme-machine en Francais", Rapport Groupe Intelligence Artificielle, Universite d'Aix Marseille, Luminy (1973).

[10] Colmerauer, A., "Metamorphosis Grammars", in G. Goos and J. Hartmanis(eds.): Lecture Notes in Computer Science, Springer-Verlag, Berlin, pp. 133-189 (1978).

[11] Hill, R., "LUSH Resolution and its Completeness", DCL Memo #78, University of Edinburgh, School of Artificial Intelligence (August, 1974).

[12] Horn, A., "On Sentences which are True of Direct Unions of Algebras", Journal of Symbolic Logic, Vol. 16. pp. 14-21 (1951).

[13] Kowalski, R., "Search Strategies for Theorem Proving", in B. Meltzer and D. Michie(eds.): Machine Intelligence, 5, Edinburgh University Press, New York, pp. 181-201 (1969).

[14] Kowalski, R., "And-Or Graphs, Theorem Proving Graphs and Bi-directional Search", in B. Meltzer and D. Michie(eds.): Machine Intelligence, 7, Edinburgh University Press, New York, pp. 167-194 (1972).

[15] Kowalski, R., "A Proof Procedure Using Connection Graphs", Journal of the ACM, vol. 22, pp. 572-595 (1974).

[16] Kowalski, R., "Predicate Logic as a Programming Language", Proceedings of IFIP 74, North-Holland, Amsterdam, pp. 569-574 (1974).

[17] Kowalski, R., Logic for Problem Solving, North-Holland, Amsterdam (1979).

[18] Kowalski, R. and P. Hayes, "Semantic Trees in Automatic Theorem Proving", in B. Meltzer and D. Michie(eds.): Machine Intelligence, 4, Edinburgh University Press, New York, pp. 87-101 (1968).

[19] Kowalski, R. and D. Kuehner, "Linear Resolution with Selection Function", Artificial Intelligence, Vol. 2, pp. 227-260 (1971).

[20] Kuehner, D., "Some Special Purpose Resolution Systems", in B. Meltzer and D. Michie(eds.): Machine Intelligence, 7, Edinburgh University Press, New York, pp. 117-128 (1972).

[21] "MProlog Language Reference", Logicware, Inc., Toronto (1984).

[22] "micro-PROLOG Programmers Reference Manual", Logic Programming Associates, London (1983).

[23] Pereira, F. and D. Warren, "Definite Clause Grammars for Language Analysis - A Survey of the Formalism and a Comparison with Augmented

Transition Networks", Artificial Intelligence, Vol. 13, pp. 231-278
(1980).

[24] Pereira, L., F. Pereira and D. Warren, "User's Guide to DECsystem-10
Prolog", Laboratorio Nacional de Engenharia Civil, Lisbon, Portugal
(1979).

[25] "PROLOG-2 Reference Manual", Expert Systems International, King of
Prussia, Pa (1985)

[26] "Prolog-86 User's Guide and Reference Manual", Micro-AI, Rheem Valley, CA
(1984).

[27] Robinson, J., "A Machine Oriented Logic Based on the Resolution
Principle", Journal of the ACM, Vol. 12, pp. 23-41 (1965).

[28] Robinson, J., "Logic Programming - Past, Present and Future", New
Generation Computing, Vol. 1, pp. 107-124 (1983).

THE LISP REVOLUTION

BY PATRICK H. WINSTON

LISP *is no longer limited to a lucky few*

A LITTLE MORE than five years ago, a friend from a major computer corporation came into my office to talk about developing artificial-intelligence (AI) packages. "How should we get started?" he asked. My answer was gloomy:

> First, get together a million dollars or so and buy one of Digital Equipment Corporation's (DEC's) big mainframe computers. Next, decide what dialect of LISP to run, choosing from MacLISP, InterLISP, Portable Standard LISP, Franz LISP, and many others. Then try to get a tape from somewhere and find someone who can install it. You'll probably find that the documentation is not particularly complete, and software maintenance will be a problem. And if you bet on the wrong dialect now, changing to another will certainly take a lot of work.

Today, by contrast, I wrote this article using an editor written in LISP. The editor is part of a $500 LISP system that I use on a $4000 personal computer. I wrote and tested a program in the $500 LISP that I will be able to run without change on a supersophisticated, superpowerful Symbolics 3670. Two things have made this progress possible. First, the recent availability of personal computers with 512K bytes of memory, which is enough to learn LISP and to start experiencing the excitement of its applications in AI. Second, Common LISP emerged as the heir apparent to all previous LISP dialects. The same Common LISP program you write on a personal computer can be transferred later to a heftier machine, as needs and resources permit.

Data General, DEC, Hewlett-Packard, LISP Machine, Symbolics Inc., Texas Instruments, and Xerox all sell versions of Common LISP for their own machines, and Common LISP is available for personal computers as well. Suddenly, serious LISP programming is no longer limited to a lucky few.

LISP MEANS SYMBOL MANIPULATION

The reason that LISP is different from most other languages is that LISP focuses on symbol manipulation rather than on numbers. To highlight the difference, I'll lay out some examples of symbol manipulation taken from the Mover program, one that moves toy blocks like those shown in figure 1. Specialized problem-solving procedures inside the Mover program enable it to get rid of obstacles that are in the way. These problem-solving procedures use and maintain information about what each object supports. For example, B3 supports B1 and B4. The Mover program knows this because the symbols B1 and B4 are found in a list obtained from B3 by the get instruction:

(get 'B3 'things-supported)
—> (B1 B4)

Now suppose we have attached the list of things that B3 supports to a variable called obstacles. LISP's symbol-manipulation primitives allow for quick answers to basic questions:

How many obstacles are there?
(length obstacles) —> 2

Patrick Henry Winston, MIT Artificial Intelligence Laboratory, 545 Technology Square, Cambridge, MA 02139.

Reprinted with permission from the April 1985 issue of *BYTE* magazine.
Copyright © by McGraw-Hill, Inc., New York 10020. All rights reserved.

What's the first obstacle?
(first obstacles) —> B1
Is B1 an obstacle?
(member 'B1 obstacles) —> t
Is B4 the first obstacle?
(eq 'B4 (first obstacles)) —> nil

Note that t is LISP notation for true, and nil is LISP notation for false. Other symbol-manipulation primitives facilitate changes to the list and test to see if it is empty:

Remove B4 from the list:
(setf obstacles
   (remove 'B4 obstacles)) —> (B1)
Add B7 to the list:
(setf obstacles
   (cons 'B7 obstacles)) —> (B7 B1)
Is the obstacle list empty?
(endp obstacles) — NIL

Once changed, the obstacle list can be reattached to the symbol B3 from which it came:

(setf (get 'B3 'things-supported)
   obstacles)

All these questions and changes are simple, low-level examples of the symbol manipulation for which LISP is famous. Similar symbol-manipulation feats enable the Mover program to keep track of what is done. Mover's history-maintaining procedures contain instructions that examine and change symbolic expressions describing every move. Those symbolic descriptions make it possible to answer questions like: Did you move block B7? How did you move block B7? Why did you move block B7? When did you move block B7?

Thus symbol manipulation enables Mover to exhibit a humanlike, introspective ability to explain itself. Symbol manipulation is so intimately associated with AI, it's no wonder that LISP is the key language used in AI applications.

COMPUTER PROFESSIONALS SHOULD KNOW LISP

LISP experts argue endlessly about why LISP remains the primary language for AI and about why it is becoming a language for general-purpose programming as well. Some say LISP's primitives and features explain all. Others claim LISP owes its power to its tradition of interactive programming and powerful debugging tools. Still others cite its simple hierarchy-encouraging procedure-definition mechanism. [Editor's note: for a short introduction to LISP, see "LISP for the IBM Personal Computer" by Jordan Bortz and John Diamant, July 1984 BYTE, page 281.]

Increasingly, LISP is becoming a more generally used language, not strictly limited to applications in AI. Because many of the systems of AI are large, LISP has become a language suited to large-system implementation. For example, it has been used with outstanding success in building the entire operating systems of the LISP machines now offered by a growing number of major companies.

Such successes are one reason why many computer-science educators believe that an understanding of LISP is de rigueur for computer science majors. Another is that LISP has been proven an excellent language for illustrating computing concepts. At MIT, for example, a dialect of LISP called Scheme has been used for years as the primary language in the basic introductory subject on programming languages.

LISP IS BOTH OLD AND NEW

Before you learn any computer language, you should ask if the language is too old to be modern or too new to be mature. What about LISP? Is it too old or too new? Many people are surprised to learn that the history of LISP goes back to the late 1950s, making LISP nearly as old as FOR-

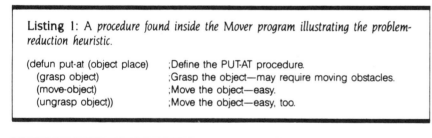

Listing 1: A procedure found inside the Mover program illustrating the problem-reduction heuristic.

```
(defun put-at (object place)    ;Define the PUT-AT procedure.
   (grasp object)               ;Grasp the object—may require moving obstacles.
   (move-object)                ;Move the object—easy.
   (ungrasp object))            ;Move the object—easy, too.
```

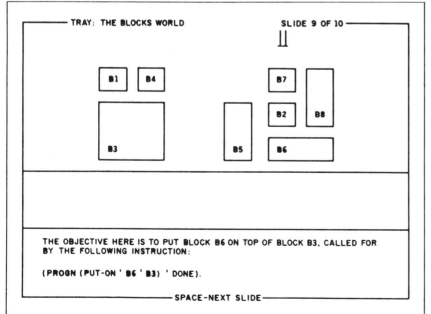

Figure 1: A picture of the blocks world in which the Mover program operates.

TRAN. Unlike FORTRAN, however, the LISP of today is much different from the LISP of 25 or even 5 years ago. Why did FORTRAN calcify while LISP continued to evolve vigorously? The principal reason is that FORTRAN was suited to commercial applications early on, whereas LISP was not. LISP re-

quires a lot of memory, and in the days when memory was expensive, there was no commercial purpose served by early standardization of LISP. Consequently, LISP dialects proliferated, LISP innovations thrived, and cross-fertilizations from one dialect of LISP to another kept each

about as powerful as any other. Now, however, memory is relatively cheap, which is attracting many commercial users to LISP, thus increasing the need for a standardized LISP for applications and instruction. Fortunately, the 25 years LISP has had to mature means that many new features have been incorporated into the Common LISP standard. Here are some of my favorites:

• a powerful structure-defining primitive that automatically generates procedures for accessing record fields
• a generalized assignment primitive that works for values, properties, arrays, and structures
• a flexible template-filling mechanism that enables complicated expressions to be constructed easily and transparently
• a strong macrocomputer capability that enables users to dream up their own syntax
• a rich variety of argument-passing options, including optional arguments with specifiable defaults as well as arguments associated with parameters by way of key words
• a modern, stream-oriented input/output (I/O) system

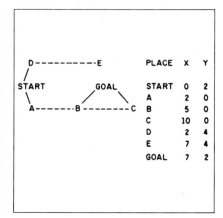

Figure 2: *Graphical description of how all the procedures in Mover work together.*

Figure 3: *An example of a maplike net.*

```
(make-rule identify16
    if      ((> animal) is a (> type))
            ((< animal) is a parent of (> child))
    then    ((< child) is a (< type)))
```

Figure 4: *A rule ready for inclusion in a LISP-based animal-recognition system.*

```
Rule IDENTIFY1 asserts  (ROBBIE IS A MAMMAL)
    because (ROBBIE HAS HAIR)
Rule IDENTIFY5 asserts  (ROBBIE IS A CARNIVORE)
    because (ROBBIE EATS MEAT)
Rule IDENTIFY9 asserts  (ROBBIE IS A CHEETAH)
    because (ROBBIE HAS DARK SPOTS)
            (ROBBIE HAS TAWNY COLOR)
            (ROBBIE IS A CARNIVORE)
            (ROBBIE IS A MAMMAL)
Rule IDENTIFY16 asserts (BOZO IS A MAMMAL)
    because (ROBBIE IS A PARENT OF BOZO)
            (ROBBIE IS A MAMMAL)
Rule IDENTIFY16 asserts (BOZO IS A CARNIVORE)
    because (ROBBIE IS A PARENT OF BOZO)
            (ROBBIE IS A CARNIVORE)
Rule IDENTIFY16 asserts (BOZO IS A CHEETAH)
    because (ROBBIE IS A PARENT OF BOZO)
            (ROBBIE IS A CHEETAH)
```

Figure 5: *Output fragment showing how a forward-chaining rule moves from facts to conclusion.*

HOW TO LEARN LISP

I think the best way to learn LISP is interactively. There are quite a number of reasons why such interactive learning is good. For instance: It's fun to do on-line puzzles; it's boring to do exercises in a book. It's easy to demystify difficult points by trying things out immediately. It's motivating to watch interesting programs work.

In any case, one factor stands undisputed: LISP programming is fun. Let's look at a few taken from an on-line, interactive instruction package known as the San Marco LISP Explorer. [*Author's note: The San Marco LISP Explorer package is sold by Gold Hill Computers Inc., 163 Harvard St., Cambridge, MA 02139.*] We will examine the Mover blocks-manipulation program, the search program, the rule-based ex-

LISP REVOLUTION

Listing 2: *A search program that finds paths through maplike nets such as the one in figure 3.*

```lisp
(defun start-depth (start goal))
   (depth (list (list start))      ;Make a one-partial-path queue.
          goal))                    ;Pass along name of goal place.

(defun depth (queue goal)
   ;;If no other partial paths, quit:
   (if (null queue)
       nil
       ;;Otherwise, if goal found, quit:
       (if (equal goal (first (last (first queue))))
           (first queue)
           ;;Otherwise, expand first partial path
           ;;and add to FRONT of queue:
           (depth (append (expand (first queue))
                          (rest queue))
                  goal)))))

(defun expand (path)
   (let ((reversed-path (reverse path)))
      ;;Turn the new partial paths right way around:
      (mapcar 'reverse
         ;;Get rid of partial paths that close on themselves:
         (remove-if '(lambda (new-path)
                        (member (first new-path) (rest new-path)))
            ;;Make one new partial path for each neighbor:
            (mapcar '(lambda (neighbor) (cons neighbor reversed-path))
               ;;Get neighbors:
               (get (first reversed-path) 'neighbors))))))
```

Listing 3: *The expression-matching procedure in any rule-based expert system must compare expressions and produce a list of pattern-match pairs.*

```lisp
* (match '((> animal) is a (> type))    ;First argument is a pattern.
          '(Robbie is a Cheetah)         ;Second argument is an assertion.
          nil)                           ;Third is a list of prior pattern-match
                                         ; pairs, none in this example.

((animal robbie) (type cheetah))         ;The answer—a list of pattern-matches.
```

Listing 4: *A matcher program for a rule-based expert system.*

```lisp
(defun match (p d matches)
   (cond ((and (endp p) (endp d))         ;Succeed.
          (cond ((endp matches) t)
                (t matches)))
         ((or (endp p) (endp d)) nil)     ;Fail.
         ((equal (first p) (first d))     ;Identical first elements.
          (match (rest p) (rest d) matches))  ;Match the rest.
         ((atom (first p)) nil)           ;Losing atom.
         ((equal (first (first p)) '>)    ;Match > variable.
          (match (rest p) (rest d)
                 (shove-value (second (first p))
                              (first d)
                              matches)))
         ((equal (first (first p)) '<)    ;Substitute variable.
```

(continued)

pert system, and the natural-language interface.

PLANNING IN THE BLOCKS WORLD

LISP programs are generally examples of the problem-reduction heuristic; that is, to solve a hard problem you must break it up into simpler subproblems. The problem-reduction heuristic can be seen in the simple Mover program. Listing 1 is a procedure found inside the Mover program that breaks the problem of putting an object somewhere into three subproblems: grasp it, move it, and ungrasp it. Figure 2 is a graphical description of how all of the procedures in Mover work together. LISP encourages the creation of layered programs, like Mover, wherein big problems are broken down successively into smaller and smaller problems.

SEARCHING IN THE MAP WORLD

Search techniques are commonly used in AI to solve problems. Here are some examples:

- finding a route through a highway net
- finding a way to put together a motor
- understanding a written database request
- learning to recognize a plant disease

Abstractly, search problems all amount to finding a way through some sort of maplike net. Figure 3 is a sample of such a net. The goal is close to place E, but there is no direct connection; E is a dead end. There are two ways to go from B to the goal: directly, and indirectly, through C. Listing 2 shows a page of LISP defining a search program that finds paths through these maplike nets. Although you won't understand much of the program if you don't know LISP yet, you may enjoy looking at its overall structure and simplicity. With a little more effort, you can define a search

```
        (match (cons (pull-value (second (first p) matches)
                     (rest p))
               d
               matches)))))
```

This matcher happens to use two auxiliary procedures:

```
(defun pull-value (variable a-list)
   (second (assoc variable a-list)))

(defun shove-value (variable item a-list)
   (append a-list (list (list variable item))))
```

Listing 5: *A program that matches sentences against a suitable representation of semantic grammars and activates the appropriate search procedure.*

```
(record question
     ((branch ((parse present)
          (branch (THE (parse attributes) OF (parse tools)
               (parse-result-if-end
                (report-attributes attributes tools)))
          ((parse tools) S (parse attributes)
               (parse-result-if-end
                (report-attributes attributes tools)))))
          (HOW MANY METERS IS (parse tool1) FROM (parse tool2)
           (parse-result-if-end
            (report-distance tool1 tool2)))
          (IDENTIFY (parse tools)
               (parse-result-if-end
                    (report-identity tools)))
          (COUNT (parse tools)
               (parse-result-if-end
                    (report-number tools))))))
```

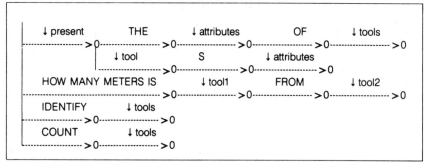

Figure 6: *The top level of a semantic grammar capable of handling queries about the color, weight, length, and position of some tools.*

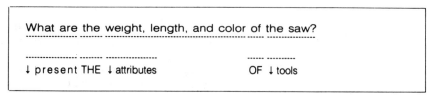

Figure 7: *An example of a question that matches the top level of the semantic grammar in figure 6.*

procedure that finds the guaranteed-shortest path.

ANALYSIS IN THE ZOO WORLD

Rule-based expert systems are the hottest thing in the commercialization of AI. All of them are built on the idea that some kinds of knowledge can be reduced to simple rules. Figure 4 shows one rule that is ready for inclusion in a LISP-based animal-recognition system, which expresses the fact that an animal's children are animals of the same kind. LISP does not have any built-in primitives that handle such rules, but it is a splendid language in which to embed a rule-exploiting program. LISP's symbol-manipulating power is well suited to the task of examining the symbols that make up a rule, comparing them to the symbols that make up the existing facts, and reacting accordingly. One kind of rule-exploiting program is a forward-chaining rule interpreter, which is a program that uses rules to move forward from facts to conclusions. Figure 5 is an output fragment showing what such a program does with facts about Robbie, knowledge about the relationship between Robbie and Bozo, and a few rules. There is always an expression-matching procedure buried inside any rule-based expert system like the animal-identification procedure. While the entire system is too lengthy to show, the matcher is short and straightforward. Its task is to compare expressions and to produce a list of pattern-match pairs, as shown in listing 3. Listing 4 is the matcher program.

INTERACTION IN THE TOOL WORLD

The pattern matcher shown previously is not just an important part of a rule-based system. It is also just about all you need to make the famous Doctor program, the one that pretends it is a psychiatrist responding with apparent sympathy as you pour your heart out over family traumas. More importantly, the pattern matcher has a family resemblance to natural-language interface programs built on what is called a semantic grammar. Basically, a semantic grammar is a model of what can be said in tightly constrained conversations about a narrow database. Suppose that you are interested in the color, weight, length, number, and position of some tools. The natural queries are:

• Identify the hammers.
• Count the red screwdrivers.
• Show me the color of the wrenches.
• Present the small red screwdriver's weight.
• What is the length and weight of the large saw?
• How many meters is the small red screwdriver from the big blue screwdriver from the big blue one?

The top level of a semantic grammar capable of handling all these queries is shown in figure 6. A semantic-grammar interpreter finds paths through such a net using input sentences as a guide. Each branch

marked with a > symbol requires traversal of a subnet. Each complete path from the entry to an exit is associated with its own data-searching procedure. For example, the sentence in figure 7 matches the topmost path in the top-level net. Three subnets are traversed in addition to the top-level net. Once again, LISP's symbol-manipulating power makes it easy to write a program that both matches sentences against a suitable representation of semantic grammars and activates the appropriate search procedures. Listing 5 shows what such a representation looks like when it is rendered in LISP-oriented notation.

CONCLUSION

We really don't need any new examples to demonstrate why professionals need to know about LISP. The examples presented are all elementary, but they indicate the sorts of

things done by their bigger brothers. LISP is the foundation for expert systems of all kinds, many of which have progressed far beyond the simple rule-based paradigm. LISP is the language for most natural-language development efforts. Indeed, LISP is the language of choice for most people working in AI—supporting work that includes learning, instruction, speech, vision, robotics, and all sorts of reasoning. ∎

BIBLIOGRAPHY
Abelson, Harold, and Gerald Jay Sussman. *Structure and Interpretation of Computer Programs*, Cambridge, MA: MIT Press, 1984.
Winston, Patrick H. *Artificial Intelligence*, 2nd ed. Reading, MA: Addison-Wesley, 1984.
Winston, Patrick H., and Berthold K. P. Horn. *LISP*, 2nd ed. Reading, MA: Addison-Wesley, 1984.
Winston, Patrick H., and Karen A. Prendergast. *The AI Business: The Commercial Uses of Artificial Intelligence*. Cambridge, MA: MIT Press, 1984.

A COMPARISON OF THREE LISP INTERPRETERS
FOR MS-DOS-BASED MICROCOMPUTERS

Stephen N. Kahane, M.D.
Richard S. Johannes, M.D.

The Departments of Medicine and Biomedical Engineering
The Operational and Clinical Systems
The Johns Hopkins Medical Institution

ABSTRACT

We report a comparison of three commercially available LISP
interpreters running on MS-DOS-based microcomputers. Marked
differences were found between the different products' memory
addressing abilities, error handling and debugging facilities. Editing tools,
tutoring environments, windowing, graphic capabilities, operating system
and port call facilities are also contrasted. Speed was tested via a group
of LISP functions (benchmarks) that attempt to isolate list manipulation,
iteration, function calling, recursion and mathematical calculation
performance.

INTRODUCTION

There has been growing attention focused on the field of Artificial
Intelligence (AI). The 1984 Symposium on Computer Applications in
Medical Care (SCAMC) Meeting saw unprecedented interest in this area;
those sessions dealing with Artificial Intelligence in Medicine were
attended to capacity.

Historically, builders of systems utilizing the concepts and techniques
of Artificial Intelligence have been forced to develop applications on
mainframes and/or special purpose hardware. LISP, a traditional
programming language in the AI community, requires a fast processor
and a large amount of memory (1). Such speed and size were never
before available on microcomputers.

Recently, microcomputer users have seen substantial growth in terms
of their machine's power, speed, and storage capacity. The increase in
interest in AI and the growth in the power and size of microcomputers
has lead to a heightened interest in the feasibility of placing AI
development systems and applications on microcomputers.

Last year we reported our experience with a nine workstation
Corvus Omninet Local Area Network running under MS-DOS (2). In
this paper, we look closely at some of the resources available for
building and running AI systems on existing microcomputers

LISP DIALECTS

LISP is not a standardized language. Differences between dialects
may be substantial and are most often the result of function set variability
as well as data typing idiosyncrasies (3). As pointed out by Touretsky
(4), even the most basic functions, such as CAR or CDR, have no
universal definition. In addition, functions that do the same thing may
have different names in different dialects, while functions that do
different things, may have the same name in different dialects. Syntax
for defining functions and scoping conventions differ as well (5).
Dialects with significant followings include:

- InterLISP

- FranzLISP (6)

- ZetaLISP (a derivative of MacLISP)

- Lisp Machine LISP (uses same syntax as MacLISP)

- Common LISP (7,8)

- MacLISP

- UCI-LISP

- P-LISP

- X-LISP (9)

The MS-DOS-based products have dialects of their own. The three
products we examined are:

- muLISP-83 Vers. 4.11 (upward compatible with McCarthy's LISP
1.5)

- IQLISP Vers. 1.4

- GOLDEN COMMON LISP Vers. 1.00 (compatible subset of
Common LISP)

Incompatibilities between dialects may significantly limit portability. To help deal with this, muLISP provides two "Utility Library
Files." Interlis.lib contains approximately 100 InterLISP functions
written in muLISP, while Maclisp.lib has approximately 125 MacLISP
(and ZetaLISP) functions written in muLISP. Many of the functions
provided are powerful, and it is convenient to have these functions
available during the development process. In addition, some of these
functions are very basic to development in LISP. For example, the
mapping functions (eg. mapcar) are found in the supplemental librarys
and are not in the base package itself. GCLISP is a "compatible subset"
of Common LISP core specification. It does incorporate a variety of
ZetaLISP concepts. The developers of GCLISP plan to provide a full
implementation of the Common LISP standard sometime in the future.
The developers of IQ make no explicit claims regarding dialect
similarities or compatibility with an established version of LISP running
on either a mainframe or a LISP machine.

COMPARISON OF THREE PRODUCTS

INTRODUCTION

muLISP, developed at The Software House in Honolulu, Hawaii is
distributed by the Microsoft Corporation. The system comes with an
interactive tutorial and an indexed 160+ page reference manual. The
manual has a function and variable name index and is packaged in an
8.5" x 11" three-ring binder. The material is well-organized and easy to
read. The entire system currently lists for $250.

IQLISP is a product of Integral Quality Corporation. No tutorial is
provided. Though well organized, their manual, packaged as a full-sized,
three-ring binder, does not have a general index and the Table of
Contents does not provide page numbers. An index of the primitive

Reprinted from *Proc. IEEE Ninth Annual Symp. on Computer Applications in Medical Care,* pp. 186–192, Nov. 1985.

function names is provided, but, despite this, the manual is difficult to use for reference. The example code segments provided are very good and may mitigate the absence of a tutorial. The systems suggested retail selling price is $175.

GCLISP is a product of Gold Hill Computers in Cambridge, Massachusetts. Within a single sturdy and partitioned case is a well organized and well indexed 6" x 8.5" three-ring binder providing a 20 page installation guide, a 3 page tutorial guide, a 120 page user's guide, and a 223 page reference manual. Winston and Horn's LISP and Steele's Common LISP are included within the case as well. In addition, the San Marco Lisp Explorer, supplied on two floppy disks, is provided as an interactive tutorial. The package sells for $495.

HARDWARE REQUIREMENTS AND CAPABILITIES

muLISP-83 can run on a variety of microcomputers including a subset of machines running CP/M-80 as well as all those running MS-DOS or PC-DOS. We had little trouble running this package on the IBM AT. Sixtyfour Kb of RAM is required for the 8086 or 8088 based machines while 48 Kb suffice in 8080, 8085 or Z80 based micros. Facilities are provided for console customization. muLISP can address 256 Kb of memory.

IQLISP runs on the IBM PC with DOS 1.1, 2.0, or 3.0. To use DOS 2.0 or greater, or to allow ample room for the development package, RAM requirements increase to 144 Kb. It is crucial to point out however that IQLISP will use all the installed RAM from its load site to 640 Kb. Sufficient technical details are provided so that software utilizing RAM for virtual disk emulation would not necessarily interfere with IQLISP implementation. In addition, despite the lack of any formal announcement regarding compatibility, we had little trouble running this package on the IBM AT.

GCLISP is capable of running on the entire IBM Personal Computer Series or any other 100%-PC-compatible computer. MS-DOS or PC-DOS versions 2.0 or higher is required. Five hundred and twelve Kb of RAM is required, though GCLISP is capable of handling 1 Mb if available.

MEMORY SUPPORT CAPABILITIES

As mentioned above, IQLISP can handle the full 640 Kb of memory supported by the DOS. GCLISP goes further; a full megabyte of contiguous RAM can be addressed (this takes full advantage of the 8088). Though not stated explicitly in their manual, muLISP appears capable of addressing 256 Kb of RAM. Column two of Table 1 shows the amount of usable memory each system has available after loading the development system facilities (interpreter, primitives, debugging and error handling facilities, and editor). Column three shows the amount of usable memory available after loading just the runtime system (interpreter and primitive functions). Finally, column four shows the maximum amount of usable RAM available at runtime for interpreted applications.

MEMORY SUPPORT SUMMARY			
	Direct Memory Addr. Capabil.	System Size (with development)	Runtime System Size	MAXIMUM APPLICATION SIZE *
muLISP	256 Kb	⁻32 Kb	⁻19 Kb	⁻237 Kb
IQLISP	640 Kb	⁻68 Kb	⁻68 Kb	⁻572 Kb
GCLISP	1000 Kb	⁻359 Kb	⁻180 Kb	⁻820 Kb

Table 1

MEMORY MAINTENANCE

The facilities provided for the removal of unwanted atoms, lists, property values, and functions play an important role in memory conservation. All three products provide automatic garbage collection and memory reallocation functions. These functions may also be called explicitly. Destructive or modifier functions capable of eliminating the relationship between a function name and its definition are provided as primitives only in IQLISP and GCLISP. These types of facilities become extremely important in real-time applications so that excessive garbage collections and memory reallocation calls (known as "thrashing") is avoided.

DEVELOPMENT SYSTEM FACILITIES

ERROR CHECKING AND DEBUGGING - Much time is developing a LISP application. The error handling and debugging facilities provided by the development system will significantly affect the speed with which an application can be developed. Error handling in muLISP is shallow providing little feedback to the programmer regarding the type of error that was made. IQLISP however opens a window that provides the programmer with a description of the problem and where it occurred eg. "UNBOUND VARIABLE "A"" or "UNDEFINED FUNCTION "A"". GCLISP provides similar feedback. This is extremely helpful for debugging applications.

All three systems provide a function tracing and backtracing facilities. GCLISP, in addition, provides a STEP function. This allows tracing by single steps through the execution of a function. At each level, the STEP function dynamically displays the bindings of variables and returned functions. In our experience, this has proven to be the single most powerful debugging tool in any of these LISP environments.

EDITOR - All three products provide editors for system development. The muLISP and GCLISP editors, muSTAR and GMACS respectively, are full screen editors. Both may be memory resident and both have facilities that aid the programmer with parentheses organization. muSTAR uses an auto-indentation technique that we found less helpful than the parenthesis matching routine supported by GMACS. Nevertheless, muSTAR is easy to use and provides ample facilities for function editing.

GMACS is an offshoot of the popular EMACS, a full screen editor that commonly runs in the UNIX environment. Like muSTAR, GMACS may be loaded in RAM during development. Consequently, interpreter-to-editor transition time is almost instantaneous. Unlike either of the other two editors, GMACS is capable of editing files. Full support for cut and paste editing is provided. Edited files may be stored on disk and the reloaded into the "environment."

IQLISP does not support a memory resident full screen editor. Instead, a full-featured structure-editor is provided which may be memory resident. A structure editor edits a function definition or identifier value as a structure of atoms and cons cells. This maintains the structure as a valid IQLISP object. In the process, it eliminates the possibility of parentheses becoming unbalanced. The structure editor forces the user to think in terms of proper LISP syntax. Conceptually, the structure editor is extremely appealing. Unfortunately, this type of editing significantly limits flexibility and despite much time and effort, we found the lack of a memory resident full screen editor a major drawback of this system's development facilities. Provision for saving source text files is provided by the "package" facilities of IQLISP.

GRAPHICS - With three primitive functions, point, line and fill, a basic graphics system can be developed. IQLISP provides two of these as primitive functions, POINT and LINE. These functions accept a window file in their argument list, thereby providing the capacity for window based graphic applications. muLISP provides a tutorial that enables the user to build a variety of graphic functions. It also provides a full Turtle Graphics library. This is the most complete set of graphics functions currently provided by any of the three products. Though not documented in the GCLISP manual, an example program with source code provides support for line, point and fill. GCLISP also provides support for the Mouse Systems three button optical mouse. Recently, Media Cybernetics Inc. released bindings for their HALO graphics package to run under GCLISP.

BENCHMARKS

INTRODUCTION - Using a group of selected LISP functions (see Appendix A for function listings), we attempted to isolate list manipulation, iteration, function calling, recursion and mathematical calculation in order to study each systems abilities and limitations. A subset of our work support the findings of previous work in this area (7). Specifically, we found muLISP the fastest of the three interpreters in most areas. However, GCLISP was not far behind.

LIST MANIPULATION - We tested each system's list manipulation ability by running ITREVERSE and ITREVERSE2, functions that calls the function REVERSE on a seven element list 1000 times. In ITREVERSE2, we utilized the PROG construct in order to avoid confusing differing iterative construct availabilities between products with list manipulation capabilities. All functions with names ending with a "2" utilize constructs found in all three packages, namely the PROG construct. Their counterparts without the "2" make use of iterative facilities provided in that particular package. For example, ITREVERSE, used the DOTIMES construct in GCLISP and the FOR construct in IQLISP. Because muLISP provides no analogous facility, no ITREVERSE function is defined.

ITERATION - Iterative capabilities were tested in two ways. First, utilizing the function IT2 we ran an empty loop constructed with the PROG syntax provided in each of these products. Second, utilizing the ITF function, we ran the same size empty loop making use of the DOTIMES construct provided in GCLISP and the FOR construct provided in IQLISP. muLISP does not provide iterative constructs other than PROG. We found the DOTIMES construct provided in GCLISP optimum for iteration. The PROG construct in GCLISP was significantly faster than this same construct in the other products, though not nearly as fast as iteration invoked with the GCLISP DOTIMES facility.

FUNCTION CALLING - Function calling was isolated by defining a function DONOTHING that does exactly that, nothing. Then, in ITF2, we use the PROG construct to call DONOTHING 1000 times. After correcting for the differences in iteration speed, we found GCLISP to be the fastest at function calling. When coupled with the iterative construct DOTIMES, as is done in ITF, GCLISP is almost an order of magnitude faster than IQLISP and more than six times faster than muLISP.

RECURSION - Recursion tests a system's facility with stack operations. Classically, the factorial function is used to demonstrate the concept of recursion. While this is appropriate, it is important to understand that double recursion will stress the stack manipulation techniques of a system much more than its single tail counterpart. We utilized the APP and REV functions described in the paper by Bortz and Diamont. As they point out, these functions are slow versions of their more universal counterparts APPEND and REVERSE. muLISP and GCLISP outperformed IQLISP in both tail and double recursion. Because IQLISP utilizes large pointers, it is forced to place more information on the stack. This is likely to slow execution though there appear to be other factors involved as well.

GARBAGE COLLECTION - We ran our iterative function ITER-TEST which utilizes the PROG construct and, instead of calling DONOTHING, explicitly called garbage collection. We did this in an attempt to determine the efficiency of this function in each of the products reviewed. Since garbage collection may be called numerous times during an application or even during a complex function, it is important that this function perform efficiently.

Unfortunately, we were unable to control for memory size and thus it remains unclear which product handles memory upkeep most efficiently. Nevertheless, both muLISP and GCLISP appear to be significantly faster than IQLISP. For a variety of reasons, testing the garbage collection facilities is difficult; a complete discussion of the reasons is beyond the scope of this paper.

FLOATING POINT - IQLISP and GCLISP are capable of utilizing the 8087 or 80287 math co-processors. IQLISP provides facilities for the testing of taxing floating point operations. At present IQLISP is the only of the three interpreters examined which provides a full set of floating point operations including exponentials and trigonometric functions. GCLISP does not yet provide the trigonometric functions, although they are included in the documentation. The only floating point operations supported in Version 1.00 of GCLISP are addition, subtraction, multiplication and division. Consequently we have not yet finished our testing in this area.

SUMMARY - Table 2 summarizes our findings. A full listing of the average time for each function may be found in Appendix B.

Table 2

LISP BENCHMARKS RANKINGS BY SPEED *			
PROCESS BEING TESTED	muLISP	IQLISP	GCLISP
LIST MANIPULATION	1 **	3	2
ITERATION			
PROG CONSTRUCT	2	3	1
OTHER LOOPS	2	N/A ***	1
FUNCTION CALLING	2	3	1
RECURSION	1	3	2
GARBAGE COLLECTION	1	3	2

*   Appendix A has listings of all functions tested. Appendix B shows mean times for each function in each environment.

**   Rank 1 is fastest
Rank 2 is intermediate
Rank 3 is slowest

***   No iterative construct other than PROG is provided

CONCLUSION

The growth in power, speed and memory size of the microcomputer has led to a variety of LISP products that attempt to provide a development and runtime environment similar to that of systems historically confined to mainframes or special LISP machines. We compared three commercially available LISP interpreters (see Table 3) running on MS-DOS-based microcomputers and found a number of differences.

muLISP, though only capable of addressing 256 Kb of memory, has an attractive assortment of tutorials and provides the listings of two libraries containing the major functions of two popular LISP dialects. muLISP functions run fast and efficiently demonstrating special abilities at list manipulation. The development environment features a full screen editor that is easy to use but not capable of editing files. muLISP provides a full set of graphics primitives (turtle graphics). We found the error and debugging facilities in muLISP not as full-featured as those provided in either IQLISP or GCLISP though TRACE and BREAK facilities are provided. Certain conventions such as auto-quoting and automatic local variable definition in lambda functions lighten the responsibilities of the programmer but, at the same time, increase the possibility of runtime errors that are difficult to debug. For the beginner LISP programmer, this product offers features well worth its cost. The system, as it is available now, has significant limitations for the serious programmer interested in developing a robust LISP application.

IQLISP can address the full 640 Kb of memory handled by DOS. No tutorials are provided, probably because the developers appear to assume a serious and LISP aware user. IQLISP proved to be the slowest of the three interpreters tested. Nevertheless, it does have windowing facilities (including graphics windows) and is the only one of the three interpreters currently supporting a full library of floating point calculations. It supports an 8087 math co-processor if one is installed. The IQLISP manual provides some of the best code segments, but is difficult to use owing to its lack of an index. Perhaps the most difficult part of using IQLISP is the use of a structure editor as opposed to a full screen editor, although there are those who prefer the structure editor approach.

GCLISP is a subset of Common LISP. In general, its speed benchmarks were intermediate between muLISP and IQLISP. GCLISP provides the most extensive library of functions including functions which allow full access to low level DOS functions. In addition, mouse support and graphics primitives are provided. Floating point support is present in rudimentary form and full implementation has been deferred to the next release. GCLISP is capable of handling a 1 Mb address space and a large memory model, capable of addressing approximately 15 Mb, should be available in the Fall. The editor (GMACS) is easy to use and its parentheses matching feature is extremely useful when writing LISP. The package is well documented and comes with two of the major reference texts to the LISP language. A compiler has been announced (currently in beta test) and will be part of the next update. Early reports suggest that compilation enhances execution speed by a factor of five.

REFERENCES

[1] Hirsch, A., "Tagged Architecture Supports Symbolic Processing", *Computer Design*, June 1984.

[2] Johannes RS., "One Year's Experience with Corvus Omninet Local Area Network", *Proceedings of the Seventh Symposium on Computer Applications in Medical Care*, pp 775-778, May 1984.

[3] Barr, A. and Feigenbaum, E.A., "Programming Languages in AI Research" *The Handbook of Artificial Intelligence*, Volume 2, HeurisTech Press and William Kaughmann, Inc. pp 1-76. 1982.

[4] Touretsky, D.S., *LISP: A Gentle Introduction to Symbolic Computation*, Harper & Row, New York 1984.

[5] Steele Jr., G.L., *Common LISP The Language*, Digital Press, 1984.

[6] Wilensky, R., *LISPcraft*, W. W. Norton & Co., New York, 1984.

[7] Winston, P.H. and Horn, B. K. P., *LISP* Second Edition, Addison Wesley 1984.

[8] Betz, D., "An XLISP Tutorial", *BYTE*, pp 221-236, March, 1985.

[9] Bortz, J. and Diamont, J. "LISP for the IBM Personal Computer" *BYTE* pp 281-291, July, 1984.

Table 3

Features of MSDOS LISP Products				
		muLISP	IQLISP	GCLISP
General	Company	MicroSoft Soft Warehouse	Integral Quality	Gold Hill
	Cost	$250	$175	$475
	Size	256 Kb	640 Kb	1000 Kb
Memory Support Capability	Pointers	2 bytes-atom pointer stack 1 byte-strings binary 0	3 bytes	
	Mem. Mgmt. Functions	++	+	+++
	Hardware Interface	Supported	Supported	Supported
Interpreter	Error Checking	+	++	+++
	Debug	Trace Backtrace Break,Statistics	Trace Backtrace	Trace Backtrace Step,Describe
Editor	Type	Full Screen	Structure	Full Screen Handles Files
Functions Provided	Total	>100	>200	>300
	Other	InterLISP macLISP library		
Help Facilities	Online	None	Provided	Provided
	Tutorial	Provided	None	Provided
Input/Output	Windows	None	Window files	Window files
	Graphics	Points,lines & Turtle graphics	Points,lines	Points,lines Fill
Calls	Operating System	Supported	Supported	Supported
	Ports	Supported	Supported	Supported
Datatypes Provided	Infinite Length Integers	Present	Present	None
	Floating Point	None	Present	Present
	Arrays	None	Present	Present
	Others	Name, Number Node	Short Integer Strings Lists	Various Common LISP Data Types
Miscellaneous	Accessories	Utility Libraries with InterLISP & MacLISP muLISP Runtime License Agreement available for Lisp.com files		Compiler Announce Mouse Support
	Miscellaneous Idiosyncracies	Explicitly CR Auto-quoting Extended Cond Implied Cond Automatic local variables in lambda fxn (2-5)	Explicit CR	Auto-CR
	Scoping (Binding)	Dynamic	Dynamic	Dynamic & lexical
	Documentation	++	+	+++

+++   Excellent

++   Good

+   Fair

APPENDIX A

BENCHMARK FUNCTIONS FOR GCLISP

We use the TESTER function to automatically time execution of the different benchmarks. Obviously one must have a clock installed.

```
(DEFUN TESTER (L)
(GC)
(TIME (EVAL L)))
```

ITER-TEST is used to facilitate our capturing the benchmark data.

```
(DEFUN ITER-TEST (L NUM)
(DOTIMES (I NUM)
(PRINT (LIST 'VALUE 'OF 'RUN I))
(TESTER L)))
```

The DONOTHING function is an empty function that is used in functions that follow for "dummy" function calls. It is not passed arguments and performs no function.

```
(DEFUN DONOTHING ())
```

The IT function utilizes the Common LISP DOTIMES construct to iterate an empty loop N times, N being the integer argument passed.

```
(DEFUN IT (N)
(DOTIMES (I N)))
```

The ITF function utilizes the Common LISP DOTIMES command and calls the DONOTHING function N times, N being the argument ITF is passed.

```
(DEFUN ITF (N)
(DOTIMES (I N)
(DONOTHING) ))
```

The ITCAR function, like the ITF function, utilizes the Common LISP DOTIMES. Instead of calling DONOTHING, it calls CAR.

```
(DEFUN ITCAR (N)
  (DOTIMES (I N)
   (CAR A) ))
```

The ITREVERSE function, like the ITF function, utilizes the Common LISP DOTIMES command but calls the REVERSE function supplied in Common LISP as well. The REVERSE function is chosen as since it performs a significant amount of list manipulation.

```
(DEFUN ITREVERSE (N)
(DOTIMES (I N)
(REVERSE A) ))
```

IT2 utilizes the PROG construct to test iteration. The function is passed an integer argument, N, and runs its empty loop N times.

```
(DEFUN IT2 (N)
(PROG (COUNT)
(SETQ COUNT 0)
LOOP
(SETQ COUNT (+ 1 COUNT))
(COND ((= COUNT N) (RETURN T))
(T (GO LOOP)))))
```

ITF2 uses the PROG construct to iterate N times a loop containing a function call to DONOTHING. It is used to test the systems function calling capability.

```
(DEFUN ITF2 (N)
(PROG (COUNT)
(SETQ COUNT 0)
LOOP
(SETQ COUNT (+ 1 COUNT))
(DONOTHING)
(COND ((= COUNT N) (RETURN T))
(T (GO LOOP)))))
```

The ITCAR2 function, like the ITF2 function, utilizes the PROG. Instead of calling DONOTHING, it calls CAR.

```
(DEFUN ITCAR2 (N)
 (PROG (COUNT)
  (SETQ COUNT 0)
  LOOP
   (SETQ COUNT (+ 1 COUNT))
   (CAR A)
   (COND ((= COUNT N) (RETURN T))
     (T (GO LOOP)))))
```

ITREVERSE2, like IT2 utilizes the PROG construct and loops n times, n being the integer argument it is passed. Within its loop however, ITREVERSE2 runs the REVERSE function on A, in our benchmarks defined as a seven element list A..G.

```
(DEFUN ITREVERSE2 (N)
(PROG (COUNT)
(SETQ COUNT 0)
LOOP
(SETQ COUNT (+ 1 COUNT))
(REVERSE A)
(COND ((= COUNT N) (RETURN T))
(T (GO LOOP)))))
```

The FACT function returns the value of the factorial of the integer it is passed. The function is written utilizing single tail recursion.

```
(DEFUN FACT (X)
(COND
((< X 2) 1)
(T(* X (FACT (SUB1 X)))))))
```

The ITER-FACT function utilizes an iterative algorithm to calculate the factorial of the integer passed.

```
(DEFUN ITER-FACT (M)
(PROG (N)
(SETQ N 1)
LOOP
(COND ((ZEROP M) (RETURN N))
(T (SETQ N (* M N))
(SETQ M (- M 1))))
(GO LOOP)))
```

The REV and APP functions are included to demonstrate two tail recursion. The return exactly what REVERSE and APPEND do respectively.

```
(DEFUN REV (X)
(COND
((NULL X) NIL)
(T (APP(REV(CDR X))(LIST(CAR X))))))
```

```
(DEFUN APP (X Y)
(COND
((NULL X) Y)
(T (APP (REV(CDR(REV X))) (CONS (CAR(REV X)) Y ))) ))
```

The remaining functions are useful as LISP benchmarks as well. They are self-explanatory and use the GCLISP (Common) dialect.

```
(DEFUN FIB (X)
(COND
((< X 2) 1)
(T (+ (FIB (SUB1 X)) (FIB (- X 2)))) )
```

```
(DEFUN PRIMES (MAX)
(LET ((NUMBERS (REVERSE (LISTNUMS MAX)))
(COUNT 0))
```

```
(PRIME-AUX NUMBERS)
COUNT))

(DEFUN PRIME-AUX (NUMBERS)
(LET ((PRIME NIL))
(COND
((NULL NUMBERS) NIL)
((NULL (CAR NUMBERS)) (PRIME-AUX (CDR NUMBERS)))
(T (SETQ PRIME (+ 3 (+ (CAR NUMBERS) (CAR NUMBERS))))
(SETQ COUNT (ADD1 COUNT))
(ELIMINATE PRIME NUMBERS PRIME)
(PRIME-AUX (CDR NUMBERS))))))
(DEFUN ELIMINATE (NUM NUMBERS FLAG)
(COND
((NULL NUMBERS) NIL)
((ZEROP FLAG)
(RPLACA NUMBERS NIL)
(ELIMINATE NUM (CDR NUMBERS)(SUB1 NUM)) )
(T (ELIMINATE NUM (CDR NUMBERS)(SUB1 FLAG))) ) )

(DEFUN LISTNUMS (NUM)
(COND
((NOT (ZEROP NUM))
(CONS NUM (LISTNUMS (SUB1 NUM))) )
(T (LIST NUM))))

(DEFUN PRIMES2 (MAX)
(LET
((J MAX)
(K 0)
(PRIME 0)
(COUNT 0))
(SETQ NUMBERS
(MAKE-ARRAY (+ 1 MAX) :INITIAL-ELEMENT 1
LEADER-LENGTH (+ 1 MAX)))
(DOTIMES (J MAX)
(COND ((= (AREF NUMBERS J) 1)
(SETQ PRIME (+ 3 (+ J J)))
(SETQ COUNT (ADD1 COUNT))
(DO ((K (+ J PRIME) (+ K PRIME)))
((>= K MAX) T)
(SETF (AREF NUMBERS K) 0)))))
COUNT))
```

```
(DEFUN TIMER (LAMBDA (FXN)
(GC)
(SETQ START (DTIME))
(EVAL FXN)
(SETQ FINISH (DTIME))
(- FINISH START)))

(DEFUN ITER-TEST (LAMBDA (FXN N)
(FOR I FROM 1 TO N
(PRINT (LIST 'VALUE 'OF 'RUN I))
(PRINT (TIMER FXN)))))

(DEFUN DONOTHING (LAMBDA ()))

(DEFUN IT (LAMBDA (N)
(FOR I FROM 1 TO N)))

(DEFUN ITF (LAMBDA (N)
(FOR I FROM 1 TO N (DONOTHING))))

(DEFUN ITCAR (LAMBDA (N)
(FOR I FROM 1 TO N (CAR A))))

(DEFUN ITREVERSE (LAMBDA (N)
(FOR I FROM 1 TO N (REVERSE A))))

(DEFUN IT2 (LAMBDA (N)
(PROG (COUNT)
(SETQ COUNT 0)
LOOP
(SETQ COUNT (+ COUNT 1))
(COND ((EQUAL COUNT N) (RETURN N))
(T (GO LOOP))))))

(DEFUN ITF2 (LAMBDA (N)
(PROG (COUNT)
(SETQ COUNT 0)
LOOP
(SETQ COUNT (+ COUNT 1))
(DONOTHING)
(COND ((EQUAL COUNT N) (RETURN N))
(T (GO LOOP))))))

(DEFUN ITCAR2 (LAMBDA (N)
(PROG (COUNT)
(SETQ COUNT 0)
LOOP
(SETQ COUNT (+ COUNT 1))
(CAR A)
(COND ((EQUAL COUNT N) (RETURN N))
(T (GO LOOP))))))

(DEFUN ITREVERSE2 (LAMBDA (N)
(PROG (COUNT)
(SETQ COUNT 0)
LOOP
(SETQ COUNT (+ COUNT 1))
(REVERSE A)
(COND ((EQUAL COUNT N) (RETURN N))
(T (GO LOOP))))))
```

```
(DEFUN TIMER (LAMBDA (FXN)
(RECLAIM)
(SETQ START (TIME))
(EVAL FXN)
(SETQ FINISH (TIME))
(DIFFERENCE FINISH START)]
(DEFUN ITER-TEST (LAMBDA (FXN N)
(PROG (COUNT)
(SETQ COUNT 0)
LOOP
(SETQ COUNT (PLUS COUNT 1))
(PRINT (LIST 'VALUE 'OF 'RUN COUNT))
(PRINT (TIMER FXN))
(COND
((EQUAL COUNT N) N)
(T (GO LOOP)]

(DEFUN DONOTHING (LAMBDA ()]

(DEFUN IT2 (LAMBDA (N)
(PROG (COUNT)
```

```
        (SETQ COUNT 0)
        LOOP
        (SETQ COUNT (PLUS COUNT 1))
        (COND ((EQUAL COUNT N) (RETURN N))
           (T (GO LOOP)]

(DEFUN ITF2 (LAMBDA (N)
   (PROG (COUNT)
        (SETQ COUNT 0)
        LOOP
        (SETQ COUNT (PLUS COUNT 1))
        (DONOTHING)
        (COND ((EQUAL COUNT N) (RETURN N))
           (T (GO LOOP))))))

(DEFUN ITCAR2 (LAMBDA (N)
   (PROG (COUNT)
        (SETQ COUNT 0)
        LOOP
        (SETQ COUNT (PLUS COUNT 1))
        (CAR A)
        (COND ((EQUAL COUNT N) (RETURN N))
           (T (GO LOOP))))))

(DEFUN ITREVERSE2 (LAMBDA (N)
   (PROG (COUNT)
        (SETQ COUNT 0)
        LOOP
        (SETQ COUNT (PLUS COUNT 1))
        (REVERSE A)
        (COND ((EQUAL COUNT N) (RETURN N))
           (T (GO LOOP))))))

(SETQ A '(A B C D E F G))
```

LISP BENCHMARK STATISTICS (in seconds)						
	IBM PC			IBM AT		
FUNCTION NAME	muLISP	IQLISP	GCLISP	muLISP	IQLISP	GCLISP
IT	NA	4.90	0.05	NA	1.84	0.00
ITF	NA	5.60	0.59	NA	2.12	19.60
ITCAR	NA	5.82	0.68	NA	2.19	24.00
ITREVERSE	NA	52.83	1.64	NA	1.96	59.60
IT2	3.62	5.28	2.93	1.28	1.99	1.10
IT2F	4.61	6.05	3.43	1.64	2.26	1.30
IT2CAR	4.50	6.27	3.52	1.59	2.36	1.26
IT2REVERSE	4.94	53.28	4.51	1.74	19.77	1.59
REV	11.66	57.11	36.03	4.19	21.20	14.57
APP	35.01	173.81	108.13	12.56	74.29	43.75
FACT	0.07	0.17	0.16	0.03	0.06	0.06
ITER-FACT	0.15	0.27	0.16	0.05	0.27	0.07
PRIMES	17.82	92.37	48.06	6.35	34.32	17.41
PRIMES2	15.16	13.15	1.53	5.43	4.90	0.55
FIB	8.19	22.70	17.30	2.96	8.51	6.23
GC*	0.23	11.46	1.82	0.22	4.55	0.85

*   The garbage collections were benchmarked with only runtime facilities present using
ITER-TEST. Five calls to garbage collect were made.

NA not applicable since muLISP does not provide a DO loop syntax.

PROLOG - THE LANGUAGE AND ITS IMPLEMENTATION COMPARED WITH LISP

David H D Warren
Department of Artificial Intelligence
University of Edinburgh
Scotland

Luis M Pereira
Fernando Pereira
Divisao de Informatica
Laboratorio Nacional de Engenharia Civil
Lisbon, Portugal

Abstract

Prolog is a simple but powerful programming
language founded on symbolic logic. The basic
computational mechanism is a pattern matching
process ("unification") operating on general
record structures ("terms" of logic). We briefly
review the language and compare it especially with
pure Lisp. The remainder of the paper discusses
techniques for implementing Prolog efficiently;
in particular we describe how to compile the
patterns involved in the matching process. These
techniques are as incorporated in our DECsystem-10
Prolog compiler (written in Prolog). The code it
generates is comparable in speed with that produced by existing DEC10 Lisp compilers. We argue
that pattern matching is a better method for
expressing operations on structured data than
conventional selectors and constructors - both for
the user and for the implementor.

Introduction

Prolog is a very simple, but surprisingly powerful, programming language developed at the University of Marseille [Roussel 1975], as a practical
tool for "logic programming" [Kowalski 1974]
[Colmerauer 1975] [van Emden 1975]. From a user's
point of view the major attraction of the language
is ease of programming. Clear, readable, concise
programs can be written quickly with few errors.

We have been concerned with implementing a Prolog
system [Pereira 1977] [Warren 1977] specifically
for the DECsystem-10 [DEC 1974]. Our implementation includes an interpreter and a compiler, both
written in Prolog itself. The main aim of this
paper is to describe some of the novel aspects of
the work, especially the concept of compiling a
"pattern matching" language such as Prolog. However, since Prolog is not widely known, we shall
begin with a brief description of the language
itself, drawing attention to the special features
which make its implementation interesting and worth-
while. The discussion will cover the basic language, but not various built-in procedures for
input-output hardware arithmetic, etc. Please
note that we have not made (nor wanted to make) any
original contribution to the basic language design.

The Language

Prolog has many parallels with Lisp. Both are
interactive languages designed primarily for symbolic data processing. Both are founded on formal mathematical systems - Lisp on Church's lambda
calculus, Prolog on a subset of classical logic.
Like pure Lisp, the Prolog language does not
(explicitly) incorporate the machine-oriented concepts of assignment and references (pointers).
Furthermore, pure Lisp can be viewed as a special-
isation of Prolog, where procedures are restricted
to simple functions and data structures are restricted to lists. Let us therefore start by
translating some elementary Lisp functions into
Prolog:-

```
append[x;y]=
    [null[x] -> y;
     T -> cons[car[x];append[cdr[x];y]]]

nreverse[x]=
    [null[x] -> nil;
     T -> append[nreverse[cdr[x]];cons[car[x];
                                            nil]]]
```

These functions for list concatenation and (naive)
list reversal are equivalent to the following two
Prolog procedures:

```
append(nil,Y,Y).
append((A.B),Y,(A.B1)) :- append(B,Y,B1).

nreverse(nil,nil).
nreverse((A.B),Y):-
nreverse(B,YO),append(YO,(A.nil),Y).
```

Each procedure comprises a number of clauses
corresponding to the branches of the conditional(s)
in the Lisp function definition. The procedure
name is called a predicate, and has an arity one
greater than the corresponding Lisp function. The
extra argument expresses the result of the function.
The leftmost part of a clause is its head or
procedure entry point, and displays a possible form
of the arguments to the predicate. The remainder
of the clause, its body, consists of a number
(possibly zero) of goals or procedure calls, which
impose conditions for the head to be true. If the
body is empty we speak of a unit clause.

We see that the Prolog formulation does not
require data selectors (car and cdr) or constructors (cons). Instead, the form or "pattern" of
the procedure's input and output is displayed as
explicit data structures. In this example these
correspond to Lisp S-expressions. In general,
Prolog data objects are called terms. A term is
either a variable (distinguished by an initial
capital letter), an atom (such as 'nil') or a
compound term (such as '(A.B)'). A compound

Reprinted with permission from *Proc. Symp. on Artificial Intelligence and Programming Languages,* vol. 12, no. 8, pp. 109–115, Aug. 1977.

term comprises a <u>functor</u> of some <u>arity</u> N >= 1, with a sequence of N terms as <u>arguments</u>. For instance the functor of '(A.B)' is '.' of arity 2 and the arguments are A,B. We have written this term using an optional infix notation. The standard notation would be '.(A,B)'. One should think of a functor as a record type and the arguments of a term as fields of a record. An atom is treated as a functor of arity 0. The head and goals of a clause are considered to be terms, so a predicate is merely a functor which occurs in a particular context.

To make use of the Prolog procedure for reversing a list, one might <u>execute</u> (or solve) a goal such as:-

    nreverse((1.2.3.nil),X)

Note that (1.2.3.nil) is merely a shorthand for (1.(2.(3.nil))). The effect of the procedure call will be to give the variable X a value which is the term:-

    (3.2.1.nil)

Prolog differs from most programming languages in that there are two quite distinct ways to understand its semantics. The <u>procedural</u> semantics is the more conventional, and describes in the usual way the sequence of states passed through when executing a program. In addition a Prolog program can be understood as a set of descriptive statements <u>about</u> a problem. The <u>declarative</u> semantics which Prolog inherits from logic provides a formal basis for such a reading. Informally, one interprets terms as shorthand for natural language phrases by applying a uniform translation of each functor. e.g.:-

    nil = "the empty list"
    (A.B) = "the list whose first element is A
           and remaining elements are B"
    nreverse(X,Y) = "the reverse of X is Y"

A clause 'P :- Q, R, S.' is interpreted as:-

    "P if Q and R and S"

Each variable in a clause should be interpreted as some arbitrary object.

The declarative semantics simply defines (recursively) the set of terms which are asserted to be true according to a program. A term is <u>true</u> if it is the head of some clause instance and each of the goals (if any) of that clause instance is true, where an <u>instance</u> of a clause (or term) is obtained by substituting, for each of zero or more of its variables, a new term for all occurrences of the variable.

Thus the only instance of the goal:-

    nreverse((1.2.3.nil),X)

which is true is:-

    nreverse((1.2.3.nil),(3.2.1.nil))

In this way the declarative semantics gives one some understanding of a Prolog program without looking into the details of how it is executed.

It is the declarative aspect of Prolog which is responsible for promoting clear, rapid, accurate programming. It allows a program to be broken down into small, independently meaningful units (clauses).

The procedural semantics describes the way a goal is executed. The object of the execution is to produce true instances of the goal. It is important to notice that the ordering of clauses in a program, and goals in a clause, which are irrelevant as far as the declarative semantics is concerned, constitute crucial <u>control information</u> for the procedural semantics.

To <u>execute</u> a goal, the system searches for the first clause whose head <u>matches</u> or <u>unifies</u> with the goal. The unification process [Robinson 1965] finds the most general common instance of the two terms, which is unique if it exists. If a match is found, the matching clause instance is then <u>activated</u> by executing in turn, from left to right, each of the goals of its body (if any). If at any time the system fails to find a match for a goal, it <u>backtracks</u>, i.e. it rejects the most recently activated clause, undoing any substitutions made by the match with the head of the clause. Next it reconsiders the original goal which activated the rejected clause, and tries to find a subsequent clause which also matches the goal.

Let us now briefly look at how the goal:-

    nreverse((1.2.3.nil),X)

is actually executed. The goal only matches the second of the two clauses for 'nreverse'. The body of the matching clause instance is:-

    nreverse((2.3.nil),Y0), append(Y0,(1.nil),X)

The result of executing the first of these two goals is to instantiate Y0 to (3.2.nil) leaving the second goal as:-

    append((3.2.nil),(1.nil),X)

This matches only the second clause for 'append', instantiating X to (3.X1) and producing a recursive procedure call:-

    append((2.nil),(1.nil),X1)

(The name chosen for the new variable X1 is arbitrary). Eventually we hit the bottom of the recursion with the goal:-

    append(nil,(1.nil),X2)

This now matches only the first clause for 'append', instantiating X2 to (1.nil) thus completing the final result:-

    X = (3.2.1.nil)

Prolog owes its simplicity firstly to a <u>generalisation</u> of certain aspects of other programming languages, and secondly to <u>omission</u> of many other features which are no longer strictly essential. This generalisation gives Prolog a number of novel properties (compared in particular with Lisp). We shall briefly summarise these and then give two illustrative examples.

(1) General record structures take the place of Lisp's S-expressions. An unlimited number of different record types may be used. Records with any number of fields are possible, giving the equivalent of fixed bound arrays. There are no type restrictions on the fields of a record.

(2) Pattern matching replaces the use of selector and constructor functions for operating on structured data.

(3) Procedures may have multiple outputs as well
as multiple inputs.

(4) The input and output arguments of a procedure
do not have to be distinguished in advance, but may
vary from one call to another. Procedures can
thus be multi-purpose.

(5) Procedures may generate, through backtracking,
a sequence of alternative results. This amounts
to a high level form of iteration.

(6) Unification includes certain features which
are not found in the simpler pattern matching
provided by languages such as Microplanner. We
sum this up in the "equation"-
    unification = pattern matching
                  + the logical variable

The characteristics of the "logical" variable are
as follows. An "incomplete" data structure (ie.
containing free variables) may be returned as a
procedure's output. The free variables can later
be filled in by other procedures, giving the effect
of implicit assignments to a data structure (cf.
Lisp's rplaca, rplacd). Where necessary, free
variables are automatically linked together by
"invisible" references. As a result, values may
have to be "dereferenced". This is also performed automatically by the system. Thus the programmer need not be concerned with the exact status
of a variable - assigned or unassigned, bound to a
reference or not. In particular, the occurences
of a variable in a pattern do not need any prefixes
to indicate the status of the variable at that
point in the pattern matching process (contrast
Microplanner etc.). In short, the logical
variable incorporates much of the power of assignment and references in other languages. This is
reminiscent of the way most uses of goto can be
obviated in a language with "well-structured"
control primitives.

(7) Program and data are identical in form.
Clauses can usefully be employed for expressing
data.

(8) As we have already seen, there is a natural
declarative semantics in addition to the usual
procedural semantics.

(9) The (procedural) semantics of a syntactically
correct program is totally defined. It is
impossible for an error condition to arise or for
an undefined operation to be performed. This is
in contrast to most programming languages including pure Lisp (cf. cars and cdrs of atoms,
unbound variables). A totally defined semantics
ensures that programming errors do not result in
bizarre program behaviour or incomprehensible
error messages.

The following example illustrates the identity of
program and data in Prolog, and shows the language's potential as a natural medium for database
interrogation. A "database" of unit clauses
provides information on the populations (in
millions) and areas (in thousands of square miles)
of various countries. A procedure 'density'
supplies "virtual data" on population densities
(per square mile):-

```
pop(china,825).    area(china,3380).
pop(india,586).    area(india,1139).
pop(ussr,252).     area(ussr, 8708).
pop(usa, 212).     area(usa, 3609).
    :
```

```
density(C,D):-
    pop(C,P), area(C,A), D is (P*1000)/A.
```

The following clause represents a database query to
find countries of similar population density
(differing by less than 5%):-

```
ans(C1,D1,C2,D2) :-
    density(C1,D1), density(C2,D2),
    D1>D2, 20*D1 <21*D2.
```

Executing the goal 'ans(C1,D1,C2,D2)' will supply,
through backtracking, the sequence of solutions
required. Notice how the density procedure
generates multiple results. The two calls to
'density' have exactly the same effect as nested
iterations in a conventional language. In implementation terms, a sequence of different values is
assigned to the variables C1,D1,C2,D2; cf. the
following Algol-style procedure:-

```
for C1 from 1 to N do
    int D1 := pop[C1]*1000/area[C1];
    for C2 from 1 to N do
        int D2 := pop[C2]*1000/area[C2];
        if D1>D2 and 20*D1 <21*D2
        then output(country[C1],D1,
                    country[C2],D2);
    repeat
repeat
```

The second example displays many of the characteristics which make Prolog an agreeable language for
compiler writing (as applied in the case of our own
Prolog compiler). The task is to generate a list
of serial numbers for the items of a given list,
the members of which are to be numbered in alphabetical order eg.

    (p.r.o.l.o.g.nil) -> (4.5.3.2.3.1.nil)

As with many Prolog programs, the key to arriving
at the required algorithm is to first conceive a
procedure which checks whether a proposed list of
serial numbers is a correct solution. This can
be done by pairing up the items of the input list
with their proposed serial numbers as an
"association list", arranging these pairs in
alphabetical order, and then finally checking
whether the serial numbers are in the correct
consecutive order. i.e.-

```
serialise(L,R) :-
    pairlists(L,R,A),
    arrange(A,T),
    numbered(T,1,N).
```

The pairing is done by a procedure very similar to
the pairlis function of the Lisp 1.5 manual, but
with the pairs represented as terms 'pair(X,Y)':-

```
pairlists((X.L),(Y.R),(pair(X,Y).A)) :-
    pairlists(L,R,A).
pairlists(nil,nil,nil).
```

The arrangement in alphabetical order and checking
of the numbers could be done using only lists, however it is much more convenient to use binary trees.
We represent a tree as a term of the form 'void'
("the void tree") or 'tree(T1,X,T2)' (" a tree
with X at the root and subtrees T1 and T2").

```
arrange((X.L),tree(T1,X,T2)) :-
    partition(L,X,L1,L2),
    arrange(L1,T1),
    arrange(L2,T2).
arrange(nil,void).
```

```
partition((X.L),X,L1,L2) :- partition(L,X,L1,L2).
partition((X.L),Y,(X.L1),L2) :-
    before(X,Y), partition(L,Y,L1,L2).
partition((X.L),Y,L1,(X.L2)) :-
    before(Y,X), partition(L,Y,L1,L2).
partition(nil,Y,nil,nil).

before(pair(X1,Y1),pair(X2,Y2)) :- X1 < X2.

numbered(tree(T1,pair(X,N1),T2),N0,N) :-
    numbered(T1,N0,N1),
    N2 is N1+1,
    numbered(T2,N2,N).
numbered(void,N,N).
```

This procedure for verifying a solution illustrates
the advantages of having more general record
structures and of manipulating them by pattern
matching.   Notice also how the partition procedure
returns two outputs.

Now it happens that the 'serialise' procedure is
multi-purpose - it can be used not only for verification, but will also actually construct the
required list of serial numbers if the initial
goal does not provide one.   This remarkable
property owes something to judicious design, but
is made possible by the characteristics of the
"logical" variable.   Let us consider what happens
when a goal such as:-

    serialise((d.a.t.a.nil),R)

is executed.   The call to 'pairlists' returns two
outputs (thus 'pairlists' can also serve more than
one purpose):-

    R = (X1.X2.X3.X4.nil)
    A = (pair(d,X1).pair(a,X2).pair(t,X3).
        pair(a,X4).nil)

Both these data structures are incomplete. i.e.
In implementation terms, they contain references
to 4 empty cells created by 'pairlists'.   The
list R is the partially completed output for
'serialise'.   Next the call to 'arrange' generates a tree of the form:-

Notice that variable X4 has become bound to X2
(it could equally well be the other way round).
The implementation has created a reference to
X2's cell and assigned it to X4's.   Finally the
call to 'numbered' completes the tree returned
by 'arrange' and causes X2,X1,X3 to be bound to
1,2,3.   This has the effect of assignments to
a data structure.   One should also note that
the finally completed list returned by 'serialise' still contains a reference (i.e. the field
corresponding to X4 will require an extra step
of indirection when accessed).

It is difficult to see how this algorithm could
be simulated in pure Lisp.   Use of rplaca and
replacd would almost certainly be called for,
resulting in a less transparent program.   Notice
how the Prolog programmer is spared all the
intricate implementation details.

Implementation

The first experimental interpreter for Prolog was
written in Algol-W by Philippe Roussel [1972].
This work led to better techniques for implementing
the language, incorporated in the more widely used
Marseille interpreter written in Fortran by
Battani and Meloni [1973].   More recently, Maurice
Bruynooghe [1976] has implemented a Prolog interpreter in Pascal.   He gives a good introduction
to the fundamentals of Prolog implementation and
describes a space saving technique using a "heap".
Other Prolog interpreters have been implemented at
the University of Waterloo, Canada (for IBM 370)
and at Budapest (in CDL for ICL 1900).

Our implementation is based on a compiler from
Prolog to DECsystem-10 assembly language.   Like
Bruynooghe, we use many of the same techniques as
were developed at Marseille.   The main innovations
are:-

(1)   the concepts for compiling Prolog into a
machine language;

(2)   indexing of clauses within a procedure;

(3)   some particular measures to economise on space
required during execution.

The most important innovation is compilation.
Recall that a Prolog computation is essentially
just a sequence of unifications or "pattern
matching" operations.   Each unification involves
matching two terms or "patterns", one a goal or
"procedure call", the other a clause head or
"procedure entry point".   The principal effect
of compilation is to translate the head of each
clause into instructions which will do the work
of matching against any goal pattern.   Of the
two patterns involved in a matching, we choose to
compile the clause head because it is initially
uninstantiated, unlike the goal.   Also the uninstantiated form of the goal which appears in
the source program typically has little structure
that can be compiled.

In any clause head, the first occurrence of a
variable can be translated into a straightforward
assignment, since the variable will be initially
uninstantiated.   If the variable is at the outermost level of the pattern, e.g.

    append((A.B),Y,(A.B1)) :- append(B,Y,B1).
            *

it will be assigned an argument of the procedure
call.   Otherwise the assignment will have the
effect of selecting a component of a data structure, e.g. in the case of:-

    append((A.B),Y,(A.B1)) :- append(B,Y,B1).
             *

Now in practice most of the symbols in a clause
head are first occurrences of variables, so much
of the pattern just translates into conventional
assignments.   The code for the rarer case of a
subsequent occurrence of a variable, e.g.

    append(nil,Y,Y).
                *

is more complex, and may involve calling a
recursive subroutine to do the matching.   If a
variable has just a single occurrence in a clause,
no executable code need be generated for it.

The code generated for a compound subterm (or subpattern), e.g.

```
append((A.B),Y,(A.B1)) :- append(B,Y,B1).
          ******
```

has to distinguish between two cases. If the subterm matches against a variable, a new data structure has to be constructed (cf. cons) and assigned to the variable. The variable assigned to will usually have to be remembered on a pushdown list (called the "trail") to allow backtracking to "undo" the assignment later. This first case is handled by an out-of-line subroutine.

The other case concerns matching against a nonvariable. This is performed essentially by inline code. It comprises a test for matching functors (record types), followed by the compiled form of each of the subterms of the compound term. This code will be responsible for accessing subcomponents of the matching data structure (cf. car and cdr).

In describing the various unification steps, we have so far passed over the creation of references and their subsequent dereferencing. If a variable matches against another variable, a reference to one of the variable's cells is created and assigned to the other. Each unification step has to be prepared to dereference an arbitrarily long chain of these references. In practice, however, constructed data structures usually contain no references, and chains of references are even rarer. Our implementation is such that a single test suffices to determine the required action for the commonest cases of most unification steps.

A useful function performed by our compiler, and not found in previous implementations of Prolog, is to index the different clauses in a procedure, giving the effect of a "switch" or "computed goto". If the clauses would conventionally be considered as data, the effect is to store this data in an array or "hash table". For simplicity of implementation, the indexing is only on the form (i.e. principal functor) of the first subterm in the head of each clause, but this is perfectly adequate for most actual Prolog programs. For example the clauses for 'pop' and 'area' in the populations example are indexed by country (the first argument) but not by the numeric value which is the second argument. Effectively, the clauses are compiled into two arrays of numbers with "nonnumeric" subscripts.

Our implementation uses the same "structure-sharing" technique for the internal representation of constructed data as was introduced by the Marseille interpreter. The technique is a novel and elegant alternative to the "literal" representation based on linked records in "heap" storage which is conventional for other languages (including Lisp). The basis of the technique is to represent a compound data object by a pair of pointers called a "molecule". One pointer indicates a "skeleton" structure (i.e. a compound term) occurring in the source program, the other points to a vector of cells called a "frame". The frame contains the values of variables occurring in the skeleton. This representation facilitates very rapid creation of structured data at the expense of somewhat slower access to its components. A further advantage is greater compactness in most cases.

Although structure-sharing entails extra work to access the components of a data structure, the overhead is small on a machine with good "indirect addressing" facilities. The architecture of the DEC10 is particularly favourable, as a variable in a skeleton can be nicely represented by a DEC10 "address word". This specifies the address of the variable's cell as an offset relative to the contents of an index register. Any DEC10 instruction can obtain its operand indirectly by referring to an address word. This means that, once the frame address for a molecule has been loaded into an index register, each of the fields of the structure-shared record can be accessed in just one instruction. The impact on overall performance is substantial.

The main drawback of the Marseille interpreter is its tendency to require unacceptable amounts of working storage. The source of the problem is that Prolog views non-determinate computation as the rule rather than the exception. A procedure cannot "return" in the conventional way until after it has generated all of its alternative results (i.e. until backtracking occurs). When just one of the results has been completed (i.e. the end of a clause is reached), the implementation can't "pop" the stack in the usual way. Instead the effect is to immediately invoke the caller's "continuation". Our space economy measures rely, like Bruynooghe's technique, on the fact that in practice most Prolog procedures produce just a single result. The major step is to classify Prolog variables into "locals" and "globals". This is performed by the compiler and need be of no concern to user. Storage for the two types is allocated from different areas, the local and global stacks, analogous to the "stack" and "heap" of Algol-68. Now when the end of a clause is reached, and provided the procedure can generate no further results, the local storage for the procedure is recovered automatically by a stack mechanism, as for a conventional language. No garbage collector is needed for this process, unlike Bruynooghe's method. Note that clause indexing helps the system to detect when a procedure can produce no more results.

Most Prolog procedures are not in practice used in a multi-purpose way. For example the 'append' procedure might only be used to concatenate two given lists, and not, say, to generate pairs of lists which when concatenated give a specified third list. In our implementation, the user can notify the system of such restrictions on the usage of procedures through optional "mode declarations". These enable a higher proportion of variables to be placed in the more desirable "local" category, and also help to improve the compactness of the compiled code.

In addition to these measures, our system can also recover storage from the global stack by garbage collection, cf. Algol-68's heap. The garbage collector used has to be quite intricate even by normal standards. After what is in principle a conventional "trace and mark", space is recovered by compacting global storage still in use to the bottom of the stack. This involves "remapping" all addresses pointing to the global stack.

It is important to notice that a garbage collector is not essential for our system (unlike for example Lisp implementations). If the user restricts himself to tasks smaller than a certain size, the garbage collector need never be used. This is because a general stack mechanism recovers <u>all</u> storage on backtracking, or when each task is complete, as for the Marseille interpreter.

We may finally remark that our implementation automatically adjusts the sizes of the different storage areas during execution.

Performance Comparisons

Some detailed performance comparisons have been made on a DEC10 (K1 processor) of compiled Prolog with interpreted Prolog (Marseille), and also with compiled Lisp (Stanford, with NOUUO option).

(a) Speed

There is a 15 to 20-fold improvement over the Marseille interpreter. Simple functions over lists (e.g. the naive reverse example) run quite uniformly at about 50% to 70% of the Lisp speed. Note that the compiler treats lists no differently from other terms. Simple functions over more general data structures can equal or better the speed of the corresponding pure Lisp function operating on data encoded as lists. For example, the following differentiation procedure:-

```
d(U+V,X,DU+DV) :- d(U,X,DU),d(V,X,DV).
d(U-V,X,DU-DV) :- d(U,X,DU),d(V,X,DV).
d(U*V,X,DU*V+U*DV) :- d(U,X,DU),d(V,X,DV).
d(U/V,X,(DU*V-U*DV)/V^2) :- d(U,X,DU),d(V,X,DV).
d(U^N,X,DU*N*U^N1) :-
    integer(N), N1 is N-1,d(U,X,DU).
d(X,X,1).
d(C,X,0) :- atomic(C), C ≠ X.
```

runs (depending on the data) 1.1 to 2.6 times faster then the equivalent Lisp DERIV function given on p. 167 of Weissman's [1967] Lisp primer.

(b) Space

The saving on working storage relative to Marseille depends greatly on the degree of determinacy of the program. At worst it is 2-times better due simply to tighter packing of data into the machine word. Figures for the compiler itself indicate roughly a 10-fold improvement. Recall that the compiler is a Prolog program, originally "bootstrapped" using the Marseille interpreter. It now rarely requires more than 5K words total for the trail and two stacks.

The compiled code itself is relatively compact at about 2 words per source symbol.

It is difficult to make meaningful space comparisons with Lisp and we have not so far attempted to do so.

(c) Comments

The tests show that Prolog speed compares quite well with pure Lisp, especially where a wider range of record types is really called for. Of course such a comparison only evaluates a limited part of Prolog and can't be entirely fair since Lisp is specialised to just this area. Moreover, Lisp systems do not provide complete security against program error - <u>car</u> and <u>cdr</u> are allowed to apply indiscriminately to any object. As a result no run-time checks are needed, and the fundamental selectors reduce to very simple machine-oriented operations - effectively hardware instructions on the DEC10. One might therefore have expected Lisp to be considerably faster than Prolog. There are two main factors acting in favour of the Prolog implementation.

Firstly, and perhaps surprisingly, there are good reasons to expect pattern matching to promote better implementation than conventional selectors and constructors. Productive computation is easily integrated with procedure call so minimising the overheads of argument passing, a process which is usually "red tape" in other languages, including Lisp. In particular, no location needs to be set up for an argument to a procedure if only its components are to be referred to. These are selected once and for all by pattern matching, in a single efficient process without having to re-load index registers for each component. No optimisation is necessary to avoid duplication of work brought about in Lisp, when, for example, <u>car</u> of an object is repeatedly referred to, or <u>caddr</u> and <u>cdddr</u> are applied to the same object. These points apply <u>a fortiori</u> for a language such as Pop-2 with multiple data types requiring run-time type checking, since the type of an object is only checked once in pattern matching. Finally, pattern directed invocation of the different clauses of a procedure enables and encourages the implementation to incorporate computed <u>gotos</u> automatically where appropriate.

The second factor favouring Prolog is structure-sharing. Ironically, this technique was first devised by Boyer and Moore [1972] as a means of saving space. However it is even more important for its contribution to Prolog's speed. Essentially it enables a "cons" to be effected faster than in Lisp. Partly this is because the nature of Prolog permits storage to be allocated in stacks, so there are none of the costs associated with allocating records individually from a "heap". Neither need there be any garbage collection overheads, since global storage can normally be recovered by the stack mechanism. Both these advantages have even greater force if one compares with a language allowing more than one record size. An additional feature of the stack regime is the avoidance of random memory accesses, enabling better exploitation of a paged machine. The other main reason for the speed of the structure-sharing "cons" is the avoidance of the copying of information which occurs when a conventional <u>cons</u> initialises a new list cell. The greater the number of symbols in a "skeleton" term, the greater is this saving. Essentially, structure-sharing replaces copying in "cons" by extra indirection in "<u>car</u>" and "<u>cdr</u>". As we have already seen, the extra indirection costs very little on suitable machines such as the DEC10, with its "effective address mechanism".

Conclusion

Pattern matching should not be considered an "exotic extra" when designing a programming language. It is the preferable method for specifying operations on structured data, both from the user's <u>and</u> the implementor's point of view. This is especially so where more than one record

92

type is allowed. Hoare [1975] makes a similar case for a more limited form of pattern-matching in the context of an Algol-like language.

For applications requiring an easy-to-use and transparent language for "symbol processing", Prolog seems to offer significant advantages over Lisp. Even ignoring Lisp's unfortunate syntax and variable binding mechanism, a major barrier to its readability is the size and complexity (degree of nesting) of typical function definitions. Prolog allows a program to be formulated in smaller units, each having a natural declarative reading. In addition it gives the programmer generalised record structures with an elegant mechanism for manipulating them. The pure Lisp view of computation as simple function evaluation is too restrictive for typical applications, so extensive use is normally made of lower-level extensions to the language (prog, rplaca etc.) resulting in less transparent programs. Prolog allows programs with similar behaviour to be written without having to resort to machine- or implementation-oriented concepts. For example, our compiler is written almost entirely in "pure" Prolog (i.e. clauses with a valid declarative interpretation). Finally, our work shows that the use of Prolog as opposed to (pure) Lisp need involve no great loss of efficiency, if indeed any.

Acknowledgements

We are indebted to members of the Groupe d'Intelligence Artificielle, Marseille, for developing both the Prolog language and the fundamental structure-sharing technique. The work was supported by a British Science Research Council Grant B/RG 9972 and by L.N.E.C., Lisbon.

References

Battani G and Meloni H [1973]
   Interpreteur du langage de programmation Prolog.
   Groupe d'Intelligence Artificielle, Marseille-Luminy, 1973

Boyer R S and Moore J S [1972]
   The sharing of structure in theorem proving programs.
   Machine Intelligence 7 (ed. Meltzer & Michie), Edinburgh U. Press, 1972.

Bruynooghe M [1976]
   An interpreter for predicate logic programs: Part 1. Report CW 10, Applied Maths & Programming Division, Katholieke Univ Leuven, Belgium, Oct 1976.

Colmerauer A [1975]
   Les grammaires de metamorphase.
   Groupe d'Intelligence Artificielle, Marseille, Marseille-Luminy, Nov 1975.

DEC [1974]
   DECsystem10 System Ref Manual (3rd edition)
   Digital Equipment Corporation, Maynard, Mass. Aug 1974.

van Emden M H [1975]
   Programming with resolution logic.
   Report CS-75-30, Dept. of Computer Science, University of Waterloo, Canada. Nov 1975.

Hoare C A R [1973]
   Recursive data structures.
   Stanford AI Memo 223, Calif. Oct 1973.

Kowalski R A [1974]
   Logic for problem solving.
   DCL Memo 75, Dept of AI, Edinburgh. Mar 1974.

McCarthy J et al. [1962]
   LISP 1.5 Programmer's Manual.
   MIT Press, MIT, Cambridge, Mass. Aug 1962.

Pereira L M [1977]
   User's Guide to DECsystem-10 Prolog.
   Forthcoming publication, Divisao de Informatica, Lab. Nac. de Engenharia Civil, Lisbon. 1977.

Robinson J A [1965]
   A machine-oriented logic based on the resolution principle.
   JACM vol 12, pp. 23-44. 1965.

Roussel P [1972]
   Definition et traitement de l'egalite formelle en demonstration automatique.
   These 3me. cycle, UER de Luminy, Marseille. 1972.

Roussel P [1975]
   Prolog: Manual de reference et d'utilisation.
   Groupe d'Intelligence Artificielle, Marseille-Luminy. Sep 1975.

Warren D H D [1977]
   Implementing Prolog - compiling predicate logic programs.
   Forthcoming report, Dept of AI, Edinburgh. 1977.

Weissman C [1976]
   Lisp 1.5 Primer.
   Dickenson Publishing Co. 1967.

The Smalltalk-80 System

The Xerox Learning Research Group
Xerox Palo Alto Research Center
3333 Coyote Hill Rd
Palo Alto CA 94304

The Smalltalk-80 system represents the current state of the object-oriented point of view as it has been reduced to practice by the Xerox Learning Research Group. The Smalltalk-80 system is composed of objects that interact only by sending and receiving messages. The programmer implements a system by describing messages to be sent and describing what happens when messages are received.

The Smalltalk-80 system is the latest in a series of programming environments that have applied the object-oriented point of view more and more uniformly to the design and production of software systems. The fundamental ideas of objects, messages, and classes came from SIMULA. (See reference 1.) SIMULA allows users to create object-oriented systems, but uses the standard data/procedure-oriented ALGOL language to provide numbers, booleans, basic data structures, and control structures. The Flex system, the Smalltalk-72, Smalltalk-74, and Smalltalk-76 (see references 5, 2, and 4, respectively) systems extended the object-oriented point of view to an increasing number of the elements of a programming environment. For example, in Smalltalk-72, arithmetic, list structures, and control structures were represented as objects and messages, but classes were not. In Smalltalk-74, class descriptions as objects were introduced. The Smalltalk-76 system added the capability to express relationships between classes, and extended the object-oriented point of view to the programmer's interface.

This article presents the central semantic features and most of the syntactic features of the Smalltalk-80 system. It was prepared by Dave Robson and Adele Goldberg as scribes for the group effort of designing and implementing the system. Two forthcoming books (see reference 3) provide the full specification of the Smalltalk-80 system; in particular, the books describe the implementation of the interpreter and storage manager, and the graphical user interface.

Sending Messages—Expressions

Messages are described by *expressions*, which are sequences of characters that conform to the syntax of the Smalltalk-80 programming language. A message-sending expression describes the *receiver, selector,* and *arguments* of the message. When an expression is *evaluated,* the message it describes is transmitted to its receiver. Here are several examples of expressions describing a message to an object. (Note: color has been added to help identify the receivers, selectors, and arguments in the following examples.)

1. | frame | center |

2. | origin | + | offset |

3. | frame | moveTo: | newLocation |

4. | list | at: | index | put: | element |

Key: □ Receiver
□ Selector
▨ Argument

Each expression begins with a description of the receiver of the message. The receivers in these examples are described by *variable names:* frame, origin, frame, and list, respectively. Generally, at least one space must separate the parts of an expression.

Messages without arguments are called *unary messages*. A unary message consists of a single identifier called a unary selector. The first example is a unary message whose selector is center.

A *binary message* has a single argument and a selector that is one of a set of special single or double characters called *binary selectors*. For example, the common arithmetic symbols (+ , − , * , and /) are binary selectors; some comparison operations are represented as double characters (eg: = = for equivalence, ~ = for not equal). The second example is a binary message whose argument is offset.

A *keyword message* has one or more arguments and a selector that is made up of a series of *keywords*, one preceding each argument. A keyword is an identifier with a trailing colon. The third example is a single-argument keyword message whose selector is moveTo: and whose argument is newLocation. The fourth example is a two-argument keyword message whose selector is made up of the keywords at: and put: and whose arguments are index and element. To talk about the selector of a multiple-argument keyword message, the keywords are concatenated. So, the selector of the fourth example is at:put:.

The message receivers and arguments in the examples are described by variable names. In addition, they can also be described with *literals*. The two most common kinds of literals are integers and strings. An *integer literal* is a sequence of digits that may be preceded by a minus sign (eg: 0, 1, 156, −3, or 13772). A *string literal* is a sequence of characters between single quotes (eg: 'hi', 'John', or 'the Smalltalk-80 system'). A binary message with an integer literal as its receiver is

45 + count

A keyword message with a string literal as its argument is

printer display: 'Monthly Payroll'

When a message is sent, it invokes a method determined by the class of the receiver. The invoked method will always return a result (an object). The result of a message can be used as a receiver or argument for another message. An example of a unary message describing the receiver of another unary message is

window frame center

Unary messages are parsed left to right. The first message in this example is the unary selector frame sent to the object named window. The unary message center is then sent to the result of the expression window frame (ie: the object returned from window's response to frame).

Binary messages are also parsed left to right. An example of a binary message describing the receiver of another binary message is

index + offset * 2

The result of sending the binary message + offset to the object named index is the receiver for the binary message *2. All binary selectors have the same precedence; only the order in which they are written matters. Parentheses can be used to change the order of evaluation. A message within parentheses is sent before any messages outside the parentheses. If the previous example were written

index + (offset * 2)

the result of the binary message * 2 to offset would be

used as the argument of a binary message with receiver index and selector + .

Unary messages take precedence over binary messages. If unary messages and binary messages appear together, the unary messages will be sent first. In the example

frame center + window offset − index

the result of the unary message center to frame is the receiver of the binary message whose selector is + and whose argument is the result of the unary message offset to window. The result of the + message is, in turn, the receiver of the binary message − index. Parentheses can be used to explicitly show the order of evaluation, eg: ((frame center) + (window offset)) − index. Parentheses can also be used to alter the order of evaluation. In the example

(center + offset) x

the binary message + offset would be sent before the unary message x.

Whenever keywords appear in an unparenthesized message, they compose a single selector. The example

window showText: 'Title' inFont: helvetica
    indented: 15

is a single message whose selector is showText:inFont:indented:. Because of this concatenation, there is no left-to-right parsing rule for keyword messages. If a keyword message is to be used as a receiver or argument of another keyword message, it must be parenthesized. The expression

frame scale: (factor max: 5)

describes two keyword messages. The result of the expression factor max: 5 is the argument for the scale: message to frame.

Binary messages take precedence over keyword messages. When unary, binary, and keyword messages appear in the same expression without parentheses, the unary messages are sent first, the binary messages next, and the keyword messages last. The example

bigFrame height: smallFrame height * 2

is evaluated as if it were parenthesized as follows:

bigFrame height: ((smallFrame height) * 2)

A *cascaded message expression* describes a sequence of messages to be sent to the same object. A simple message expression is a description of the receiver (ie: a variable name, literal, or expression) followed by a message (ie: a unary selector, a binary selector and argument, or a set of keywords and arguments). A cascaded message expres-

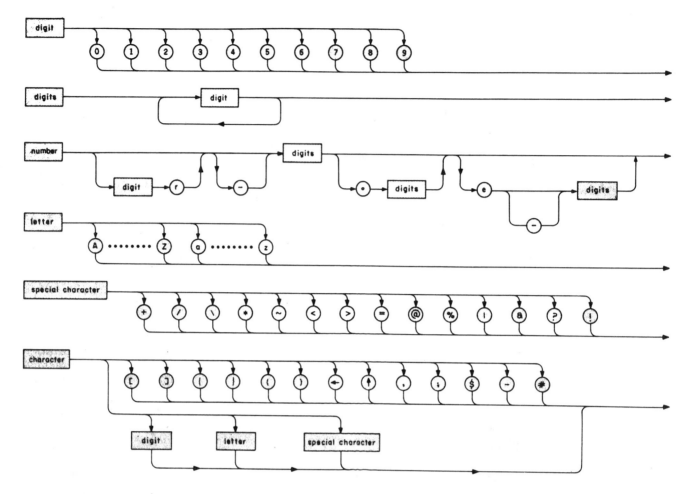

Figure 1: *Syntax diagrams for the Smalltalk-80 language.*

sion is a single description of a receiver followed by several messages separated by semicolons. For example, in the expression

    printer newLine; print: reportTitle; space;
        print: Date today.

four messages are sent to the object named *printer*. The selectors of the four messages are *newLine*, *print:*, *space*, and *print:*. In the expression

    window frame center: pointer location;
        width: border + contents; clear

three messages are sent to the object returned from the frame message to *window*. The selectors of the three messages are *center:*, *width:*, and *clear*. Without cascading, this would have been three expressions

    window frame center: pointer location.
    window frame width: border + contents.
    window frame clear

Assigning Variables

The value of a variable can be used as the receiver or

argument of a message by including its name in an expression. The value of a variable can be changed with an *assignment expression*. An assignment expression consists of a variable name followed by a left arrow (←) followed by the description of an object. When an assignment expression is evaluated, the variable named to the left of the arrow assumes the value of the object described to the right of the arrow. The new value can be described by a variable name, a literal, or a message-sending expression. Examples of assignments are

    center ← origin
    index ← 0
    index ← index + 1
    index ← index + 1 max: limit

In the last example, the message + 1 is sent to the value of the variable *index*, the message *max: limit* is sent to the result of the + 1 message, and the result of the *max: limit* message becomes the new value of the variable *index*.

A number of variables can be assigned in the same expression by including several variable names with left arrows. The expression

    start ← index ← 0

makes the value of both *start* and *index* be 0.

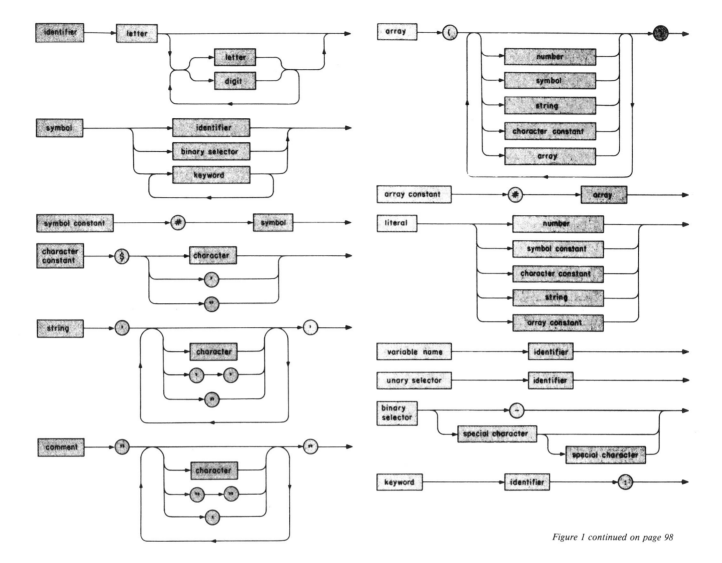

Figure 1 continued on page 98

The syntax table in figure 1 is a diagram for parsing well-formed Smalltalk-80 expressions. This table does not specify how *spaces* are treated. Spaces must not appear between digits and characters that make up a single token, nor within the specification of a number. Spaces must appear

• between a sequence of identifiers used as variables or unary selectors
• between the elements of an array in an array constant
• on either side of a keyword in a keyword expression

Spaces may optionally be included between any other elements in an expression. A carriage return or tab has the same syntactic function as a space.

Receiving Messages—Classes

A *class* describes a set of objects called its *instances*. Each instance has a set of *instance variables*. The class provides a set of names that are used to refer to these variables. A class also provides a set of *methods* that describe what happens when its instances receive messages. A method describes a sequence of actions to be taken when a message with a particular selector is received by an instance of a particular class. These actions consist of sending other messages, assigning variables, and returning a value to the original message.

To create a new application, modify an existing application, or to modify the Smalltalk-80 system itself, a programmer creates and modifies classes that describe objects. The most profitable way to manipulate a class is with an interactive system. Much of the development of the Smalltalk-80 system has been the creation of appropriate software-development tools. (See Larry Tesler's article "The Smalltalk Environment," on page 90.*) Unfortunately, to describe a system on paper, a noninteractive linear mode of presentation is needed. To this end, a *basic class template* is provided as a simple textual representation of a class. The basic class template in table 1 shows the name of the class, the names of the instance variables, and the set of methods used for responding to messages.

In table 1, the italicized elements will be replaced by the specific identifiers or methods appropriate to the

* Page number refers to the August 1981 issue of *BYTE* magazine.

97

Figure 1 continued:

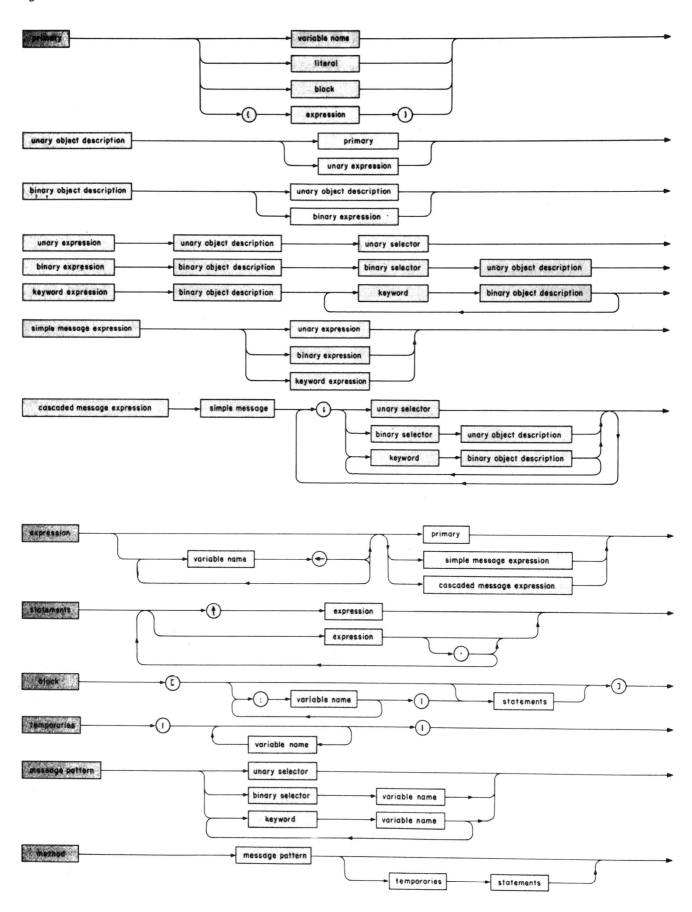

98

class name	identifier		
instance variable names	identifier	identifier	identifier
methods			
method			
method			
method			

Table 1: *The basic class template.*

class. Names of classes begin with an uppercase letter, and names of variables begin with a lowercase letter. As an example, figure 2 shows the basic template form of a class named Point whose instances represent points in a two-dimensional coordinate system. Each instance has an instance variable named x that represents its horizontal coordinate and an instance variable named y that represents its vertical coordinate. Each instance can respond to messages that initialize its two instance variables, request the value of either variable, and perform simple

arithmetic. The details of methods (in particular, the use of '|', '.' and '↑') are the subject of our next discussion.

Methods

A method has three parts:

- a *message pattern*
- some *temporary variable names*
- some *expressions*

The three parts of a method are separated by vertical bars (|). The message pattern consists of a selector and names for the arguments. The expressions are separated by periods (.) and the last one may be preceded by an up arrow (↑). In the method for selector + in figure 2, the message pattern is + aPoint, the temporary variable names are sumX and sumY, and there are three expressions, the last one preceded by an ↑.

Line breaks have no significance in methods; formatting is used only for purposes of aesthetics. The vertical bars and periods are delimiters of significance.

As stated earlier, each message pattern contains a selector. When a message is received by an instance, the method whose message pattern contains the same selector will be executed. For example, suppose that offset were an

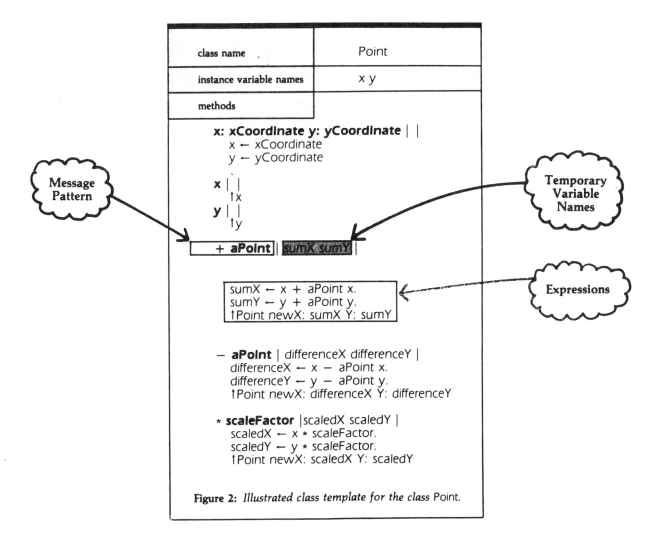

Figure 2: *Illustrated class template for the class* Point.

class name	DepositRecord
superclass	Object
instance variable names	date amount
methods	

of: depositAmount on: depositDate | |

    date ← depositDate.
    amount ← depositAmount

amount | |
    ↑ amount

balanceChange | |
    ↑ amount

Table 2: *Class template for class DepositRecord.*

class name	CheckRecord
superclass	DepositRecord
instance variable names	number
methods	

number: checkNumber for: checkAmount on: checkDate | |
    number ← checkNumber.
    date ← checkDate.
    amount ← checkAmount

of: anAmount on: aDate | .|
    self error:
      'Check records are initialized with
    number:for:on:'

balanceChange | | ↑ 0 − amount

Table 3: *Class template for class CheckRecord.*

instance of Point in the expression

offset + frame center

The method whose message pattern is + aPoint would be executed in response. For selectors that take arguments, the message pattern also contains *argument names* wherever arguments would appear in a message. When a method is invoked by a message, the argument names in the method are used to refer to the actual arguments of that message. In the above example, aPoint would refer to the result of *frame center*.

class name	identifier
superclass	identifier
instance variable names	identifier identifier identifier
class variable names	identifier identifier identifier
class messages and methods	

   method

   method

   method

instance messages and methods	

   method

   method

   method

Table 4: *The full class template.*

Following the message pattern, a method can contain some *temporary variable names* between vertical bars. When a method is executed, a set of variables is created that can be accessed by the temporary variable names. These temporary variables exist only while the method is in the process of execution.

Following the second vertical bar, a method contains a sequence of expressions separated by periods. When a method is executed, these expressions are evaluated sequentially.

So, there are three steps in receiving a message, corresponding to the three parts of the method. Smalltalk will

1. *Find* the method whose message pattern has the same selector as the message and *create* a set of variables for the argument values.
2. *Create* a set of temporary variables corresponding to the names between the vertical bars.
3. *Evaluate* the expressions in the method sequentially.

Six kinds of variables can be used in a method's expressions:

- the instance variables of the receiver
- the pseudo-variable self
- the message arguments
- temporary variables
- class variables
- global variables

The instance variables are named in the message receiver's class. In the example, x and y refer to the values of the instance variables of offset.

There is an important *pseudo-variable* available in every method, which is named self. self refers to the

100

receiver of the message that invoked the method. It is called a pseudo-variable because its value can be accessed like a variable, but its value cannot be changed using an assignment expression. In the example, *self* refers to the same object as *offset* during the execution of the method associated with +.

Arguments and temporary variables are similar, in that the names for both are declared in the method itself and they both exist only during the method's execution. However, unlike arguments, temporary variables are not automatically initialized. The values of temporary variables can be changed with an assignment expression.

Class variables are shared by all instances and the class itself. Names for the class variables are shown in the full class template in an entry called "class variable names" (see table 4). Although they are variables and their values can be changed, they are typically treated as constants, initialized when the class is created, and then simply used by the instances. For example, if the class of floating-point numbers wanted to provide trigonometric functions, it might want to define a variable called pi to be used in any of its methods.

Global variables are shared by all objects. A global dictionary, called Smalltalk, holds the names and values of these variables. The classes in the system, for example, are the values of global variables whose names are the class names. With the exception of variables used to reference system resources, few global variables exist in the Smalltalk-80 system. Programming style that depends on user-defined globals is generally discouraged.

If the last expression in a method is preceded by an ↑, the message that invoked the method takes on the value of this expression. If an ↑ does not precede the last expression, the value of the message is simply the receiver of the message. For example, the x:y: message to a *Point* (see figure 2) behaves as if it had been written

x: xCoordinate y: yCoordinate | |
    x ← xCoordinate.
    y ← yCoordinate.
    ↑ self

Methods can contain comments anywhere. A *comment* is a sequence of characters delimited by double quotes. Two consecutive double quotes are used to embed a double quote within a comment. The methods in class *Point* were purposely written in a verbose style to provide examples. The messages for + could have been written

    + aPoint | |
      ↑ Point newX: x + aPoint x Y: y + aPoint y

The basic class template presents only the most important attributes of a class. The complete description of a class is provided by the *full class template*, described in the next section.

Inheritance

The basic template allows a class to be described in-dependently of other classes. It ignores inheritance among classes. The full class template, however, takes inheritance into account. (See table 4.) With it, a class can be described as a modification of another class called its *superclass*. All classes that modify a particular class are called its *subclasses*. A subclass inherits the instance variable names and methods of its superclass. A subclass can also add instance variable names and methods to those it inherits. The instance variable names added by the subclass must differ from the instance variable names of the superclass. The subclass can *override* a method in the superclass by adding a message with the same selector. Instances of the subclass will execute the method found in the subclass rather than the method inherited from the superclass.

To assemble the complete description of a class, it is necessary to look at its superclass, its superclass's superclass, and so on, until a class with no superclass is encountered. There is only one such class in the system (ie: without a superclass), and its class name is Object. All classes ultimately inherit methods from *Object*. Object has no instance variables. The set of classes linked through the superclass relation is called a *superclass chain*. The full class template has an entry called "superclass" that specifies the initial link on the class's superclass chain.

As an example, we might describe a class, *DepositRecord*, whose instances are records of bank account deposits. Each instance has two instance variables representing the date and amount of the deposit. The class template is shown in table 2.

class name	CheckRecord
superclass	DepositRecord
instance variable names	number
class messages and methods	

number: checkNumber for: checkAmount on: checkDate | |
    ↑ self new number: checkNumber
        for: checkAmount
        on: checkDate	

instance messages and methods	

number: checkNumber for: checkAmount on: checkDate | |
    super of: checkAmount on: checkDate.
    number ← checkNumber
 	
of: anAmount on: aDate | |
 	
    self error: 'Check records are initialized with
      number:for:on:'
balanceChange | | ↑ 0 − amount	

Table 5: *Full class template for class CheckRecord.*

A class, CheckRecord, whose instances are records of checks written on an account is a subclass of DepositRecord; this new class adds an instance variable that represents the check number. The class template is shown in table 3.

An instance of CheckRecord has three instance variables. It inherits the amount message, adds the number:for:on: message, and overrides the balanceChange and of:on: messages. The of:on: method contains a single expression in which the message error: 'Check records are initialized with number:for:on:' is sent to the pseudo-variable self. The method for error: is found in the superclass of DepositRecord, which is the class Object; the response is to stop execution and to display the string literal argument to the user.

An additional pseudo-variable available in a method's expressions is super. It allows a subclass to access the methods in its superclass that have been overridden in the subclass description. The use of super as the receiver of a message has the same effect as the use of self, except that the search for the appropriate message starts in the superclass, not the class, of the receiver.

For example, the method associated with number:for:on in CheckRecord might have been defined as

number: checkNumber for: checkAmount on: checkDate | |
    super of: checkAmount on: checkDate.
    number ← checkNumber

Metaclasses

Since a class is an object, there is a different class that describes it. A class that describes a class is called a *metaclass*. Thus, a class has its own instance variables that represent the description of its instances; it responds to messages that provide for the initialization and modification of this description. In particular, a class responds to a message that creates a new instance. The unary message new creates a new instance whose instance variables are uninitialized. The object nil indicates an uninitialized value.

The classes in the system might all be instances of the same class. However, each class typically uses a slightly different message protocol to create initialized instances. For example, the last expression in the method associated with + in class Point (see figure 2) was

  Point newX: sumX Y: sumY

newX:Y: is a message to Point, asking it to create a new instance with sumX and sumY as the values of the new instance's instance variables. The newX:Y: message would not mean anything to another class, such as DepositRecord or CheckRecord. So, these three classes can't be instances of the same class. All classes have a lot in common, so their classes are all subclasses of the same class. This class is named Class. The subclasses of Class are called *metaclasses*.

The newX:Y: message in Point's metaclass might be implemented as

newX: xValue Y: yValue | |
    ↑ self new x: xValue y: yValue

The new message was inherited by Point's metaclass from Class. One reason for having metaclasses is to have a special set of methods for each class, primarily messages for initializing class variables and new instances. These methods are displayed in the full class-template form shown in table 4; they are distinguished from the methods for messages to the instances of the class. The two categories are "class messages and methods" and "instance messages and methods," respectively. Methods in

class name	Point
superclass	Object
instance variable names	x y
class variable names	pi
class messages and methods	

instance creation
newX: xValue Y: yValue | |
    ↑ self new x: xValue
            y: yValue
newRadius: radius Angle: angle | |
    ↑ self new x: radius * angle sin
            y: radius * angle cos

class initialization
setPI | | pi ← 3.14159

instance messages and methods

accessing
x: xCoordinate y: yCoordinate | |
    x ← xCoordinate.
    y ← yCoordinate
x | | ↑x
y | | ↑y
radius | | ↑$((x * x) + (y * y))$ squareRoot
angle | | ↑(x/y) arctan

arithmetic
+ aPoint | | ↑Point newX: x + aPoint x
                  Y: y + aPoint y
− aPoint | | ↑Point newX: x − aPoint x
                  Y: y − aPoint y
* scaleFactor | | ↑Point newX: x * scaleFactor
                    Y: y * scaleFactor
circleArea | r |
    r ← self radius.
    ↑ pi * r * r

Table 6: *Full class template for class Point.*

the category "class messages and methods" are associated with the metaclass; those in "instance messages and methods" are associated with the class.

If there are no class variables for the class, the "class variable name" entry is omitted. So, CheckRecord might be described as shown in table 5.

It is often desirable to create subcategories within the categories "class messages and methods" and "instance messages and methods." Moreover, the order in which the categories or subcategories are listed is of no significance. (The notion of categories is simply a pretty printing" technique; it has no semantic significance.)

Returning to the example of class Point, if the instance methods of class Point include subcategories *accessing* and *arithmetic*, the template for Point might appear as shown in table 6.

When the class Point is defined, the expression

Point setPi

should be evaluated in order to set the value of the single class variable.

A Point might be created and given a name by evaluating the expression

testPoint ← Point newX: 420 Y: 26

The new Point, testPoint, can then be sent the message circleArea:

testPoint circleArea

or used in a more complex expression:

(testPoint * 2) circleArea

Primitive Routines

The response to some messages in the system may be performed by a *primitive routine* (written in the implementation language of the machine) rather than by evaluating the expressions in a method. The methods for these messages indicate the presence of such a primitive routine by including < primitive > before the first expression in the method. A major use of primitive methods is to interact with the machine's input/output devices.

An example of a primitive method is the new message to classes, which returns a new instance of the receiver.

new | | < primitive >

This particular primitive routine always produces a result. If there are situations in which a primitive routine cannot produce a result, the method will also contain some expressions. If the primitive routine is successful in responding to the message, it will return a value and the expressions in the method will not be evaluated. If the primitive routine encounters difficulty, the expressions will be evaluated as though the primitive routine had not been specified.

Another example of a message with a primitive response is a message with the selector + sent to a SmallInteger

+ **aNumber** | | < primitive >
self error: 'SmallInteger addition has failed'

One reason this primitive might fail to produce a result is that the argument is not a SmallInteger. In the example, this would produce an error report. In the actual Smalltalk-80 system, an attempt is made to check and see if the argument were another kind of number for which a result could be produced.

Indexed Instance Variables

An object's instance variables are usually given names by its class. The names are used in methods of the class to refer to the values of the instance variables. Some objects also have a set of instance variables that have no names and can only be accessed by messages. The instance variables are referred to by an integral *index*. Indexable objects are used to implement the classes in the system that represent collections of other objects, such as arrays and strings.

The messages to access indexed instance variables have

class name	Array
superclass	IndexedCollection
indexable instance variables	
class messages and methods	

instance creation
with: anElement | |
↑(self new: 1) at: 1 put: anElement
with: firstElement with: secondElement
| anArray |
anArray ← self new: 2.
anArray at: 1 put: firstElement.
anArray at: 2 put: secondElement.
↑anArray

instance messages and methods	

accessing
at: anInteger | |
< primitive >
self error: 'index out of range'

at: anInteger put: anElement | |
< primitive >
self error: 'index out of range'

funny stuff
embed | |
↑Array with: self

Table 7: *Full class template for class Array.*

selectors at: and at:put:. For example

list at: 1

returns the first indexed instance variable of *list*. The example

list at: 4 put: element

stores *element* as the value of the fourth indexed instance variable of *list*. The at: and at:put: messages invoke primitive routines to load or store the value of the indicated variable. The legal indices run from one to the number of indexable variables in the instance. The at: and at:put: messages are defined in class *Object* and, therefore, can be understood by all objects; however, only certain classes will create instances with indexable instance variables. These classes will have an additional line in the class template indicating that the instances contain *indexable instance variables*. As an example, we show a part of the template for class *Array* in table 7.

Each instance of a class that allows indexable instance variables may have a different number of them; such instances are created using the *new:* message to a class, whose argument tells the number of indexable variables. The number of indexable instance variables an instance has can be found by sending it the message *size*. A class whose instances have indexable instance variables can also have named instance variables. All instances of any class will have the same number of named instance variables.

Control Structures and Blocks

The two control structures in the Smalltalk-80 system described so far are

●the sequential execution of expressions in a method
●the sending of messages that invoke other methods that eventually return values

All other control structures are based on objects called *blocks*. Like a method, a block is a sequence of expressions, the last of which can be preceded by an up arrow (↑). The expressions are delimited by periods; they may be preceded by one or more identifiers with leading colons. These identifiers are the *block arguments*. Block arguments are separated from expressions by a vertical bar.

Whenever square brackets are encountered in a method, a block is created. Evaluation of the expressions inside the square brackets is deferred until the block is sent the message *value* or a message whose selector is a concatenation of one or more occurrences of the keyword *value:*. Control structures are implemented as messages with receivers or arguments that are blocks. The methods for carrying out these control-structure messages involve sending the blocks patterns of *value* messages.

In the Smalltalk-80 system, there are two types of

primitive control messages: conditional selection of blocks, *ifTrue:ifFalse:*, and conditional iteration of blocks, *whileTrue:* and *whileFalse:*.

The representation of conditions in the Smalltalk-80 system uses distinguished boolean objects named *false* and *true*. The first type of primitive control message provides for conditional selection of a block to be executed. This is similar to the IF . . . THEN . . . ELSE of ALGOL-like languages. The expression

queue isEmpty ifTrue: [index ← 0]
        ifFalse: [index ← queue next]

evaluates the expressions in the first block if the receiver is *true* and evaluates the expressions in the second block if the receiver is *false*. Two other forms of conditional selection provide only one alternative

queue isEmpty ifTrue: [index ← 0].
queue isEmpty ifFalse: [index ← queue next].

When *ifTrue:* is sent to *false*, it returns immediately without executing the block. When *ifFalse:* is sent to *true*, the block is not executed.

The second type of primitive control message repeatedly evaluates the expressions in a block as long as some condition holds. This is similar to the WHILE and UNTIL statements in ALGOL-like languages. This type of control message is a message to a block; the receiver, the block, evaluates the expressions it contains and determines whether or not to continue on the basis of the value of the last expression. The first form of this control message has selector *whileTrue:*. The method for *whileTrue:* repeatedly executes the argument block as long as the receiver's value is *true*. For example,

[index < = limit] whileTrue: [self process: list at: index.
        index ← index + 1].

The binary message < = is understood by objects representing magnitudes. The value returned is the result of comparing whether the receiver is less than or equal to (< =) the argument.

The second conditional iteration message has selector *whileFalse:*. The method for *whileFalse:* repeatedly executes the argument block as long as the receiver's value is *false*. For example,

[queue isEmpty] whileFalse: [self process: queue next]

The messages *whileTrue* and *whileFalse* to a block provide a shorthand notation for messages of the form *whileTrue: aBlock* and *whileFalse: aBlock*, if the argument *aBlock* is an empty block.

Block arguments allow one or more of the variables inside the block to be given new values each time the block is executed. Instead of sending the block the message *value*, messages with selectors *value:* or *value:value:*, and so on, are sent to the block. The arguments of the value: messages are assigned to the block arguments (in order) before the block expressions are evaluated.

As an example, classes with indexed instance variables could implement a message with selector do: that takes a block as an argument and executes it once for every indexed variable. The block has a single block argument; the value of the appropriate indexed variable is passed to it for each execution. An example of the use of such a message is

list do: [:element | self process: element]

The message might be implemented as

```
do: aBlock | index |
    index ← 1.
    [index < = self size] whileTrue:
        [aBlock value: (self at: index).
         index ← index + 1]
```

Similar control messages can be implemented for any class. As an example, a simple repetition could be provided by a timesRepeat: aBlock message to instances of class Integer

```
timesRepeat: aBlock | index |
    index ← 1.
    [index < = self] whileTrue:
        [aBlock value.
         index ← index + 1]
```

Examples of implementing other control messages are given in L Peter Deutsch's article "Building Control Structures in the Smalltalk-80 System," on page 322.*

The Smalltalk-80 System: Basic Classes

The Smalltalk-80 *language* provides a uniform syntax for retrieving objects, sending messages, and defining classes. The Smalltalk-80 *system* is a complete programming environment that includes many actual classes and instances. In support of the uniform syntax, this system includes class descriptions for Object, Class, Message, CompiledMethod, and Context, whose subclasses are BlockContext and MethodContext. Multiple independent processes are provided by classes ProcessorScheduler, Process, and Semaphore. The special object nil is the only instance of class UndefinedObject. These classes comprise the *kernel* Smalltalk-80 system.

The system also includes class descriptions to support basic data structures; these are numerical and collection classes. The class Number specifies the protocol appropriate for all numerical objects. Its subclasses provide specific representations of numbers. The subclasses are Float, Fraction, and Integer. For a variety of reasons, there are both SmallIntegers and LargeIntegers; of these, there are LargePositiveIntegers and LargeNegativeIntegers.

Class Collection specifies protocol appropriate to objects representing collections of objects. These include Bag, Set, OrderedCollection, LinkedList, MappedCollection, SortedCollection, and IndexedCollection. The latter provides protocol for objects with indexable instance variables. It has subclasses String and Array. Elements of a string are instances of class Character; bytes are stored in instances of ByteArray. A subclass of String is Symbol; a subclass of Set is Dictionary (a set of Associations).

Interval is a subclass of Collection with elements representing an arithmetic progression. Intervals can be created by sending the message to: or to:by: to Integer. So, the expressions 1 to: 5 by: 1 and 1 to: 5 each create a new Interval representing 1, 2, 3, 4, 5. As a Collection, Interval responds to the enumeration message do:. For example, in

(1 to: 5) do: [:index | anArray at: index put: index * 2]

the block argument index takes on successive values 1, 2, 3, 4, 5.

For programmer convenience, an Integer also responds to the messages to:do: and to:by:do:, allowing the parentheses in interval enumeration expressions to be omitted.

The ability to stream over indexed or ordered collections is provided by a hierarchy based on class Stream, including ReadStream, WriteStream, and ReadAndWriteStream. A file system, local or remote, is then implementable as a subclass of these kinds of Streams.

Since instances of the system classes described above are used in the implementation of all applications, an understanding of their message protocol is as necessary to understanding an implementation as an understanding of the language syntax. These system classes are fully described in the forthcoming Smalltalk books.

In addition to the basic data-structure classes, the Smalltalk-80 system includes class descriptions to support interactive graphics (forms and images and image editors, text and text editors), networking, standard files, and hard-copy printing. A complete Smalltalk-80 system contains about sixty class definitions, not including a variety of windows or views, menus, scrollbars, and the metaclasses. Many of these are discussed in companion articles in this issue. (See Daniel H H Ingalls's 'The Design Principles Behind Smalltalk,'' page 286,* and Larry Tesler's "The Smalltalk Environment," page 90.*)

The important thing to note is that each of these class descriptions is implemented in the Smalltalk-80 language itself. Each can be examined and modified by the programmer. Some of the class descriptions contain methods that reference primitive methods; only these methods are implemented in the machine language of the implementation machine. It is a fundamental part of the philosophy of the system design that the programmer have such complete access. In this way, system designers, such as members of the Xerox Learning Research Group, are able to build the next Smalltalk in the complete context of Smalltalk itself. ■

* Page number refers to the August 1981 issue of *BYTE* magazine.

References

1. Birtwistle, Graham; Ole-Johan Dahl; Bjorn Myhrhaug; and Kristen Nygaard. *Simula Begin*. Philadelphia: Auerbach, 1973.
2. Goldberg, Adele and Alan Kay, editors. *Smalltalk-72 Instructional Manual*. Xerox PARC technical report, March 1976 (out of print).
3. Goldberg, Adele; David Robson; and Daniel H H Ingalls. *Smalltalk-80: The Language and Its Implementation* and *Smalltalk-80: The Interactive Programming Environment*, 1981 (books forthcoming).
4. Ingalls, Daniel H H. "The Smalltalk-76 Programming System: Design and Implementation." In *Proceedings of the Principles of Programming Languages Symposium*, January 1978.
5. Kay, Alan. *The Reactive Engine*. Ph.D. Thesis, University of Utah, September, 1969 (University Microfilms).

Glossary

Editor's Note: *This glossary provides concise definitions for many of the keywords and concepts related to Smalltalk-80. These definitions will be most useful if you first read the introductory Smalltalk articles. . . . GW*

General Terminology

object	a package of information and descriptions of its manipulation
message	a specification of one of an object's manipulations
method	a procedure-like entity; the description of a sequence of actions to be taken when a message is received by an object
class	a description of one or more similar objects
instance	an object described by a particular class
method dictionary	a set of associations between message selectors and methods; included in each class description
metaclass	a class whose (single) instance is itself a class
subclass	a class that is created by sharing the description of another class, often modifying some aspects of that description

Syntax Terminology

message receiver	the object to be manipulated, according to a message
message sender	the object requesting a manipulation
message selector	a symbolic name that describes a desired manipulation of an object
message argument	one of the objects specified in a message that provides information needed so that a message receiver can be manipulated appropriately
unary message	a message without arguments
binary message	a message with a single argument and a selector that is one of a set of special single or double characters
keyword message	a message that has one or more arguments and a selector made up of a series of identifiers with trailing colons, one preceding each argument

block	a literal method; an object representing a sequence of actions to be taken at a later time, upon receiving an "evaluation" message (such as one with selector value or value:)

Semantics

instance variable	a variable that is information used to distinguish an instance from other instances of the same class
class variable	a variable shared by all instances of a class and the class itself
named variable	an instance variable that is given a name in the class of the instance; the name is used in methods of the class
indexed variable	an instance variable with no name, accessed by message only; referred to by an integer (an index)
global or pool variable	a variable shared by instances of several classes; a system example is Smalltalk, a dictionary that includes references to all the defined classes
temporary variable	a variable that exists only while the method in which it is declared is in the process of execution
pseudo-variable	a variable available in every method without special declaration, but whose value cannot be changed using an assignment. System examples are self, super and thisContext.
nil	a special object, the only instance of class UndefinedObject

Implementation Terminology

field	the memory space in which the value of an object's variable is stored
bytecode	a machine instruction for the virtual machine
object pointer	a reference to an object
reference count	of an object, is the number of objects that point to it (ie: that contain its object pointer)

USER DEFINED PARALLEL CONTROL STRATEGIES IN NIAL

J.I. Glasgow, M.A. Jenkins and C.D. McCrosky

Department of Computing and Information Science
Queen's University, Kingston, Canada

ABSTRACT

Nial is an interactive, general purpose programming language that has data structure concepts based on a theory of nested rectangular arrays. This paper discusses the integration of logic programming with the functional style of Nial. It also illustrates how the language captures the notion of parallelism using transformers that map operations to new operations. Utilizing the ability to express concurrent computations and the basic logic functions of the language, it is demonstrated how a variety of parallel and sequential control strategies can be implemented in Nial.

INTRODUCTION

There is currently increasing interest in the development of parallel inference machines. Much of this work is focused on designing parallel implementations of the language Prolog. Conery[1] has described several types of parallelism that can be implemented in Prolog: AND-parallelism, OR-parallelism, stream parallelism and search parallelism. Augmented Prolog systems such as Epilog[2] and Concurrent Prolog[3] have also been designed to take advantage of parallel architectures.

Another approach to extending logic programming is the integration of logic and functional programming environments. Funlog[4] is a computational model based upon first-order predicate logic that provides the notion of functions. Languages that combine properties of logic and Lisp also exist. Robinson and Sibert's Loglisp[5] is a system that consists of a Lisp-like environment offering both Lisp and logic.

Similar to Loglisp, we describe in this paper a programming language that combines logic with functional programming. Other features of Loglisp that we have encorporated are user access to the search strategy and functional reduction of data within logical terms. Unlike most of the current work in functional logic programming, we are also considering concurrency in our language. The language is the Nested Interactive Array Language (Nial). Nial is considered to be a candidate language for fifth generation systems[6] because:

- it captures a powerful notion of parallelism.
- it allows a natural and useful implementation of resolution logic.
- it is very high level and mathematically tractable.

This paper will concentrate on the underlying features of the language that support parallel processing and demonstrate how these features can be used to develop logic control strategies for OR-parallelism. We also emphasize the importance of allowing the the user the flexibility of defining inferencing techniques.

The organization of the paper is as follows: The three sections following the introduction describe the language Nial, the logic component of Nial, and concurrency in the language. Section 5 discusses how parallel logic control strategies can be defined in Nial.

NIAL

Nial is an interactive, general purpose programming language that has data structure concepts similar to those of APL and Lisp. It is based on array theory, a theory of nested rectangular arrays. This theory was introduced by T. More[7,8] of the IBM Cambridge Scientific Centre and was later extended to the language Nial by More and Jenkins[9].

Array Theory

Array theory consists of a universe of data of one sort: finite, nested, rectangular arrays. Similar to set theory, array theory involves concepts of aggregation and membership of objects within a collection. The theory is one-sorted in that every data object is an array. The items of an array, that are gathered together in rectangular arrangement along any number of axes of various lengths, may themselves be arrays to any depth of nesting. A table of coefficients, such as a matrix or multiplication table, a list of letters, such as a word, and a single object, such as a number or truth-value, are examples of rectangular arrays having 2,1, and 0 axes respectively.

In array theory there are seven types of atomic objects, four numeric types (Boolean truth-values,

Reprinted from *Proc. IEEE Symp. on Logic Programming*, pp. 22–28, July 1985.

integers, reals, complex numbers) and three literal types (characters, phrases and faults). Arrays are nested collections that contain atomic objects at the deepest level. For mathematical convenience atomic objects are viewed as self-nesting arrays.

An operation in array theory is a function that maps arrays to arrays. The basic operations of the theory are total in that they are defined for all arrays. User-defined operations can be constructed in several ways (e.g., by means of composition, transformation, currying, aggregation or lambda abstraction).

Operations and Transformers

The operations of Nial are primarily designed for the manipulation of nested arrays. These operations can be considered in several subclasses including: those that are applied to lists, logical operations, selectors and arithmetic operations. Nial also contains many operations to construct and decompose arrays. Below are a few simple examples of the application of Nial array operations.

shape (4 5 6)

3

tell 4

0 1 2 3

hitch (1 2) (3 4 5)

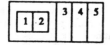

2 2 reshape (tell 4)

Nial provides several ways to construct new operations. Two or more operations can be composed by juxtaposition. Thus,

foo is first rest

defines foo to be the composition of first with rest. The resulting operation selects the second item of a list. Curried operations can be formed by placing an array to the left of an operation. The resultant operation follows the rule (A foo) B = foo A B.

The operations of Nial can be grouped into atlases, similar to a combining form used by Backus[10]. Each operation in an atlas is applied to the array argument and the result of the application of the atlas is the array formed by all the individual function applications.

The abstraction mechanism for defining an operation from an expression in Nial is called an operation-form. An example that defines the average function:

Average is OPERATION Numbers
(Sum Numbers div tally Numbers).

Transformers in Nial allow the mapping of operations to new operations. In particular EACH is a transformer that applies an operation to all items of an array. For instance

EACH foo (A B C)

is the array with three items: the values of foo A, foo B and foo C.

FORK is another example of a transformer that expects an atlas of three operations. The first operation is applied to the argument and if it evaluates to true, then the second operation applied to the argument is returned. If it is false then the application of the third operation is returned.

LOGIC IN NIAL

In this section we describe a logic programming system based on array theory. Unlike most systems, the Nial approach is functional in that three basic "logic" functions are built into the language: substitution, unification and resolution. Embedded arrays are used to represent the syntactic objects of logic to which these functions are applied. The state of a logic proof is represented by an array corresponding to the tree generated by the and-or tree problem reduction method [11].

Substitution and Unification

Nial primarily supports Horn-clause resolution but also provides the tools to define other forms of logical inferencing. Unification is a function that determines the most general unifier of two atomic formula represented as embedded arrays. For example P(x,y,y) and P(a,b,z) would correspond to the arrays

and unification of these two atomic formulae would result in the list of substitution pairs

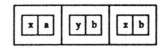

Such a substitution list can be applied to logic formulae expressed in Horn clause or other logic syntactic forms. For instance the above substitution list applied to the array representing the clause

P(x,y,y) – Q(x), R(v,y)

would result in the array:

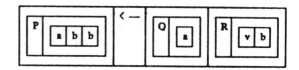

Resolution

Resolution in Nial is a generalized form of Prolog Horn clause resolution. Prolog assumes that resolution is performed only on a goal clause of the form

$$-C_1, ..., C_n \ (n \geq 1)$$

and a procedural clause of the form

$$A - B_1, ..., B_m \ (m \geq 0)$$

to get a resolvent which is a new goal clause (assuming A and C_1 are unifiable). This can be considered as a form of top-down problem solving. Nial allows resolution to be applied to any two Horn clauses. Thus we could also apply resolve to clauses of the form

$$A \leftarrow . \text{ and } B \leftarrow A.$$

to derive B.

This implies that Nial allows for the construction of top-down, bottom-up or bi-directional [12] problem solving techniques.

Nial does not restrict the user to resolution logic. Including substitution and unification as built-in functions enables the programmer to define other inference rules. For example, an array could be interpreted as a disjunction of atomic formula and the rule of disjunctive syllogism could be easily be defined using the unification function and array operators.

State Information

Many authors have noted the relationship between top-down inferencing and problem reduction. Kowalski [12] demonstrates how an and-or tree representation for problem reduction corresponds to the Horn clause representation for a problem reduction task. This tree representation is a generalization of the implication tree which illustrates the state of a Prolog proof. An implication tree is a conjunctive subtree of the and-or tree where backtracking is used to consider alternative disjunctions. Since only a leftmost depth-first strategy is used in Prolog such a representation is sufficient.

In Nial we wish to be able to construct a variety of logic control strategies. These include depth-first, breadth-first and combinations of depth and breadth precedence. Thus we choose the and-or tree representation for the state of a proof. It can be shown that for any such tree we can produce an equivalent disjunctive normal form (DNF) and-or tree [13]. There then exists a mapping onto a disjunctive normal form array:

| C1 | C2 | . . . | Cn |

where C_i is a subarray representing a conjunction of subgoals. We interpret the array then as a disjunction of the conjunctive subarrays. In section 5 it is demonstrated how this array representation of a DNF and-or problem reduction tree allows for the simple construction of a logic control strategy.

Logic, Functions and Arrays

Resolution logic defines predicates that may be applied to terms which are functions. Although some recent Prolog implementations permit this, they do not provide useful mechanisms for defining new functions. Being primarily a functional language, Nial allows this facility. As well, Nial permits information within an array to be considered either as data or a program. This implies that functions within predicates can be evaluated and thus unification can be extended to include a limited version of equality of terms [14].

The only data structure that is supported by Prolog is the logical term. Because of the computational overhead and the difficulty in manipulating more general data structures in the language, attempts have been made to add structures such as arrays to logic programming languages [15]. Since the basic structure of Nial is the embedded array, it supports many built-in functions defined to operate on these objects. Thus a Nial logic clause can be viewed in two ways: as a theorem that can be used in a deduction step of a logical proof or as an embedded array to which any of the array operations of Nial can be applied. This provides the user with increased flexibility and power in constructing logic programs.

PARALLELISM IN NIAL

In this section we discuss the parallelism which can be present in the evaluation of array-theoretic expressions. For the purposes of this section, we consider only the applicative subset of the Nial language, as the imperative features prohibit the free exploitation of parallelism.

We begin by identifying potentially parallel constructs in Nial. The EACH transformer is the most obvious parallel construct. EACH applies an operation to every item of the argument:

$$\text{EACH } f \ [A, B, C] = [f \ A, f \ B, f \ C].$$

Clearly, if the operation has no side effects, the applications can proceed in parallel. This application corresponds to Flynn's SIMD architecture [16], in which a single instruction stream (f) is applied to multiple data streams (A, B, and C).

Nial operations can be collected into array-like structures which are themselves operations, for example [first, rest]. Such collections of operations are called atlases (they are collections of maps, or functions), and are similar to the operation collections of FP [10]. Their importance is due to their application rule. When an atlas is applied to an argument, each operation in the atlas is applied to the argument, and the results of the applications are collected into an array with shape equivalent to the shape of the atlas:

$$[f, g, h] \ A = [f \ A, g \ A, h \ A].$$

This pattern of application corresponds to the MISD category of Flynn. Though it was not considered an important category by Flynn, it is of importance to array theory.

Flynn's MIMD architecture corresponds to the TEAM transformer of Nial. This transformer takes an atlas and an equivalently shaped argument, and applies the operations to the items of the argument in a pairwise manner:

$$\text{TEAM } [f, g] \ [A, B] = [f \ A, g \ B]$$

The above three parallel forms correspond to the three parallel architectures in Flynn's classification.

We have proposed that practical implementations of the paracomputer model [17] can serve as the basis for a task-oriented parallelism for these Nial forms [6]. In our proposed architecture, the parallel constructs cause the creation of task descriptions. A collection of task descriptions is kept to supply processors with work.

Effective parallel logic computation may require other forms of parallelism [1]. Array theory responds to such demands with a variety of other potentially parallel transformers. A simple example is the LEAF operation that applies an operation to every atom in the argument. We say potentially parallel because both in the theory and the implementation, parallelism must be assumed (or constructed) for selected constructs. For instance, EACH could be parallel or could be a non-parallel tail recursion (iteration). The choice of which constructs should be parallel depends upon the architecture and the anticipated work load.

A primary task of our research is to identify the appropriate forms of parallelism for logic programming. We feel some combination of AND-parallelism and OR-parallelism will eventually be the most effective form. In section 5 we introduce a user defined control strategy that relates to OR-parallelism. AND-parallelism, where multiple literals within a single clause are attempted concurrently, requires a more complicated algorithm and will not be considered in this paper. We can demonstrate, though, a simple notion of applying AND parallelism. Assuming A is an array of data objects and has_property_P is a predicate that computes whether an item of A has property P, then the expression
    and EACH has_property_P A
determines if all items of A have the property. This description implies that the predicate is applied to all items of A and the resulting overall predicate is achieved by anding the results.

In a sequential machine, the evaluation of the predicate to the items of A would occur sequentially. Once one returns falsehood, the entire process could stop and return falsehood. This suggests a new transformer ANDEACH that combines the application of the predicate with accumulating the result.

ANDEACH is also meaningful in a parallel implementation based on task queues. In this case all unfinished applications of the predicate would be aborted once one returned falsehood. A similar consideration leads to an OREACH transformer that terminates as soon as a predicate becomes true.

These techniques can be used in conjunction with a heuristic that reduces the size of A prior to applying ANDEACH has_property_P.

PARALLEL SEARCH STRATEGIES IN NIAL

Resolution logic programming in Nial consists of determining a strategy for applying the function resolve to an array of logic clauses. Assuming the description of the logic functions and applying the concepts of parallelism discussed in earlier sections, we define control strategies in Nial that correspond to OR-parallelism of Prolog implementations. Con-

currency is implied by the logic programmer in terms of the transformers EACH and EACHLEFT. The use of these allow function applications to each item of an array either sequentially or in parallel, depending on the implementation.

OR-parallelism eliminates the need for backtracking by resolving a goal clause with all clauses whose conclusions can be _____ with the current goal. If there are n such suitable clauses then n processes can be spawned to solve the resulting subgoals. If we again apply OR-parallelism to each of these subgoal lists we are implementing a form of breadth-first search. This implies an exponential growth in the number of subgoals generated by the technique and thus we would rapidly run out of processors. We require then some way of controlling OR-parallelism. We do this by introducing the notion of a heuristic applied to a conjunction of subgoals. This allows us, at any stage in a proof, to apply OR-parallelism to the m "best" (or perhaps m "good") conjunctive subtrees in our and-or tree. It is also necessary to stop processes once a goal has either been proven or disproven. A goal succeeds if a state contains a contradiction denoting a conjunction of goals. No proof exists if the disjunction is itself an empty array that semantically is interpreted as a vacuous disjunction, or falsehood. If neither of these cases holds then the proof procedure can continue in parallel.

A discussion of heuristic search strategies is not within the scope of this paper. We do wish to impress though that the array operations of Nial allow us to implement a variety of such strategies. We can count the number of subgoals to be solved or determine the depth of the search as examples of simple strategies. Since we can also consider our goals as data, we are able to define heuristics determined by manipulating information given in the goal. This corresponds more closely to techniques employed in artificial intelligence problem solving.

We break down the problem of defining our strategy into several functions. The function *newgoals* takes as its parameters a goal clause and an array containing a list of clauses. *newgoals* applies the built-in function resolve to the goalclause and each element of clauses (i.e. each clause in the knowledge base) by use of the transformer EACHLEFT.

newgoals IS OPERATION goalclause clauses
    (prune (clauses EACHLEFT
    resolve goalclause))

The function *prune* removes any empty arrays resulting from unsatisfied unifications.

We wish our control functions to be applicable to any proof strategy that may be defined. Thus a predefined function *strategy* is assumed that returns 1 (true) if a particular goalist should be attempted in a given environment, otherwise *strategy* returns o (false). The environment for such a function consists of a current state and a set of clauses. A few simple examples of possible *strategy* functions are given below:

% strategy for breadth-first search

strategy IS OPERATION goalist environment (l)

% strategy for depth-first left-most search

strategy IS OPERATION goalist environment
    (equal (goalist (first first environment))

% heuristic strategy that only attempts goalists with
the minimum number of goals

strategy IS OPERATION goalist environment
    (equal (shape goalist)
    (min EACH shape (first environment)))

Assuming that a strategy function has been defined, we define the function *nextstate* that maps a state and a set of clauses onto a new state as a result of applying *newgoal* to only those goalists that meet the requirements of the predefined strategy as determined by function *applystrategy*.

    applystrategy IS OPERATION goalist environment
      (IF strategy (goalist environment)
        THEN newgoal goalist (second environment)
        ELSE [goalist]
      ENDIF)

      nextstate IS OPERATION state clauses
        (link (state EACHLEFT applystrategy
        (state clauses)))

Our final control function determines when a proof has been completed. Assuming our representation of contradiction is of the form o ← (empty conjunction implies false) the function *prove* halts if the empty state is reached (proof fails) or the state contains a contradiction (proof succeeds). If neither of these cases holds, *prove* continues generating new states.

    prove IS OPERATION state clauses
      (IF empty state
        THEN o
        ELSE
        IF (o "<--) in state
          THEN l
          ELSE prove (nextstate state
            clauses) clauses
        ENDIF
      ENDIF)

    To illustrate our user defined strategy we trace through a couple of steps of a proof using the function *nextstate* and a breadth-first search strategy. Given a list of simple clauses represented by the array:

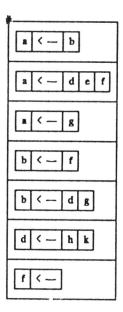

Assume we have the goal ← a to prove. We initialize our state array to be:

The function application
    nextstate state clauses
would generate the state:

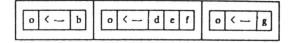

If apply *nextstate* twice more we derive the succeeding states:

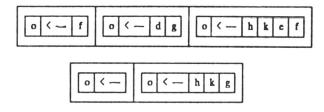

Since the final state above contains the contradiction array, our goal has been proven. Normally we would simply apply the function *prove* to the initial state and the list of clauses and get a result that denotes whether the proof was successful or not without displaying the intermediate states. The function *nextstate* is useful though if the programmer wishes to trace through a proof.

CONCLUSIONS

The control strategy described in this paper is only one example of the flexibility in manipulating knowledge using Nial. It illustrates a concurrent algorithm for defining an OR type of parallel proof technique. The built-in logic functions also provide for the construction of forward inferencing techniques, production rules, semantic networks and many other tools for artificial intelligence problem solving [18].

The work being carried out in Nial has similar intent to Loglisp, which also combines logic programming with a functional environment. Our approach to logic contrasts with the work of Robinson and Sibert in that we attempt to provide high-level operations for performing logical inferences rather than a completed proof system. We are also concerned with capturing a useful notion of parallelism in Nial. This enables the programmer to express parallel computations without explicit specification. It also allows for a natural implementation of logic that does not restrict the user to a particular control strategy. Heuristics can be defined to control concurrency in the search.

FUTURE AND RELATED WORK

Nial is currently implemented by a conventional, single-process interpreter written in C, and running on several machine/operating system combinations. Some of these are VAX/UNIX, VAX/VM, DEC 20/TWENIX, SUN/UNIX, MC6800/XENIX, IBM PC/DOS and IBM/VM. The language is used in teaching and research at a dozen institutions in North America and Europe.

There are many areas of research underway involving the language Nial. These include:

- work on the theory of arrays and the design of Nial
- development of a single-process VLSI-compatible Nial architecture
- design of a parallel architecture based on the language Nial
- investigation of logic programming techniques and how they can be implemented in Nial, particularly heuristic search strategies
- array theory based models for expert systems, theorem proving, vision and natural language understanding and their implementation in Nial
- application of Nial in intelligent office automation environments including inferencing data base systems

We feel that the combination of functional programming, embedded arrays and logic provides a powerful problem solving and proof system in Nial. The current state of the language and research offer evidence of its suitability for artificial intelligence and general purpose applications.

REFERENCES

[1] J.S. Conery and D. F. Kibler, "Parallel interpretation of logic programs", *Proc. of the ACM Conference on Functional Programming Languages and Computer Architecture*, October 1981, pp. 163-170.

[2] M.J. Wise, "A parallel prolog: the construction of a data driven model", *Proceedings of the 1982 Symposium on LISP and Functional Programming*, pp. 56-66.

[3] E.Y. Shapiro, "A subset of concurrent prolog and its interpreter", *ICOT Technical Report TR-003*, Tokyo, January 1983.

[4] P.A. Subrahmanyam and J.H. You, "Conceptual basis and evaluation strategies for integrating functional and logic programming," *1984 International Symposium on Logic Programming*, pp. 144-153.

[5] J.A. Robinson and Sibert, "Loglisp: motivation, design and implementation," in *Logic Programming*, K.L. Clark and S.A. Tarnlund (eds.), Academic Press, 1982, pp. 315-324.

[6] C.D. McCrosky, J.I. Glasgow and M.A. Jenkins, "Nial: a candidate language for fifth generation systems", *Proceedings of the 1984 ACM Annual Conference*, October 1984, pp. 157-165.

[7] T. More, "The nested rectangular array as a model of data," *APL79 Conference Proceedings*, 1979, pp. 55-73.

[8] T. More, "Notes on the diagrams, logic and operations of array theory," in *Structures and Operations in Engineering and Management Systems*, Oyvind Bjorke and Ole I. Franksen (eds.), Rapir Publishers, Trondheim, Norway, 1981, pp. 497-666.

[9] M.A. Jenkins, *Q'Nial Reference Manual*, Queen's University, Kingston, Ontario.

[10] J. Backus, "Can programming be liberated from the von Neumann style? a functional style and its algebra of programs," *Communications of the ACM 21(8)*, 1978, pp. 613-641.

[11] H. Gelenter, "Realization of a geometry theorem proving machine," in *Computers and Thought*, Feigenbaum and Feldman (eds.), McGraw Hill, New York, 1963, pp. 134-152.

[12] R.A. Kowalski, "Logic for problem solving," *Artificial Intelligence Series*, Ed. Nilsson, North Holland, 1979.

[13] J. Glasgow, "Logic programming in nial," *Queen's University Technical Report 84-158*, Department of Computing and Information Science, Queen's University, Kingston, Ontario, 1984.

[14] W.A. Kornfeld, "Equality for prolog," *Proceedings Eighth International Joint Conference on Artificial Intelligence,*" 1983.

[15] L. Eriksson and M. Rayner, "Incorporating mutable arrays into logic programming" *Proceedings of the Second International Logic Programming Conference,* 1984.

[16] M.J. Flynn, "Very high-speed computing systems," *Proceedings of the IEEE,* 54,112, Dec. 1966, pp. 1901-1909.

[17] J.T. Schwartz, "Ulracomputers," *ACM Toplas,* 1980, pp. 484-521.

[18] J. Glasgow and R. Browse, "Programming languages for artificial intelligence", to appear in *Int. Journal of Computers and Mathematice,* special edition on practical A.I. systems, 1985.

IN THE previous part, various languages for implementing expert systems were described. In addition to Prolog and Lisp, the discussion covered newer approaches such as Smalltalk and Nial. Because of their broader approach and their support of facilities designed exclusively for expert systems, Smalltalk and Nial are sometimes classified as tools rather than languages.

As compared to the development of a new language, the development of a new tool involves much less time and effort. New tools for expert systems continue to be introduced, many quite similar in design to tools introduced previously, but with improvements in specific areas.

We begin this part with a brief, rather than exhaustive, guide to microcomputer-based software for expert systems work. This directory includes products that can be used in a typical microcomputer or personal computer environment.

In the second paper, Harmon stresses the fact that small systems are in essence "intelligent job aids." Written in an informal style, his paper divides expert system building tools into five categories as follows:

    (i)   induction tools,
    (ii) simple rule-based tools,
    (iii) structured rule-based tools,
    (iv) object-oriented hybrid tools, and
    (v) logical tools.

He gives examples for each category and discusses the issues of problem characteristics, end-user interface, development interface, systems interface, and support facilities.

The third paper, by Milman, describes the Expert-Ease software package. This was among the first products designed for the IBM Personal Computer. Expert-Ease differs from traditional rule-based systems because it "learns" from experience.

In the fourth paper, Turpin describes Personal Consultant, a product of Texas Instruments. This product offers explanation facilities, natural language processing, reasoning with uncertainty, window-oriented interface, and full development support.

Williams describes the Knowledge Engineering System (KES) in the next paper. This system supports three types of inference mechanisms: (i) backward chaining of rules, (ii) statistical inferences based on Bayes' Theorem, and (iii) minimal set covers to simulate a hypothesize-and-test approach.

In the sixth paper, Rappaport and Perez describe NEXPERT, which is a rule-based expert system building tool that runs in a Macintosh environment. The rule format, the inference mechanism, and the architecture of this product are described.

In the seventh paper, Konopasek and Jayaraman describe TK!Solver. This product was launched by Software Arts

Products Corporation, the developers of Visicalc. Unfortunately, the collapse of that company has prevented this product from receiving the attention that it deserves.

The next paper, by Neiman and Martin, describes rule-based programming in the OPS83 environment. This product was designed to solve problems heuristically. At the same time, it supports algorithmic, or imperative, coding modes. The internal data structure is optimized to allow efficient matching of production rules against the working memory.

Next Michie et al. describe RuleMaster, which features a hierarchically ordered system of inductive learning for the acquisition of expert knowledge. This product supports both diagnostic- and procedure-oriented approaches.

The tenth paper, by Reddy et al., describes LASER. This system features an object-oriented knowledge representation kernel and a set of packages for knowledge-based simulation, rule-based programming, and a network inference engine.

The next paper, by Lehner and Barth, covers 11 products, but the primary focus is on AL/X (abbreviated from Advice Language/X). This system, modeled after Prospector and EMYCIN, can run on very small systems, containing as little as 64K bytes of memory.

The last paper in this part attempts to identify major trends and features of expert system tools. Gilmore et al. evaluate leading products and conclude with the observation that their organization "did not purchase a single Expert System Tool mentioned in the paper as their combined cost easily exceeds half a million dollars."

All designers of expert systems are faced with this dilemma. It is extremely important to make the right choice of the expert system shell, as this is a lasting commitment and an error cannot be easily remedied [1]. Selection implies careful evaluation, which is possible, in the true sense, only through hands-on experience with all the tools and this involves nontrivial investments. Given these problems, most designers are constrained to make a decision based on the feelings of their peers and a less-than-thorough comparison of different alternatives. Hopefully, the contents of this part will help in facilitating the evaluation process.

The next part of this book will look at several examples of expert systems built for different operating environments.

REFERENCE

1. Firdman, H. E., "The importance of being earnest in selecting an expert system shell," *AI Expert,* pp. 75–77, Oct. 1986.

BIBLIOGRAPHY

Burns, N. A., T. J. Ashford, C. T. Iwaskim, R. P. Starbird, and R. L. Flagg, "The portable inference engine: Fitting significant expertise into small systems," *IBM Syst. J.,* vol. 25, no. 2, pp. 238–243, Feb. 1986.
Finn, G. A. and J. J. Connor, "'IMAC': An intelligent method of rule processing," *Microsoftware for Engineers,* vol. 1, no. 2, pp. 82–90, 1985.

Gilmore, J. F. and K. Pulaski, "A survey of expert system tools," in *Proc. of the IEEE Second Conf. on AI Applications,* Dec. 1985, pp. 498–502.

Harmon, N. P., "Small expert systems building tools," *Expert Syst. Strategies,* vol. 1, no. 1, pp. 1–13, Sept. 1985.

Hays, N., "AI programs permit development of expert systems on PCs," A Special Feature on New Products, *Computer,* vol. 19, no. 7, pp. 130–132, July 1986.

Kaplan, M. A. and S-C. Jen, "SMALL-X: An environment for constructing expert systems on a microcomputer," in *Proc. of the ACM SIGSMALL Symp. on Small Systems,* Danvers, MA, May 1985, pp. 169–178.

Karna, A. and A. Karna, "Evaluating the existing tools for developing expert systems in PC environment," in *Proc. of the IEEE Expert Systems in Government Symp.,* McLean, VA, Oct. 1985, pp. 295–300.

Naef, F. E., "An artificial intelligence system for a restricted memory microcomputer," in *Proc. of COMPCON Fall '84,* Sept. 1984, pp. 4–10.

Perrone, J., "Expert systems get personal: Modeling expertise with the IBM PC," in *Proc. of the First Annual AI & Advanced Computer Technology Conf.,* Apr. 1985, pp. 172–175.

Sawyer, B., "Inductive front ends to rule-based expert systems," in *Proc. of the Second Annual AI & Advanced Computer Technology Conf.,* May 1986, pp. 208–210.

Symonds, A. J., "Introduction to IBM's knowledge-systems products," *IBM Syst. J.,* vol. 25, no. 2, pp. 134–146, Feb. 1986.

Valdes-Perez, P., "Inside an expert system shell," *AI Expert,* pp. 30–42, Oct. 1986.

Directory of microcomputer-based software for expert systems work

Introduction

This is a brief guide to software available for developing expert systems (and other artificial intelligence systems) on personal computers. It is intended to supplement the three articles in this issue of *Expert Systems: the International Journal of Knowledge Engineering* on the theme of expert systems on small computers. It is not intended to be a comparative assessment or evaluation of the software, and we have decided to arrange it as a directory rather than a table for that reason. Comparisons are almost impossible in this field and we consider that potential purchasers should use the directory to decide which software may be of interest to them and then contact the suppliers for further information that would allow them to make the necessary comparisons before purchase.

We have defined 'microcomputers' and 'personal computers' to be any small computer commonly found in businesses, up to an IBM PC AT with 640K random-access memory and twenty megabyte hard disk. We do not cover the majority of the advanced workstations based around the Motorola 68000 series processor, nor does it include dedicated Lisp machines.

This seems to be a reasonable dividing line: few general computer users have access to a Sun or Apollo workstation, whereas many have access to machines in the IBM PC AT or Apple Macintosh classes. The directory is intended for computer-users who are interested in experimenting with expert systems but who have to work within the limitations of a conventional computer and cannot requisition a specialist AI machine.

Almost all the software listed for the IBM PC runs on other MS-DOS-based personal computers.

As can be seen from even this short directory (which is certainly not comprehensive) there is a wide variety of personal computer-based development tools. We have excluded systems which are delivery-only versions of larger systems. There is also a wide choice of versions of the high-level programming languages used in artificial intelligence generally, so we have included information on the PC versions of Lisp and Prolog about which we know. Although many expert systems and expert systems development tools have been built in conventional computer languages (Pascal and C seem popular) we have not listed these as information about them is already easily available.

We have separated development tools that use rule-induction techniques from other shell systems. Several of the rule-induction systems do offer shell-like facilities though but we believe that as rule-induction is still a controversial issue they make up a separate category of their own.

We have also separated rule-based programming languages from other systems, as they are not expert systems shells but offer more than most programming languages. In fact, all the rule-based programming languages are implementations of OPS5, the language used to build Digital Equipment Corporations Xcon and Xsel expert systems.

We would like to keep this directory up-to-date. Any suppliers not listed are welcome to contact us with details of their products. Suppliers who have added new products or developed enhanced versions of their software should also contact us so that we can change the entries if we publish an updated version. We have tried to be as accurate as possible, but if there are any errors in the information please inform us so that we can correct it in future.

The name of the supplier is given in the information for each system. The addresses are listed separately at the end.

PROGRAMMING LANGUAGES

LISP

Byso Lisp

A full Lisp interpreter with Maclisp and Common Lisp functions. Includes 'Visual Syntax' interface for designing programs graphically.
$150
IBM PC (128K minimum)
Levien Instrument Co.

ExperLisp

Lisp interpreter with incremental compiler. Makes use of Macintosh interface facilities. Includes Editor and graphics.
$495
Apple Macintosh (512K minimum)
ExperTelligence Inc.

Golden Common Lisp

Subset of Common Lisp: interpreter with compiler option. Includes GMACS editor and interactive tutorial system.
$495
IBM PC (512K minimum)
Gold Hill Computers.

IQ Lisp

Lisp interpreter: dialect resembles Franz Lisp. Interfaces to assembly language. Supports 8087 processor and graphics.
$175
IBM PC (192K minimum)
Integral Quality.

MacScheme

Lisp interpreter with integrated editor. Supports some features of Common Lisp. Based on MIT's Scheme language.
$125
Apple Macintosh (512K minimum)
Semantic Microsystems.

muLisp-85

Compiler and interpreter with window-based programming environment. Claimed to be similar to Common Lisp.
$250
IBM PC (128K minimum)
Microsoft Corporation.

UO-Lisp

Interpreter and compiler with debugger and three editors. Tutorial options available.
$150
IBM PC (128K minimum)
Northwest Computer Algorithms.

Waltz Lisp

Similar to Franz Lisp and compatible with MacLisp. For use with external editors but includes full debuggers available at all times.
$169
IBM PC (90K minimum)
ProCode International.

PROLOG

Arity/Prolog

Prolog interpreter with optional compiler. Large set of built-in predicates. Interfaces to other programming languages.
$495 (interpreter only)
$1950 (interpreter and compiler)
IBM PC (256K minimum)
Arity Corporation.

MProlog P-500

Prolog interpreter. Large number of built-in predicates, including DEC-10 Prolog compatibility. Includes interactive program development environment.
$725
IBM PC (512K minimum)
Logicware Inc.

micro-Prolog Professional

Interpreter with optional compiler. Two different forms of syntax supported, including Edinburgh Prolog. Built-in window manager and editor.
£350 (IBM PC)
£395 (Apple Macintosh)
IBM PC (256K minimum)
Apple Macintosh (512K minimum)
Logic Programming Associates.

Prolog-86

Edinburgh syntax Prolog interpreter with tutorial features. Includes online help system.
$125
IBM PC (128K minimum)
Solution Systems.

Prolog 1

Interpreter using Edinburgh Prolog syntax.
£390
IBM PC (128K minimum)
Expert Systems International Ltd.

Prolog 2

Interpreter with optional compiler and full DEC-10 compatibility. Includes built-in editor, help system and windowing system.
£2,000
IBM PC (256K minimum)
Expert Systems International Ltd.

SMALLTALK

Methods

PC implementation of Smalltalk object-oriented programming system. Smalltalk source code for system supplied.
> $250
> IBM PC (512K minimum)
> Digitalk Inc.

NIAL

Q'Nial

Implementation of Nested Interactive Array Language. Includes logic programming features. Interpreter with compiler under development.
> $395 (IBM PC)
> $995 (IBM PC/AT, Xenix)
> IBM PC (512K minimum)
> Starwood Corporation.

EXPERT SYSTEMS DEVELOPMENT TOOLS

Apes

Apes (Augmented Prolog for Expert Systems) is a set of Prolog-based development tools that can be used to build expert systems. In particular, it offers automatic generation of dialogues and reasoning explanations.
> £395
> IBM PC (128K minimum)
> Logic Based Systems Ltd.

ESP Advisor

Prolog-based expert systems shell specifically designed for 'text animation' (turning pre-written texts into an expert system). Includes interface to Prolog itself.
> £600
> IBM PC (128K minimum)
> Expert Systems International Ltd.

Expert Edge

Expert systems shell using production rules with Bayesian statistics for handling probabilities. Supports other data formats (Lotus, dBase etc) for data entry. (System formerly known as TESS.)
> £650
> IBM PC (256K minimum)
> Helix Expert Systems Ltd.

Exsys

Rule-based expert systems shell that can handle probabilities. Can interface to database systems. Can call external programs to control equipment.
> $395
> IBM PC (minimum not specified)
> Exsys Inc.

Inference Manager

Inference net mechanism for processing probabilistic hypotheses. Based on AL/X. Allows degrees of belief to be expressed on a simple scale.
> £500
> IBM PC/XT (128K minimum)
> Intelligent Terminals Ltd.

Insight 1 and Insight 2

Expert systems shell. Production-rule based. Some forward-chaining ability. Supplied in two versions: Insight 1 is entry-level system, Insight 2 full version.
> $95 (Insight 1)
> $485 (Insight 2)
> IBM PC (Insight 1: 128K minimum,
>   Insight 2: 256K minimum)
> Level 5 Research Inc.

KES II

Frame (or schema) based expert systems development tool originally developed for Lisp workstations and rewritten in C. Bayesian statistics and production rule facilities incorporated.
> $4,000
> IBM PC/XT (512K minimum)
> Software Architecture and Engineering Inc.

M1 and M1A

Prolog-based development system that will allow reasoning about objects as well as rules. Basically backward-chaining inference mechanism with limited forward-chaining. M1 can interface to other programs, M1A cannot. M1 user interface can be configured by a knowledge engineer.
> $5,000 (M1)
> $2,000 (M1A)
> IBM PC (128K minimum)
> Teknowledge Inc.

Nexpert

Rule-based expert system development tool. Nexpert automatically creates a graphic image of the relationship between the rules. Knowledge can also be represented using 'categories' which allow an inheritance mechanism.
> $5,000
> Apple Macintosh (512K minimum)
> Neuron Data Inc.

Personal Consultant and Personal Consultant Plus

Rule-based system that is able to accept any knowledge base created under Emycin, as well as under Personal Consultant itself. Personal Consultant Plus adds frame and meta-rule facilities.
> $950 (Personal Consultant)
> $2,950 (Personal Consultant Plus)
> Texas Instruments PC
>   (Personal Consultant),
>   TI PC and IBM PC
>   (Personal Consultant Plus)
>   (512K minimum)
> Texas Instruments.

Reveal

Numerical modelling system which allows expert system rules to be incorporated into the model. Approximate reasoning is permitted.
> £1,900
> IBM PC/XT or AT with 8087 co-processor (640K minimum)
> Tymshare UK Ltd.

Savoir

Rule-based expert system shell. Permits 'fuzzy' reasoning to be incorporated. Compiler checks consistency of knowledge base. Savoir includes a videotex (viewdata) interface that can be used for end-users of the finished system.
> £3,000
> IBM PC or PC/AT (512K minimum)
> ISI Ltd.

Series PC

Production rule system that will support both forward- and backward-chaining reasoning. Lisp can be used within the rule-base. Friendly interface for end-users. Price includes training.
> $15,000
> IBM PC/XT (256K minimum)
> SRI International.

Xi

Prolog-based expert system shell that supports both backward- and forward-chaining. End-user interface can be dialogue or menu driven and includes 'what-if' facility.
> £495
> IBM PC (384K minimum)
> Expertech Ltd.

Xsys

Rule-based expert system shell with uncertainty handling. Menu-driven end-user interface. Lisp can be used directly within the knowledge-base.
> $1,000
> IBM PC (640K minimum)
> California Intelligence.

RULE-BASED LANGUAGES

ExperOPS5

Complete implementation of the OPS5 language for Apple Macintosh computers. Requires ExperLisp.
> $325
> Apple Macintosh (512K minimum)
> ExperTelligence Inc.

OPS5+

Complete implementation of OPS5 for IBM PCs and Apple Macintosh. Includes window-based development system.
> $3000
> IBM PC (256K minimum),
> Apple Macintosh (512K minimum)
> Artelligence Inc.

OPS83

Compiled version of OPS that supports access to other languages. Incorporates conventional imperative programming as well as rule-based programming.
> $2,500
> IBM PC/XT (512K minimum)
> Production Systems Technologies Inc.

TOPSI

Version of OPS5 for small computers. Enhanced version with expanded rule capacity available.
> $75 (basic version), $175 (enhanced version).
> CP/M systems, IBM PC (256K minimum)
> Dynamic Master Systems Inc.

RULE-INDUCTION SYSTEMS

Ex-Tran 7

Expert system construction tool and rule induction system written in Fortran. Rules can be supplied explicitly or induced from examples. Rules are generated as Fortran.
> £1,995
> IBM PC/XT or AT with maths co-processor
> (512K minimum), Grid PC
> Intelligent Terminals Ltd.

Expert-Ease

User-friendly induction system that uses spreadsheet format. Run-time system for interrogating finished expert system.
> £695
> IBM PC (128K minimum)
> Intelligent Terminals Ltd.

Knowledge Development System

Induction-based expert system development tool written in assembly language. Interfaces to other programs and devices. Requires both development system and playback system.
> $795 (development system),
> $150 (playback system)
> IBM PC (512K minimum)
> KDS Corporation.

Micro In-Ate

Expert system shell intended specifically for fault diagnosis. Generates rules from CAD data and component reliability tests. Pascal version of system written in Lisp for larger machines.
> $5,000
> IBM PC (512K minimum),
> Apple Macintosh (512K minimum)
> Automated Reasoning Corporation.

RuleMaster

Inductive rule-generator combined with Radial rule-language to allow rules to be entered explicitly. Can handle uncertainty and 'fuzzy'

attributes. Primitive attributes for the problem domain can be coded in C.
> £1,995
> IBM PC/XT and AT (512K minimum)
> Intelligent Terminals Ltd.

TIMM

Induction-based system that can form generalised as well as specific rules. Knowledge can also be added explicitly. Has 'terse' and 'verbose' dialogue modes for user interface.
> $9,500
> IBM PC/XT (640K minimum)
> General Research Corporation.

Arity Corporation
358 Baker Avenue
Concord
MA 01742
USA.
(617) 371-1243

Artelligence Inc.
14902 Preston Road
Suite 212-252
Dallas
TX 75240
USA.
(214) 437-0361

Automated Reasoning Corporation
290 West 12th Street
Suite 1-D
New York
NY 10014
USA.
(212) 206-6331

California Intelligence
912 Powell Street
San Francisco
CA 94108
USA.
(415) 391-4846

Digitalk Inc.
5200 West Century Boulevard
Los Angeles
CA 90045
USA.
(213) 645-1082

Dynamic Master Systems Inc.
PO Box 566456
Atlanta
GA 30356
USA.
(404) 565-0771

ExperTelligence Inc.
559 San Ysidro Road
Santa Barbara
CA 93108
USA.
(805) 969-7874

Expert Systems International Ltd.
9 West Way
Oxford
OX2 0JB
England.
0865 242206

Expertech Ltd.
Expertech House
172 Bath Road
Slough
SL1 3XE
England.
0753 821321

Exsys Inc.
PO Box 75158
Albuquerque
NM 87194
USA.
(505) 836-6676

General Research Corporation
Software Sales and Marketing
7655 Old Springhouse Road
Maclean
VA 22102
USA.
(703) 893-5915

Gold Hill Computers
163 Harvard Street
Cambridge
MA 02139
USA.
(617) 492-2071

Helix Expert Systems Ltd.
St. Bartholomew House
92 Fleet Street
London
EC4Y 1DH
England.
01 583 9391

ISI Ltd.
11 Oakdene Road
Redhill
Surrey
RH1 6BT
England.
0737 71327

Integral Quality
6265 Twentieth Avenue NE
Seattle
WA 98115
USA.
(206) 527-2918

Intelligent Terminals Ltd.
George House
36 North Hanover Street
Glasgow
G1 2AD
Scotland
041-552 1353

KDS Corporation
934 Hunter Road
Wilmette
IL 60091
USA.
(312) 251-2621

Level 5 Research Inc.
4980 South A-1-A
Melbourne Beach
FL 32951
USA.
(305) 729-9046

Levien Instrument Co.
Sittlington Hill
PO Box 31
McDowell
VA 24458
USA.
(703) 396-3345

Logic Based Systems Ltd.
40 Beaumont Avenue
Richmond
Surrey
TW9 2HE
England.
01-940 9563.

Logic Programming Associates Ltd.
Studio 4
The Royal Victoria Patriotic Building
Trinity Road
London
SW18 3SX
England.
01-871 2016

Logicware Inc.
1000 Finch Avenue West
Toronto
Ontario
M3J 2V5
Canada.
(416) 665-0022

Microsoft Corporation
10700 Northup Way
Bellevue
WA 98004
USA.
(206) 828-8080

Neuron Data Inc.
444 High Street
Palo Alto
CA 94301
USA.
(415) 321-4488

Northwest Computer Algorithms
PO Box 90995
Long Beach
CA 90809
USA.
(213) 426-1893

ProCode International
15930 SW Colony Place
Portland
OR 97224
USA.
(503) 684-3000

Production Systems Technologies Inc.
642 Gettysburg Street
Pittsburgh
PA 15206
USA.
(412) 362-3117

SRI International
Advanced Computer Systems Department
333 Ravenswood Avenue
Menlo Park
CA 94025
USA.
(415) 859-2859

Semantic Microsystems
1001 Bridgeway Suite 543
Sausalito
CA 94965
USA.
(415) 332-8094

Software Architecture and Engineering Inc.
1500 Wilson Boulevard
Suite 800
Arlington
VA 22209
USA.
(703) 276-7910

Solution Systems
335-B Washington Street
Norwell
MA 02061
USA.
(617) 659-1571

Starwood Corporation
PO Box 160849
San Antonio
TX 78280
USA.
(512) 496-8037

Teknowledge Inc.
525 University Avenue
Palo Alto
CA 94301
USA.
(415) 327-6600

Texas Instruments
Data Systems Group
PO Box 809063
H-809
Dallas
TX 75380
USA.
(800) 527-3500

Tymshare UK Ltd.
Heron House
Guildford Road
Woking
Surrey
England.
048 62 26761

THE USE OF SMALL EXPERT SYSTEMS IN BUSINESS

by

Paul Harmon
Harmon Associates
San Francisco, California

Intelligent Job Aids

I became aware of Artificial Intelligence (AI) and expert systems during 1982. At first I was fascinated by the analysis techniques that underlay expert systems and the potential for large, powerful new computer systems. In 1984, however, with the introduction of expert system building tools that could operate on personal computers, the market split into two major segments, and my interests became firmly focused on the potential of small expert systems.

Large expert systems are systems that truly attempt to emulate world—class human experts. The most successful of these systems use AI techniques that allow their designers to construct systems that it would be hard to build using conventional programming techniques.

Small expert systems, on the otherhand, do not try to capture true expertise. Instead, they aid the user in the analysis of a small but difficult problem and they usually provide the user with specific advice on how to deal with the problem. They rely on AI techniques, but not to the degree that the larger systems do. Their main advantage over conventional approaches lies in the fact that users with only a minimal knowledge of computers can quickly learn to develop very useful small systems.

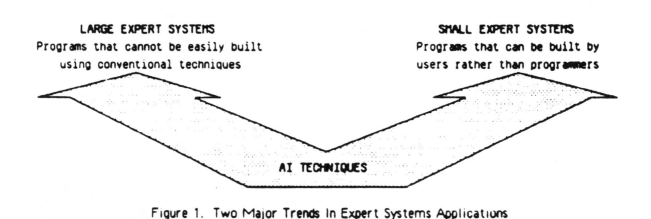

LARGE EXPERT SYSTEMS
Programs that cannot be easily built
using conventional techniques

SMALL EXPERT SYSTEMS
Programs that can be built by
users rather than programmers

AI TECHNIQUES

Figure 1. Two Major Trends In Expert Systems Applications

Perhaps I should not call these small systems "expert systems". Some prefer to call them "knowledge systems", but I prefer "intelligent job aids".

The idea of a job aid is well established among training professionals. A job aid is a device that one consults when one wants assistance in performing a task. Job aids have become very popular because they reduce training time while simultaneously increasing the quality of the performer's work. They minimize memorization and maximize accurate responses. And, in many cases, they allow a less trained employee to perform tasks that previously required a more highly trained, and hence more expensive individual.

Reprinted with permission from *Proc. First Annual AI and Advanced Computer Technology Conf.*, pp. 317–328, Apr. 1985.

Job aids have generally consisted of checklists, step—by—step assembly procedures, cookbooks, or other paper devices. To some extent computers have already begun to act as job aids. The bank teller who uses a small terminal to determine a customer's balance is using a job aid. And, of course, help screens and menus are job aids for conventional computer programs. Until recently, however, job aids could not be effectively designed to help individuals perform really complex jobs. Complex tasks require a performer to consider a large number of different facts and apply many different heuristics to determine a correct response. Moreover, complex tasks often require individuals to make intelligent guesses. Job aid design has been limited to algorithmic analyses of problems in the same way that conventional computer programming has been limited. A job aid that contained enough information to help a performer with a complex task usually turned out to be so complex that it could not be used. Conventional wisdom holds that you are better off hiring someone how already knows how to perform such tasks or providing classes to teach individuals how to perform such tasks. For this reason, job aids to assist bank loan officers in the evaluation of loan applicants have generally been dismissed as impractical.

Intelligent job aids will rapidly change the way we analyze such problems. The existence of small expert system building tools will allow skilled individuals to record their knowledge in a manner that will provide practical assistance to new performers.

Consider, for example, the problem of helping clerks process insurance applications. The knowledge required for such a task would not normally be compared with the knowledge possessed by a highly specialized physician. Yet there is quite a bit that the clerks must know and mistakes can be costly. In a typical insurance company, knowledge of application processing is usually possessed by one or more senior application examiners. New clerks receive a week or two of training and a procedures manual. Once they begin to work at the task, they slowly acquire additional knowledge and heuristics by asking questions to the senior examiners whenever they encounter unusual cases.

Now, by using a small expert system building tool, a senior clerk can develop an intelligent job aid to help new clerks evaluate applications. The new clerks will be able to turn to the intelligent job aid whenever they might otherwise leaf through a procedures manual or ask questions of a senior clerk.

The senior examiner might not get the system right on the first try, but that is one of the flexible virtues of small expert systems; they are highly modularized and can be quickly revised. Every time the system fails to help a new clerk and the clerk is forced to ask the senior examiner a question, the senior examiner is prompted to add some new knowledge to the system. Like large expert systems, intelligent job aids do not need to be "finished" to be used. They are used, revised, updated and maintained by the people who use them. In the case of our insurance examiners, the Application Advisor System could become a responsibility of the senior examiner in the department. In a reasonably short time, of course, the system should save the senior examiner the time that would previously have been used in answering questions and allow everyone in the department to be more accurate and productive.

Obviously an effort like the one I just described could not happen if the senior examiner had to learn how to program in LISP or use a mainframe computer. It probably could not even be done if it required the assistance of data processing personnel, since the task is rather small and not nearly as pressing as the many larger tasks waiting for the attention of the data processing department. The success of the small effort I have described depends on user friendly small expert system building tools that are at least as easy to use as the better electronic spreadsheet programs. Moreover, the tools must run on personal computers. Programs of this type first became available in the summer of 1984 and they are rapidly increasing in number and quality while their prices are declining.

In the remainder of this article I want to describe some of these tools to you and discuss how you might select an application appropriate for one of these tools.

Identifying Appropriate Applications

Although some of the small expert system building tools currently available are quite powerful and flexible, they are still very limited when compared with the wide range of problems that humans routinely confront and solve. Extreme care must be exercised in choosing problems that lend themselves to small tool solutions.

There must be a human expert or senior technician who can currently solve the problem. If the expert currently relies on a policy or procedures manual, so much the better. No expert systems have yet been built that did not initially obtain their knowledge from a human expert. If a human can not solve the problem then you can not build an expert system to solve it.

The solution to an appropriate problem should rely on specific, formal knowledge, not on common sense. More formalized areas like engineering and medicine lend themselves to expert system development because people have already developed precise vocabularies in which to discuss problems. Common sense refers to a vast amount of knowledge that we all acquired experientially in the process of growing up. Its not formalized and its very hard to encode it in an expert system. Assertions like: "There is dirt in a garden" or "People get upset when they are told that they are to be fired" depend on our knowledge of common sense. We can all imagine exceptions, but we assume that such statements are true in situations in which we anticipate that they will apply unless we know that they will not apply in some specific case. Trying to capture and formalize such common sense knowledge, however, is beyond the current generation of expert system building tools.

At the moment the appropriate problems are largely found in one general area: diagnosis and prescription. These tasks are characterized by a limited set of possible recommendations which are chosen as a result of reasoning about evidence for and against various recommendations. A physician employs this approach when diagnosing a disease and deciding what drugs to prescribe. An engineer uses the same general strategy when considering a construction problem and deciding what structural materials to employ. A senior clerk uses this approach in reviewing an application and deciding which of several agencies should review it. An automotive technician uses diagnostic/prescription approach when he or she asks questions and conducts checks to determine the specific cause of an auto malfunction.

In addition to choosing a problem that depends on a diagnostic and prescriptive approach, the task should be narrowly defined. Its much easier to develop three small systems than to develop one with a large number of rules. Start by picking a very specific, narrowly defined problem and expand the system only after you have a system that handles the narrow domain well.

Existing tools rely on typed input. Thus you should avoid problems that require a physical examination. The system can ask the user to make an examination and report the results, but unless the user knows what to look for you will not be using an intelligent job aid to maximize the reduction of training and to avoid errors. In otherwords, choose a problem that a human expert could solve over the telephone by asking questions and suggesting additional things to check before suggesting how to solve the problem.

Finally, the solution to the problem should depend primarily on informal reasoning. The expert should be drawing on past cases and rules of thumb to help in solving the problem. The problem should not require a large amount of mathematical calculation. Most of the small systems can handle mathematics, but they are optimized for judgmental reasoning not mathematical calculation. (There are many conventional (non-expert) systems that can be used to solve problems that are essentially mathematical in nature.)

Characteristics of Small Expert System Building Tools

An expert system building tool is a constrained programming environment designed to facilitate the rapid development of small expert systems. In otherwords, small expert system building tools are like electronic spreadsheet programs; the developer inserts data and the program manipulates it. In the case of expert system building tools, however, the developer inserts facts and rules rather than numbers. The best of the tools allow the developer to input facts and rules in an almost English syntax.

Figure 2 illustrates a spectrum that runs from languages like LISP and Pascal on one side to tools on the other. A programmer might enjoy developing a small expert system with LISP or PROLOG.

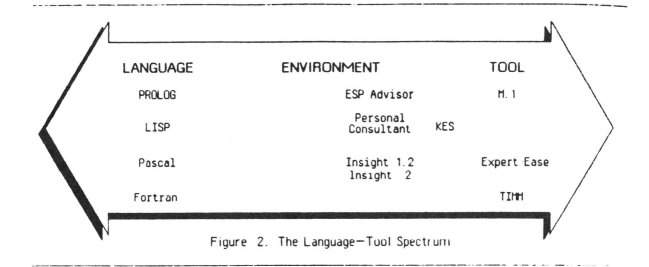

Figure 2. The Language—Tool Spectrum

These languages have recently become available for personal computers and will undoubtedly result in some interesting new software. I assume that most of you, like myself, will prefer tools to languages. Even among tools, however, an important distinction can be made between those that are designed to be more open and flexible and those that completely constrain the developer to a single paradigm. Some tools, for example, prohibit the developer from accessing the language that underlies the tool. Developers with more programming experience will probably tend to prefer the more open or "environment—like" tools while non—programmers will probably be happy to simply use the tools surface utilities.

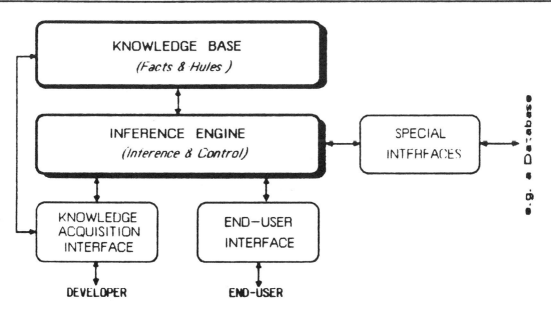

Figure 3. The Architecture of an Expert System Building Tool

Figure 3 provides an overview of the architecture of a typical expert system. The inference engine guides the system in reasoning about the facts and rules that apply to a particular type of problem. The knowledge that a system needs to solve a problem is stored in a separate knowledge base. Tools lack any knowledge. The developer must create a knowledge base about a particular task in order to change the tool into an expert system. Most tools are designed to allow the user to switch knowledge bases just as someone using an electronic spreadsheet can go from one set of data to another spreadsheet with a different set of data. Most tools have a collection of utilities that help developers create knowledge bases. Likewise tools have utilities that help end-users actually run the system once the knowledge base has been created. The developer and user interfaces share a set of utilities that allow either to ask questions of the system and to trace its reasoning. Some tools have utilities that allow the system to obtain information from other databases. Likewise, some tools allow the developer to design hooks into other programming languages in which certain operations can be more easily accomplished.

Tables 1a and 1b summarize the characteristics of the small expert system building tools that I know are currently available. My knowledge of some of these tools is limited. Moreover, most of these tools have been rushed to market and will be revised in the coming months. The pricing, for example, is totally irrational with some poor tools selling for a lot while one of the best tools sells for the least. In addition, everyone is inventing their own terms so its hard to know exactly what a particular tool will or will not do until you try it out. All of the information on Tables 1a and 1b must be regarded as tentative until you can confirm it with the manufacturer.

Types of Tools

Expert system building tools can be divided into five general categories:

Induction Tools. These friendly but weak and inflexible tools are derived from experiments in machine learning. The developer enters a large number of examples. The tool converts the examples into a rule and then applies an algorithm to the rule to determine the order in which to ask the user questions in order to determine a recommendation. These tools are useful for very simple tasks; they are certainly quick and easy to develop. They can not be used for more complex tasks however, or their inflexibility will rapidly become apparent. In the near future these tools will probably be used primarily as front-ends for rule-based tools.

Simple Rule-based Tools. These tools use If...Then rules to represent knowledge. They are "simple" only in contrast to "structured" rule systems that allow the developer to subdivide the rules into various sets that can be arranged into a hierarchy. If the knowledge necessary for a task can be captured in 50 to 200 rules, these tools quite adequate. Moreover, if the task itself is rather unstructured, these tools are quite equal to the structured tools.

Structured Rule-based Tools. These tools use If...Then rules that are arranged into sets that are, in turn, arranged into hierarchies One set of rules can inherit information acquired when other sets of rules were examined. These systems are more desirable when a large number of rules are involved and are especially efficient if the problem lends itself to a structured analysis.

Object-oriented Hybrid Tools. These tools use object-oriented programming techniques to represent the problem elements as objects. An object, in turn, can contain facts, If...Then rules, or pointers to other objects. There tools are much more complex to use and typically require a knowledge of LISP. They usually facilitate the development of complex, graphically oriented user interfaces. They are very powerful, but only justified when the problem is complex enough to justify the considerable effort.

Logical Tools. These tools use horn clauses and resolution strategies derived from Predicate Calculus. They are more popular in Europe than in the U.S. and are much more difficult to use. They are powerful if one is dealing with very complex problems that lend themselves to a rigorous logical analysis.

CHARACTERISTICS	ESP ADVISOR	EXPERT-EASE	INSIGHT 1	INSIGHT 2	KES	M.1	PERSONAL CONSULTANT	TIMM
TYPE OF TOOL	Simple Rule Logical	Induction	Simple Rule	Simple Rule	Simple Rule	Simple Rule	Structured Rule	Induction
PROBLEM CHARACTERISTICS								
Single/Multiple Objects	Single	--	Single	Single	Single	Single	Multiple	--
Single/Multiple Values	Multiple	Single	Single	Multiple	Multiple	Multiple	Multiple	Single
Explanation Expansion	Yes	No	Yes	Yes	Yes	Indirectly	Indirectly	Yes
Math Calculations	Yes	No	No	Yes	Yes	Yes	Yes	No
Certainty Factors	No	No	Yes	Yes	Yes	Yes	Yes	Yes
Fast/Slow Interaction	Medium	Fast	Fast	Fast	Slow	Medium	Slow	Medium
END-USER INTERFACE								
Line/Menu Screen	Menu	Menu	Menu	Menu	Line	Line	Menu	Line
Initial Pruning	No	No	Yes	Yes	No	Indirectly	No	No
Multiple & Uncertain Answers	Yes	No	Yes	Yes	Yes	Yes	Yes	Yes
DEVELOPMENT INTERFACE								
Knowledge Base Creation	Word processor	Line entry	Word processor	Word processor	Word Processor	Word processor	Line entry	Line entry
How/Why Explanations	Yes	No	No	Yes	No	Yes	Yes	No
Inference Tracing	Yes	No	Yes	Yes	No	Yes	Yes	No
Locates Specific Attributes	Indirectly	--	Indirectly	Indirectly	Indirectly	Yes	Yes	--
On-line KB Editor	No	No	No	No	No	Yes	Yes	No
Cases Saved	Yes	No	No	Yes	Yes	Yes	Yes	Yes
Screen Format Utilities	Indirect	No	Indirect	Yes	No	Indirect	Indirect	Indirect

Table 1a. Characteristics Of Small Expert System Building Tools

Table 1b. Characteristics Of Small Expert System Building Tools

CHARACTERISTICS	ESP ADVISOR	EXPERT-EASE	INSIGHT 1	INSIGHT 2	KES	M.1	PERSONAL CONSULTANT	TIMM
SYSTEMS INTERFACE								
Hooks to Databases	Indirect	No	Indirect	Yes (Dbase II)	Indirect	Yes	Indirect	No
Hooks to Other Languages	Yes (Prolog)	No	Yes (Pascal)	Yes (Pascal)	No	No	Yes (LISP)	No
SOFTWARE								
Language of Tool	Prolog	Pascal	Pascal	Pascal	Lisp	Prolog	Lisp	Fortran
Can be Compiled	Yes	Yes	Yes	Yes	No	No	No	Yes
Other Language Required	No	No	No	No	Yes (IQLISP)	No	Yes (IQLISP)	No
Operating System	MS-DOS	UCSD-P	MS-DOS	MS-DOS	MS-DOS	MS-DOS	MS-DOS	MS-DOS
Locked	Yes	Yes	No	Yes	No	Yes	Yes	No
HARDWARE REQUIREMENTS								
Computer	IBM	IBM, DEC, Victor	IBM, DEC, Victor	IBM, DEC, Victor	IBM PC XT	IBM	TI Prof.	IBM PC XT (10M Hard Disk)
RAM Req (Recommended)	128	128	128	192 (256)	540	192	512 (768)	640
Other (Recommended)	-	-	-	(2 drives)	8087 Math Co-fro	(Color monitor)	(10M Hard disk)	8087 Math Co-Pro
TRAINING/SUPPORT								
Course Available	No	No	Yes	Yes	Yes	Yes	Yes	No
Documentation	Yes	Yes	Yes	Yes	Yes	Extensive	Yes	Yes
COST (Circa 1/85)								
Tool (& Documentation)	$895	$695	$95	$495	$4,000	$10,000 *	$3,000	$9,500
Training Course	-	-	$1,200	$1,200	$500	$2,500	$1,500	-
Run-Time Versions	Negotiable	Negotiable	(unlocked)	Negotiable	Negotiable	Negotiable	Negotiable	Negotiable

(* A $2,000 version - M.16 - is available with unspecified limitations)

130

Table1a identifies the general type of each tool. Various small tools employ Inductive, Simple and Structured Rule paradigms. One simple rule system allows the developer to access the underlying PROLOG and hence has the capability of incorporating logical techniques. To date no object—oriented hybrid tools have become available on personal computers. There are rumors that an object—oriented tool may become available for the Macintosh, but you can not build a system with a rumor.

Problem Characteristics

The key to the successful use of the current crop of expert system building tools is to only use the tools on appropriate problems. I have already argued that the appropriate problems for the current crop of tools are narrowly defined tasks that involve diagnosis and prescription. Some of the specific problem characteristics that are facilitated by the existing tools are described below.

Single/Multiple Objects. In the sense that I am using it here, an "object" refers to a set of facts and rules that are closely related. If a tool allows multiple objects that means the developer can divide the knowledge base up into various sets of rules and create hierarchies that allow one set of rules to inherit information from another object. Multiple objects imply structured rule systems (or object—oriented systems). Multiple objects are valuable when building large systems in areas where the problem can be easily subdivided into parts. Systems that only support a "single object" simply keep all the rules together as one group. Various tools have devices that make it more or less easy to manipulate sets of rules in a "single object environment".

Single/Multiple Values. If a tool only supports single values, it means that it will stop reasoning when it has found one answer. Thus, if asked to recommend a restaurant, it will stop once it has found one satisfactory restaurant. A tool that supports multiple values will continue to search its knowledge base until it has found every possible acceptable solution. Most tools allow the developer to determine whether a particular goal will be satisfied when one acceptable answer is found or when all possible values have been identified. Most problems that developers will tackle will require a tool that can handle multiple values.

Explanation Expansion. Most tools allow the developer to include information that can be provided if the user asks for a more elaborate explanation. Thus, if the user is asked if the client is "non—exempt", and the user dopes not understand the term, the user can quickly obtain an elaboration. While most tools allow explanation expansion, however, some facilitate it while others do not. Some problems will typically require this feature and in such cases, other things being equal, the developer will want to use a tool that makes it quick and easy to add explanations.

Math Calculations. All small tools perform "logical operations with numbers" (e.g. greater than, less than), but some do not perform normal arithmetic operations and thus can not do addition, etc. Those that allow the developer to enter into a conventional language like Pascal permit the developer to use any conventional mathematical operation desired.

Certainty Factors. "Certainty Factors" are "probability—like" numbers that are attached to facts and rules to indicate the certainty the expert has in the rule. A system that uses certainty factors can make several recommendations and indicate its confidence in the various recommendations. In some cases the system may indicate evidence both for and against a decision and assign weights to the conflicting recommendations. Not all problems require the use of "probabilistic" knowledge, but most of the small problems that developers will be facilitated by having such a technique available.

Fast/Slow Interaction. This is a somewhat subjective evaluation and certainly depends on exactly what a job aid is designed to do. In general, however, the tools written in conventional languages go very fast and would be quite adequate in most job environments. The tools that are written in LISP and that can not, as yet, be compiled go too slow for most practical purposes.(There is no LISP for a personal computer that can be compiled though a compiler has been promised for quite a while by at least two vendors). The rest of the tools fall in the middle and may or may not be fast enough, depending upon the specific application.

End-User Interface

At the same time that one is considering the nature of the problem itself, most analysts will want to consider the way in which the end-user will need to interact with the resulting system. Features that effect the user interface include the following:

Line/Menu Screen. Some tools interact with users via menus while others prompt line entries. While the latter can be used in some cases, the increased friendliness and speed of menu oriented tools makes them desirable if the problem will require that the system be built or used by individuals who are not very familiar with computers or the subject matter of the problem.

Initial Pruning. "Initial Pruning" refers to techniques that allow the end-user to quickly indicate which aspects of a problem he or she wants assistance with. Thus, if an auto technician starts to consult a system on auto problems and he already knows that the problem is an electrical problem rather than a mechanical problem, he would like to be able to begin the consultation by pruning the system so that it only considers electrical problems. If a tool lacks this feature and the problem situation will frequently require the user to answer questions that he or she knows are irrelevant, the job aid will not be well received and will probably fall into disuse.

Multiple and Uncertain Answers. Imagine a situation in which the end user is asked if he or she would prefer a solution that involved the use of technique A or technique B. The user might not be prepared to express a clear preference or might want to reserve judgment until later. Likewise, the user might not know the answer. A tool that allows multiple or uncertain answers allows the user to answer: "Technique A, 40%, Technique B, 60%". Or, the user can simply answer "unknown". If the problem is tightly structured and involves analyzing documents that are always complete, multiple answers and "unknown" might not be necessary. Most problems involving judgment, however, will require this facility.

Development Interface

The development interface refers to the facilities that the tool provides to facilitate the initial development and subsequent modification of the knowledge base. Import developmental facilities include:

Knowledge Base Creation. All tools provide some facilities for the creation and storage of knowledge bases. Some tools provide internal utilities for writing and editing a knowledge base. Most small tools allow the developer to create the knowledge base in a conventional word processor and then simply load the word processor file into the tool when the knowledge base is required. This means that the developer must own a word processing program to use the tool, but it also means that the developer probably already knows all of the editing commands and can create and edit large sets of rules quite rapidly.

How and Why Explanations. If a developer or user is running a system and is asked a question, a "why" probe (usually a function key on a menu driven system), asks the system to explain why it is asking that question. Tools that provide "why" explanations respond by printing the rule that the system is seeking to confirm. A "how" probe asks the system how it arrived at a particular conclusion. In this case the system indicates if it reached a conclusion by applying a particular rule, or by obtaining the information from a database or from the user. These explanation facilities can be useful to the end-user, but they are especially important to a developer who is trying to debug a large knowledge base.

Inference Tracing. "Inference Tracing" refers to a detailed list of the inferences a system made during a consultation. The developer will use this facility frequently while creating a new knowledge base.

Locates Specific Attributes. Imagine that you have developed a small knowledge system about auto parts and that now one part is to be replaced by another. You need to find every fact and rule in the knowledge base that refers to the former part and replace it with the name and characteristics of the new part. A Specific Attribute Editor allows you to identify every reference to any particular attribute (e.g. the old part) in your knowledge base. Obviously you can do this indirectly if you have the knowledge base stored in a conventional word processing program by simply using the "Find/Replace" command. Some tools allow you to do it "on-line".

On-line Knowledge Base Editor. A knowledge base editor allows the developer to quickly examine and change items in the knowledge base. Some tools allow this even when the knowledge base was created via an external word processing system. Others, that compile the knowledge base do not allow this "on-line" editing and the developer is forced to return to the word processor to change a knowledge base entry.

Cases Saved. The most important technique used in the evaluation and improvement of most expert systems is to simply run well-known cases until the system can consistently and correctly solve them. Thus, time is saved if the developer can store a library of cases and automatically re-enter them after making modifications in the knowledge base. Some tools provide utilities for storing and quickly re-entering cases.

Screen Format Utilities. All tools provide some approach to creating the screen that the end-user will interact with when using the system. Some tools make it easy for the developer to create a good interface and handle such things as displaying titles and copyright information and some do not.

Systems Interface

Hooks to Databases. Some tools make it possible to access information in other databases by creating programs in the language that underlies the tool. Some facilitate the use of a specific external database program (e.g. Dbase II). Others do not provide such hooks. Obviously the nature of the problem will indicate if it is important to draw data from conventional databases. In some cases database hooks will prove very valuable.

Hooks to Other Languages. Just as some tools allow the developer to exit the system to obtain information in external databases, some tools facilitate the use of external languages and others do not. If one is considering using an expert system as a front end to an already developed system this could be a very important consideration.

Software

Language of Tool. Tools are written in various languages and they are noted on the chart. Obviously if the developer can gain access to the language the tool is written in he or she will need to be able to program in that language if he or she is to take advantage of the access.

Can the System be Compiled. Some systems can be compiled and some can not. As a rule, those that can run much faster. On the otherhand, compiling tends to limit on-line editing during development.

Other Language Required for Tool Use. Some tools require that a separate language be running on the computer before the tool will function. Other tools are complete packages and do not require that any "underlying" languages be available.

Operating System Required for Tool. The operating system required for the use of the tool is specified on the chart. Most of the tools run on an IBM personal computer under MS-DOS. Exceptions can require that you partition a disk and that can be a hassle.

Hardware Requirements

Computer. The chart indicates the hardware on which the tool vendor supports the tool. Expert system tools are more "delicate" than most programs and are less likely to run on "clones" than more conventional software.

RAM Required (Recommended). The chart indicates the active memory required by the vendor. A figure in parentheses is the RAM recommended by the vendor. As a rule, tools written in LISP need lots of RAM and the recommended figure turns out to be the minimum you would want for a large system.

Other (Recommended). Some vendors require special cards or recommend color monitors to take advantage of color that highlights system activities. Required and recommended additional hardware are noted.

Training/Support

Course Available. The great promise of small expert systems will only be realized if large numbers of people who would not attempt to program a system using any conventional programming language use these tools to develop intelligent job aids. If that happens, then small expert system building tools will change the ordinary decision making processes in business in a more profound way than electronic spreadsheets have changed financial decision making. If this promise is to be realized, however, lots of people who do not know anything about programming are going to have to learn how to use these tools to develop intelligent job aids. The tools themselves are programmed in a near—English syntax and are really not very difficult to learn to use. The analysis of a problem and the decision—making process necessary to solve it, however, can be quite a challenge. A new developer who is already in programming will probably find the manuals quite useful. Most new developers, however, will find a workshop a great help[in learning how to analyze problems and use a tool to represent the resulting knowledge. Some vendors have created workshops to provide this initial training and support and it is certainly valuable, though most vendors have so far overpriced their training.

Documentation. Most tools come with a manual and most manuals tell you how to use the tool. Since most of the tools are relatively friendly, the manuals work well enough in a narrow sense. The real trick to getting a lot of value out of these tools, however, lies in selecting appropriate problems and analyzing those problems in an effective manner. Here, most of the manuals do not tend to help. Some vendors provide "extensive" documentation, which includes several step—by—step examples and several knowledge bases for study. This is a help, though ultimately the workshop is the way to go.

Cost

The chart indicates the cost of the tool, the cost of any training and the cost of run—time versions if they are available. (A "run—time version" is a job aid that has a knowledge base and it compiled or locked in such a way that the user can no longer modify the knowledge base. For certain purposes, businesses will want to develop the intelligent job aid on a tool and then convert it into a "run—time version" before distributing it to the field.) All prices should be considered very tentative. The market is just being created and many of the entries are grossly overpriced. The prices will probably be much more reasonable by the end of 1985 when there will be more competition.

The addresses of the vendors of the tools mentioned on the chart are included at the end of this article.

Recommendations

The important thing is to get started. The potential for improving employee effectiveness and efficiency is huge. The market is very confused at the moment and it will take some time to settle. When it does there will probably be more cost/effective options than there are now. The next generation of small tools will probably offer induction—like front—ends to help developers generate an initial set of rules more rapidly. Moreover, sometime soon, there probably will be an object—oriented hybrid tool available.

But the availability of cost—effective tools is really only about a third of the whole picture. The rest of the effort involves identifying the proper problems in your company and learning how to analyze expertise and convert such knowledge into formalisms that can be used by small expert system building tools. In otherwords, the tools are not as important as the overall analysis and design that leads to an intelligent job aid. Do not be confused about the "knowledge engineering bottleneck" issue; that only applies to large expert systems. You do need think about "knowledge engineering" issues when you design a small system , but your concerns will be much more pragmatic than those normally considered to be "knowledge engineering". The key characteristic of small system building tools is that they can be used by non—programmers! Get started right away with whatever tool makes sense for your organization. I personally recommend you begin with one of the less expensive tools and concentrate on identifying problems that you want to solve with such tools. By the time you learn how to develop intelligent job aids, there will be several better, cheaper tools available to use when you actually want to field your intelligent job aids.

Vendors of Small Expert System Building Tools

ESP ADVISOR. Expert Systems International, 1150 First Ave., King of Prussia, PA 19406. (215) 337-2300

EXPERT-EASE. Jeffrey Perrone & Assoc. Inc., 3685 17th Street, San Francisco, CA 94114. (415) 431-9562

INSIGHT 1 and INSIGHT 2. Level 5 Research, 4980 S A 1 A, Melbourne, FL 32951. (305) 729-9046

KES. Software Architecture & Engineering, 1500 Wilson Blvd., Suite 800, Arlington, VA 22209. (703) 276-7910

M. 1 and M. 1a. Teknowledge, Inc., 525 University Ave., Palo Alto, CA 94301. (415) 327-6600

PERSONAL CONSULTANT. Texas Instruments, 12501 Research Blvd., MS 2223, Austin, TX 78769. (512) 250-7533

TIMM. General Research Corp. 7655 Old Springhouse Road, McLean, VA 22102. (703) 893-5900

Bibliography

The overall best source on new developments is The AI Magazine published by the American Association for Artificial Intelligence. ($25/year. 445 Burgess Drive, Menlo Park, CA. 94025)

Harmon, Paul and King, David. Expert Systems: Artificial Intelligence in Business. New York, John Wiley, 1985.

Hayes-Roth, Frederick, Waterman, Donald A. and Lenat, Douglas B. (Eds.). Building Expert Systems. Reading, Mass., Addison-Wesley Pub. Co., 1983.

Weiss, Sholom M. and Kulikowski, Casimir A. A Practical Guide to Designing Expert Systems. Totowa, New Jersey, Rowman & Allanheld, 1984.

DO-IT-YOURSELF EXPERT SYSTEMS WITH ARTIFICIAL INTELLIGENCE ON A MICROCOMPUTER

Jeffrey O. Milman, President

Expert Systems Inc.
868 West End Avenue, Suite 3A, New York, New York 10025
(212) 662-7206

ABSTRACT

A new microcomputer program called Expert-Ease
(tm) can assist in building expert systems for
medical diagnosis, troubleshooting and repair
of machinery, capturing the experience of
retiring personnel, developing department
knowledge bases for training, and discovering
trends in stock and commodity data. Expert-
Ease's artificial intelligence "inference
engine" was designed by Professors Donald
Michie and Ross Quinlan. Expert-Ease requires
128K RAM and one DS/DD disk drive on an IBM PC
or compatible. The software automatically
generates a single multibranch 'if... then'
rule from a matrix of up to 31 different numeric and word attributes by 255 examples of
values of those attributes leading to 31
different conclusions or decisions. At the
user's option the rule can be converted to
multiple choice questions and answers in any
natural language. Expert-Ease requires no
computer experience or knowledge engineering
to build or inquire of its expert systems.

For many years, artificial intelligence has been
like the weather: everyone talks about it, but
no one has done anything useful with it for less
than $100K on a minicomputer. Now, for the first
time, a new software package, called Expert-Ease
(tm), allows anyone with a standard IBM PC (128K
RAM) or compatible to create expert systems, in
any field, in a short period of time.

In this paper I will discuss the state of the art
in artificial intelligence and expert systems
before Expert-Ease, the theory and operation of
Expert-Ease, the design of several expert systems
using the software, general methods of extracting
knowledge from experts, and the shape of the
foreseeable future beyond the current version of
Expert-Ease.

THE STATE OF THE ART

Artificial Intelligence (AI) has been described
in many ways. For our discussion, a useful frame
of reference is to consider as AI any technique
that resembles human reasoning. Currently
expressive of AI techniques are computer programs
that mimic natural languages, those we speak.

These natural language interfaces permit the
inquiry from existing data bases by non-technical
personnel in day-to-day English without having to
know anything about the underlying file structures. Natural language programs contain rules
of grammatical structure that convert natural
English sentences through artificial intelligence
algorithms into program calls that are recognized
by the underlying data base. Natural language
interfaces, however, do not reason with the data
base. They merely call up existing data requested by the user in a conversational manner.

Another current set of AI techniques is embodied
in robotics. AI algorithms are harnessed to
recognize patterns not only in the primary
movements of the robot, but in the feedback from
tactile and vision sensors incorporated in the
circuitry. Robots have been "trained" to
recognize repetitive and new situations and to
adjust their movements accordingly. In a sense,
then, the robot reasons about its surroundings in
the same manner as a human might.

The third, and currently the most intensely
developed area of AI is in expert systems,
sometimes called knowledge-based systems. These
systems consist of a body of knowledge in a
specific area and an AI inference engine that
"reasons" about the knowledge base to apply only
the pertinent facts constituting expert advice to
a new inquiry. Until Expert-Ease, expert systems
were rule-based, that is, they contained as their
base of knowledge, condition-action rules provided by experts in a specific domain. A condition-action rule is simply a set of one or more
conditions, which when detected, demand a specific action or conclusion. For example, one rule
from a medical diagnosis expert system is: IF
the infection type is primary bacteremia and the
suspected entry point is the gastrointestinal
tract and the site of the culture is one of the
sterile sites, THEN the organism is Bacteroides.

Several successful expert systems, each
incorporating hundreds of these rules have been
applied to medical diagnosis, oil prospecting,
and repair and maintenance of complex machinery.
To build such systems, however, a discipline
called knowledge engineering has been necessary
to ferret out expert knowledge from the people
who have that knowledge and then incorporate that

Reprinted from *IEEE COMPCON*, pp. 20–26, Sept. 1984.

knowledge in computer programs which when inquired by a user give expert level advice. Knowledge engineers are rare, since they must combine both a significant knowledge of the expert's domain and the AI languages like LISP or Prolog that must be programmed to contain and impart that knowledge.

The process necessary to extract knowledge from an expert, even by a knowledge engineer, is no easy task. In fact, it is so arduous it has been given the name of the "Feigenbaum Bottleneck" after Edward Feigenbaum, Chairman of the Computer Science Department at Stanford University. Experts do not always know the specific rules by which they practice their craft. They apply years of experience, integrated, rationalized, and sometimes in intuitive leaps to new problem definitions. Yet, for the rule-based expert system to operate effectively, almost every conceivable rule must be nailed down and incorporated into the knowledge base. Knowledge engineers must often spend years observing and interacting with the experts to uncover all the pertinent rules. The combination of the "Feigenbaum Bottleneck" and the vast computer storage requirements of LISP and Prolog has meant that expert systems were confined to large mainframe or minicomputers and huge budgets, often well into the millions of dollars.

At this point, you might ask "Why bother with expert systems at all if they are this difficult and expensive to produce?" Because true experts in any field are limited. They are also mortal. Their expertise, in many cases, dies with them. In high value disciplines, like oil field geology and medical diagnosis, the payback from being able to incorporate the knowledge of several experts forever is well worth the investment.

If expert systems could be developed faster and cheaper, they promise to bring the very best expert advice in every field to bear on every problem.

Expert-Ease, as I will demonstrate, is a means to inexpensive, rapidly producible, reliable and valuable expert systems.

THEORY AND PRACTICE OF EXPERT-EASE (tm)

Expert-Ease differs from rule-based systems because it "learns" from experience, not previously discovered rules, in the form of successful examples of an expert's actual practice of his craft. If the expert can state his experience in the form of conditions (called Values of Attributes in the Expert-Ease environment) and the actions (called Decisions) he took as a result of the conditions, then the AI algorithms in Expert-Ease will induce an 'if...then' rule that underlies the mass of the examples. The 'if...then' rule (pictured on the computer screen as a stairstep) can be converted with 2 keystrokes into simple English questions with multiple choice answers. This Q&A format is the user interface through which new inquiries requiring expert advice are entered.

The induction of a single 'if...then' rule from a matrix of examples of expert activity or experience is performed through algorithms designed by Dr. Donald Michie, Director of the Machine Intelligence Research Unit of the University of Edinburgh and Dr. Ross Quinlan, Professor of Computer Science at the University of New South Wales, Australia. These algorithms are programmed in Pascal and constitute the "inference engine." The inference engine is a concept of logical reduction that begins with the universe of final actions or decisions taken by the expert and works backwards over all the expressed values of the conditions encountered by the expert that caused him to select these actions. In working backwards, the algorithms are sorting and comparing each value of each condition to determine exactly which values and conditions, without exception, always lead to one or more of the actions. If a value and/or a condition is found to be less than 100% necessary to produce the action listed, it is dropped from the 'if... then' rule. The final 'if...then' rule contains the absolute minimum number of conditions and values necessary to point to each and every action.

Conditions and values are prioritized and chained in order of relevance depending upon their relationship to the universe of all actions. For example, if a particular condition and value, such as warm-blooded temperature above 98 degrees Fahrenheit relates to all the actions, in this case, a listing of various mammals and birds, then this condition and value will take precedence over a second condition and value, such as four-footed, which would only apply to some of the mammals to distinguish them from birds and whales. Colors of the birds and mammals, although valid data, would probably serve only to make a distinction between certain birds on the list, and if they did not serve to do even that, would not appear at all in the final rule.

The algorithms essentially classify the minimum and maximum number of conditions and values that correlate in every case to each action. By adding more examples of new conditions and values that relate to existing or new actions, the algorithms will reclassify these new conditions and values together with the previous entries, re-prioritize and cull them. This culling and re-prioritization constitute learning by example, or if the examples represent experience, learning by experience.

The power of this technique will be demonstrated in a real-world expert system we will build now. This system is a simple kidney diagnosis expert system designed by a radiologist who diagnoses kidney disease by reading x-rays. The same principle demonstrated here can be applied to any type of diagnosis or expertise that relies upon expert experience.

The design of the system begins in the Attribute screen (Exhibit A). Note the screen layout resembles a spreadsheet cell structure. The far right column of the grid is the Decision column,

```
ZDDDDDDDDDDDDDDDDDDDDDDDDDDDDDDDDDDDDDDDDDDDDDDDDDDDDD1
3 EXPERT-EASE   file: KIDNEY      45094 bytes left
CDDDDDDDDDDDDDDDDDDDDDDDDDDDDDDDDDDDDDDDDDDDDDDDDDDDDD1
3          logical   logical    logical
3          Kidsize   Contour    Density    Diagnosis
3   1      small     smooth     increased  ischemia
3   2      large     regular    decreased  maligtmr
3   3      normal    irreg      normal     stone
3   4                                      benign
3   5                                      normal
3   6                                      venobstr
3   7                                      arterobs
3   8                                      infection
3   9
3   10
3   11
3   12
CDDDDDDDDDDDDDDDDDDDDDDDDDDDDDDDDDDDDDDDDDDDDDDDDDDDDD
3 Malignant tumor
3
CDDDDDDDDDDDDDDDDDDDDDDDDDDDDDDDDDDDDDDDDDDDDDDDDDDDDD
3 editing attributes
3 , , ,  ', new, value, delete, change, text ? ('+' fo
3 >
eDDDDDDDDDDDDDDDDDDDDDDDDDDDDDDDDDDDDDDDDDDDDDDDDDDDDD
```

Exhibit A

in this case the doctor's diagnosis of kidney
disease. There are eight different diagnoses of
kidney disease that this doctor normally encounters. To the left of the diagnosis column are
three Attribute columns with headings that denote
the conditions whose values must be determined
for each x-ray before the doctor can make his
diagnosis. The three conditions, kidney size,
kidney contour, and tissue density, on the x-ray
are headed by the word 'logical.' This is
because these conditions are expressed as values
in words, such as "small," "large," "normal,"
"irregular," instead of numbers. But Expert-Ease
can process integer (numeric) values of Attributes as easily as word values (symbolic logic),
as we will see further on. For the time being,
however, this doctor is telling the system that
by just knowing the word values of each of the
three Attributes for an x-ray, he can arrive at
one of the eight diagnoses.

You can think of the Attribute screen as the
dictionary or lexicon of terms that will be acted
upon by the AI algorithms. Note toward the
bottom of the screen the words "malignant tumor."
These words are entered into a wordprocessing
window built into the Attribute screen and can be
chained to any word on the grid, in this case, to
the diagnosis "maligtmr," so that a non-expert
inquiring of the system later can understand what
the doctor meant. The only limit to the amount
of the text that can be chained to any single
word in the grid is your microcomputer disk
storage space. This endlessly scrolling wordprocessing window is also the area where we
build the questions and answers that are the
output of the expert system.

Exhibit A is a small Attribute screen for the
purposes of demonstration. In practice, this
screen can contain up to 31 different diagnoses
or Decisions, 31 different Attributes, and 255
word Values of each Attribute. Numeric integer

Values of each Attribute can range from negative
32,000 to positive 32,000.

Having established the universe of terms in this
kidney expert system and their definitions in the
wordprocessing window, we move (with a single
keystroke) to the Example screen (Exhibit B). In

EXPERT-EASE Example Listing, Problem: KIDNEY

	Kidsize logical	Contour logical	Density logical	Diagnosis logical
	-------	-------	-------	-------
1	small	smooth	increased	ischemia
2	large	regular	increased	stone
3	normal	irreg	decreased	maligtmr
4	normal	regular	decreased	benign
5	normal	smooth	normal	normal
6	large	smooth	increased	venobstr
7	large	irreg	decreased	maligtmr
8	small	regular	decreased	arterobs
9	small	irreg	normal	infection

Exhibit B

this screen, which automatically reproduces the
column headings built in the Attribute screen,
the doctor enters examples of 9 patient x-rays
for which he has made successful diagnoses. Note
that when the doctor sees a small kidney on the
x-ray, a smooth contour, and increased tissue
density, he always diagnoses ischemia. One
Example screen can contain up to 255 examples of
such experience.

At this point, with another keystroke, Expert-
Ease will generate a Rule using the AI algorithms
in about 10 seconds. The Rule is shown in
Exhibit C. It is read from top to bottom, left

EXPERT-EASE Rule Listing, Problem: KIDNEY

```
Contour
     smooth : Kidsize
              small : ischemia
              large : venobstr
             normal : normal
    regular : Kidsize
              small : arterobs
              large : stone
             normal : benign
      irreg : Kidsize
              small : infection
              large : maligtmr
             normal : maligtmr
```

Exhibit C

to right. It says that the most important
Attribute for the doctor to consider is kidney
contour. Then depending upon whether the contour
is smooth, regular or irregular, the next question that must be asked is kidney size. Depending on the kidney size, one of the eight diagnoses is 100% indicated. Note that all the
diagnoses shown in the Example screen are accoun-
ted for. Note also that tissue density turned
out not to be a defining factor for any of the
diagnoses. This is the power of artificial
intelligence over linear programming or regression analysis which require or give a numeric

factor to every variable. Expert-Ease will automatically exclude redundant or irrelevant logic from the Rule, whether denoted in words or numbers.

Now, we will return to the Example screen and add a new example to see the effect of new experience on the learning algorithms. You should keep in mind that a Rule is only as valid as the expert's experience. The choice of expert and that expert's choice of his most successful experience will determine the long-term validity or general applicability of the rule generated. In our example, now, however, we will put in some inexpert experience to highlight the ability of the software to think and to diagnose gaps in the knowledge base. In Exhibit D, we have added a

EXPERT-EASE Example Listing, Problem: KIDNEY

	Kidsize logical	Contour logical	Density logical	Diagnosis logical
1	small	smooth	increased	ischemia
2	large	regular	increased	stone
3	normal	irreg	decreased	maligtmr
4	normal	regular	decreased	benign
5	normal	smooth	normal	normal
6	large	smooth	increased	venobstr
7	large	irreg	decreased	maligtmr
8	small	regular	decreased	arterobs
9	small	irreg	normal	infection
10	small	irreg	normal	maligtmr

Exhibit D

new Example on line 10 with the same Values of Attributes as line 9 but with a different diagnosis. When we generate the Rule in Exhibit E, we find that when the contour is irregular and the kidney size is small, the Rule signals a "clash." It cannot determine from the example matrix, or knowledge base, whether to diagnose an infection or a malignant tumor. To eliminate a clash, the expert system designer would take the same steps as a real life expert: he would call for more information to distinguish between the two plausible diagnoses. In real life, a doctor unable to choose between two diagnoses, will ask his patient to undergo another medical test. We will do the same in Exhibit F.

EXPERT-EASE Rule Listing, Problem: KIDNEY

```
Contour
      smooth : Kidsize
              small : ischemia
              large : venobstr
              normal : normal
      regular : Kidsize
              small : arterobs
              large : stone
              normal : benign
      irreg : Kidsize
              small : clash (infection maligtmr)
              large : maligtmr
              normal : maligtmr
```

Exhibit E

Exhibit F returns us to the Attribute screen where we have just added a new Attribute called Blood Test which we will express in integers. We

EXPERT-EASE Attribute Listing, Problem: KIDNEY   Date: 11

	Bloodtest integer	Kidsize logical	Contour logical	Density logical	Diagnosis logical
1		small	smooth	increased	ischemia
2		large	regular	decreased	maligtmr
3		normal	irreg	normal	stone
4					benign
5					normal
6					venobstr
7					arterobs
8					infection

Exhibit F

switch back to the Example screen in Exhibit G to enter the results of blood tests for the two patients with conflicting diagnoses. Note the

EXPERT-EASE Example Listing, Problem: KIDNEY   Date: 11-

	Bloodtest integer	Kidsize logical	Contour logical	Density logical	Diagnosis logical
1	*	small	smooth	increased	ischemia
2	*	large	regular	increased	stone
3	*	normal	irreg	decreased	maligtmr
4	*	normal	regular	decreased	benign
5	*	normal	smooth	normal	normal
6	*	large	smooth	increased	venobstr
7	*	large	irreg	decreased	maligtmr
8	*	small	regular	decreased	arterobs
9	30	small	irreg	normal	infection
10	130	small	irreg	normal	maligtmr

Exhibit G

asterisks on lines 1 thru 8 under the Blood Test column. The asterisks indicate a "don't care" or not important Value for these patients. The Blood Test values are important for patient 9 and patient 10, where we have entered widely different numeric findings. Now when we regenerate the Rule in Exhibit H, the clash is eliminated and a Rule for distinguishing between infection and malignant tumor is disclosed. Note that the

EXPERT-EASE Rule Listing, Problem: KIDNEY

```
Contour
      smooth : Kidsize
              small : ischemia
              large : venobstr
              normal : normal
      regular : Kidsize
              small : arterobs
              large : stone
              normal : benign
      irreg : Kidsize
              small : Bloodtest
                      <80 : infection
                      >=80 : maligtmr
              large : maligtmr
              normal : maligtmr
```

Exhibit H

inference engine added the numeric values together and divided by two to come up with ranges.
If you argue that this approach is too crude for
life and death, reflect again that the Rule is
only as valid as your knowledge base. The more
complete the knowledge base, the more examples of
successful experience entered therein, the better
the Rule will be. In the Example screen, if you
now added two additional cases for highest and
lowest blood test values that would still indicate infection or malignant tumor, then the
Rule will display a finer range of Values for
discrimination.

In Exhibit I, we have entered two new patients'
x-rays (lines 11 and 12) arbitrarily to show you
another self-diagnosing feature of the Rule

EXPERT-EASE Example Listing, Problem: KIDNEY   Date: 11-

	Bloodtest integer	Kidsize logical	Contour logical	Density logical	Diagnosis logical
	-------	-------	-------	-------	-------
1	*	small	smooth	increased	ischemia
2	*	large	regular	increased	stone
3	*	normal	irreg	decreased	maligtmr
4	*	normal	regular	decreased	benign
5	*	normal	smooth	normal	normal
6	*	large	smooth	increased	venobstr
7	*	large	irreg	decreased	maligtmr
8	*	small	regular	decreased	arterobs
9	30	small	irreg	normal	infection
10	130	small	irreg	normal	maligtmr
11	*	large	irreg	increased	normal
12	*	small	smooth	decreased	benign

Exhibit I

generated in Exhibit J. Note in Exhibit J,
because of the complexity of the new patients'
histories, the Rule now contains 3 stages in-

EXPERT-EASE Rule Listing, Problem: KIDNEY

```
Contour
      smooth : Kidsize
              small : Density
                     increased : ischemia
                     decreased : benign
                         normal : null
              large : venobstr
              normal : normal
      regular : Kidsize
              small : arterobs
              large : stone
              normal : benign
       irreg : Density
           increased : normal
           decreased : maligtmr
              normal : Bloodtest
                      <80 : infection
                      >=80 : maligtmr
```

Exhibit J

cluding tissue density as well as contour and
size before a diagnosis with 100% assurance can
be reached. But note also on line 6 of the Rule
the diagnosis called "null." A null indicates an
incomplete 'if...then' chain. Values of critical
Attributes are included as part of the lexicon,
but are nowhere to be found in the knowledge base
of the expert's experience. Our Example screen

in Exhibit I shows not one example of a combination of smooth contour, small kidney size and
normal density. This null tells the doctor he
needs more examples to cover this set of conditions if he wishes to complete the Rule. He may
know that this combination is never to be found
in nature and will leave the Rule as is. Or he
may inquire of his colleagues as to what they
have found in this circumstance and add their
experience to his Example screen, regenerate the
Rule and eliminate the null. This example
demonstrates the power of Expert-Ease to communicate what it doesn't know so that the expert can
fill in the gaps in his knowledge base.

If, after these adjustments, we think that the
Rule in Exhibit J is a good Rule by which to
diagnose kidney disease from x-rays (and an
occasional blood test), with two keystrokes,
Expert-Ease will convert the Rule into simple
English questions with multiple choice answers,
which when selected by the non-technical user,
will give the same expert advice as if the doctor
himself were in attendance. Scan the four
screens of questions and answers in Exhibits K
through N. We have chosen answers 1. (for smooth
contour), 1. (for small kidney size) and 2. (for
decreased density), respectively, which gives us
the diagnosis Benign Tumor, exactly as the Rule
path which governs, indicates in Exhibit J.
Notice how simple the Q&A technique is for a
non-technical user. A power user of Expert-Ease
would probably scan the Rule directly for advice.

Expert-Ease Query Screen

```
ZDDDDDDDDDDDDDDDDDDDDDDDDDDDDDDDDDDDDDDDDDDDDDDDDDDDD.
3 EXPERT-EASE    file: KIDNEY        44710 bytes left
CDDDDDDDDDDDDDDDDDDDDDDDDDDDDDDDDDDDDDDDDDDDDDDDDDDDD.
3
3 Is the contour-
3
3
3    1. smooth
3
3    2. regular
3
3    3. irregular
3
3
3
3
3
3
3
3
CDDDDDDDDDDDDDDDDDDDDDDDDDDDDDDDDDDDDDDDDDDDDDDDDDDDDI
3 running KIDNEY
3 Enter value 1..3
3 >I
@DDDDDDDDDDDDDDDDDDDDDDDDDDDDDDDDDDDDDDDDDDDDDDDDDDDDI
```

Exhibit K

Is the kidney size-

    1. small

    2. large

    3. normal

Exhibit L

```
Is the density-

   1. increased

   2. decreased

   3. normal


        Exhibit M


ZDDDDDDDDDDDDDDDDDDDDDDDDDDDDDDDDDDDDDDDDDDDDDDDDDDDDDDDI
3 EXPERT-EASE   file: KIDNEY      44710 bytes left
CDDDDDDDDDDDDDDDDDDDDDDDDDDDDDDDDDDDDDDDDDDDDDDDDDDDDDDDI
3 The diagnosis is -
3 Benign Tumor
3
3

        Exhibit N
```

The texts in the Q&A screens result from being
chained to the keywords in the wordprocessing
section of the Attribute screen, and as noted
above, can be as voluminous as your disk storage.

It is important to explain at this point, that
any single Rule screen in Expert-Ease can be
chained to any number of other separate Rules
supported by their own Example matrices. This
sub-Rule chaining feature permits an extremely
large or unwieldy knowledge domain that would not
fit within 31 different Attributes or 255 examples to be broken down into subsets of the domain
for Rule generation and then stitched together
seamlessly into a very large expert system of
extreme complexity.

OTHER EXPERT-EASE EXPERT SYSTEMS

The demonstration above of the kidney expert
system is an example of one of three major
classifications of expert systems, called diagnosis, which are easily built with Expert-Ease.
Diagnosis-type expert systems can apply not only
to medicine, but also to autos, factory plant and
equipment, and administrative approval steps or
repetitive departmental activities. Another
major classification is communication. Corporations which have large corporate policy manuals
that are expensive, rarely read, and require long
lead times for review and revision, printing,
distribution and interleaving can use Expert-Ease
instead. Its wordprocessing window and Q&A
format easily and swiftly disseminate corporate
policy to employees, who have only to boot the
"expert system" for the policy, say T&E, they are
interested in and answer the very few questions
posed about their corporate status, travel
destination, etc., to get the latest and most
pertinent corporate policy.

The third major classification which I call
prediction is at once the most intriguing and the
most dangerous. Expert-Ease is a pattern finder
or detector. In our demonstration, it detected
thru its Rule-making function gaps and inconsistencies in the doctor's knowledge called nulls

and clashes. The Rule learned to eliminate these
ambiguities with the addition of new experience
to the Example screen. What if we just enter
streams of unconnected Values of Attributes and
their experimental or historical results without
any forethought? What would the resulting Rule
tell us then?

Some users of Expert-Ease already apply this
approach. One trader entered 19 different
variables of stock market activity as Attributes
and tracked the Values of these variables for 52
prior weeks of history. In the Decision column
he posted the trend of the Dow Jones stock market
averages the following week. The Rule generated
pointed to a 100% correlation among many of the
variables and the trend. By answering the Q&A
with a new week's variables the trader was able
to achieve an impressive record of successful
predictions of future stock market activity. The
danger is, of course, that a new week's activity
in the market may have no relation at all to the
prior 52 weeks. But this same approach can be
applied by law enforcement agencies to find
connections among crimes, clues, victims and
suspects from among a jumbled mass of data.

I predict, somewhere, sometime, someone will use
this technique to discover a new law of physics,
chemistry or human psychology from among a mass
of experimental values not otherwise analyzable.
Unfortunately, we will probably also be innun-
dated with 100% correlations, such as the foot-
ball team with at least three running backs with
living grandmothers always wins the Super Bowl,
until, just when you bet the ranch, it doesn't
happen the next Super Bowl Sunday.

GENERAL METHODS OF EXTRACTING
EXPERT KNOWLEDGE

My experience with Expert-Ease has taught some
valuable lessons about the techniques that can be
applied to debrief an expert. Even experts using
Expert-Ease themselves find it difficult to
extract from their heads and their records all
the Attributes and Values they must have considered before they took their actions or gave
their advice. The process usually involves
generating several Expert-Ease Rules, analyzing
them, testing them in the field, adding new
Values, Attributes, and Decisions and reworking
the entire process again.

I have found the following technique to speed
this process considerably. Have the expert, in a
stream of consciousness frame of mind, list the
significant nouns, verbs and adjectives jargon at
random that are encountered in his field. Add to
this list day by day. Then separate these terms,
with the expert's assistance, into classifications for Expert-Ease: Decisions, Attributes or
Values. Set up the Attribute screen with these
terms, and present it together with an empty
Example screen. Now ask the expert to try to
complete some successful combinations of these
terms in the Example screen that represent his
experience in practice. Having the expert's mind

triggered by all the jargon of his craft in Expert-Ease format appears to considerably improve the feedback process to the expert and makes him comfortable with the computer environment because it seems to speak his language.

THE SHAPE OF THE FORESEEABLE FUTURE

Expert-Ease is sometimes criticized for not having a self-commenting or backchaining feature to explain its reasoning to the user. I find this feature is just not necessary with an experience-based system like Expert-Ease. With a rule-based expert system, it is vital to know that no important rule was omitted from the expert advice or a ridiculous rule somehow incorporated. But Expert-Ease begins with the very best experience or examples of successful practice from the most proficient expert. If the expert is recognized for his talent and his experience has been validated in practice, the Rule generated by Expert-Ease is absolutely logically impeccable. The best way to assure yourself of a good Rule is to apply it prospectively to new cases. But I expect some future version of Expert-Ease will include a self-commenting feature.

Another so-called enhancement of the system may be the addition of probabilistic Attributes, Values, and Decisions. Expert-Ease is a deterministic system that when completely "tuned" gives only 100% correlations. Most users, I find, prefer the best advice without ambiguity. Most rule-based expert systems, however, have probabilistic values and produce weighted results. But what will a doctor do when confronted with a diagnosis of .60 flu and .40 cancer? Send the patient home with two aspirin to sleep it off and bet on the odds? Perhaps, however, for some applications there may be imperative reasons for including a probabilistic feature.

More exciting then these possibilities is the promise of interfaces between the expert system generator and giant data bases of historical or experimental data. The data will feed directly into the Example screen and generate Rules dynamically. The output Rules will be automatically analyzed statistically against the data base by another subsystem like TK!Solver(tm), an existing product from Software Arts, Inc. By deletion of inappropriate examples and addition of new ones to the Example screen, Expert-Ease will produce the best fit Rule without constant human intervention. Output ports from the system will be connected to instruments, robots, sensors or machines to constantly adjust them in line with its new learning. With existing voice-chip technology, even the current version of Expert-Ease is capable of being commanded by and express its output in speech. If Expert-Ease in its current version is considered first generation microcomputer artificial intelligence, then by the speed of development in this industry, we can expect the fourth generation to arrive about 1991. I predict the fourth generation of Expert-Ease will make HAL in the movie 2001 seem retarded.

REFERENCES

P. Kinnucan, "Computers That Think Like Experts," High Technolgy Magazine, pp. 30-42, 71, January 1984.

P. Michalski, J. Carbonnell and T. Mitchell (Editors), Machine Learning: The Artificial Intelligence Approach, Tioga Press, Palo Alto, CA (1983).

TEXAS INSTRUMENTS - PERSONAL CONSULTANT (TM)
EXPERT SYSTEM DEVELOPMENT TOOLS

by

William M. Turpin
Manager, Knowledge Systems
Texas Instruments Incorporated
Austin, Texas

This paper is an introduction to the Texas Instruments Personal Consultant (TM) Expert System Development Tools. Personal Consultant is one of the first commercial development environments for rule-based expert systems on personal computers. It supports many of the features usually found in larger, more expensive computer environments such as explanation facilities, natural language processing, reasoning with uncertainty, window-oriented interface, and full development support. This paper describes what Personal Consultant is and who should use it. It lists the important features and capabilities of the product. A few examples of current applications using Personal Consultant are also included.

INTRODUCTION

Expert system applications depend on the combination of two factors to be useful: 1) an "expert" exists that can perform a valuable service in some domain, and 2) other people would like to benefit from or perform that same service, but are less proficient for some reason. An expert system can help fill this gap by substituting for the human "expert."

Figure 1 illustrates the two primary uses of the Personal Consultant: development and delivery. The development environment is used by the creator(s) of the expert system application. The Personal Consultant development environment contains a set of tools to help prototype, refine, test, and validate knowledge bases. These development tools are used by the knowledge engineer (programmer/ analyst) and/or domain expert (possessor of knowledge) to transfer knowledge about a particular domain into the Personal Consultant formalism. These tools are similar in concept to an editor, compiler, and debugger in a more traditional programming environment.

Once a knowledge base has been created and validated, it can then be presented to the end-user through use of the commercial delivery environment. The delivery environment contains an inference engine which helps the user interact with the knowledge base. This environment asks the user questions, explains lines of reasoning, and provides advice to the end-user. It does not allow the end-user to modify the knowledge base, except for ways which the creator intended. The Personal Consultant delivery environment is smaller than the development environment since it does not contain the development tools. The delivery environment is similar to a run-time package for a traditional programming language.

TARGET MARKET

The Personal Consultant development tools are primarily intended for an experienced computer programmer. Experience with one or more programming languages and microcomputer systems is highly beneficial. Knowledge of Lisp and AI techniques is also helpful, but not required. The development environment is targeted at the creation of expert system applications -- not basic research into alternative AI techniques.

The Personal Consultant delivery environment is more targeted for the general population. It does not require any prior computer experience or in-depth knowledge in the application domain. It can provide on-line help, natural language translations, cursor selection, and labeled function keys to increase the usability of the application.

Personal Consultant is appropriate for three different market segments: 1) Corporate research and development, 2) Third party software developers, and 3) University education. Corporations can

Personal Consultant™

SYSTEM COMPONENTS

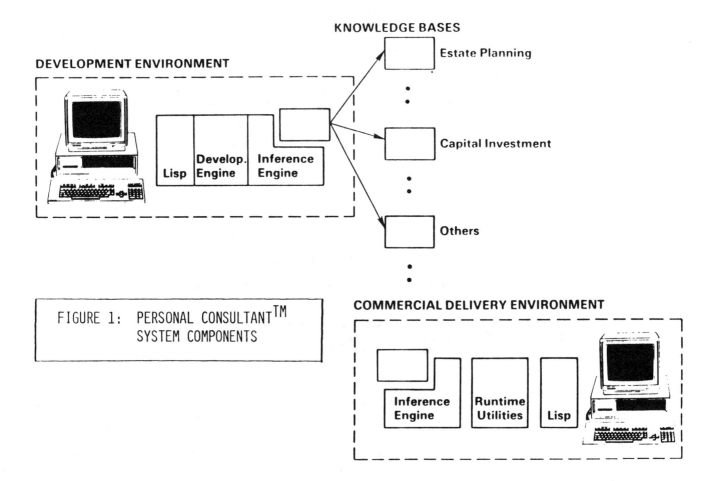

KNOWLEDGE BASES

Estate Planning

Capital Investment

Others

DEVELOPMENT ENVIRONMENT

Lisp | Develop. Engine | Inference Engine

COMMERCIAL DELIVERY ENVIRONMENT

Inference Engine | Runtime Utilities | Lisp

FIGURE 1: PERSONAL CONSULTANT™ SYSTEM COMPONENTS

use Personal Consultant to learn about and apply expert system techniques toward solving company problems. They can rapidly test the feasibility of and create applications which help save money and/or produce better results using their existing personal computer resources. Third party software developers can more easily create high-value applications for specific vertical markets using standard, high-volume microcomputers. Universities can use Personal Consultant to help teach the principles of AI or to explore new uses for expert systems in business, medical, and engineering schools.

PRODUCT FEATURES

Personal Consultant was designed to leverage from the many previous years of expert system research and development that went on at universities and large corporations. It uses the same knowledge representation scheme as was used by the MYCIN, and later the EMYCIN, projects at Stanford University. This formalism was chosen because it had been used to create several successful expert systems (MYCIN, PUFF, NEWTAX, etc.). It was also being used at many locations nationwide and was amenable to microcomputer implementation. Because of this compatibility, Personal Consultant provides a set of migration utilities to help transport EMYCIN knowledge bases into the personal computer environment.

The primary knowledge representation technique in Personal Consultant is production (if/then) rules. A production rule in a knowledge base describes an inference that can be made about a certain situation. The scope of a knowledge base depends on the number and types of situations which are covered by the production rules. This rule structure has several advantages:

* Humans can relate to production rules as "rules-of-thumb."

* Rules are very modular, and therefore easy to modify

* Rule specification is non-procedural (system links them together)

* Rules allow for explanation of reasoning as a sequence of inferences

Production rules are selected and applied during a consultation by Personal Consultant based upon a goal-oriented control strategy (backward chaining). This control strategy only considers rules which can infer the value of a current goal for possible application. Benefits of this strategy include asking a fewer number of questions and reduced processing requirements. Personal Consultant also provides a forward-chaining mechanism for certain rules where the backward-chaining is inappropriate. Forward-chaining rules can help eliminate unnecessary questions or restrict the scope of a problem solution.

Personal Consultant is capable of dealing with applications involving uncertainty through the use of certainty factors. A certainty factor is associated with each data item as a measure of belief or disbelief. Imprecise knowledge can be specified by the creator of the knowledge base by placing a certainty factor in rule conclusions. Uncertain and unknown answers can be entered by the end-user during a consultation. Certainty factors are accumulated and combined by Personal Consultant automatically during a consultation and reflected in any recommendations it makes.

In addition to production rules, Personal Consultant supports a class-inheritance mechanism to represent relationships between aspects of a problem. Personal Consultant allows a knowledge base to be divided into sub-domains, called contexts, to represent physical structures or events. Contexts are related to each other in a hierarchical manner and can inherit rules and data from contexts above them. Personal Consultant automatically creates instances of a context as required during a consultation. Multiple instances of a context can be created when needed to apply a set of rules to several similar situations.

Both the development and delivery environments of Personal Consultant employ several features to simplify interaction with the user. Dynamically-sized windows divide the display into several information zones. Color is used to help differentiate between various types of information. The available function key operations are listed on the lower portion of the display. Function keys are used to provide help, obtain explanations, change an answer, or stop the system. Menu items can be selected by positioning the cursor or typing the first letter of the desired response. These features all help make interacting with Personal Consultant applications easier to learn and simpler to operate.

Personal Consultant always interacts with the end-user through a natural language dialog. The knowledge base creator has full control over the wording of prompts, helps, and messages. Simple formatting commands can also be used to control how information is presented. Personal Consultant automatically translates all explanations and rule listings into natural language for the end-user.

The Personal Consultant development environment contains all of the tools necessary to create and test knowledge bases. It contains a simplified rule entry language, an editor, a listing facility, debug aids, and regression testing support. Personal Consultant prompts the developer for any needed information and provides default values whenever possible. The development environment also provides extensive on-line help and error checking. Because the development environment is completely self-contained, it supports the highly productive code/test/modify programming style associated with AI programming.

In addition to its standard features, Personal Consultant supports a Lisp programming environment so that a sophisticated developer can create and add user-defined functions to a knowledge base. User-defined functions can be fully integrated into Personal Consultant including the explanation sub-system.

User defined functions have been used to read and write data to files, display graphics, interface to a speech synthesis board, create higher-level data types, and perform advanced calculations.

Personal Consultant can take advantage of all of the memory that is available in the microcomputer it is running on. This allows it to develop and deliver substantial expert system applications. In a system with 768K bytes of memory, Personal Consultant can develop a knowledge base containing about 1,000 entries (rules plus parameters). Personal Consultant can also use an 8087 numeric coprocessor for performance improvement in floating point intensive applications.

PRODUCT AVAILABILITY

Personal Consultant was announced on July 27, 1984 and demonstrated at the 1984 American Association for Artificial Intelligence Conference. It was available to beta test customers in the fourth quarter of 1984 and production shipments started in January, 1985. A demonstration diskette is planned for April, 1985.

Personal Consultant is available for the Texas Instruments Professional Computer family, the IBM Personal Computer family, and its compatibles. For development, we recommend maximum memory configurations (640K bytes for IBM and 768K bytes for TI), a 10 Mbyte hard disk, a double sided diskette drive, and 80 column display. A printer is also suggested.

The delivery environment requires at least 512K bytes (depending on knowledge base), double sided diskette drive, and 80 column display. Both environments support color monitors and an 8087 numeric coprocessor.

CURRENT APPLICATIONS

Since its introduction, Personal Consultant has been readily accepted by major corporations and universities. Although many of these applications are proprietary, there are several that can be discussed.

The first external application of Personal Consultant was at the InfoMart in Dallas, Texas. Personal Consultant was used to implement a Simplified Needs Analysis System (SNAP) in the InfoMart Resource Center. This system helps first-time computer system buyers determine what sort of hardware and software they should investigate. Personal Consultant was particularly well suited for this application because of its easy-to-learn user interface. The application was programmed by Boeing Computer Services.

Other large corporations, including Texas Instruments, are developing Personal Consultant applications to assist in design and manufacturing areas. One company has a Personal Consultant application which helps configure electrical panel boards for large buildings. Its output is a recommended model number complete with pricing information. Other companies are developing applications to help diagnose failures of complex manufacturing machinery. The time and money saved by quickly getting a manufacturing process restarted can often pay for the development costs of the expert system the first time it is used.

Dr. Bruce Buchanan and Dr. Ted Shortliffe have selected Personal Consultant as the teaching vehicle for their course on medical applications of expert systems at Stanford. They felt that the personal computer environment improved the accessibility of the tool to the students. University of Texas has also used Personal Consultant in several courses in the Computer Science Department on expert systems. Ten other colleges and universities are currently working on research projects using Personal Consultant funded by a grant from Texas Instruments.

Several smaller knowledge bases have been created at Texas Instruments to help demonstrate Personal Consultant. These applications help show various features of the product and possible application domains. Current demonstration systems include:

* Individual Retirement Account (IRA) investment advice

* Stock performance analysis

* Will writing

* Real estate loan qualification

* Tomato gardening diagnosis

* Capital investment analysis

SUMMARY

We at Texas Instruments believe that Artificial Intelligence will make a major contribution to the computer industry. We are producing high performance development systems such as the Explorer for research in AI and economical delivery environments such as Personal Consultant for the commercial deployment of AI. Personal Consultant should help to greatly increase the accessibility of artificial intelligence to the broader computer market. Because of its advanced features and friendly user interface, Personal Consultant can provide the catalyst for a new era of practical applications of AI.

MICRO KES

by

Robert S. Williams
Software A&E, Inc.
Arlington, VA   22209

ABSTRACT

This paper describes the KES expert system development tool, and discusses the recent conversion of KES to the format of an IBM-PC personal computer. Although LISP was used for the initial implementation, it has been decided that re-engineering in the C language is necessary to make KES a robust production tool in the PC environment.

1.   INTRODUCTION

One of the main goals in the study of artificial intelligence (AI) is the creation of computer programs that perform actions which, when performed by humans, can be said to require intelligence [7]. In the past, this goal could only be achieved (to the extent that it has been achieved at all) through implementations which were restricted, by their memory and computing time requirements, to run on mainframes, sophisticated minicomputers, or special purpose single user machines. Recently, however, it has become possible to realize AI applications on personal computers (see, e.g., [1]).

With the emergence of several good LISP interpreters designed to run on personal computers, it is now possible to port an AI application system designed on a larger computer over to a personal computer. Certain constraints point, however, to the C language as a better eventual implementation language for these applications, both on larger computers and on personal computers (where problems that might have been encountered on larger computers tend to become magnified).

This paper describes development currently underway to convert KES, an expert system development tool, to run on an IBM-PC personal computer. Section 2 gives a brief overview of expert systems, while section 3 describes the KES expert system development tool in detail. Section 4 gives some details of the conversion of KES to an IBM-PC version of LISP. Section 5 evaluates the results of this conversion. FInally, section 6 discusses the decision to reimplement KES in C, in the context of the personal computer.

2.   EXPERT SYSTEMS

Expert systems can be defined as those AI systems that solve complex problems in specialized areas by emphasizing the domain-specific knowledge that underlies human expertise in those areas, rather than any domain-independent formal reasoning methods [3]. Like many AI applications, they can be seen as consisting of two major components: a knowledge base and an inference mechanism [8]. A knowledge base can be thought of as a repository of expert knowledge, while an inference mechanism can be viewed as the means of putting the stored knowledge to use in the process of solving a particular problem.

By far the most popular of the current approaches to building expert systems involves the rule-based system [11]. In a rule-based system, the knowledge base consists of a set of rules, generally of the form:

        if   antecedent
        then   consequent

Here, both the antecedent and the consequent denote collections of relations between elements in the rule-based system's domain of expertise. For example, if we were to describe a set of rules for animal classification (as in [13]), some of them might be expressed (informally) as follows:

> if an animal has hair
> then the animal is a mammal

> if an animal is a mammal,
>   and the animal eats meat
> then the animal is a carnivore

The inference mechanism for this type of system is generally a procedure that chains together a series of rules such that the antecedent of any given rule matches (or partially matches) the consequent of the previous rule in the chain. Such a chain can be constructed either through antecedent driven application of rules (forward chaining) or through consequent driven application of rules (backward chaining).

Though the rule-based approach is the most ubiquitous in the literature on expert systems (practically every system discussed in [3], for example, is essentially a rule based system), there are other methods of representing and using knowledge that are worth mentioning. Other forms of knowledge representation have included formulae in predicate logic (more or less a generalization of the rule-based approach), sets of probabilities, and frames [6]. Other inference mechanisms have included formal inference rules for predicate logic (such as resolution [2]), statistical pattern classification techniques [8], and techniques based on theories of cognition [8].

3.   THE KES EXPERT SYSTEM DEVELOPMEMT TOOL

KES (Knowledge Engineering System [10]) is a tool designed to assist in the creation of expert systems. The system was designed to allow even people inexperienced with computers to build sophisticated expert systems.

KES is capable of constructing knowledge bases for three types of inference mechanisms. KES.PS is a rule-based system which uses backward chaining of rules as its inference engine. KES.BAYES is a system that uses statistical methods (specifically Bayes' Theorem) to infer results. Finally, KES.HT is a system that uses a method based on the concept of minimal set covers [9] to simulate a hypothesize-and-test approach to diagnostic problem solving.

Representing knowledge is fairly straightforward in KES. To build a rule-based system, for example, one needs to define two collections of information: a collection of attributes representing the elements in the system's domain of expertise, and a collection of rules representing the associative knowledge that ties the attributes together. To represent the example in the previous section, for instance, one would first define the attributes used. Four attributes are needed to describe the relations captured in the informal rules in that example. We can call these attributes "type of coat", "type of animal", "eats meat" and "type of mammal":

> type of coat: hair, feathers.
> type of animal: bird, mammal.
> eats meat: yes, no.
> type of mammal: carnivore, ungulate.

These are the actual attribute declarations, as they would appear in a KES knowledge base. Likewise, the knowledge that associates these attributes in the way described in the previous section can be expressed by the rules:

> mammal classification
>   if type of coat = hair
>   then type of animal = mammal.   (1)

```
carnivore classification
    if type of animal = mammal
      & eats meat = yes
    then type of mammal = carnivore.                    (2)
```

Here, "mammal classification" and "carnivore classification" are merely names associated with rules (1) and (2), respectively.

Once a knowledge base like the one above has been created and used to generate an expert system via KES, the backward chaining inference engine could be used to infer values for attributes declared in the knowledge base. We could, for instance, cause the expert system to obtain a value for the "type of mammal" attribute by giving it the following command:

       obtain type of mammal

The system would then look for rules containing the "type of mammal" attribute in the consequent, and would find rule (2). It would then examine the antecedent of the rule to determine its truth. Discovering that the attributes in the antecedent of the rule ("type of animal" and "eats meat") had not yet been obtained, the system would recursively attempt to obtain values for them. Rule (1) would be discovered to contain the "type of animal" attribute in its consequent, and so its antecedent would be examined for its truth. Again, since the attribute in the antecedent of rule (1) ("type of coat") had not yet been obtained, the system would attempt to obtain a value for it. Finding no rules in which the "type of coat" attribute appeared as a consequent, the system would ask the user for the value of that attribute. If the user indicated that "hair" was the value for "type of coat", the antecedent of rule (1) would be proven true, and this event would cause the consequent of the rule to be verified (and thus the "type of animal" attribute would get the vaue "mammal"). The attention of the system would then turn to the "eats meat" attribute. Since it appears as the consequent in no rules, the system would once again resort to asking the user for a value. If now the user indicated that "yes" was the value for "eats meat", the antecedent of rule (2) would be proven true, and as a result the "type of mammal" attribute would acquire the value "carnivore".

Currently (in addition to the PC version, to be described presently), KES runs in FRANZ LISP, PSL, and ZETA-LISP. It has been run on a variety of UNIX-based computers, as well as on the Apollo and LISP Machine. Also, work is currently underway to convert KES to SPICE LISP, a dialect of COMMON LISP which runs on PERQ computers.

4.   KES ON THE IBM-PC

Until recently, it has been difficult (if not impossible) to find the appropriate hardware and software to run a system such as KES on a microcomputer. But this situation is changing, thanks to the emergence of small computers with fairly large amounts of onboard memory, greater availability of mass-storage devices, and the introduction of microcomputer implementations of LISP with many of the features found in their mainframe relatives.

In particular, the IBM-PC/XT computer has 16 bit internal architecture, a 10MB hard disk, and can be equipped with as much as 640K random access memory (this turns out to be sufficient for the needs of KES). To complement the IBM-PC, IQLISP (Integral Quality, Inc. [4]) is a micro implementation of LISP which is able to address the full 640K of RAM available for that machine, and in addition offers some LISP features (such as read/splice micros and access to the LISP scan table) which until recently have been difficult to find in the versions of LISP available for micros. This combination of the IBM-PC/XT and IQLISP has made it feasible to convert KES to a personal computer environment.

The process for converting KES to IQLISP for the IBM-PC has turned out to be a rather straightforward one, and differs little from the process that has been developed for converting to the other LISPs that KES runs under (this is due to two factors: the general merits of IQLISP as a LISP execution environment, and (perhaps more importantly) the relatively small subset of FRANZ LISP that KES actually uses). The process consists basically of two steps. In the first step, mapping code is applied to the original FRANZ LISP source code to make simple lexical transformations from one LISP to the other. This step covers such things as converting lower case function names to upper case (since lower case is assumed in FRANZ LISP and upper case is assumed in many other LISPs) and converting FRANZ LISP functions to functions in other LISPs whose names are different but whose effects are the same (for example, "plus" in FRANZ LISP must be mapped to "+" in IQLISP).

The second step of the conversion process can become slightly more involved (and in fact was fairly time consuming in the conversion to IQLISP). In the second step, mapping routines are created which will become part of the LISP environment under which KES will run. The purpose of these routines is twofold. First, the routines can simulate functions which are defined in FRANZ LISP but not in IQLISP. For example, FRANZ LISP contains a function called "tyipeek" (the purpose of which is to peek at a character in the input stream without actually reading it) which has no analog in IQLISP. Therefore an IQLISP version of "tyipeek" must be defined.

The second purpose of these routines applies to a rather more subtle type of problem that can occur in translating from one LISP to another: in some cases there will be a function that has the same name in both dialects, but which performs slightly differently (or in some cases, dramatically differently) in each dialect. An illustration of this problem is the "setq" function, which in FRANZ LISP can take as arguments any number of symbol-value pairs, and will bind the values to their respective symbols in order. For example,

$$(\text{setq a 1 b 2 c 3}) \tag{3}$$

will bind the value 1 to the symbol a, 2 to b, and 3 to c. In contrast, the IQLISP version of "setq" expects only two arguments, a symbol and a value, and will simply ignore any other arguments that may appear. So in IQLISP, expression (3) above wil have the effect of assigning the value 1 to the symbol a and leaving the symbols b and c unbound. This type of inconsistency between dialects can manifest itself in rather unusual ways (of course, these problems generally arise because erroneous assumptions are made as to which functions can safely be converted via the lexical mappings of the first step of the conversion process, described above).

In addition to converting KES to IQLISP, the IQLISP version of KES contains some extensions that are specific to the IBM-PC environment. For instance, windowing capabilities [12] have been added in order to make the interface between KES and the end user more friendly. In addition, a special interface has been designed that allows KES to execute external processes from within an expert system, allowing, for example, one expert system to request the services of another expert system (this capability already exists in KES, but its implementation proved not to be portable to the IBM-PC environment). Finally, a memory management scheme has been incorporated into the system, which allows knowledge bases of indefinite size to be handled by KES (this tends not to be a problem in most other KES environments, since they as a rule run on virtual memory machines or on machines with massive internal memory).

5. EVALUATION OF THE LISP-IMPLEMENTED SYSTEM

The conversion of KES to the IBM-PC has been a valuabe experience. We have learned that it is indeed possible to run a sophisticated piece of AI software on a very small computer. But we have also uncovered a number of limitations in the resulting software.

On the plus side, we have reproduced on a microcomputer a large piece of software, designed to be run on machines in a completely different class with regards to capabilities (and of course, with regards to price also). It is important to keep in mind that the micro version of KES is functionally equivalent to the KES that runs on VAX computers: there are no features of KES that exist on the VAX but not on the IBM-PC.

Additionally, we have found that once a knowledge base has been parsed from the description language discussed in section 3 into a form that can be used by one of the KES inference engines, the performance of the resulting expert system is at least adequate (more or less comparable to a heavily loaded VAX). This suggests that the micro version of KES can be used as an expert system execution environment, with development being done on a larger machine.

Unfortuanetly, we have found some rather serious limitations to the LISP micro version of KES. One of these limitations is a limitation exemplified by our rather elaborate conversion process: LISP is not a portable language. It is a fairly time-consuming process to convert a large piece of software from one dialect of LISP to another; such a process should not be necessary every time one wants to run one's software on a new machine.

A more serious limitation is that imposed by the part of KES that is responsible for parsing a knowledge bases into its internal form. This process is significantly slower on the IBM-PC than it is on the VAX, and makes expert systems development with micro KES difficult (though, as stated above, the micro version is an adequate execution environment).

Still another limitation is the dependence of KES on the surrounding LISP environment. This dependence restricts KES from being embedded in other software systems. This restriction is becoming more and more important as people move from prototype expert sytems to production level systems for use in real applications.

6.   THE DECISION TO RE-IMPLEMENT

Several months ago, the decision was made to implement a small subset of the KES.PS subsystem in the C language for use on an IBM-PC or compatables. This decision resulted in MICRO-PS, a system capable of generating expert systems containing around 20 attributes and 20 rules. Though only small expert systems can be generated via MICRO-PS, it is possible for these small systems to contain many of the capabilities that are available in KES. Most attractively, the system is compact enough to be able to fit in 128K of memory.

One of the most enlightening insights gained from the MICRO-PS experience is that expert systems on a microcomputer don't have to be slow. In fact, the knowledge base parser in MICRO-PS compares favorably with thee parser for the VAX version of KES. Likewise, the resulting expert systems execute at a rate comparable to simlar sized systems on the VAX. This favorable performance of a C-implemented expert system generator (though admittedly small in scope) caused us to begin to think seriously above re-implementing all of KES in C.

In fact, work is now underway to completely re-engineer KES in C, keeping all present functionality intact. And while it is expected that re-engineered KES will allow swift development and execution of expert systems, excellent performance is only one of several factors that will make re-engineered KES a production quality system rather than a prototype or educational tool (as most current systems on the PC seem to be).

First, since implementations of C are quickly becoming available on all levels of computer, re-engineered KES is expected to be extremely portable. And while it may be true that there are minor discrepancies among different versions of C, most versions are basically compatable with the Kernighan and Ritchie standard [5]. Unfortunately, no such standard yet exists for LISP.

Second, re-engineered KES will be embeddable in other systems. This is extremely important if one is designing a system containing many components, one of which happens to be an expert system component, and one wishes to have the expert system component interact with the rest of the system in a reasonable way. This type of embeddability is at best difficult with LISP, where the LISP environment cannot help but be a part of every program written in LISP (thus forcing the LISP environment to be part of what is embedded).

In a similar vein, re-engineered KES will allow inexpensive external interfaces to routines written in C. The capability for interfacing with external programs is actually available in KES now (as alluded to in section 4), but it is extremely expensive since it involves spawning a child process from within the currently running LISP process. On the IBM-PC, which does not really facilitate concurrent processes, the situation is in fact much worse. In that environment, "spawning a child process" actually means saving the current LISP environment by writing it to disk, suspending the LISP environment (forcing a costly garbage collection), running the child process, and finally restarting the suspended LISP environment. In a C-implemented system, the KES object code could be linked with any external C routines at SYSGEN time, thus avoiding the above run-time overhead.

Finally, re-engineered KES will allow much greater flexibility than the current KES in tailoring the user interface to a particular expert system application. Currently, KES knowledge base authors are limited in their design of user interfaces to what is provided with KES. With re-engineered KES, knowledge base authors will be able to use the provided interface facilities or, if they wish, design their own interface facilities specific to their application.

The original conversion of KES to an IBM-PC demonstrated the possibility of running sophisticated expert systems software on a microcomputer. Now, with re-engineered KES, it will be possible to create modular, efficient, production quality applications utilizing expert systems technology, and to run those applications in a microcomputer environment.

SELECTED REFERENCES

[1] Artificial Intelligence Report, 1, 3, 1984
[2] Chang, C., and R.C. Lee: Symbolic Logic and Mechanical Theorem Proving, Academic Press, New York, 1973
[3] Hayes-Roth, R., D.A. Waterman, and D.B. Lenat (eds.): Building Expert Systems, Addison-Wesley, 1983
[4] Integral Quality, Inc.: IQLISP Reference Manual, 1983
[5] Kernighan, B.W. and D.M. Ritchie, The C Programming Language, Prentice-Hall, Inc., 1978
[6] Minsky, M.: "A framework for representing knowledge" in P. Winston (ed.): The Psychology of Computer Vision, McGraw-Hill, 1975, 211-277
[7] Nilsson, N.J.: Principles of Artificial Intelligence, Tioga Publishing Co., 1980
[8] Reggia, J.A.: "Knowledge-based decision support systems: development through KMS", TR-1121, University of Maryland (Ph.D. thesis), 1981
[9] Reggia, J.A., D. Nau, and P. Wang: "Diagnostic expert systems based on a set covering model", Int. J. Man- Machine Studies, 1982
[10] Software Architecture and Engineering, Inc.: KES Knowledge Base Author's Manual, 1984
[11] Waterman, D.A. and E. Hayes-Roth (eds.): Pattern-Directed Inference Systems, Academic Press, 1978
[12] Whaley R.: "Menu specification for SAM/WS", Software A&E internal memo
[13] Winston, P.W. and B.K.P. Horn: LISP (first edition), Addison-Wesley, 1981, pp. 239-250

Knowledge Design Environment for Domain-Experts

A Rappaport & P Perez
Neuron Data Corporation
444 High St Palo Alto CA 94301

The Problem

From the cognitive standpoint, a problem may be defined as an unexpected event requiring from the human facing it a substantial amount of resources. Since the first part of this definition is related to a state of expectation, and the second to a resource allocation problem, one sees that the observer is clearly part of the problem. In fact, the detection of a problem per se and its consequent handling brings important information for the formalization of this problem. Thus, it is necessary to use a technology which can take into account the nature of both the problem and the cognitive task it triggers.

A New Functionality

Although AI research is at the cutting edge of Computer Science, part of its image in the real world is linked to the level of investment necessary to demonstrate one's interest in the field. The technology itself has shown to be quite stable over the past few years. In task-oriented environments, the notion of problem-solving should become a common activity. Thus, tools must be available to enable the domain experts themselves to progress in this direction. A problem-solving technology must be close to both the expert and the end-user. Reducing this distance represents a scientific challenge. Indeed, the environments must be powerful, and yet reachable by non-AI minds. It is certainly possible to make an already existing software technology more difficult to use by adding new features. But the obscurity of the tool and the development time of productive applications increases even faster than the power of the tool.

Hence, the development of true desktop intelligent systems (on microcomputers and workstations) should follow directions which may be qualified as strategic. These notions are illustrated in the NEXPERT AI environment.

1) An understanding and integration of AI methodologies and elements of human cognitive psychology. This leads to the definition of adaptive environments in the sense that they can be adapted to the task from both the knowledge and the problem-solving behavior standpoints, taking into account for instance "physiological" information, or deep knowledge, as well as relatively unexplained variations of the expert's reasoning (intuition-based knowledge). Different types of reasoning are available, dealing with complete and/or uncertain knowledge, using various methodologies within the same knowledge base. Whatever their underlying representation, knowledge bases in NEXPERT are a composite image of both structural and behavioral information (knowledge and agenda), each with its different qualitative components. In this environment, the same rules are used for the forward and backward chaining mechanisms, greatly simplifying the construction.

2) The development of a powerful man-machine cognitive continuum. Mainly, we are concerned here with the design of new interfaces [1], which, beyond affecting the user-friendliness of a system become a factor of power and performance. A typical issue is the synthesis of graphical tools allowing the automatic reconstruction of a macroscopic structure of the system's knowledge in a visible form. The term macroscopic is in opposition to the microscopic level at which the design and integration of each unit of knowledge is normally made. The visual thinking paradigm applied to knowledge-base browsing mechanisms is essential in keeping the attention of the domain-expert on the cognitive task of representing problems (using the system). At the knowledge edition level, mechanisms to prevent lexical inconsistencies from occuring and various levels of syntactic and type checking are implemented. Communications with the user are based on an automatic dialog system and includes graphics as well as text. Communications are also established with external databases and allow the execution of external programs.

Following these two directions, cited among others, much progress can be done for problem-solving (or problem-structuring) environments to reach a widespread use. Obviously, cognitive sciences and AI have to meet at both the fundamental and applied research levels [1,2]. This cooperation leads to another consequence, where the knowledge acquisition activity becomes available to the experts themselves and is not restricted to the so-called knowledge engineer. Hence, it is necessary to work in parallel on the knowledge acquisition methodologies.

The Philosophy

Current AI technology for knowledge-based systems are centered around two principal philosophies, namely object-oriented and rule-based programming. Far from being exclusive, they present a high degree of complementarity. However, a successful implementation of the two philosophies integrated in the same tool remains to be made (on any hardware).

A key issue is whether highly complex tools do not increase the programming difficulty to an unbearable extent. We view the AI tools as systems in permanent evolution. What then is the basic granularity to adopt, the elementary unit of knowledge? The object perspective is useful for descriptions of the world in question, but they delay the phase of development dealing with the inference mechanism and rule system. On the other hand, the rules have the advantage of being elementary units of representation that are more dynamic than static. In effect they intrinsically possess a direction, a sense of progression which can be easily captured by any domain-expert, and represent also the minimum level of control structure, a notion which develops with the increasing size of the knowledge base. If simple rules are inefficient, they can be augmented by giving them a wide range of possibilities for either controlling the reasoning process or relating to the user. Furthermore, they can reason upon progressively complex data structures which can become objects. Thus, there is a gradient of representations rather than an opposition but the central point is to give a dynamic sense to the elementary "chunk". From the first few rules, knowledge can be expanded and, provided that the system is flexible enough, complex tasks can be modelled.

Knowledge Transfer

The transfer of knowledge from the human to the machine requires means with which the user can effectively formalize his own knowledge. This crucial phase, also refered to as the knowledge acquisition process (not to be confused with autonomous learning capabilities), is deeply modified by results in the directions and the "philosophical" approach mentioned above. Much of this work is currently spent on learning the tools and trying to understand, the overall structure of the knowledge and the system's resulting behavior, and on translating a problem into rigid formalisms with constrained logics. Rather, the possibility to adapt the different methods to one's problem greatly increases the ability to formalize an initial set of rules. The decompilation of the human knowledge is also greatly facilitated by the interface. The delineation of knowledge on the graphic browser (e.g. the NEXPERT Network) and interactive rule editor allows to increment the knowledge base easily from an initial nucleus. These mechanisms help buid better techniques for the knowledge analysis and transfer, which will progressively be embedded in the systems themselves.

Illustration: The Knowledge Design Task in NEXPERT

The NEXPERT AI environment is the outcome of research and development in this direction. NEXPERT is a rule-based expert system building tool with an augmented rule format, a new inference mechanism and an open architecture, currently running on the Macintosh™ desktop personal computer.

Knowledge design is the task of building applications with NEXPERT. The knowledge acquisition interface has been designed using bit-map graphics and menu/mouse-driven access to functions on top of an incremental rule compiler for the interactive knowledge debugging and maintenance. Optimization of visual control and mouse-driven access to the already present universe of knowledge for edition purposes leads to the rapid automation of the user-machine relation. Thus, more resources can be allocated to "what to write" rather than be distracted by "how to write" subtask (figure 1). This greatly enhances, the accessibility of the rule concept to non-AI-aware domain-experts.

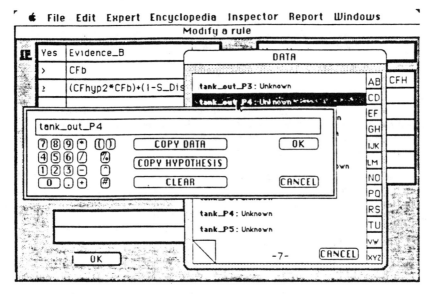

The following is the content of the figure window shown:

File Edit Expert Encyclopedia Inspector Report Windows

Modify a rule

IE	Yes	Evidence_B
	>	CFb
	?	(CFhyp2*CFb)+(1-S_Dis

DATA

tank_out_P3 : Unknown
tank_out_P4 : Unknown

tank_out_P4

7 8 9 * ( )   COPY DATA   OK
4 5 6 / %   COPY HYPOTHESIS
1 2 3 - ^   CLEAR   CANCEL
0 . + #

tank_P4 : Unknown
tank_P5 : Unknown

OK   -7-   CANCEL

AB CFH
CD
EF
GH
IJK
LM
NO
PQ
RS
TU
VW
XYZ

figure 1

This interface constitutes the user-interface for the edition of new chunks of knowledge, a microscopic level task not directly related to an overall understanding of the knowledge base. To grasp the latter, a unique graphic knowledge-base browsing mechanism was designed, called the Network. It is conceived as a *navigational* tool allowing to explore a knowledge base in both a deductive and evocative fashion (figure 2).

While exploring the knowledge base, the Rule Editor is at a "two-click distance". With the incremental rule compiler, the user benefits from a truly interactive knowledge debugging environment. Furthermore, this capacity can be used during a runtime, when the network allows to visualize the lines of reasoning and the system's focus of attention. Another influence of such advanced interfaces is that the concept of problem-solving and its underlying mechanisms are much better understood by the user, in this case the domain expert. Eventually, the expert can better envision what the end-user interface should and will be.

Part of the role of the expert in the problem's definition and description is the treatment of uncertain knowledge. There are two types for the latter: *(i)* the expression of uncertain knowledge in the domain and *(ii)* the expectation that the user/device may not be able to provide the adequate information, which should not necessarily stop the reasoning process. Furthermore, different types of knowledge may intervene in the knowledge base, in a complementary fashion (deep, surface or default knowledge for instance).

The NEXPERT environment allows this mixed and adapted approach to uncertainty. It allows to formalize reasonings ranging from classical architectures to more sophisticated ones (notions of knowedge islands and strategies for instance).

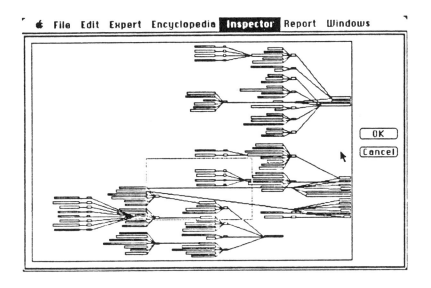

figure 2

Knowledge Processing in NEXPERT

Since there exists such a wide variety of problems, the inference mechanisms must be flexible, offering both a powerful default methodology and the ability to make local modifications through declarative access to the control mechanisms. Moreover, not only the nature of the knowledge varies but also the presentation of problems, i.e. it may be a data-driven or goal-driven presentation or even a mixture of both. The inference mechanism, working both forward and backward in an integrated fashion, has an automated goal generation process, and allows a flow of control between the so-called knowledge islands. It allows a new approach to the volunteering or suggestion of information to the system during a session, from an external program or device.

Visualization tools allow to trace the dynamics of problem solving and thus the debugging of the knowledge bases (figure below).

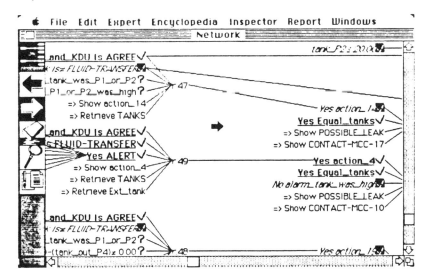

Perspectives and Organizational Impacts

While trying to blaze new ways in the design of AI tools, a preoccupation naturally arises which deals with the effects of the availability of such tools. First and foremost, heavy applications can be undertaken by domain-experts, possibly assisted by more knowledgeable people for refinement and assistance (the latter can be a corporate or university laboratory). The obvious second consequence is the spreading of the notion of AI, or automated problem-solving or design aid, to a large population of scientists, engineers, managers etc... The knowledge based system appears now not only as a productivity tool but as a media. Such flows of knowledge will certainly have an impact on organizations in general, in particular in the decision making processes. Furthermore, there is little doubt that the availability of such a functionality induces a permanent self-criticism of the very knowledge involved. The difficulty of problems encountered in a very wide range of domains is essentially measured by the size of resources needed to deal with the problem, and most importantly with the efficiency of the methods used to do so [3]. Such aspects are particularly relevant in systems built for environmanents as complex and constrained as activities in space [4, and Rappaport, A., NASA Ames Research Center AI Forum, unpublished communication, Dec. 85.]. Both issues can considerably benefit from a widespread use of automated problem-solving tools. As stated before, they must allow rapid and efficient transfer of knowledge, and continuous maintenance and update of the knowledge (the turnover rate of knowledge is increasingly high). From today's isolated projects we can start envisioning local or large knowledge banks.

Systems following the previous directions, running on small and affordable desktop hardware, will modifiy the organization of groups around AI tools. First and foremost graphical representation can be printed while disks are easily passed, thus making knowlegde available to many and allowing multiple expert interaction for the development phase. Non-AI-experts will be able to suggest modifications. On the other hand, the so-called knowledge engineer becomes an internal (or external) consultant to refine present work or provide advise concerning the cognitive aspect of the problem. The key emerging concept is that the knowledge engineer is not the sole relator to the machine, and domain-experts also become knowledge designers.

REFERENCES

1.   Card, S.K., Moran, T.P. and Newell, A. (1983) The Psychology of Human-Computer Interface, Lawrence Erlbaum Associates, Hillsdale NJ.

2.   Ericsson, K.A. and Simon, H.A. (1984) Protocol Analysis, MIT Press, Cambridge MA.

3.   Simon, H.A. (1978) Rationality as Process and as Product of Thought, American Economic Review 68:1-16.

4.   Georgeff M.P. and Firschein O. (1985) Expert Systems for Space Station Automation, IEEE Control Systems, 5:3-85.

Acknowledgements: many thanks to Albert Gouyet and Chris Shipley for their helpful comments.

Expert Systems for Personal Computers: The TK!Solver Approach

MILOS KONOPASEK AND SUNDARESAN JAYARAMAN

The advancements in the fields of artificial intelligence (AI) and microcomputer technology are converging to a point where it is becoming feasible to implement some of the AI concepts in the inexpensive personal computer environment. One such example of a software package that makes the personal computer a more intelligent partner in the problem-solving and decision-making process is TK!Solver. Aside from being an expert system in its own right, TK!Solver can be used by noncomputer and non-AI professionals as a framework for building and tailoring personalized expert systems in disciplines with quantifiable knowledge bases.

The Editors

I. HISTORICAL NOTE

Early research in artificial intelligence (AI) was aimed at producing domain-independent reasoning techniques. As a classic example, GPS [35] could prove theorems, and solve a variety of problems and puzzles. However, it was inadequate for larger real-world problems. By the mid-1960s the research efforts had shifted to the building of expert systems with large stores of domain-specific knowledge, such as DENDRAL at Stanford University and MACSYMA at MIT. This marked the beginning of increased research interest in the development of applied AI systems, and the philosophy behind it is reviewed in literature [2], [4], [8], [20], [44]. Further interest in expert systems triggered by the proliferation of computing power is reflected in popular reviews by Duda and Gaschnig [17] and Nau [34].

The fundamental issue of problem representation [1] became more important in the context of these expert systems. Efforts were directed at determining proper structures for representing the knowledge applicable to the problem domain in an efficient manner, with the difficulty increasing as the domain broadened. Goldstein and Papert characterized these efforts as a paradigm shift in AI [23].

The knowledge bases for the expert systems were hand assembled—requiring many man-years of effort and mediation of a knowledge engineer. According to Feigenbaum, this was the principal bottleneck in the development of expert systems [20]. TEIRESIAS was the first step towards the elimination of this bottleneck [12]. Although it was limited to helping debug and fill out the knowledge base of MYCIN that had already been largely codified, it separated the two basic components of an expert system—the knowledge base and the problem-solving or inference part. This was also a step towards domain independence, i.e., realization of the idea of removing the current knowledge base and "plugging in" a different one [10].

The authors are with Software Arts Products Corp., 27 Mica Lane, Wellesley, MA 02181, USA.

Reprinted from *Insights into Personal Computers*, pp. 301–314, IEEE PRESS, 1985.

More recently, because of the increasing cost of development of expert systems and experimentation with them, a trend towards the development of design tools for building expert systems is emerging. These tools also facilitate easy modifications of and experimentation with the constructed expert systems. EMYCIN [47], OPS [21], AGE [38], EXPERT [48], and HEARSAY III [3] are some examples of this trend.

TK!Solver (TK for Tool Kit) developed in 1981–1982, and commercially available since the spring of 1983, is one such framework for building and experimenting with expert systems in various fields of knowledge. It is a realization of many of the concepts expounded by research in AI, human–computer interface design, and problem solving by humans. The system has no built-in knowledge of any particular discipline, but provides a framework that makes it easy for the user to construct expert systems with such knowledge. The knowledge engineer—the bottleneck mentioned earlier—is eliminated.

There are strong links between the prehistory of TK!Solver and the developments in AI. Prior to elucidating these links we have to mention the efforts outside the mainstream of AI aimed at creating special purpose languages/frameworks for computer-assisted problem solving in specific areas. ICES for Civil Engineering [41], statistical package SPSS [37], and simulation package GPSS [24] are typical examples. These programs lacked "knowledge" in the AI sense and on the surface they just simplified the noncomputer professional's task of using computers. They naturally reflected the then state of the art in commercially available hardware and software. Yet, a large amount of domain-specific and mathematical knowledge went into the design of constituent subprograms and command structures. Running these programs is equivalent to accessing the embedded knowledge and using it for solving a variety of problems.

The development of these and scores of similar packages (for CAD, operations research, forecasting, etc.) was facilitated by application programmers' grasp of particular fields of expertise, coupled with experts' grasp of programming in high-level languages. The high utility of these packages, their complexity and their relative efficiency still present a challenge to AI techniques proper and to the methodology of expert system design.

In the late 1960s, Milos Konopasek, then at University of Manchester Institute of Science and Technology, was assigned the task of developing what in present terminology would be equivalent to an expert system for a textile professional. The knowledge base in question included (but was not limited to) components from mechanical, industrial, and chemical engineering. He faced a dilemma: on one hand the nature of the knowledge base did not justify or require the ICES/GPSS/SPSS approach; the AI approach, on the other hand, looked promising in principle, but unlikely to yield quick results because of lack of practical tools at that time.

Most of the knowledge under consideration dealt with relationships which could be described in terms of algebraic equations and empiric functions. This fact, and the desire to increase both quantitatively and qualitatively the computer's share in the problem-solving process, led to the idea of making the user communicate with the computer at the level of relationships (represented by equations) rather than at the level of sequential programs and assignment statements. In 1972, a "GPS," limited in scope but suitable for solving a large variety of real world problems inexpensively, was born. It was called "Question Answering System on mathematical models and related data bases" or QAS for short [27], [29]. It was implemented first on PDP-10 and other mainframe timesharing systems, and much later on microcomputers [28].

In QAS the expert sets up (i.e., types in or loads) the domain-specific knowledge as a "model" consisting of a set of relationships in the form of equalities

$$\langle expression \rangle = \langle expression \rangle$$

and empiric functions defined by lists of pairs

$$(\langle argument\ value \rangle, \langle function\ value \rangle).$$

He or she then assigns the values of any combination of variables as input, and lets the computer find its way of solving for the unknowns using either the consecutive substitution procedure or iteration.

Interestingly enough, the intended role of QAS as an expert system naturally brought about the separation of the knowledge base and control strategy—a key factor in the design of expert systems.

The strong points of QAS were fast response to any question, high power/resources ratio, and its knowledge-carrying potential. Its weak point, especially in the light of recent developments in human–computer interface, was the line-oriented dialogue.

This shortcoming is remedied in TK!Solver which represents a substantially enhanced implementation of the QAS ideas. This development was made possible by the rapid proliferation of inexpensive microcomputers with a direct memory to screen mapping which facilitates screen-oriented dialogues and results in an improved human–computer interface. Along another line of reasoning we may view TK!Solver as an answer to the need for easy-to-build and easy-to-use expert systems which would fit the mass-produced professional class personal computers.

II.   OVERVIEW OF TK!SOLVER

Fig. 1 shows the architecture of TK!Solver. The domain specific knowledge responsible for the high performance of the system is contained in the knowledge base. The problem-solving tools embodying the control strategy—the *direct and iterative solvers*—utilize the knowledge base in the process of solving particular problems. For interaction (or I/O) TK!Solver provides "sheets" displayed through one or two windows on the screen.

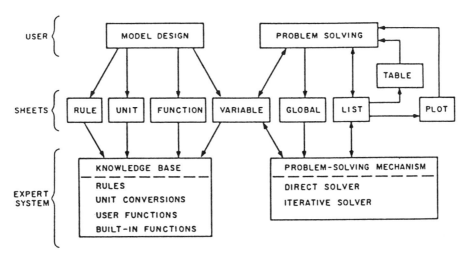

Fig. 1.   Functional diagram of TK!Solver—user interface (the arrows indicate predominant flow of information, all links are actually bidirectional).

The main feature of the architecture is the explicit division between the knowledge base and the control strategy. Consequently, the expert/user deals only with issues of domain specific knowledge, and is insulated from the details of the implementation of the control strategy.

In the following paragraphs we describe the four components of the knowledge base, the characteristics of a model and the problem-solving mechanism. We will illustrate these concepts by examples for which we have chosen an oversimplified knowledge base that has information about Ohm's law, Joule's law, and resistivities of materials. Obviously, the kind of interaction shown here is not restricted to this particular knowledge base.

Rules

The rule is the basic component of the domain-specific knowledge. It expresses the underlying mathematical relationship in terms of the equality of left-hand and right-hand side

161

expressions. Equations, constraints, or definitions may all be represented as rules. Fig. 2 shows the *rule sheet* with the set of rules in our sample knowledge base. The set of rules can be represented in the form of a network of relationships called the *R*-graph (for relationships graph) as shown in Fig. 3. A variable is represented by a node in the *R*-graph and each subgraph or polygon corresponds to a rule in the knowledge base.

```
==================== RULE SHEET =====
S Rule
- ----
    I = V / R          " Ohm's Law
    I^2 = P / R        " Joule's Law
    P = V * I
    U = P * t
    rho = fun(MC)
    R / rho = L / A
    A = pi()/4 * D^2
```

Fig. 2. "Laws of electricity..." knowledge base: rule sheet.

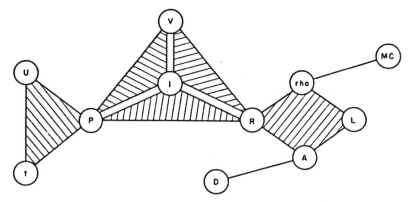

Fig. 3. *R*-graph for equations in Fig. 2.

Unit Conversions

Units of measurement are associated with most measurable quantities. Conversions between them are frequently encountered in problem solving and have to be defined in the knowledge base. Fig. 4 shows the *unit sheet* with the unit conversions in the knowledge base of our example.

```
==================== UNIT SHEET ==============
```

From	To	Multiply By	Add Offset
hour	min	60	
min	sec	60	
kW	W	1000	
J	cal	.239	
W	cal/sec	.239	
kWh	J	3600000	
hp	W	746	
m	cm	100	
m^2	cm^2	10000	

Fig. 4. "Laws of electricity..." knowledge base: unit sheet.

Function Definitions

Empiric relationships between sets of values are expressed in the form of (user-defined) functions, and make up the third component of the knowledge base. Fig. 5 shows the *user function subsheet* relating the materials and their resistivities as a part of our knowledge base example.

```
==================== USER FUNCTION: fun =========
Comment:          Electrical Properties of Matter
Domain List:      material
Mapping:          Table
Range List:       resistivity
Element Domain       Range

------- ------       -----

   1      'aluminum  .0000000263
   2      'copper    .0000000162
   3      'gold      .0000000222
   4      'iron      .00000011
   5      'platinum  .000000111
   6      'silver    .000000016
```

Fig. 5. "Laws of electricity..." knowledge base: user function subsheet.

Built-In Knowledge

Irrespective of the domain-specific knowledge, TK!Solver can solve problems involving basic arithmetic operations and a large variety of built-in mathematical functions. A standard variety of these is supplemented by a few special ones like "element" for retrieving list components or "apply" for associating empiric functions with arguments (it may, for instance, associate the function defining the stored load-deformation characteristics with a particular type of material).

Model

The model encompasses the first three components of the knowledge base in Fig. 1 (rules, unit conversions, user functions) as contained in the *rule, variable, unit*, and *user function* sheets. In more general terms, the model can be seen as a compact, high-level representation of structure, organization, and content of the domain knowledge. The composition of the model coupled with its elegant internal representation allow for a simple yet powerful control strategy. The model also serves as a user-friendly guide during the problem-solving process.

The model usually reflects a certain part of the knowledge base in a particular discipline. The models may be easily merged by the subsequent loading of some or all of the knowledge base components into TK!Solver, in order to create larger models capable of addressing more complicated problems. There is also the concept of TK!SolverPacks or sets of models from particular disciplines; these are available for mechanical engineering, financial analysis, building design, and other areas. Creating and using more comprehensive knowledge bases are within reach.

Problem-Solving Mechanism

The direct solver is the workhorse of the problem-solving mechanism. In it lies the grace and power of TK!Solver. It manipulates the equations depending on the problem formulation and solves for the unknowns. The solution process goes through the *R*-graph and "fires" all polygons with only one unknown node. It continues until as many unknowns as possible are evaluated. This "propagation of solution" strategy actually simulates the consecutive substitution procedure. If an inconsistency error or an illegal operand is detected, the solution process is terminated, and the rule causing the problem is flagged with the appropriate error message. Since the solution path depends on the problem formulation, the control strategy may be regarded as forward chaining or data-driven.

Whenever the direct solver cannot match the nature and complexity of a given problem, the iterative solver can be used. The heart of the iterative solver is a modified Newton–Raphson procedure which handles sets of simultaneous linear and nonlinear equations. It can be either explicitly invoked or automatically called when the direct solver fails to produce a solution.

A detailed account of the workings, features and applications of TK!Solver may be found in the book by Konopasek and Jayaraman [30].

Examples

Figs. 6 through 8 show the variable sheets with the formulations and solutions of a few problems concerning the sample knowledge base defined in Figs. 2–5. The so-called "calculation units" (i.e., units implied in rules in Fig. 2) are specified and used in Fig. 6 for all the variables except *t*. In the next two figures the units for *U*, *D*, and *A* were changed respectively to kWh, cm, and cm^2, and the values changed accordingly.

```
==================== VARIABLE SHEET ============================

St Input      Name    Output      Unit      Comment
-- -----      ----    ------      ----      -------
   4          I                   amp       current
   110        V                   volt      voltage
              R       27.5        ohm       resistance
              P       440         W         power
              U       3168000     J         energy
   2          t                   hour      time
              MC                            material of conductor
              rho                 ohm-m     resistivity of material
              L                   m         length of conductor
              D                   m         diameter of conductor
              A                   m^2       cross-sectional area
```

Fig. 6. Variable sheet with list of variables used in the rules in Fig. 2. It shows the solution of a problem concerning the energy supplied to a motor drawing 4 A from a 110 V line over a period of 2 h.

In Fig. 7 the user overconstrained the model by assigning *U* = 1.25 without releasing *I* from the set of input variables. The partial view of the variable and rule sheets shows the offending rule and related variables marked by > . Bringing the cursor over the > mark in the rule sheet causes the error message "inconsistent" to be displayed in the status line.

The asterisks in front of the last three rules in Fig. 7 indicate that those rules were not used in the attempted solution. The solution of the problem in Fig. 8 involved all the rules, the function relating the type of material and resistivity, and the unit conversions.

The ease with which the knowledge base may be changed is demonstrated by the example in Fig. 9. In order to solve a few simple problems concerning the elements of a triangle (after finishing with electrical properties of matter), the user has to type /RA (for reset all) and load the "Triangle" model. To set up the problem in Fig. 9 and solve it is a trivial matter.

Somewhat more complicated situations are exemplified in Figs. 10–13. The results in Figs. 11 and 13 had to be arrived at using the iterative solver. Fig. 12 shows an impromptu modification of the knowledge base: the desire to solve for an isosceles triangle is expressed simply by adding the rule *a* = *b* to the rule sheet.

In Fig. 14 the knowledge base is again changed for one dealing with simple projectile problems.

(3s) Status: > Inconsistent

```
==================== VARIABLE SHEET ===
St Input       Name      Output    Unit
-- -----       ----      ------    ----
    4          I                   amp
    110        V                   volt
               R         27.5      ohm
 >             P         440       W
 > 1.25        U                   kWh
 > 2           t                   hour


==================== RULE SHEET =======
S Rule
- ----
   I = V / R
   I^2 = P / R
   P = V * I
 > U = P * t
 * rho = fun(MC)
 * R / rho = L / A
 * A = pi()/4 * D^2
```

Fig. 7. What must have been the current if, in the example in Fig. 6, the energy supplied was 1.25 kWh? (See text for the explanation of the inconsistency.) The solution, after removing the value of *I* from input, is *I* = 5.68 A, *R* = 19.36 Ω, and *P* = 625 W.

```
==================== VARIABLE SHEET ============================
St Input     Name    Output     Unit      Comment
-- -----     ----    ------     ----      -------
             I       10         amp       current
             V       1.5        volt      voltage
   .15       R                  ohm       resistance
   15        P                  W         power
             U       .0075      kWh       energy
   30        t                  min       time
   'copper   MC                           material of conductor
             rho     1.62E-8    ohm-m     resistivity of material
             L       7.2722052  m         length of conductor
   .1        D                  cm        diameter of conductor
             A       .00785398  cm^2      cross-sectional area
```

Fig. 8. Variable sheet with the solution of the following problem: What would be the current and the voltage across a 0.15 Ωcopper resistor producing 15 W of heat? What is the energy supplied in 30 min if the wire diameter is 0.1 cm?

In short, the demonstrated power of TK!Solver comes from the ease with which a particular knowledge base may be set up or selected, problems formulated, assumptions varied, and results generated.

III. TK!SOLVER AND EXPERT SYSTEMS

It follows from the previous section that TK!Solver by itself may be considered an expert system primarily in the area of numerical problem solving. As such it does the following:

1) parses entered algebraic equations and generates a list of variables;
2) solves sets of equations using consecutive substitution procedure (direct solver);

```
==================== VARIABLE SHEET ============================
St Input      Name    Output      Unit       Comment
-- -----      ----    ------      ----       -------
              alpha   36.869898   deg        angle opposite to side a
              beta    53.130102   deg        angle opposite to side b
              gamma   90          deg        angle opposite to side c
   3          a                              side a
   4          b                              side b
   5          c                              side c
              P       12                     perimeter
              A       6                      area
==================== RULE SHEET ================================
S Rule
- ----

* alpha + beta + gamma = pi ()          " sum of angles equals pi
* a^2 = b^2 + c^2 - 2*b*c*cos(alpha)     " cosine theorem
* a / sin(alpha) = b / sin(beta)         " sine theorem
* P = a + b + c                          " perimeter
* A = a * b * sin(gamma)/2               " area
```

Fig. 9. The variable and rule sheets for the triangle model showing the solution of a right-angle triangle with sides 3, 4, and 5.

```
==================== VARIABLE SHEET ===
St Input      Name    Output      Unit
-- -----      ----    ------      ----
              alpha               deg
   55         beta                deg
              gamma               deg
 G 3          a
 G 4          b
   5          c
              P
   7          A
```

Fig. 10. What would be the elements of a triangle given angle $\beta = 55°$, side $c = 5$, and area $A = 7$? Direct solver failed. Partial variable sheet shows a and b set as guesses for iterative solver.

```
==================== VARIABLE SHEET ===
St Input      Name    Output      Unit
-- -----      ----    ------      ----
              alpha   42.652161   deg
   55         beta                deg
              gamma   82.347839   deg
              a       3.4181688
              b       4.1325618
   5          c
              P       12.550731
   7          A
```

Fig. 11. Solution of the problem in Fig. 10.

166

```
==================== VARIABLE SHEET ===
St Input      Name    Output    Unit
-- -----      ----    ------    ----
              alpha   42.652161 deg
              beta              deg
              gamma   82.347839 deg
 G 3.7753653  a
              b       4.1325618
    5         c
              P       12.550731
    7         A
==================== RULE SHEET =======
S Rule
- ----
* alpha + beta + gamma = pi ()
* a^2 = b^2 + c^2 - 2*b*c*cos(alpha)
* a / sin(alpha) = b / sin(beta)
* P = a + b + c
* A = a * b * sin(gamma)/2
* a = b
```

Fig. 12. What would be the elements of an isosceles triangle with side *c* and area *A* as in Fig. 11 and no angle given? Constraint *a* = *b* is added to the rule sheet. Guess value for *a* arrived at by typing in (*a* + *b*)/2 (rationale: expected value must lie between previous values of *a* and *b*). Values in output field left from previous solution do not count.

```
==================== VARIABLE SHEET ===
St Input      Name    Output    Unit
-- -----      ----    ------    ----
              alpha   48.239700 deg
              beta    48.239700 deg
              gamma   83.520599 deg
              a       3.7536649
              b       3.7536649
    5         c
              P       12.507330
    7         A
```

Fig. 13. Solution of the problem in Fig. 12.

```
==================== VARIABLE SHEET ==============================
St Input   Name    Output    Unit      Comment
-- -----   ----    ------    ----      -------
   100     VO                m/sec     initial velocity
   30      alpha             deg       angle of departure
   32      a                 ft/sec^2  accln. due to gravity
           time    10.252625 sec       time taken
           maxht   128.15781 m         maximum height reached
           range   887.90334 m         horiz. dist. travelled
==================== RULE SHEET =================================
S Rule
- ----
  maxht = VO^2 * sin(alpha)^2 / (2 * a)
  range = VO^2 * sin(2*alpha) / a
  time = sqrt(8 * maxht / a)
  (range/time)^2 = VO^2 - 2*maxht*a
```

Fig. 14. The variable and rule sheets for the projectile model with the solution of the following problem. A baseball is thrown with an initial velocity of 100 m/s at an angle of 30°. How far does it travel and how long does it take before it hits the ground?

3) solves sets of simultaneous algebraic equations by a modified Newton—Raphson iterative procedure when consecutive substitution procedure fails (iterative solver);

4) searches through tables of data and evaluates either unknown function values or arguments when required in the process of 2) or 3);

5) performs unit conversions;

6) detects inconsistencies in problem formulation and domain errors;

7) generates series of solutions for lists of input data and displays results in tabular and graphical forms.

More importantly, however, TK!Solver with the above (and a few more) features and capabilities may be considered as a general framework for setting up expert systems in a whole class of disciplines; this class is defined by the heavy dependence of human experts on the use of mathematical and logical skills provided by TK!Solver and listed above.

We prove our point by reviewing the position of TK!Solver in the light of the attributes of expert systems as they evolved and as they have been discussed in literature. In the following paragraphs the typical or desired characteristics of expert systems are juxtaposed with current features of TK!Solver.

(1) The domain-specific knowledge (Knowledge Base) and problem solving methodology (Inference Engine) should be separated [8], [13], [17], [34], [36], [47].

TK!Solver: The domain specific knowledge is represented by relationships in terms of equations and optionally, domain-related empiric functions and unit conversion tables. Problem solving methodology is embodied in the direct and iterative solvers.

(2) The expert system should think the way the human expert does [20].

TK!Solver: The expert solving problems in the domain of his interest thinks in terms of relationships and constraints and in terms of "knowns" and "unknowns." This is exactly how TK!Solver handles the input information and generates results.

(3) Bias towards telling the computer "what" the problem is rather than "how" to solve it [19].

TK!Solver: The user tells the computer "what" by selecting a model and by typing in the values of known variables. The control strategy knows "how" to make use of the knowledge base in order to arrive at the response to the query.

(4) Dynamic knowledge base—should be expandable, modifiable, and should facilitate "plugging in" different knowledge modules [8], [10], [11], [13], [17], [20], [25], [47].

TK!Solver: The models consisting of rules, equations, constraints, empiric relations, etc. are easy to edit, amend, and merge. Different knowledge modules may be "plugged in" by simply loading another model or typing it in.

(5) Interactive knowledge transfer; minimize the time needed to transfer the expert's knowledge to the knowledge base [12], [32], [34].

TK!Solver: In the highly interactive environment resulting from the uniform internal representation of knowledge, and good human-engineered I/O, building and maintaining the knowledge base is fast and easy.

(6) Addition of a new rule results in a new competency for the system and, conversely, the absence of the rule marks the absence of the related ability [31].

TK!Solver: The addition or removal of rules is a major feature of the model design and problem solving process.

(7) Interaction in the language "natural" to the domain expert; allow the user to think in problem-oriented terms. System should adapt to the user and not the other way around. User should be insulated from the details of the implementation [7], [8], [12].

TK!Solver: Interaction in terms of mathematical relationships pertaining to the domain of interest represents a major advancement as compared to programming in conventional languages.

(8) The principal bottleneck in the transfer of expertise—knowledge engineer—should be eliminated [20].

TK!Solver: Expert communicates directly with TK!Solver; no need for knowledge engineer.

(9) Control strategy should be simple and user-transparent, the user should be able to understand and predict the effect of adding new items to the knowledge base. At the same time it should be powerful enough for solving complex problems. [8], [12], [16], [40].

TK!Solver: The direct and iterative solvers are easy to grasp because their design reflects the human problem solving strategy. At the same time TK!Solver allows for a level of complexity which makes manual approach impossible, and dedicated programming inefficient.

(10) Computationally fast and not demanding on the resources. Avoiding the situation when, according to Gerring *et al.,* interactive intelligent systems suffer from a basic conflict between their computationally intensive nature and the need for responsiveness to a user [22].

TK!Solver: Response ranges from immediate to a few seconds thanks to the thoughtful design of internal knowledge representation and control strategy.

(11) Inexpensive framework for building and experimenting with expert systems [8], [34], [47].

TK!Solver: The ease, with which the rules may be added or removed, and the distribution of the known and unknown variables changed prove to be of exceptional help in the building, verification, and use of the system.

(12) Human engineering aspects are important for making the system understandable, for keeping experts interested and for making users feel comfortable [8], [34].

TK!Solver: The command structure strikes a fine balance between simplicity and sophistication depending upon the individual user's needs. He can easily modify (tailor) the knowledge base to suit his changing interests.

(13) Provision for help and English language dialogue [8].

TK!Solver: On-line help facility provides information on features and commands as requested. No need for natural language communication, see (7).

(14) Display-oriented interface (e.g., INTERNIST [40], with additional advantage of window concept as in SMALLTALK [45].

TK!Solver: Exploits the direct memory-screen mapping for an instantaneous display-oriented interface. User communicates with the system via well laid-out information sheets displayed through windows (one or two at a time). Sheets can also be scrolled in the windows.

(15) Reasoning under conditions of uncertainty and insufficient information, and probabilistic reasoning [11], [16], [25], [43].

TK!Solver: generally not applicable; in particular situations, however, TK!Solver can be used for determinacy and dependency analyses. Also, probability measures may be easily attached to the rules and their components.

(16) System should be able to explain "why" a fact is needed to complete the line of reasoning and "how" a conclusion was arrived at [11], [20].

TK!Solver: Underlying laws of algebra make transparent both "why" and "how." In addition it points out "what" was responsible for the termination of solution under error conditions.

(17) Pragmatic systems are needed—should be robust, general, and efficient for routine use [8].

TK!Solver: Well debugged; meets other characteristics as well.

(18) Available for users in properly sized and properly packaged combinations of hardware and software; chronic absence of cumulation of AI techniques in the form of software packages that can achieve wide use [20]; proliferation should lead to expert systems at everyone's disposal [17].

TK!Solver: Available on affordable microcomputers and priced for mass consumption; supplemented with extensive documentation.

(19) Usefulness of the system, i.e., responsiveness to the practical needs of professional communities; real-world systems [8], [34].

TK!Solver: By virtue of the perfect match between adopted control strategy and most commonly used mathematical techniques, TK!Solver is gaining acceptance in a wide range of disciplines.

(20) Expert systems should be capable of learning from experience [11], [33].

TK!Solver: In a narrow sense, it "learns" from experience to the effect of speeding up repetitious solution processes. In a broader sense the symbiotic relationship between the user and TK!Solver results in extensive complementary "learning from experience."

It should be mentioned in addition to the above points that we experimented extensively with the use of TK!Solver for building expert systems in a variety of disciplines. We were able to quickly set up a large number of models and use them for solving, for instance, whole sets of problems in Schaum's Outline Series on physics, chemistry, finance, etc.

Several publishers are contemplating, or are in the process of converting reference literature and standard textbooks into the format of TK!Solver models. The first of them is McGraw-Hill's *TK!SolverPack to Accompany Hicks: Standard Handbook of Engineering Calculations,* by Ross [42].This is a practical example of knowledge representation in a framework that allows for utilization, and modification when necessary.

The TK!Solver concept also comes out extremely strong particularly when covering a whole body of well-structured knowledge as embodied, for example, in the classic engineering manual by Hudson [26] consisting of 1029 "chunks" of knowledge and 30 accompanying tables of empiric relationships, functions, constants, unit conversion factors, etc. (with the exclusion of about 10 percent of the text dealing with concepts beyond the scope of the control strategy of the current version of TK!Solver). This experience compares favorably with the domain limitations of systems like MECHO [9], [31] or NEWTON [15]; the latter also faced difficulties in interfacing the quantitative knowledge with the mathematical expertise provided by MAC-SYMA.

IV. Conclusion and Further Developments

It follows from the description of the TK!Solver design in Section II and from the comparison of its features with the widely accepted characteristics of expert systems in Section III that

TK!Solver in its present form provides a general framework for building expert systems in a wide class of scientific, engineering, and other disciplines. In that sense it falls in the category of knowledge representation languages like KRL [5], NETL [18], Klone [6], or Prolog [11], [25].

It may be argued that TK!Solver falls short of learning capabilities, analogical reasoning, reasoning under conditions of uncertainty, and some other features stipulated by the theoreticians of expert systems or proclaimed, for instance, in the grand design of the Japanese 5th generation computers [46]. There are other "standards" set for work in AI and for design of expert systems, which TK!Solver seems to ignore: natural language interface, restriction to problems which are "not algorithmic or totally understood" [8], and "representation of symbolic knowledge for use in machine inference" (Buchanan and Feigenbaum in [14]). Finally, there is the implicit notion of the need to use a list processing language for AI work (incidentally, TK!Solver is implemented in a LISP-like language; on the other hand, even if it had not been it would still have had all the attributes qualifying it as a meta-expert system).

In fact all these advanced attributes are present in TK!Solver to a small or embryonic extent, and it would serve no purpose to argue to what extent they have to be present in order to classify the system one way or another.

We would rather point to what TK!Solver can do in its present form (which is a lot!), and stress the fact that it provides a solid basis for implementing additional features and capabilities as the advances in hardware permit and as the mass user requires. In its further development TK!Solver should look two ways: first, at concepts and tools emerging from research in AI, and second at the time-proven "non-AI" program packages that have become a part of human experts' lives. TK!Solver will naturally continue to take maximum advantage of the state of the art in human–computer interface.

ACKNOWLEDGMENT

An adapted version of this chapter appeared in the May 1984 issue of *BYTE* magazine. The authors wish to thank McGraw-Hill, Inc. for permission to publish this full version.

REFERENCES

[1] S. Amarel, "On representation of problems of reasoning about actions," *Machine Intell.*, vol. 3, pp. 131–171, 1968.

[2] S. Amarel, B. G. Buchanan, C. Kulikowski, and H. Pople, "Reports of panel on applications of artificial intelligence," in *Proc. IJCAI-77*, pp. 994–1006.

[3] R. Balzer, L. Erman, P. London, and C. Williams, "HEARSAY—III: A domain independent framework for expert systems," in *Proc. 1980 AAAI Conf.*, Stanford, CA, 1980.

[4] A. Barr and E. A. Feigenbaum, *The Handbook of Artificial Intelligence*, Vol. 2. Los Altos, CA: Kaufmann, 1982.

[5] D. G. Bobrow and T. Winograd, "An overview of KRL, a knowledge representation language," *Cognitive Sci.*, vol. 1, pp. 3–46, 1976.

[6] R. J. Brachman, "On the epistemological status of semantic networks," in *Associative Networks: Representation and Use of Knowledge by Computer*, N. V. Findler, Ed. New York: Academic, 1979, pp. 3–50.

[7] R. J. Brachman and H. J. Levesque, "Competence in knowledge representation," in *Proc. 1982 AAAI Conf.*, Pittsburgh, 1982, pp. 189–192.

[8] B. G. Buchanan, "New research on expert systems," *Machine Intell.*, vol. 10, pp. 269–299, 1982.

[9] A. Bundy, L. Byrd, G. Luger, C. Mellish, and M. Palmer, "Solving mechanics problems using meta-level inference," in *Proc. IJCAI, 1977*, pp. 1017–1027.

[10] J. R. Carbonell and A. M. Collins, "Natural semantics in artificial intelligence," in *Proc. 3rd IJCAI*, 1973, pp. 344–351.

[11] K. L. Clark and F. G. McCabe, "PROLOG: A language for implementing expert systems," *Machine Intell.*, vol. 10, pp. 455–470, 1982.

[12] R. Davis, "Applications of meta-level knowledge to the construction, maintenance and use of large knowledge bases," Ph.D. dissertation, Stanford University, Stanford, CA, 1976.

[13] _____, "Interactive transfer of expertise: Acquisition of new inference rules," in *Proc. IJCAI-77*, pp. 321–328.

[14] R. Davis and D. B. Lenat, *Knowledge-Based Systems in Artificial Intelligence.* Hightstown, NJ: McGraw-Hill, 1982.

[15] J. de Kleer, "Multiple representations of knowledge in a mechanics problem-solver," in *Proc. IJCAI-77,* pp. 299–304.

[16] R. O. Duda, J. Gaschnig, P. E. Hart, K. Konolige, R. Reboh, P. Barrett, and J. Slocum, "Development of the PROSPECTOR consultation system for mineral exploration," Final report, SRI Projects 5821 and 6415, Artificial Intelligence Center, SRI International, Menlo Park, CA, 1978.

[17] R. O. Duda and J. G. Gaschnig, "Knowledge-based expert systems come of age," *BYTE,* pp. 238–281, Sept. 1981.

[18] S. E. Fahlman, *NETL: A System for Representing and Understanding Real-World Knowledge.* Cambridge, MA: MIT, 1979.

[19] E. A. Feigenbaum, "Artificial intelligence research: What is it? What has it achieved? Where is it going?" (Invited paper), presented at Symp. on Artificial Intelligence, Canberra, Australia, 1974.

[20] _____, "The art of artificial intelligence: Themes and case studies of knowledge engineering," in *Proc. IJCAI-77,* pp. 1014–1029.

[21] C. Forgy and J. McDermott, "OPS, A domain-independent production system language," in *Proc. IJCAI-77,* pp. 933–939.

[22] P. E. Gerring, E. H. Shortliffe, and W. van Melle, "The interviewer/reasoner model: An approach to improving system responsiveness in interactive AI systems," *AI Magazine,* pp. 24–27, Fall 1982.

[23] I. Goldstein and S. Papert, "Artificial intelligence, language and the study of knowledge," *Cognitive Sci.,* vol. 1, 1977.

[24] G. Gordon, *System Simulation.* Englewood Cliffs, NJ: Prentice Hall, 1969.

[25] P. Hammond, "Appendix to PROLOG: A language for implementing expert systems," *Machine Intell.,* vol. 10, pp. 471–475, 1982.

[26] R. G. Hudson, *The Engineers' Manual,* 2nd ed.   New York: Wiley, published originally in 1917.

[27] M. Konopasek, "An advanced question answering system on sets of algebraic equations," in *Proc. European Conf. on Interactive Syst.,* D. Lewin, Ed.   Uxbridge, England: Online Publications, 1975.

[28] M. Konopasek and M. Kazmierczak, "A question answering system on mathematical models in microcomputer environments," in *Proc. First West Coast Computer Fair Conf.,* San Francisco, CA, 1977, pp. 182–186.

[29] M. Konopasek and C. Papaconstadopulus, "The question answering system on mathematical models (QAS): Description of the language," *Computer Languages,* pp. 145–155, 1978.

[30] M. Konopasek and S. Jayaraman, *The TK!Solver Book: A Guide to Problem-Solving in Science, Engineering, Business and Education.* Berkeley, CA: Osborne/Mc-Graw-Hill, 1984.

[31] G. F. Luger, "Mathematical model building in the solution of mechanics problems: Human protocol and the MECHO trace," *Cognitive Sci.,* vol. 5, pp. 55–77, 1981.

[32] W. S. Mark, "The reformulation approach to building expert systems," in *Proc. IJCAI-77,* pp. 329–335.

[33] R. S. Michalski, J. G. Carbonell, and T. M. Mitchell, *Machine Learning: An Artificial Intelligence Approach.* Palo Alto, CA: Tioga Publishing, 1983.

[34] D. S. Nau, "Expert Computer Systems," *Computer,* pp. 63–85, Feb. 1983.

[35] A. Newell and H. A. Simon, "GPS, A program that simulates human thought," in *Computers and Thought,* E. A. Feigenbaum and J. A. Feldman, Eds.   New York: McGraw-Hill, 1963.

[36] _____, *Human Problem Solving.* Englewood Cliffs, NJ: Prentice Hall, 1972.

[37] N. H. Nie, C. H. Hull, J. G. Jenkins, K. Steinbrenner, and D. H. Bent, *Statistical Package for Social Sciences.* Hightstown, NJ: McGraw-Hill, 1975.

[38] H. P. Nii and N. Aiello, "AGE (attempt to generalize): A knowledge-based program for building knowledge-based programs," in *Proc. IJCAI, 1979,* pp. 645–655.

[39] G. S. Novak, "Representations of knowledge in a problem for solving physics problems," in *Proc. IJCAI-77,* pp. 286–291.

[40] H. E. Pople, "The formation of composite hypotheses in diagnostic problem solving and exercise in synthetic reasoning," in *Proc. IJCAI-77,* pp. 1030–1037.

[41] D. Ross, *ICES Systems Design.* Cambridge, MA: MIT, 1967.

[42] S. S. Ross, *McGraw-Hill's TK!SolverPack to Accompany Hicks: Standard Handbook of Engineering Calculations.* New York, McGraw-Hill, 1984.

[43] E. H. Shortliffe, *Computer-Based Medical Consultations: MYCIN.* New York: American Elsevier, 1976.

[44] M. Stefik, J. Aikin, R. Balzar, J. Benoit, L. Birnbaum, F. Hayes-Roth, and E. Sacerdoti, "The organization of expert systems: A tutorial," *Artificial Intell.,* vol. 18, pp. 135–173, 1982.

[45] L. Tesler, "The Smalltalk environment," *BYTE,* pp. 90–147, Aug. 1981.

[46] P. C. Treleaven and I. G. Lima, "Japan's fifth-generation computer systems," *Computer,* pp. 79–88, Aug. 1982.

[47] W. van Melle, "A domain independent system that aids in constructing knowledge based consultation programs," Ph.D. dissertation, Stanford University, Stanford, CA, 1980.

[48] S. Weiss and C. Kulikowski, "EXPERT: A system for developing consultation models," in *Proc. IJCAI-79,* pp. 942–947.

Rule-Based Programming in OPS83

OPS83 is designed to be an efficient, portable language for writing and delivering rule-based systems

The design of expert systems is becoming an increasingly important area of programming. In the course of specifying a system, a designer must consider not only the development and implementation aspects, but also the mechanism for delivering the system to the end user. Current tools for developing expert systems provide an impressive functionality but require equally impressive amounts of computing power and memory. Unfortunately, the ideal delivery vehicle for an expert system is the mini or microcomputer, which is unable to support serious implementations of these development tools.

A particularly popular language for implementing expert systems has been OPS5, which is typically written in a dialect of LISP and runs in an interpretive environment. (See sidebar for a brief history of the OPS family of languages). This article introduces OPS83, the latest version of OPS.

Developed by C. Lanny Forgy at Carnegie-Mellon University, OPS83 was implemented in C with the goal of producing an efficient, portable language for writing and delivering rule-based systems.[1] This article will give a brief overview of the OPS83 language and its applications, present examples of how to approach writing a production system in OPS83, and discuss some of the advantages and disadvantages of OPS83 as compared with other available expert system development tools.

ALGORITHMS VS. HEURISTICS

Most problems currently solved by computer have a purely algorithmic solution. The method of solving the problem is well-known and can be specified easily in a conventional programming language. A trivial example of a problem with an algorithmic solution is balancing a checkbook. The sum remaining in the account is equal to the amount at the beginning of the month plus the sum of all deposits minus the sum of all checks written.

Some problems can not be solved so easily. Many can be solved only by using heuristics, or rules of thumb. Such a problem might be taking an integral of a complex equation. The integral might be common, in which case it can be looked up in a table. If the integral is not well-known, it is often possible to reduce the equation to a more manageable form by performing a transformation such as a substitution or an integration by parts. There is no well-defined algorithm to determine which method to apply to the equation; instead, the integration is performed using trial and error guided by the experience gained in doing many previous integrations.[2]

So what is OPS83 good for? OPS83 was designed to solve problems heuristically, using rules, which are also known as productions. However, few tasks can be designated as purely heuristic. Therefore, OPS83 is also designed to allow the programmer to slip easily into an algorithmic, or imperative, coding mode when necessary.

Tasks for which OPS83 might be suitable are: diagnosing faulty mechanical or electrical systems such as cars and computers, performing the routing on a printed circuit board, or playing games of strategy such as chess and cribbage. All of these tasks contain an algorithmic component, whether it be the collection of symptoms for a diagnostic program or the scoring of a hand in cribbage.

WORKING MEMORY

An OPS83 program consists of a combination of procedures, functions, and rules. During the execution of procedures and functions, the control flow of the program is deterministic, moving sequentially from one statement to another. During the execution of productions, the control flow is data-driven and any one of a number of rules is allowed to fire

Reprinted with permission from *AI Expert,* pp. 54–65, Premier 1986.

OP83's internal data structure is constructed for extremely efficient matching of productions against working memory

depending on the current contents of memory.

Most AI languages have one or more principal data structures. In LISP, for example, the basic data structures are the atom and the list. The basic data structure of OPS83 is the working memory element. A working memory element has the form of a record or structure. The first field of the record identifies the type of the working memory element. The following fields represent attribute-value pairs. A typical working memory element representing a person might be printed as:

```
(person name = Ron; age = 75;
        job = president;salary = 200,000.00)
```

The fields of the working memory element are strongly typed. The basic types are *integer*, *real*, *boolean*, *char*, and *symbol*. All of these types except *symbol* will be familiar to a C or Pascal programmer. A *symbol* is similar to the LISP atom; it consists of characters and symbols concatenated together and is represented internally by a unique pointer. A field of a working memory element can also contain more complex types such as records and arrays, although these require special care when pattern matching.

Working memory elements must be declared before being used in the program. A typical declaration would be:

```
type person = element
(name : symbol;
 age : integer;
 job : symbol;
 salary : real;);
```

Working memory is used to represent the "state of the world" of a production system. As the current state of the system changes, working memory elements are added, deleted, or modified to correspond with these changes.

An OPS83 programmer uses working memory for several different purposes. Knowledge about the problem being solved is stored in working memory. Information about the status of the program itself is also stored in working memory as well as knowledge about intermediate goals and information used for explanation facilities. In general, any information likely to be mutable or dependent on a particular set of input values is stored in working memory. In a typical (hypothetical) blocks world example, we can see several different uses of working memory.

—control information
```
(goal is = move;name = block1;x = 5;y = 4;
       tag = goal1)
(goal is = clear;name = block1;tag = goal2);
```
—state of the world
```
(object shape = block;color = red;name = block1;
       x = 1;y = 1)
(on obj1 = block1;obj2 = triangle13)
```
—history or explanation data

```
(createdby job = goal2;
       ... = clear_block_to_move)
```

Working memory in the OPS83 system is constantly monitored by a set of rules. Each rule consists of a left-hand side (LHS) and a right-hand side (RHS). The left-hand side of a rule consists of a set of patterns, or condition elements. The right-hand side of the rule contains an arbitrary number of executable statements or actions. When all the condition elements on the left-hand side of a rule are satisfied by the contents of working memory, then the rule is eligible to fire. When a rule fires, all the actions on the RHS are executed.

A typical rule has the form:

```
rule < name >
(condition element₁
 condition element₂

 condition elementₙ
 -->
 action₁
 action₂

 actionₘ
);
```

The left hand side contains an arbitrary number of condition elements. It is helpful to think of the condition element as a pattern that is matched against working memory. A condition element has the form:

```
&var      (type      term₁ term₂ . . . termₙ)
```

The &var represents a condition element variable. When the condition element matches a working memory element, the variable is bound to that working memory element. Any component of the working memory element can be referred to by using the condition element variable. Condition element variables can be referred to in both the LHS and RHS of a rule. Their bindings are valid only during the matching and firing of that rule.

The terms of a condition element can be any of three flavors.

1. A test of a field of a working memory element.

```
(person job = president);
```
—find a person whose job is president

2. An arbitrary logical expression enclosed in parentheses. If a term must reference the current working memory element being matched, the self-referential notation @.field is used.

```
&1 (person (@.job = president \/ @.job = actor));
```
—find a person whose job is president or actor

3. A function call. A function call cannot

access global variables, cannot change the working memory element being matched, and must return a logical value.

```
&1 (person is_tax_bracket(@.salary,35));
—find a person in the 35 percent tax bracket
```

Condition elements can be negated by use of the ~ operator.

```
~ (person name = Richard;job = president);
—Matches only if there is no such working
—memory element
```

When the LHS of a rule is satisfied by existing working memory elements, the rule is eligible to be fired. When a rule is fired, it executes the statements in the RHS. The RHS will typically perform one or more of the following:
■ Add to, delete from, or modify working memory
■ Perform I/O
■ Perform calculations on data extracted from matched working memory
■ Make a call to a foreign language subroutine or the operating system.

Working memory elements are created using the *make* command.

```
make (person name = Ron; job = actor; age = 30);
```

The *modify* command is used to change one or more fields of a working memory element; it requires a condition element variable that refers to the working memory element.

```
modify &1 (job = president; age = 75);
```

The *remove* statement is used to completely delete a working memory element.

```
rule two_terms
{ &pres (president name = Ron);
  (date year = 1988;month = November);
--)
remove &pres;}.
```

The RHS resembles a procedure in that it can contain any executable OPS83 statement, local variables, and calls to foreign language subroutines.

CONFLICT RESOLUTION

It is possible for the left-hand sides of more than one rule to be satisfied at one time. It is not possible to fire more than one rule at a time. Therefore, there must be a method of deciding which of the competing rules is to be given priority. When the LHS of a rule is satisfied, the rule is not fired immediately but is placed in a conflict set. After all rules have been tested for eligibility, the OPS83 system examines the conflict set and selects which rule to fire. The algorithm for selecting the rule to fire is called conflict resolution.

Conflict resolution can be performed in several ways. The concerns in choosing the algorithm are to fire the most appropriate rule, to avoid looping behavior in the program, and to avoid intensive computation (because conflict resolution must be performed during every cycle of the OPS83 interpreter).

A typical conflict resolution scheme used in the OPS5 interpreter is the MEA strategy. This ensures:
■ A rule will only fire once per working memory element
■ The most specific rule (judged by number and complexity of the LHS elements) will take precedence
■ The most recently added working memory elements will be most likely to cause a rule to fire.

A modified version of MEA is the default conflict resolution strategy provided in the shell included in the OPS83 system.

While suitable in many cases, the MEA algorithm is occasionally unsatisfactory. For example, an OPS83 programmer might wish to do away with conflict resolution entirely and cause all eligible rules to fire, one after another. Less drastic changes in the conflict resolution scheme can dramatically alter the performance of the production system. OPS83 gives the programmer the ability to build in a conflict resolution scheme tailored for a specific application.

The two productions that follow illustrate a use of conflict resolution. Both will be eligible to fire whenever a working element of the form (*goal is = process_data*) exists. The rule *process_data* will take precedence as long as any data remains unprocessed, because it is the more specific rule. The rule *end_process_data* serves the role of demon, firing when all data has been processed and the *rule process_data* is no longer eligible to fire. Note that this use of conflict resolution is necessary because the OPS language cannot express the condition "All working elements of type data have *state = processed.*" Condition elements cannot refer to aggregates of working memory.

```
rule process_data
{ &state  (goal is = process_data);
  &d      (data state = unprocessed);
  - - )
call handle_data(&d.info);
modify &d (state = processed);}.
rule end_process_data
{ &state (goal is = process_data);
  - - )
modify &state (is = process_input);
}.
```

INTERNAL STRUCTURE

The internal data structure of OPS83 is constructed for extremely efficient matching of

Most types, including arrays and structures, are represented in the same format in OPS83 and C

productions against working memory. This data structure is called a rete net. (The term rete net is actually redundant; the word rete is defined as a net, web, or neural network).

The rete net is a modified implementation of a discrimination net, which is a programming technique frequently used in AI programming. It is a tree consisting of a number of (usually) binary nodes. Each of these nodes contains a test. Note that this definition differs from the standard notion of a tree in that nodes contain executable code that acts on the data being entered, as opposed to the nodes of a standard tree in which only data is stored, and only one test criterion is used to position the data.

When data is entered into a discrimination net, its position is determined by the results of the tests encountered at each node. Because each test eliminates approximately half of the remaining nodes in the tree, a discrimination net is a very efficient way to store information.

A rete net differs from a discrimination net in that it stores partial results in the nodes of the tree. This results in a large gain in efficiency because only new or modified working memory elements cause a traversal of the tree to be performed.

The OPS83 compiler parses the condition elements in the LHS of each rule and assigns them to one or more nodes in the rete net. When a working memory element is added (or deleted) from the system, it is compared against nodes in the rete net. Each time a token arrives at a terminal production node, that node fires, placing its name and data in the conflict set.

The preceding discussion has grossly simplified an extremely complicated data structure. A complete discussion of the net is beyond the scope of this article. For the authoritative reference, see Forgy's *Rete: A Fast Algorithm for the Many Pattern/Many Object Pattern Match Problem.*[3]

It is not necessary to understand the rete net to program in OPS83. However, knowledge of the underlying data structure makes clear some otherwise puzzling behaviors of the OPS83 system and will allow the programmer to construct more efficient systems.

One of these behaviors is that increasing the complexity of rules may improve the performance of the system. Systems with many productions with undifferentiated left-hand sides will run less quickly than systems in which the productions have condition elements of sufficient specificity to allow them to be discriminated quickly. More complex left-hand sides will cause the tree structure of the rete net to become broad and shallow, rather than narrow and deep. This will allow working memory elements to very quickly arrive at the correct node.

Nodes in the rete net are shared between productions. Therefore, as more rules are added, the size of the system increases slowly and the speed of the system is relatively unaffected (Figure 1).

An underlying assumption of OPS is that working memory will change only incrementally. If we examine the rete net, we can see why this is so. Every time a working memory element is added, deleted, or modified, a traversal of the rete net must be performed. This tree traversal involves many tests and can be time consuming. It is only the fact that the rete net stores previous working memory matches that allows matching to be done efficiently. If many working memory elements must be added and deleted on each cycle, the speed of the system would be greatly degraded.

AN OPS83 PROGRAM

An OPS83 program is constructed in terms of modules. Each module contains an arbitrary number of type declarations, procedures, functions, and rules. By convention, each module must have a name with the .ops suffix. Each module must begin with the module statement, which identifies the module to the OPS83 compiler and which also specifies the start procedure for the system.

```
module ops_program(start_routine)
      { module text }
```

Modules may be dependent on type declarations or procedure/function definitions contained in another module. This is specified by means of the *use* statement.

FIGURE 1. Graphic representation of two productions entered into a rete net. Tokenized representations of working memory elements are stored in the two input nodes.

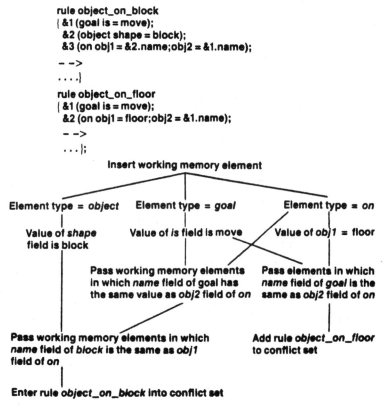

```
rule object_on_block
{ &1 (goal is = move);
  &2 (object shape = block);
  &3 (on obj1 = &2.name;obj2 = &1.name);

 - ->
 . . . .}
rule object_on_floor
{ &1 (goal is = move);
  &2 (on obj1 = floor;obj2 = &1.name);

 - ->
 . . . };
```

Insert working memory element

Element type = *object*   Element type = *goal*   Element type = *on*

Value of *shape* field is block   Value of *is* field is move   Value of *obj1* = floor

Pass working memory elements in which *name* field of goal has the same value as *obj2* field of *on*   Pass elements in which *name* field of *goal* is the same as *obj2* field of *on*

Pass working memory elements in which *name* field of *block* is the same as *obj1* field of *on*   Add rule *object_on_floor* to conflict set

Enter rule *object_on_block* into conflict set

On a VAX 11/780 running UNIX, production firing speeds ranged from 8 to 140 rules/ sec

```
use mytoplevel;
use typedefs in |\ ops \ sys \ typedefs|;
```

Each module is compiled separately by the OPS83 compiler. The result of the compilation is a synopsis (.syn) file and an assembler file. The synopsis file is used by the compiler to enforce the dependencies implied by the *use* statement. The assembler file is assembled by the standard assembler supplied with the system in which the version of OPS83 is written. After assembly, all the resulting object modules are linked together with the OPS83 C run-time system. This produces an OPS83 program.

It is to the programmer's advantage to keep all modules relatively small to avoid lengthy recompilations. In general, the compile-assemble-link sequence is somewhat complex and should be handled by use of a configuration control program such as the UNIX *make* command.

Users of OPS5 have become accustomed to an interactive top level from which it is possible to examine and modify the contents of working memory and prettyprint productions, monitor the conflict set, and step through production executions. OPS83 is delivered with a primitive shell that provides a subset of OPS5 functionality and a set of hooks whereby programmers who desire a more powerful environment may "roll their own."

The built-in functions *wtype* and *wextract* can be used to determine the type and contents of working memory elements. Similar commands are provided for examining the conflict set and for firing productions. There are, however, several limitations caused by the noninterpretative nature of OPS83. It is impossible to add or build productions on the fly; they must be compiled in separate modules and linked.

To implement a full ppwm (prettyprint working memory), it is necessary to create an auxiliary file containing the fields and types of the working memory elements. A typical auxiliary file might have the format:

```
person name symbol
person age integer
person salary real
person job symbol
etc . . .
```

It would be a fairly tedious job to create such files by hand. Fortunately, it is possible to create shell or C programs to generate them automagically from the synopsis files created by the OPS83 compiler. While it is possible for an ingenious programmer to create an arbitrarily powerful environment for OPS83, it is unfortunate that this effort must be duplicated by so many developers.

INTERFACING TO C

The ability to interface with foreign language systems is one of the most vital features in an expert system language that will be used in real world applications. An OPS83 program might be only one small part of a larger system and will thus have to interface with existing data bases, analysis programs, and graphical front-ends.

Interfacing can be done quite easily, particularly if the foreign system is implemented in C. Foreign language calls are declared as external. Thereafter they are treated as any other OPS83 procedure or function call. Arguments are passed by reference; it is usually necessary to write a small filter routine that converts the argument to the appropriate format. For example, to call the graphics command *lineto(x,y)* from OPS83, the following code would be necessary:

```
—In OPS83
external procedure lineto(&x: out integer,&y : out
                            integer);
call oline(5,10);

/* In C */
olineto(x,y)
integer *x,*y;
{
lineto(*x,*y);
}
```

Most types, including arrays and structures, are represented in the same format in both OPS83 and C. Symbols have no analog in C and must be converted to an array of characters before being passed.

Some applications may require that OPS83 be used as an embedded application. While the OPS83 run-time system is always the main procedure, it is possible to call a C procedure immediately after invocation. It then becomes the master procedure. OPS83 procedures can then be called from within C. The only restriction is that it is not possible to call procedures that take an arbitrary number of arguments, for example, *make* and *modify*. The following is an example of an embedded OPS83 application:

```
module ops_example(start)
{
procedure start()
{
call C_master_procedure()
};
procedure ops83_calls()
{
    . . . ops83 calls . . .
};
/* C coroutine */
C_master_procedure()
{
```

```
for(;;)   {
   . . . program . . .
ops83_calls();
   . . . program . . .}
}
```

OPS83 has been implemented under VAX VMS, UNIX on VAXs and Suns, Apollo Aegis, and MS-DOS. Other implementations are currently underway. Pure OPS83 programs can be compiled and run on any of these systems. Most foreign language routines linked with OPS83 will be written in C and will thus be reasonably portable with the obvious exception of system calls.

EXAMPLE
A small program is included in this article as an example of OPS83 structure and function (Listing 1). The program Ohms uses Ohm's

Production Systems and the OPS Family

OPS83 is the latest member of the OPS family of production system interpreters. The most well-known and successful of the OPS family is OPS5, which was written by Dr. Charles L. Forgy at Carnegie-Mellon University.[4]

OPS5 was originally written in LISP, and most of the LISP versions are in the public domain. OPS5 and a previous implementation, OPS4, were used by researchers at Carnegie-Mellon and Digital Equipment Corp. to implement the well-known R1 expert system that configures VAX computers.[5] Over the years, much work has been conducted at Carnegie-Mellon on speeding up production system interpreters by means of both hardware and software. The result is that OPS5 is a mature and popular language for implementing expert systems. An excellent reference for OPS5 programming is Brownston et al.'s *Programming Expert Systems in OPS5*.[6]

In principle, OPS production systems are very simple. A production system has three main entities: the set of productions or rules; the data structures, which are called working memory elements; and the interpreter itself. A rule consists of a left-hand side (LHS) of patterns and a right-hand side (RHS) of actions. Actions include addition, deletion, and modification of working memory elements, reading and writing to the user, and escapes into another language, often LISP. Conceptually, the interpreter looks at all of the LHSs of rules, and those that are completely matched against the working memory become members of the conflict set . The strength of the OPS languages is that the interpreters are very clever about this matching process, and perform it very quickly.

While OPS5 is very popular for implementing expert systems, it has a number of well-known deficiencies. LISP-based OPS5 programs tend to be memory intensive and are of limited use on microcomputers. The use of the production system paradigm to perform simple tasks such as I/O is awkward and inefficient. Interfaces to other programs and data bases tend to be difficult to develop. In general, these problems are shared with other popular AI languages, notably PROLOG.

Law and basic circuit knowledge to solve very simple resistor networks.

In this micro world, a circuit consists of devices that can be either resistors or voltage sources. Each device has a current which may or may not be known and a value. Each device has two terminals connected to junctions. Two or more terminals are connected to each other if they are connected to the same junction. Each junction has a voltage which may or may not be known. The initial state of the system is represented in working memory.

The goal of the program is to completely identify the value of and current through each device and the voltage at each junction. Three rules represent each of the basic permutations of Ohm's Law, $V = IR$, $I = V/R$, and $R = V/I$. Two rules represent knowledge about combining resistors. Two resistors in series or in parallel may be replaced by one resistor with the appropriate value (Figure 2). A special working memory type is provided for performing this substitution. In effect, the program will remove the two resistors from the network and replace them with an equivalent resistor. When values for that resistor are known, it is in turn replaced by its constituent resistors.

Please note that there are several possible configurations for resistor networks which can not be solved by this simple reduction/replacement paradigm. More complex networks must be solved by setting up loop equations and using Kirchoff's Law. This enhancement is left as an exercise for the reader.

BENCHMARKS
In general it is difficult to benchmark a production system due to the large number of variables to be considered. There is no convenient analogue to PROLOG's LIPS (Logical Inferences Per Second). A single production firing involves a considerable amount of pattern matching and conflict resolution. The right-hand side of a production can contain an arbitrary amount of computation unrelated to the inference process. Benchmarks must consider the number and complexity of condition elements on the left-hand side of productions, the number of rules in the system, and the number of working memory elements in memory at any given time.

On a VAX 11/780 running UNIX we have seen production firing speeds ranging from 140 rules/sec for very simple productions with simple right-hand sides to 8 rules/sec for rules that do significant right-hand side processing. OPS83 programs running on a PC tend to run at approximately one-tenth the speed of a VAX implementation. The same program running on an IBM AT will run at 50-80% of the speed on a VAX. In general, these speeds seem to be approximately an order of magnitude faster than a LISP-based

OPS5. Users used to running OPS5 will perceive OPS83 to run quite quickly.

PLUSES AND MINUSES

OPS83 lacks many features to which users of some AI languages have become accustomed. The most significant deficit is the lack of a rule interpreter. By the nature of production systems, the development of a rule set is a heuristic and error-prone process. The need to recompile the system when changes are made can produce lengthy delays in the development process.

The syntax of OPS83 seems to be derived equally from Pascal and C and is not always intuitive. Users of C will be confused by the use of call statements for procedures and the lack of pointers and unions.

The OPS83 system is proprietary and source code for everything except the shell is unavailable. While this is not an unusual state of affairs for compiled languages, the lack of source code will prove frustrating to LISP developers who are used to hacking code to suit their purposes.

Although priced competitively with other expert system development tools, the cost of OPS83 is quite high compared to software such as C compilers, which can be sold in high volume. Fortunately, extremely generous educational discounts are available.

In conclusion, OPS83 occupies a unique niche in the domain of AI languages. The ability to write imperative code means the developer is not limited to a specific problem-solving paradigm. The compiled nature of the code leads to small object modules and fast execution speeds. OPS83 code is portable, so implementations can be developed and debugged on powerful machines but delivered on micros. Due to the small size of the language, training time for programmers is minimized. A competent programmer with no prior knowledge of rule-based programming can be producing useful code within a week.

Our expert systems group at the ITT Advanced Technology Center has been serving as a beta test site for OPS83. In the course of our research, we have also experimented with LISP-based versions of OPS5, PC-based expert system tools, various versions of PROLOG, and a large LISP-based deductive retriever. Our conclusion is that the qualities of OPS83 listed in this article make it the tool of choice for the creation of small to medium size expert systems that are expected to advance beyond the prototype stage and to be delivered as products to clients in the real world. ∎

Inquiries about OPS83 should be sent to: Diana Connan, vice president of marketing, Production Systems Technologies, 642 Gettysburg St., Pittsburgh, Pa. 15206.

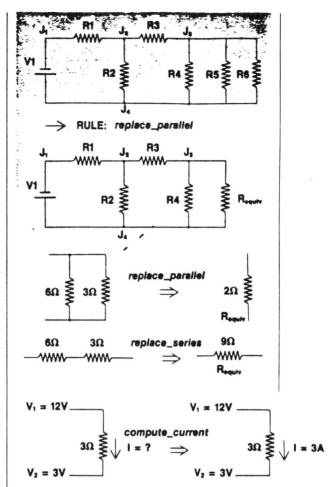

FIGURE 2. Example of a production application. Compute_current's LHS conditions—a resistor exists of known value with a known voltage drop—are satisfied. The rule fires, computing the value of the amperage through the resistor.

REFERENCES

1. A full description of the OPS83 language may be found in C.L. Forgy's The OPS83 User's Manual and Report, *available from Production Systems Technology.*

2. Many programs solve mathematical problems in a symbolic manner, the most well-known of which is MACSYMA. A very early integration program was described in:

Slagle, J.R. "A Heuristic Program that Solves Symbolic Integration Problems in Freshman Calculus." Journal of the Association for Computing Machinery 10 (1963) 507-520.

3. Forgy, C.L. "Rete: A Fast Algorithm for the Many Pattern/Many Object Pattern Match Problem." Artificial Intelligence 19 (1982): 17-37.

4. Forgy, C.L. OPS5 User's Manual. Carnegie-Mellon University, CMU-CS-78-116, 1981.

5. McDermott, J. A Rule-Based Configurer of Computer Systems. Carnegie-Mellon University, CMU-CS-80-119, 1981.

6. Brownston et al. Programming Expert Systems in OPS5. Addison-Wesley, 1985.

Dan Neiman—ITT Advanced Technology Center, Shelton, Ct.

John Martin—Philips Laboratories, Briarcliff Manor, N.Y.

LISTING 1

Rule-Based Programming in OPS83

This abridged OPS83 program uses Ohm's Law to solve simple DC circuits

```
module ohms (start_ohms)
{
use shell;
--First we have to model the circuit.
--Devices look like this:
type device = element
   (type : symbol;        -- resistor, voltsource
    tag : symbol;         -- tag identifies each unique device
    i : real;             --current through device
    istat : symbol;       --status of i, solved or unknown
    val : real;           -- value of device in ohms or volts
    valstat : symbol;     --is value known?
    );
--All devices are connected to junctions.  Two devices connected
--to the same junction are connected to each other.
 type connect = element
    (dev : symbol;
     trm   : integer;
     junct : symbol;);
--All junctions have a voltage.  Implicitly, this means that
--all terminals connected to a given junction are at the same potential.
 type junct = element
    (tag : symbol;
     volts : real;
     vstat : symbol);
-- An equivalent resistor is one which is substituted for
-- a resistor using one of the combining forms.  The values
-- and connections of the replaced resistors are stored in
-- the working memory element for future use.
type equiv_r = element
(type : symbol;
 tag : symbol;
 r1 : symbol;  -- connections for r1
 r1t1 : integer; r1t2 : integer; r1j1 : symbol; r1j2 : symbol;
 r2 : symbol;   -- connections for r2
 r2t1 : integer; r2t2 : integer; r2j1 : symbol; r2j2 : symbol;
 );
--The start procedure.  In this procedure, the circuit is modeled,
--and whatever values are known are set.
procedure start_ohms()
{
 make (device type=voltsource; tag=v1;val=12.0;i=12.0;istat=unknown);
 make (device type=resistor;tag=r1;val=10.0;valstat=known;i=12.0;istat=unknown);
 make (connect   dev=v1;trm=1;junct=j1);
 make (connect   dev=v1;trm=2;junct=j4);
 make (connect   dev=r1;trm=1;junct=j1);
 make (connect   dev=r1;trm=2;junct=j2);
 make (junct volts=12.0;vstat=known;tag=j1);
 make (junct vstat=unknown;tag=j2);
 make (junct vstat=unknown;tag=j3);
 make (junct volts=0.0;vstat=known;tag=j4);
            :         :        :
            :         :        :
 call run(100);   -- run the production system
};
--Some simple rules derived from Ohms Law
--If you know the voltage across a device and the resistance of the
--device, then you know the current through the device.
--Rules compute_voltage and compute_resistance are similar.
rule compute_current
  { &1 (device type=resistor;istat=unknown;valstat=known);
    &2 (connect   dev=&1.tag;trm=1); -- get the junctions involved
    &3 (junct tag=&2.junct;vstat=known);
    &4 (connect   dev=&1.tag;trm=2);
    &5 (junct tag=&4.junct;vstat=known);
  -->
       -- I = V/R
       -- Establish convention, current flows from t1 to t2 in
       -- each device.  A negative sign indicates the inverse.
       modify &1 (i= (&3.volts - &5.volts)/&1.val;istat=known)
       };
```

Rule-Based Programming in OPS83

```
--Resistor manipulations
-- Two resistors in parallel can be replaced by one resistor with
-- value (R1 * R2)/(R1 +R2)
-- Rule replace_series is similar
rule replace_parallel
{    &1   (device type=resistor;istat=unknown;valstat=known); --find device
     --find both connections to that device.
     &2   (connect dev=&1.tag;trm=1);
     &3   (connect dev=&1.tag;trm=2);
     --now, find another device connected to both junctions
     &4   (device type=resistor;istat=unknown;valstat=known;tag<>&1.tag);
     &5   (connect dev=&4.tag;junct=&2.junct); --find common junction
     &6   (connect dev=&4.tag;junct=&3.junct); --find common junction
     -->
     local &equiv : symbol;
     &equiv = gensym(equiv); --create name for new device
     make(equiv_r type=parallel;tag=&equiv;r1=&1.tag;
                  r1t1=&2.trm;r1t2=&3.trm;r1j1=&2.junct;
                  r1j2=&3.junct;r2t1=&5.trm;r2t2=&6.trm;
                  r2j1=&5.junct;r2j2=&6.junct;r2=&4.tag);
     make(device type=resistor;tag=&equiv;istat=unknown;
                  val = (&1.val * &4.val)/(&1.val + &4.val);valstat=known);
     --substitute new device into circuit
     modify &5 (dev=&equiv;trm=1);
     modify &6 (dev=&equiv;trm=2);
     remove &2;
     remove &3;
     };
--After an equivalent resistor has been solved, it can be replaced
--by its constituent parts
```

181

RULEMASTER™: A SECOND-GENERATION KNOWLEDGE-ENGINEERING FACILITY

Donald Michie* - Stephen Muggleton** - Charles Riese† - Steven Zubrick†

* Intelligent Terminals Ltd., George House 36, North Hanover Street, Glasgow G1 2AD, Scotland, UK
** University of Edinburgh, Hope Park Square, Edinburgh EH8 9NW, Scotland, UK
† Radian Corporation, P.O. Box 9948, Austin, Texas 78766, USA

Abstract

A new expert system building kit called RuleMaster implements a hierarchically ordered system of inductive learning for the acquisition of expert knowledge. RuleMaster allows the development of both diagnostic and procedurally oriented expert systems. A powerful facility is provided for interfacing rules to other knowledge sources.

HOW THIS PAPER IS WRITTEN

First, we describe some of the knowledge engineering issues which RuleMaster addresses. Following this are implementation details of the approach taken. Next is a description of two significant expert systems built using RuleMaster. We conclude with some remarks concerning how well the research goals have been met.

SOME ISSUES IN KNOWLEDGE ENGINEERING

The following aspects distinguish expert systems from other computer programs:

o   Explanation. Expert systems are capable of inspecting their own reasoning in order to explain "why" certain factors are being investigated and "how" particular conclusions are reached.
o   Problem type. Expert systems are more suitable than an algorithmic approach for problems which involve a large amount of branching.
o   Partial certainty. Expert systems are usually able to deal with a set of values between true and false which represent the partial certainty of a proposition.

The bottleneck of expert system building lies in knowledge acquisition from experts. A key issue here is the difference between dialogue acquisition and the use of machine learning. The latter approach relieves the expert of much of the burden of authoring rules directly, allowing him/her to present merely instances of correct decision making, while the machine produces generalisations of these examples of correct decision making.

One of the goals of AI programming language design (e.g., as pursued, though not yet fully attained, by the logic programming school) is to allow the user to tell the machine relevant facts, theories, advice, etc., in any order they occur to him rather than in some fixed sequence (as demanded by traditional programming languages). What has so far eluded every Prolog interpreter can be supplied by a new style of programming based on inductive rather than deductive mechanisms.

Large knowledge bases can become unwieldy and difficult to understand. Experts tend to organise their knowledge as a set of interrelated factors. By making a hierarchy of attributes explicit[11], it is possible to make the interrelationship of problem attributes easier to understand and maintain. Even though this approach appears to involve overheads in terms of structure formation, its advantages outweigh this disadvantage.

Expert systems can be broadly divided into two main categories: those which do classification (e.g., MYCIN), and those which carry out a task (e.g., R1). Often expert systems require a combination of these abilities. In many systems, the knowledge representation form supports one of these approaches while impeding the other.

Most practical expert systems require information sources other than the rules which the expert uses for decision making. For instance, a medical diagnostic system might read biomedical sensors, access patient records and do mathematical modeling of organic processes. Facilities for linking to external routines may, therefore, be considered as an essential component of modern expert system software.

RULEMASTER IMPLEMENTATION

Overview

RuleMaster is a general purpose expert system building tool. It consists of two major components: RuleMaker™ and Radial™. RuleMaker is an inductive generator of decision trees expressed as code in a rule language called Radial. RuleMaker is discussed in the knowledge acquisition section below, while some of the special features of Radial are described in further sections.

RuleMaster is motivated by a desire to solve the knowledge engineering issues involved in building large expert systems (described in the previous section). The original basis for the inductive techniques used in RuleMaker are those of Quinlan's ID3 algorithm.[7] This method was later refined and improved by Shapiro and Niblett[10] and

Reprinted from *Proc. IEEE First Conf. on Artificial Intelligence Applications*, pp. 591–597, Dec. 1984.

Paterson and Niblett.[6] A basis for structuring inductively generated rule sets was developed and tested by Shapiro.[11] The explanation facility used by the Radial interpreter is derived from a proposal by Michie, Bratko and Shapiro.[12] Radial is the commercial name of Mugol designed by one of us as part of an academic project.[4]

RuleMaster is written as a set of interrelated programs written in C under the UNIX* operating system. There are current working versions running on DEC VAX, SUN Microsystems and IBM PC/XT computers.

Two sizeable expert systems built with RuleMaster are described in this paper.

Knowledge acquisition

The approach taken in RuleMaster differs considerably from that of using production rules. It is well known that experts explain complex concepts to human apprentices implicitly by way of examples rather than explicitly by stating principles. The apprentice generalises these sample decisions to more widely applicable rules. A computer can learn in the same way as the human apprentice if it is able to produce general rules from specific instances.

RuleMaster allows the expert system builder to use rules authored either by an expert or by the machine. The machine builds rules by a process called *rule induction*. In induction of classification rules, rules are induced by generalisation over *examples* of expert decision-making. An example is expressed as a vector of values pertaining to attributes of the decision, together with the expert's classification. For instance, in a very simple case, if we are trying to build a rule to classify animals, the attributes of the decision might be "color" and "size". A possible classification is "ELEPHANT". Given the example:

Colour	Size	Class
gray	big	ELEPHANT

The induction algorithm would generalise this example to the rule:

irrespective of color and size, the class is always ELEPHANT

In order to get a more accurate generalisation, more examples would need to be added, and a more complex rule would be induced. For instance, with the following example set:

Colour	Size	Class
grey	big	ELEPHANT
yellow	big	GIRAFFE
grey	small	TORTOISE

the following decision tree is generated:

* UNIX is a trademark of Bell Laboratories.

If the animal's colour is:

   a) yellow, then it is a GIRAFFE
   b) grey, then if the animal's size is
     i) big, then it is an ELEPHANT
     ii) small, then it is a TORTOISE

In RuleMaster, the class is comprised of an action and a next-state. The action specifies what to do in the example situation, and the next-state says which context must be entered after the action has been carried out. The induction subsystem which supports this is known as RuleMaker.

An illustration of the power of inductive inference is shown in the following example taken from the WILLARD expert system. Contained within a widely used meteorological manual[17] is a table (Figure 1) of three attributes used to determine the expected change of lapse rate.

Flow	Vertical Motion	Thickness		Change in Lapse Rate
divergent	descent	shrinking	=>	more stable
divergent	ascent	shrinking	=>	more stable
divergent	ascent	stretching	=>	less stable
convergent	descent	shrinking	=>	more stable
convergent	descent	stretching	=>	less stable
convergent	ascent	stretching	=>	less stable
divergent	none	shrinking	=>	more stable
convergent	none	stretching	=>	less stable
divergent	ascent	no change	=>	no change
convergent	descent	no change	=>	no change
none	ascent	stretching	=>	less stable
none	descent	shrinking	=>	more stable

Figure 1
Table (found in AWS, 1969) of examples
used in lapse rate determination.

The rule generated from these examples used only one of the three given attributes. This rule was as follows:

if the thickness (distance between the two constant pressure surfaces)

a) *shrinks then the lapse rate becomes more stable*
b) *stretches then the lapse rate becomes less stable*
c) *does not change then the lapse does not change*

This rule was found to be correct and consistent with a physical model of the atmosphere (based on the hypsometric equations[14]), although this is not readily apparent from inspection of the table.

Entering rules by examples has several distinct advantages over writing production rules. When the example set has insufficient information to cover the entire problem space, RuleMaker will generalise these examples in order to produce a decision tree which covers all the possible situations. If the knowledge is entered directly as rules, no generalisation is carried out. When too many attributes are present (as in the case shown in Figure 1), redundant information will be ignored by RuleMaker. Again, production systems do not have this ability to compact knowledge.

The knowledge is given as examples in a more implicit declarative form than production systems, and this is automatically transformed into a more explicit procedural form than that of production systems. Thus, an expert can enter and revise knowledge without regard to order, while reviewing and executing an economical procedural form constructed for him by the system.

Structuring

A key feature of the RuleMaster rule language, Radial, is the ability to structure large expert systems. The method of doing so follows that of structured algorithmic programming languages such as Pascal.

A Radial program[4,16] consists of a collection of inter-related modules. An individual module can represent either an executable procedure or a piece of data. In order to aid the imposition of a structure on these modules, they are arranged as a tree of modules. The scope of referencing a module from any other is limited by a recursive scope rule called "visibility". Visibility is defined as follows:

> Module   X is visible to module A iff
>
> X is a child of A
> or
> X is visible to the parent of A

Figure 2 represents a hypothetical program tree with modules named by the letters of the alphabet.

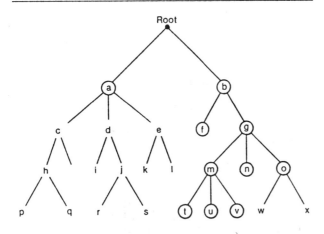

Figure 2
Modules Visible to Module m (see text)

Note that the highest module in the tree, "root", by the definition of visibility cannot be referenced by any module in the tree. The circled modules are those visible to module "m". Rather than using block bracketing in the code to indicate the tree structure (as in Pascal), each module is identified using its unique path from the root in the program tree (e.g., module m's complete name is "b.g.m").

Explanation

The rule language, Radial, has the ability to explain its line of reasoning at any time during a session. When an expert system is consulted, the reasoning behind a piece of advice may influence its acceptance. For example, if the explanation indicates that a critical factor has been ignored, the user may decide to reject the advice. Requests for explanation during hypothetical test cases can also be used to instruct novices. Explanation has additional value at development time. In explanation driven development, the expert checks that correct decisions are reached, and that they are reached for the right reasons. This increases the likelihood that situations outside the training set will be dealt with correctly. Different explanations from possibly conflicting expert sources can be used to refine the knowledge base, or to further research in the field. Our implementation follows that described in Shapiro and Michie.[12]

Each Radial module requires a text segment containing optional slots for run-time substitution of the input arguments of that module. These pieces of text are combined in a standard set of masks to produce English phrases. An algorithm orders the individual phrases to form a theorem-like proof which justifies the reasoning by building from axiomatic facts towards the final conclusion. The explanation is given piecemeal, the most relevant portion being presented first, with further elaboration on demand. Actions and tests are dealt with differently by the presentation algorithm. A user can ask for explanation at any time that he/she is asked a question or given advice. In addition, the user can interrupt the system at any time to find out what is happening. Furthermore, a full report of the line of reasoning leading to some final conclusion can be produced at the end of a session.

An example of automatically generated explanation can be found in the section on the Willard expert system.

Partial certainty

Values of belief between absolute truth and falsity have been used in many domains to model an expert's method of reasoning. Several techniques have been developed for dealing with this.[9,13] This has caused a certain amount of controversy over the use of numerical representations of belief.[1,2,8]

Two techniques for dealing with partial certainty are supported by RuleMaster. Firstly, the Rule-Maker subsystem uses a multi-valued logic as a method of providing finite sets of qualitative attribute values. Secondly, Zadeh's fuzzy set operators[15] have been built into the Radial language, for use with either discrete or continuous belief values. Radial provides computational mechanisms for the implementation of additional uncertainty schemes.

For example, WILLARD (described below) represents the probability of severe thunderstorm occurrence as low, slight, moderate or high. These are meteorological terms and are each ascribed numerical probability ranges. However, the rules used for selecting a level are predominantly heuristic, and only partially based on numerical calculation.

Types of expert systems supported

A wide range of approaches may be classified as expert systems. The best understood of these are diagnostic in nature. However, expert system packages made by emptying diagnostic applications (e.g., EMYCIN) often have difficulty handling procedural actions. RuleMaster was designed from the start to incorporate a wide range of control strategies, so that the system could be applied to a broad set of problem types.

An expert system application built with RuleMaster consists of a set of Radial modules. The Radial language has its formal basis in finite automata theory.[3] Each module consists of a transition network of states, each of which contains a single decision tree. When invoked, each decision tree carries out a sequence of tests until a decision is reached to perform an action. After execution of this action, control is passed to a new state within the same module. The ability to do conditional branching together with that of calling modules recursively allows the building of arbitrarily complex control structures.

The two large expert systems which have been built with RuleMaster are primarily diagnostic and only use a subset of the Radial language. However, small but effective procedural expert systems have been built. For example, an expert system which builds an arch out of a set of blocks from an arbitrary starting position to a given goal position was inductively constructed from sample arch-building action-decisions.[5] Although this was only a demonstration of RuleMaster's capabilities, the domain contains several of the features of non-diagnostic applications (e.g., design and scheduling).

External information sources

Virtually all large expert system applications will require access to external information sources, such as sensors, files, data bases, and specially written or existing programs. External resources can also be used to incorporate alternate reasoning approaches into a system. External output to control devices or update data bases may also be desired.

To deal with these demands, RuleMaster allows the developer to set up separate processes under the operating system. Communication with these other processes is defined by a simple interface which allows external programs to be called in the same manner as Radial modules. At execution time, instructions and data are passed across a UNIX pipe between RuleMaster and the external programs. These programs can be written in any language supported by UNIX (e.g., FORTRAN, C, LISP, Prolog).

SOME CASE STUDIES OF REAL EXPERT SYSTEMS BUILT USING RULEMASTER™

WILLARD

WILLARD forecasts the likelihood of severe thunderstorms occurring in the central United States. Annually, storms in this region cause the loss of many lives and billions of dollars of property damage.

Severe thunderstorm forecasting for the entire United States is currently done by skilled meteorologists at the National Severe Storms Forecast Center (NSSFC). This time consuming task entails continuous analysis of vast amounts of raw data and numeric modeling results, much of which may turn out to be irrelevant. An expert system might automatically screen the data, providing meteorologists with suggested forecasts together with their justifications.

Full Explanation of the forecast

Since upper level cold air advection causing increased upwards vertical velocities is present
    it follows that the upper-level destabilization potential is sufficient
Since the K Index is strong
    when the Lifted Index is strong
    it follows that the stability indices condition is favorable
Since daytime heating acting as a possible trigger mechanism for potential instability release is strong
    when the stability indices condition is favorable
    it follows that low-level destabilization potential is favorable
Since an approaching 500 millibar short wave trough is present
    it follows that the vertical velocity field is favorable
Since a high 850 mb dew point is present
    when surface dew point classification is moderate
    it follows that the low-level moisture field is marginal
Since the upper-level destabilization potential is sufficient
    when low-level destabilization potential is favorable
    and the vertical velocity field is favorable
    and the low-level moisture field is marginal
    it was necessary to advise: 'There's a SLIGHT CHANCE thunderstorms occurring 12 hours from now will be severe at this location.'

Figure 3
Sample WILLARD forecast explanation

A large number of specific case studies of occurrences of severe thunderstorms have been documented and analysed in the meteorological literature. However, no coherent system of rules covering all possible cases has yet been synthesised. For this reason, an inductive rule generator is a powerful tool for generalising this accumulated knowledge.

For the purposes of rapid development, subjectively selected examples were used to build the prototype expert system. Objective cases of real weather data have subsequently been applied in the ongoing refinement of WILLARD. An illustration of the use of inductive inference in the development of WILLARD is given in Figure 1.

The WILLARD expert system is composed of a hierarchy of thirty modules, each containing a single decision rule (Figure 4). This hierarchy is on average four levels deep. All modules' rules were developed using inductive generalization. About 140 examples out of a possible nine million situations were used in building WILLARD.

For the top level module, inductive generalization was able to order the critical meteorological factors in a manner consistent with the way forecasters perform their analysis. For example, if the key factors are unfavorable, then a rapid decision can be made, otherwise, more parameters are investigated until a decision can be reached.

Although, WILLARD is essentially a diagnostic expert system, RuleMaster facilitates the use of control loops required for top level control and the monitoring of incoming data (see previous section on "Types of Expert Systems Supported").

WILLARD can operate in manual or automatic forecast mode. In the manual mode, the system asks questions of the meteorologist about pertinent weather conditions for the forecast area and produces a complete, reasoned forecast.

In the automatic mode, WILLARD obtains all necessary information from National Meteorological Center data files. External FORTRAN functions were interfaced to WILLARD to access and operate on these data files. The user may specify an area, in which WILLARD will generate a grid of nodal values for the chance of severe thunderstorms for that area.

For preliminary validation of the expert system, a region including west and central Texas, Oklahoma, and Colorado was chosen. During a one-week period in late spring (May 22-29, 1984), five severe storm systems passed through that region.

WILLARD's forecasts were compared against the convective outlook forecasts prepared by NSSFC. Both systems use similar data, forecasting approach, and prediction format, both forecasting the probability of severe thunderstorms as being none, approaching, slight, moderate, or high.

Table 1 gives forecast comparisons in the vicinity of each of the storm systems which occurred in the test set.

We are continuing to add to the knowledge base, to enlarge both the depth and the scope of the forecasting system. The particular goals are: more refined diagnoses, localized forecasts, better discrimination in borderline situations, and increased use of computer data bases and existing numerical models.

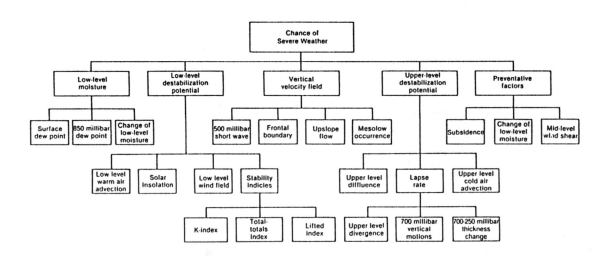

Figure 4
WILLARD Structure

Table 1
SEVERE STORM FORECASTING RESULTS

Case	Willard	NSSFC	Actual
North Texas 23May1984	slight	none	none (1"/hr. rain)
NE Colorado 24 May 1984	moderate	slight	Yes 1-3/4" hail tornado
Oklahoma 26 May 1984	slight	slight	Yes 1-3/4" hail
West Texas 27 May 1984	slight	none	Yes 1-3/4" hail
SW Texas 28 May 1984	approach	none	Yes 1-3/4 " hail

Transformer fault diagnosis

When large power distribution transformers begin to fail, some form of heating of the oil and/or insulation occurs. These materials decompose when heated to produce hydrogen and hydrocarbon gases which dissolve in the oil. Over the past 20 years, expert techniques to diagnose transformer condition from dissolved gas concentrations have been developed.

Service interruption and repair or replacement costs for failed transformers may run into the millions of dollars. This provides financial incentive to detect the onset of failures before catastrophic damage occurs. Hartford Steam Boiler Inspection and Insurance Company (HSB) insures industrial equipment and has sponsored the development of an expert system which utilizes oil sample analyses to prepare transformer condition and recommended action reports.

The diagnostic portion of the expert system contains 27 modules, each containing one or more induced rules. Since this is a developing field, the theory relating gas concentrations to faults is not well worked out or documented. It was necessary to rebuild the expert system structure several times, as better organizations of the knowledge became apparent. The induction of rules from examples proved valuable in this rule construction and testing process.

The expert system was verified with a set of ten transformer failures for which dissolved gas analysis and failure causes were both available. The expert system arrived at the same diagnosis as the expert on all ten cases. The fault diagnosis system is now being integrated into HSB's transformer testing procedure.

Conclusion

RuleMaster is an expert system building package intended to solve many of the problems involved in the construction of large knowledge based programs. An inductive learning system (RuleMaker) allows rapid and effective acquisition of expert knowledge. The success of the inductive rule acquisition approach is indicated by the fact that although hand-crafting of rules is allowed by the RuleMaster system, the builders of all the expert systems described in this paper preferred to construct all their rules by induction. The Radial language allows structured organisation of large quantities of knowledge acquired in such a manner. Radial also provides a facility for presenting ordered explanation of reasoning to the level of elaboration required.

Typical expert system applications contain aspects of both diagnostic and sequential processing. RuleMaster provides a consistent knowledge representation for these disparate problem elements. Furthermore, an interface to external sources and sinks of information is provided.

Acknowledgments

This research was conducted as a cooperation between Radian Corporation, Intelligent Terminals Ltd., the University of Edinburgh, and Hartford Steam Boiler Insurance and Inspection Company. Thanks are due to these bodies for resources and facilities.

We also thank Dr. Alen Shapiro and Dr. Timothy Niblett for their valuable contributions.

REFERENCES

[1] P. R. Cohen and M. R. Grinberg, "A framework for Heuristic Reasoning About Uncertainty," *Proceedings of the Eighth International Joint Conference on Artificial Intelligence*, Los Altos, CA: William Kaufmann, Inc., 1983.

[2] R. O. Duda, P. E. Hart, and N. Nilsson, "Subjective Bayesian Methods for Rule-based Inference Systems," Technical Note 124, Artificial Intelligence Center, Menlo Park, CA: Stanford Research Institute, 1976.

[3] J. E. Hopcroft, and J. D. Ullman, *Introduction to Automata and Formal Languages*, Reading, MA: Addison-Wesley, 1979.

[4] S. H. Muggleton, "A Process Description Language," Private Communication, Edinburgh: Machine Intelligence Research Unit, 1983.

[5] S. H. Muggleton, "An Inductively acquired strategy for building an arch in a blocks world," Private communication, 1984.

[6] A. Paterson and T. Niblett, *ACLS Manual*, Edinburgh: Intelligent Terminals, Ltd., 1982.

[7] J. R. Quinlan, "Discovering rules from large collections of examples: a case study," *In Expert Systems in the Micro-electronic Age*, (D. Michie, ed.), Edinburgh Univ. Press, 1979.

[8] J. R. Quinlan, "INFERNO: A cautious Approach to Uncertain Inference," RAND Note N-1898-RC, Santa Monica, CA: RAND Corporation, 1982.

[9] G. Shafer, *A Mathematical Theory of Evidence*, Princeton, NJ: Princeton Univ. Press, 1976.

[10] A. D. Shapiro and T. B. Niblett, "Automatic induction of classification rules for a chess endgame," *Advances in Computer Chess 3*, 1982.

[11] A. D. Shapiro, *The Role of Structured Induction in Expert Systems*, Ph.D. thesis, Edinburgh: Machine Intelligence Research Unit, 1983.

[12] A. D. Shapiro and D. Michie, "A self-commenting facility for inductively synthesised endgame expertise," to appear in *Advances in Computer Chess 4* (in press).

[13] E. H. Shortliffe and B. G. Buchanan, "A Model of Inexact Reasoning in Medicine," *Mathematical Biosciences 23:351-379*, 1975.

[14] M. Wallace and P. V. Hobbs, *Atmospheric Science*, New York, NY: Academic Press, 1977.

[15] L. A. Zadeh, "A theory of approximate reasoning," *Machine Intelligence 9* (ed. Hayes, Michie, Mikulich), 1979.

[16] *RuleMaster System User Manual*, Technical Report, DCN 84-141-603-01. Austin: Radian Corporation, 1984.

[17] "Use of the Skew T, Log P Diagram in Analysis and Forecasting," *Air Weather Service Manual AWSM 105-124*, NTIS AD695603. Springfield, VA: National Technical Information Service, 1969.

LASER:
A HIGH PERFORMANCE A.I. PROGRAMMING ENVIRONMENT

R. Reddy, R. Raman, R. Dziedzic, and A. Butcher
Artificial Intelligence Laboratory
West Virginia University
Morgantown, West Virginia 26506

LASER is a highly efficient, portable programming environment that provides a unified approach to Artificial Intelligence Programming. It consists of an object oriented knowledge representation kernel and a series of horizontally integrated packages for Knowledge Based Simulation, Rule Based Programming and a PROSPECTOR like network inference engine.

1. Introduction

The prime motivation to develop yet another knowledge representation environment was:

- to incorporate the achievements of existing systems into one package while eschewing their individual inadequacies.

- to enable research into interesting inference knowledge mechanisms.

- to develop a complete environment wherein simulation, expert systems, and other knowledge-based applications can co-exist.

- to provide an environment which is capable of running on a variety of computers ranging from desktop PRO350's to

- super-mini VAX 780's, as well as different operating systems like Unix, VMS, etc.

- to be fast (a significant disadvantage of quite a few of the existing knowledge representation systems).

These objectives resulted in the design of LASER (Laboratory for Simulation, Evaluation and Representation of systems)). Laser is a C-language based knowledge-representation and, as its name might imply, it is quick and clean. The choice of C as the implementation language, rather than one of the many flavors of Lisp, was based on the speed that C provides, as well as the fact that few mutations of C exist.

The choice of the implementation language (C), does not restrict LASER-based applications from being developed in other languages. It is expected that this environment will encourage the utilization of the user's existing software in conjunction with LASER.

The LASER environment provides a knowledge representation environment, as well as software packages like:

- generic expert system shells for:

    * Production systems

    * Network systems

- a Knowledge Based Simulation package

- utilities, such as:

    * hierarchical command system

    * graphical model builder

    * knowledge base

    * template filler

With such tools, a user can develop expert systems, knowledge-based decision support systems, simulation programs, and so on.

Reprinted from *Proc. IEEE Expert Systems in Government Symp.*, pp. 16–23, Oct. 1985.

189

There are many ways of interacting with LASER:

- Writing C-language programs which LASER library functions

- Writing Lisp programs with the aid of the Lisp/Laser interface

- Interacting directly with LASER by means of the LASER top-level user-interface

The development of LASER will, eventually, provide all four programming paradigms: Object Oriented, Procedure Oriented, Data Oriented, and Rule Oriented. During the course of this manual, each of these paradigms will be examined, detailing its implementation in LASER, as well as the approach used in utilizing that paradigm in developing typical software applications.

In this paper we will briefly introduce the concepts of object oriented knowledge representation followed by a discussion of its implementation in the LASER system.

2. Objects, Properties, and Values

LASER is a knowledge representation environment wherein knowledge is stored in the form of frame-style entities called objects. Each object is a simple data structure having zero or more elements called properties, each of which contains zero or more data known as values. With the aid of this data representation mechanism it is possible, for instance, to put together a descriptive symbolization of a dog:

```
dog:
  genus:      "Caninus_Dogus"
  diet_type:  "carnivore"
  food:       "rabbit" "dog_food"
  legs:       4
```

In the above example, "dog" is an object having 4 properties (genus, diet_type, food, and legs). The property "food" has two values -- the character strings "rabbit" and "dog_food" -- while the property "legs" has the single value -- the integer number 4.

Typically, an object contains knowledge of the type: concepts, processes, situations, and facts. The properties of the object indicate the taxonomy, structure, attributes, and methods pertinent to that object. A number of different data-types can be stored as values. This is enabled by the use of a catch-all data cell called a value-unit. Value-units contain information about the data being stored in them:

- the data-type,

- the data itself (or a pointer to where it can be found),

- a pointer to the next value-unit, if any

Value units can contain a variety of data-types:

- integer numbers,

- long integers,

- real numbers,

- double,

- strings,

- function pointers,

- objects,

- user-defined pointers,

- lists

Objects can be created by one of two ways: using the Top-Level command interpreter (a la Lisp), or by writing a C language program with the appropriate function invocations. Either way, one has to make use of LASER library functions which allow objects to be created, modified, deleted, accessed, and so on. For example, the LASER function "mkobj" can be used to create objects. And "mkprop" can be used to create the properties of an object. The "setval" function allows values to be assigned to properties.

The Top-Level Interpreter of LASER allows the user to interactively create and manipulate objects. Objects can be printed, with the aid of the "print" command, which prints out the object, its properties, values, as well as any associated meta-information. A "help" command causes a list of commands, to be printed. Elaborate help on each of the commands is available. For example, "help mkobj" will invoke a sub-process which causes the Unix manual entry corresponding to "mkobj", to be printed on the screen. Error detecting routines, trap most errors and report them to the user. The top-level interpreter facilitates user-interaction by eliminating the need for parentheses, commas, and so on.

An example of using the Top-Level is shown below:

```
mkobj dog
mkprop dog genus
mkprop dog diet_type
mkprop dog food
mkprop dog legs
setval dog genus "Caninus_Dogus"
setval dog diet_type "carnivore"
setval dog food "rabbit"
addval dog food "dog_food"
setval dog legs 4
```

The same process could have been performed in a C language program as follows:

```
mkobj("dog");
mkprop("dog", "genus");
mkprop("dog", "diet_type");
mkprop("dog", "food");
mkprop("dog", "legs");
setval("dog", "genus",
 MKSTRVAL("Caninus_Dogus"));
setval("dog", "diet_type",
 MKSTRVAL("carnivore"));
setval("dog", "food",
 MKSTRVAL("rabbit"));
addval("dog", "food",
 MKSTRVAL("dog_food"));
setval("dog", "legs",
 MKINTVAL(4));
```

In the above example for the C-language creation of the "dog" object and its associated properties and values, use has been made of a few macros (MKSTRVAL and MKINTVAL).

Other LASER library functions allow the user to delete objects ("delobj"), delete properties ("delprop"), access the current data in a property ("getval"), and so on.

3. Meta Information

Meta information is, typically, information about information. It allows the user to include specific information which can be accessed by other programs and allow data-validation and other checks to be performed on an automatic basis. It also is the basis of "data-oriented" programming. This meta-information is available in LASER as meta-objects, meta-properties, and meta-values. A "meta-object" is an "object" containing information about a particular "object". Similarly, a "meta-property" is an "object" containing information about a specific "property" of a specific "object". And so on...

So, in order to put together meta-information, you have to:

1. create the object about which meta-information is to be stored.

2. create the object containing the meta-information

3. connect the meta-information to the appropriate part of the object

An example of creating meta information is shown below: In this example, the first step (of creating the object and its properties) is skipped, for the sake of brevity. We will, therefore, assume that the object "dog" exists.

```
mkobj dog_diet_type_meta
mkprop dog_diet_type_meta
 valid_types
setval dog_diet_type_meta
 valid_types "carnivore"
addval dog_diet_type_meta
 valid_types "omnivore"

setmprop dog diet_type
 dog_diet_type_meta
```

In the above example, the meta-information associated with the property "diet_type" can be used by any function which is performing data-validation checks, to ensure that the data to be entered is of the type "carnivore" or "omnivore".

4. Methods

As mentioned earlier, function pointers can also be stored in objects. This allows for objects to contain both data and programs. Data can be stored in the manner shown in the previous section, but programs require a slightly different form of handling. This is necessitated because the programs are, typically, C programs, pointers to which have been created in advance by the user.

example:

```
mkobj("dog");
mkprop("dog", "bark_method");
mkprop("dog", "voice");
setval("dog", "voice",
 MKSTRVAL("bow-wow"));
addval("dog", "voice",
 MKSTRVAL("woof_woof"));
addval("dog", "voice",
 MKSTRVAL("grrr_ruff"));
```

191

```
addval("dog", "voice",
 MKSTRVAL("yelp"));
setval("dog", "bark_method",
 MKMTDVAL(bark_fn));
```

```
............................................
............................................
bark_fn()
/* bark_fn is a function which
determines the voice used by
the dog depending upon the
dog's objective:

  to greet another male dog
                  ==> bow_wow
  to sound macho near attractive females
                  ==> woof_woof
  to bluff intruder by fierce-sounds
                  ==> grrr_ruff
  to get another dog biscuit from master
                  ==> yelp
*/
```

In the above example, the property "bark_method" gets the address of the function "bark_fn". The function can be invoked by means of the LASER function "evalobj". This is synonymous to passing messages between objects. If such an object had been created, the function bark_fn could be invoked as follows:

```
  /* from within a C-language program as: *

     evalobj("dog", "bark_method");

  /* and from the LASER top-level by: */

     message dog bark_method
```

5. Relations

The interaction of the knowledge stored in objects can be carefully regulated and even enhanced by the use of "relations" to show their interconnections. This mechanism is known as "relation", and allows a hierarchy of structures to be created. This hierarchy allows for generic and specific object creation, which allows for local refinement of generic objects. Three relations have been defined: isa, instance, and partof.

Objects which are related by the "isa" relation inherit information which is not available locally (i.e., within the object itself). Such information is accessed, by traversing the inheritance path, as defined, by the "isa" relations of connected objects. For the sake of efficiency, once such information is accessed, it is recreated at the local level.

Objects which are related by the "instance" relation inherit information in a manner similar to the "isa" related objects. The major difference lies in the fact that the use of the "instance" relation causes that object to be a terminal node in the inheritance path of that particular relationship. In other words, an object which is an "instance" of some other object cannot have any other object beneath it (hierarchically speaking).

An example of the use of relations is shown below: Again, for reasons of brevity, the steps involved in creating the object "dog" have been left out.

```
mkobj poodle
mkprop poodle bark
mkprop poodle utility
setval poodle bark "YELP"
setval poodle utility "pet"

relate poodle isa dog

mkobj fifi
mkprop fifi owner
mkprop fifi color
setval fifi owner "Zsa_Zsa_Gabor"
setval fifi color "black"

relate fifi instance poodle
```

In the above example, fifi is an "instance" of a poodle, which "isa" dog. So fifi has all the characteristics of a poodle which in turn has all the characteristics of a dog. So, whereas there can be other objects which are "isa" related to "dog" and "poodle", there cannot be any object which is "isa" related to "fifi".

Besides the standard relations: "isa", "instance", and "partof", user-defined local relations can also be employed to show the interconnection between objects. In order to use a local relation, one must, of course, define the relationship. This is performed by the LASER function "mkrel". It should be understood that local relations show the interconnection between the one object (for which the relationship is defined) and the other objects to which it is being related to. In other words, the same relation cannot then be employed by two other objects without redefinition.

```
  example:
```

```
mkobj Zsa_Zsa_Gabor
mkrel Zsa_Zsa_Gabor owns owned_by
relate Zsa_Zsa_Gabor owns fifi
```

In the above example, a new object Zsa_Zsa_Gabor has been created, and a local relationship with name "owns" (and inverse-name "owned_by") has been created. The "relate" statement then causes Zsa_Zsa_Gabor to "own" fifi (and automatically causes fifi to be "owned_by" Zsa_Zsa_Gabor).

Incidentally, if Zsa_Zsa were to own some other entity, say fido, then that fact could be incorporated by:

```
addrel Zsa_Zsa_Gabor owns fido
```

Note that "addrel" was used and not "relate". This is due to the fact that relate is a destructive operation, i.e., it is similar to "setval" in that any previous values are erased, and the single new value is inserted in that place. So, if "relate" had been employed, rather than "addrel" in the above example, then poor "fifi" would have been left without an owner.

A side-effect of the "relate" function is the automatic creation of the object to which the current object is being related. Example:

```
mkobj king_tut
relate king_tut isa mummy
```

This will cause an object called "mummy" to be created, if it doesn't already exist. Finally, relations can be destroyed by the use of the "delrel" function. It eliminates all values associated with that relationship in the object in question, as well as the corresponding inverse links in its relatives. example:

```
delrel king_tut isa
```

6. Reasoning in Alternate Worlds

In rule based programming using the forward/backward chaining as well as simulation it will be necessary to make temporary changes to a knowledge base.

These incremental changes may be organized as a tree of data bases which can be used to store the effects of applying alternate rules or to show the performance of alternate scenarios in case of a simulation model.

6.1. General information

The world mechanism in LASER permits the user to organize objects in in a hierarchical manner. Each world acts as a separate object data base. worlds are organized in a tree i.e. initially only a root world exists, each newly created world will be a child of an already existing one. The search for objects is performed in the current world and its ancestors. Identical objects may exist in different worlds but all objects in a given world must have unique names. The removal of a world causes the removal of all its siblings.

Here is a brief description of the world commands:

- delete_world - remove a world (all siblings will also be removed)

- child_world - find names of all children worlds

- get_world - get name of currently seted world

- is_world - check if a world exits

- join_world - join world with its parent, resolve conflicts in favor of child's objects

- make_world - create a world, the user will have to specify a name and the name of the parent world.

- parent_world - find parent world name

- set_world - set world, by default the root world will be set.

6.2. Implementation

Object names in a given world are hashed and the resulting value is the address of a hash table entry that is the root of a tree of objects. worlds are a hierarchy of hash tables with "ROOTW" as a root. worlds are described by a "world" object :

```
world
   parent :
   children :
   objects :
```

This is an example of a world, ROOTC its parent is "ROOTW" and children are world1 and worldA21.

```
ROOTC
  instance:world
  parent : "ROOTW"
  children : "world1" "worldA21"
  objects: "foo1" "foo2" "foo3"
```

The current world can be changed using the set_world command. By default the current world is "ROOTW".

6.3. Inheritance mechanism.

Destructive LASER commands[1] have the following behavior :

- If the object to which a command is referring to exists in the current world, there is no change in behavior.

- If the object to which a command is referring to is not present in the current world, parent worlds will be searched.

- If the property to which a command is referring to is not present in the current world, parent worlds will be searched.

- If an object is related to an object from an ancestral world, the parent object is moved to the current world and an inverse property is created. The possibility of searching for properties through related objects from other worlds is preserved.

Non-destructive LASER commands such as evalobj, getnth, getval and message search for objects and properties in ancestral worlds.

Meta information is local to a world and will not be moved across worlds.

_____

[1]
    addrel, addval, delnth, delval, mkprop, mkrel, popval, pushval, relate, setval, unmkrel

6.4. Super Root

The concept of a super root world is introduced. This world holds all system related objects which are otherwise invisible to the normal user. The super root world cannot be set or deleted and acts as a write only memory.

7. Software Development with LASER

7.1. C language based programs

In the previous sections, it has been shown how to create and modify objects. This ability would be of little value were it not for the fact that this data manipulation capability can be combined with functions to produce meaningful programs. C is the language of choice when interacting with LASER. By using C, the user can manipulate and exploit LASER, at a very low level, if necessary. However, other functions which do not directly access LASER objects can be written in other languages and compiled/linked with LASER routines. This will be specified in a later section.

In order to invoke LASER functions from the user's program, the following steps are necessary:

- include a laser.h file

- link with a laser library

The following example shows a C language program which utilizes some LASER functions.

```
%include <laser.h>
%include <string.h>

main{
mkobj("dog");
mkprop("dog", "diet_type");
mkprop("dog", "prey");
mkprop("dog", "taste");
mkprop("dog", "size_up");
setval("dog", "diet_type",
 MKSTRVAL("carnivore"));
setval("dog", "prey",
 MKSTRVAL("moose"));
setval("dog", "taste",
 MKMTDVAL(to_eat_or_not_to_eat));
setval("dog", "size_up",
 MKMTDVAL(fight_or_run));
..............
..............
}
to_eat_or_not_to_eat()
{
```

```
. . . . . . . . . . . . . . . . . .
/* function which determines
   whether the dog should eat
   its prey */
}

fight_or_run()
{
. . . . . . . . . . . . . . . . . .
/* function which determines
   whether the dog should
   fight or run */
}
```

In the above example, the address to the functions "fight_or_run", and "to_eat_or_not_to_eat" are stored in the object "dog" by means of the macro MKMTDVAL. In order to invoke these functions, the corresponding object and property need to be evaluated. This can be done as follows:

```
evalobj("dog", "taste");
```

This will cause the function "to-eat_or_not_to_eat" to be invoked.

8. Foreign Function access

Even though only C language functions may directly interact with LASER objects, procedures written in other languages can be used to help in the program development process. These programs can be separately compiled, and then linked with the rest of the programs. In fact, with the use of the "getaddress" and "cfasl" routines, it is possible to dynamically load object modules of foreign functions (non-C language functions). This mechanism can also be used to get the address of functions (foreign or C) at run-time and store them in objects. Whereupon, they can be invoked by evaluating that property of the object where they are stored.

9. Lisp based programs

It is now currently possible to combine aspects of LISP and LASER programming to produce an environment with the benefits of both systems. This is achieved by initially invoking the LISP environment, then employing LISP's own "cfasl" and "getaddress" mechanisms to load in the LASER image along with other LISP/LASER interface routines. At this stage, it is possible to create LASER objects using the LISP top-level, then invoke the LASER top-level and manipulate them, as necessary. This transition from LISP-LASER-LISP will allow practically unlimited power to the user. Work is in progress to allow LISP functions to be defined on the fly, inserted in LASER objects, so as to be invoked when needed.

10. Debugging with the Top_level Interface

During program development and debugging, it is easier to employ the Top-Level interpreter than elaborate test/print statements. In fact, as part of the debugging process, the top-level interpreter can be invoked from within the program, so that the user can temporarily examine and modify, if necessary, the object-space.

The predefined C function "laser" invokes the top-level. An example of its use, in a debugging mode, is shown below:

```
main()
{

. . . . . . . . . . . .
. . . . . . . . . . . .
user defined C initialization routines
. . . . . . . . . . . .

laser();

<use print, getval, setval, etc to
 examine/modify  the object space
 exit top-level by "quit">


. . . . . . . . . . . . .
other complex user-defined routines
. . . . . . . . . . . .

laser();

. . . . . . . . . . . . .
<enter top-level of laser in order
 to examine/modify  the object space;
 quit top-level when satisfied>
. . . . . . . . . . . .

<continue this process as often
 as necessary>

}
```

In addition to the ability of examining the state of the program (i.e.the collection of objects) using the LASER top-level function, we can also "instrument" selected objects to display themselves whenever they are accessed or modified. This facility may be useful in constructing "self disclosing" programs which facilitates managing large programs which get continuously modified over a long period of time by diverse groups.

195

11. Conclusion

In this paper we have briefly touched upon the knowledge representation features of the LASER system which plays a central role in representing concepts involved in different programming paradigms. Further work is under way to further generalize the concept of object relations presented here.

12. Acknowledgement

We wish to thank A. Patil and N. Husain who built the original prototype of LASER and other members of the Artificial Intelligence Laboratory and numerous graduate students who helped debug the system. Thanks are also due Digital Equipment Corporation and the Energy Research Center at West Virginia University for supporting several related projects in the A.I. Laboratory.

Expert systems on microcomputers*

Abstract: *The increasing popularity of expert systems has led to a demand to apply expert systems technology in a wide variety of computing environments. As a result, various efforts have been made to implement expert systems on microcomputers. This article reviews some of the ongoing work on tools for the development of microcomputer-based expert systems. Some specific application areas are noted, and a brief discussion of the advantages and disadvantages of implementing expert systems on microcomputers is presented.*

PAUL E. LEHNER STEPHEN W. BARTH

*PAR Technology
Corporation
PAR Technology Park
220 Seneca Turnpike
New Hartford
NY 13413
USA*

Introduction

One popular area within Artificial Intelligence today involves the development of knowledge-based expert systems. Expert systems are designed to assist users with domain specific problem solving expertise, by encoding the same problem solving heuristics that are used by human experts. Expert systems have been developed for a wide spectrum of problem areas including chemical spectrogram analysis [1], medical diagnosis [2], mineral exploration [3], genetic engineering [4] and computer system configuration [5]. Many other applications of this technology have been developed or are currently in progress. Most of these systems were or are being developed using versions of the Lisp programming language on large main frame computers (e.g., the DEC-10), or, in recent years, machines with specialized Lisp processors.

With the increasing popularity of expert systems, there has been a corresponding increase in the demand to apply expert system technology in a wide variety of computing environments. This demand has resulted in various efforts to implement expert systems on microcomputers. Several of these efforts have demonstrated that certain knowledge-based programming techniques can be taken out of the Lisp environment in which they were originally developed and moved into the more standardized and structured programming environment needed to make efficient use of the limited capabilities of microcomputers.

This article reviews some of the ongoing work in the development of microcomputer-based expert systems. Some specific application areas are noted, and a brief discussion of the advantages and disadvantages of implementing expert systems on microcomputers is also presented.

An earlier version of this paper appears in Applications in Artificial Intelligence, *ed. S. Andriole, Petrocelli Books, Princeton, 1984.*

2. Microcomputer-based expert system tools

A number of different software systems have been designed for implementing expert systems on microprocessor-based computer systems. All are problem independent tools for building expert systems. They use a variety of inference mechanisms and knowledge representation schemes. All are currently being used for a wide variety of expert system applications, and are undergoing enhancements or improvements for future releases. They run on a variety of microcomputer-based computer systems, including the more popular personal computers with mini-floppy or Winchester disk storage capabilities. Some of the systems can run in as little as sixty-four Kbytes of memory with small knowledge bases, but with more memory larger knowledge bases are possible. The systems to be described, and their developers are listed in Table 1, along with hardware and memory requirements. Hardware is described in terms of some of the kinds of microcomputer systems on which the software has been installed. Memory requirements are listed as the minimum or recommended amount of bytes of memory required to run the software. Most of these systems are commercially available. AL/X, in fact, was the first expert system building tool to be commercially licensed. Some of the specific application areas of the systems are described in Table 2.

2.1 AL/X

The first significant effort in the implementation of expert system capabilities on microcomputers was AL/X (Advice Language/X) [6, 7]. It was developed by Intelligent Terminals Ltd., under the direction of Professor Donald Michie and sponsorship of British Petroleum Development Ltd., at the Machine Intelligence Research Unit of the University of Edinburgh, Scotland. AL/X which operates on computer configurations as small as an Apple II+ with sixty-four Kbytes of memory, provides an inference engine, rule description language and consultation system capability that is modeled after Prospector [3] and EMycin [8]. The original application was for fault diagnosis on North Sea oil production platforms. AL/X is designed to be used with any set of rules supplied to it in the format of the AL/X rule description language. It can be applied to a particular problem domain by simply creating a file with domain specific rules that represent the relevant problem solving expertise.

For comparison purposes, AL/X will be described in some detail. Its design illustrates the microcomputer implementation of some techniques, drawn from early successful work in expert systems, that are also incorporated in several of the other microcomputer-based systems described below.

With AL/X, as in Prospector, rules are represented in the form of an inference network. As illustrated in Figure 1, an inference network contains top level hypotheses, called goal hypotheses, which are decomposed into various

Reprinted with permission from *Expert Syst.*, vol. 2, no. 4, pp. 198–208, Oct. 1985.

Table 1. *Selected Microcomputer-based Expert System Tools*

System	Developer	Hardware	Required Memory
AL/X	Intelligent Terminals Ltd. 15 Canal St., Oxford OX2 6BH, UK	APPLE II + LSI 11/02 IBM PC	64K
ACLS	Intelligent Terminals Ltd. (see address above)	APPLE II + IBM PC	64K
APES	Dept. of Computing, Imperial College University of London, 180 Queens Gate, London SW7 2BZ, UK	IBM PC (any machine with Micro-PROLOG	128K
ERS	PAR Technology Corp. 220 Seneca Turnpike New Hartford, NY 13413	IBM PC/XT	256K
DELTA	General Electric Research and Development Center Schenectady, NY 12345	PDP-11/23	
GEN-X	General Electric Research and Development Center (see address above)	IBM PC LSI-II	256K
K:base*	Gold Hill Computers 163 Harvard St. Cambridge, MA 02139	IBM PC	512K
M.1*	Teknowledge Inc. 525 University Ave. Palo Alto, CA 84301	IBM PC	128K
Personal Consultant*	Texas Instruments Inc. P.O. Box 809063 Dallas, TX 75380	TI Professional Computer	512K
RuleMaster*	Radian Corp. P.O. Box 9948 Austin, TX 78766	IBM PC/XT	512K
TIMM*	General Research Corp. P.O. Box 6770 Santa Barbara, CA 93160	IBM PC/XT IBM PC/AT	640K

* M.1 and T.1 are trademarks of Teknowledge Inc.,
  K:Base is a trademark of Gold Hill Computers Inc.,
  The Personal Consultant is a trademark of Texas Instruments Inc.,
  RuleMaster is a trademark of Radian Corporation
  TIMM is a trademark of General Research Corporation

levels of sub-hypotheses that are further broken down into specific items of evidence that can support those hypotheses. Directed arcs in Figure 1 indicate the antecedent-consequent relationships in the rules. For example, the arc from H3 to G1 indicates a rule of the form

IF H3 THEN (to some degree) G1

and the arcs from E1 and E2 to A1 indicate a rule of the form

IF E1 AND E2 THEN (to some degree) A1

Each node in the inference net has an associated prior degree of belief. The prior degrees of belief for evidence nodes are updated by asking the user for an observation on the evidence that the node represents. Rules are defined for combining degree of belief values of antecedent nodes into updated degrees of belief for consequent nodes. Available combination rules, using the inference net example in Figure 1, are illustrated in Figure 2. The nodes labeled A1, 01, and N1 have their degrees of belief updated respectively by the *and*, *or*, and *not* combination rules, using the degrees of belief of the nodes linked to them as antecedents. All other links between nodes in Figure 1 indicate the use of the Bayesian updating rule. The link from E5 to H2 illustrates this rule. The Bayesian weights of evidence, pw, the positive weight, and nw, the negative weight, are used to determine, by interpolation on the degree of belief of E5, the weight of evidence W. W is

Table 2. *Some Microcomputer-based Expert System Applications*

System	Applications
AL/X	oil production platform fault diagnosis
ACLS	induction of rules for classifying chess and game positions
APES	determining eligibility for social security benefits, pipe corrosion diagnosis, suitability of sites for dam construction, care for terminally ill patients
ERS	interpreting military sensor information, aircraft design for maintainability evaluation
DELTA	troubleshooting for diesel locomotives, plastic injection molding equipment process controller design
GEN-X	troubleshooting for jet engines, industrial process control
RuleMaster	severe storm forecasting transformer fault detection
TIMM	financial analysis personnel management insurance underwriting for yachts tuning the Vax VMS operating system
K:base	financial analysis of interest rate swaps
M.1	various demonstration systems for the knowledge engineering tutorial, T.1

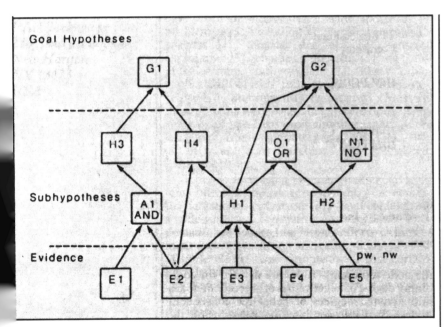

Figure 1. *Sample Form of an Inference Network*

AL/X, during a consultation session, consist primarily of answering system questions, and occasionally requesting an explanation of the inference process. For example, for the simple inference net in Figure 3, from a rule base for diagnosing automobile engine problems, a consultation session such as listed in Figure 4 is representative. User responses are listed in bold type. Italicised comments are added to describe AL/X operation. (This example is a portion of one developed in [7] to illustrate knowledge engineering with AL/X).

AL/X was originally developed on a PDP 11/34 under the Unix* operating system. It was written in standard Pascal (as defined in [9]). AL/X has been installed on an Apple II+ and an LSI-11/02 under UCSD Pascal, a Cromemco Superbrain under Pascal/M, all with sixty-four Kbytes of memory, and on an IBM PC, which can have in excess of 512 Kbytes of memory. AL/X has also been installed on a number of larger main-frame computers under various operating systems and Pascal language implementations. Since Pascal is available for most microcomputers, transferring AL/X to other microprocessor environments does not present any difficulties.

With sixty-four Kbytes of memory, AL/X can process about one hundred rules in a single consultation session. It is possible, however, to process a much larger rule base by decomposing it into smaller rule sets and storing each rule set in a separate file. AL/X would then proceed through several consultation sessions, one for each rule

then added to the degree of belief for H2 to obtain an updated value for the latter.

In a consultation session, AL/X attempts to evaluate the degree of belief of a goal hypothesis by chaining down the inference net, identifying the evidence items that affect the goal hypothesis, and querying the user about each relevant item of evidence. Consequently, user interactions with

★ Unix is a trademark of Bell Laboratories.

Type of Rule	Degree of Belief Calculation
AND	Deg[A1] = min[Deg[E1], Deg[E2]]
OR	Deg[O1] = max[Deg[H1], Deg[H2]]
NOT	Deg[N1] = −Deg[H2]
Bayesian	Degree[H2] = W + Deg[H2], where W is calculated by a linear interpolation on Deg[E5] between the positive and negative weights, pw and nw, linking E5 to H2.

Figure 2. *AL/X Degree of Belief Propagation Rules*

set. In this way, for instance, AL/X could process a rule base of the same size and structure as Prospector's, although extra processing time would be required for transitions between rule bases.

2.2 ERS

A second system that supports expert system implementation on microcomputers is ERS (Embedded Rule-based System) [10]. ERS is like AL/X in that both systems have inference engines similar to the one found in Prospector, and both systems can be used to implement expert systems in multiple problem domains. However, unlike AL/X, ERS is not simply a consultation system building tool, but is also designed to support development of expert systems that function as 'intelligent interfaces'. Specifically, instead of asking the user questions to ascertain basic pieces of evidence, ERS can call up any of a set of application specific primitive functions to evaluate evidence nodes. These primitive functions, in turn, can consult (get input from) various databases for factual information.

An example of an expert system that operates as an intelligent interface is the Dart decision aid [11], which provides expert advice to an analyst on interpreting information from various sources. At the heart of the Dart system, which operates on a Vax 11/780, is the same application independent inference engine component found

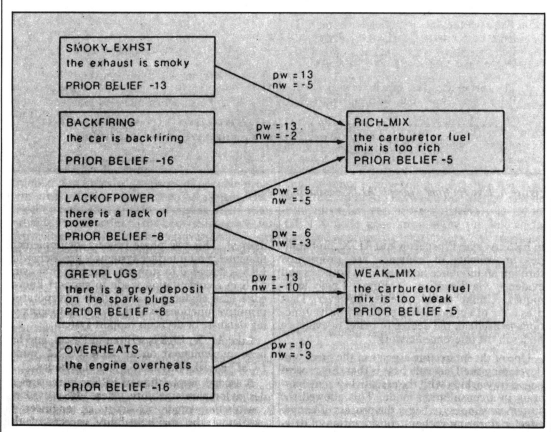

Figure 3. *A sample inference network*

```
The current goal is whether or not
the carburettor fuel mix is to rich (rich-mix)
Current degree is -5.0.

How certain are you that the exhaust is smoky?
>5

How certain are you that the car is backfiring?
>c
              (The c command provides the "chain of reasoning", the node path
              from a particular question to the current goal).

The car is backfiring (backfiring)
with degree -16.0
     is evidence for (pw =  13.0  nw =  -2.0)
The carburettor fuel mix is toorich (rich-mix)
with degree 8.0


How certain are you that the car is backfiring?
>-5

...that there is a lack of power?
>3

After considering all significant questions,
the degree that the carb fuel mix is toorich (rich-mix)
initially was -5.0. It is now  11.0.


There are no more significant questions for the current goal

************************************************************************************
Investigated goals with degree of belief >=  0.0 are:

The carb fuel mix is toorich (rich-mix)
Prior degree was  -5.0. Current degree is  11.0.

Other goals with degree >=  0.0 are:

The carburettor fuel mix is tooweak (weak-mix)
Prior degree was  -5.0. Current degree is  1.0.

************************************************************************************
              (At this point, AL/X would begin to consider yet unanswered evidence
              for the weak-mix goal).
```

Figure 4. *Excerpt from a sample AL/X consultation session*

in ERS. As with Prospector and AL/X, probabilities or weights of evidence are propagated through an inference network of hypotheses and evidence via Bayesian or Fuzzy Logic techniques. Unlike those systems, however, Dart uses a set of application specific primitive functions to evaluate the degree of belief of evidence nodes in the inference network.

One of the interesting aspects of the process of developing the Dart rule base is that this process began by working with the essential system operating in a consultation mode. This allowed the system developers to begin the process of knowledge engineering without consideration of database interfaces. Primitive functions for the evidence nodes encoded in the inference network were gradually incorporated as they became well defined. This two phase process for implementing intelligent interface systems is precisely what ERS is designed to support. Namely, first using ERS in a consultation made to support knowledge base engineering, and then incorporating primitive functions to tie the system into an existing database or decision support system.

Like AL/X, ERS is written in Pascal, and has been implemented on an IBM PC/XT under UCSD Pascal, with 256 Kbytes of memory.

A second, application of ERS is in the area of design for maintainability, where ERS is used in a consultation mode to assist an engineer in evaluating the maintainability aspects of the designs for a large complex system. The Maintainability Design Expert System [12] performed this application for a particular kind of aircraft.

2.3 Delta

Delta, Diesel-Electric Locomotive Trouble-shooting Aid, is an expert system to assist maintenance personnel in isolating and repairing diesel train engine problems [13]. It has been developed by General Electric Corp. at its Research and Development Center in Schenectady, NY. While it was developed with a particular application in mind, the architecture and software of Delta is flexible and general purpose and can be applied to a variety of fault diagnosis or troubleshooting problems. In fact, Delta is also being applied to troubleshooting for plastic injection molding equipment and, in a Sacon-like [14] system to provide expert assistance for using computer software for process controller design.

Like AL/X, Delta is a consultation system and incorporates a software architecture consisting of a domain independent inference engine with a domain specific knowledge base. Delta, however, uses a hybrid inference mechanism that allows both forward reasoning, from facts to conclusions, and backward reasoning, to confirm or disprove hypotheses. The overall reasoning of the system is based on a troubleshooting paradigm that involves finding a fault, repairing it, and checking to see that no problems remain, repeating the cycle if necessary. Troubleshooting knowledge is represented as *and/or* rules that describe the conditions for detecting faults. A sample diagnostic rule in simplified form, for the diesel locomotive application is

IF:

      engine-set-idle
      AND
      fuel-pressure-below-normal
      AND
      fuel-pressure-gauge-ok

THEN:

      fuel-system-faulty.

The rules may contain necessary or sufficient conditions for detecting faults, and are partitioned into knowledge spaces of possible problem areas, such as the mechanical system, electrical system, etc., of a diesel engine. Meta-rules provide a smart index to the knowledge spaces for retrieving the relevant rule sets given an initial set of user specified fault symptoms. When a fault is isolated a treatment or repair prescription is provided. When the user has completed the prescribed repairs the system asks questions to confirm that the problem has been fixed, and continues on to check for other faults if problems remain.

Delta uses over 500 rules to assist a technician in locating and repairing problems with diesel engines. Diagnostic and repair knowledge is contained in approximately 300 rules, and the other rules provide· a Help system to answer user queries and provide additional information. A unique feature of the Delta system is an optional interface provided for a videodisc. The videodisc system provides visual and audio segments of training films to assist the technician in carrying out repair instructions and collecting the information to answer system queries. Also, Delta can use CAD files, stored in Tektronix standard format for providing help to the user; for example, schematics of the diesel engine system or its parts that are being analyzed.

The Delta system was originally implemented in Lisp but was translated into the Forth language for installation on microcomputers. The diesel locomotive troubleshooting application uses an PDP-11/23 microcomputer with a ten Mbyte Winchester disk, a portable videodisc player and a graphics display terminal. Field testing of Delta has begun at General Electric's locomotive repair facilities.

2.4 GEN-X

GEN-X, a Generic Expert system, is designed to assist a user with the knowledge engineering task for building an expert system, and produce an efficient compilation of the system for downloading to a variety of microcomputer environments [15]. It also was developed at General Electric's Research and Development Center. Like Delta, GEN-X is designed to be applied to troubleshooting or fault diagnosis problems. Applications of GEN-X are currently underway for troubleshooting in jet engines and industrial process control.

GEN-X provides a different approach to expert systems implementation than systems like AL/X. The GEN-X system consists of a knowledge manager, interpreters, and code generators. The knowledge manager provides an interactive graphics facility for knowledge base creation and editing. The user can choose among *and/or* networks, and inheritance network, or decision tables as a knowledge representation scheme. Interpreters use the knowledge base and user interface specifications to drive a consultation session. During the knowledge engineering phase, GEN-X is used to provide consultation sessions, and maintains separate knowledge base and inference engine components, like the architecture used in AL/X. When knowledge base development has reached a satisfactory level, the GEN-X code generators allow the knowledge base and appropriate interpreters to be translated into compact C, ADA, Pascal, and Fortran programs for execution in more constrained environments.

GEN-X is implemented in C using the portable C library and can itself be run on an IBM PC with a color graphic display terminal. Ideally, however, it would be used in a mainframe environment to generate code for downloading to target microcomputer-based systems. It is estimated that a knowledge base as large as 1000 *and/or* rules could be compiled by GEN-X for implementation on systems with 256 Kbytes of memory, and that non-trivial rule bases could be loaded into systems with as little as thirty-two Kbytes. Current applications contain approximately 100 rules and have been generated for IBM PC's and LSI-11's.

2.5 Apes

Apes, a Prolog expert system shell, is an expert system user interface, or shell, for the Micro-Prolog logic programming language [16, 17, 18]. Along with Micro-Prolog it was developed at Imperial College, London, under the direction of Professor Keith Clark.

Prolog is a programming language based on mathematical first order logic, that has been used for a number of AI applications and research [19]. It has been very popular with researchers in the European AI community, and, in addition, has been selected to play a major role in the development of the well-known Japanese Fifth Generation Machine project [20]. It has built-in mechanisms for deductive inference, and has a uniform representation for the facts and rules that make up a knowledge base. New facts can be derived from existing facts and the rules, via the built-in backtracking and efficient theorem proving mechanisms. Apes has been designed to provide explanation capabilities and other user interface features for Prolog to facilitate expert consultation system development.

Like AL/X, Apes has separate inference engine and knowledge base components, but allows the user to define the way that uncertain reasoning is handled. The user can select an inference mechanism like that used in EMycin, or a Bayesian one, (like AL/X). Other inference techniques are currently being incorporated into Apes. The mechanisms for uncertain reasoning can be combined with the logical deductive reasoning capability that the system derives from Prolog. An Apes knowledge base is a collection of Prolog statements, or clauses as they are called, representing the expert rules and facts of the problem domain.

Micro-Prolog is available for nearly any microprocessor-based system with sixty-four Kbytes of memory. The first Micro-Prolog release of Apes does not contain modules for uncertain reasoning, because sixty-four Kbytes is too small for the full Apes implementation, but the basic system has been implemented in Micro-Prolog systems on North Star Horizons, IBM PC's and IBM PC look-alike machines, all with mini-floppy disk drives.

Applications with Apes so far have used up to 400 Micro-Prolog clauses, (facts and rules). Some of the applications have been expert consultation systems for determining Social Security benefits, suitability of sites for dam construction, determining proper care for terminally ill patients, and pipe corrosion diagnosis. The application for determining proper care for terminally ill patients was sponsored by the Imperial Cancer Research Fund, and involved implementation of an EMycin-like system in Apes. An example of a rule from the Social Security benefits application, as formated by the Apes explanation facility, is

```
IF      not (david is-disqualified-by sex) and
        not (david is-a-juvenile) and
        david (study-status-OK) and
        david is-a-GB-resident and
```

```
        david  is-excused-or-registered-for-
            work and
        david needs-financial-help and
        not (david is-disqualified-by-trade-
            dispute)
THEN    david is-entitled-to sup-ben
```

where "david" was initially entered as the name of the person being considered for supplementary benefits. This formated version of an Apes rule is a straightforward translation of its Prolog form.

2.6 ACLS

ACLS, Analog Concept Learning System, allows a user to generate classification rules from examples or cases of a rules application [21]. It was developed at the Machine Intelligence Research Unit at the University of Edinburgh under the direction of Professor Donald Michie, and is based upon earlier work in inductive learning [22, 23]. ACLS is different from the other systems described so far in this article in that it requires a different kind, and, in some sense a lower level, of participation from an expert or domain specialist building the knowledge base.

ACLS provides a capability for describing the basic features or attributes of a classification problem, using them to describe a set of examples that illustrate the application of an as yet unknown classification rule, and from the examples generating a rule that accommodates them. In expert systems like AL/X, knowledge engineering involves obtaining the rules for problem solving directly from the domain specialists; in ACLS the expert descriptions of the important features of a problem are used to derive the rules for solving it.

Using ACLS involves first defining a set of primitive attributes and the set of classes upon which the classification problem depends. These are obtained from the expert and need not be complete or entirely relevant to the problem in the early iterations of the system. Next, a training set of examples is composed by the expert in the form of records with the values for the attributes of the example and the resulting class that the expert would assign to them. These are fed to ACLS and the system induces a rule in the form of a decision tree that accounts for the set of examples. Attributes that turn out not to be relevant are not used in the classification rule. ACLS can produce executable Pascal code, embodying the logic of the induced decision tree in the form of nested *if-then-else* expressions, that can then be used for classification of other data described by the set of attributes.

ACLS can be used interactively or in a batch mode to analyze the training set of examples. Interactively, the system allows the user to review the decision rule as it is revised by each new example that is provided. The role of the expert, aside from supplying the necessary attributes and training examples, is to evaluate whether the ACLS induced rule expresses his classification expertise accurately. ACLS essentially uses the list of examples to 'observe' the expert's behavior as a classifier and construct the simplest rule it can to describe that behavior. If initial attempts fail to derive a satisfactory rule, new examples or new sets of attributes can be added to the system.

The ACLS program has been written in UCSD Pascal, and has been implemented on the Apple II+ and IBM PC. An improved version of ACLS, called Expert-Ease, with a graphics and menu oriented user interface is being marked by Human Edge Corp. in USA and Thorn-EMI Computer Software Ltd. in Europe [24]. ACLS has been applied to derive rules for classifying chess end game positions as won, lost, or drawn.

2.7 RuleMaster

RuleMaster [25] incorporates the same inductive learning algorithm as found in ACLS into a broader expert system framework. It has mechanisms for hierarchical organization of the induced decision trees or rules, and for explanation of system reasoning. Induced rules are automatically coded as modules in the Radial language [25]. Radial provides mechanisms for linking modules together controlling rule execution, accessing external information sources, adding fuzzy set operators and adding explanation text.

The Radial language for representing rules offers a general purpose control mechanism based on finite automata theory. Each rule or decision tree corresponds to a state within a transition network in a module. After a rule is fired, control is passed to a new state within the same module. State transitions can be included as part of the examples from which a rule is induced. Control is passed between modules by hierarchical invocation.

Two applications of RuleMaster have demonstrated its utility. Willard [25] is a system for forecasting the likelihood of severe thunderstorms in the central United States. It consists of thirty modules each of which is a single induced decision tree. Using the mechanisms available in Radial, Willard can run in either a consultative or automatic mode. In the latter case, it obtains all the necessary information from National Meteorological Center files. The diagnosis for a storm is in terms of a high, low, or moderate likelihood, similar to that produced by the National Severe Storms Forecast Center (NSSFC). Preliminary performance tests of Willard, by comparing its predictions with those of the NSSFC, indicate that the system does as well if not better. Further testing and expansion of the system is currently underway.

Another application of RuleMaster aids in the analysis of transformer oil for transformer fault detection [25]. This system consists of twenty-seven modules, each with one or more rules. This latter system is nearing deployment as an expert system for use in an industrial environment by Hartford Steam Boiler Insurance and Inspection Company, the parent company of Radian. The system would aid insured customers in maintaining their transformers, and inspectors in early diagnosis of potential problems.

RuleMaster is written in C and runs under versions of the Unix operating system on IBM PC/XTs, Sun Microsystems, and DEC Vax computers.

2.8 TIMM

TIMM, The Intelligent Machine Model, [26] combines a knowledge engineering tool capable of automatic rule definition with an inference mechanism that uses inexact reasoning. An expert uses TIMM to first define the problem domain in terms of a set of attributes and their possible values or range of values. Sets of attributes may be grouped into cooperating blocks each with a unique decision factor, reflecting the structure of the problem domain. Decision factors can take on a range of values that indicate the potential advice of the system. For example, in a system for advice on loan applications, one current debt and income might be two attributes with ranges of values, and a decision factor might have values representing approval or rejection of the loan.

After problem domain definition, an expert trains TIMM to form production rules. The system uses the definition of the domain to generate plausible event conditions for which the expert presents the correct decision or advice. Also, the expert can specify attribute values that define interesting cases and record the correct decision factor value for those. The expert's decisions are recorded as production rules. TIMM provides facilities for checking the completeness of the rules by looking for situations where there are few rules to cover particular ranges of attribute values. Consistency checking is performed by searching for rules with similar conditions but inconsistent or contradictory results, and presenting them to the expert for consideration.

Once a rule base has been defined, TIMM can execute the rules to provide advice on a problem. The inference mechanism uses partial matching of rule conditions and a metric for determining similarity of conditions to determine which rules should be executed. Partial matching allows that not all of the conditions of a rule be matched exactly by the data of the current situation. Rule conditions that are specified as attributes having an ordered range of values are used to define a partial metric across the knowledge representation space. Using this metric allows closeness of match of the current situation data with rule conditions to be determined. In this way the TIMM inference mechanism is 'analogical'; if the current situation is similar to conditions described in the rule base, the rules that match it best will be used to infer advice on the problem.

Applications with TIMM, developed for its IBM PC versions, include systems developed for financial analysis, insurance underwriting for yachts, and personnel management. The TIMM/Tuner [26] applies TIMM to the problem of tuning the DEC Vax VMS operating system to yield maximum performance. A sample rule of the kind of rule used in TIMM/Tuner, without some of the detailed commentary which can be easily added to elucidate rules further, is

IF there is excessive swapping
AND there are free balance set slots
AND there is not enough available memory for all working slots
AND the page cache is not too large
AND big compute-bound processes consume the system
THEN use the command MOD username/ WSQUOTA = nnn/WESEXTENT = nnn to lower WSQUOTA and WSEXTENT which will reduce the amount of memory being used up by large processes so that other processes will not be swapped out as frequently.

TIMM/Tuner was used to obtain an average of 15% performance improvement in the Vax systems to which it was applied during beta testing.

TIMM is written in Fortran and runs on the IBM PC/XT with the 8087 Math processor chip, and on the IBM PC/AT with the 80287 Math processor chip, as well as larger computer systems with Fortran capabilities. On the IBM PC it requires 640 Kbytes of memory and a ten Mbyte Winchester disk, of which about five Kbytes is used for the TIMM software and knowledge base.

2.9 The Personal Consultant

The Personal Consultant, [27] a recent release by Texas Instruments, is an expert system development tool designed for the TI Professional Computer. Personal Consultant implements control procedures and rule structures essentially identical to those found in EMycin [8]. As a result, The Personal Consultant can be used to transfer EMycin applications to the TI Professional Computer environment.

The Personal Consultant is written in Lisp. The recommended configuration is the TI Professional Computer, operating under MS-DOS 1.1 or 2.1 with a ten Mbyte Winchester, and a minimum of 512 Kbytes memory. Using this configuration Personal Consultant can execute up to 400 rules.

2.10 M.1

M.1, [28] a recent release by Teknowledge, Inc., is also a tool for exploring and developing expert system applications. M.1 also implements control procedures and rule structures similar to those found in EMycin. As a result, it has the same advantage that the TI system has, namely that it can be used to transfer EMycin applications to a microcomputer environment. M.1 has been used to provide demonstration systems for Teknowledge's knowledge engineering tutorial package, T1. One of these systems is Sacon [14] for advice to engineers on the use of a complex structural analysis simulation program.

M.1 is written in Micro-Prolog. The recommended minimum configuration for M.1 is an IBM PC operating under DOS 2.0 with at least 128 KBytes memory. A color monitor and board is recommended. Using this configuration, M.1 can handle a knowledge base of up to 200 rules.

2.11 K:base

All of the microcomputer-based expert systems described above use more or less the same knowledge representation scheme. Specifically, they all require that domain knowledge be encoded as a set of independent rules to represent the heuristics used by experts, or that such rules be induced from examples given by experts.

One system that does not follow this common thread is K:base [29] K:base uses a knowledge representation format called frames. Frames are essentially static data structures that combine declarative information about objects with procedural information for using or manipulating those objects [30]. As compared to the rule-based approach, the frame-based approach may be more suitable for applications in which the knowledge base can be highly structured, and it also may facilitate the use of graphic displays for depicting the contents of a knowledge base.

K:base is a joint product, presently under development by Gold Hill Computers, Symbolics Inc. and Lehman Brothers. The initial application area for which K:base is being developed is the financial analysis of the desirability of an interest rate swap between two companies.

K:base is being developed in common Lisp. The target hardware environment is either a Symbolics 3600 Lisp machine, or an IBM PC configuration with at least 512 Kbytes of memory.

3. Advantages of microcomputer-based expert systems

Although the systems described above represent only a subset of the work on microcomputer-based expert systems it is clear from the variety and success of these systems that implementing expert systems on microcomputers is a serious option for potential users of this AI technology. The issue to be addressed, then, is that of determining the contexts under which it is desirable, or even feasible, to use microcomputers for expert system implementation.

Clearly, the primary motivations for implementing an expert system on a microcomputer involve the same factors that make microcomputers popular for other types of applications. Among them, their low cost, availability and transportability. The low cost and availability of microcomputer systems makes it possible to distribute cost effectively multiple copies of the same system. This, for instance, makes it possible for General Electric to distribute multiple copies of Delta for use at different centers.

With regard to transportability, the small size and robust design of microcomputer systems make them appropriate for applications where physical space is limited and harsh environments may be encountered, such as the North Sea oil platforms that AL/X was intended for. The physical convenience of a small microcomputer system also makes interactive, online knowledge engineering with experts at remote sites more feasible.

Overall, it appears that a primary advantage of implementing expert systems on microcomputers is that these computers provide potential users with a low risk opportunity to bring expert system capabilities in-house, and, as a result, determine the probable value of this technology for their applications.

4. Issues for implementing expert systems on microcomputers

With regard to determining the feasibility of a microcomputer-based expert system application, an important characteristic to note about the systems described in this article is that all of them implement capabilities and techniques that were previously developed and tested by the AI research community. Consequently, implementing expert systems on microcomputers appears to be most feasible where a good prototype of the proposed system already exists in the AI research domain. This makes it possible to generate precise specifications for re-implementing the system software on microcomputers with memory and storage space limitations.

Another issue is the size of the knowledge base, and hence the size and kinds of problems, that can be handled by microcomputer-based expert system tools. Clearly, microcomputer-based expert systems face the memory and disk storage restrictions imposed by microcomputer systems, and thus face limitations on the size of problems that can be addressed. The expert system applications described in this article have been directed toward what the AI community now recognizes as small or low medium sized problems, requiring in the order of hundreds of rules. Being able to estimate the size of knowledge bases required for a problem domain is thus a critical issue for the designer considering a microcomputer-based expert system as a final product. Making such estimates is very difficult, to say the least, although the base of experience for such

judgements is widening with the increasing number of expert system applications. If, however, the trend of decreasing hardware costs resulting in increased microcomputer system capabilities continues, with desktop Vaxes or ruggedized, inexpensive Lisp machines becoming commonplace, then microcomputer-based expert systems should be able to keep pace with the development of larger expert system applications, and the issue of estimating the size of knowledge bases will remain only as important as it is for applications developed on larger mainframes.

Another issue to be considered for any particular application, is the amount of knowledge engineering required during the different development phases of the system. Most of the systems described in this article take the approach of implementing the full range of expert system capabilities in a microcomputer environment, including explanation mechanisms and knowledge engineering tools. GEN-X, however, offers the approach of knowledge base compilation and downloading, leaving explanation and knowledge engineering tools to be used in the development environment on a larger machine. RuleMaster and ACLS offer a similar potential capability, in that the rules are coded in a programming language that could be executed independently of the portion of the program for inducing rules. For some applications, e.g. real time processing tasks, explanation and online knowledge engineering capabilities may be not important in the mature phases of system development, and may in fact hinder system performance if they require additional memory and processor cycles for maintaining data structures. Other expert system applications will require online explanations of system reasoning and tools for upgrading the knowledge base throughout their life cycle. Since very few expert system applications have gone beyond prototype or developmental stages, it remains to be seen whether current microcomputer-based expert system tools, enhancements to existing systems, or different kinds of microcomputer-based expert system tools will be developed to provide resolution of this issue.

References

[1] B.G. Buchanan and E.A. Feigenbaum, 'DENDRAL and Meta-DENDRAL: Their Applications Dimension,' *Journal of Artificial Intelligence*, 11, 1978; pp. 5–24.

[2] E.H. Shortliffe, B.G. Buchanan and E.A. Feigenbaum, 'Knowledge Engineering for Medical Decision Making: A Review of Computer-Based Clinical Decision Aids,' *Proc. IEEE*, 67, 1979 pp. 1207–1224.

[3] R.O. Duda, P.E. Hart and J. Gaschnig, 'Model Design in the PROSPECTOR Consultant System for Mineral Exploration', *Expert Systems in the Micro-electronic Age*, ed. D. Michie, Edinburgh University Press, Edinburgh, 1979.

[4] M.J. Stefik, 'Planning with Constraints', PhD Dissertation, Report No. STAN-CS-80-784, HPP-80-2, Computer Science Department, Stanford University, 1980.

[5] J. McDermott, 'R1: A Rule-Based Configurer of Computer Systems' Department of Computer Science, Carnegie-Mellon University, Report CMU-CS-80-119, 1980.

[6] J.E. Reiter, 'AL/X: An Inference System for Probabilistic Reasoning', M.S. Thesis, Department of Computer Science, University of Illinois, Urbana, Illinois 61801, 1981.

[7] A. Paterson, *AL/X User Manual*, Intelligent Terminals Ltd., 15 Canal St. Oxford, OX2 6BH, UK, 1981.

[8] W. van Melle, 'A Domain-Independent System that Aids in Constructing Knowledge-Based Consultation Programs', PhD Dissertation, Report No. STAN-CS-80-820, Computer Science Department, Stanford University, 1980.

[9] K. Jensen and N. Wirth, *Pascal User Manual and Report*, Springer-Verlag, New York, 1974.

[10] S.W. Barth, *ERS User Manual*, PAR Technology Corp., PAR Technology Park, 220 Seneca Turnpike, New Hartford, New York 13413, 1983.

[11] T. Figgins, S.W. Barth and K. Gates, *Functional Description for the Duplex Army Radio/Radar Targeting Aid (DART)* PAR Report 83-117, written for RADC Contract F30602-81-C-0263, PAR Technology Corp., PAR Technology Park, 220 Seneca Turnpike, New Hartford, New York 13413, 1983.

[12] P.E. Lehner and M.L. Donnell, 'Maintainability Design Expert System', PAR Technology Corporation Report, 1983.

[13] P.P. Bonissone and H.E. Johnson, 'An Expert System for Fault Diagnosis in Diesel Electric Locomotives', General Electric Corporate Research and Development Center, Schenectady, New York 12345, 1983.

[14] J. Bennet, L. Creary, R.S. Engelmore and R. Melosh, 'SACON. A Knowledge-Based Consultant in Structural Analysis', Heuristic Programming Project Report No. HPP-78-28, also Report No. STAN-CS-78-699, Computer Science Department, Stanford University, 1978.

[15] Personal communication from John W. Lewis, General Electric Corporate Research and Development Center, Schenectady, New York 12345, 1983.

[16] P. Hammond, 'APES: a detailed description', Research Report 82/10, Department of Computing, Imperial College of Science and Technology, University of London, 180 Queens Gate, London SW7 2BZ, UK, 1982.

[17] M. Sergot, "A Query-the-user facility for Logic Programming', *Integrated Interactive Computing Systems*, eds. P. Degano and E. Sandwell, North Holland, New York, 1983.

[18] F.G. McCabe, *Micro-PROLOG Reference Manual* Logic Programming Associates, 10 Burntwood Close, London SW18 3JU, UK, 1981.

[19] W.F. Clocksin and C.S. Mellish, *Programming in PROLOG*, Springer-Verlag, New York, 1981.

[20] E.A. Feigenbaum and P. McCorduck, *The 5th Generation*, Addison-Wesley, Reading, Massachusetts, 1983.

[21] A. Paterson, *ACLS User Manual*, Intelligent Terminals Ltd., 15 Canal St. Oxford, OX2 6BH, UK, 1982.

[22] E.B. Hunt, J. Martin and P. Stone, *Experiments in Inductive Learning*, Academic Press, New York, 1966.

[23] J.R. Quinlan, 'Discovering Rules by Induction from Large Collections of Examples', *Expert Systems in the Micro-electronic Age*, ed. D. Michie, Edinburgh University Press, Edinburgh 99.

[25] D. Michie, S. Muggleton, C. Riese and S. Zubrick, 'RuleMaster: A Second Generation Knowledge Engineering Facility' presented at the First Conference on Artificial Intelligence Applications, sponsored by the IEEE Computer Society, Denver, Colorado, 5–7 December 1984, also Radian Technical Report MI-R-623, 1984, Radian Corp., P.O. Box 9948, Austin TX 78766

[26] J. Kornell, 'A VAX Tuning Expert Built Using Automated Knowledge Acquisition', *Proceedings of the First Conference on AI Applications*, IEEE Computer Society, pp. 38–41, December, 1984.

[27] Texas Instruments Inc., P.O. Box 809063, Dallas, TX 75380- 9063, 1984, tel. 800-527-3500.

[28] Teknowledge Inc., 525 University Ave., Palo Alto, CA 84301, 1984, tel. 415-327-6640.

[29] Gold Hill Computers, 163 Harvard St., Cambridge, MA 02139, 1984, tcl. 617-492-2071.

[30] M. Minsky, 'A framework for representing knowledge'. In P.H. Winston (ed.) *The Psychology of Computer Vision*. McGraw-Hill, New York, 1975.

A Comprehensive Evaluation of Expert System Tools

John F. Gilmore, Kirt Pulaski, and Chuck Howard

Artificial Intelligence Branch
Georgia Tech Research Institute
Atlanta, Georgia 30332

1.0 ABSTRACT

Current trends in knowledge-based computing have produced a large number of expert system building tools. This onslaught of high-tech software stems from the discovery that expert systems can be effectively applied to a variety of industrial and military problem domains. A variety of vendors provide expert system prototyping and development tools which greatly accelerate the construction of intelligent software. Today's expert system tool generally provides the user with a friendly interface, an efficient inference engine, and formalisms that simplify the creation of a domain knowledge base. This paper presents a formalism for expert system tool evaluation and critiques an exhaustive variety of commercially available tools.

2.0 INTRODUCTION

The multitude of Expert System Tools (ESTs) available in today's marketplace combine to form an elite repertory of artificial intelligence software that can be used to construct prototype expert systems in a wide range of application areas. These prototypes are then progressively refined, eventually evolving into operative expert systems tailored to specific problem domains. Given any application area, the chances that one of today's ESTs will address the problem are quite high. It is worth noting, however, that the converse is not always true (i.e., given an EST, one should not expect to be able to tackle problems in all application areas).

State-of-the-art ESTs, by virtue of their design and artificial intelligence capabilities, possess certain inherent constraints which better suit them to particular problem areas. The more constrained an EST is, the greater the chance that it will only function in a single problem domain. An analogy exists to Heisenberg's Law of Uncertainty, which states that as the certainty in location of a particle is increased, the certainty of its momentum decreases, and vice versa. In terms of ESTs, offering more constrained ways of representing and manipulating knowledge decreases the applicability of the expert system tool. If a wide applicability is desired, then a tool offering flexibility in representation and control should be sought. The problem with this idea is that no one EST will be able to maximize both.

The spectrum of today's ESTs ranges along a dimension of constraint in knowledge representation and manipulation. At one end of the spectrum is the almost totally unconstrained environment afforded by the LISP programming language. At the other end is the highly constrained environment that a full-fledged expert system tool offers. This paper surveys all software packages claiming to be an expert system building tool. Tools at the unconstrained end of the EST spectrum have not been included since they are essentially symbolic programming languages, and not actually expert system building tools by our definition. This survey thus covers the spectrum from production rule languages like ROSIE and OPS5, to hybrid tools such as KEE and ART.

Perhaps the most limiting factor of an expert system tools' computing power is its host machine. Embedded in this dimension is a price trade-off between the machine and the tool. The most powerful ESTs run on expensive machines and tend to be large and expensive themselves. Alternately, an abundance of computing power may not be desired, or the user may wish to integrate the EST into existing small scale hardware such as a PC. These ESTs are not extremely powerful but run on inexpensive machines and are for the most part small and inexpensive. Although some ESTs run on both small and large computers, the very fact that one version runs on a PC, and another version on a LISP machine indicates that these tools will have differing capabilities (i.e., just because the name is the same does not mean you get the same product).

This paper is divided into two parts. First, a number of EST evaluation criteria are presented in order to expose potential users to the broad range of features available in current expert system tools. Second, an overview of thirty seven expert tools is presented to familiarize the user with the wide spectrum of current commercially available EST's. The goal of this paper is to provide the reader with the evaluation methodolgy and specific tool characteristics required to narrow the expert system tool selection process down to a small number of systems. The summary advises the reader on how to make the final choice, and includes references to sources of more specific technical details on some of today's best expert system tools.

3.0 Small Scale Expert System Tool Evaluation Criteria

In order to differentiate small scale ESTs, a set of discriminating dimensions is required. These dimensions should refer to features that define the ideal EST. The set of dimensions chosen for our comparative analysis is an extended version of the set compiled by Harmon [7]. For this paper all the known tools were gathered for which there was sufficient information, and measured them against our chosen set of dimensions. Table 1. shows how the top eight ESTs fared. A discussion of each dimension follows.

A. Methods of Reasoning

Generally speaking, five distinct methods of reasoning may be employed in an expert system tool. Methods of reasoning may be interpreted to mean the way in which knowledge is acquired, stored, and manipulated by an EST. Some ESTs use more than one method which is possible because eventually all the methods converge to the same underlying paradigm of rule-based knowledge. A discussion of the actual kinds of rules ESTs offer is located elsewhere in this work.

1. Simple Rule-Based Tools - These ESTs simply store an aggregation of IF-THEN rules input by the knowledge engineer. The rules all co-exist in a single knowledge base. The inference engine essentially searches sequentially to find which ones are applicable to the current situation. If a problem can be solved with fifty to two hundred rules then a simple rule-based tool may be adequate.
2. Structured Rule-Based Tools - A tool of this type utilizes IF-THEN rules input by the knowledge engineer. Unlike simple rule-based tools, the rules are subdivided into knowledge base partitions arranged in a structured hierarchy. This structure allows each partition to inherit information inferred by its ancestors. These ESTs are well suited to problems requiring a large number of rules, or problems that can be decomposed into subproblems.
Another advantage of structured rule base reasoning is in the area of non-monotonic reasoning. In essence, the firing of a knowledge base partition establishes a current belief by the system. Beliefs being worked on in lower levels of the hierarchy depend on the beliefs established at higher levels. Since the path of the inference engine can be viewed as a tree traversal through the hierarchy of rule partitions, inferential dependencies are easier to track. In this manner, truth maintenance applied to each rule partition can be utilized to consider a variety of hypotheses. Some of the more elaborate ESTs that employ structured rule bases do in fact exploit structured knowledge and offer the user an efficient and powerful non-monotonic reasoning capability.
3. Induction Tools - Out of the machine learning research labs has come a unique method of performing the knowledge entry phase of knowledge base construction. As an alternative to the two preceeding methodologies requiring a KE to compile his/her own rules then add them to the system, induction tools allow the KE to input a number of domain examples. The domain examples are then analyzed by the tool to produce a consistent set of rules to elicit end solutions equal to the examples when fired. While this permits the system to compile its own set of rules, current algorithms severely limit the complexity and usefulness of the knowledge representation that the examples are mapped into. Only when the domain permits an absolutely perfect set of examples to be constructed is this kind of tool useful. The use of an induction tool requires that the KE spend much time modifying and adding examples in an attempt to get the system to demonstrate the correct behavior. Induction tools are good for very simple domains that can be well described by examples, however when numerous exceptions and many interdependencies exist the KE will want more control over what rules are used by the system.
4. Logical Tools - These tools have rules in the form of Horn clauses. Rule firing is actually goal resolution, as dictated by predicate calculus. Logical tools operate fast and efficiently, although acquiring the logic rules may be a major problem. If the problem at hand lends itself to a rigorous logical analysis, a knowledge engineer capable of performing the analysis and producing good rules, then this is the desired system. These kinds of tools are more popular in Europe than the United States, and are more difficult to use.
5. Object-Oriented, Hybrid Tools - Tools of this type are the most sophisticated and difficult to use, although they are becoming easier to operate as new versions are released. These tools attack a problem from an object-oriented point of view. Problem elements, as well as rules, graphics procedures and menus, are all represented as some type of object. An object may contain facts, procedures, rules or pointers to other

Table 1a. Small Scale Expert System Tool Evaluation

Tool vs. Criteria Method	ES/P Advisor	Expert-Ease	Insight 2	M.1	PC Plus	TIMM	Nexpert	SeRIES-PC
Method of Reasoning								
* Simple	X		X	X			X	X
* Structured					X		X	
* Induction		X				X		
* Logic	X							
Problem Characteristics								
* Pools	S		S	S	M		M	S
* Solutions	M	M	M	M	M	S	M	M
* Certainty			X	X	X	X	X	
* Arithmetic	X		X	X	X		X	X
End User Interface								
* Screen	M	M	M	L	M	L	M	M
* Input	C	C	C	T	C	T	C	C
* M&U Answers	X		X	X	X	X	X	X
* Pruning			X				X	
* OnLine Help	X		X		X	X	X	X
* Interaction	M	F	F	M	S	M	F	M
Development Interface								
* KB Creation	WP	LE	WP	WP	LE	LE	WP	WP
* KB Editing				X	X		X	X
* KB Graphics					X		X	
* HOW & WHY	X		X	X	X		X	X
* Inf Tracing	X		X	X	X		X	X
* Apropos				X	X		X	X
* Saved Cases	X		X	X	X	X		
* Formatting			X		X			
Systems Interfaces								
* Embeddable					X			
* Data Hook			X	X				
* Other Lang	P		Pa		L			
Software Considerations								
* Language	P	Pa	Pa	P	L	F	A	L
* Compilation	X	X	X		X	X	X	
* Other Lang					L		L	
* Op. Sys	DOS	UCSD-P	DOS	DOS	DOS	DOS	DOS	DOS
* Lockable	X	X	X	X	X			

objects. The entire system then becomes a multitude of object hierarchies, where control is in the form of data-driven messages passing between objects.

Object-oriented hybrid tools usually require that the KE have a good understanding of both LISP and object-oriented programming. They are particularly useful in creating a complex graphical user interface, and when the problem is monitoring, modeling or simulating some ongoing process. These tools are very powerful but are difficult to build. Vendors typically have to extensively train clients just to get them to the point of creating a prototype. They are recommended for the most complex of problems where the prodigous effort required can be justified.

B. Problem Characteristics

Problem characteristics are a primary consideration in selecting an expert system tool except when the problem is not well known, or if the tool is to be applied to multiple problems with varying characteristics. Four factors should be considered in this area.

Table 1b. Small Scale Expert System Tool Evaluation

Tool Vs. Criteria Method	ES/P Advisor	Expert-Ease	Insight 2	M.1	PC Plus	TIMM	Nexpert	SeRIES-PC
Hardware Requirements								
* Host	P	PDV	PDV	PX	PXT	PX	M	P
* RAM (rec)	128	128	192 (256)	192	512 (768)	640	512	384 (640)
* Other (rec)	(C)		(2D)	(C)	(10M)	M (10M)		
Training and Support								
* Workshop			X	X	X			X
* Elec Mail								
* Hot Line				X				
* Consulting					X			
* Document.	X	X	X	X	X	X	X	X
Knowledge Representation								
* Uncertainty			X	X	X	X	X	
* Frames					X			
* Facts	X		X	X	X	X	X	X
Rule Firing								
* Forward			X	X			X	
* Backward	X		X	X	X		X	X
* Both							X	
Conflict Resolution								
* First Found	X			X	X		X	X
* Antecedent			X					
* Global					X			
Cost	$895	$695	$495	10K	$3K	$9.5K	$5K	$5K

Legend

```
Any Language  --- P  = Prolog; Pa = Pascal; L = LISP; F = Fortran
Pools         --- S  = Single; M  = Multiple
Solutions     --- S  = Single; M  = Multiple
Screen        --- M  = Menu  ; L  = Line-oriented
Input         --- C  = Choose; T  = Type
Interaction   --- S  = Slow  ; M  = Medium; F = Fast
KB Creation   --- WP = Word Processor  ;LE  = Line Entry
Host          --- P  = IBM PC; D  = DEC; V  = Victor;
                  X  = IBM XT; M  = Macintosh
Other         --- C  = Color Monitor  ; 10M = 10M Hard Disk;
                  2D = 2 Disk Drives  ; M   = 8087 Math Co-Processor
```

1. **Single/Multiple Partitions** - A partition is a grouped set of facts, data, rules, procedures, etc. The knowledge in a partition may be syntactically diverse while semantically the partition elements are closely related. If a problem lends itself to multiple partitions, it can typically be arranged into a hierarchy for a structured approach to solving the problem. As was mentioned before, using multiple partitions allows focusing of computation on subproblems and allows inheritance of information from ancestoral pools.

2. **Single/Multiple Solutions** - Some problems require only a single solution, while other problems may have numerous solutions from which the "best" one is desired. A tool supporting single solutions will halt upon finding the solution, whereas a tool supporting multiple solutions will continually search until all possible solutions are found and then determine a rank order of solutions according to a predetermined criterion.

3. **Certainty Factors** - Sometimes a problem will necessitate probabilistic knowledge as a means of assigning certainty to decisions and recommendations. In addition, a knowledge engineer may wish to attach confidence measurements both for and against

hypotheses and conclusions. Problems such as these require that the EST be capable of dealing with certainty factors. Because the world does not behave in a a strictly Bayesian or stochastic fashion, a number of ESTs exploit decision theory to supplement the inference process. These ESTs have ways of manipulating certainty factors so that conflicting information may be contrasted [1].

4. <u>Arithmetic Requirements</u> - Certain problems require the use of mathematical operations. While all ESTs offer at least comparison operations (e.g., less than, greater than, etc.), most tools are limited in their mathematical capabilities. Tools that allow calls to external languages such as Pascal or Fortran will no doubt satisfy whatever mathematical needs a problem may have.

C. End User Interface

A number of features are required to evaluate how the end user will interact with the resulting system. While it is true that the user interface may be constructed independently and independently call processes within the expert system, some ESTs simplify this construction by integrating its development with that of the expert system itself. The following features are helpful in determining the usability of the end user interface.

1. <u>Line/Menu Screen</u> - Convention line editors are the simplest interface while menu-oriented interaction with a system is both faster and friendlier.

2. <u>Multiple and Uncertain Answers</u> - Expert systems most often need to prompt users for answers to questions, or for recommendations with respect to courses of action. The user may not always know or be certain of an answer, or he/she may wish to give multiple answers. If the problem is tightly structured and single answers will always be known, then there is no need for a system with these capabilities. Most problems that involve judgment require this facility.

3. <u>Initial Pruning/Directed Search</u> - This refers to the ability that the user has to minimize the search space that the expert system must process to reach a solution. For example, if an auto mechanic knows that the car he/she is working on has an electrical problem, then he/she could relate this fact to the system at the outset of the session. Initial pruning would allow the system to concentrate on electrical problems and not be burdened with having to consider all other types of problems.

Directed search is the same idea as initial pruning, except it can be performed at any time during the session. Some tools allow the user to introduce new paths for the system to consider, in addition to simple pruning. This may be an important point to consider when evaluating an EST. If an expert system application requires that many questions be asked of the user, then not having any form of directed search would be cumbersome. The user would have to answer many irrelevant questions, waiting for the system to home in on the correct subproblem.

4. <u>On-Line Help</u> - Depending on the end user, there may be a need for explanation of the technical jargon and protocols used in presenting and solving the problem. Most tools allow the knowledge engineer to associate explanation information with the terms and protocols being used. When a user prompts for the explanation of a term not known to him/her, the information is readily available. This point would probably not make or break the decision on whether to buy an expert system tool or not, unless it were a very important problem characteristic.

5. <u>Fast/Slow Interaction</u> - This dimension heavily depends on exactly what the expert system's is intended use is. Most tools are written in conventional algorithmic languages or LISP, and can be compiled. These tools are serviceable in most applications. ESTs such as ART were designed for speed and problems that require the fastest possible feedback. Other tools use a LISP dialect that cannot be compiled and are quite slow. This is the case with a number of ESTs designed to run on personal computers.

D. Development Interface

In addition to considering how a resulting expert system will interact with its end users, one needs to weigh the development interface as well. This feature greatly affects the time required to attain a first prototype, and to make successive refinements of the evolving expert system. A good development interface offers the KE many aids in creating, manipulating and testing the knowledge. The following features are helpful in appraising an EST with respect to its development interface.

1. <u>Knowledge Base Creation</u> - All ESTs provide some method of creating and storing one or more knowledge bases. Tools that run on personal computers will usually require that the knowledge base (KB) be created outside of the development environment. For example, line editors, screen editors or full scale word processors may be used. This permits the KE to use an editor that he/she is already familiar with. Other ESTs provide an internal facility for creating and storing a KB.

2. <u>Knowledge Base Editing</u> - Once a KB has been created it is likely that many changes will have to be made. This feature is more important than the preceeding one because the time spent editing a KB will exceed the time it takes to initially create it. In the worst scenario, the KE will have to leave the development environment totally to make

changes to a KB. Upon returning to the development environment after using an external general purpose editor to make changes in a KB, the state of the EST is lost and the KE must test his changes from scratch. For this reason some small ESTs and most large ones provide some sort of on-line KB editing, even if the KB was created via an external editor. This maintains the state of the development environment.

Another point to consider is that an EST may perform compilation of its KB, and editing cannot be performed without recompiling the KB. Inductive tools fall into this category, as well as tools that map knowledge representations into Prolog-like assertions to attain speed-up.

3. <u>Graphically</u> <u>Displayed</u> <u>Knowledge</u> <u>Bases</u> - One of the nicest features to appear in current ESTs is a graphical representation of the KB. For example, some ESTs display a KB of frames by enclosing the given name of each frame in a box, and then connecting all the boxes by lines to show the structure of the hierarchy. The user can then browse through the KB, using the mouse to click on the boxes to display and edit the contents of a frame. This feature of displaying the KB graphically and being able to edit it at the same time imparts to a KE the ability to refine the expert system more rapidly.

4. <u>HOW</u> <u>and</u> <u>WHY</u> <u>Explanations</u> - Explanations in expert systems have received quite a lot of attention. It is generally agreed that giving an expert system the ability to answer HOW and WHY questions makes the system more usable. By asking these questions, the user has a chance to interrogate the expert system's line of reasoning, thereby establishing confidence in the system's correct conclusions. The ability to answer questions becomes even more important in the development of the expert system for debugging purposes. Hence, an EST that provides an explanation facility will offer faster development of an end system and will be able to gain the confidence of its end users.

The user may type "why" in response to a question that the system has posed. Tools usually answer this type of question by outputting some form of the current rule it is considering. So, the "why" can be interpreted as, "Why do you ask this question?", and the answer is, "Because I am trying to determine if X." The user may type "how" in response to a conclusion or recommendation that the system has made. This question usually is answered by outputting the rules and/or data that has led to the conclusion. Better ESTs may even allow additional types of questions to be asked, such as counterfactuals. In this type of question the user asks something like, "What would happen if X?", or "What if X were true?" Tools that can answer this type of question will usually forward chain from the given X, then output the conclusion that is reached.

5. <u>Inference</u> <u>Tracing</u> - A tool that extends inference tracing to the user will provide more sophisticated techniques of querying the system's performance. Usually a detailed list of the inferences made, and where they came from will be output to the user. Additionally, some way of further probing the inference chain for more detail is provided as well. Some of the large ESTs will even output a graphical representation of the inference chain, allowing the user to use the mouse to probe deeper.

6. <u>Apropos</u> <u>Facility</u> - Often times a KB will contain multiple references to an object or one of its attributes. For example, a KB that represents the parts that make up a machine might refer to some part number several times in rules, facts, frames, or any kind of knowledge structure. If the user wishes to know what knowledge structures are affected by changing the machine part, he would want some type of apropos facility. This type of facility lists all the knowledge structures that mentioned the part number so that the KE could see how changing the part might propagate a change of behavior in the system. This also allows a universal replacement to be performed as well, such as changing all references to part number A714 to A767. Some tools allow even more sophisticated apropos facilities, such as listing all the rules that conclude X, or all the frames that are children of Z. A good apropos facility can indeed speed up the development of an expert system.

7. <u>Saved</u> <u>Cases</u> - A useful method of incrementally developing an expert system is to have a store of cases. Cases are representations of well-known domain problems. The KE runs test cases on the system being developed, making the appropriate modifications to the expert system until the system can solve all the cases correctly and consistently. An EST that facilitates the storing and re-use of test cases saves a considerable amount of time.

8. <u>Screen</u> <u>Format</u> <u>Utilities</u> - Part of developing a usable expert system is specifying the interaction screens that will be encountered by the end user. Some tools provide format utilities that simplify the KE's task of engineering good interfaces. Icon editors, and utilities for specifying screen titles, window size and window placement, are among some of the desired format utilities.

E. System Interfaces

An EST will be powerful if it can be embedded into an existing system. The EST can then be treated as a kind of library module that can solve complex problems for the rest of the environment. Moreover, the EST will itself be made more powerful if it can call external modules to solve some of its information problems.

1. <u>Embeddable</u> - If an EST is embeddable, then it can be integrated into some pre-existing external environment. Embeddable ESTs are usually written in a system applications language like C and therefore embed into systems like a VAX; or they may be

written in LISP and are embedded into the LISP environment of the LISP machine they run on.

    2. Hooks to Databases - Considering the nature of a tool's information requirements, a decision must be made as to whether a conventional database would serve the expert system faster than its own KB. A large part of the knowledge that is to be fed to the EST may actually pre-exist in databases. Rewriting the database information into the EST's KB may be too much work to prove cost effective. For cases like these, some ESTs automatically provide calls to external databases (such as Dbase II). Other ESTs can be programmed to access external databases if the hook is created using the language underlying the EST.

    3. Hooks to Other Languages - In the same way that certain ESTs provide external calls to databases, they may also support calls to external languages as well. An EST with this feature might prove useful if much number crunching of input data needs to be done. For example, if the EST is written in LISP it would be desirable to call Fortran functions to act on the raw numerical data allowing the system to continue running in LISP with the computed results.

F. Software Considerations

An expert system tool by definition is a intelligent software package used to build an expert system. For this reason, consideration must be given to a tools software environment.

    1. Language of the Tool - This refers to the programming language that the tool is written in. ESTs will usually obscure the underlying language somewhat and offer the user a restrictive form of the language. If the developer wishes to extend the capabilities of the EST, then he/she must [a] be familiar with the underlying language, and [b] make sure that the EST provides access to the language.

    2. Compilation - ESTs that can be compiled run faster than ones that cannot, but a compiled system tends to limit on-line editing during development.

    3. Other Language Required for Tool Use - Some tools will require that another language already be running on the host machine before the EST will work. Other tools come as a complete package and do not require that an underlying language be available.

    4. Operating System Required for the Tool - Most small ESTs run on IBM PCs under MS-DOS. Large ESTs are embedded into the LISP environment of a LISP machine and do not require an operating system.

    5. Is the Tool Lockable? - If a tool can be locked, then an end user will not be able to alter the system's knowledge base (i.e. therefore its performance) once it has been established. This is desirable for an application where a KE creates a runtime version for distribution and use by designers.

G. Hardware Requirements

Expert system tools are originally made with a specific hardware configuration in mind. As they market increases, version of a tool developed for for machines arise. For these reasons, the host machine, memory requirements, and additional hardware options need to be explored.

    1. Host Machine - ESTs tend to be more delicate than most other programs, and may not run on "clones" of the machine they were designed on. For this reason, the manufacturer will usually guarantee support for their EST only if it is run on the intended host machine.

    2. RAM Required - Table 1 shows the RAM that is required to run each EST. The values in parenthesis are the RAM sizes recommended by the vendor and should be taken as the minimal RAM required for the EST to create a large expert system.

    3. Other Requirements - Some vendors require additional hardware to run their expert system tool. These recommendations are also located in Table 1.

H. Training and Support

The success of an EST depends on being able to train individuals unknowledgeable of programming in general (and AI in particular) to effectively use the tool. ESTs will be more cost efficient if the price for knowledge engineering consulting goes down. Moreover, some companies are working on additional AI tools that aid in the knowledge acquisition and engineering phases of constructing an expert system. Outside of these facts, vendors offer a variety of training methods to their customers in addition to basic software support.

    1. Workshops - The price of workshop attendance for some number of people is included in the purchase price of some ESTs when their EST is purchased. Workshops introduce the user to knowledge engineering, and may even guarantee continued assistance until a first prototype is constructed. For the most part, the buyer is usually on his own after the first prototype. If development personnel did not learn enough from the workshop, then refining the prototype to attain a working expert system will become costly since professional KEs may have to be contracted.

2. <u>Electronic Mail</u> - Several vendors provide electronic mail lines to the buyer so that ongoing support during the development of the expert system may occur.

3. <u>Phone Hot Line</u> - There are vendors who support their EST by means of a telephone hot line, so that developers may call in with questions concerning their EST problems, and converse with a trained technician.

4. <u>Consulting</u> - Vendors also may provide consulting to help the buyer develop his expert system. This is easily the most expensive option and for the most part develops <u>no</u> internal capability.

5. <u>Operating System Required for the Tool</u> - Most small systems always come with manuals. Manuals usually tell how the EST works, and how to use the tool. This is one extreme. Many vendors fail to provide documentation with sets of real life, well thought out, well drawn out examples. This is the other extreme, whereby reading the documentation a developer gets a good idea about how to take a real world problem and solve it with an expert system.

I. Cost

Cost is the limiting factor for a number of applications. In particular, if the final expert system is to be distributed throughout an organization, multiple EST licenses must be purchased. What is included in the purchase price is as important as what is not included.

1. <u>Tool (Plus Documentation)</u> - The cost of the EST is the most exorbitant part of the total licensing fee. This price includes the EST and some form of basic documentation.

2. <u>Training</u> - Personnel training may be included in the licensing fee or bought for an additional cost.

3. <u>Academic Prices</u> - Some vendors offer their software and/or services at a greatly reduced rate to academic institutions, providing the tool is used for educational (and not developmental) purposes.

4. <u>Maintenance</u> - Vendors usually specify a time period over which they will provide maintenance for their EST. For the buyer this usually includes receiving new releases of the software, new documentation, and patching bugs. Software maintenance beyond this period is available at an additional cost.

J. PC-Based Expert System Tools

To make this survey as complete as possible, a short description of several other small ESTs is included below. The tools listed here either were not rated in the top eight, or sufficient information was not available from the vendor to rate it against all the others.

o **INSIGHT 1.2** - This tool is the same as INSIGHT 2 without explanations or saved cases. It looks for single values and stops computing when it finds it. It only needs 128K and sells for $95.

o **APES** - APES is a set of Prolog modules. By combining the different modules one can obtain the environment that best suits the problem at hand. APE features meta-queries and automatic menu generation. Also, it runs on any system that supports Micro-Prolog and costs $395.

o **EXSYS** - Written in C, it includes a rule editor and mathematical functions. Though runtime copies are free, the actual tool costs $295.

o **TOPSI** - A small version of OPS5, TOPSI is a forward chaining production rule tool. It is not easy for a non-programmer to use, and runs on Z80 CP/M system or IBM PC with 128K and costs only $80.

o **Advice Language/X (AL/X)** - Uses attribute-value pairs, IF-THEN rules, forward chaining, and Bayesian probabilities. Written in Pascal, it runs on an APPLE II.

o **The Knowledge WorkBench** - Operates on UNIX machines, has a natural language interface, hooks to external databases and programs, and has a Prolog-based inference engine which runs on the PC, XT, and AT.

o **Ex-Tran** - An inductive tool that also permits direct entry of rules. It hooks to Fortran, and runs on a VAX (VMS or UNIX) or an IBM PC.

o **K:base** - Runs on a Symbolics, IBM PC, or a combination of the two. Example-driven like TIMM and Expert-Ease, it falls somewhere between the two in sophistication.

o **Personal Consultant (PC)** - This tool is the predecessor of TI's Personal Consultant Plus. It does not have good on-line help or interface formatting utilities. It is not embeddable and cannot be compiled. The largest difference between PC, and PC Plus is that PC Plus has a frame knowledge representation facility. PC sells for $950. Users who already have PC may apply the $950 towards the $3000 dollar price of PC Plus.

4.0 Large Scale Expert System Tool Evaluation Criteria

Most of the ESTs that run on large computers are of the hybrid type previously discussed. These tools are generic in nature, which makes it harder to find a set of dimensions to differentiate them. All run on LISP machines (some may run on UNIX machines) and are embedded into the machines' LISP environments. Because of this, it is hard to say whether any of these tools actually lack any given feature that we looked at for the small tools. Since the tool is embedded into a LISP environment, any feature that it lacks can be programmed by the KE. Of course this is easier in some tools than others. Rating large tools using the dimensions from Table 1 is not extremely enlightening since they all possess the features introduced for evaluating small tools. Therefore, a different method of discriminating these ESTs is required. First, the characteristics that are common among most of the hybrid tools are presented. Second, a discussion of how each of the top eight large scale ESTs based upon all of the EST features described in this paper is presented. Table 2 summarizes these findings by rating the top eight large ESTs on dimensions that they differ the most on.

A. Hybrid Tool Characteristics

Hybrid tools blend together several disparate areas of AI technology. This merging of strategies stems from the belief that no single AI technique is versatile enough to solve all problems in AI. Each known technique has characteristics that suit it to some applications and deters performance in others. In order to provide a truly generic expert system building tool, a product must provide a working union of all renowned strategies. Hence, state-of-the-art hybrid tools offer more than one method to accomplish knowledge representation and manipulation. This frees the KE to use any subset of strategies or to employ all of them at once. This dimension introduces the different schemes for knowledge-based computation that exist in today's ESTs.

1. _Reasoning with Uncertainty_ - A good EST will provide a mechanism for reasoning with uncertainty. Belief percentages or probabilities are usually associated with the uncertain knowledge. An algorithm is applied to manipulating knowledge to compute a probability to the resulting (uncertain) inference. This continues until the final conclusions are drawn with each having an assigned probability depending on the knowledge that was used to conclude it. Allowing the user to attach probabilities to the knowledge endows an EST with the ability to consider differing hypotheses.

Two methods are used to reason with probabilities. Bayesian techniques are used to compute probabilities of results. Often a variation of Shafer's mathematical theory of evidence is used. Shafer's formalism is more general than a Bayesian approach, but provides Bayesian inferencing when the appropriate information is available.

Certainty Factors are a second method designed to handle more complex AI problems where straightforward probability theory could not be applied. This approach has been referred to as "ad hoc" but its success cannot be ignored as Shortliffe's method [1] of using certainty factors to compute other certainty factors is widely accepted and utilized in many expert system tools.

2. _Types of Rules_ - The phrase "IF-THEN rule" is actually a generic term covering a variety of rule types. Since the term is now commonplace, vendors have begun to use the IF-THEN syntax to construct rules that have different semantics claiming that they offer more kinds of rules which is misleading. Below is a list of a variety of rule types. Though the semantics of the rules that are different, the underlying mechanism is still the same.

o **Inference Rule** - This is probably the most common type of IF-THEN rule. If the clauses in the antecedent are all true, then the clauses in the consequent are added to the knowledge base. This kind of rule has also been called Modus Ponens.

o **Production Rule** - If the clauses in the antecedent are all true, then the clauses in the consequent are used to change the knowledge base. These rules are prominent in generate-and-test systems and are also used for implementing opportunism. Clauses in the consequent may actually be function calls.

o **Hypothesis Rule** - An IF-THEN rule where its associated probablilities deal with using certainty factors.

o **Bayesian Rule** - A hypothesis rule where the probabilities deal with using straight-forward probability theory. Since Baye's Theorem is applied, the alternatives introduced must be probabilistically independent of each other.

o **Constraint Rule** - A variation of a production rule, constraint rules are used for constraint propagation by means of these function calls. If a portion of the knowledge base satisfies the antecedent conditions then consequent function calls are made to test that portion of the knowledge base in order to verify that it complies with known constraints.

o **Belief Rule** - Employed by tools that support parallel hypotheses validation; belief rules equate a measure of belief with each rule firing. If one of the competing hypotheses is validated, the consequent condition transfers control to a mechanism that "poisons" all competing hypotheses, thereby believing the one validated.

3. _Semantic Frames_ - Frames are a method of knowledge representation that groups together conceptually related information. If only one element of a frame is specified, the whole frame may still be brought into focus making more knowledge available for the current task. Minimal attributes underlying an effective frame system are as follows.

Table 2. Large Scale Expert System Tool Evaluation

Large Scale EST	KES	S.1	ART	KEE	LOOPS	KC	DUCK	GEST
Structured	X	X					X	X
Object-Oriented			X	X	X	X		
Non-Monotonic			X	X		X		
Interaction	F	M	F	M	M	M	F	F
Line/Menu Screen	L	M	M	M	M	M	L	M
Tool Language	C	C,L	L	L	L	L	P,L	L
Hosts								
* Symbolics		X	X	X		X		X
* LMI			X	X		X		
* VAX	X	X	X	X		X	X	
* TI			X	X		X		
* Xerox			X	X	X	X		
* Other	X	X					X	
Rule Types								
* Inference		X	X	X	X	X	X	X
* Production	X		X	X	X	X	X	X
* Hypothesis	X	X	X			X		X
* Bayesian	X							
* Constraint			X					X
* Belief	X		X					
Rule Firing								
* Forward	X		X				X	X
* Backward	X	X	X	X		X	X	X
* Both			X				X	X
Conflict Resolution								
* First-Found	X	X	X	X	X	X	X	
* Least Recent								X
* Most Recent								X
* Antecedent	X							X
* Consequent								X
* MostComplex								X
* LeastComplex								X
* Global								X
* User-Defined		X	X	X	X	X		X
Cost	25K	45K	80K	60K	$300	50K	6K	9.5K

Legend
```
Interaction        --- F = Fast; M = Medium
Line/Menu Screen   --- L = Line; M = Menu
Tool Language      --- C = C   ; L = LISP ; P = Prolog
```

   o **Declarative Knowledge** - Static knowledge conforming to a representational standard, this knowledge may be changed, but it is always declarative in nature.

   o **Procedural Knowledge** - Constraint propagation, graphics interface, error handling, computing values with dynamically changing data, just to name a few. An excellent technique for implementing data-driven systems procedures which are invoked by referring to some part of the frame. Procedures that are activated by data are called "demons."

   o **Multi-valued Slots** - All frames have slots and their associated values. One differentiating feature is whether or not a slot can have more than one value. Each value is associated with the slot using a different relation, or aspect. Relations are one way of attaching a procedure to a slot. In this manner a slot may have multiple relations, defining multiple values and/or procedures. Relations are also a useful mechanism of attaching meta-knowledge to a slot (e.g. how many times the slot has been accessed, what entity added the slot).

o **Frame Types** - Though a frame may be typed by a slot and value, some frame systems provide the user with pre-existing frame types. The only thing different between frames of differing types is how the frame gets treated. For example, a tool might offer general-type frames that hold general information and specific-type frames that hold specific information. They might be treated differently because of the generality of the knowledge embedded in them (i.e. matching incomplete data to a general frame should be easier than matching to a specific one). Other tools offer meta-frames which hold meta-knowledge about the regular frames.

o **Facts** - Another means of representing/manipulating knowledge is facts. Facts are embedded in a frame as declarative knowledge and provide a faster access than inheritance in a frame hierarchy.

4. Control Strategies - Existing ESTs usually use forward or backward chaining to control the search for rules. Forward chaining matches elements of the knowledge base with rule antecedents in order to fire consequent actions. Backward chaining matches elements of the KB to rule consequents in an attempt to verify rule antecedents. Advanced ESTs use both strategies in searching for a solution because a solution is easier to find if the search space is minimized. Forward chaining from observed facts and backward chaining from probable hypotheses minimizes the search space.

There are ESTs that claim to use backtracking with/without forward chaining at the same time. What these systems actually do is use their ability to forward chain multiple hypotheses in "parallel." When the correct one is reached, the others are poisoned, yielding the same result as backchaining [6]. Other ESTs claim to use both forward and backward chaining at the same time when actually they only use backward chaining. In this case, special backward chaining rules called "when-found" rules are constructed, limited forward chaining is performed during backward chaining if a when-found rule is encountered. This does minimize the search space, but it doesn't really use backward and forward chaining simultaneously.

5. Conflict Resolution Strategies - A control strategy produces a subset of knowledge base rules with validated antecedent conditions that may be fired. Known as the conflict rule set, a conflict resolution strategy attempts to select the most applicable control strategy in order to reach a solution at the earliest possible time. Some of the more widely used strategies are as follows:

A) First-Found - The first applicable rule that is found is used. This is a rather simplistic approach and furthermore requires that the KE pay attention to the order of the rules in the KB. This method also greatly inhibits the KE's ability to modify the KB on-line, since new rules are usually added to the end of the KB.

B) Least Recently Used - The applicable rule least recently used is chosen.

C) Most Recently Used - The applicable rule most recently used is chosen.

D) Antecedent Ordered - Priorities attached to the antecedents of rules are used to resolve conflicts. This is helpful if there is a natural ordering of importance amongst the antecedents.

E) Consequent Ordered - The same as the previous strategy except that priorities are attached to the consequents of the rules.

F) Most Complex First - The rule that has the most antecedent or consequent clauses (depending on whether the inference engine is chaining backward or forward, respectively), will be fired first.

G) Simplest First - Same as the previous strategy, except the rule with the least number of clauses is chosen.

H) Global Priority - As well as assigning priorities to the antecedents and consequents of rules, a rule may be assigned a priority as a whole.

I) User-defined - The user directs the inference engine, defining his/her own conflict resolution strategy

A specific example of each of these strategies for conflict resolution can be found in [13]

B. Hybrid Tools Evaluation

Hybrid tools are generic in nature, so it is therefore hard to find a set of dimensions that differentiates between them. On this subsection only the features that are different from our notion of the ideal tool are mentioned (i.e. only the strong limitations and advantages of each tool are discussed).

1. Knowledge Engineering System (KES II)

KES II is written in C and runs on any system that supports C. It was developed as a product for commercial users who do not possess a LISP machine but still have a desire for an expert system development tool.

One disadvantage of KES II is that it is limited to line-oriented input. Other disadvantages include no graphics capabilities, and no ability to create procedures to control the knowledge inference process.

Good features of KES II include its rule types (bayesian, hypothesis, and production; with a separate inference engine for each one), its conflict resolution strategy (antecedent ordered), and its embeddability into any system supporting the C programming language. KES II also hooks to databases and other languages.

2. S.1

S.1 is modeled after EMYCIN by Teknowledge and is primarily applicable to the diagnosis/prescription domain. S.1 was designed mainly to handle classification problems. Therefore, it can often offer a cleaner solution than a more generic EST. S.1 does not allow forward chaining nor variables, therefore S.1 is not appropriate for planning, designing, constraint-satisfaction or modeling problems. On the other hand, S.1 has many good points. For example, S.1 allows certainty factors, procedural attachments and backward chaining. Cases can be saved and used again for system testing, and the user can override answers to questions in saved cases. Also, S.1 has user friendly interfaces, help windows, KB editing, event tracing, and system monitoring. Another advantage of S.1 is its availability in two languages (LISP and C), its ability to hook to databases and other languages with the C version.

3. Automated Reasoning Tool (ART)

ART is one of the more powerful ESTs on the market today, and is implemented by Inference Corporation. ART has a couple of limitations including the manner in which backward chaining is implemented. ART's hypothesis mechanism (called Viewpoints) actually forward chains "in parallel" to find the backward chaining rules. Control then proceeds backwards from the goal, "poisoning" the other hypotheses. Though this solution works it is slightly unorthodox. ART transforms its frame-based knowledge into Prolog-like assertions. This increases ART's speed but inhibits complexity, readability and changeability of its knowledge bases. Another disadvantage is the price of ART. A good point of ART is its rules which include inference, production, constraint, hypothesis, and belief rules. ART Studio, ARTIST (ART Interface Synthesis Tool) and Viewpoints facilities provide the developer with a sophisticated programming workbench. These added features simplify the implementation of temporal reasoning, planning and scheduling, and assumption-based truth maintenance. In addition, ART uses a blackboard architecture for control. This facility allows efficient management of ART's search space, and provides nesting up to nine levels deep. Finally, Inference Corporation provides good support but at a cost. They provide two weeks of training for two people. Additionally, they provide three days of knowledge engineering support at the customer site.

4. Knowledge Engineering Environment (KEE)

Available through IntelliCorp, KEE does not differ much from the ideal EST that were defined. "With the purchase of KEE, two people may take three IntelliCorp training courses. Other support includes ten days of on-site consulting, updates to KEE and technical support up to a year after purchase, as well as access to a telephone hot line and consultations through electronic mail." (Richer, 1985). The price of each successive copy of KEE goes down considerable after the original purchase (1st 60K, 2nd 20K, 3-5th 15K, and 6-10th 10K). Since KEE is totally object-oriented, it tends to be slow. This happens when excessive page-swapping is performed while retrieving objects from different parts of memory. KEE and ART tend to be the most expensive ESTs available. KEE's ActiveImages helps to provide applications in Discrete Event Simulation and Process Management. KEE's 2D bitmapped graphics are outstanding and provide an icon editor. Icons may be constructed by the user, then associated with some process. By using the mouse to click on icons, the user can stop and start processes in KEE whenever and wherever he/she likes. Icons may also be declared as an object and animated by rules. This permits a data-driven means of simulation.

5. LOOPS

LOOPS was designed to be a knowledge engineering environment rather than an actual expert system building tool and leaves much to the KE as far as developing an operational expert system. This usually requires that much code must be written. However this does add flexibility and a trained KE may make good use of this environment. One major drawback is that LOOPS is not at all supported. Xerox apparently regards LOOPS as a research tool and for this reason sells it for only three hundred dollars for Xerox 1100 series workstations.

6. Knowledge Craft (KC)

Knowledge Craft does not possess any strong limitations or advantages, though it does manifest all the basic features of an ideal EST. One advantage is KC's underlying frame system upon which the entire object-oriented environment is built. The frame system is similar to Fox's SRL (Schema Representation Language), and allows the KE to tailor frames to exhibit desired inheritance, control and search. KC, like KEE, has a 2-D graphics facility that supports icon editing. KC uses CRL-OPS to perform forward chaining, and CRL-Prolog for backward chaining. These are Carnegie Group's own versions of OPS5 and Prolog, and make for a good working combination. KC comes with an agenda mechanism, a window/canvas interface, and an embedded database for large applications on a DEC VAX. Items placed on the agenda are "events," also represented as frames. A multi-queue event manager can schedule these events to occur in either a simulated or actual operating mode.

"Contexts" are provided, which are analogous to ART's Viewpoints. Since KC is written in Common LISP, it may prove to be more portable than other ESTs. Carnegie Group Incorporated provides continuing support for KC and its purchase includes a two week hands-on tutorial in Pittsburgh.

7. DUCK

DUCK has been in use in the Yale Cognitive AI Research Lab since the late seventies and was acquired for commercial license by Smart Systems Technology. It's user and development interface are minimal, offerring no graphics or attractive menus and screens. DUCK does have all the reasoning capabilities of a good large tool. Its uses non-monotonic reasoning capabilities which apply dependency-directed backtracking through truth maintenance of its data pools. It performs forward and backward chaining in unison, at the same time allowing user-directed search. A portable LISP dialect called NLISP provides the bridge of control between the rule firing, logic programming and non-monotonic reasoning in DUCK. DUCK is embeddable in most LISP environments. Training for the DUCK system is available at an additional cost while extra copies are $1200 each.

8. Generic Expert System Tool (GEST)

GEST was developed by the Artificial Intelligence Branch of the Georgia Tech Research Institute. It encompasses specifications abstracted from past internal projects, and manifests advancements resulting from on-going research. The GEST project team continues to incorporate state-of-the-art EST technology into its product with new versions passed on to the licensee as they are created. The most important aspect that was adhered to during the design of GEST was its generality. A strongpoint of GEST is its user interface which makes extensive use of the Symbolics windowing system. GEST can be instantiated any number of times, allowing multiple users to solve multiple problems on the same machine. The state of any one problem solving process is saved upon switching to a new one. GEST offers three choices for rule firing (forward chaining, backward chaining, or both), and eight choices for conflict resolution strategies (least recently used, most recently used, antecedent ordered, consequent ordered, most complex, simplest, global priority and user-defined). GEST also offers a choice of "gears" for its inference engine. The user may call for a single sweep through the current rule base, then fire the most applicable rule, discarding it from consideration if further sweeps. A single sweep version which does not discard rules is also provided. Finally, a multiple sweep with rule replacement can be initiated. GEST also provides four mechanisms for representing knowledge: rules, frames, facts, and functions.

C. Other Large Tools

As was done for the small ESTs, descriptions of other large ESTs are included for completeness. Unlike the previous eight ESTs, the reader should not assume that these ESTs possess the characteristics of our ideal model.

1. EXPERT

Written in Fortran, EXPERT possess attribute-value pairs, three kinds of IF-THEN rules and confidence factors, a line-oriented screen, traces and probes of the knowledge base, and statistical analysis of performance. EXPERT is best suited for consultation tasks where the system engages in an interactive dialogue with the user for deciding among a fixed set of alternative conclusions.

2. OPS5 Family

Several tools have been modeled after the original OPS which gained much attention when it was used to write the R1 system for configuring VAX computers. The basic mechanisms act on a rule base of production rules, which is called working memory. The inference engine features a recognize-act cycle which uses pattern-matching techniques to find an applicable rule (this could indeed be quite helpful, however probably too slow due to overhead for run-time applications), then uses the RETTE algorithm to chose the best applicable rule, and finally fires the rule and looks for another. OPS83 is the successor to OPS5 and is now commercially available. It includes additional data structures (records, user-defined types), programming language features (if, while, for, call), and facilities for manipulating files, symbols, and working memory. Several problems exist in terms of OPS5 being an effective expert system tool. Facts are restricted to lists of atoms and numbers restricting the user from taking advantage of nested sublists. Antecedent evaluation is limited to equality matching or binary comparisons while consequents are limited to predefined OPS5 semantics. Since all these problems can readily be surmounted with the proper focus of attention, some tool developers have written their own version of OPS5 to do forward chaining.

3. Rule-Oriented System for Implementing Expert Systems

ROSIE is written in INTERLISP and requires a XEROX LISP machine, a DEC20, or a DEC VAX running ISI-VAX Interlisp as a host machine. It accepts English-like syntax to make programming easier. Not a powerful knowledge engineering environment, ROSIE may be easier for non-programmers to use since a complete English-like programming language is provided that insulates the user from INTERLISP.

4. EMYCIN

The forerunner of many expert system building tools, EMYCIN has explanation, IF-THEN rules, object-attribute-value triples, certainty factors, backward chaining, saved cases, knowledge base editor, and event history.

5. Rule Master

Rule Master is an example-driven induction tool capable of representing knowledge in facts, rules and frames. It runs on UNIX machines as well as IBM PCs. Logic-based Rule Master supports Zadeh's fuzzy logic.

6. ENVISAGE

Prolog-based Envisage supports fuzzy logic, Bayesian inferencing, explanation, and external hooks. Training and consultancy are available. It runs on a VAX/VMS system.

7. Expert System Environment (ESE)

ESE consists of two sections: the Expert System Consultation Environment (ESCE), and the Expert System Development Environment (ESDE). ESE's features include backward chaining, forward chaining, user-defined rule firing, structured rule base editor, customized displays, and fuzzy logic. Runs on IBM System/370 processors under VM/CMS.

8. PORTAL

This expert system shell is similar to EXPERT and was developed by Chang, McNeely, and Gamble at the University of Victoria for use in medical expert systems experiments. PORTAL includes a structure editor for the editing rules and is primarily written in FRANZLISP to perform screen updating functions. One drawback of PORTAL is that the user cannot make calls to the underlying LISP system. Designed for classification problems, PORTAL uses highly constrained rule syntax and data typing. There is no built-in way to do arithmetic, so it can only deal with variables in ranges. It runs on a DEC VAX system.

9. OPS5+.

This is an enhanced version of the OPS5 forward chaining production rule system. It is window-based supports, has rule editing, and runs on Apollo Workstations, IBM PC's and MacIntosh's.

10. YAPS - Yet Another Production System

YAPS is the University of Maryland's product rule system alternative to Carnegie-Mellon's OPS5 system. Part of the Maryland Software Distribution is a package of tools that include a Flavors system for FRANZLISP running in a UNIX environment, this tool addresses many of the problems that OPS5 possesses. Within YAPS rules can be compiled, DEFSTRUCTS may be used within facts, discrimination net techniques match productions with facts. In addition, YAPS has recently been ported to a Common LISP version [11].

11. HEARSAY-III

This tool is the shell extracted from HEARSAY-II, the speech understanding system. It features a blackboard control structure, and complex scheduling and planning capabilities for rule firing from distributed knowledge sources. HEARSAY-III is written in the AI database language AP3 which requires the ISI-VAX INTERLISP compiler. The tool is not well supported.

5.0 SUMMARY

This paper has provided both a mechanism for evaluating expert system tools and a synopsis of all available as of January 1986. In determining the final system to purchase, the buyer will probably want to give more weight to resource-limited considerations (e.g. hardware and money) than any other single factor. In addition to the EST descriptions provided in this paper, the user should be aware that most vendors will sell the documentation for their EST for a reasonable price. Carefully reading of the functional and technological descriptions of each candidate EST would help immensely. Though marketing literature can also be helpful, one must realize that it is biased. For a more focussed look at several of today's best ESTs, the user is directly to Harmon [7] and Gilmore [6].

This study was based materials gathered from a variety of sources including references listed on the following page, vendor provided expert system tool descriptions, and discussions with EST sales representatives. It should be noted that Georgia Tech did not purchase a single EST described in this paper as their combined cost easily exceeds half a million dollars.

6.0 REFERENCES

[1] Buchanan,B.G., and Shortliffe, E. H.
     Rule-Based Expert Systems
     Addison-Wesley Publishing Company
     Reading, MA 1984

[2] Cross, G.R.
     "Tools for Constructing Knowledge-Based System"
     Report WA 99164-1210
     Department of Computer Science, Washington State University 1985

[3] Dunn, R. J.
     "Expandable Expertise for Everyday Users"
     InfoWorld
     September 30, 1985

[4] Fikes, R., and Kehler, T.
     "The Role of Frame-Based Representation in Reasoning"
     Communications of the ACM, July 1985

[5] Garvey, T. D., Lowrance, J. D., and Fischler, M. A.
     "An Inference Technique for Integrating Knowledge from Disparate Sources"
     Proceedings of 7th IJCAI
     Vancouver, B.C., Canada   August 1985

[6] Gilmore, J.F., and Pulaski, K.
     "A Survey of Expert System Tools"
     IEEE Proceedings of the 2nd Conference on Artificial Intelligence Applications
     Miami Beach, FL. December 1985

[7] Harmon, P., and King, D.
     Expert Systems
     John Wiley & Sons, Inc.
     New York, New York 1985

[9] Hayes-Roth, F., Waterman, D., and Lenat, D.
     Building Expert Systems
     Addison-Wesley Publishing Company, Inc. 1983

[10] Richer, M.
      "Five Commercial Expert Systems Tools: An Evaluation"
      The Artificial Intelligence Report
      Volume 2, Number 8   August 1985

[11] Steele,Guy, L.
      Common LISP Reference Manual
      Digital Press
      Bedford, MA. 1984

[12] Weiss,S.M.,and Kulikowski, C.A.
      A Practical Guide to Designing Expert Systems
      Rowman & Allanheld
      Totowa, NJ 1984

[13] Gilmore, J.F., Ho, D., and Howard C.
      "GEST - The Generic Expert System Tool"
      SPIE Applications of Artificial Intelligence
      Orlando, FL April 1985

Part IV
Case Studies

THE earlier parts of this book covered the wide array of powerful languages and tools available to the developer of expert systems. We now present actual case studies covering a spectrum of application scenarios.

The first paper, by Rogers and Barthelemy, pertains to the automated design environment. Developed under the aegis of a NASA grant, the Automated Design Synthesis (ADS) general-purpose optimization program provides approximately 100 combinations of strategy, optimizer, and one-dimensional search. Since it is difficult for a nonexpert to select the correct combination, an expert system called EXADS has been developed. In the latter system, the knowledge base has been divided into three categories. The inference engine and the rules have been written in Lisp. The software can run either on DEC-VAX or on IBM Personal Computers.

The second paper, by Wright et al., deals with real-time control. Hexscon (the name is derived from Hybrid Expert System Controller) is an experimental knowledge-based expert system designed to deal with control problems encountered in defense and industrial applications. The design goals were: (i) a capacity of 5000 rules in a microcomputer with 512K bytes of memory; (ii) a response time of 10 to 100 ms; (iii) the ability to handle 1000 objects; and (iv) the ability to function even under conditions of high uncertainty.

The third paper, by Seiler and Seiler, covers two case studies, both involving Insight 2. The first study describes the effort to monitor and diagnose an environmentally regulated biological system. The second study relates to a nuclear power generation environment. In the latter case, one of the authors took less than 4 hr to encode the knowledge base which is comprised of less than 75 production rules. This new set of rules replaced 14,000 lines of Fortran code. The authors emphasize that the time required to code decision logic into a rule-based system is trivial compared to that required when encoding it into a conventional language.

The fourth paper, by Ragheb and Gvillo, deals with identification of faults in engineering systems. Instead of rule-based systems which use rules based exclusively on human expertise, the authors have developed model-based production-rule analysis systems that model devices based on knowledge of their structure and past behavior. The concept of fault-tree analysis has been used, and this analysis system has been developed with a "backward-chaining deduction-oriented antecedent-consequent logic."

The next paper, by Pandit and Sriram, relates to civil engineering. To aid in the field inspection of augered, cast-in-place, concrete pile installations, an expert system called AUGERPILE was implemented using Insight. However, the latter does not permit handling of multiple instantiations. This implies that the user must start the program and run it,

repeating the input of data, for each segment. Because of this problem, the authors decided to replace Insight by Personal Consultant. Their experiences, in the two cases, are described in this paper.

Next, Miyasato et al. deal with a different issue in civil engineering. The Seismic Risk Evaluation System, developed at Stanford University, provides a preliminary analysis of seismic risk for different types of buildings. Theories about the many factors involved in a seismic risk evaluation are not well defined, and measurements are difficult to verify. Using heuristics based upon experience, the authors have developed and implemented a set of rules on "Deciding Factor," a microcomputer program for developing expert systems.

The next paper, by Ohler, relates to water purification. The water treatment process includes a water softening stage. At a particular company, this stage was operating at a suboptimal level because of the low skill and knowledge level of the regular plant operators. A system, developed in Micro-Prolog, enables these operators to secure immediate expert advice and assistance at all times.

The following paper, by Turpin, covers four case histories: (i) Campbell Soup Cooker Diagnosis; (ii) Texas Instruments Epitaxial Reactor Diagnosis; (iii) Westinghouse Corrosion Expert; and (iv) Purdue Grain Market Advisor. A common thread in all these cases is their use of Personal Consultant. The number of rules varies between 150 and 1000. The level of education of the end user differs significantly across the four cases. The fourth case relates to marketing and business.

The next expert system supports auditors in the field. It uses the development tool called AL/X which was described in Part III of this book. Dungan and Chandler cover the details of the development process from initial interviews to validation studies. The system was originally developed to run on a CYBER 175 mainframe computer, and later modified to operate in a personal computer environment.

The following paper, by Barber et al., describes the Interactive Critical Path Analysis (ICPA) system, which allows project networks to be drawn on the screen via a joystick. The system, designed to operate in a BBC microcomputer environment, allows a network of up to 100 nodes and 150 links. The system has been written in Basic language. The authors emphasize the fact that interactive graphics capabilities are becoming increasingly important.

In continuation of these ideas, the next paper, by Prasad et al., deals specifically with the issues of graphs, pictures, and images, and how to use them effectively in a microcomputer environment. Given a set of thousands of graphs and images, it is indeed a challenge to pick out the desired subset in an acceptable period of time. Until recently, only the expert who created and stored the information could do so. The system, implemented entirely in "C" language, extends concepts from conventional data base technology to allow novices to retrieve information of all types as efficiently as experts.

The following paper, by Chapman, holds special appeal for persons involved in the computing business. It describes a system that assists engineers and managers in estimating software development efforts and schedules. There are four separate knowledge bases, each based on a different COCOMO software cost model. The system has been implemented using the Insight shell, and it can be run in an IBM Personal Computer environment.

The last paper, by Dankel and Russo, deals with medical diagnosis. The Verifier I system contains sets of well-classified pathological entities. The system displays algorithms detailing the correct analytical steps. In most cases, the system simply acts as a reminder to the physician. The full intelligence of the system is applied only in the case of discrepancies and inconsistencies.

We have now seen examples of expert systems in various fields of engineering, in business, and in the medical field. These case studies were selected because they relate specifically to the microcomputer domain.

We hope that the readers of this book will build expert systems in their respective areas, and that they will publish case studies of their work. These case studies will in turn serve as the starting point for the next generation of professional endeavors.

BIBLIOGRAPHY

Bradley, S., R. Buys, A. Elsawy, and A. Siper, "Developing a microcomputer-based intelligent planning system," in *Proc. of the IEEE Expert Systems in Government Symp.*, McClean, VA, Oct. 1985, pp. 56–60.

Cochran, E. L. and B. L. Hutchins, "Testing, verifying, and releasing an expert system: The case history of Mentor," in *Proc. of the IEEE Third Conf. on Artificial Intelligence Applications,* Kissimmee, FL, Feb. 1987, pp. 163–169.

Harmon, N. P., "Inventory and analysis of existing expert systems," *Expert Syst. Strategies,* vol. 2, no. 8, pp. 1–17, Aug. 1986.

An Expert System for Choosing the Best Combination of Options in a General Purpose Program for Automated Design Synthesis

James L. Rogers
Interdisciplinary Research Office, NASA Langley Research Center, Hampton, VA 23665

Jean-Francois M. Barthelemy
Virginia Polytechnic Institute and State University, Blacksburg, VA 24061

Abstract. An expert system called EXADS has been developed to aid users of the Automated Design Synthesis (ADS) general purpose optimization program. ADS has approximately 100 combinations of strategy, optimizer, and one-dimensional search options from which to choose. It is difficult for a nonexpert to make this choice. This expert system aids the user in choosing the best combination of options based on the users knowledge of the problem and the expert knowledge stored in the knowledge base. The knowledge base is divided into three categories; constrained problems, unconstrained problems, and constrained problems being treated as unconstrained problems. The inference engine and rules are written in LISP, contains about 200 rules, and executes on DEC-VAX (with Franz-LISP) and IBM PC (with IQ-LISP) computers.

1 Introduction

An expert system to aid a user of the Automated Design Synthesis (ADS) general purpose optimization program has recently been developed. Because ADS has three levels of options (strategies, optimizers, and one-dimensional searches), the user has approximately 100 combinations from which to choose. This could easily overwhelm a novice user of the program. According to the developer, a principal difficulty with a program of such broad capability as this is the development of a concise set of guidelines identifying the best choice of a combination of strategy, optimizer, and one-dimensional search options for a given problem. In view of this fact and the anticipated high usage of ADS throughout industry, a decision was made to develop an expert system for ADS (EXADS).

In general, an expert system consists of two major components, the knowledge base and the in-

ference engine. The knowledge base for EXADS was developed from contributions from the author of ADS, a literature search, and discussions with optimization experts; and currently contains 98 different hypotheses and approximately 200 rules. It is divided into three distinct sets of rules and hypotheses: (1) for constrained problems, (2) for unconstrained problems, and (3) for constrained problems being treated as unconstrained problems. The inference engine asks questions about, makes decisions from, and determines the consequences implied by the knowledge built into the knowledge base. It is written in LISP and currently executes on DEC-VAX and IBM PC computers.

The purpose of this paper is to discuss how this expert system came into being and to describe its major components. Also discussed are the problems encountered during the testing and verification of the system and solutions to those problems. A listing from a sample session is included.

2 The Origin of the Expert System for ADS

The ADS (Automated Design Synthesis [1]) computer program, developed under a NASA grant, is a general purpose, numerical optimization program containing a wide variety of algorithms. ADS requires a three-level decision to select an algorithm for solving a general optimization problem. These levels are strategy, optimizer, and one-dimensional search. ADS allows the user to have great flexibility in solving a problem by providing eight strategy options (Table 1), five optimizer options (Table 2), and eight one-dimensional search options (Table 3). Table 4 shows the large number of possible combinations of options available.

One difficulty with a program like ADS which provides so many options is choosing the best pos-

Reprint Requests: J.L. Rogers, Interdisciplinary Research Office, NASA Langley Research Center, Hampton, VA 23665.

Table 1. Strategy options

No.	Strategy to be used
0	None. Go directly to optimizer.
1	Sequential unconstrained minimization using the exterior penalty function method.
2	Sequential unconstrained minimization using the linear extended interior penalty function method.
3	Sequential unconstrained minimization using the quadratic extended interior penalty function method.
4	Sequential unconstrained minimization using the cubic extended interior penalty function method.
5	Augmented Lagrange multiplier method.
6	Sequential linear programming.
7	Method of centers (method of inscribed hyperspheres).
8	Sequential quadratic programming.

Table 2. Optimizer options

No.	Optimizer to be used
0	None. Go directly to the search. This option should only be used for program development.
1	Fletcher–Reeves algorithm for unconstrained minimization.
2	Davidon–Fletcher–Powell (DFP) variable metric method for unconstrained minimization.
3	Broydon–Fletcher–Goldfarb–Shanno (BFGS) variable metric method for unconstrained minimization.
4	Method of feasible directions (MFD) for constrained minimization.
5	Modified method of feasible directions for constrained minimization.

sible combination of options to solve a given problem. This choice requires knowledge of the problem to be solved and experience in optimization. Typically, an engineer has sufficient knowledge of the problem to be solved in his or her discipline but lacks the necessary experience in optimization to make a proper choice among the several options available at each of the three levels in ADS. The development of an expert system to aid an engineer in this selection is one solution.

It is generally recognized that the development of an expert system rests on satisfying the following prerequisites [2]:

1. There must be at least one human expert acknowledged to perform the task well using special knowledge, judgment, and experience. Within the Interdisciplinary Research Office (IRO) at NASA's Langley Research Center, we have access to a renowned expert in the optimization field as well as several other regular, in-house users of optimization techniques. In addition, several optimization experts are currently working under grants and contracts for the IRO, including the author of ADS.

2. The expert must be able to explain the special knowledge and experience and the methods used to apply them to a particular problem. Many of the available experts also teach optimization techniques and are accustomed to explaining difficult concepts to novices.

3. The task must have a well-bounded domain. The domain for this task is bounded by the number of possible combinations available for ADS.

4. The problem does not require common sense and should take an expert from a few minutes to a few hours to solve. Common sense will not be very helpful to an engineer in selecting the best combination of options. Experience with ADS has shown that a choice can almost always be made within the required time frame.

5. The problem should be nontrivial but tractable, with promising avenues for incremental expansion. Within the subject domain the problem is nontrivial and tractable. It can be expanded to accommodate new combinations of options as strategies, optimizers, and one-dimensional searches are added to ADS.

Since the present application appeared to meet the required prerequisites, it was decided to proceed with building an expert system for ADS. The first step was to begin acquiring the expert knowledge for the knowledge base.

3 Knowledge Acquisition

The acquisition of the expert knowledge for the knowledge base portion of the expert system proved to be a difficult task as discussed by Hayes-Roth et al. [3]. Initially, Rogers, acting as knowledge engineer, met with the in-house expert and Barthelemy to discuss what rules they would follow in choosing from a small subset of the possible combinations of options in ADS. These rules were then coded into production rules similar to those described by Winston [4]. Concurrently, a questionnaire was sent to engineers, knowledgeable

Table 3. One-dimensional search options

No.	One-dimensional search to be used
1,5	Find the minimum of an (1) unconstrained or (5) constrained function using the Golden Section method.
2,6	Find the minimum of an (2) unconstrained or (6) constrained function using the Golden Section method followed by polynomial interpolation.
3,7	Find the minimum of an (3) unconstrained or (7) constrained function by first finding bounds and then using polynomial interpolation.
4,8	Find the minimum of an (4) unconstrained or (8) constrained function by polynomial interpolation/extrapolation without first finding bounds on the solution.

Table 4. Program options

	Optimizer				
Strategy	1	2	3	4	5
0	X	X	X	X	X
1	X	X	X	0	0
2	X	X	X	0	0
3	X	X	X	0	0
4	X	X	X	0	0
5	X	X	X	0	0
6	0	0	0	X	X
7	0	0	0	X	X
8	0	0	0	X	X
One-D Search					
1	X	X	X	0	0
2	X	X	X	0	0
3	X	X	X	0	0
4	X	X	X	0	0
5	0	0	0	X	X
6	0	0	0	X	X
7	0	0	0	X	X
8	0	0	0	X	X

in optimization, to solicit their input. This did not prove to be beneficial because no usable knowledge was returned, possibly attributed to the fact that many of the engineers surveyed use only one combination, and use it as a "black-box." The main benefit from the questionnaire was that it reinforced our belief that an expert system would be very beneficial to most engineers using ADS. The remainder of the knowledge that currently resides in the knowledge base came from two primary sources. First, Barthelemy performed a literature search to identify rules for each strategy, optimizer, and one-dimensional search option in ADS. Second, the developer of ADS included a set of rules in his documentation [1]. The collection of rules from these sources provided sufficient rules to begin developing the expert system.

4 The Expert System for ADS

EXADS, the expert system developed for ADS, like most expert systems, consists of two major components, an inference engine and a knowledge base. These two components are discussed in detail in this section.

4.1 The Inference Engine

The inference engine described [4] was used to help us get started with this project. This engine is written in LISP. Users respond to a question with either a "yes" or a "no." This proved to be very helpful in learning some of the basics about building expert systems with production (if–then) rules. However, the inference engine lacked some useful capabilities, such as confidence levels and dealing with uncertainty. About the time a search was begun to find

or develop a new inference engine, one, which appeared to meet our needs, was delivered to another organization at Langley. This engine, called AESOP (An Expert System engine Operative with Probabilities), was developed under a NASA grant. AESOP is a rule-based inference engine written in LISP that can make decisions about a particular situation using user-supplied hypotheses (potential solutions), rules (guidelines to finding the correct solution), and answers to the questions drawn from the rules. It is a backward chaining problem solver, that is, works from hypotheses to facts.

One of the important features of AESOP is that questions do not have to be answered with only a "Yes" or a "No." A confidence level ranging from 0 (no) to 10 (yes) may be given instead, depending on how certain the user is about a particular piece of information. The user can also respond with a "maybe" (5), "probably" or "likely" (7), "not-likely" (3), or "don't know" (dk). If the user responds "dk," AESOP checks the knowledge base to determine if rules exist that deal with this uncertainty. The "dk" capability is very powerful, allowing several levels of rules to exist, with each level containing more specific rules to help decide the appropriate response to a higher-level question. The rules must be structured top–down so that the rules for resolving a "dk" response are located below the original rules because AESOP will not jump backward through the rules to resolve a "dk" response. If no rules exist for resolving a "dk" response, the default is "no." However, the user is given an opportunity to override the default.

AESOP has an "explanation" feature and a "help" command. When any hypothesis reaches a confidence level of 90% or more, it is deemed confirmed as the best choice and displayed to the screen. If all rules have been exhausted and no hypothesis has been confirmed, then the status of all hypothesis with a confidence level greater than 10% are displayed on the screen. The user can choose a combination of options based on the confidence levels or examine the explanation of the hypotheses that appear promising and determine why they failed to reach the 90% level. The "help" command displays the choices currently available to a user.

Other reasons for choosing AESOP are its availability and its portability. The program is in the public domain and available from COSMIC, NASA's software dissemination center at the University of Georgia. It executes on both the DEC-VAX (Franz-LISP) and the IBM PC (IQ-LISP) at Langley and should be portable to any computer running a version of LISP with little or no modification.

4.2 The Knowledge Base

The knowledge base contains: (1) the rules to be used in the decision making; (2) the hypotheses to be investigated; (3) the list of mutually exclusive rules (opposites) to avoid giving essentially the same information twice; and (4) detailed information about specific rules. The general format of the knowledge base is:

```
(setq *rules '(
     ((hypothesis1)
          (or
               (confidence-level1 rule1)
               (confidence-level2 rule2)
                    .
                    .
                    .
               (confidence-levelN ruleN))
     ((hypothesis2)
          .
          .
          .
     ((hypothesisN)
          (or
               (confidence-level1 rule1)
```

```
               (confidence-level2 rule2)
                    .
                    .
                    .
               (confidence-levelN  ruleN))))
(setq *hypotheses '(
     (hypothesis1)
     (hypothesis2)
          .
          .
          .
     (hypothesisN)))
(setq *opposites '(
     ((ruleA) (ruleB))
     ((ruleC) (ruleD))
          .
          .
          .
     ((ruleY) (ruleZ))))
(setq *details '(
     ((ruleA) (details about ruleA))
     ((ruleB) (details about ruleB))
          .
          .
          .
     ((ruleZ) (details about ruleZ))))
```

The confidence level assigned to each rule by the expert works in conjunction with the confidence level the user expresses about how well the rule applies to his or her problem. This combination is divided by 10 before it is stored. For example, if the expert has placed a confidence level of 8 on a rule and the user responds to a question about that rule with a confidence level of 5, then the combined confidence level is (8*5)/10 or 4. The confidence level for the hypothesis is computed by again dividing by 10, resulting in a value between 0 and 1 given as a percentage. When this confidence level exceeds 90%, the hypothesis is deemed confirmed as the best choice. The rules can be expressed in two ways, as "and" or as "or." An example of an "and" rule follows:

```
((strategy 1 optimizer 2 and 1d-search 3
          is best for *)
     (or
          (10 and (* requires a strategy of 1)
               (* requires an optimizer of 2)
               (* requires a 1d-search of 3))))
```

The * serves as a "wild card" for describing the problem on which the user is working and is discussed in more detail subsequently. The 10 shows that the expert is certain that this hypothesis is correct if the facts enclosed in the parentheses are true. The user responds with a confidence level to each of the three questions included in the "and" portion of the rule. For example, the engine would ask: "Does * require a strategy of 1?" The user responds "1" (or likely or 7). If the user responds "y" (yes or 10) to the remaining two questions, the 10 preceding the "and" would only be multiplied by 7 because in an "and" rule the engine chooses the minimum of all responses. After the two divisions by 10 the confidence level for this hypothesis is at 70%.

An "or" rule looks like the following:

```
((* requires a strategy of 4)
    (or
        (8 * requires starting from a feasible
            design space)
        (7 * is a second order problem)
        (6 * has more than 50 design variables)
        (5 analytical gradients are available
            for *)))
```

Each of the "or" rules works in combination with the others. A confidence level is computed for the first time by multiplying the confidence level of the expert by the confidence level of the user and dividing by 10. The confidence level of the second rule is computed likewise. These two confidence levels are then combined according to the computation:

new_confidence = confidence1
    + ((1 − confidence1) * confidence2)

This process (replacing confidence1 with new_confidence and confidence 2 with the confidence level of the next rule) is repeated until all of the rules in the "or" have been used or, after another division by 10, a 90% confidence level has been attained for that hypothesis.

AESOP allows the knowledge engineer to store an initial prompt function in the knowledge base. This function, which is contained on a file loaded into memory by the inference engine, lets the user describe the problem being solved (e.g., building bridges). This description replaces the wild card (*) in the remainder of the knowledge base.

5 Problems Encountered and Their Solutions in Developing the Expert System

Testing and verificiation of the knowledge base proceeded along several different lines. First, we tried numerous test cases to test the validity of the rules and the associated confidence levels. This step eliminated most of the simple problems and errors. Next, five students taking a graduate level optimization course were invited to test the system. Each of these students had an optimization problem to solve and used EXADS as would a typical optimization novice. They responded to questions with answers based on their particular problem. In two cases a combination of options for ADS was deemed confirmed as the best choice for that student's problem. In the other three cases no hypothesis was confirmed, but the students were given 2 to 4 combinations from which to choose. New problems were discovered and solved at this step also. Finally, the EXADS system has been sent to ADS users for testing and evaluation in the field. It is expected that new and modified rules and confidence levels will be added as a consequence of the evaluation by the ADS users.

The remainder of this section discusses the problems we and the students discovered during the first two levels of testing and evaluation. The solutions to these problems are also considered because these problem-solving experiences may be important to potential developers of expert systems.

The original knowledge base contained 98 hypotheses (the possible combinations for ADS) and about 550 rules in a single file. Many of the "or" rules were combined into "and" rules, thereby reducing the total number of rules to near 200. AESOP works with frames [4]. A frame is a list of poperties about an entity, similar to relations and attributes in a relational data base management system. To reduce the excessive amount of time AESOP was taking to create the frames and not ask the user questions that possibly did not pertain to the problem, we decided to divide the rules into three separate categories depending on whether the problem to be solved is unconstrained, constrained, or constrained but being treated as unconstrained. The categories were then further divided into levels for strategy, optimizer, and search rules. The rules corresponding to each category and level were then written as eight separate files (an unconstrained problem has no strategy). Some of the rules overlap in the files because, for example, a single optimizer may be used for an unconstrained problem as well as for a constrained problem being treated as an unconstrained problem.

To handle these three categories of problems, we expanded the initial prompt function to ask additional questions about which category is to be used.

229

Once the category is determined, then the appropriate file is loaded from the knowledge base. After initialization of certain variables, the initial prompt function queries the user for a description of the problem to be solved. This description replaces the "*" wild card in the rules as before.

Because of the way the original AESOP system was written, the user was required to answer redundant questions. "Remember" and "recall" features from the original inference engine [4] were added to AESOP to let the inference engine store and recall user responses, thus minimizing the number of questions a user is asked. In addition, there are a number of rules in the knowledge base that are exact opposites, such as (iterative analysis is available for *) as opposed to (iterative analysis is not available for *). An "opposites" feature was added so that the user would not be asked about both rules. Using this feature, when a user responds to a question and its opposite is in the knowledge base, the corresponding inverse confidence level is given to its opposite. For example, if a user responds "probably" (7) to a question, then its opposite is automatically given a "not-likely" (3) confidence level. The students found that responding to rules stated negatively proved to be a problem. The addition of the "opposites" feature and a slight reordering of the rules and hypotheses seems to have helped here because, except in rare occasions, the user not only sees a positively stated question.

The addition of the "opposites" feature to AESOP led to a problem with the default of "no" for a "dk" (don't know) response. Since "dk" defaults to a "no," its opposite defaults to a "yes" without the user ever seeing the question. Obviously, the opposite of "dk" is not "yes." The engine was modified so that the opposite of "dk" is "dk," with both defaulting to "no." A feature to allow the user to override the default was added.

We found that the "explanation" feature tended to generate quite a bit of output that really did not help in understanding what rules were being used to find the best combination. All combinations of strategy, optimizer, and one-dimensional search options with their rules were displayed even though there may have been no evidence that that combination was best. To reduce the amount of output, only hypotheses and rules having a confidence level of greater than 10% are now displayed, eliminating the hypotheses and rules with little or no evidence.

Because some users may not be familiar with the optimization terminology used in the rules, a "detail" feature was added. This feature allows users to type "detail" if they do not understand a rule, and details for that rule are displayed on the screen if they are available in the knowledge base.

6 Concluding Remarks

An expert system, called EXADS, has been developed to aid a user of the Automated Design Synthesis (ADS) general purpose optimization program. Because of the general purpose nature of the program, it is difficult for a nonexpert to select the best choice of a combination of strategy, optimizer, and one-dimensional search options from among the many combinations that are available. An expert system for ADS (EXADS) consisting of an inference engine (AESOP) and a knowledge base of approximately 200 rules was developed to aid an engineer in determining the best combination based on the his or her knowledge of the problem and the expert knowledge stored in the knowledge base. After in-house testing and verification, EXADS was delivered to ADS users for their evaluation. Upon completion of this evaluation, the system will be modified to correct any errors, problems, or "holes" in the knowledge base. It will then be expanded periodically to account for any new ADS options.

Sample Session
```
lisp
Franz Lisp, Opus 38.79
→ (load 'aesop.src)
[load aesop.src]
t
→ (start)
```
****
A E S O P
An Expert System engine Operative with Probabilities
****

Enter name of rules/hypotheses file →trules.
[load trules.]

Respond with y or n.

Is this problem unconstrained?

> n
****

Do you know that your problem has local minima?

Are the objective function and/or constraints nonlinear or strongly nonlinear?

Is it true that analytical gradients are not available?

Is it true that the objective function and constraints are not expensive i.e. explicit or approximate?

Are equality constraints involved in this problem?
****

Type y if the answer to one or more of these questions is yes. Otherwise type n.

> y
Recommendation: Treat as an unconstrained problem.

Even though the problem is constrained, do you
           want to treat it as if it were unconstrained?

> y
This problem is constrained, but is being treated as unconstrained.

Do you know what strategy to use?

> n

[load custrat.]

what kind of problem are you solving?
      Please enter as a single string, with no spaces

      > building-bridges

           You may answer the following questions with a
      y (yes), n (no), m (maybe), l (likely), nl (not
      likely), p (probably), dk (don't know),
      or a probability factor ranging from 0
      (least certain) to 10 (most certain).

           Enter a how or a why to see an explanation,
      enter detail to see details about a rule,
      and to get help, type HELP or ?

      Please wait. . .

      With what certainty can you assert:
      intermediate designs may have violated constraints for
       building-bridges ?

      > y
      With what certainty can you assert:
      final design may have slightly violated constraints for
       building-bridges ?

      > p
      With what certainty can you assert:
      constraint values increase sharply in feasible domain for
       building-bridges ?

      > detail

      A feasible domain is a region of design space where
       all constraints are satisfied

      With what certainty can you assert:
      constraint values increase sharply in feasible domain for
       building-bridges ?

> nl
    With what certainty can you assert:
final design must have precisely satisfied constraints
    for building-bridges ?

    > n
No hypothesis can be confirmed with certainty

Hypothesis   building-bridges requires a strategy of 1
    has certainty 0.7

        Strategy 1 uses the exterior penalty function method

Hypothesis   building-bridges requires a strategy of 2
    has certainty 0.3

        Strategy 2 uses the linear extended interior penalty
            function method

Hypothesis   building-bridges requires a strategy of 3
    has certainty 0.3

        Strategy 3 uses the quadratic extended interior penalty
            function method

Hypothesis   building-bridges requires a strategy of 4
    has certainty 0.3

        Strategy 4 uses the cubic extended interior penalty
            function method

        Options are next, done, how, why, help

        > why
    there was strong evidence that building-bridges
        requires a strategy of 1
    this followed from 2 things:

    there was strong evidence that final design may have
        slightly violated constraints for building-bridges

    there was very strong evidence that intermediate
        designs may have violated constraints for
        building-bridges

    there was weak evidence that building-bridges requires
        a strategy of 2
    this followed from 1 things:

    there was weak evidence that final design must be
        feasible for building-bridges

    there was weak evidence that building-bridges requires
        a strategy of 3
    this followed from 1 things:

    there was weak evidence that final design must be
        feasible for building-bridges

    there was weak evidence that building-bridges requires
        a strategy of 4
    this followed from 2 things:

    there was weak evidence that constraint values increase
        sharply in feasible domain for building-bridges

    there was weak evidence that final design must be
        feasible for building-bridges

        Options are next, done, how, why, help

        > next
Respond with y or n.

do you want more rules?

        > y

232

Do you know what strategy to use?

> y

Do you know what optimizer to use?

> n

[load cuopt.]

what kind of problem are you solving?
Please enter as a single string, with no spaces

> building-bridges

You may answer the following questions with a
y (yes), n (no), m (maybe), l (likely), nl (not
likely), p (probably), dk (don't know),
or a probability factor ranging from 0
(least certain) to 10 (most certain).

Enter a how or a why to see an explanation,
enter detail to see details about a rule,
and to get help, type HELP or ?

Please wait. . .

With what certainty can you assert:
computer storage is very limited for building-bridges ?

> n

With what certainty can you assert:
analytical gradients are available for building-bridges ?

> y

does building-bridges involve more than 50 design
variables ?

> nl

does building-bridges involve more than 200 design
variables ?

> 2

With what certainty can you assert:
building-bridges has a well-conditioned objective function and/or
constraints ?

> detail

A problem with smoothly varying objective function
constraints and derivatives eg polynomials

With what certainty can you assert:
building-bridges has a well-conditioned objective function and/or
constraints ?

> p

is analysis iterative for building-bridges ?

> dk

There are no subrules for the rule you
don't know about. The default is NO!
Do you wish to accept the default,
y or n?

> n

is analysis iterative for building-bridges ?

> m

With what certainty can you assert:
optimizer 3 has been tried unsuccessfully fo
building-bridges ?

> n

No hypothesis can be confirmed with certainty

Hypothesis   building-bridges requires an optimizer of 1
  has certainty 0.3

    Optimizer 1 is the Fletcher-Reeves conjugate gradient
    algorithm

Hypothesis   building-bridges requires an optimizer of 3
  has certainty 0.85

    Optimizer 3 is the Broydon-Fletcher-Goldbarb-Shanno
    variable metric or quasi-Newton method

    Options are next, done, how, why, help

    > next
Respond with y or n.

do you want more rules?

    > y

Do you know what strategy to use?

    > y

Do you know what optimizer to use?

    > y

[load cusearch.]

what kind of problem are you solving?
    Please enter as a single string, with no spaces

    > building-bridges

    You may answer the following questions with a
y (yes), n (no), m (maybe), l (likely), nl (not
likely), p (probably), dk (don't know),
or a probability factor ranging from 0
(least certain) to 10 (most certain).

    Enter a how or a why to see an explanation,
enter detail to see details about a rule,
and to get help, type HELP or ?

    Please wait. . .

  With what certainty can you assert:
function evaluations are expensive for building-bridges ?

> 8
  With what certainty can you assert:
building-bridges has a well-conditioned objective function and/or
  constraints ?

> p
No hypothesis can be confirmed with certainty

Hypothesis   building-bridges requires a oned-search of 3
  has certainty 0.7

    A oned-search of 3 first finds bounds then uses
    polynomial interpolation

Hypothesis   building-bridges requires a oned-search of 2
  has certainty 0.2

    A oned-search of 2 uses the golden section method
    followed by polynomial interpolation

Hypothesis   building-bridges requires a oned-search of 1
  has certainty 0.2

    A oned-search of 1 uses the golden section method
    Options are next, done, how, why, help

Options are next, done, how, why, help

    > done
$

References

1. Vanderplaats, G.N. (1984) ADS—A FORTRAN Program for Automated Design Synthesis—Version 1.00, NASA CR 172460, October

2. Gevarter, W.B. (1982) An Overview Of Expert Systems, NBSIR 82-2505, May

3. Hayes-Roth, F., Waterman, D.A., Lenat, D.B. (1983) Building Expert Systems. Reading, MA: Addison-Wesley

4. Winston, P.H., Horn, B.K.P. (1981) LISP. Reading, MA: Addison-Wesley

An Expert System for Real-Time Control

M. Lattimer Wright, Milton W. Green, Gudrun Fiegl, and Perry F. Cross
SRI International

Microcomputers can host real-time control expert systems. As Hexscon shows, the key is combining the best of conventional and expert-system controllers.

Real-time control computers — ranging from small, simple controllers in home appliances to large, complex systems for industrial and military purposes — are used in more applications than ever before. Both small and large controllers perform increasingly complex tasks. The complexity is increasing not only in the number of functions controlled but also in the kinds of factors that must be considered before a correct decision can be made.

This increasing complexity has caused considerable interest in using knowledge-based techniques in controller applications. Proper application of these techniques can result in more sophisticated control strategies for advanced applications.

The evolutionary development of Hexscon (for Hybrid Expert System Controller), an experimental knowledge-based expert system intended to deal with control problem encountered in military and advanced industrial applications, shows how these more sophisticated strategies can be achieved.

The real-time nature of most control applications, as well as the desirability of using microcomputer-scale machines, distinguishes the controller application from more traditional knowledge-based systems such as the Mycin medical evaluator. Real-time means a decision is available at or before the time it is needed, although it usually implies a real-time system design philosophy as well.

When Hexscon development began in 1983, knowledge-based systems running in microcomputer environments did not appear to exist for real-time control applications. Newer real-time systems such as Picon[1] use a Lisp machine for intelligence but lack the microcomputer-based representation structures of Hexscon. Systems requiring a Lisp machine cannot now be used for embedded military applications.

Military applications for controllers often combine the need for a high degree of sophistication with strict requirements for small size and high speed. Some general features and requirements of such applications are

- Conclusions must be formed and actions must be taken in real time as they respond to the sensors' perceptions of an unpredictable and changing environment.
- Data from sensors must be interpreted and reasoned about to identify types of events and objects known to the knowledge base. In addition, temporal and spatial properties and relationships of objects and events must be reasoned about.
- The system must operate reasonably and safely on inaccurate or uncertain data inputs.
- The system must work with very limited hardware resources (for example, a microcomputer with a modest amount of fast storage as the host machine).

A sample problem domain is that of a partially autonomous satellite that participates in early warning missile tracking and countermeasures, and possibly in self-defense activities. Here the objects known to the knowledge base are such things as missiles, satellites, submarines, missile sites, ground-based emitters (radars and lasers), and geographical landmarks. Events consist of missile launch detection, missile track identification, observation of geographical features, message reception, and the like.

The Hexscon design includes several sophisticated features often associated with military and advanced commercial applications. Although the satellite example provides an illustrative case with complex requirements, none of the domain knowledge about the satellite problem is encoded into the system. Thus, Hexscon can be used for a wide range of problems in commercial, industrial, and military applications.

Hexscon's design goals included (1) a capacity of 5000 rules in a microcomputer system with 512K memory, (2) a response

Reprinted from *IEEE Software*, vol. 3, no. 2, pp. 16–24, Mar. 1986.

John W. Backus:
Fortran

Photo courtesy Annals of the
History of Computing

time of 10 ms to 100 ms, (3) the ability to handle many objects (about 1000), and (4) the ability to continue functioning despite a lot of uncertainty.

Knowledge representation

Many real-time operational decisions, particularly the simpler ones, are now made quite adequately and rapidly by conventional logic controllers. To preserve this capability, the hybrid Hexscon system uses both conventional logic and knowledge-based techniques. During development, it became apparent that both parts of the system were significantly affected by having to work together.

Many of these design differences were caused by the need for compatible knowledge representations in the two parts. For example, the internal representation of knowledge about objects is quite different in conventional controllers than it is in knowledge-based controllers.

General-purpose conventional controllers are often table-driven; that is, information about objects is stored in table form. The knowledge of what the tables contain and how to manipulate the information in the tables is contained in the conventional code.

The knowledge-based part, on the other hand, does not represent data in tabular form. Instead, it represents data as variables associated with particular chunks of knowledge in the knowledge base. Hexscon computer code is really an inference engine that knows only how to run a knowledge base. It has no information or knowledge about the problem domain.

The knowledge base, rather than the inference engine, contains knowledge of how various variables interrelate and how they are connected to the domain knowledge. These two approaches normally lead to very different internal representations for both knowledge and data.

Representation translator. To make a completely integrated hybrid system,

knowledge and data representations for both conventional and knowledge-based parts would have to be identical or at least fully compatible. During the early stages of development, the knowledge representation issues were not as clear as they were later, so a representation translator was used in the initial hybrid design.

This representation translator lets the conventional and knowledge-based parts exchange information freely without requiring full representational compatibility. The translator knows how knowledge and information are represented in both parts and how to convert back and forth.

Because information had to flow through the representation translator, it slowed down the system somewhat. As greater degrees of representation compatibility were achieved in successive generations, the representation translator had less and less to do and therefore hindered the system performance less and less.

The performance slowdown was not as great as originally expected, so the translator remained part of the Hexscon design. The advantage of the representation translator was that it allowed both parts to use techniques that had been developed and proven in stand-alone systems of both kinds.

Control flow. Another major difference between Hexscon and stand-alone conventional or knowledge-based systems concerned the flow of control in the real-time sense. Real-time systems are usually partitioned into highly modular tasks, communicating under the control of a real-time operating system. However, it proved difficult to implement the knowledge-based part this way.

Straightforward applications of conventional real-time techniques were extremely expensive in scarce memory resources. More sophisticated partitioning of the inference engine introduced significant problems in implementing efficient knowledge representations that had been developed in stand-alone knowledge-based

systems. The solution was to let the knowledge-based portion run as a single task in the real-time system.

A distinction was made, at the control-flow level, between processor interrupts and logic interrupts. A processor interrupt is essentially identical to the interrupts in conventional real-time operating systems. Logic interrupts refer to the interruption of the knowledge-based portion part way through its reasoning process.

In a machine with a lot of available memory, this partially reasoned process could be stored temporarily and a new set of data could be reasoned about until the stored problem is resumed. This queuing technique proved too expensive in memory resources, however, and was abandoned. Instead of queuing, a logic interrupt would cause the knowledge-based portion to forget the current state of reasoning completely and begin on a new problem.

Progressive reasoning. Decision times envisioned for Hexscon ranged from about 10 ms for rapid reflex-like responses to about 20 minutes for very complex decisions involving future possibilities. Interviews with experts indicated that many problems could be reasoned at several different levels and that human response time was quite different at these different levels of reasoning.

A similar capability for reasoning at different levels was designed into Hexscon and called progressive reasoning. This progressive reasoning lets Hexscon obtain the best possible decision within the time available.

Assume that a new piece of information comes into the system, producing a processor interrupt and causing the system to analyze the data and determine, as quickly as possible, the best action to take and how much time is available before an action must be taken. This analysis is done by the first level of progressive reasoning.

The system then asks, "Do we have more time to think about this problem?" If not, the system executes the currently designated actions. If time is available, the system goes to the second level to determine a more well-thought-out, and presumably better, course of action.

At the end of the second level, the system again asks the same question. If the answer is no, the revised currently designated actions are executed. If the answer is yes, additional levels of reasoning are invoked. Each successive level will use data that are more time-consuming to retrieve and process than the previous level. The current implementation allows four levels, with the first implemented in conventional logic, followed by three levels of reasoning in the knowledge-based part.

Task priorities. Since Hexscon may have to reason about several different objects or situations at the same time, and each of these objects or situations may be reasoned about at any of the progressive reasoning levels, the choice of the most important problem to work on next can get rather complex. For this reason, both the knowledge-based part and the conventional part share the responsibility for determining the priority of problems the knowledge-based part should handle.

Priorities are kept on an ordered list, and either part of the system can change the order of the list. Determining priorities in complex situations can take a long time — in some cases longer than the decision takes. For this reason, prioritization can also be handled with the progressive reasoning technique to provide the best prioritization in the time available.

Reasoning

The basic representation framework is a production system using if-then rules. These rules contain the heuristic knowl-

edge of the problem domain. This choice, to a large extent, determines not only the overall Hexscon system design but also the way it represents other concepts, such as multiple objects and time reasoning.

This choice was strongly influenced by the relatively large body of knowledge available about building production systems. Also, we believed that knowledge in this form could be written so it would be easily understood by both knowledge engineers and experts.

Rule format. Figure 1 shows an example of the information contained in the rule format. Figure 1a shows the heuristic knowledge represented by English-like if-then statements. Each line consists of a

word ("if," "and," or "then") followed by a fact. Each fact contains three phrases, each enclosed by parentheses. Each phrase contains one or more words.

The third fact (third line) in Figure 1a contains a named variable. The variable name is "current jeopardy" and its value is tested to see if it is less than 10. Variables can represent numbers or strings.

Rules in the form shown in Figure 1 are too wasteful of space for modest-sized microcomputers. To minimize the size of the working knowledge base and to speed execution time, the English-like rules are compiled into a more compact form for the inference engine. This rule compilation is handled by a separate piece of software used for knowledge acquisition and management.

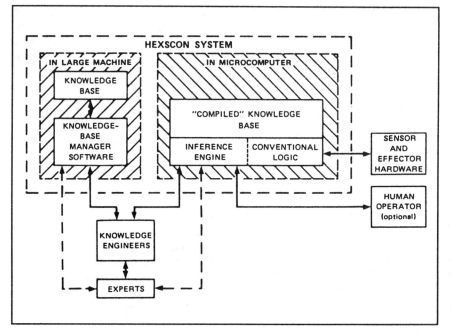

Figure 2. Composition of a microcomputer-based expert system.

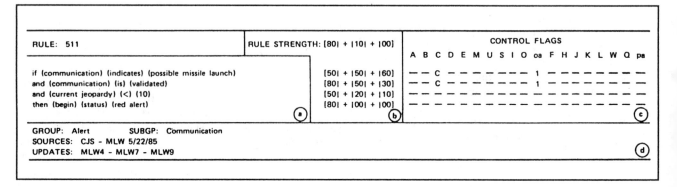

Figure 1. Example of rule format information.

Grace M. Hopper:
automatic programming—Cobol

The complete Hexscon system includes the three major parts shown in Figure 2: the inference engine, the knowledge base, and the knowledge-base management software. The knowledge-base management software and the English-like knowledge base can be in a large machine such as a Lisp machine.

However, a very capable microcomputer-resident knowledge-base manager has been developed for modest-sized problems (about 500 to 1000 rules). The microcomputer contains the permanent inference engine and conventional logic parts and, for a particular problem domain, the compiled knowledge base produced by the knowledge-base manager.

Multiple objects. Hexscon can reason about multiple objects. A basic assumption is that the entire knowledge base applies to the object being reasoned about. Thus, the inference net implied by the knowledge base can be assumed to apply to each object. If this inference net is represented geometrically as a plane, additional objects can be represented by additional inference net planes, as Figure 3 shows.

Additional inference net planes are created dynamically by the inference engine to accommodate the number of objects being reasoned about simultaneously. Relations between objects can be represented graphically as links between planes as shown in Figure 3.

Each inference net plane represents the entire knowledge base. An actual replication of the knowledge base would be far too wasteful of space in microcomputer systems. In Hexscon, only the absolutely essential parts of the knowledge base are replicated, although logically the entire knowledge base appears to be replicated for each object.

At runtime, each object is assigned a unique object number by the system. This object number is used to distinguish multiple occurrences of the same object or kind of object and is used by both the knowledge-based part and the conventional part. This number allows data stored in one representation in the knowledge-based part to be associated correctly with data stored in a different representation in the conventional part.

Hexscon can handle basic reasoning about time. Time is partitioned into past, present, and future frames. The present

time frame is defined by one or more object planes in memory about which the system is currently reasoning. Past and future time frames are resident on disk files, since information on the maximum number of objects (1000) is far too much to store in microcomputer memory.

Information stored for past and future times is highly compressed to save space but is logically equivalent to the object planes used in the present. Thus, if something has been thought about in the past, that entire line of reasoning is available in these files without having to repeat the reasoning.

A time stamp is associated with each object plane. Different occurrences of the same object at different times will have the same object number but different time stamps. They may or may not contain the same data. Different objects of the same type, seen at different times, will have different object numbers and time stamps.

These time stamps are accessible from rules and are the basic data used in time reasoning.

Control knowledge

In addition to heuristic knowledge, the system must also represent control knowledge. As the name implies, this knowledge controls how the inference engine operates on the heuristic knowledge. In Hexscon, control knowledge is divided into two categories.

Part of the control knowledge is implicit in the design of the inference engine and is not under the control of the knowledge engineer. Part is explicitly available to the knowledge engineer within the rule constructs.

The built-in (implicit) control knowledge includes the general capabilities for reasoning about the knowledge concepts implemented by the system.

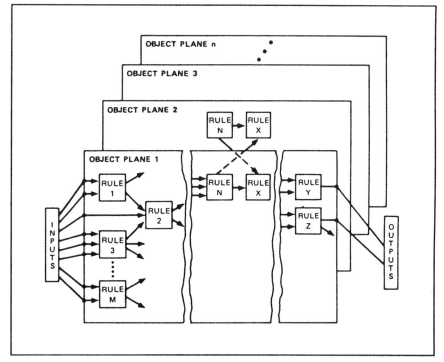

Figure 3. Logical representation of multiple objects.

Search strategies. Search strategies used in traversing the inference net are fundamental to the inference engine's operation. Hexscon starts searching the inference net at points determined by the available input data. In this sense, it is a data-driven, or forward-chaining, system. In the course of traversing the inference net forwards, the system back-chains to obtain relevant or missing pieces of information.

This back-chaining may include requests to sensors to provide details that are not ordinarily volunteered. This assumes that the sensors allow some interactive processing.

Systems that do both forward-chaining and back-chaining are susceptible to looping in the inference net. The detection of such loops is a function of the knowledge-base manager. Early versions of the inference engine that did not incorporate a multiple-object capability had a built-in, effective loop detection and suppression algorithm. We removed it to improve runtime performance after the loop-detection function of the knowledge-base manager became operational.

The loop-detection function operates effectively only in one object plane. Problem domains with a lot of multiple-object interaction will have many possible links between object planes. Because these dynamic links are set up at runtime, they can introduce formation of multiplane loops not detectable by a single-plane static loop analysis. With richly interconnected object planes, the number of possible loops becomes extremely large, and exhaustive search techniques don't detect such loops well.

Nonbinary inferencing. Another built-in control structure is the inferencing technique that determines when a rule will fire. In Hexscon, a key consideration in choosing an inferencing technique is explicitly representing uncertainty. In many military applications, high degrees of uncertainty are associated with both data and reasoning processes.

An enemy may deliberately try to fool us. This introduces elements that are more difficult to deal with than ordinary uncertainty in a cooperative environment. In such cases, the uncertainty itself is part of the reasoning process and must be explicitly represented.

Commonly used Bayesian techniques do not help distinguish uncertainty with complete information from a lack of information. In Hexscon, this distinction is achieved with two inferencing parameters: belief and confidence.

The belief parameter ranges from +100, at the "yes" end of the scale, to −100 at the "no" end of the scale. The midpoint, 0, represents the "don't know" between the two. The confidence parameter ranges from +100, meaning "absolutely certain," to 0, meaning "I have no information."

In deciding whether to fire a multifact rule, a third inferencing parameter — importance — indicates the relative importance of the facts in a rule. These importance parameters weight the other parameters to determine when a rule fires. They can also guide the search path in the most important direction.

Inferencing parameters are propagated from one rule to the next. The inference engine uses parameters coming from a previous rule (or an input) into the "if" parts (antecedents) of a rule to determine if the rule will fire. If the rule does fire, parameters are passed from the "then" parts (consequents) of the rule to the next rule. In linear inferencing, the parameters passed to the next rule are calculated as the average of the input parameters weighted by the importance values.

Inferencing

Knowledge engineering sessions with experts show they use both linear and nonlinear inferencing. Linear inferencing propagates inferencing parameters through a rule using a fixed algorithm. Nonlinear inferencing propagates parameters that are not necessarily related in a fixed way to a rule's antecedent parameters, but instead are set by values in the rule itself.

Belief parameters. To partially accommodate both types of reasoning, the knowledge engineer can choose whether belief parameters are set by the consequent or propagated through a rule. If propagated through a rule, the consequent belief parameter values passed to the next rule are the weighted averages of the input beliefs. Confidence is always propagated through a rule.

If the belief parameters are set rather than propagated, the parameter values in the rule are propagated to the next rule if the rule fires. For example, Figure 1b shows that the fourth fact (in the consequent of the rule) would pass a belief of 80 to the next rule if this rule were to fire.

Another aid to modeling nonlinear reasoning is a flag indicating which of two ways inferencing parameters interact to fire a rule. In one case, each fact is treated independently. The inferencing parameters coming into each fact must be above the threshold for the fact to be true. Furthermore, all facts in the antecedent of the rule must be true for the rule to fire.

The second case combines the inferencing parameters for all facts in the rule and compares this result to an overall rule-strength inferencing parameter. This case is closer to the more linear reasoning techniques found in such programs as Emycin[2] and Prospector.[3]

Multiple reasoning lines. Interviews with experts indicate that there are often several different lines of reasoning leading to a particular conclusion. In such cases, it is common that different lines of reasoning do not produce the same belief and confidence in the final conclusion — and may even produce opposite conclusions. Some systems have no mechanism to resolve these disparate views about the same subject produced by different lines of reasoning.

In Hexscon, different reasoning lines are combined (and possible conflicts resolved) with a technique based on a combination of evidence developed by Shafer and Dempster.[4] The technique can produce a single, overall composite value of belief and confidence for different and perhaps conflicting results. The Shafer-Dempster technique is used in combining multiple lines of reasoning because it can deal with the explicit representation of lack of knowledge.

Multiple objects. Multiple-object referencing is another important function of control knowledge. A basic assumption underlying the representation of knowledge in rule form is that each rule should not depend on any other rule for proper execution. With that assumption, each rule can be considered as an independent chunk of knowledge and object references can be done entirely within a rule. Referencing is done by object-association numbers, as Figure 4 shows.

The rule in Figure 4 reasons about three objects: a new object, an enemy platform, and a set of sensors used for decoy

Kenneth E. Iverson:
APL

detection. The association numbers permit the correct facts to be associated with each object. This approach is similar to the use of subscripted variables in systems where heuristic knowledge and control knowledge are less separated. This approach makes rule parsing easier and more efficient in microcomputers with limited capabilities.

With the rule set in Figure 4's example, the inference engine would set up at runtime at least three logical object planes. If the status of the decoy sensors is not known, the inference engine would backchain to determine status only in the object plane associated with object 3 (the sensors).

Because the back-chaining to obtain this status takes place entirely in a single object plane, the correct object association for other rules in this plane is implicitly maintained. Using multiple object planes allows correct object referencing to take place between rules, even though the only explicit object referencing takes place within a single rule. The object referred to by an object association number in one rule is not necessarily the same object referred to in another rule by the same object association number.

Another number is used to reference the same object at different times or at different occurrences. Since each reasoning process about an object occurs in one logical object plane, these numbers are called plane association numbers. Figure 5 shows an example of plane association numbers.

A single object reference number (1) is used for all facts associated with the enemy satellite, indicating that we are referring to a single object. At some earlier time, Hexscon reasoned that this object was tracking us on an intercept course. This reasoning was done in a plane associated with a plane association number of 1.

At a different time associated with a different plane, the inference engine reasoned that this same object is still tracking us and is still on an intercept course. This later reasoning is done in a different plane with a plane association number of 2. The earlier line of reasoning is in the history file and will have the same object number as in the later plane.

The enemy platform object reference number (1) in Figure 5 need not be the same as the object reference number (2) in Fig-

ure 4 for the same object because object numbers are local to a single rule.

Algorithms. Procedural knowledge seems quite extensive in many applications of controllers, particularly those for which conventional logic controllers now exist. Much of this information is in the form of algorithms and other numeric processes. Many such algorithms already exist for conventional controllers. The Hexscon design keeps these algorithms within the conventional portion but allows free access to these algorithms by the knowledge-based part.

Algorithms are accessed by a function identifier in the rule structure. Figure 6 illustrates such a function. The function "attack course" is a numeric algorithm

that knows the current spatial location of the two platforms and the geometric positions and movements of each. This algorithm resides in the conventional part and is activated when a fact beginning with (fn attack course) is encountered in any rule.

It is possible to pass parameters from within rules to this numeric algorithm. In the Figure 6 example, the type of attack course, collision, is passed to the numeric algorithm, which evaluates only the collision possibility. Other possible attack courses could include intercept, stand-off, and so forth.

If the algorithm finds it is on a collision course, the algorithm terminates and the fact associated with that function is declared to be true. The inference engine

	OAN*
if (enemy platform) (is) (approaching)	1
and (new object) (is) (detected)	2
and (decoy sensors) (are) (operational)	3
and (decoy sensors) (are not) (shielded)	3
then (begin) (decoy) (discrimination)	

*Object Association Number

Figure 4. Multiple-object referencing by object association number.

	OAN	PAN*
if (enemy radar) (was) (tracking us)	1	1
and (enemy course) (was) (intercept)	1	1
and (our satellite) (has) (maneuvered)	2	--
and (enemy radar) (is) (tracking us)	1	2
and (enemy course) (is) (intercept)	1	2
then (enemy platform) (has) (maneuver capability)	1	--
and (our maneuver) (is not) (effective)	2	--
and (consider) (launching) (active decoy)	2	--

*Plane Association Number

Figure 5. Example of reference to multiple occurrences of the same object.

then continues normal rule execution.

The association of the conventional part to named functions in rules is now done manually, although procedures for automating the process have been devised. The next generation of knowledge-based managers could include a capability to not only simplify the knowledge-base acquisition and management but also eliminate errors caused by manual transfer techniques.

Development framework

It is often easier to build an application with an existing expert system tool if the tool can deal with the problem domain. When we began the development, we found few expert system tools that ran on microcomputers. Those that could included only simple concepts. They could not handle sophisticated applications. Even tools that could be ported to microcomputers did not contain the required concepts, so we could not build on an existing framework.

Lisp is a preferred language for building knowledge-based systems and thus was the first language considered for this development. However, Lisp languages for microcomputers tend to use a lot of memory and execute significantly more slowly than other microcomputer languages. The need for periodic garbage collection was an especially serious problem for real-time systems because the system is inoperative while collecting garbage. These combined difficulties made Lisp unattractive for our application.

Pascal chosen. After investigating Pascal, Ada, C, Forth, Basic, and several other languages, we chose Pascal because it simplified construction of large programs, produced compact, fast code in the target environment, could be easily

converted to Ada later, and was well-known by the developers. We chose a dialect of Pascal native to the microcomputer's own 8086 processor that has a particularly rich array of extensions.

The Hexscon development clearly showed that the techniques used to implement knowledge-based systems on microcomputers are quite different from the techniques used on larger machines, especially Lisp machines. Once the details of such implementation techniques are developed, however, the Lisp machine becomes the ideal choice for production software development of the same or similar kinds of systems.

Programmers using the Lisp machine must be very careful to use only those constructs known to be convertible to compact, efficient microcomputer code in another language. Lisp machines in particular have a very rich language and powerful constructs. Experience has shown that some of these constructs are difficult to realize in a fast, compact form in the microcomputer runtime environment. The ideal development language for this type of system is a Lisp subset containing only those constructs effective in real-time microcomputer systems.

Knowledge acquisition. The knowledge we acquired from experts was divided into two categories: conceptual knowledge and operational knowledge. Conceptual knowledge focuses on the concepts necessary for effective operation in the desired domain. Possible concepts include multiple objects, time reasoning, spatial reasoning, multiple lines of reasoning, planning, analysis, conflict resolution, and truth maintenance.

Conceptual knowledge. Conceptual knowledge indicates the kinds of capabilities that must be designed into the system.

After the system is built, heuristic knowledge is obtained with concepts and representational techniques built into the system.

Within each broad concept area, necessary details of each concept must be identified to determine what must be built into the system. For example, if reasoning about multiple objects is required, several questions must be answered:

What is the total number of objects to be reasoned about? If the total number is very large, is it enough to reason about a smaller subset of objects at any one instant? Are there multiple instances of the same kind of object that must be distinguished? Is the same object reasoned about several times or under several different circumstances?

Similar detailed questions must be answered about each required concept. The detailed answers to these questions indicate how the concept is used in the problem domain and what capabilities the system must have.

Conceptual knowledge was acquired almost exclusively through interviews with experts. An effective technique was to have the expert run through a number of typical problems and describe his high-level reasoning techniques at each point. Experts tended to focus on lower-level details, so it fell to the knowledge engineer to keep the interview focused on high-level, conceptual processes.

As high-level concepts are identified by the knowledge engineer and the expert continues to describe problem scenarios, it is appropriate for the knowledge engineer to direct the discussion to successively lower-level conceptual details on subsequent problem descriptions. After several iterations, this should net enough details about the required concepts to permit an initial design of a knowledge base and an inference engine.

Operational knowledge. The second category of knowledge acquired from the experts, operational knowledge, is the experts' detailed working knowledge that will be incorporated into the final knowledge base. Operational knowledge was gathered at both high and low levels. High-level information was gathered first so that simplified — but complete — problems could be run on early prototype systems.

These early prototypes let the high-level logic, as expressed by the expert, be checked out early. As with the conceptual

```
if (enemy platform) (is) (approaching)
and (platform velocity) (is) (high)
and (fn attack course) (is) (collision)
then (attack type) (may be) (ramming)
and (consider) (maneuver type) (anti-ram)
```

Figure 6. Example of function reference in a rule.

242

Niklaus Wirth:
Pascal

knowledge, gaps were found in the high-level operational knowledge and could be corrected before proceeding to lower-level operational knowledge. This high-level to low-level development is a little like a top-down approach to knowledge-base development.

Early collection of low-level operational knowledge (that is, knowledge associated with inputs and outputs from both the conventional part and sensors and effectors) eased the design of the interface between the conventional part and the knowledge-based part of the hybrid Hexscon system.

This portion of the knowledge-base development was similar to a bottom-up approach. Early collection of this low-level knowledge also permitted early demonstration of a system incorporating both conventional and knowledge-based parts. This, in turn, helped reveal a number of interface problems at an early stage.

Expert variability. Experts seem to express knowledge in different ways in different situations. These situations can be divided into two categories: in the interview, in which the expert interaction is largely verbal or written, and in a simulation of an actual situation where the expert must provide inputs, interact with the machine, and examine lines of reasoning.

The differences between these two situations are both qualitative and quantitative. When interviewed about military battlefield applications, for example, the experts were relaxed and offered knowledge from a theoretical point of view. Later, when running realistic simulated problems on a small knowledge base, these same experts were less relaxed and focused their attention on somewhat different issues — and often seemed to express knowledge differently.

In addition to these qualitative differences, quantitative differences in inferencing parameters were observed as well. In interviews, experts would consistently give higher estimates for inferencing thresholds than they would for runs of simulated problems. These differences were more noticeable in military situations where one's personal safety would be threatened. In other domains, the effect was absent or less pronounced.

Knowledge engineers working on military problems may have to modify their usual knowledge acquisition techniques to avoid the significant inconsistencies introduced by this effect. The use of rapid prototypes provides early checkpoints that help identify the nature and extent of the problem.

User interfaces. The primary expert interface during development is a knowledge engineer. In later stages of knowledge base development, some experts can interact effectively with both the knowledge-base manager and the inference engine. When the knowledge base becomes operational, users can easily interact directly with the inference engine in an interactive mode, if required.

For controller applications, the nature of the interaction with the human user is significantly different from that of the more familiar knowledge-based systems. In real-time control systems, most of the inputs come from sensors while many of the outputs go to effectors.

In many applications, the only interface to the user are messages telling the user what the machine is doing. The usual question/answer dialogue of many knowledge-based systems is inappropriate for a large number of real-time control applications.

In developing the knowledge base, however, it is essential to interact with the machine. Because of this dichotomy, the system is designed to operate in both an interactive simulation mode and a real-time control mode.

Hexscon status

We have developed and demonstrated a prototype real-time knowledge-based control system running on a microcomputer. During development, we tried to minimize the encoding of a particular problem domain into either the inference engine or the knowledge-based manager. Problem domains for military applications, international banking, puzzles, and games have been implemented. This range of demonstrated problem domains indicates that the system contains minimal information about any specific problem domain.

Our effort focused on developing a prototype Hexscon controller system, not on including an operational rule base for a particular application. The demonstrated knowledge bases varied from very rudimentary, for an international banking case, to a moderately complete subset, as in selected military applications. Knowledge bases for the games were generally complete but not as large as most applications would require.

During development, we investigated several variations of the system. The results of these experiments are shown in Figures 7-9. Figure 7 shows the results of an experiment whose goal was to squeeze as much knowledge as possible into a small computer. Allowing a longer response time and minimizing the sophistication achieved the large rule capacity. We

Computer	8-bit micro (8085), 64k memory
Max. number of rules	About 2000 (1650 actually used)
Response time	10–30 s (knowledge-based part only)
Sophistication	Minimum

Figure 7. Results with emphasis on maximum squeeze.

243

Computer	16-bit micro (8086), 256k memory
Max. number of rules	About 5000 (250 actually used)
Response time	0.25–0.5 s (knowledge-based part only)
Sophistication	Moderate

Figure 8. Results with emphasis on maximum speed.

Computer	16-bit micro (8086), 512k memory
Max. number of rules	About 4000 (350 actually used)
Response time	1–10 s (knowledge-based part only)
Sophistication	Maximum

Figure 9. Results with emphasis on maximum expertise.

achieved fast response time by selecting only those concepts that can be implemented in ways that execute quickly, as Figure 8 shows.

The maximum expertise experiment (Figure 9) implemented all concepts we investigated. The rule capacity for the maximum expertise experiment was slightly reduced compared to the speed experiment, even though the memory size was doubled. The larger range of response times reflects the greater range in possible complexity of solutions.

We also demonstrated the maximum expertise version as a hybrid system incorporating a conventional-logic part. This hybrid system was connected to a separate computer to provide simulated real-time inputs to the system and successfully controlled a number of hardware devices connected to the outputs of the system.

This work has shown we can build a knowledge-based controller that runs on a microcomputer and has enough sophistication and capacity to be effective for real-world problems. ☐

Acknowledgments

The authors gratefully acknowledge the many contributions Bette Webb, Steve Miner, Leann Sucht, and Len Karpf have made to the success of this project.

References

1. R.L. Moore et al., "A Real-Time Expert System for Process Control," *Proc. Conf. AI Applications*, Denver, Dec. 1984.

2. W. van Melle et al., *The Emycin Manual*, Report STAN-CS-81-885, Dept. of Computer Science, Stanford University, Stanford, Calif., Oct. 1981.

3. R.O. Duda et al., "Development of the Prospector Consultation System for Mineral Exploration," final report, SRI Projects 5821 and 6415, SRI International, Menlo Park, Calif., 1978.

4. G. Shafer, *A Mathematical Theory of Evidence*, Princeton University Press, Princeton, N.J., 1976.

The authors' address is SRI International, 333 Ravenswood Ave., Menlo Park, CA 94025.

PROCESS CONTROL AND MONITORING
USING MICRO-COMPUTER BASED EXPERT SYSTEMS

by

H.B. Seiler and K.E. Seiler
Level Five Research, Inc.
503 Fifth Avenue, Indialantic, FL

Abstract

This paper discusses the uses of micro-computer based expert systems for real-time process monitoring and control. Expert system technology provides a readily available solution to real-time process applications where ease of development and maintenance are primary design constraints. In situations where, because of cost or development schedule constraints, a real-time application must be prototyped and developed without the aid of programmer/analysts, expert systems provide the scientist or engineer the ability to develop and deploy a process control application using the higher level problem representation provided by off-the-shelf microcomputer expert systems.

A discussion of the comparative merits of real-time vs. highly-interactive vs. batch computer systems is presented in relation to expert systems and process control. Two case studies are presented which demonstrate how expert systems can be used for effective real-time diagnosis and control of time critical processes. The first case study presents a description of the implementation of an expert system used to monitor and diagnose an environmentally regulated biological system. The second case study discusses an implementation of a Critical Safety Parameter Display System (CSPDS) for nuclear power plants implemented via conventional means. An analysis of the project life cycle illustrates where the use of expert systems by plant engineers to prototype the overall system decision logic would have reduced costs and reduced the project implementation time.

Introduction

In keeping with the way things are done here at Level Five, this paper will not be a metaphysical diatribe on the best of all possible worlds but rather a discussion of observations gleaned from our experiences in the field and with our users. These observations will describe what is being attempted with micro-computer based expert systems in small scale applications and will offer our projections of where this technology needs to be utilized in large scale industrial applications. The paper will define various terms related to the discussion and briefly describe design constraint conditions in process control. Two methodologies of application development cycles will be developed and then later described in relation to a actual case histories.

Real-Time Process Monitoring and Control

A real-time computer system is a combination of software and hardware for which the sense-evaluate-response time matches or exceeds the event cycle time of the real-world process the computer system must interact with. Real-time computer systems can generally be characterized by a high-speed computer interfaced to analog and digital sensing devices under the control of software which is time slice and interrupt driven. These systems are commonly used to monitor and control certain real-world processes where failure to diagnose and initiate prompt corrective action can result in either outright damage to the physical process and/or loss of production time and revenues.

Historically, real-time process control and monitoring systems have been implemented on minicomputers, mainframes and more recently on super-micros. The real-time process is modeled by the process engineers and is generally designed and coded into FORTRAN software by programmer/analysts. These systems tend to be monolithic in nature, requiring one centralized computer with a large complex operating system and a highly integrated set of programs controlling the entire system. As a result of their history of development and entrenched methodologies, such process monitoring and control computer systems generally lack several important characteristics as noted below.

1) Process knowledge isolation: The knowledge of the process to be monitored and/or controlled is often obscured by the real-time control logic of the program.

2) Difficulty in the representation of heuristic knowledge: Conventional algorithmic programming languages such as FORTRAN and C lack the ability to represent the qualitative decision processes required for fault isolation and diagnosis. Thus, the heuristic knowledge of the process that is routinely possessed by the engineers and operators is not integrated into the control system.

3) Alarm minimization: When a process undergoes a dramatic state transition or a failure occurs, a large number of sensors of sub-processes will usually generate alarms due to side effects or sub-system dependencies. At the time of the failure the plant operators are consequently flooded with alarms. During the first critical moments of a failure the operator must rely on past experiences to filter through extraneous alarms to determine the true point of failure.

4) Ease of development and maintenance: When modifications in the process require new control logic, the process engineers must re-define control program specifications for implementation in a conventional programming language by the programmer/analysts. The requirement for programmers to translate a process engineer's specifications into programs is time consuming, costly, and prone to logic errors.

Highly-Interactive Systems

Micro or personal computers are not usually considered useful in real-time process control because their sense-evaluate-response time is geared to conform to the human perceptual needs of reasonableness. Events that occur in conventional PC applications are user initiated. The user answers a question or invokes a command causing the computer to perform some task. The computer then waits for the next user direction. We define this type of interaction and its associated stimulus-response time cycle as "highly-interactive" but not as a real-time system. However, as we are seeing more and more often, it is possible for the personal computer to be relegated to some advisory role in a real-time process control system. With the addition of sensor hardware and software for the polling of devices, personal computers are being used to monitor and control small manufacturing systems, laboratory environments, and serving as diagnostic aids in industrial applications.

Micro-computer Based Expert Systems

Most micro-computer based expert system development tools ("shells") do not possess the basic real-time capabilities necessary to perform process control. This is not to say that an expert system created with one of the popular development tools should be expected to perform all the various duties of a real-time process control system. However, there does exist a minimum criteria set that these systems require for performing an advisory role. The expert systems that are the products of these tools are typically highly-interactive systems. These systems receive a majority of the input data interactively from a human user as answers to direct questions. Results are presented in the form of static display screens and printed or filed reports. The event cycle time of a PC based expert system is dependent upon human response time, which could range from seconds to hours, and the problem under evaluation is generally not dependent upon the timeliness of the results. Thus, we often see personal computer based expert systems used for evaluation and diagnostics which can be conducted independently of the process under evaluation.

In order for an microcomputer based expert system to serve as an executive for a process control system several features are essential:

1) Forward chaining. The expert system inference engine must be capable of forward chaining. The inference engine must be able to cyclically execute the knowledge base at definable time rates in order to continuously monitor the real-time process.

2) Backward chaining. The expert system's inference should also be able to perform backward chaining goal-driven logic upon invocation by the forward chaining constructs. This capability is called upon for fault isolation and diagnosis when required. The best architecture would allow the forward chaining knowledge base and the backward chaining knowledge base to execute asynchronously and communicate via messages. One could envision an executive forward chaining knowledge base continuously monitoring the process and calling or activating other knowledge bases when a fault is detected. These knowledge bases could be either forward chaining or backward chaining.

3) Quantitative evaluation and computation. The knowledge representation capabilities of a real-time expert system would have to include access to functions and operating system services traditionally found in conventional software architectures. They must be able to perform arithmetic, trigonometric and logarithmic evaluations and have access to communication channels and the computer systems resources (disk, memory, screens, etc.).

4) Access to existing data bases and tables of application specific static or near static information. The heuristic process needs immediate access to all relevant information. As this generally resides in conventional data base systems, built-in data base access facilities are required.

5) External program activation and communication. As the expert system is not expected to perform the tasks of sensor polling and point value characterization, access to and some control of external programs is required.

6) Time keeping functions or access to them. This is required for synchronization of the expert system with the time-based process and monitoring processes.

7) An appropriately rich knowledge representation scheme. The knowledge representation scheme of the tool must be adequate to capture the control logic of the system and its operation. Also if a diagnostic role is anticipated the diagnostic models of the plant operators and engineers must be able to be accurately represented.

8) Maintainable knowledge. The captured control logic and/or diagnostic expertise must be inherently maintainable. Process control systems change. They break, sub-systems are taken out of service, new devices

are added or replaced, new control requirements are invented by the engineers and plant managers. If the captured knowledge is hard-coded somewhere in 42,000 lines of FORTRAN, it is a black box. The essence of modern knowledge representation schemes whether they use production rules or frames, is making the knowledge readable and able to be comprehended.

Advantages of Expert Systems in Process Control Architectures

The availability of powerful and inexpensive microcomputers and expert system development tools now make it feasible to implement process control applications without the costly and time consuming development cycle typical of conventional real-time process control. We have observed that a number of process control applications which were being implemented via traditional means can now be successfully and economically implemented using microcomputers and expert systems. This conclusion is drawn from the successful implementation of these tools in the control and monitoring of small processes such as laboratory environmental control, network-node monitoring and small industrial manufacturing applications. The following is an outline of some of the benefits of expert system based process control.

1) Adaptive process control. Expert system based process control has the advantage of adaptive process control. This is defined to be the ability of the system to readily adapt to changes in the process configuration and process state. Because of many factors such as readability of the control logic embodied in knowledge bases, short prototype and development cycles and qualitative reasoning capabilities, these systems are much easier to modify and upgrade. Also, expert system based process control has the advantage of being able to detect, differentiate and diagnose multiple simultaneous process failures, which is typically very difficult for conventional systems.

2) Autonomous and asynchronous data collection. By using a mixture of expert system technology with conventional data acquisition and point characterization hardware and software one can utilize the most efficient machinery appropriate for specific problem domains. By separatin the part of the system that interfaces to the real-world of sensors, and that is therefore subject to high failure rates and caustic environments, from the expert system advisor one ensures data integrity and survivability of the critical sub-systems.

3) Isolation of process knowledge from real-time control structure. With the knowledge representation schemes embodied in most expert system development shells, the expertise of how a plant should operate and how to diagnosis failures can be isolated from the nuts-and-bolts of the detailed real-time control logic of the process. This results in clarity of the overall system design and, of course, the added spin-offs of ease of maintenance.

4) Ease of development and modification. Because a much higher symbolic representation is used in an expert system in comparison to FORTRAN, the development can be performed by the plant engineers without the programmer/analysts intermediaries. Also, because the captured logic is readable, in a natural language, its comprehension survives across generations of plant personnel.

5) Incorporation of the heuristic knowledge of process engineers and operators. There is a wealth of knowledge in any industrial or laboratory environment contained in the brains of plant operators and engineers. This knowledge is captureable by expert systems and is therefore available as decision making criteria to the computer controlling the process.

Controlling a Biological Environment

The following example describes a micro-computer based expert system performing in a highly-interactive mode. It was developed using a commercially available expert system development shell for the control of a laboratory process. This system was developed by Dr. Pierce Jones and his associates at the Irrigation Research and Education Park of the University of Florida using the INSIGHT 2 knowledge engineering environment (Jones et al., 1985). It is just one example of many that we at Level Five Research are seeing in which users of PC based expert system tools are successfully creating small integrated process control systems.

The system being monitored and controlled is an environmental growth chamber for a biological system and therefore requires critical control of the process, reliable data acquisition, and correctly implemented and speedy control actions. When a system such as this fails in the traditional scenario, the central task of the systems operators is the quick and effective diagnosis of the problem and correct repair of the fault. This operation of course requires thoroughly trained and experienced operators. Since expert systems had demonstrated to the developers of this system the ability to capture this kind of expertise from the best of operators and had the ability to provide the expertise in a very usable and operational form, they attempted to automate the control and diagnosis process. The additional benefits they perceived were that the captured expertise would also be available to the newer operators in a training capacity. Normally this task had involved a network of expert operators that supported the system and passed their knowledge to novice operators via tutorials and ongoing documentation of the system. The new system was hoped to perform these function autonomously.

The central operational requirements of the environmentally controlled chamber was the accurate and perpetual long term control of CO_2 concentration, dry bulb temperature and dew point temperature. If a change in these conditions was detected the systems functioned to alert the operator only if a problem condition was discerned and then to parse a decision tree as far as possible without user observational input in order to recommend remedial action and to correctly report on the nature of the failure. Turbo Pascal programs are used to check the sensor values by communication with a remote computer. If the program detects out-of-range conditions it returns to the expert system inference engine for the failure determination. The system´s knowledge base uses forward chaining functionality to broadly eliminate failure classes followed by using the backward chaining functionality for best guess diagnosis of the specific causative failures.

Figure 1.   Structure of the Biological Control System

Biological Plant Chamber
|
Sensors
|
Remote Data Collection Computer
|
RS-232 Phone Line Communication Connection
|
Turbo Pascal Program for Communication
and Data Transfer to the Expert System
|
INSIGHT 2 Expert System
|
Knowledge base for Monitoring,
Diagnosis of Problems,
Display of Results,
and Recommendations of Remedial Solutions

249

Figure 2. <u>Logic Flow of the Biological Control System</u>

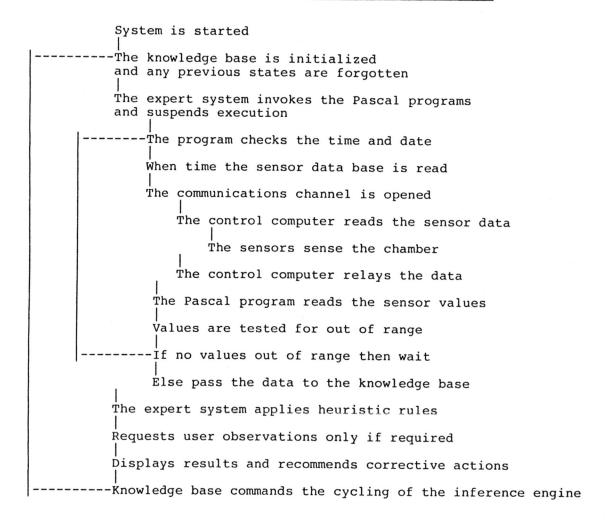

Critical Safety Parameter Display Systems

One of the authors was recently involved in the design and implementation of a Critical Safety Parameter Display Systems (CSPDS) for Maine Yankee Atomic Power Co. The CSPDS is responsible for monitoring critical functions of the core and related safety systems and alert the plant operators of any possible challenge to plant safety. From a high level functional perspective, i.e. that of the plant engineering group, the system consists of a series of six decision trees used to determine the status of the critical safety functions and eighteen color graphic displays that show in alpha-numeric and bar graph format the data related to each safety function. From a completed application perspective, i.e. that of the plant computer group, the system consists of 70 modules totaling over 14,000 lines of FORTRAN IV program code and 36 color graphic displays integrated into the existing plant monitoring and display software which exists as over 100 real-time program tasks consisting of over 800 modules totaling over 100,000 lines of FORTRAN code.

The initial requirements specification of the CSPDS were developed by the plant engineers and then passed to the plant computer group for implementation. Part way through implementation the decision trees and alarm setpoints were redefined by the engineers which required the development group to go back through the 14,000 lines of FORTRAN determine where in the code the affected decision processes were and make the changes. Once the software was completed and went into unit testing it was discovered by the plant operations group that although the FORTRAN worked as specified, the decision tree logic contained errors. They had to dive back into the FORTRAN ...

The author was sufficiently amused by how six decision trees could become over 14,000 lines of FORTRAN that he decided to implement the CSPDS decisions trees within an off the shelf microcomputer expert system shell, INSIGHT 2+. The completed knowledge base required less than 4 hrs to write comprising less than 75 production rules. The resulting expert system prompts the operator for specific data point values and and concludes which if any safety functions are challenged. From a high-level decision perspective the conclusions reached by the two systems are identical. Obviously the micro-based expert system CSPDS does not have any of the data linkages to the real-time process data and thus could not be used to do the job, but an expert system could have made a real contribution to shortening the development cycle of the CSPDS project.

The plant engineers could have used a microcomputer based expert system shell to prototype the decision processes of the CSPDS and used the resulting knowledge base as an part of an interactive design review process. The knowledge base could have been reviewed internally by the engineering group, the computer group as well as by the plant operations personnel. Working with the expert system interactively would allow the plant's experts very quickly to see just where the specified decision trees varied from Nuclear Regulatory Commissions specifications and plant requirements.

Use of expert systems as a prototyping tool before going to implementation can allow system designers to see how their application will behave. The time required to code decision logic into a rule based system is trivial compared to coding and implementation in a conventional language. The design engineers themselves can develop these prototype expert systems without requiring the use of programmers. The expert system in effect can become a part of the critical design review phase of a project.

Summary

We have seen that real-time processes have specific operational requirements that limit the types of computer systems that can be used to control and monitor them. In order for expert systems to perform advisory, diagnostic or monitoring roles in these systems, they must contain functionality that addresses these limiting criteria. Also, it is very important that the expert system technology be able to interact with and integrate into conventional hardware and software environments. As we have seen there are many applications in process control that require the assistance of expert system based process control. But what are some of the characteristics of a process control domain that would make it appropriate for this technology ?

1) The process should be subject to failures.

2) Failures in the process should require diagnosis.

3) Diagnosis of the failures should require special expertise and that expertise must be available for capture.

4) The process should require adaptive control upon failure detection.

5) The computer system should capable of performing speedy adjustment of the process to avoid loss or damage.

The nature of expert system development environments is perceived to have many advantages over conventional development methodologies. With PC based expert systems in their present state one gains the advantages of rapid prototyping, the ability to capture the plant operator's and engineer's diagnostic expertise, an easier method of maintaining the documented and operational control logic of the system and the ability to create systems that perform adaptive control. The spin-off benefits of the expert system based knowledge representation are in training tools, lowered development costs, lowered training time in the development system itself and lowered maintenance costs.

In the future we anticipate that micro-computer based expert systems will be allowed to play increasingly critical roles in large industrial applications as the fear factor of new technologies wears off and as hardware and software capabilities increase in power. Currently, we maintain that state-of-the-art expert systems can be used in large process control environments as prototyping tools for the design of the control logic of systems. They can be used to capture the expertise of the best operator and engineers at a plant site to be used as a training tool for new personnel. And finally, they can be used in distributed process control control networks as intelligent nodes for diagnostic and monitoring roles.

From our observations of our expert system development environment user base we perceive more and more applications are being developed in the process control arena and anticipate that this will be a rapidly expanding area of interest in the near future.

References

1.   Budzinski, M., "Distributed Intelligence Moves Into Industrial Control Applications," Computer Technology Review, Fall, 1985.

2.   Burg, B., Foulloy, L., Heudin, J., Zavidovique, B., "Behavior Rule Systems for Distributed Process Control," Proceedings of The Second Conference of Artificial Intelligence Applications, December 11-13, 1985.

3.   Evers, D.C., D.M. Smith, and C.J. Staros. 1984. Interfacing an intelligent decision-maker to a real-time control system. Proceedings SPIE Applications of Artificial Intelligence. 485:60-64.

4.   Goff, K., "Artificial Intelligence in Process Control," Mechanical Engineering, p.53-57, October, 1985.

5.   Jones, P., "Interfacing an Expert Diagnostic Tool to Real Time Data," Proceedings of the 1985 Winter Meeting of the American Society of Agricultural Engineers, December 17, 1985.

6.   King, M., Brooks, S., Schaefer, R., "Knowledge-based Systems", Mechanical Engineering, p.58-61, October 1985.

7.   Level Five Research, Inc. 1985. INSIGHT 2. 503 Fifth Avenue, Indialantic, Florida 32903.

8.   Mayer, R., Young, R., Phillips, D., "Artificial Intelligence - Applications in Manufacturing," Proceedings of AUTOFACT 6 Conference, October 1-4, 1984.

9.   Moore, T., "Artificial Intelligence: Human Expertise From Machines," EPRI Journal, p.6-15, June 1985.

10.   Nelson, W.R. 1982. REACTOR: An expert system for diagnosis and treatment of nuclear reactor accidents. Proceedings of Am. Assoc. for Artificial Intelligence, Carnegie-Mellon University, Pittsburg, PA.

11.   Jamieson, C. E., Delaune, C., "A FAULT Detection and Isolation Method Applied to Liquid Oxygen Loading for the Space Shuttle," Proc. 9th Int. J. Conf. Art. Intell. (IJCAI-85), Los Angeles, 1985.

Development of Model-Based Fault-Identification Systems on Microcomputers

Magdi Ragheb and Dennis Gvillo

Nuclear Engineering Program, and National Center for Supercomputing Applications (NCSA)
The University of Illinois at Urbana-Champaign, 103 S. Goodwin Ave., Urbana, Illinois 61801

Abstract

The development of Model-Based Production-Rule Analysis Systems for the identification of faults in Engineering Systems is discussed. Model-Based systems address the modelling of devices based on knowledge about their structure and behavior in contrast to Rule-Based systems which use rules based solely on human expertise. The exposed methodology uses the Fault-Tree Analysis technique for problem representation to generate Goal-Trees simulating the behavior of system components. Application of the methodology to a Knowledge-Base for the identification of the dominant accident sequences, consequences, and recommended recovery and mitigation actions for a Pressurized Water Reactor (PWR) is demonstrated. The accident sequences were generated using probabilistic risk analysis methods and analyzed with the Transient Reactor Analysis Code (TRAC). The Analysis System uses a backward-chaining deduction-oriented antecedent-consequent logic. Typical case results are given, and the aspects of using the methodology for Fault-Identification are discussed.

Introduction

A methodology for developing Model-Based Production-Rule Analysis Systems for the identification of Faults in engineering systems is exposed.[1,2] The methodology of Fault-Tree Analysis[3-6] is used for representation of the failure states of a given system and the generation of a Goal-Tree, which is translated into a Knowledge-Base. We demonstrate the methodology by constructing a Model-Based Production-Rule Analysis Systems for the identification of the dominant accident-sequences in a Pressurized Water Reactor (PWR). Once an accident sequence is identified, its consequence is assessed, and then an appropriate course of action for recovery and/or mitigating the consequences of the accident is suggested.

One of the main current thrusts of Artificial Intelligence (AI) work is in the area of Rule-Based or Production Rule Analysis Systems[7,8]. These systems use user-supplied information as basic facts, IF/THEN rules as part of a Knowledge-Base, and an Inference Engine to deduce facts about the status of a physical system, such as a complex machine. Production-Rule systems use heuristics and symbolic programming to provide useful diagnostics and/or consultation in complex logic problems that cannot be addressed using procedural programming techniques. We here demonstate a methodology for the development of Model-Based Production-Rule Analysis Systems in conjunction with the formal methodology of Fault-Tree Analysis for problem representation.

Deductive methods for system analysis

The operation and design of complex engineering systems requires the analysis of their possible mechanisms of failure and the estimation of the expected rates of such failures. When faults occur, they need to be identified, and possible courses of action for recovery and mitigation of their consequences must be available to the system operators. The analytical methods by which such analyses can be conducted can be classified into Inductive and Deductive Systems Analyses Methods[3]. In Inductive System Analysis, one assumes some possible component condition or initiating event and tries to determine the corresponding effect on the overall system. In deductive system analysis, one postulates that the system itself has failed in a certain way, and attempts to find out what modes of system/component behavior contribute to this failure. Deduction constitutes reasoning from the general to the specific. Fault-Tree Analysis is an example of this method[4]. It is a graphical method for tracing back from an undesirable event to any of its many possible causes. It can be defined as a deductive failure analysis which focuses on one particular undesired event and which provides a method for determining the causes of this event. The undesired event constitutes the top event in a Fault-Tree diagram constructed for the system.

In Fault-Tree construction, the system failure event that is to be studied is called the Top Event. Successive subordinate, i.e. subsystem, failure events that may contribute to the occurrence of the Top Event are then identified and linked to the Top Event by logical connective functions. The subordinate events themselves are then broken down to their logical contributions, and, in this manner, a failure Event-Tree structure is created.

Progress in the synthesis of the tree is recorded graphically by arranging the events into a tree structure using logical gates[5].

The use of a Fault-Tree to evaluate the system failure probability requires that the tree roots be developed to finer and finer detail. The tip of each root must be an equipment failure or human error for which it is possible for reliability engineers familiar with the components to assign component failure rates and experts on human factors to assign probabilities of human errors[6].

The top event expression can be written in the general form,

$$T = M_1 + M_2 + \ldots + M_n \tag{1}$$

where T is the top event,

M_i, i = 1, 2, ..., n are minimal cut sets

(+) denotes the Union or OR operation

Each minimal cut set consists of a conclusion of specific component failures, and hence the general n-component minimal cut set can be expressed as:

$$M_i = X_1 * X_2 \ldots X_m \tag{2}$$

where X_1, X_2, ..., X_m are basic component failures on the tree,

(*) denotes the Intersection or AND operation.

An example of a top event expression is:

$$T = A + B * C \tag{3}$$

where A, B, and C are component failures. This top event has a one-component minimal cut set A and a two-component minimal cut set B * C.

Deductive methods of analysis are applied to determine "how" a given state (usually a failed state) can occur. This bears a close analogy to the methodology of backward-chaining in the AI field. In this situation, the system hypothesizes a conclusion and uses the antecedent-consequent rules to work backward toward the hypothesis-supporting facts. This analogy allows us to readily adapt the AI methodology of Rule-Based Systems for Analysis[7] to the identification of engineering system failures. Typical of deductive analysis in real life are accident investigations: what chain of events caused the sinking of an "unsinkable" ship such as the Titanic on its maiden voyage, or what failure processes (humans or instrumental), contributed to the crash of a plane, or to the Three-Mile-Island Reactor accident? With symbolic programming and high speed computations, one could foresee the possibility of averting and avoiding these accident situations, and whenever they happen, provide the alternatives for recovering from them, or acting in ways so as to mitigate their consequences. Fault Tree Analysis is here used to symbolically represent the different operational states of an engineering system.[8] In this way, they represent the hypotheses in an equivalent Goal-Tree[9] on which an Inference Engine can check the validity of these hypotheses. The Inference Engine operates on a Knowledge Base comprising a set of facts represented by the basic events at the roots of the tree, and by the logical gates in the tree. We consider a case where a Model-Based system is constructed using the Fault-Tree analysis technique for problem representation.

System description

For the sake of demonstrating the methodology, we consider the faults occurring in a complex engineering system: a Pressurized Water Reactor (PWR). To treat a realistic situation, we consider the Oconee-1 reactor located at Lake Keowee, South Carolina. It is an 886 MWe, two-loop, four-cold leg Babcock & Wilcox PWR. The reactor coolant system (RCS) of Oconee-1 is shown in Fig. 1. The RCS is arranged in two heat transport loops, each with two shaft-sealed reactor coolant pumps (RCPs) and one vertical once-through steam generator (SG). An electrically heated pressurizer is used to maintain the RCS pressure. It is equipped with a with a safety relief valve (SRV) and a power operated relief valve (PORV). The emergency core cooling system (ECCS), which is designed to prevent core damage over the entire spectrum of Loss of Coolant Accidents (LOCAs) break sizes consists of the high-pressure injection system (HPIS), the low-pressure injection system (LPIS), and the core flooding tanks (CFTs) or accumulators, containing borated water.

We consider the dominant accident sequences identified by the Reactor Safety Study Methodology Applications Program (RSSMAP).[10] These are summarized in Fig. 2 with the corresponding radioactive release categories and the containment failure modes. The accident sequences are caused by a combination of Accident Initiating Events and System Failures shown in Figs. 3 and 4 respectively. The consequences of the release categories corresponding to the accident sequences of Fig. 2 are shown in Table I, as well as the recommended emergency action levels corresponding to these release categories.

Generation of production-rule knowledge base and typical case results

Dearing et al.[10] have determined for the Oconee-1 reactor the dominant accident sequences that, when followed by a failure of the containment vessel, would cause radiation releases capable of large consequences in terms of property damage and loss of life. These scenarios are grouped into release categories based on the predicted impact of the radiation release. The purpose of this Model-Based system is to recommend a course of action to the regulatory agencies and the control room operator during an accident. Therefore, the goal states of this system are the emergency action levels of the Nuclear Power Plant: Normal Operation, Alert, Site Area Emergency, and General Emergency. Those release categories with the most damaging radiation releases will call for a General Emergency while less serious accidents will warrant a lower Emergency Action Level. According to Ref. 10, a radiation release can be caused by the progression of an accident sequence coupled with an ensuing failure of the containment. The accidents that are capable of such damage have been determined. The accidents themselves are the result of an accident initiating event, such as a small loss of coolant accident, followed by one or more particular system failures, such as the containment spray recirculation system failure and the emergency coolant recirculation system failure. This would be the accident sequence S_2FH as shown in Fig. 2. The manner in which the containment fails also determines the release category, whether it be by penetration leakage (beta mode), base mat melt through (epsilon mode), or some other mode. The Fault-Tree corresponding to the Declare-Alert top event is shown in Fig. 5. Other Fault-Trees are constructed for the other top events and then combined to yield Fig. 6. This is translated into a knowledge base where each logical gate is translated into an IF/THEN Rule. A typical programmed rule is shown in its LISP version as well as its English Translation through the Natural Language Interface in Fig. 7. The Fault Tree branches run from the failure states (release categories) at the top, down through the accident sequences and to the user-supplied facts, the accident initiating events, system failures, and containment failure modes. This, with the addition of the recommendations to the top of tree represents the goal tree that models the device at hand.

The Personal Consultant[1,11] Expert System building-tool was used for construction of the knowledge base. It is structured along the same line as the E-MYCIN system[9] with an added Natural Language interface. Figure 8 shows a typical screen where the system queries the operator about the existence of any accident initiating events. Figure 9 queries about the containment failure modes, and Fig. 10 shows the identification of the particular fault at hand and the corresponding recommendation for action. The system is capable of explaining the logic behind its inferences by accessing the appropriate rule in the Knowledge base and answering WHY and HOW questions by the user.

Conclusions and recommendations

We demonstrated a methodology for Model-Based systems construction by coupling the Methodologies of Fault-Tree Analysis from the System-Analysis area and of Production-Rule Analysis Systems from the Knowledge Engineering field. Implementation on a microcomputer was undertaken. When the execution time is not a limitation, the methodology provides a relatively inexpensive way of generating Model-Based systems for fault identification. Since the modelling amounts to a logical simulation of the system at hand, the complexity of the Goal-Trees increases quite rapidly as the number opf logical gates in the Fault-Trees increases. Methods for handling this situation for more complex cases, such as Computer-Aided-Design (CAD) techniques, will probably need to be adapted. Future development will be directed towards developing these Model-Based systems to run on a real-time basis accepting sensors input and sending signals to modify the settings of the monitored devices. Improved methodologies for assessing the uncertainties involved in the deduction process and for adaptive learning will further enhance the usefulness of this Model-Based systems methodology.

Acknowledgements

The support from L. Berry, G. Miley and M. Abdel-Hai, the University of Illinois at Urbana-Champaign, is appreciated. Funding was partly provided by the University of Illinois Alumni Association and Texas Instruments.

255

References

1. Mishkoff, H. C. et al., "Understanding Artificial Intelligence," TI Information Publishing Center (1985).

2. Davis, R. et al., "The Hardware Troubleshooting Group," Artificial Intelligence Laboratory, Massachusetts Institute of Technology, Cambridge, MA (1985).

3. Robert, N. H., Beseley, W. E., Haasl, D. F., and Goldbert, F. F., "Fault Tree Handbook," U.S. Nuclear Regulatory Commission, NUREG-0442 (1981).

4. McCormick, N. J., "Reliability and Risk Analysis Methods and Nuclear Power Applications," Academic Press, Inc., New York, (1981).

5. Apostolakis, G. and Lee, Y. T., "Methods for the Estimation of Confidence Bounds for the Top-Event Unavailability of Fault Trees," Nucl. Eng. Des., 41, p. 411 (1977).

6. Lewis, E. E., "Nuclear Power Reactor Safety," John Wiley and Sons, Inc., New York (1977).

7. Winston, P. H. and Horn, B. K. H., "LISP," Second Edition, Addison-Wesley Publishing Co. (1984).

8. Salem, S. L., Apostolakis, G. E. and Okrent, D., "A New Methodology for the Computer-Aided Construction of Fault Trees," Am. Nucl. Energy, 4, p. 417 (1977).

9. Buckerman, B. G. and Shortliffe, E. H., "Rule Based Expert Systems, the Mycin Experience of the Stanford Heuristic Programming Project," Addison-Wesley Publishing Co. (1984).

10. Dearing, J. F., Henninger, and Nassersharif, B., "Dominant Accident Sequences in Oconee-1 Pressurized Water Reactors," NUREG/CR-4140, LA-10351-MS, Los Alamos National Laboratory, April (1985).

11. Sims, H. A., "Knowledge Engineering with the TI's Personal Consultant," TI Professional Computing, Dec. (1985).

Table I. Consequences and Emergency Action Levels corresponding to different release categories

Category	Early Fatalities	Latent Cancer Fatalities per year	Property Damage $(10^6 S)$	Action Level
1	45	118	2130	General Emergency
2	7	67	2440	" "
3	0.4	55	990	" "
4	0	18	340	Site-Area Emergency
5	0	6	200	" "
6	0	1	170	" "
7	0	~0	170	" "

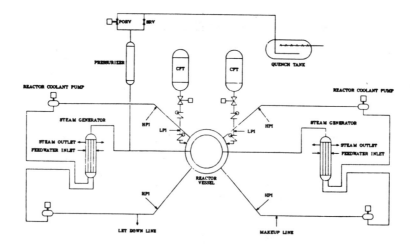

Fig. 1 Physical Configuration of Reactor Coolant System.

Accident Sequence	Radioactive Release Category						
	1	2	3	4	5	6	7
T_2MLU			γ		β		ε
T_1MLU			γ		β		ε
V		∨					
$T_1(B_3)MLU$			γ		β		ε
T_2MQ-H			γ		β		ε
S_3H			γ		β		ε
S_1D	α		γ		β		ε
T_2MQ-FH		γ		β		ε	
S_3FH		γ		β		ε	
S_2FH	α			β		ε	
T_2MLUO			γ		β		ε
T_2KMU			γ		β		ε
S_2D	α		γ		β		ε
S_3D			γ		β		ε
T_1MLUO			γ		β		ε
T_3MLUO			γ		β		ε
T_2MO-D			γ		β		ε

Containment Failure Modes: α - Vessel Steam Explosion
β - Penetration Leakage
γ - Overpressure Due to Hydrogen Burning
ε - Base Mat Melt Through

Fig. 2   Dominant Accident Sequences and the associated release categories.

T_1	Loss of Offsite Power (LOSP) Transient
T_2	Loss of Power Conversion System Transient Caused by Other Than a LOSP
T_3	Transients with the Power Conversion System Initially Available
S_1	Intermediate Loss of Coolant Accident (LOCA)
S_2	Small LOCA (4" < Pipe Diameter ≤ 10")
S_3	Small-Small LOCA (Pipe Diameter ≤ 4")
V	Interfacing Systems LOCA

Fig. 3   Accident Initiating Events

(B_3)	Emergency Power System Failure
D	Emergency Coolant Injection System Failure
F	Containment Spray Recirculation System Failure
H	Emergency Coolant Recirculation System Failure
K	Reactor Protection System Failure
L	Emergency Feedwater System Failure with Recovery of Power Conversion System and High Head Auxiliary Feedwater System
M	Power Conversion System Failure
Q	Reclosure of Pressurizer Safety/Relief Valves
U	High-Pressure Injection System Failure
O	Failure of Reactor Building Cooling System

Fig. 4   System Failures

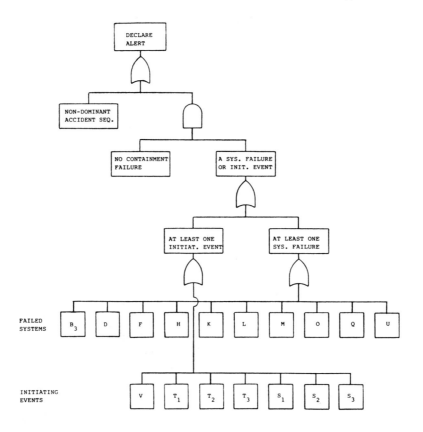

Fig. 5   Fault-Tree for the Declare-Alert Top Event.

RULE033 [PWR-ACCIDENTS-ANALYSISRULES]

If 1) the accident initiating event is INITIATING-EVENT-S3, and
   2) status of the Emergency Coolant Injection System is
      FAILED,
Then 1) it is definite (100%) that the identified accident
        sequence in progress is SEQUENCE-S3D, and
     2) Inform the user of this decision.

PREMISE: ($AND
              (SAME CNTXT INITIATING-EVENTS
              INITIATING-EVENT-S3)
              (SAME CNTXT SYSTEM-FAILURE-D FAILED))
ACTION: (DO-ALL
              (CONCLUDE CNTXT ACCIDENT-SEQUENCES SEQUENCE-S3D
              TALLY 1000)
              (SPRINTT "Accident Sequence S3D is in progress."))

Fig. 7   A typical rule in its LISP and Natural
         Language form.

```
┌─────────────────────────────────────────────────────────────────┐
│ Knowledge Base :: Simulating Dominant Accident Sequences in Oconee-1 PWR │
│                                                                   │
│ Please check the instrument readings and identify the             │
│ existence of any of the following accident initiating             │
│ events: No Initiating Event; T1 - Loss of Off-Site Power (        │
│  LOSP) Transient; T2 - Loss of Power Conversion System            │
│ Transient caused by other than a Loss of Off-Site Power (         │
│  LOSP) ; T3 - Transients with the Power Conversion System         │
│ initially available; S1 - Intermediate Loss of Coolant            │
│ Accident (LOCA) (10 inches < pipe diameter < 13.5 inches) ;       │
│ S2 - Small Loss of Coolant Accident (LOCA) (4 inches < pipe       │
│  diameter < 10 inches) ; S3 - Small-Small Loss of Coolant         │
│ Accident (LOCA) (pipe diameter < 4 inches) ; V - Interfacing      │
│ Systems Loss of Coolant Accident (LOCA)                           │
│ Select one of the following:  (Press 'F3' for selection help.)    │
│           NO-INITIATING-EVENT                                      │
│           INITIATING-EVENT-T1                                      │
│           INITIATING-EVENT-T2                                      │
│           INITIATING-EVENT-T3                                      │
│           INITIATING-EVENT-S1                                      │
│           INITIATING-EVENT-S2                                      │
│  Up   Down  CF Unknwn    Done  ---  Why  How   Help Undo    Stop   │
│  F1   F2    F3  F4       F5    F6   F7   F8     F9   F10    ESC    │
└─────────────────────────────────────────────────────────────────┘
```

Fig. 8   System-operation interaction regarding the
         existence of any accident initiating events.

```
┌─────────────────────────────────────────────────────────────────┐
│ Knowledge Base :: Simulating Dominant Accident Sequences in Oconee-1 PWR │
│                                                                   │
│ Please identify whether the containment has failed or not,        │
│ and if it has failed, please identify the containment             │
│ failure mode: ALPHA (Vessel Steam Explosion) , BETA (             │
│  Penetration Leakage) , GAMMA (Overpressure due to Hydrogen       │
│  burning) , EPSILON (Base Mat Melt Through)                       │
│ Select one of the following:  (Press 'F3' for selection help.)    │
│           NO-FAILURE                                               │
│           ALPHA                                                    │
│           BETA                                                     │
│           GAMMA                                                    │
│           EPSILON                                                  │
│                                                                   │
│                                                                   │
│                                                                   │
│                                                                   │
│                                                                   │
│                                                                   │
│  Up   Down  CF Unknwn    Done  ---  Why  How   Help Undo    Stop   │
│  F1   F2    F3  F4       F5    F6   F7   F8     F9   F10    ESC    │
└─────────────────────────────────────────────────────────────────┘
```

Fig. 9   System-operator interaction concerning
         containment failure modes.

```
┌─────────────────────────────────────────────────────────────────┐
│ Knowledge Base :: Simulating Dominant Accident Sequences in Oconee-1 PWR │
│                                                                   │
│ This accident falls under Release Category 3.  The expected consequences │
│ are:  0.4 Early Fatalities, 55 Latent Cancer Fatalities per year, │
│ and $990 million in Property Damage.                              │
│ Due to the extremely high loss of life as well as severe property │
│ damage expected from the consequences of this radiation release,  │
│ it is recommended that a GENERAL EMERGENCY be declared.           │
│     ... end   --  press RETURN                                     │
│                                                                   │
│                                                                   │
│                                                                   │
│                                                                   │
│                                                                   │
│                                                                   │
│                                                                   │
│                                                                   │
│  Up   Down  CF Unknwn    Done  ---  Why  How   Help Undo    Stop   │
│  F1   F2    F3  F4       F5    F6   F7   F8     F9   F10    ESC    │
└─────────────────────────────────────────────────────────────────┘
```

Fig. 10   The recommendation reached for the
          identified fault and its consequences.

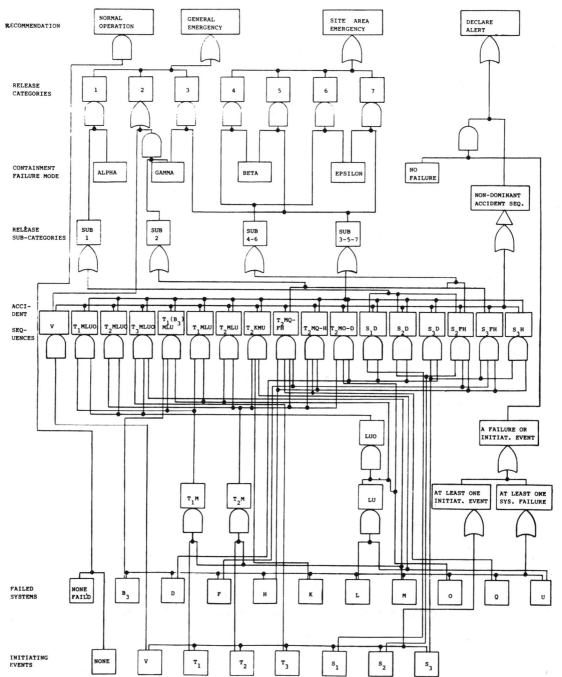

Fig. 6   Total system representation using Fault-Tree modelling

MICRO-COMPUTER BASED EXPERT SYSTEMS
IN ENGINEERING: AN EXAMPLE

Nitin S. Pandit and D. Sriram

Department of Civil Engineering
Carnegie-Mellon University
Pittsburgh, PA 15213

Abstract

Development costs of knowledge-based expert systems are very high. A number of inexpensive micro-computer based tools were considered for the design of an expert system. Based on the availability, cost and appropriateness to the task, INSIGHT was used to develop the first version of AUGERPILE, an expert system to aid in the field inspection of augered, cast-in-place, concrete pile installation. Despite its numerous limitations, INSIGHT can be used to model an important part of the highly judgement prone inspection process. It is felt that such micro-computer based tools should be used to rapidly build small, low-cost prototype expert systems to assess the suitability of a major developmental effort.

1. Introduction

The proliferation of Expert System (ES) tools on micro-computers is changing the design philosophy ·of many Knowledge-Based Expert Systems (KBES). These personal computer-based ES (PCES) tools provide an environment for rapid prototyping of KBES, thus avoiding costly investment in the preliminary stages of the system development. In recent years there has been an increased interest in the engineering field in the development of KBES[1]. However, most of these systems were implemented on mini-computer systems that typically cost around $50,000 to $100,000. A large number of these systems were prototypes and were built to study the feasibility of ES technology. The authors feel that it is better to build low-cost, simple prototypes on micro-computers, before venturing into a major developmental effort (some micro-based expert systems can handle large problems). The tools currently available on micro-computers are ideally suited for building classification-type systems, although with the availability of object-oriented languages the problems of design can also be addressed. In this paper we describe the implementation of a prototype KBES on a micro-computer in geotechnical engineering. The problem is described in Section 2. In Section 3, features of INSIGHT-the PCES tool used in this study-are described. Section 4 discusses the knowledge-base. Finally, an evaluation of the prototype and the tool is performed in Section 5.

2. System Overview

The system, called AUGERPILE, is being developed to aid in the field inspection of augered concrete cast-in-place piles (ACCP). The piling process is described in Section 2.1, while the suitability of KBES to this problem is explored in Section 2.2.

2.1. Pile System Description

The piles considered in this report are typically considered as a specialized form of deep foundations. They are typically used to provide buildings and other superstructures with sufficient bearing to rest on the ground, subject to some design requirements and criteria, such as settlement. They are normally classified as friction piles which transfer the load from the superstructure to the soil through the frictional resistance between the soil and the pile wall. Occasionally their end bearing capacity is also utilized. Currently, these piles are typically used in areas where the soils are too soft to enable the usage of other foundation types which are primarily end bearing in nature, such as caissons. Although the load carrying capability of the piles is in the typical load ranges encountered in practice (10 to 100 tons), their use is limited mainly because of the reluctance of designers, architects and owners in using them. The reluctance arises from a well founded belief that the installation of such piles requires considerable skill and therefore may not always be reliable.

The installation of the piles requires a special - yet relatively inexpensive - rig, one operator, one foreman, one inspector and materials. The process of installation involves the following steps (see Figure 2-1):

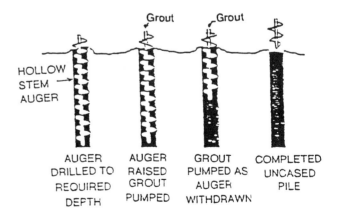

Grout   Grout

HOLLOW
STEM
AUGER

AUGER	AUGER	GROUT	COMPLETED
DRILLED TO	RAISED	PUMPED AS	UNCASED
REQUIRED	GROUT	AUGER	PILE
DEPTH	PUMPED	WITHDRAWN	

Figure 2-1: Pile Installation Procedure[2]

Reprinted from *Proc. IEEE Expert Systems in Government Symp.*, pp. 10–15, Oct. 1985.

1. An auger is drilled into the ground in a manner that avoids excavating any soil. This is possible with an auger which is formed like an Archimedes screw and a little practice.
2. The auger is then raised and grout (A mixture of cement, aggregate, other fluidifiers, additives and water) is <u>simultaneously</u> pumped through the hollow stem of the auger into the cavity made in place of the excavated soil.

This process is essentially very simple and can be very expeditious. However, the uncertainties of the subsurface conditions, equipment performance, material quality and faulty installation can lead to a number of situations that lead to a pile that undergoes "necking", where the cross section of the pile becomes smaller than that required for supporting the design load. This has often led to failures in the past. Some noteworthy conditions when "necking" occurs are in fact in soft/loose water bearing soils where the surrounding soil squeezes in, and in man made fill where the grout spreads out suddenly into voids.

2.2. Expert System Suitability

The difficulty in controlling this process, in addition to dealing with the inherent uncertainty in the knowledge of the subsurface conditions, arises from the fact that there is no easy way of knowing for sure as to how the pile was formed in place. The only observations and measurements that can be made to judge the pile integrity are at the ground surface. Other methods such as load tests, pullout tests are usually very elaborate and expensive. Further, some testing methods, such as acoustic monitoring and the family of geophysical methods themselves contain uncertainties in the interpretation of their data. In any event, the data are gathered and used by the people at the surface to infer whether the pile is installed properly or not. This is a tricky and a highly judgment prone process, which makes the entire process unreliable, especially in the hands of novices and new inspectors/contractors.

It is noteworthy, however, that the cost of installation of the piles is quite low as compared to other forms of deep foundations because of the speed with which they can be installed. This allows for cost savings in the otherwise expensive items, such as equipment rental and labor. This is particularly noteworthy when the contractor and the inspector are experienced enough to perform the task in smaller time schedules leading to major cost savings for the entire project. Another advantage of using such piles is that the rig is usually light, versatile and it can operate with small side clearances, i.e. fairly close to an existing structure. The authors believe that if the expertise of expert operators/inspectors can be made available to the system at all times, the reliability of installation will be significantly higher. Perhaps, enough to persuade the hesitant decision makers to use such piles more often and benefit from it!!

3. PCES Tools - INSIGHT

A large number of PCES tools were released this year. Since it is beyond the scope of this paper to review all these tools, only a brief description of some tools is provided below (see[3]):

- **DECIDING FACTOR** is a PC version of KAS, which is a domain independent version of PROSPECTOR.

The system has very nice user interface and is reasonably priced. It can be obtained from Software Publishing Corporation, 1901 Landings Drive, Mountain View, CA 94043.
- **EXPERT-EASE** is a programming tool for building KBES. The sales personnel claim that it formulates rules based on examples provided by the expert (essentially it is a decision table evaluator). It can be used for developing prototype systems for a wide range of problems including policy making, training and diagnosis. Its applicability to engineering design is not clearly known. It is marketed by Human Edge Software, 2445 Faber Place, Palo Alto, CA 94303, Tel. No: (800) 624-5227 and costs $695.
- **EXSYS** is written in C. The 256K IBM machine can handle up to 700 rules. Performs backward chaining. Registered users can distribute the runtime program with their expert systems without royalty. Costs $295 and marketed by EXSYS Inc., P. O. Box 75158, Contr. Sta., 14 Albuquerque, NM 87194.
- **EX-TRAN77** is implemented in Fortran-77 and is a ruled based system. It can induce rules from examples (same as Expert-Ease and RuleMaster) and offers a good environment for building classification-type systems. Facilities to call Fortran-77 sub-routines are provided. It is marketed by Jeffrey Perrone & Associates, Management Consultants, 3685 17th Street, San Francisco, California 94114.
- **INSIGHT** is a backward chaining expert system tool for the personal computers. It is on of the cheapest PCES tools available in the market. Although it is priced low, it can be used to build prototype expert systems for many applications. It also provides means to incorporate inexact reasoning. An extended version of INSIGHT (costs around $500) that can be interfaced with dbase-II is also available. The bare version costs $95.00 and can be obtained from Level Five Research, Inc, 4980 South A-1-A, Melbourne Beach, Florida 32951.
- **MPROLOG** is based on the logic-based language Prolog. Since Prolog was selected as the fifth generation language by the Japanese, Prolog has gained increased popularity in Europe and US. MPROLOG seems to be supported well by Logicware. US contact address: Ian MacLachlan, The Koll Center, 500 Birch Street, Suite 333, Newport Beach, CA, USA 92660.
- **OPS5 +** is a PC version of OPS5, a production language system developed at C-MU and used in the development of a large number of KBES. It can handle 1500 rules for the 640K IBM PC. A nice mouse-menu interface is provided. It is sold by Artelligence Inc., 14902 Preston Rd., Suite 212-252, Dallas, Texas 75240 and costs $3000.00
- **PERSONAL CONSULTANT** is a PC version of EMYCIN and implemented in IQLISP. The number of rules that the systems can handle is restricted to 500. However, the system has nice user interfaces, allows numerical computations and user defined functions. It is marketed by Texas Instruments and costs $3000.00.

Other PCES tools include KES, M. 1, MicroExpert, RuleMaster, TOPSI, ES/P, LightYear, Reveal, SeRIES-PC and TIMM-PC.

3.1. INSIGHT

INSIGHT provides the PC user with a tool for rapid prototyping of KBES. It consists of an inference system and a knowledge-base compiler. The inference mechanism is called INSIGHT. It searches the knowledge-base in a backward chaining mode to establish the final goal. The knowledge-base compiler, PRGEN, creates a compiled knowledge-base from the knowledge-base developed by the user using the Production Rule Language (PRL). The PRL is briefly described below:

3.1.1. PRL

PRL was developed such that the expert can input his knowledge using a restricted "natural language". PRL rules are of the form

```
IF Condition1
AND Condition2
....
THEN ACTIONS CONFIDENCE X
```

The Conditions and Actions are English statements, not exceeding 60 characters. The right hand side may also contain the key words DISPLAY and EXPAND to tell the user of the current status of the system. The confidence factors allow the incorporation of uncertain knowledge.

The overall PRL text file should contain the following elements in the specified order:

1. the TITLE of the knowledge-base
2. the THRESHOLD value of the confidence level necessary for conclusions
3. the GOALS of the knowledge-base
4. the RULES that support the goals
5. the word END

The THRESHOLD statement indicates the cut-off limit for uncertainty measures. A few arithmetic comparison operators, such as >, <, = , etc, are also provided. A set data type to accommodate input of constant values is also provided. A condensed version of AUGERPILE's PRL file is shown below.

```
!••••••••••••••••••••••••••••••••••••••••••••••
!-----------------------------------------
!
!AUGERPILE : An Augercast Pile
!                 Inspector's Assistant
!
!Programmer: Nitin S. Pandit
!
!Date      : 3 May 1986.
!
!Abstract  : This knowledge base cont-
!            ains the basic insight
!            to assist you in the field
!            inspection of  augered
!            cast in place concrete piles.
!
!••••••••••••••••••••••••••••••••••••••••••••••
!
```

otherwise be a measured/observed quantity or the site geotechnical engineer's opinion.

It is noteworthy that in ACCP construction, the site geotechnical engineer is required to judge the integrity of the ACCP at every point along the entire length of the pile. Faulty installation, e.g. necking, at any point in the ACCP is unacceptable. Fortunately, the installation at any one point at a particular time is not significantly influenced by installation requirements above that point or by installation practices before that time. Therefore, the site geotechnical engineer needs to consider primarily the local conditions at every point/instance.

```
TITLE AUGERPILE - The Augercast Pile
                         Inspector
    •••••••••••• AUGERPILE ••••••••••••

    An Augercast Pile Inspector Assistant

                     by

             Nitin S. Pandit
      Department of Civil Engineering
         Carnegie-Mellon University
         Pittsburgh,  Pennsylvania.


Nomenclature :

Augerpile == The augered cast in place
             concrete pile.
grout     == A mixture of cement, aggregate
             fluidifiers  and other special
             purpose additives.
rig stroke== The amount, in ft., that a rig
             can lift an auger without
             having to stop.

THRESHOLD = 60
CONFIDENCE ON
!
!
!••••••••••••••••••••••••••••••••••••••••
!                             GOAL
!••••••••••••••••••••••••••••••••••••••••
!
1. Augerpile Installation Passed
!
2. Augerpile Installation Failed
!
!
!••••••••••••••••••••••••••••••••••••••••
!                             RULES
!••••••••••••••••••••••••••••••••••••••••
< SETS OF RULES>
END
```

4. AUGERPILE - Knowledge Decomposition

AUGERPILE's knowledge base was designed to simulate the actions of a site geotechnical engineer who is charged with the responsibility of either accepting or rejecting the ACCP during or immediately after its installation. This overall task of judging the ACCP integrity is subdivided into five smaller tasks. Further subdivisions of these tasks ultimately lead to the deepest level, where AUGERPILE asks the user for data which would

To judge the ACCP integrity at even one instance is a very challenging task and forms the core of the expertise required of the site geotechnical engineer in the ACCP inspection process. Due to the lack of formalized, documented data and expertise, it was felt that AUEGRPILE be made capable of judging the ACCP integrity at a single instance. Extensions of AUGERPILE for simulating the complete task of the site geotechnical engineer are discussed later in this paper.

In the framework offered by INSIGHT, the top level goal is decomposed in a form shown in Figure 4-1. To assess the validity of the top level actions/goals, INSIGHT tries to assess the validity of each of the conditions noted below (the words enclosed in the square brackets are acronyms used as nodes in the partial inference network).

```
RULE Final judgment
IF equipment was ok [eqpok]
AND starting conditions were ok [srtok]
AND grout mix ok [grtok]
AND installation so far ok [insok]
AND steel installation ok [stlok]
THEN Augerpile Installation Passed [aupok]
AND DISPLAY pass
ELSE Augerpile Installation Failed
AND DISPLAY fail
```

To assess if *equipment was ok*, one out of two sets of conditions have to be satisfied. Such an "OR" condition is represented as shown below.

```
RULE equipment checked
IF equipment was recently checked [eqchk]
AND all subsystems were ok [subchk]
AND there was no need to check again
                              [nochk]
THEN equipment was ok [eqpok]
```

```
RULE auger equipment
IF pumping system ok [pmpok]
AND augering system ok [augok]
THEN equipment was ok [eqpok]
```

To assess if *starting conditions were ok*, a similar set of rules have been formulated.

```
RULE start check
IF pile specs were checked on site [spechk]
AND pile specs matched field conditions
                              [speok]
AND there is no need to check again [chkno]
THEN starting conditions were ok [strok]
```

```
RULE starting augering
IF pile location was ok [locok]
AND pile design made sense [desok]
THEN starting conditions were ok [strok]
```

To assess if *grout mix ok*, the following rules were developed.

```
RULE grout checked
IF grout mix was recently checked [grtchk]
AND no significant changes expected in
                              batch [nochng]
THEN grout mix ok [grtok]
```

```
RULE grout quality
IF materials quality was acceptable [matok]
AND grout mix consistency was ok [conok]
AND temperatures were ok [temok]
AND mixing of grout was ok [mixok]
AND grout standby time was acceptable
                              [stdok]
THEN grout mix ok [grtok]
```

The assessment of the steel reinforcement installation practices were not as thoroughly incorporated, due to the dirth of information on acceptability of various practices in different conditions. The following rules indicate this limitation.

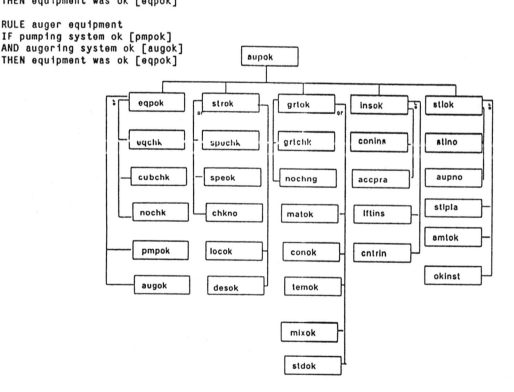

Figure 4-1: Partial Inference Network

264

```
RULE no steel yet
IF steel has not been placed yet [stlno]
AND augerpile is not complete [aupno]
THEN steel installation ok [stlok]

RULE steel placement
IF steel has been placed [stlpla]
AND amount placed more than minimum
                        required [amtok]
AND steel installed properly [okinst]
THEN steel installation ok [stlok]
```

Most of the conditions noted in the rules above are in fact subgoals which are expanded in AUGERPILE to the lowest level making practical sense. In some cases, the input associated with the lowest condition was a measurable data item; in other cases it was an observable data item. Both types of inputs are associated with uncertainties in some cases. In other cases, the application of a rule to inputs was associated with a confidence level. The following set of rules are exemplary of AUGERPILE's capability in handling such features in the knowledge base.

```
RULE continuous installation
IF installation method was continuous
                            [conins]
AND installation practice was accept-
                        able [accpra]
THEN installation so far ok

RULE installation in lifts
IF installation was done in lifts [lftins]
AND installation was well controlled
                            [cntrin]
THEN installation so far ok

RULE smooth installation
IF positive grout pressure was maintained
AND auger withdrawal was done properly
AND other evidence shows no problems
THEN installation practice was acceptable

RULE other evidence
IF volume of grout pumped was acceptable
AND pressure head was ok
AND pressure variations were not erratic
THEN other evidence shows no problems

RULE grout volume
IF enough grout was pumped in
AND did not find big void
THEN volume of grout pumped was acceptable

RULE minimum grout
IF grout volume pumped is more than
                    (1.1*volume of hole)
THEN enough grout was pumped CONFIDENCE 85

RULE void found
IF grout volume pumped was less than
                    (2.2*volume of hole)
AND underground cavity not encountered
THEN did not find big void

RULE cavity
IF pressure did not drop suddenly near zero
AND sudden, large volume of grout flow not
                                    noted
AND long term pressure drop not seen
AND tunnels/sewers/cables/sinkholes not
                                suspected
THEN underground cavity not encountered
                        CONFIDENCE 85
```

5. Evaluation and Extensions

Based on this exercise, some salient features of INSIGHT are now better understood from a practical standpoint. Its evaluation as a prototyping tool for ES development and some thoughts on making a more elaborate prototype are discussed in Sections 5.1 and 5.2.

5.1. Evaluation of INSIGHT

INSIGHT is a handy tool for developing diagnostic, rule-based ES prototypes similar to AUGERPILE. The limitations of INSIGHT and some noteworthy peculiarities of AUGERPILE's task are discussed below.

- It was preferable to make AUGERPILE on a small personal computer. INSIGHT requires only 128 K bytes of RAM with a single disk drive, and runs on the IBM PC. In addtion, the compilation and execution times were relatively fast.

- In INSIGHT's framework, AUGERPILE is very easy to learn, use, maintain and modify. This is further enhanced by its common, natural language-like interface which allow its use by practitioners, such as geotechnical engineers, who may not be specialists in ES development.

- INSIGHT uses only backward chaining as its control strategy, which is normally the strategy used in most diagnostic expert system frameworks. For a purely diagnostic system with few goal states, such as AUGERPILE, this was quite appropriate. For a problem requiring forward chaining or mixed control strategy, INSIGHT is not very useful.

- The numerical computations required for AUGERPILE's task were limited in number and complexity. Most of the data could be categorized and described in a linguistic format; INSIGHT does not have facilities to handle numerical calculations. And although AUGERPILE, as a prototype, needs only a few, this is a handicap. On the other hand, INSIGHT handles linguistic variables quite effectively.

- Perhaps the most serious limitation of INSIGHT is that it does not allow multiple instantiation, i.e. looping structures/strategies for the evaluation of pile integrity at various depths can not be made. Each time the entire network has to be traversed again.

- It was necessary to give AUGERPILE an explanation facility, since it will inevitably be asked to justify its judgement on pile integrity. INSIGHT does provide a reporting facility. At the end of a run, a report of the session can be obtained. This report consists of the user inputs, and the interpretation sequence followed by AUGERPILE.

- It was essential to give AUGERPILE a way of handling uncertain information and uncertainties in the application of rules. This is accomplished in INSIGHT by assigning a "confidence" on any rule's conclusion and the "threshold" confidence value for the entire system, as described in Section 3.1.1.

- INSIGHT does not have the facility to enable building of decision tables. Therefore, multiple rules have to be written. Sometimes, this is inconvenient.

- INSIGHT (the smaller version used here) does not allow access to databases. Therefore, information based on typical or previously encountered soil conditions, pullout tests, load tests, or failures can not be directly used. For instance, a number of heuristics can be added for taking special precautions where the stratigraphy is stiff clay over sand in contrast to a stratigraphy which has very soft clay overlying loose silty sand).

The above mentioned pros and cons of INSIGHT (and similarly those of other micro-computer based KBES tools) affect not only the limitations of the ES prototype developed, but also the choice of the development tool itself. Factors which are likely to guide the choice of the ES developer are availability, cost, and appropriateness for the scope of the task that the prototype was chosen to model. In the case of AUGERPILE, it is noteworthy that a lack of formalized data/rules makes it very difficult to judge pile integrity at any one instance. Therefore, it is likely that prototypes like AUGERPILE will be used to assess whether a larger KBES development effort is appropriate, and to make a skeletal framework if such an effort is justifiable. A skeletal framework, such as AUGERPILE, can also be used to check and modify the appropriate uncertainty values so that more data may be gathered only in the larger developmental effort, but only where it is needed.

5.2. Extensions

It was noted in the previous section that INSIGHT does not provide facilities for handling multiple instantiations. Hence, the user has to start the program and run it - repeating the input of data - for each segment. This problem is being resolved by using PERSONAL CONSULTANT, which is a fairly powerful tool for building a large class of classification KBES. Other extensions to AUGERPILE are also being considered.

6. Conclusions

A micro-computer based expert system, AUGERPILE, to aid in the field inspection of augered concrete cast-in-place piles (ACCP) is described. The first version of AUGERPILE was implemented in INSIGHT. Since INSIGHT lacked some of the capabilities needed for AUGERPILE, it is being implemented on PERSONAL CONSULTANT. The authors believe that prototypes for certain class of problems, such as classification-type, should be developed on micro-computers, before venturing into a major developmental effort.

7. Acknowledgments

This work was conducted as part of the course work for *Expert Systems in Civil Engineering*. We would like to thank Professor Fenves for his comments. The authors would also like to thank Jim Garrett for his helpful suggestions.

8. Bibliography

1. Sriram, D., "A Bibliography on Knowledge-Based Expert Systems in Engineering", July, 1984, SIGART newsletter

2. Fuller, F. M., *Engineering of Pile Installations*, McGraw-Hill, New York, 1983.

3. Sriram, D., "A Survey of AI Tools in Industry", Forthcoming Publication

Implementation of a knowledge based seismic risk evaluation system on microcomputers

Glenn H. Miyasato, Weimin Dong, Raymond E. Levitt and **Auguste C. Boissonnade**

John A. Blume Earthquake Engineering Center, Department of Civil Engineering, Stanford University, Stanford, CA 94305, USA

The introduction of microcomputers to the civil engineering community has gone hand in hand with an ever increasing population of engineering software. The recent development of microcomputer expert system shells opens the path to yet a new set of applications. This article reports on the use of an expert system to determine the level of risk a building may face due to seismic hazard. The risk level is dependent on the building use, design, construction, and the ground motion level to which the building may be exposed. Theories about the many factors involved in a seismic risk evaluation are not well defined. Measurements are difficult to verify. However, seismic risk experts do have judgemental and heuristic rules based upon their broad knowledge and experience. Using heuristics based upon such experience, a set of rules was developed and implemented on *Deciding Factor*$^{(TM)}$, a microcomputer program for developing expert systems. An internal validation performed over several buildings showed that the system evaluation corresponded favourably with the expert's opinion. When further validated and refined, this seismic risk evaluation system could be used to aid in city planning, insurance assessment, and disaster mitigation.

Key words: microcomputers, expert systems, seismic risk, buildings, earthquake engineering

INTRODUCTION

Most civil engineering problems are solved by combining a formal technical approach with engineering experience and know-how. While formal technical methods can usually be modelled through algorithmic programs, the same cannot be said for engineering know-how. Knowledge based expert systems provide a methodology to achieve the performance level of a human expert, using the same type of experience-based heuristics which an expert employs when solving problems.

The expert system contains a large amount of knowledge gathered from experts that is specific to the domain of the problem. The knowledge in an expert system can be represented as rules which are manipulated by a processor in the system. Based upon the facts of an individual case, this processor determines the applicability of the rules, tests the premises, and invokes the corresponding actions in the appropriate sequence. The expert system can deal with rules that are not complete or unique or with incomplete or uncertain data. Also, although it uses the type of premise-action rules used in algorithmic programs, the order in which rules are entered is not important. Hence, rules and therefore knowledge can be added in a much simpler manner.

A hallmark characteristic of expert systems is that they explicitly represent the knowledge that they use as rules which are easily seen and understood by the expert in creating the knowledge base and by subsequent users who consult it. Graphical representation of the knowledge base futher enhances this 'glass box' (vs. black box) characteristic of expert systems. Although the knowledge is used to perform problem solving tasks in a manner similar to experts, the system is not creative or innovative. However, it is designed to overcome shortcomings of algorithmic computer applications.

The intent of this study was neither to develop expert system software nor to advance the state of the art in seismic risk evaluation but instead to use a commercial, readily available expert system development package or 'shell'. The expert system tool *Deciding Factor*$^{(TM)}$ was investigated for use in building a seismic risk evaluation system. The resulting system was then internally validated in several case studies taken from the city of Palo Alto, California.

SEISMIC RISK EVALUATION

This study is an outgrowth of an ongoing project at Stanford University involving risk analysis and seismic safety of existing structures. A preliminary step of the project was to select from a group of buildings certain buildings that were suspect in terms of seismic risk criteria. The expert system was one tool investigated as a means to accomplish this particular task. Experts at the John A. Blume Earthquake Center at Stanford University involved in the project were consulted for the knowledge base development.

The problem of assessing a level of seismic risk of a building is appropriate for expert system development because much of such an assessment involves expert opinion and knowledge from past experience. Also, the fact that many criteria involved in a seismic risk evaluation are not well defined or that measurements are

Received December 1985. Discussion closes September 1986.

Reprinted with permission from *Int. J. for Artificial Intelligence in Engineering*, vol. 1, no. 1, pp. 29-35, July 1986.

267

difficult to verify makes judgemental and heuristic rules even more important.

Specifically, this study details the use of an expert system approach to assign a relative risk level to an individual building based on certain seismic risk criteria. Seismic risk is defined as the likelihood of loss due to earthquakes and involves four basic components: hazards, exposure, vulnerability and location. These factors are further defined below[1].

1. The hazards or dangerous situations may be classified as follows:

   1.1. Primary hazards (fault break, ground vibration);
   1.2. Secondary hazards which are potentially dangerous situations triggered by the primary hazards. For example, a fault break can cause a tsunami or ground shaking can result in foundation settlement, foundation failure, liquefaction, landslides, etc.;
   1.3. Tertiary hazards produced by flooding by dam break, fire following an earthquake and the like.

   All these hazards lead to damage and losses. They may be expressed in terms of severity, frequency and location.

2. The exposure is defined as the value of the structures and contents, business interruption, lives, etc.
3. The vulnerability is defined as the sensitivity of the exposure to the hazard(s) and the location relative to the hazards(s).
4. The location is defined as the position of the exposure relative to the hazard.

Losses resulting from seismic hazard are numerous and can be categorized as follows:

1. Life and injury.
2. Property.
3. Business interruption.
4. Lost opportunities.
5 Contents.
6. Tax base.
7. Other losses.

A seismic risk analysis requires the identification of the losses to be studied as well as the indentification of the hazards, exposures and their locations and vulnerability. For the purposes of this study, life and injury losses resulting from seismic hazard were the major considerations in the evaluation of the risk level. Some aspects of the four components affecting risk were not included in the evaluation. The parts of the four components that were used in this evaluation are organized as shown in Fig. 1. The hierarchy starts with the main idea at the top and progresses to the supporting levels below. The main idea appears as: 'Seismic Risk Level'. At the next level, three key ideas, 'Seismic Hazard', 'Building Vulnerability', and 'Building Importance' support the main idea. These ideas have additional sub-levels of increasingly specific support.

The 'Seismic Hazard' idea includes some aspects of the hazards and the location components. The supporting ideas considered below this idea consisted of the primary and secondary hazards. The primary hazard of ground vibration along with the location component was included in the 'Ground Shaking' supporting idea. A severity parameter (peak ground acceleration, modified mercalli intensity) was used to measure the ground shaking level. This parameter implicitly included the location of the exposure relative to the hazard. Two secondary hazards, liquefaction and landslides, were selected for inclusion below the 'Ground Failure Potential' supporting idea along with the primary hazard of fault break. Due to the fact that landslides tend to occur where the natural grade is relatively steep and where top soil layers are underlain by differing materials or

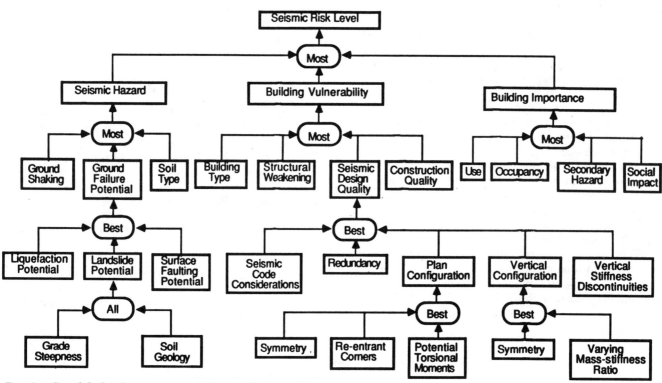

Fig. 1. Simplified inference network for the Seismic Risk Evaluation System

lubricating layers, landslides were further supported by grade steepness and soil geology. The last supporting idea involved was 'Soil Type' where extreme soil types can affect the seismic hazard level.

The 'Building Vulnerability' idea reflects the vulnerability component by taking into account the sensitivity of a particular structure to the seismic hazard. Thus, supporting ideas below 'Building Vulnerability' include structure characteristics such as building type (structural system and type of material used), structural alteration or weakening, quality of construction and seismic design quality. Seismic design quality refers to specific areas in the design which may affect the building's seismic performance. This category includes seismic code considerations, vertical stiffness discontinuities, structural system redundancy and architectural configuration factors such as plan and vertical symmetry, significant re-entrant corners, etc.

The 'Building Importance' idea reflects one aspect of the exposure component; the value of human life. 'Building Importance' reflects the utility value that is placed on the structure; where utility is measured in terms of public safety. High importance suggests that damage or destruction of the building due to an earthquake would be detrimental to public safety. Therefore the supporting ideas are concerned mainly with how building use and occupancy affect the possible loss of human life during and after an earthquake.

HARDWARE AND SOFTWARE TOOLS USED IN THE SEISMIC RISK EVALUATION SYSTEM

A computer-based damage assessment system has been developed at Purdue University[2,3]. The system uses observation data and other deep knowledge to assess a level of damage to an existing structure that has been subjected to earthquake excitation. The study described in this paper intends to develop an evaluation system which assigns a level of risk to a building before an earthquake occurs. Much of the knowledge used in this determination was heuristic.

The Deciding Factor program was chosen for application since the risk evaluation methodology fitted the framework. The program uses a decision model formulation, where ideas are organized in a hierarchical tree from the general to the specific.

This problem decomposition approach to building an expert system was first employed by the team at SRI International that developed the PROSPECTOR mineral resource evaluation expert system[4,5]. Deciding Factor, authored by Dr Alan Campbell, one of the scientists on the SRI team, is a direct outgrowth of this research.

Deciding Factor is a production rule based expert system shell which contains a backward-chaining inference engine to flexibly connect facts provided by the expert. It is composed of two parts called the *Editor*[TM] and the *Consultant*[TM]. The Editor guides the builder in the construction of a graphic model of ideas that support a proposed goal. The Consultant directs questions to the user and issues a report on the proposed goal based on the responses to the questions. Because the questions are derived from the ideas, each idea must be a statement that can be either supported or denied during consultation.

All ideas at the bottom of the hierarchy are examined by the Consultant. These ideas, called factors, are converted into questions which are answered in degrees of belief between yes and no inclusive. For example, if the factor is liquefaction potential, the question becomes: to what degree do you believe the liquefaction potential is very high? Numerical values ranging between $+5.00$ (yes) to -5.00 (no) to each response are multiplied by the numerical weights for positive or negative belief that the expert has assigned to each factor. The resulting product is then posted to the above idea called a hypothesis. The value is truncated if necessary so that it lies between $+5.00$ and -5.00. This value represents the numerical degree of belief in the hypothesis. Thus, the hypotheses are examined indirectly by evaluation of the supporting factors and hypotheses below them until the top hypothesis or main idea is examined.

The weighting factor which ranges between -1.0 to 1.0 is actually two weighting factors. A positive weighting factor is used when the user's response to the question is positive and a negative weighting factor is used when the response is negative. This is a significant departure from the Bayesian likelihood factors for sufficiency and necessity used in PROSPECTOR. In this application we found that it simplified the knowledge representation and gave essentially equivalent results.

Each question was also assigned an importance value which was used by Deciding Factor to calculate a reliability estimate of the conclusion. The importance varied from 0 (low importance) to 99 (high importance) and measured the extent to which the user needed to answer a question with a great deal of certainty.

For certain questions, user responses ($+5.00$ to -5.00) were assigned as categories (e.g., type of structure) instead of degrees of belief. The system prompts the user for a value and refers to a table. The user then picks the value assigned to the appropriate category, where the assignments were made by an expert. The assignment of values to these questions replaces the concept of 'degree of belief' in the answers. Therefore the reliability estimate as calculated in the conclusion of Deciding Factor no longer gave an accurate measure of the reliability of the final answer. For instance, an answer of 0.0 was taken by Deciding Factor to be a very uncertain response when in fact it corresponded to an exact category (e.g., medium soil). To remedy this, the importance of these 'value' class questions was set to zero so that they would not affect the reliability estimate.

The system can be run on an *IBMPC, XT, AT*[TM], or equivalent computer with at least 128 K of memory. Deciding Factor is very easy to use as no external editor is needed to input the knowledge base. Built-in logic screens display relationships between rules to show why a particular question is being asked. Deciding Factor also prints out a decision tree showing the overall logic as well as the weights assigned to each factor. This capability makes it very convenient for knowledge base development. The system also provides the ability to attach text or extended character set graphical explanations to variables or questions. Thus, questions or hypotheses can be clarified or expanded using explanation screens.

KNOWLEDGE REPRESENTATION

Each group of factors below a hypothesis must be linked together so that they can be evaluated and a conclusion can be reached about the hypothesis. Deciding Factor provides several relationships to express the logic between factors. The most appropriate relationship was chosen and fit to each situation.

One such situation shown in Fig. 2 involved the factors of grade steepness (x_1) and soil geology (x_2) below the landslide hypothesis (y), where both factors support the hypothesis equally. Of the logical relationships provided by Deciding Factor, the 'ALL' relationships was found to be the most appropriate.

For the 'ALL' logic, the sum of the numerical values of the factors $(x_i, -5.00 \leqslant x_i \leqslant +5.00)$ multiplied by the corresponding weights $(w_i, -1.0 \leqslant w_i \leqslant +1.0)$ becomes the numerical value of the hypothesis:

$$y = w_1(x_1) + w_2(x_2) \qquad (1)$$

The relative weights are normalized so their sum is 1.0. Therefore the strongest support the hypothesis can receive is 5.00 (definite yes) to -5.00 (definite no). Since both factors counted equally towards supporting the hypothesis, w_1 and w_2 were set to 0.5. As an example of is logic, consider the following case. The grade is steep; therefore $x_1 = 5.00$. The top soil layers are underlain by differing materials; therefore $x_2 = 5.00$. The value of (y) is:

$$y = 0.5(5.00) + 0.5(5.00) = 5.00$$
(the landslide potential is high)

Unequal weights can be used if one factor affects the hypothesis more than the other. Similar differing positive and negative weights account for prior probabilities above or below 0.5 in a Bayesian sense.

Another situation involved evaluating the seismic hazard (y). The expert considered three supporting factors: ground shaking (x_1), soil type (x_2), and ground failure potential (x_3). Fig. 3 shows this particular case. The problem involved finding a way to link these three factors which all supported the seismic hazard to some degree. Through the expert, it was found that when the ground motion level is very high, the seismic hazard level would certainly be high regardless of the other two factors. However, when the ground motion level is moderate or low, then the other two factors do contribute to the determination of the seismic hazard level. Therefore, a relationship was sought which weighted some factors more than others and allowed one factor to govern the situation in extreme cases. In order to fit this knowledge structure, the following combination logic was chosen.

$$y = w_1(x_1) + w_2(x_2) + w_3(x_3) \qquad (2)$$

This logical relationship is called 'MOST' in Deciding Factor. The weights are not normalized; therefore their sum could be greater or less than 1.0. However, the numerical answer for the hypothesis is truncated so that it still ranges between 5.00 and -5.00. Since information

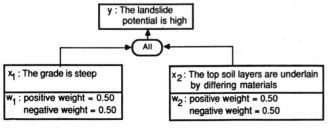

Fig. 2. *Landslide hypothesis and supporting ideas*

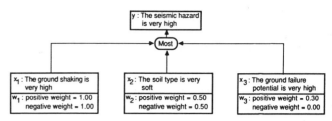

Fig. 3. *Seismic hazard hypothesis and supporting ideas*

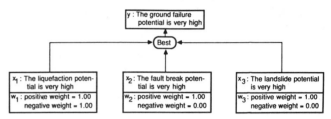

Fig. 4. *Ground failure potential hypothesis and supporting ideas*

about ground shaking should govern the evaluation of the hypothesis, w_1 was set to 1.0. The weight w_2 was set to 0.5 and the positive weight for w_3 was set to 0.3. The unequal weights were used because some factors affected the hypothesis more. Factors which could only add support but not reduce support for the hypothesis were given negative weights of 0.0. For instance, since a high ground failure potential can increase seismic hazard but a low potential for ground failure will not decrease the hazard, ground failure potential was assigned a negative weight of 0.0.

Consider an example of the 'MOST' logic for the following specific case of seismic hazard. The ground shaking level is very high; therefore $x_1 = 5.00$. The soil type is moderately soft; therefore $x_2 = 2.50$. The ground failure potential is very low; therefore $x_3 = -5.00$. The value of (y) is:

$$y = 1.0(5.00) + 0.5(2.50) + 0.0(-5.00)$$

$$y = 6.25 > 5.00$$

$$y = 5.00 \quad \text{(the seismic hazard is very high)}$$

The logical relationship 'MOST' and unequal weights were also used to combine the three supporting ideas below the main idea. The seismic hazard factor was given the highest weight of 1.0 so that it would govern the assignment of a risk level over the other two factors. This weighting gave good results except in the case where hazard was very low and both of the other factors were very high. However the possibility that both of the other factors will be high at the same time is extremely unlikely so for practical purposes the weighting used was appropriate.

The logical relationship 'MOST' was used whenever it was decided that one factor should influence the decision much more than the others. The possibility of using conditional logic (where out of range answers cause pruning or branching in the tree) should be investigated as an alternative to the 'MOST' relationship in some cases. For the remaining cases a relationship was needed where any one factor by itself could prove the hypothesis. For example, ground failure (y) is caused by the occurrence of any one of the three factors: liquefaction (x_1), fault break (x_2), and landslide (x_3). In other words, the most strongly supported factor below the ground failure potential will support it. Fig. 4 shows this case.

The relationship used by Deciding Factor that was deemed most appropriate was the relationship 'BEST'. 'BEST' uses the following combination logic:

$$y = \max[(x_1), (x_2), (x_3)] \qquad (3a)$$

In the case where certain factors may qualify as being more important than others, weighting factors can be introduced:

$$y = \max[w_1(x_1), w_2(x_2), w_3(x_3)] \qquad (3b)$$

The following calculation shows the use of the 'BEST' logic with a specific case of evaluating the ground failure potential. The liquefaction potential is very high; therefore $x_1 = 5.00$. The fault break potential is very low; therefore $x_2 = -5.00$. The landslide potential is high; therefore $x_3 = 2.50$. The value of (y) is:

$$y = \max[1.0(5.00), 0.0(-5.00), 1.0(2.50)]$$

$$y = \max[5.00, 0.00, 2.50]$$

$$y = 5.00 \quad \text{(the ground failure potential is very high)}$$

For most 'BEST' cases, all factors were equally weighted. However, for the building importance case as shown in Fig. 5, the factors were unequally weighted because each factor was actually a category of building types. The categories with the more important buildings were given more weight relative to the other categories. For instance, essential facilities (hospitals, fire stations, other buildings necessary for post-earthquake recovery) must function during and immediately after an earthquake, so they are considered more important than secondary hazards (buildings which pose an immediate health hazard if damaged). Therefore, the essential facilities weight is greater than the secondary hazard weight. The fuzzy logic type of flexibility in Deciding Factor was found to be advantageous in this application.

Although the main idea was to determine if the building was a high risk building, the conclusion was not to

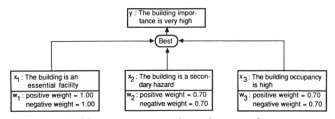

Fig. 5. Building importance hypothesis and supporting ideas

determine clearly whether or not the building was at high risk, but rather to determine the level of risk. Therefore a grading system based on the final numerical conclusion was developed. For instance, a range of 5.00 to 3.75 indicated a very high risk, a range of 3.75 to 1.25 indicated a high risk, 1.25 to -1.25 indicated moderate risk, -1.25 to -3.75 indicated low risk and -3.75 to -5.00 indicated very low risk.

SYSTEM VALIDATION

Several structures were evaluated by the system and compared to evaluations made by an expert whose knowledge was used in constructing the system. The internal validation was performed on five buildings in the city of Palo Alto, California. For the purpose of this study the buildings were labelled alphabetically from A to E.

Building A is a nine storey office building with approximately 500 occupants during commercial hours. The structure, built in 1972, has a reinforced concrete core wall with cast-in-place interior columns, precast exterior columns, precast beams, and precast floor planks. The building exhibits both plan symmetry and elevation regularity.

Building B is a one storey hospital housing approximately 500 occupants during commercial hours. during the night. The structure was built in 1966. It is of mixed construction comprising of concrete buttresses, interior box steel tube columns and wood roof framing. The building is square in plan with buttresses on three sides.

Building C was originally a single storey unreinforced masonry building constructed in the 1890's. The structure is used to house a retail outlet and has a daytime occupancy of approximately fifteen people. The building is rectangular in plan and originally had a tin roof supported by timber trusses. However the building was modified by adding a new floor at the truss lower chord level. Timber columns were added to take care of additional loads but show no sign of anchorage to roof trusses or to the existing floor.

Building D, constructed in 1963, consists of a combined shear wall, reinforced concrete column, and wood truss roof system. The building is a fire station with an occupancy of three. The one storey structure is composed of a hanger housing the fire trucks flanked by an adjoining room on either side. The building is cross shaped in plan.

Building E is a large church constructed in 1959. It holds approximately 150 people on Sunday mornings and

Table 1.

		Comparison of Risk Levels		
Building	Internal Expert Assigned Level	System Assigned Level (I)	System Assigned Level (II)	External Expert Assigned Level
A	low-moderate (-3.75 to 1.25)	moderate (1.1)	moderate (-0.4)	moderate (-1.25 to 1.25)
B	moderate (-1.25 to 1.25)	high (1.6)	moderate (0.1)	high (1.25 to 3.75)
C	high (1.25 to 3.75)	high (3.2)	high (1.7)	high (1.25 to 3.75)
D	high (1.25 to 3.75)	high (3.3)	high (1.8)	high (1.25 to 3.75)
E	low (-3.75 to -1.25)	low (-1.3)	low (-2.8)	low (-3.75 to -1.25)

is usually empty otherwise. The structure is primarily a wood frame with diagonal columns that join at the roof peak. The church is rectangular in plan with a large dormer on one side.

The results of the separate evaluation by the system and by the internal expert are shown in Table 1 and Fig. 6. The evaluations compared favourably with each other. Most buildings were assigned the same risk category by both system and expert and both evaluations ranked the buildings in the same order from the highest risk level to the lowest.

The comparison between the answers of the expert and the system represented in Table 1 and Fig. 6 are represented in a scattergram (Fig. 7). Each interval representing the expert's answer was represented by its mean value. From Fig. 7 we can see that version I of the system consistently assigned slightly higher risk levels. Calibration on the weighting factors were then performed such that all points were as close as possible to the straight line passing through the origin point. This resulted in version II of the system.

The five structures were also evaluated separately by an external expert. Comparison with the system evaluation showed a favourable correlation. As can be seen in Table 1, the external expert assigned the same risk categories as version I of the system for all five buildings.

The seismic risk evaluation system was also tested with the help of building officials in the city of Palo Alto. A tilt-up structure located in the downtown area was chosen for evaluation. During consultation, the system asked the user to provide information about the specific building being evaluated. The system provided explanations as to why the information was needed. The user could also ask the system to further explain how it wanted the user to respond.

Table 2 shows the answers provided by the city building officials along with the implications of each answer. The

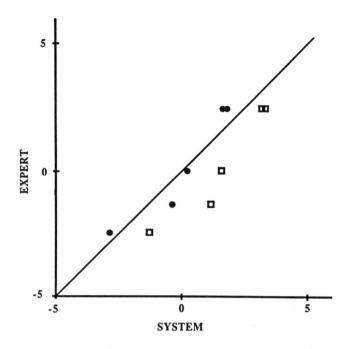

Fig. 7. Seismic risk evaluation system

final conclusion reached was that the building is at the moderate to high risk level. ($y = 3.4$, where y is the conclusion value). This corresponded to their own evaluation, considering the questionable performance of this type of building in an earthquake.

While extensive modification and validation must be performed if the system is to provide useful and accurate information, the present system does have value as a teaching aid. It is currently being considered for use as an information tool to expose building owners to seismic risk factors.

CONCLUSION

The Seismic Risk Evaluation System provides a preliminary evaluation of seismic risk for different types of existing buildings. The possible applications of this type of evaluation include assessments for possible seismic upgrading of buildings, city planning, disaster mitigation, and insurance feasibility studies. The system could also be implemented as an informational aid to educate the general public about seismic risk. As the system runs on a microcomputer, it is easily accessible and economical to develop and use. The Deciding Factor Shell provides a flexible, easy to use development and consulation package. Besides the consultation, the user can also receive some insight on how the risk assessment is reached.

However, this risk model is by no means complete. First of all, only a limited number of factors affecting risk were taken into consideration by the model. Some factors, such as liquefaction potential, fault break potential, ground shaking level, and quality of construction, could have been expanded several more levels downward. These factors themselves are of sufficient complexity that individual systems can be developed for each of them. Secondly, factors such as building type and seismic considerations, which have assigned values as input

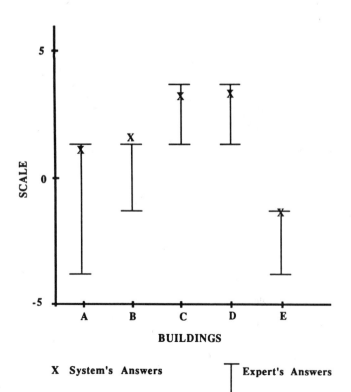

Fig. 6. Risk levels assigned by expert and system

Table 2

Data for Seismic Risk Evaluation of a Tilt-up Structure

Idea	Response	Implication
ground motion	+2.5	Intensity = 9
soil condition	−1.5	Medium to hard
liquefaction potential	−5.0	low
fault break potential	−5.0	low
slope of natural grade	−5.0	flat
soil underlain	−3.0	slight
building type	+2.0	tilt-up structure
structural system is weakened	−5.0	not weakened
quality of construction	−2.5	relatively good
seismic considerations included	−2.5	not to great extent
redundancy	−5.0	no redundancy
discontinuities in vertical stiffness	−5.0	no discontinuities
symmetrical plan configuration	+5.0	symmetrical
re-entrant corners	−5.0	no re-entrant corners
potential for large torsional moments	−5.0	no potential
significant changes in diaphragm strength	−5.0	no changes
mass and seismic resisting system are coincident	+5.0	coincident
Change of mass-stiffness ratios between adjacent stories	−5.0	no significant change
symmetric vertical configuration	+5.0	symmetric
essential facility	−5.0	not an essential facility
will cause secondary hazard	−5.0	will not
high occupancy	+1.0	about 100 persons
high-rise building	−5.0	single storey
serious social impact	−5.0	no serious social impact

needed to be improved so that values exist for every possibility. The current values are not compatible with the broad range of observed facts. Some inputs are quite subjective as they are in the form of linguistic descriptions. Fuzzy set theory should be investigated as a means to deal with this kind of linguistic information.

Finally, extensive validation with existing data must be done to calibrate the values and weights with the ranges assigned to the final answer. This way, the system can provide consultation comparable with an expert's performance.

ACKNOWLEDGEMENTS

The authors wish to express their appreciation to Professors Haresh Shah, James Gere and graduate students of Stanford's Department of Civil Engineering who contributed to the expert knowledge embodied in the system described in this paper. Partial support was attained from the National Science Foundation Grant No. CEE-8403516.

REFERENCES

1 Boissonnade, A. C. and Shah, H. C. Seismic Vulnerability and Insurance Studies, *The Geneva Papers on Risk and Insurance*, 1984, **9**, No. 32, 223–254

2 Ogawa, H., Fu, K. S. and Yao, J. T. P. SPERIL-II – An Expert System for Damage Assessment of Existing Structures, *Report No. CE-STR-84-11*, School of Civil Engineering, Purdue University, 1984

3 Ishizuka, M., Fu, K. S. and Yao, J. T. P. SPERIL-I: Computer Based Structural Damage Assessment System, *Report No. CE-STR-81-36*, School of Civil Engineering, Purdue University, 1981

4 Campbell, A. N., Hollister, V. F., Duda, R. O. and Hart, P. E. Recognition of a Hidden Mineral Deposit by an Artificial Intelligence Program, *Science*, 1982, **217**, No. 3

5 Duda, R., Gaschnig, J. and Hart, P. Model Design in the Prospector Consultant System for Mineral Exploration, *Expert systems in the Micro-electronic Age*, Edinburgh University Press, 1979, 153–167

BIBLIOGRAPHY

Applied Technology Council, Tentative Provisions for the Development of Seismic Regulations for Buildings, *ATC*, Vol. 3-06, ATC, June 1978

Boissonnade, A. C., Dong, W. M., Shah, H. C. and Wong, F. S. Identification of Fuzzy Systems in Civil Engineering, *Proceedings of the International Symposium on Fuzzy Mathematics in Earthquake Engineering*, 1985

Buchanan, B. G. and Shortliffe, E. H. *Rule-Based Expert Systems: The MYCIN Experiments of the Stanford Heuristic Programming Project*, Addison-Wesley, 1984

Campbell, A., Fitzgerrell, S. and Glover, T. *The Deciding Factor User's Manual*, Power Up Software, San Mateo, California, 1985

Dym, C. L. and Mittal, S. Knowledge Acquisition from Multiple Experts, *The AI Magazine*, American Association for Artificial Intelligence, 1985, Vol. VII, No. 2, 32–37

Harmon, P. and King, D. *Expert Systems: Artificial Intelligence in Business*, John Wiley and Sons, 1985

Laird, R. T. *et al.*, Quantitative Land-Capability Analysis, *USGS Professional Paper 945*, 1979

IMPLEMENTATION OF EXPERT SYSTEMS ON MICROCOMPUTERS

by

Peter C. Ohler
Lockheed Missiles & Space Company, Inc.
Sunnyvale, California

INTRODUCTION

The purpose of the water softener troubleshooting expert system was to not only show that microcomputer based expert systems were feasible but to show that they were preferred over mini or mainframe computer expert systems in some situations. Microcomputer have some advantages over larger computers as well as some disadvantages. These features will be discussed in more detail, along with some of the methods and tools that can be used to successfully develop a microcomputer expert system.

ADVANTAGES OF MICROCOMPUTERS

The principle advantages of a microcomputer are the cost and portability. In the past these advantages were not worth considering since a micro was barely capable of executing an expert system program due to memory and time constraints. Many microcomputers are now only an order of magnitude or two away from the mainframes in speed and memory.

The typical cost of a microcomputer is about 10 percent of the cost of a mainframe or less. This lower hardware cost is somewhat offset by the higher development costs of an expert system on a microcomputer although in most cases there is a decided cost savings realized by creating an expert system on a microcomputer as compared to a mainframe. Software for microcomputers, due to the larger market is usually less expensive than the software for larger systems. If this software can be used, off the shelf with little or no modifications development costs may be reduced as well. Due to the low costs of microcomputers the cost performance of an expert system is low enough to make expert systems feasable in areas that could not afford them in the past.

The portability of some microcomputers have allowed expert systems to make some inroads into more remote and harsh environments than in the past. It is possible for a repair person of some complex equipment to take along a microcomputer with an expert system to help diagnose equipment before making repairs or taking other actions. There are many more microcomputers in use today than the larger mainframes; therefor, an expert system developed on a microcomputer has a broader base on which it can be implemented. The power requirements of a microcomputer are much easier to satisfy than larger machines. This brings expert systems into any place that has standard electrical power.

The advantages of microcomputers are allowing expert systems to enter markets in areas that could not be considered in the past. Part of the recent success and advances in expert systems are due the microcomputer, it's portability, and lower cost.

LIMITATIONS OF MICROCOMPUTERS

There are some significant advantages to using a microcomputer to implement an expert system, but the developer and user must be aware of the limitations of a microcomputer expert system. The limitations of microcomputers are the same as limitations of larger, more powerful machines. Of course these limitations are more severe on microcomputers. The limitations are in memory size and processing speed. Just a year ago microcomputers were limited to under a megabyte of RAM. Now some systems can use up to several megabytes of temporary storage. This is still far short of a mainframe computer or some of the commercial LISP machines which use virtual storage methods to gain access to hundreds of megabytes of memory. Speed is another area in which microcomputers can not compete with larger computers. Although there have been some impressive speed increases in micro computers over the last few years, they are not as fast as the LISP machines that are used in many Expert system applications. The effects of these limitations can be seen in several areas.

	Mini or Large	Micro
Initial cost	High	Low
Time to develop an expert system	Shorter	Longer
Cost to develop an expert system	Lower	Higher
Software costs (expert system shell)	High	Low
Availability of expert system shells	Many	Few
Usable memory	Large	Small
Execution speed	Faster	Slower
Portability	No	Yes

Figure 1. Advantages and Limitations of a Microcomputer

Small usable memory will limit the size of the data base as well as the knowledge base in an expert system. This will either eliminate some potential expert system applications or it will limit the complexity of the system. Lack of usable memory may reduce the quantity and quality of development tools available on a machine.

With the use of 32 bit processors in microcomputers, the processing speeds have increased considerably, yet if response times are limited a microcomputer may not be able to do the job satisfactorily. This usually keeps the microcomputer out of complex, computationally intense, real time control environments.

These limitations can be offset to some extent with efficient programing, yet this requires a skilled programmer, as opposed to an engineer, and longer development times. Both of which increase the cost of implementing an Expert system on a microcomputer. The lack of fully featured development tools will slow the development of the system if the system is developed on a micro. Developers are more likely to attempt to tax the capability of the computer with a microcomputer. To do so requires more creative coding than coding which does not try to push the machine to its limits.

The limitations of using a microcomputer are reflected in what can and cannot be included in the delivered package. Some nice to have features such as natural language interfaces may have to be sacrificed for a menu driven approach, or limits on run time and flexibily may have to be accepted. When choosing a potential application it may be necessary to look for problems that can be solved using shorter inference paths, problems that are not as highly combinatorial, or those with smaller data and knowledge bases.

DEVELOPMENT TOOLS AVAILABLE

Just a year ago there were very few expert system shells available for microcomputers, and none for small microcomputers with only 64K of memory. Most of the shells available today are somewhat limited and do not have the flexibility found in expert system shells implemented on a LISP machine. There are several AI languages available for almost any microcomputer and these can be used to create an expert system.

The tools that are available to develop an exert system vary from languages such as LISP and PROLOG to shells made by many different companies with many different features. The more developed the package is, the more memory it usually uses. Shells, being more developed require more memory than LISP or PROLOG. The additional features in most shells makes for slower execution times yet faster development times if the shell has all the features needed by the knowledge engineer. If the features the engineer needs are not included in the shell they will have to be created outside the shell in another language. If the shell allows for external patches the task may not be too difficult. If patches cannot be made easily the knowledge engineer will have to find another way to solve the problem with in the confines of the shell. The process of patching in additional routines can sometimes be slow and error prone if the shell was not designed specifically to handle them gracefully. The features of the shell that are not used still require memory in the machine. The memory used for these features is a waste of a valuable resource on a micro computer, one that may restrict the potential application as well as the speed at which the final program is executed.

If the shell fits the problem it would be wise to use it. A shell fits a problem if the method used by an expert to solve the problem are the same as the methods available in the shell. An example might be a car diagnostic expert that required backward chaining of rules to identify the source of a problem. If the expert system shell does backward chaining well it will fit the problem. If the shell used a data driven approach to arrive at conclusions it would be more difficult to use the same approach to the problem. The experience of the knowledge engineer should also be considered. An engineer who is familiar with a more primitive tool such as LISP or PROLOG may be more than capable of developing an expert system with such tools, although the maintenance of the expert system may not be as easy if an engineer with the same competence level can not be found to maintain the software. If a programmer is not readily available a shell usually has a front end that is easier, although not as flexible, that can be used to develop and maintain an expert system. The cost of this front end is less memory available for the program and slower speed.

Most real world problems are not so straight forward as to require only one method of attacking the problem. A human expert usually uses several methods to arrive at the correct solution to a given problem. The expert system does not have to solve the problem in the same way as the expert but development can be simplified if it does. The memory required for the expert system can be kept to a minimum and the flow of the system can be better understood if the methods used to solve a given problem by a human expert are the same as those used by the expert system. The algorithms used to solve the problem can be forced to conform to the algorithms that the shell supports or they may be added to the shell. If there are many additions that must be made it may have been easier to not use the shell at all. In general, the wider the variety of algorithms supported the more memory will be required. The less memory that is available on the microcomputer the more careful and creative the knowledge engineer must be.

The two most common problem solving techniques used in microcomputer expert system shells are forward and backward chaining. Most utilize some sort of frame based method for storing data and some try to keep the rule appearance close to that of a spoken sentence. Usually there is a rather strict format that must be adhered to in creating the expert system from the shell. None have the same flexibility found on larger machines with commercial development systems. The constraints on the algorithms that can be used may make it very difficult to use. As memory restrictions are eased and the speed of the microcomputer increases other features such as viewpoints, object oriented features, and others will be supported, but for now shells on microcomputers are more limited.

A computer language is more primitive than an expert system shell, is faster and uses less memory. LISP is one of the most common languages used to create expert systems. It is also used to create many of the expert system shells. To develop an expert system using LISP requires a LISP programmer and usually more time to develop than using a shell. The resulting product will usually require less memory and will solve the problem faster than using an expert system shell. LISP is more flexible but all the tools used to create an expert system must be built from scratch and this will increase the development costs as well as the time required to develop the system. The advantage is the tools will be exactly what are needed, no more and no less.

PROLOG is a language that is based on predicate logic. It utilizes pattern matching, recursion, tail recursion, and backward chaining. It's structure gives it some of the features found in a shell, yet it has much of the flexibility found in LISP. PROLOG does not require large amounts of memory yet there are some crude development tools in some versions that allow an easier syntax for entering rules. A PROLOG programmer will have to be used to develop and possibly maintain the expert system. Micro-PROLOG, an implementation of PROLOG for microcomputers has a feature that allows modules to be loaded and unload as needed. It also allows for virtual memory usage by the programmer. PROLOG is a reasonable compromise between a primitive language and a developed shell for creating an expert system for a microcomputer.

APPLICABLE TYPES OF PROBLEMS

When considering using an expert system to solve a problem the user and developer must be aware of the limitations on a microcomputer to be able to gain from the advantages of using a microcomputer. The expert system may be limited to aiding a user in a job that requires a lower level of expertise or less knowledge. These areas include helping new or inexperience individuals, or aiding a person perform a task that is done only infrequently. Although these systems may not have the notoriety of an expert system that helps keep the space shuttle on course it could save a company a substantial amount in costly repairs or down time. The key to success in creating an expert system is to choose the right application. There are three major areas that tax the capability of a computer, used to implement an expert system. They are: the size of the data base, the speed required, and the complexity of the inference paths. These are also the areas in which an expert system can be the most beneficial to a human operator.

The size of the data base needed by the expert system is restricted by the amount of memory in the machine as well as the size and access speed of the mass storage media. If a large data base is needed the the speed of execution may be reduced. The length of the inference path may have to be shorter with a large data base so that results can be derived in a reasonable amount of time. A likely example might be an application with large amounts of meaningless data in the form of numbers, tables, dates, or names are hard for people to remember yet the expert system can keep track of them more easily.

The response time of the expert system can be an important design consideration. Even if the inference paths are short and the data base small an expert system that gives reliable and consistent results in situations that would be stressful, distracting, or boring to a person may be very useful. To respond quickly, sacrifices may have to be made in the size of the data base and in the length of the inference paths required to solve a problem.

Some problems require a minimum amount of memory or speed is not important, yet they are difficult for people to solve due to the complexity or intricacy of the problem. These are the types of problems that are found in puzzle books. In these types of problems the inference path to the solution is highly combinatorial, long, or hard to follow. These types of problems can be dealt with using microcomputer expert systems as long as the data base size and time requirements are not to stringent. Highly combinatorial problems can be modeled readily on a machine as well as abstract ideas or those that deal with numbers and calculations. The logical inferences performed by these expert system are the most critical part of the system. This is the area where creativity, knowledge of the tools available, and understanding of the problem are most important.

A well designed expert system will perform better than the user in at least one of these areas or possibly all three of them. Large computer expert systems can perform well in all the areas mentioned above, yet a microcomputer may only do one or two of the areas well due to memory and speed inadequacies. If all the areas are not strictly constrained a microcomputer may be a better choice due to the lower cost. As an example, if an operator of a piece of equipment must call a repair person and wait several days for a diagnosis of that equipment by an expert, it would be more than adequate to have an expert system take as long as several minutes or even hours to respond. If the task is to retrieve several pieces of data or specifications and make a simple deduction based on that data faster than a person, an expert system on a microcomputer may do very well. A task or problem that is not overly constrained by time, data base size, and inference path length is a good candidate for a microcomputer expert system.

A SPECIFIC EXPERT SYSTEM

To demonstrate the use an expert system on a microcomputer a very small machine was used with only 64K of memory and an 8 bit Z80 processor. The problem is a real problem encountered in oil fields using steam floods to recover oil, such as those in California. The purpose of this expert system was to provide a proof of concept rather than to actually implement the system in the field. A brief background on the user, a description of the equipment, and an outline of the expert system, implemented in Micro-PROLOG is included on the following pages.

User Background:

An unnamed oil company has been employing tertiary oil recovery methods for the last ten years. This method involves creating steam in steam generators and injecting it into the ground through steam injection wells at about 1000 psi. This steam heats the oil in the formation and drives it to a production well. The water-oil mixture that is collected at the well is separated into two liquid phases. The oil is processed and shipped to a refinery. The water is sent to a water plant, conditioned, and then sent back to the steam generators to be heated to steam and reinjected to complete the cycle.

About five years ago a central water plant was built to supply the steam generators with filtered, oil free, soft water. As the water enters the plant it passes through an oil floatation clarifier which, when operating properly, removes all but 1 to 2 parts per million of the oil in the water. Then the water goes through a bank of filters which remove the remaining oil and solids. The last, most critical step in the water treatment plant is the softening portion. If the plant effluent water contains more than 1 part per million of hardness, scale will form in the steam generators. Scale in the generators will increase the fuel consumption of the generator which will be reflected in the operating cost. When the scale gets thick enough, about 1/8" to 1/4" thick, tube failure will occur. Tube failures are costly and dangerous on these steam generators which operate at a pressure of 1000 psi. Problems often arise in the water softeners and they must be handled quickly so that the water plant effluent water quality and quantity will not be degraded.

Although it is important to keep the water softeners operating properly, the operators at the water plant do not have the skill and knowledge to correct many of the problems that arise and an outside expert must be called in. This lack of skill and knowledge is due to the fast turnover of the plant operators and the low basic educational background of the operators. The delays that occur or the attempts to fix the problem without the required knowledge can lead to hardness in the water or not enough water leaving the plant to keep the generators operating. When generators are down no steam is injected which means less oil is recovered, production decreases, and profits drop.

Equipment Description:

The water softeners (Figure 2a-e) consists of two vessels, a primary and a secondary. The primary is the larger of the two units and removes most of the hardness. The secondary is the smaller of the two vessels and removes the rest of the hardness in the water. The softener operation can be divided into eight steps or modes of operation. These modes are:

Backwash of the secondary;
Backwash of the primary;
Brine cycle;
Displacement;
Fast rinse of the primary;
Fast rinse of the secondary;
Standby;
Service cycle.

Most of the time the softener is in the service cycle and is discharging soft water. Soft water is defined as water that has less than a few parts per million of calcium and magnesium ions. Each step of the softener operation has an important function in keeping the softener effluent soft. The

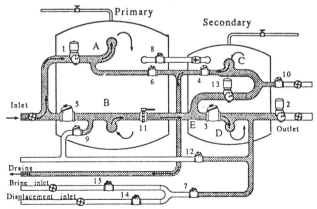

Figure 2a. Backwash of the Secondary

function of each step as well as the flow the water takes during each step is described below.

The backwash of the secondary is used to clean the secondary softener, which is the smaller of the two units. This is done by making the water flow upward in the softener vessel. This fluffs up the media in the softener and washes out any dirt and oil that has been filtered out in the softener during the normal service cycle. The water flows from the inlet, past valve number 1, through the primary, past valve number 3, up through the secondary, past valve number 4, and then to the drain.

The backwash of the primary is used to clean the primary softener. This step is similar to the previous step but cleans the primary instead. The water flows from the inlet, past valve number 5, up through the primary, and past valve number 6 to the drain.

The brine cycle removes the calcium and the magnesium from the softener resin and replace these ions with sodium ions. This is done by putting high concentrations of salt in the softener. This must be done for a specific length of time and at a specific salt concentration. The brine flows from the brine pump, to the brine valve number 15, past valve number 7, and up through the secondary. The brine is diluted with soft water which enters through valve number 10. It flows past valve number 8 into the primary. After passing through the primary the spent brine goes through valve number 9 to the drain.

The displacement cycle displaces the brine in the softener with soft water. The brine must be removed before the softener is put back in service. The dilution water follows the same path as the brine with one exception. Valve number 15 is closed and valve number 14 is opened.

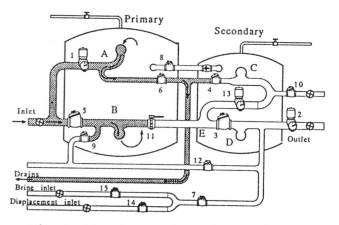

Figure 2b. Backwash of the Primary

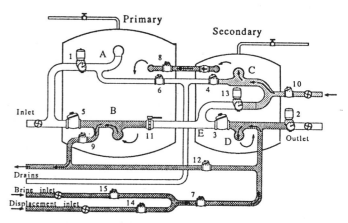

Figure 2c. Brine and Displacement

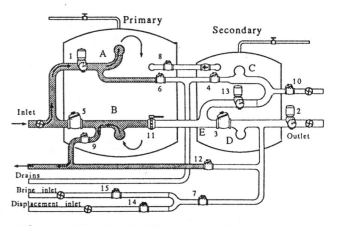

Figure 2d. Fast Rinse of the Primary

280

The fast rinse of the primary rinses out the remaining salt from the primary. The flow rate for this step is faster than for the displacement cycle. The water flows from the inlet, through valve 1, through the primary, and past valve number 9 to the drain.

The fast rinse of the secondary rinses the brine out of the secondary. The flow is from the inlet, past valve number 1, through the primary, past valve number 13, down through the secondary, and past valve number 12 to the drain.

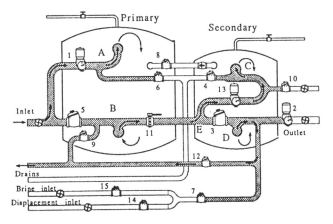

Figure 2e. Fast Rinse of the Secondary

The standby cycle is simply a standby mode where no water is flowing through the softener.

The service cycle is the normal operation of the softener. Hard water enters the set of softeners and softened water exits past valve number 2. The flow is from the inlet, past valve number 1, through the primary, past valve number 13, through the secondary, and to the outlet past valve number 2.

Each of these steps must be performed properly or a problem will occur during the service cycle and hard water will be passed to the field and to the steam generators.

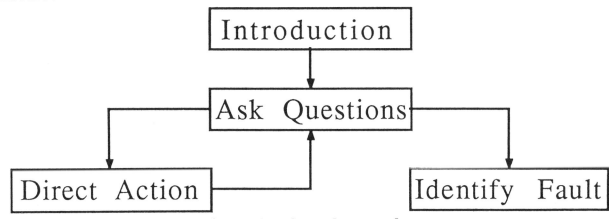

Figure 3. Flow of Control

Program Outline:

As an expert system the water softener troubleshooting system was designed to accept a variety of responses to questions. After a brief introduction and some simple instructions the system begins by asking the user questions about the water softeners. If a problem is evident from the answers the user supplies, the system will ask further questions to isolate the problem and direct the user to perform some action, while the consequences of those actions are observed. The information obtained by reading the gauges and observing the drains will be used by the system to continue troubleshooting the water softener. This process will iterate until a corrective action can be suggested (Figure 3). To implement this system Micro-

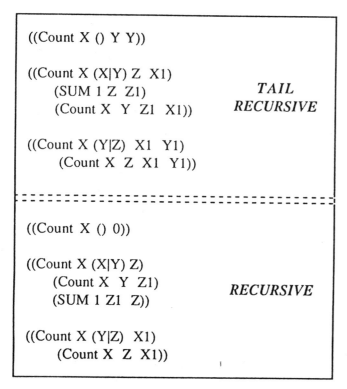

```
((Count X () Y Y))

((Count X (X|Y) Z X1)
    (SUM 1 Z Z1)
    (Count X Y Z1 X1))          TAIL
                                RECURSIVE
((Count X (Y|Z) X1 Y1)
    (Count X Z X1 Y1))

- - - - - - - - - - - - - - - - - - - - - - -

((Count X () 0))

((Count X (X|Y) Z)
    (Count X Y Z1)
    (SUM 1 Z1 Z))               RECURSIVE

((Count X (Y|Z) X1)
    (Count X Z X1))
```

Figure 4. Recursion and Tail Recursion

PROLOG was used due to it's flexibility and since it had such features as backward chaining and pattern matching built in. It also took up very little of the small 64K of memory in the machine. PROLOG was deemed to be a better choice than LISP since it had many of the tools needed for the expert system that would have had to be developed in LISP. Many shells had some of the tools needed but not all of the required tools and none of the shells could be run on a 64K computer. Some of the techniques used in the expert system were recursion, tail recursion, backward chaining, pattern matching, the use of modules to compensate for the lack of memory, and some combinatorial methods. An example of the difference between recursion and tail recursion is shown in Figure 4. A variety of methods were used to increase the efficiency of the program and to model the way an expert would go about troubleshooting the water softeners. The expert system was designed with the possibility of becoming part of an autonomous system in the future. This was reflected in the program by the use of directives given to the user by the expert system. These directives could just as easily be given to a controller which would open or close valves on command and return the values read from flow meters and pressure gauges. The techniques used are noted in the following paragraphs which briefly describe the workings of the program.

The water softener troubleshooting expert system is composed of a shell and a data base. The knowledge base is built into the shell and consists of rules that model the basic physical properties of a fluid in a system of pipes and valves. There are a few rules in the shell that are specific to the softeners that the shell was built for, but these can be changed readily. The kernal of the system consists of 14 rules and 15 facts which take up only a small amount of memory. The first module consists of 35 rules. The elution study module has 78 rules and 38 facts such as those in Figure 5. The longest time delay is when the expert system is finding the possible paths the water can take. This can take up to 40 seconds. If more memory was available many of these functions could have been kept in a more general context instead of being specific for the system modeled. Micro-PROLOG has several files included with the interpreter that allow for tracing and backtracking. These modules, not used in this implementation,

```
Flow limit and other information of each step:

    ((FLOW-LIMIT 1 FILTER 200  251 4))
    ((FLOW-LIMIT 2 FILTER 450  551 6))
    ((FLOW-LIMIT 3 BRINE 32  36  15))

Correct paths for each step:

    ((CP 1 ((FILTER A B E D C BW-DRAIN)))
    ((CP 2 ((FILTER B A BW-DRAIN)))
    ((CP 3 ((BRINE F D C A B BR-DRAIN)))

Connection between valves and nodes:

    ((LINK FILTER A 1))
    ((LINK FILTER B 5))
    ((LINK A B PRIMARY))
    ((LINK A BW-DRAIN 6))
```

Figure 5. Sample Facts

could be used to ask how a conclusion was reached if more memory was available in the microcomputer. The program is broken into two parts due to the memory constraints. The first part is structured as a simple logic tree where the user responds to questions from the expert system and is moved to different branches of the tree. This tree is used to determine if the softener is working properly and to detect some valve failures that can be detected without an elution study. An elution study is a careful monitoring of the water softener while it is in regeneration to determine if and where a fault exists. If the softener is not working properly and an elution study is required the program will lead the user through the elution study. The second part of the expert system uses several different methods to determine the problems in the system. A very simple single word pattern matching function is included to make the input more flexible and increase the number of correct responses that will be accepted. The operator will be expected to answer questions about valve positions, water hardness, flow rates, and brine concentrations. The action required to be taken by the operator include opening and closing valves, checking time between steps, and changing valves that are found to be defective.

The program begins with an introduction and then the decision tree. A decision tree was the most advantageous way to make the simple decisions that required only short and simple inference paths to arrive at the correct conclusion. Included in the first section were other functions that checked the range of an answer, compared answers to predicted parameters, and checked answers for a match with any synonym of the expected choices. If the decision tree leads to an elution study then all the branches of the tree are collasped and the new root is the start of the elution study start. All other functions are removed and the elution study module is loaded. Control is passed to the elution study function which will be true if the expert system cannot find the fault and false if the fault is found and identified. If it does not find the fault, then the final function called is one that informs the operator that a human expert will have to be consulted.

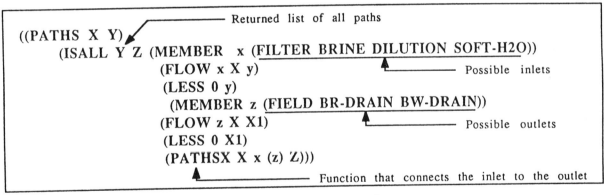

Figure 6. ISALL Example

The water softener model is created by assigning letters to different nodes in the plumbing of the softeners as indicated in Figure 2. The valves are numbered and the data base consists of facts that describe how nodes are connected to valves and to the softener vessels. The flow of control follows the execution of functions that correspond to the steps in the regeneration cycle of the softeners. In each step a combinatorial method is used to find all the possible paths the water can take that will not conflict with the observations made by the operator. The ISALL primitive of Micro-PROLOG is the backbone of this part of the program. ISALL is used to find all the possible paths the water takes given certain patterns to match (Figure 6). The observations that are asked for by the expert system are simply flow rates at each of the possible flow meters and drain pipes. At this point all the possible paths that have the correct input and output flows are found with no regard to whether or not the path is the actual path taken by the water. Paths are found by starting at the input of the softener system and checking the facts for any connection that can be made to that node and any other node through some valve. This process continues, recursively until the path arrives at an output that has some indicated flow. The expert system then uses backward chaining to eliminate paths that do not have water in them based on a valve position of either open, closed, or unknown. This is done in three parts. Each way asks the operator to observe valve positions and to open or close specific valves as changes in flow rates and pressure are recorded. The first part of the elimination process is based the outcome of closing certain valves. The next part is based on opening valves and recording flow changes. The last part eliminates paths based on pressure at a given node. The valves that can be used to eliminate paths are chosen based on which valve position changes will actually reduce the number of possible paths that are being considered. Finally after all the information needed has been collected the results are compared to the correct model of the softeners for the given step based on flow path, flow rates, and the time it took to complete the step. If the model is not correct or there is more than one path being used, the valve that is causing the incorrect flow is identified, the operator is told to replace the bad valve, the function is proved to be false, and the program stops. If the flow rate is incorrect the operator is told to adjust the flow by changing the setting of a specific valve. The step completion time is not correct the operator is told to adjust the timers and the step continues. When a step succeeds the next step is begun and the process continues until all the steps have been completed or until a step fails. In this way if a problem can be identified the recommended corrective action is suggested to the operator; if not, the program continues until it has checked as much as it can and finally gives up by calling in a human expert to solve the small number of cases that can not solve independently.

CONCLUSION

The water softener troubleshooting expert system was never installed in the field although it was tested on many of the actual problems that occurred to the equipment in the field. It performed well and was able to diagnose the failed part correctly. A microcomputer was used due to cost considerations as well as the adverse environmental conditions that exist in an oil field maintenance shed. This system was able to perform all the tasks that it was designed for using only 64K of memory. Micro-PROLOG was one of the key elements in the success of this expert system. The tools that are available in Micro-PROLOG fit the problem well and yet, being a language, Micro-PROLOG was flexible enough to be used to create the other tools needed to solve the problem efficiently. It seems apparent that on a microcomputer with limited resources it may be necessary to use a language such as LISP or PROLOG to extract the most from the computer when implementing an expert system.

DEVELOPMENT OF EXPERT SYSTEM APPLICATIONS
USING PERSONAL CONSULTANT(TM)

by

William M. Turpin
Manager, AI Applications
Texas Instruments Data Systems Group
Austin, Texas

During the past year and a half since the introduction of Personal Consultant[TM] in 1984, we at Texas Instruments have had an opportunity to work with and observe what many customers have done with the product. Additional customer understanding has been gained through our training classes and knowledge engineering services. These observations, plus our own involvement in expert system creation, have helped us to better understand the product features and management techniques which contribute to successful projects.

This paper presents four case histories of how actual expert system applications were created using Personal Consultant[TM]. They were selected from actual customer applications as being representative of various issues involved in expert system creation. These case histories show how varied expert system applications are in terms of their problem domain and intended user community. They also show different strategies for learning about and managing expert system technology. Hopefully, they can be instructive in the design and use of PC-based expert system technology.

CASE HISTORY #1 - CAMPBELL SOUP COOKER DIAGNOSIS

The first case history involves a traditional application of expert system technology. It involves a diagnostic domain which is well suited to rule-based backward chaining systems. It was also produced using a knowledge engineer working in conjunction with a single domain expert.

This application was done for manufacturing plants at the Campbell Soup Company. These plants use giant product sterilizers, commonly called cookers, in the production of soup products. Each cooker processes several hundred cans of soup at a time. So when one malfunctions, it is very important to get the problem diagnosed and fixed quickly. If a fix for the cooker is not found soon enough, then you "lose the soup".

Many routine cooker problems can be handled by plant operators on a day-to-day basis. Occasionally, however, difficulties arise that require the advise of an expert--someone who understands the design, installation, and operation of the equipment. Unfortunately, there are not enough human experts to go around. This can result in long delays while an expert is located and flown in. To make matters even worse, Campbell's best expert was nearing retirement.

Campbell's management decided to use this problem situation as a test of the viability of expert systems. They contracted with Texas Instruments to provide knowledge engineering in the creation of this expert system. Campbell supplied the domain expert, while TI provided the knowledge engineer. The two would meet three to four days a month to design and review the evolving system.

After several months, a prototype system of about 30 rules was developed. It did not have much depth of knowledge, but it demonstrated that the expert system approach was feasible. It also served as a catalyst for adding additional knowledge to the system. After about 150 rules had been entered, the system was ready for production use. At the time of this writing, the system is being used at eight of Campbell's manufacturing facilities.

The Campbell Soup expert system was created using the Personal Consultant Expert System Tools to run on IBM PC-XT computers. The Personal Consultant[TM] provides several features which were important in this application:

- An easy-to-use interface so that plant maintenance personnel can quickly learn to use the system

- English explanation facilities help facilitate working with the domain expert and provide ongoing training for the maintenance personnel

- Multiple runtime versions have been created to distribute the system to several plants while maintaining central control of the knowledge base

Another important aspect of this application was Campbell's decision to get help in the creation of their first expert system application. By using a low-cost, PC-based expert system shell and the consulting services of a knowledge engineer, they were able to significantly increase their chances for success. They were also able to get involved with expert system technology in a very timely manner. This has allowed them to prove the feasibility of an expert system approach and stay competitive in their product market.

PERSONAL CONSULTANT[TM] APPLICATION SUMMARY

CASE HISTORY	1	2	3	4
WHO	Campbell Soup	Texas Instruments	Westinghouse	Purdue/USDA
DOMAIN	Soup Manufacturing	Semiconductor Manufacturing	Powerplant Design	Grain Marketing
TASK	Equipment Diagnosis	Equipment Diagnosis	Material Selection	Marketing Advise
PROBLEM	Expert Retiring	Expert Not Available	Knowledge Transfer	Knowledge Transfer
END USER	Technician	Technician	Engineer	Farmer
KNOWLEDGE ENGINEER	Hired Consultant	Programmer/Analyst	Domain Expert	Graduate Students
SIZE	150 Rules	1000 Rules	300 Rules	150 Rules
FEATURES	Runtime	Runtime	LISP functions Frames Graphics	LISP functions Data Access Graphics
STATUS	Production Usage	Production Usage	Refinement	Refinement

CASE HISTORY #2 - TEXAS INSTRUMENTS EPI REACTOR DIAGNOSIS

The second case history involves the use of an expert system for a similar diagnostic task. However, it is quite different in the manner that it was produced. It was created using multiple domain experts and a self-taught knowledge engineer.

This system is an equipment diagnosis situation at a semiconductor manufacturing facility within Texas Instruments. The manufacturing process for semiconductors uses many different machines to produce silicon "wafers" with intricate patterns etched in layers to produce complex electronic circuits. Each machine is very expensive and operates with very small tolerance levels.

At the TI manufacturing facility in Sherman, Texas, one such machine, called an epitaxial reactor, is an essential step in the production of semiconductors. These reactors use very high temperatures and controlled mixtures of gases to grow a very thin silicon film (the epitaxial layer) on silicon wafers. Since the reactors process several wafers at a time, an equipment failure can produce a large amount of material scrap and hold up the rest of the manufacturing process.

In September 1984, this machine was selected as the most serious bottleneck in the manufacturing process, and an expert system approach was selected to help reduce downtime. It was felt that there were a large number of problems that the machine operators and local maintenance staff could remedy with appropriate help from an expert system. If successful, such a system could save thousands of dollars.

The programmer/analyst assigned to this project had no previous AI or LISP programming experience but was willing and anxious to learn. After selecting the Personal Consultant™ system as her programming tool, the new knowledge engineer attended a one-week course on the system. This gave her the initial training necessary to go back to the work environment and concentrate on her application.

To obtain the necessary expertise about the epi reactors, two committees were formed. The first was a technical committee charged with defining the scope of the system, the problems to attempt to diagnose, and the diagnostic procedures. It was composed of the knowledge engineer, a manufacturing engineer, several service technicians, and a service representative from the manufacturer of the epi reactor. They decided to initially focus on common problems which a reactor could help identify through its operator panel.

The second committee was formed of the planned users of the system. It included the knowledge engineer, service technicians, and machine operators. They helped determine how the system would fit into the actual work environment and how users would be trained. They would go in on weekends to test the operation of the prototype system in the production environment.

After six months, the development team had created a 400 rule system called the Intelligent Machine Prognosticator (IMP) which could suggest solutions to 25 common problems. By the time of this writing, the system had grown to about 1000 rules (segmented into seven knowledge bases) covering about 300 reactor problems. This system has been installed on a portable TI Professional Computer which is rolled to the epi reactors as needed on a moveable cart. The results so far have been an outstanding forty-four percent increase in average time between reactor failures. Work is also in progress on creating expert systems for other selected machines at this facility.

This application was facilitated by several Personal Consultant™ features. The easy-to-use interface and ability to make runtime versions for delivery were both essential. The product training also helped the new knowledge engineer gain experience and confidence more quickly. The English explanation of the system's operation also helps train the maintenance personnel and instill user confidence in the system.

The use of two committees was also a key element in the success of the IMP system. The pooling of several expert's knowledge helped make the system more intelligent. The inclusion of the system's eventual users during the design phase was also instrumental in getting the system accepted in the work environment. Many people overlook the fact that an expert system is useless unless the people it is intended to help come to it for advice.

CASE HISTORY #3 - WESTINGHOUSE CORROSION EXPERT

The next case history involves a domain in which the expert system gives design advise. It was produced by the domain expert himself who learned the necessary computer programming skills. The resulting system is intended to help engineers design better, longer lasting products.

This expert system was created in the Research and Development labs at Westinghouse. The subject of the system is the selection of metal alloys for the construction of steam generators in nuclear power plants. A researcher there had discovered how to combine dissimilar metal alloys to produce a component with specific corrosive properties--which were sometimes different from either of the metals alone. He was faced with the choice of how to disseminate this information to the appropriate engineers at Westinghouse. His solution was in the form of an expert system that could help further his research while providing a good medium to transfer the knowledge.

This metalurgical expert had an interest in computers but did not have any formal computer education. Therefore, after selecting Personal Consultant^{TM} as his expert system tool, his first step was to attend training classes on the product. With this training, he was able to go back to Westinghouse and create several small expert systems--one of which helped salespeople configure electrical panel boards. During this period, he also started teaching himself LISP so that he could add custom features into his expert systems.

At the time of this writing, this system is still being expanded and refined. In particular, the researchers are studying the discrepancies between theoretical relationships and empirical evidence--both of which have been encoded into production rules. When these two systems of logic produce conflicting advice, it helps suggest an area needing further research.

This project has used several features of Personal Consultant^{TM} in order to achieve its results:

- Reliance on certainty factor calculations to incorporate and report imprecise knowledge

- Extensive use of graphics has been employed to enhance the display of conclusions

- The problem domain was structured into modular components (frames) to make it more manageable

- User defined LISP functions have been written to extend the functionality of the system

- The symbolic form of the rules (not compiled) has been useful in finding and reporting conflicting knowledge

Other features, such as the easy-to-use interface and explanation facilities, will help the transfer of knowledge to other engineers at Westinghouse.

This application also demonstrates that it is sometimes possible to train the domain expert on expert system creation. The non-procedural style of rule-based expert systems can simplify the knowledge encoding process much like computer spreadsheets simplify the manipulation of tabular, numeric data. If the domain expert is willing and able to learn about expert systems, he can be very effective at creating applications in his domain.

CASE HISTORY #4 - PURDUE GRAIN MARKET ADVISOR

The last case history involves an application in the domain of marketing. It was produced in a university setting by a team of knowledge engineers and domain experts. It adds some new features to an expert system in order to make the system more capable.

In 1985, Purdue University received a grant from the United States Department of Agriculture (USDA) to study improvements that could be made in the US farm industry. As a result of this study, Purdue has created several expert systems which can help individual farmers beocme more productive. One of these systems, called the Grain Market Advisor, helps farm operators determine the best method of marketing the grain they produce.

The grain marketing process is a confusing problem to many farmers because of price uncertainties, commodity markets, and joint marketing alternatives. Yet, the marketing strategy employed by the farmer can have a tremendous impact on the selling price of a crop. A good marketing strategy can also help reduce some of the risk involved in farming. In order to give good, consistent advise on grain marketing, Purdue decided to create an expert system.

During a consultation with GMA, grain price history information is retrieved from a commercial data base via a dial-up telephone line. This price information is used to help predict future price trends. Graphics are produced from this data to help convey these price trends to the user. Given these trends, the system helps decide which risk-sharing strategies, such as selling grain futures, are relevant. These strategies are then tested to see if they can be used in the current situation.

Before starting work on GMA, Purdue sent a graduate student from the project to live and work with the Personal Consultant™ development team. During the Spring of 1985, the student was able to learn about the product and develop user interface routines which would be helpful to the project. This cooperative effort proved to be beneficial to both parties involved. Back at Purdue, this student became the lead knowledge engineer for the project. The resulting expert systems, including the GMA, were presented to the USDA last December.

Custom LISP functions were used extensively in GMA to perform the data base access and present graphical information. These additional features allow the system to be more capable and easier to understand. When combined with the standard explanation facilities, the system became very transparent and capable of explaining its reasoning. This will be very important to the user of the system who will be pricing an entire year's crop production based on advise from the system.

Certainty factors were employed to represent imprecise knowledge, determine default values, and rank competing grain marketing alternatives. The easy-to-use interface will be essential when dealing with users who do not work with computers on a day-to-day basis. The price point and availability of personal computers coupled with the ability to make runtime versions of the application make this system feasible for mass distribution within the farming industry.

SUMMARY

In addition to being successful, these four case histories share several common themes relating to PC-based expert system development. These projects, along with others, can be used to generalize the following observations:

- Many organizations are getting involved with and creating expert system applications

- Useful, cost-effective expert systems are being produced for use on personal computers

- Current expert system technology can be applied in many different problem domains

- Many successful projects start with a small prototype which is extended and refined over time

- Companies without prior AI experience are being successful by getting assistance

These case histories also demonstrate that the creation of expert systems is no longer limited to high-tech, early adopter companies. The availability of powerful PC-based tools, such as Personal Consultant™, have significantly reduced the risk and training involved in creating useful applications in many problem domains. The development of expert systems is quickly moving from AI research labs into business practice at many companies. Soon, they will be a standard method of improving quality and managing the flow of knowledge within an organization.

Auditor: a microcomputer-based expert system to support auditors in the field

Abstract: *Public accounting firms are beginning to use more sophisticated forms of decision support as competitive pressures rise and technological advances are made. One form of support is the microcomputer-based expert system. This paper describes the development of one such system to aid external auditors in estimating the dollar amount of their client's uncollectible accounts receivable. The resulting system is* Auditor, *which is based on the general inference engine, AL/X, developed by Michie. The details of the development process from initial interviews to validation are presented. Insights into the process of audit decision making and into the development of microcomputer-based expert system for auditing are discussed.*

CHRIS W. DUNGAN*
JOHN S. CHANDLER§

* University of South Florida at Sarasota 4202 E. Fowler Avenue Tampa, FL 33620, USA

§ University of Illinois at Urbana-Champaign IL 61801, USA

1. Introduction

Decision support systems for implementation on microcomputers are being developed to aid external auditors in the field. Reasons for this development are not hard to find. Increased competition among the major public accounting firms stimulates a search for more efficient and less costly audit procedures. Such procedures can yield not only greater profit from current engagements but can also provide greater flexibility in bidding for new clients. Recent advances in the cost-effective use of microcomputers by auditors in the field opens the door for sophisticated modes of support [1]. The impetus behind much of the published research — including the work reported on here — was initially provided by the Research Opportunities in Auditing program of the public accounting firm of Peat, Marwick, Mitchell and Co. [2].

Auditor is an application of the generic inference engine, AL/X (Advice Language/X) [3]. At the instigation of Donald Michie, AL/X was adapted for use in Pascal systems on microcomputers from the general design principles of Prospector [4]. It separates the domain-specific knowledge from the control program which uses the knowledge. Thus, while AL/X was originally used in one realm of application (oil rig shutdown analysis), its inference structure provides a foundation upon which expert systems in other domains can be built. This is very similar to the relationship of KAS to Prospector and EMycin to Mycin [5]. *Auditor*, however, is implemented on an IBM PC, or compatible, with 256 K.

This paper describes the development of a microcomputer-based expert system called *Auditor* to aid independent auditors in their estimation of the dollar amount of a client's uncollectible accounts receivable. The task of auditing as an application of expert systems is discussed first. The development of *Auditor* and the mechanics of its inference engine, AL/X, are described next, together with the two validation techniques to which the system was subjected. Finally, insights gained during the project are discussed, both as to auditors' decision making and to the implications of decision support for auditors via expert systems on microcomputers.

2. Auditing as a task for expert systems

2.1. Why expert systems are suited for auditing

Auditors have not been performing their function unaware of developments in decision support. Regression analysis has been applied to analytic review [6–11] and to sample size determination [12]. Other statistical techniques have been applied to sample size determination and sample analysis [13, 14]. Simulation has been used to analyze potential errors [15]. All of these approaches employ quantitative data to achieve their results. Statistical and operations research software are available for microcomputers so that many of these techniques are now being used in the field by practicing auditors.

Expert systems have been built and used in many fields. Most of these task domains have precisely characterized attributes and objective measurements as inputs to the system: mineral prospecting [16, 4], computer configuration [17], chemical structure analysis [18, 19]. Medical diagnosis and therapy is commonly driven by a mixture of objective tests and subjectively assessed values [20–29]. In auditing, as in medical diagnosis, although vast amounts of objective data exist (e.g., account balances, confirmations and cash receipts), it is the auditor's subjective interpretation of this data that is used to generate and evaluate alternative solutions. For example, it may be found that a client has a stated, tight credit policy, but it is the auditor's perception of the effectiveness of the credit manager in enforcing that policy that is significant. Thus, audit decision making is presented with a mix of objective and subjective inputs and, in general, is an appropriate task domain for expert systems.

There are several expert systems in auditing being developed on or for microcomputers. Hansen and Messier [30] are using the same AL/X used in this project to study auditor evaluations of internal controls in the EDP environment. Braun and Chandler [31] are using ACLS (Analog Concept Learning System), developed by Michie [32], to induce decision rules on bad debt evaluations in the health care industry. The resulting decision rules will then be used as a basis for constructing an expert system. ACLS is the non-commercial version of Expert-Ease. Wright and Willingham [33] are developing an expert system to aid bank auditors in evaluating the collectibility of loans. Their system is based on the M.1 system, developed by Teknowledge, and it is planned to be used in the field by auditors on microcomputers. The initial expert system in accounting, Taxadvisor [34], was built on a mainframe using EMycin. Commercial packages available now could allow Taxadvisor to be built and run on a microcomputer.

Reprinted with permission from *Expert Syst.*, vol. 2, no. 4, pp. 210–221, Oct. 1985.

2.2. The auditing task under scrutiny

A business enterprise seeks to report its financial performance according to uniform standards called Generally Accepted Accounting Principles (GAAP). A firm which deviates from these official rules finds that its financial statements have lost credibility in the eyes of bankers and stockholders. As a consequence, the ability of the enterprise to raise capital for continued operation or expansion can be seriously hampered. To report its current financial position properly, an enterprise must prepare a Balance Sheet which shows assets and liabilities. One type of asset involves claims against customers, called Accounts Receivable, which arise from credit sales of the firm's product or service. The rules state that the firm must differentiate, however, between those claims against its customer which it can reasonably expect to collect and those which it cannot reasonably expect to collect.

Because of business slowdowns, unemployment, bankruptcy, fraud, or death, some customers will not pay. Such uncollectible accounts (bad debts) cannot be individually identified, *a priori*, with precision. Their aggregate amount, however, must be estimated in order to conform to the accounting rules. The aggregate amount is referred to as the Allowance for Bad Debts (ABD), or the Provision or Reserve for Uncollectible Accounts Receivable. However titled, this is simply an estimate of the dollar value of the accounts which may not be collected.

Certified Public Accountants (CPAs) are hired to examine the enterprise's financial statements in order to enforce the accounting rules. CPA's, or external auditors, are legally liable for their negligence should the Balance Sheet be incorrect. Thus, they are vitally concerned that the Allowance for Bad Debts be estimated correctly. The expert system, *Auditor*, functions as an aid to CPAs in performing judgments as to the adequacy of the ABD.

When the external auditors begin their annual examination of a client's financial statements they are confronted with an ABD which has already been calculated by the client's management team and its in-house accountants. The auditor's responsibility is to give an opinion about the 'fairness' of the statements and their adherence to the official accounting rules, including the 'fairness' of the Allowance for Bad Debts.

Because of the tremendous volume of transactions entered into by an enterprise, for cost and feasibility considerations, the auditors resort to 'test-checking' to accomplish their audit. In the case of the ABD this test-checking consists primarily of a systematic scrutiny of those as-yet-uncollected accounts receivable which are both individually large and delinquent. Delinquent means outstanding and unpaid beyond the credit period normally extended by company policy, usually thirty days but varying with company and industry. The auditor's scrutiny includes sending letters of confirmation to the debtors, examining correspondence between the debtor and the client, making inquiries of the client's manage-ment, and investigating economic conditions. Based on these findings, the auditor then makes a professional judgment as to the likelihood of collection of that particular, individually large account. It is this judgment which is supported by the *Auditor* system, using as inputs the external auditor's reports of his findings.

2.3. Problems unique to the auditing task

Several facets of the task make it unique. For one, the auditor is not creating from whole cloth an Allowance for Bad Debts. Instead, he is seeking to verify the reasonableness of a judgment already performed, with varying degrees of good faith and competence, by his client. This aspect would seem to tolerate inexactitude on the auditor's part, since he is expected to merely corroborate via test-checks the reasonableness of the primary party's action. An additional facet, however, imbues his decision with a degree of gravity. Although the external auditor may be liable for money damages to anyone who relies upon the accuracy of the financial statements, he is hired and paid by the client whose financial statements he is examining.

Theoretically at least, both parties strive for accuracy and clarity in the statements. There are elements of an adversarial standoff, however, between the two parties. In order to enhance his own financial standing, the client normally will prefer that any doubts as to collectibility be resolved in favor of a showing of a larger asset balance, thus a smaller ABD. Individual employees will also be motivated toward optimistic predictions about the collectibility outcome; the sales manager who approved the sale and the credit manager who extended the credit. Although internal controls exist to restrict the range of their actions, both of these individuals, along with other client employees, enjoy opportunities to manipulate the data examined by the auditor.

Thus, the external auditor must not only search for data but also speculate about its credibility. Hence the need to capture uncertainty in their judgments, which is an attribute of many expert systems. Unfortunately, the ADB judgment, albeit of great importance, is only one of dozens of decisions which must be made by the external auditor in the course of rendering an opinion about a set of financial statements. In all cases, the time available to accomplish the judgment is limited.

2.4. Benefits of using expert systems

Quality control within an CPA firm is enhanced through consistency in decision making. The simultaneous conduct by hundreds of auditors in audits of a multitude of clients in locations throughout the world, however, militates against a high degree of consistency despite the firm's dedication of resources to supervision and review. The use of *Auditor* and other microcomputer-based expert systems as decision support tools can underlay a firm's judgment process with a framework of consistent methods which, to a great extent, can be independent of the biases of individual auditors. Additionally, with the aid of these micro-based systems which can carry the knowledge of the firm's experts, the locus of critical judgments can be more safely transferred to less experienced persons operating in the field.

Training in the use of such systems must be provided, which will accomplish two desirable goals as by-products. First, an enhancement of the trainee's personal understanding of the parameters of the critical decision can be expected along with his competence in the use of the system. Second, more consistent, efficient, and less costly audits will be performed by better trained employees.

3. The structure and operation of *Auditor*

3.1. Overview of Auditor and AL/X

Auditor is a rule-based expert system that applies the knowledge domain of a sub-area of auditing to the generic inference engine, AL/X. In the following discussion of the mechanics of *Auditor*, the details of knowledge representation, uncertainty propagation, hypothesis evaluation, and user interaction essentially describe the functions of AL/X as well. For the sake of clarity, however, we will refer to *Auditor* only. Operationally, *Auditor* interacts with the user; asks for items of evidence, evaluates the new evidence with respect to what the system already knows, and then responds with recommendations or by asking for new evidence. *Auditor* is very similar to Prospector and its shell system, KAS [4].

In *Auditor* knowledge is represented by an inference network of rules, hypotheses, and logical combinations of these rules and hypotheses. The strength of the links within the network (or rule base) is represented by user-defined weights. Uncertainty is handled in two ways by *Auditor*. First, each rule and hypothesis has a degree of belief (DB) assigned to it that reflects the likelihood that the evidence is true or false. A DB is a log transformation of probabilities such that a DB of $+30(-30)$ represents a probability of truth (falsity) of .999 (.001) and a DB of 0 represents a .5 probability. Second, the responses of the user are in terms of 'certainty values' (CVs) or scaled responses reflecting the user's belief in the truth or falsity of a query made by the system. A CV of $+5(-5)$ implies that the statement is absolutely true (false) while any intermediate value requires an interpolation. The initial DB values and link weights are parameters of the system that must be elicited from the user.

The software that controls the operation of the system is called the inference engine. In *Auditor* both backward- and forward-chaining techniques are used. To determine what question to ask, the system searches backward from the goal at hand until it finds that question (i.e., item of evidence) that has the greatest potential impact on the goal. Then, upon receiving the user's response, it uses Bayesian revision to update probabilities and propagates them through the network from the goal by forward-chaining.

3.2. The development of Auditor

Auditor was built in three stages: initial modeling, refinement, and validation. Initial modeling encompassed the determination of the goal of the system (i.e., what decision to support), interviews with the auditing experts to elicit rules, and polling of the experts to determine the system's internal parameters. In the refinement stage, the experts operated the model interactively and presented their suggestions for improvement. These improvements included changes in parameter values, additional interactions among rules, and the rewording of questions. Finally, the completed system was exposed to validation exercises to determine the level of its expertise.

Auditor's single goal is expressed as, 'The delinquent portion of this account should specifically be reserved for in the allowance for bad debts to a substantial degree'. (The internal name of this goal, RESERVE, as well as the names of other rules, will be written in capital letters.) The phrase, 'this account', refers to the one individually large account which is under scrutiny by the auditor. 'To a substantial degree' means a significant amount is still considered uncollectible. The wording of this goal was modified several times by the auditors themselves until they agreed on this final interpretation.

The rule base was developed from rules accumulated from eight expert auditors on the staff of an international CPA firm. Each auditor was interviewed and asked to identify which decisions they do not allow novice auditors to make and to describe how they make those decisions. From the voluminous notes taken at these interviews an initial set of fourteen rules was made. This list was sent back to the eight auditors for review. At this point four of the eight dropped out of the project. The four remaining auditors included three audit managers and one staff auditor. Their comments expanded the initial list to twenty-five rules, due mainly to the decomposition of compound rules into individual rules. The complete list can be examined in Dungan [35] and is summarized in Table 1.

The four auditors were then polled by mail as to their evaluation of this new rule list. The experts were asked to rank the rules with respect to a scale of 'strong', 'moderate', 'weak', and 'no effect'. There was a high degree of consensus among the four auditors on each rule. One of the authors, a CPA with auditing experience, translated each set of responses into a set of weights for each rule which reflected the impact of each rule on the goal, RESERVE.

The experts were then allowed to interact with this version of *Auditor* while analyzing previously-prepared sets of audit evidence (called audit work papers) to verify the logic and conclusions of *Auditor*. Because, at that point in time, *Auditor* had to be run on a mainframe, the interactions were made on a hard-copy, portable

Table 1. *List of rule base*

Rule name	Description
COLLECTED	Account is no longer delinquent by audit completion date.
NO RESPONSE	There was no response to the confirmation request nor to a follow-up request.
NONCONTACT	The confirmation request was returned by the Postal Service as undeliverable.
ACTIVE	Customer continues to be an active customer.
CREDIT MANAGER	The credit manager, or other company official, expresses a strong belief in collectibility.
PROBLEMS	Confirmations revealed serious problems.
CORRESPOND	Recent data in correspondence file supports collectibility.
WORKOUT	Recent collections are proceeding satsifactorily.
LEGAL	Legal action would be fruitless.
ALLBUTONE	All portions have been collected except for a single, large, delinquent transaction.
NOTPAY	Debtors have stated their intention to pay little or nothing of the delinquent balances.
GOOD RECORD	Debtor has a good past record of ultimately paying substantially all delinquent balances.
OUTSTANDING	The outstanding delinquent balance continues to increase.
AVG AVE	The average age of the delinquent portion is increasing.
COLLECT AGENCY	This account has been assigned to a collection agency or lawyer.
CREDITSTOP	The client has stopped credit to this debtor.
NOPAYEVER	No payments have ever been received from this customer.
WRITEOFF	Total writeoff of this account, if required, will represent a material adjustment.
BANKRUPT	The debtor is in bankruptcy-type proceedings.
LAWYER	legal counsel gives poor prospects of any significant recovery from this debtor.
ECONOMICS	Economic factors are hampering this customer's ability to pay.
RIGOROUS	The collection effort being applied by your client is inadequate.
FORMER EMPLOY	This delinquent account is from a former employee.
NEW PAID	Despite the presence of this delinquent item, newer items have been fully paid.
ISSUENOTE	This debtor has issued notes for the unpaid portions of this account.

terminal using a dial-up facility on a CYBER 175. This made testing very laborious because it was run in 'full trace' mode which allowed the auditors to observe the sequential and marginal effects of their responses on the goal, RESERVE.

After this round of evaluation, the four auditors added interactions in the form of logical *and* rules to the network. There were many new interactions specified, so many in fact, that the efficiency of the system was threatened. This growing list of rules was pared down by the authors based on their experience and on the implied low impact of certain *and* rules. How these *and* rules affected the goal of RESERVE was also specified. This new version of the system was then again tested by the auditors operating in a 'full trace' mode. Further modifications to the internal parameters resulted from this last examination.

3.3. How Auditor *works*

The inference network for *Auditor* is shown in Figure 1. Each arrow represents a logical link between rules. Each of the twenty-five primary rules (e.g., COLLECTED and ACTIVE) have direct links to RESERVE but for the sake of clarity they are not shown in the figure. There are thirteen *and* rules in the inference network, each with its own impact on RESERVE. Thus, a primary rule that is an element in an *and* rule has at least two impacts on RESERVE; one by itself

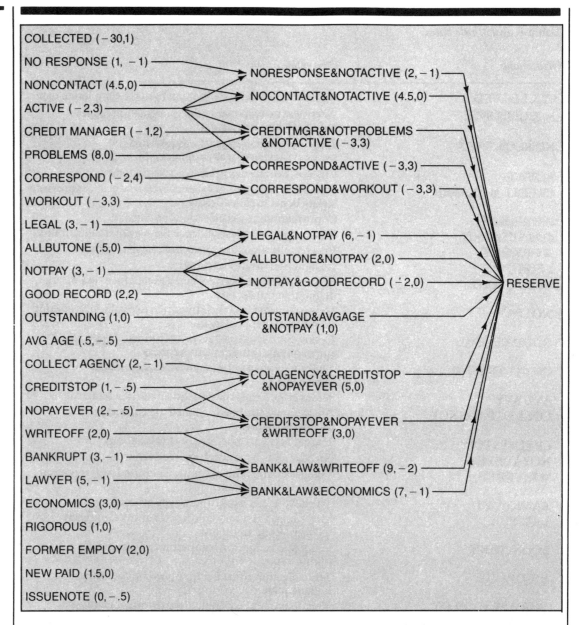

Figure 1. *Inference Network for Auditor*

and one from the *and* rule. For example, the primary rule NOTPAY (which means that the customer has stated his intention not to pay the delinquent amount) has five impacts on RESERVE; one by itself and four from associated *and* rules. The actual impact on the DB of the *and* rules is governed by the mechanics of Fuzzy logic [36].

The numbers in the parentheses are the user-specified weights associated with the links between rules and the main goal, RESERVE. They indicate how the DB value of RESERVE is to be updated based on a user response to that rule. The first number (called a positive weight or PW) indicates how the DB value of RESERVE is to be updated if the user responds with a positive 5 (absolutely true). The second number (called a negative weight or NW) indicates what the impact is if the user responds with a negative 5 (absolutely false). Any response in between, except 0, results in a piece-wise linear interpolation between PW and 0 (if the response is positive) or between NW and 0 (if the response is 0). A response of zero does nothing to the DB or RESERVE. For example, a +5 response to COLLECTED changes RESERVE from DB = 0 to DB = −30, which implies a probability of collection of .001. A −5 response, however, only changes DB of RESERVE to +1 (probability of .56). Note that very few of the PWs and NWs represent symmetrical situations. This is very common in auditing where the presence of negative evidence is much more damning than the absence of positive evidence.

In order to discuss how *Auditor* works from the user's point of view, an annotated trace of an actual interaction is shown in Figure 2. The impacts on the DBs of RESERVE and related

The current goal is whether or not the delinquent portion of this account should specifically be reserved for in the allowance for bad debts to substantial degree. RESERVE.

[*Auditor* is announcing its goal hypothesis. It has an initial DB = 0.0, i.e., probability of reserve = .5]

How certain are you that your tests of cash receipts indicate that the delinquent portions of the account in question have been collected substantially in their entirety subsequent to the date of the balance sheet?
? −5

[*Auditor* prompts the user for a response with a "?". The user's response of −5 implies that the user is certain that the account is still uncollected. The implied rule is:

IF account has been collected (i.e., CV>0)
    THEN DB(RESERVE) = DB(RESERVE) + fn(PW,CV)
ELSE IF account has not been collected (i.e., CV<O)
        THEN DB(RESERVE) = DB(RESERVE) + fn(NW,CV)
    ELSE DB(RESERVE) = DB(RESERVE)

In this case the positive weight (PW) of the rule COLLECTED is −30 and the negative weight (NW) is +1. Thus, the impact of this response is to change the DB(RESERVE) from 0 to 1 (probability of reserve = .56).]

How certain are you that the confirmation request was returned by the postal service as undeliverable and the client for several months has been unable to communicate with the debtor?
? 2

[The user has not firmly established this fact yet but has some indication that it is true, and thus responds with a + 2. From the semantic net in Figure 1 we see that NOCONTACT also impacts an AND rule. The implied rule is:
IF no contact with debtor (CV>0)
    THEN DB(RESERVE) = DB(RESERVE) + fn(4.5,CV)
        DB(NOCONTACT&ACTIV) =
            fuzzy(DB(NOCONTACT&ACTIV), CV)
ELSE IF contact with debtor (CV<O)
        THEN DB(RESERVE) = DB(RESERVE) + fn(0,CV)
            DB(NOCONTACT&ACTIV) =
                fuzzy(DB(NOCONTACT&ACTIV), CV)
    ELSE DB(RESERVE) = DB(RESERVE)
        DB(NOCONTACT&ACTIV) = DB(NOCONTACT&ACTIV)

In this case, fn(4.5,2) = 3.7 and DB(RESERVE) goes to 4.7
(probability of reserve = .70) and DB(NOCONTACT) = 3.7. Note that fn(0,2) = 0.]
and fuzzy (2) for the AND rule is 0.0.

How certain are you that recent correspondence and other data in the customer's credit file supports belief in the collectibility of this account?
? −1

[The user's initial review of this data has found some problems that may need to be investigated but still gives the user the perception of non-support so a response of − 1 is given. The semantic net in Figure 1 shows that two other AND rules are effected by a response to CORRES in a non-zero manner. Table 1 shows how the DBs for the AND rules are effected. Thus, RESERVE is updated by three rules, CORRES and the two AND rules and jumps to DB = 10 (probability of reserve = .95). Thus, by asking only three questions so far *Auditor* is already suggesting that the account should be reserved for with a high probability.]

How certain are you that although a portion of this customer's total balance is still delinquent, he continues to be an active customer?
? −1

[This customer is consistent with the CORRES response. The user has evidence indicating the possibility that the customer may not be active anymore. This question is key to the ABD decision as evidenced by its impact on the semantic net. It affects five other rules, its complement NOTACTIVE and four AND rules. In the audit situation as long as the customer remains active there may be still a chance to recover, so the major impact on ACTIVE is justified. The cumulative effect of the − 1 response is to increase DB(RESERVE) to 15.2 (probability of reserve = .97)]

How certain are you that recent collections toward the delinquent portions of this account are proceeding satisfactorily?
? −3

[This is a much stronger test of the relationship between the client and the debtor in that money is changing hands, not just correpsondence. Thus, in this case, the user can say with more certainty (i.e., − 3) that collections are not proceeding satisfactorily. Again, another AND rule is effected and in this case, its DB changes from − 1.8 to −6 (see Table 1). DB(RESERVE) is now at 19.5 which is approximately 99% certain to reserve and the user ended the session with *Auditor*.]

Figure 2. *Annotated interaction with Auditor [Annotations are in "[]" and user responses underlined]*

Table 2. *Propagation of uncertainty through inference network for actual interaction*

Rule asked	COLLECTED	NONCONTACT	CORRESPOND	ACTIVE	WORKOUT
User Response: (in CVs)	−5	+2	−1	−1	−3
Impact on:* (in DB's)					
RESERVE	1	4.7	10	15.2	19.5
COLLECTED	−100	−100	−100	−100	−100
NONCONTACT	0	3.7	3.7	3.7	3.7
CORRESPOND	0	0	−1.8	−1.8	−1.8
ACTIVE	0	0	0	−1.8	−1.8
NOTACTIVE	0	0	0	+1.8	1.8
WORKOUT	0	0	0	0	−6
CORRES&ACTIVE	0	0	−1.8	−1.8	−1.8
CORRES&WORKOUT	0	0	−1.8	−1.8	−1.8
NONCONT&ACTIVE	0	0	0	1.8	1.8
CR&NPB&ACTIVE**	0	0	0	−1.8	−1.8

* All rules had an initial DB value of 0
** ANDing of rule CREDITMANAGER(CR), NOPROBLEMS(NPB) and ACTIVE

rules are shown in Table 2. Several points demonstrated in the trace in Figure 2 deserve comment. First, the questions posed by *Auditor* to the user are in English. Second, the implied IF-THEN rules allow for uncertainty in two ways: the CV and the interpolating function that uses the CV and either PW or NW. Notice also the final ELSE clauses which handle the CV=0 case, i.e., no DB values are changed. Third, the user responses to the CORRES, ACTIVE, and WORKOUT questions are all consistent. Furthermore, although none are absolutely false (−5), the cumulative effect of this type of evidence is to push the probability of RESERVE from .75 to .97.

The propagation of DB values shown in Table 2 also deserves comment. Degrees of Belief have an absolute range of +100 to −100. Besides RESERVE, each rule, primary or *and*, also has a DB associated with it. When that rule is asked, or its component rules in the case of an *and* rule, the CV will affect the DB for that rule as well as the DB for RESERVE. For example, the first question asked, COLLECTED, received a response of −5 (absolutely false) and, as Table 2 shows, its DB went to −100, 'absolutely

false'. Another point shown in Table 2 is the ripple effect of DB through *and* rules. When CORRESPOND is answered it also sets off changes in CORRES&ACTIVE and CORRES&WORKOUT.

3.4. *Validation of* Auditor

Auditor was validated with two different procedures: 'open-book' and 'blind'. In both procedures, another external auditor, not involved in the development of *Auditor*, served as validator. His task was to compare the judgment of *Auditor* to that of the actual auditors on the job. In the 'open-book' procedure an auditor from a different office of the same CPA firm served as validator. Because the data used by the validator contained the actual judgments made by the auditors on the job, this procedure is called 'open-book'. The 'blind' validation exercise is based on a test proposed by Turing [37]. In this case, the validator was an auditor from a different CPA firm, who, during the validation, did not know the source of the ABD judgment (i.e., whether it was from *Auditor* or a human auditor). Table 3 summarizes the results of both validation procedures.

Table 3. *Summary of validation exercises*

	Acceptable Auditor judgments	Unacceptable Auditor judgments	Number of cases
"Open Book"	9(90%)	1(10%)	10
"Blind"	10(91%)	1(9%)	11
Total for all Cases	19(90%)	2(10%)	21

```
INVESTIGATING WRITEOFF
INVESTIGATING LAWYER
BEST EVIDENCE FOR BANK&WR&LAW : POS = BANKRUPT    NEG = BANKRUPT
INVESTIGATING ECONOMIC
INVESTIGATING BAN&ECO&LAW
INVESTIGATING BANKRUPT
INVESTIGATING ECONOMIC
INVESTIGATING LAWYER
BEST EVIDENCE FOR BAN&ECO&LAW : POS = BANKRUPT    NEG = BANKRUPT
INVESTIGATING GOODRECORD
INVESTIGATING LEGAL
INVESTIGATING LEGAL&NPAY
INVESTIGATING LEGAL
INVESTIGATING NOTPAY
BEST EVIDENCE FOR LEGAL&NPAY : POS = LEGAL    NEG = LEGAL
INVESTIGATING NPAY&GDREC
INVESTIGATING NOTPAY
INVESTIGATING GOODRECORD
BEST EVIDENCE FOR NPAY&GDREC : POS = NOTPAY    NEG = NOTPAY
BEST EVIDENCE FOR RESERVE : POS = PROBLEMS    NEG = COLLECTED


HOW CERTAIN ARE YOU THAT YOUR TESTS OF CASH RECEIPTS INDICATE
THAT THE DELINQUENT PORTIONS OF THE ACCOUNT IN QUESTION HAVE
BEEN COLLECTED SUBSTANTIALLY IN THEIR ENTIRETY SUBSEQUENT TO
THE DATE OF THE BALANCE SHEET?
```

Figure 3. *Portion of a DEBUG trace*

4. Conclusions

4.1. Insights into auditing from Auditor

In the process of developing *Auditor* several insights into audit decision making were revealed. First, the importance of items of evidence in practice was corroborated through an analysis of the experts' responses in the actual case situations used in the validation procedures. Second, this analysis also suggested that, to some extent, there was an inverse relationship between diagnosticity and availability. Evidence that is commonly gathered in an audit, although inexpensive to obtain, alone provides little aid in making the final decision while high diagnostic evidence is infrequently applied. Third, analysis of the inference network and the expert responses indicated that the auditors in this project formed an efficient sub-hypothesis to distinguish between 'slow-pay' and 'no-pay' debtors. Because a 'slow-pay' does not usually require a reserve, it is more efficient to initially narrow the scope of investigation to the 'no-pays' as soon as possible.

4.2. Evaluation of AL/X as a development tool

There are several built-in features of AL/X that make it a good development environment as well as a supportive, operational environment. AL/X offers several types of traces: debug, full, and partial. The debug trace is unique in that it allows one to follow the logic of AL/X in choosing the next question to ask (see Figure 3). This is very useful in the development stage of an expert system as it allows the knowledge engineer to determine how well the system is matching the reasoning of the domain expert. The other trace options provide information on the updated values of the DBs of the main goals and hypotheses of the inference network as a result of user responses. This is also important during development as it allows the domain expert to verify the values of the internal parameters by observing the impact of individual items of evidence on goals.

Another positive feature of AL/X is that it allows the user to volunteer information at anytime. Without such an ability the user must wait for the inference engine to select the corresponding question before the user can input the information. In development volunteering evidence is very important to perform localized testing of individual rules efficiently. Otherwise, the tester may have to respond to ten to fifteen meaningless questions to get to the one question that he wants to answer, wasting time and allowing for errors.

In operations, the option of volunteering information has several benefits. First, it provides a more realistic operating environment. In a non-expert-system decision environment, the decision maker does not have to wait to apply known information but can use it immediately. The same situation should apply with an expert system to promote acceptance by the user and gains in efficiency. Second, the diagnostic process of the expert system can be made faster. Because AL/X uses known information to determine what questions to ask next and what conclusions to draw, the more information AL/X has sooner, the better. In some cases, volunteering only a few key items of evidence may allow AL/X to reach a conclusion without asking further questions. And third, if the user discovers that he has made an error in a response, he can rectify it by volunteering the proper response.

One finds that with any expert system, modifications must be made all the time because decision makers change, decision situations change, and evidence changes. Thus, an ability to modify internal parameters and the network structure easily is very important. Because the network structure in AL/X can be coded as a simple text file from any line editor or word-processor, physical changes to the permanent structure can be made easily. But AL/X also provides a mechanism to modify values during a consultation. This can be used in development to perform sensitivity analysis of internal parameter values or the structure of the network.

One key characteristic of an expert system that differentiates it from a decision support system is its ability to explain its reasoning and logic [38]. AL/X offers explanation options by allowing the user to ask 'why' a question is being asked and 'how' a goal will be proven. Figure 4 shows the response of AL/X to a W(hy) query by the user concerning the WORKOUT rule. It states that WORKOUT is being asked to help determine the goal RESERVE and the *and* rule of "CORRESPOND & WORKOUT." Figure 5 shows the response of AL/X to a H(ow) query by the user concerning the *and* rule of "CORRESPOND & WORKOUT." It states that that *and* rule will be evaluated by asking about WORKOUT and CORRESPOND.

. . . THAT RECENT COLLECTIONS TOWARD THE DELINQUENT PORTIONS OF THIS ACCOUNT ARE PROCEEDING SATISFACTORILY?

? W

TYPE A SPACE NAME, <CR> TO INDICATE WORKOUT, OR ? TO LIST SPACE NAMES

<CR>

THIS QUESTION IS ASKED TO FIND OUT WHETHER OR NOT

1) THE DELINQUENT PORTION OF THIS ACCOUNT SHOULD SPECIFICALLY BE RESERVED FOR IN THE ALLOWANCE FOR BAD DEBTS TO A SUBSTANTIAL DEGREE (RESERVE)

WHICH HAS CURRENT DEGREE 11.0 (PW = −3.0   NW = 3.0)

2) CORRESPOND AND WORKOUT (CORRES&WORK)

WHICH HAS CURRENT DEGREE −6.0

Figure 4. *AL/X response to a W(hy) query*

AL/X is not without its problems, however. A main drawback is that it requires a knowledge engineer to construct the inference network. The actual physical inputting of the network can be done by anybody. But the translation of the user's problem domain into a structure of rules, weights, and degrees of belief requires an intimate knowledge of how AL/X operates. This is especially telling in the current software environment which promotes user-friendly, non-technical interfaces to expert systems (e.g., TI's Personal Consultant).

This technically-oriented interface takes some of the luster off some of the benefits discussed above. To volunteer information one must know the internal name of the associated rule. Although AL/X allows one to list these names, it can still be difficult to select the appropriate one if the rule names are abbreviated or non-associative. The explanation options can be difficult to understand. As Figures 4 and 5 show, the response can be somewhat cryptic unless one knows how knowledge and network information is stored in AL/X.

Finally, one of the intelligent advantages of AL/X can actually be an operational disadvantage. AL/X chooses the next question to be asked based on the greatest potential impact on the goal at hand. This ordering does not take into consideration, however, the cost to the user of obtaining the evidence required to answer the question. Thus, the user may incur a greater cost than needed to use the system or be forced to wade through many questions for which he has no evidence, in order to get to the ones he can answer. In either case, such an ordering of the

Figure 5. *AL/X response to a H(ow) query*

questions may not match the reality of the user's environment, making acceptance and use less likely.

4.3. Evaluation of the computing environment

One final benefit of the AL/X environment, not mentioned in the previous section, is that it can be run on a microcomputer. This project is in a unique position in that both a mainframe and microcomputer environment have been used. The original development of *Auditor* was made on a mainframe, a CYBER 175. On-site (i.e., at the auditors) interactions with *Auditor* had to be handled over long-distance telephone lines with a hard-copy terminal. Busy signals and thirty cps printers made testing very tedious and awkward. The experts sensed immediately that such an environment was inappropriate for commercial use of any expert system.

Currently, however, AL/X, and thus *Auditor*, can operate on a personal microcomputer. Continued validation and sensitivity analysis can now be made very rapidly. Demonstrations of *Auditor* can and are made anywhere that an IBM PC resides. This has convinced other auditors, who have recently tested *Auditor*, that expert systems provide feasible opportunities for auditing.

4.4. The future of Auditor

There are several directions that *Auditor* is now taking. Continued testing of *Auditor* by experienced auditors with actual case situations will result in the refinement of the existing set of rules and inference network. This effort will also aid in the calibration of the use of *Auditor.* Many of the case situations used to develop and validate *Auditor* were all or nothing cases; that is, the decision was to reserve all of the delinquent account balance or none of it. More cases are needed in the middle ground where the delinquent amount is partially reserved for. Practicing auditors have stated that this secondary ABD decision has little consistency across auditors.

Another operational goal of *Auditor* is to develop training applications for novice auditors. The use of an expert system as a simulation environment is one of the by-products of development. Plans are being made to establish an experimental training program with an international CPA firm using *Auditor* as the training vehicle.

Acknowledgements

The authors would like to thank Peat, Marwick, Mitchell and Company for their support of this research through their Research Opportunities in Auditing Program. We would also like to thank Professor Donald Michie for his encouragement and advice.

References

[1] 'Symposium on Decision Support Systems for Auditing,' University of Southern California, February, 1984.

[2] Peat, Marwick, Mitchell & Co., *Research Opportunities in Auditing Program Report*, 1983.

[3] A. Paterson, *AL/X User Manual*, Intelligent Terminals Ltd., 15 Canal Street, Oxford, 1981.

[4] J. Gaschnig, 'Development of Uranium Exploration Models for the PROSPECTOR Consultant System,' Final Report SRI Project 7856, Artificial Intelligence Center, SRI International, Menlo Park, CA, 1980.

[5] D.A. Waterman and F. Hayes-Roth, 'An Investigation of Tools for Building Expert Systems,' in *Building Expert Systems*, Hayes-Roth, Waterman and Lenat (eds.), Addison-Wesley, 1983.

[6] A.D. Akresh and W.A. Wallace, 'The Application of Regression Analysis for Limited Review and Audit Planning,' *Symposium on Auditing Research IV*, University of Illinois at Urbana, 1983, pp. 67–128.

[7] W.S. Albrecht and J.C. McKeown, 'Towards an Extended Use of Statistical Analytical Reviews in the Audit,' *Symposium on Auditing Research II*, University of Illinois at Urbana, 1977, pp. 53–69.

[8] W.R. Kinney Jr., 'ARIMA and Regression in Analytical Review: An Empirical Test,' *The Accounting Review*, January 1978, pp. 48–60.

[9] W.R. Kinney Jr., 'Integrating Audit Tests: Regression Analysis and Partitioned Dollar-Unit Sampling,' *Journal of Accounting Research*, Autumn 1979, pp. 456–475.

[10] K.W. Stringer, 'A Statistical Technique for Analytical Review,' Supplement to the *Journal of Accounting Research*, Autumn 1979, pp. 465–475.

[11] W.A. Wallace, 'Discussant's Response to 'The Effect of Measurement Error on Regression Results in Analytical Review',' *Symposium on Auditing Research III*, University of Illinois at Urbana, 1979, pp. 70–81.

[12] E. Deakin and M. Granof, 'Regression Analysis as a Means of Determining Audit Sample Size,' *The Accounting Review*, October 1974, pp. 764–771.

[13] D. Roberts, M. Shedd, and M. MacGuidwin, 'The Behavior of Selected Upper Bounds of Monetary Errors Using PPS Sampling,' *Symposium on Auditing Research IV*, University of Illinois at Urbana, 1982.

[14] D.A. Leslie, A.D. Teitlebaum and R.J. Anderson, *Dollar-Unit Sampling: A Practical Guide for Auditors*, Copp Clark Pitman and Commerce Clearing House, 1979.

[15] D.C. Burns and J.K. Loebbecke, 'Internal Control Evaluation: How the Computer Can Help,' *Journal of Accountancy*, August 1975, pp. 60–70.

[16] R. Duda, J. Gaschnig, and P. Hart, 'Model Design in the PROSPECTOR Consultant System for Mineral Exploration,' in *Expert Systems in the Micro-electronic Age*, D. Michie, Ed., Edinburgh University Press, 1979, pp. 153–167.

[17] J. McDermott, 'R1: A Rule-based Configurer of Computer Systems,' Technical Report CMU-CS-80-119, Department of Computer Science, Carnegie-Mellon University, 1980.

[18] B.G. Buchanan and E.A. Feigenbaum, 'DENDRAL and Meta-DENDRAL: Their Applications Dimension,' *Artificial Intelligence*, **11**, 1978, pp. 5–24.

[19] E.A. Feigenbaum, B.G. Buchanan and J. Lederberg, 'On Generality and Problem Solving: A Case Study Using the DENDRAL Program,' *Machine Intelligence*, D. Michie and B. Meltzer, Eds., **6**, 1971, pp. 165–190.

[20] W.J. Clancey, 'Tutoring Rules for Guiding a Case Method Dialogue,' *International Journal of Man-Machine Studies*, **11**, 1979, pp. 25–49.

[21] W.J. Clancey, E.H. Shortliffe, and B.G. Buchanan, 'Intelligent Computer-aided Instruction for Medical Diagnosis,' in *Proceedings of the Third Annual Symposium on Computer Applications in Medical Care*, 1979, pp. 175–183.

[22] L.M. Fagan, J.C. Kunz, E.A. Feigenbaum, and J. Osborn, 'Representation of Dynamic Clinical Knowledge: Measurement Interpretation in the Intensive Care Unit,' *Proceedings of the International Joint Conference on Artificial Intelligence*, 1979, pp. 260–262.

[23] C.A. Kulikowski, 'Artificial Intelligence Methods and Systems for Medical Consultation,' *IEEE Transactions on Pattern Analysis and Machine Intelligence*, 1980, pp. 464–476.

[24] S.G. Pauker, G.A. Gorry, J.P. Kassirer and W.B. Schwartz, 'Towards the Simulation of Clinical Cognition — Taking a Present Illness by Computer,' *American Journal of Medicine*, **60**, 1976, pp. 981–996.

[25] H.E. Pople Jr., 'The Formulation of Composite Hypotheses in Diagnostic Problem Solving: An Exercise in Synthetic Reasoning,' *Proceedings of the Fifth Joint International Conference on Artificial Intelligence*, 1977, pp. 119–185.

[26] H.E. Pople Jr., J.D. Myers and R.A. Miller, 'DIALOG: A Model of Diagnostic Logic for Internal Medicine,' *Proceedings of the Fourth Joint International Conference on Artificial Intelligence*, 1975, pp. 848–855.

[27] E.H. Shortliffe, *Computer-based Medical Consultation: MYCIN*, American-Elsevier, New York, 1975.

[28] S.M. Weiss and C.A. Kulikowski, 'EXPERT: A System for Developing Consultation Models,' *Proceedings of the Sixth International Conference on Artificial Intelligence*, 1979, pp. 942–7.

[29] S.M. Weiss, C.A. Kulikowski and A. Safir, 'Glaucoma Consultation by Computer,' *Computers in Biology and Medicine*, 8, 1978, pp. 25–40.

[30] J.V. Hansen and W.F. Messier Jr., 'Continued Development of a Knowledge-based Expert System for Auditing Advanced Computer Systems,' Preliminary Report submitted to Peat, Marwick, Mitchell Foundation, 1984.

[31] H.M. Braun and J.S. Chandler, 'Development of an Expert System to Assist Auditors in the Investigation of Analytic Review Fluctuations,' Research project for Peat, Marwick, Mitchell Foundation, 1983.

[32] A. Paterson and T. Niblett, *ACLS User Manual*, Department of Computer Science, Class Note.8 CS347/397D, University of Illinois at Urbana, Fall 1982.

[33] W. Wright and J. Willingham, 'Development of a Knowledge-based System for Auditing the Collectibility of a Commercial Loan,' Research Proposal, 1985.

[34] R. Michaelsen, 'An Expert System for Federal Tax Planning,' *Expert Systems*, 1, 2, 1984, pp. 149–167.

[35] C.W. Dungan, 'A Model of an Audit Judgment in the Form of an Expert System,' Ph.D. Dissertation, Department of Accountancy, University of Illinois at Urbana, 1983.

[36] L. Zadeh, 'A Theory of Approximate Reasoning,' *Machine Intelligence*, 9, J.E. Hayes, D. Michie and L. Mikulich, Eds., Wiley & Sons, 1979.

[37] A.M. Turing, 'Computing Machinery and Intelligence,' *Mind*, October, 1950.

[38] F. Hayes-Roth, D.A. Waterman and D.B. Lenat, Eds., *Building Expert Systems*, Addison-Wesley, 1983.

Interactive critical path analysis (ICPA)—microcomputer implementation of a project management and knowledge engineering tool

T. J. Barber, G. Marshall and J. T. Boardman

*Department of Electrical and Electronic Engineering,
Brighton Polytechnic, Moulsecoomb, Brighton, BN2 4GJ, UK*

The paper describes the implementation on a microcomputer of a personal level project management tool, which facilitates simple project network construction and analysis. The interactive critical path analysis system (ICPA), allows project networks to be drawn on the screen of a monitor via a joystick in a natural manner. ICPA therefore provides a powerful and easy to use planning tool for site engineers and the managers of small businesses.

The authors are engaged in a programme of AI research leading to the definition of expert systems tools for the use of project managers. Accordingly they have sought to use ICPA as a knowledge engineering tool in conjunction with the elicitations and representation of knowledge educed from expert project managers. The paper describes the ease with which ICPA lends itself to the definition of an intelligent knowledge-based system applied to the project management domain.

1. Introduction

For the past twelve months or so, the authors have been engaged in a research programme investigating the application of artificial intelligent computer systems to the project management domain. This research is concerned with the processes of project planning and control as exercised by project managers. Its aim overall is to produce tools to assist in the construction of a knowledgeable system that will make planning and control more efficient.

A specific objective of the research was to establish and implement a simple to use, highly graphical experimentation tool on which project networks could be constructed, analysed and interactively modified and updated. This requirement was confirmed by expert project managers with an interest in the research. Accordingly a system known as ICPA (interactive critical path analysis) has been developed based upon thorough consultation with engineering project management consultants.

1.1 *A history of project planning by network*

A well-established tool of project management is the representation of task dependencies in a project as a network of nodes and links. There are a number of different techniques for the construction of the network, e.g. Precedence networks and activity/event networks. In all cases, durations are assigned to tasks and the project network is analysed to estimate the completion time of the project and to indicate which paths are most time-critical.

The first project network analysis methods were called critical path method (CPM) and project evaluation and review technique (PERT), developed separately in the late 1950s. Since then numerous improved versions have been released and at present there are in excess of one hundred different systems (Woodgate, 1977). Together with a host of other tools (Gantt charts, S curves, Scheduling, etc.) CPM, PERT and their brethren form the basis of a more secure project management framework.

Although network techniques remain a huge success in industry, many companies developing small to medium-sized projects have consistently shunned the many computer-based network implementations because of the difficulties associated with their use, and their expense.

1.2 *Towards interactive systems*

The early CPM systems ran, of necessity, on mainframe computers, thereby forcing CPM analyses into a batch-type operation. Often a CPM plan would take more than seven days to input correctly; by the time the analysis arrived the project status had changed and the recommendations were no longer valid. Project network analysis is more suited to a real-time environment, in which the flow of the project status can be continually monitored and controlled.

Hardware and software capabilities have steadily increased in the intervening period, and there is now a wide range of systems available on mainframes, minicomputers and microcomputers. Each of these, and their associated software, suits a particular sector of the market; each has different capabilities and quite different price ranges.

1.3 *Towards site-sized systems*

In many organizations, project networks may consist of thousands of activities, but often these networks will be an abstract view of a project consisting of many more tasks. With this abstracted view, project managers can control the overall project with, hopefully, a comprehensible project plan. However, for the site or functional manager whose responsibility it is to manage sections of the plan at a detailed work level, there has been a dearth of tools to assist planning and control. It would be infeasible for this level of management to use the sophisticated tools of upper management for many reasons. First the machines are not easily accessible since they quite often need to be centrally located and supported. Secondly there is the time overhead to be considered, and moreover there is the inevitable penalty of delays in information transfer. As such the site manager will rely largely on his experience to manage often quite complex work loads. There remains, therefore, a definite requirement for smaller, site-sized management tools that are easy to use, compact, inexpensive and portable.

2. System definition

The idea of a small but powerful tool for the site engineer (or the manager of a small business) developed out of discussions with project managers. They were all too aware of the paucity of tools available. It is ironic that the man at the sharp end, who really needs the decision support, is left with little in the way of computer assistance to support his experience.

Recently there have been project management applications packages released on business micro machines, but the cost of the hardware and software can be prohibitive, and in most cases the use of interactive graphics as a natural method of interaction is absent.

From discussions, a set of features were drawn up which would specify the nature of the package and its capabilities. The general features describing the nature of the package are shown in Table 1 and the more specific requirements in Table 2. From these features ICPA was created. The package runs on the BBC microcomputer with a second processor, is disc based and requires a colour monitor for the graphics displays and a dot-matrix printer for screen dumps. The technical specification is shown in Table 3.

Table 1. *General features describing the nature of the package*

1. A small system which is portable in the sense that it can be transported and then set up in a few minutes

2. The use of high resolution colour graphics to portray the network

3. A simple and natural interaction using a joystick to move a graphics cursor over the screen

4. Graphical presentation of results, critical path to be highlighted on the screen plus the automatic generation of bar charts

5. A system which would be easy to learn how to use, and with on-line help facilities if required

Table 2. *Specific features describing capabilities*

1. Multiple start and end events

2. All attributes of activities to be optional except for durations

3. Scheduled times on start and end events, defaulting to be zero float convention if omitted

4. Scheduled times on any intermediate events to facilitate milestones, or special targets, etc.

5. An actual finish attribute to monitor project progress

6. The results to be listed in a user-selectable manner (e.g.: all activities in order of increasing total float, then on ties with earliest start, etc.)

3. Implementation

This section describes the implementation of the ICPA system. The major requirements specified by the project managers were in terms of ease of use. This was reflected in the amount of design effort required to perfect the user-interface. The greatest emphasis was placed on creating a vivid graphical network in order to maximize the information displayed, and on making the system robust for the novice-user.

3.1 *Microcomputer strategy*

The choice of machine was the BBC microcomputer. It has good colour graphics capabilities and a second processor option, which provides both speed and memory enhancement relatively inexpensively.

Table 3. *ICPA specification*

Network size:
 100 nodes—represent events
 150 links—represent activities

Node attributes:
 Symbol
 Scheduled time
 Earliest event
 Latest event
 Slack event

Link attributes:
 Activity name
 Activity code
 Duration
 Actual finish
 Earliest start
 Latest start
 Earliest finish
 Latest finish
 Total float
 Free float

The microcomputer has limited resources and capabilities, which will ultimately constrain the size of the network that can be processed. The three fundamental constraints are:

(1) memory usage;
(2) acceptable calculation time;
(3) graphics capabilities.

The simultaneity of these constraints limits the network size to about 100 nodes and 150 links.

3.1.1 *Memory usage.* The network is a directed graph of nodes and links, representing events and activities, respectively. The nodes and links each have a set of attributes to facilitate this representation. Both the network connectivity and the attributes require storage within the system, for which there are only two alternatives, memory (RAM) or disc. The former offers considerable increase in access time, the latter offers more storage space. To compromise, only those variables directly required for calculations reside in memory; thereby obviating further restrictions on the calculation speed.

Program storage has to compete with variables storage, the major part of which is a function of the maximum number of nodes and links. Table 4 details the utilization of memory.

3.1.2 *Calculation time.* As the network size increases, so the calculation time increases exponentially. A network of 100 nodes and 150 links has a calculation time of

Table 4. *Memory usage (Z80 2nd processor)*

	kbyte
Total available user memory	41
Program size	25
1 node storage:	
29 bytes in memory (0 bytes on disc)	
× 100 nodes	2·9
1 link storage:	
36 bytes in memory (27 bytes on disc)	
+ 150 links	5·4
Adjacency matrix	2
Remainder of variables	
+ stack	5·7

approximately 110 s, but if the network were any larger the system would soon be considered unresponsive.

3.1.3 *Graphics capabilities.* The BBC microcomputer has a graphics mode which permits a four-colour display of 320 × 256 pixels. However, due to the use of text windows in this package, the graphics area is reduced to 320 × 224 pixels. This presents a limitation to the amount of graphics information that can be displayed on the screen. To provide reasonable viewing of a network with 100 nodes and 150 links, it is necessary to use a quasi-graphics area four times larger, and display only one of the four quadrants of that area at any time.

3.2 *Network rules*

A valid CPA network must obey certain basic rules. However, the extensive error-handling facilities built into ICPA detect any such violations and report them to the user (Harrison, 1981). To enhance the process further, offending links or nodes are highlighted in red. The rules are:

(i) There must be at least one, but no more than eight starting events (nodes), i.e. an event with no predecessor activities.
(ii) There must be at least one, but no more than eight terminal (end) events, i.e. an event with no successor activities.
(iii) There must not be any loops within the network.
(iv) Every link in the network must have a value of duration assigned to it (there is no default value).

3.3 *Network conventions*

In the network, the 'scheduled time' and the 'actual finish time' attributes are optional. The following conventions govern their use:

(i) For each start node: If there has not been a scheduled time given, then the 'earliest event time' will default to zero.
(ii) For each terminal node: If there has not been a scheduled time given, then the

306

'latest event time' will default to the value of the 'earliest event time' for that node (the zero float convention).

(iii) For each intermediate node: If a 'scheduled time' is given, then the 'latest event time' for that node will be the minimum of the 'scheduled time' given, or the calculated 'latest event time' (as found by the reverse pass calculation through the network). Thus, the 'latest event time' is given by the harder target to achieve.

(iv) For any activity: If an 'actual finish time' is given then it is used in the 'earliest event time' calculations, thereby enabling the network to be updated.

3.4 *Network display*

To display the project network, events (nodes) are drawn as circles with a two-digit symbol inside, activities are drawn as directed lines (links) between nodes, with an arrow at their head to indicate the logic of the network.

The graphics cursor (driven by the joystick) moves over the network diagram allowing the user to simply identify the events and activities by pointing to them. To view and edit the activity attributes, the activity is identified, the appropriate single key-stroke command invoked whereupon a window is displayed next to the activity showing all the attributes ready for editing. When that is complete the window disappears leaving the network intact as before. Other examples of commands used with the cursor are to add new events and activities to the network and move events and activities to tidy the networks appearance.

The design philosophy adopted incorporates separate screen areas (windows) for differing information types: a large graphics area and windows for prompts, messages and warnings. Thus, the user will direct his attention to the appropriate window as required.

The prompt-window displays a menu of currently available commands; these change according to the particular situation. One such command invokes the 'Help' facility which will display a text file explaining the use of all the currently available commands. This should obviate the need to refer to the manual. The message window displays the system status and any other pertinent information of value. The warning-window highlights, in red text, alarms or errors generated as a result of misuse by the user.

For larger projects, the network may be created using four screens, of which only one can be displayed at any instant. However, the diagrams are contiguous and switching between screens is a simple operation. There is also a small window indicating which quadrant is currently being viewed.

Figures 1–7 show typical screen displays demonstrating full network manipulation and attribute examination, network based on Lockyer (1964).

3.5 *Network calculations*

The network nodes and links form a directed graph: one type of well-established data structure for representing such graphs is the adjacency matrix. Essentially, it is a two-dimensional ($n \times n$), binary matrix which defines the nodal connectivity in the graph.

On commencing the calculations, the adjacency matrix is found, thereby enabling the start and termination nodes to be determined. Subsequently, the matrix is operated on by Warshall's algorithm (Cooke & Bez, 1985), which has the effect of raising it to the power of $n-1$ (where $n = 100$). As a result, all paths of length $n-1$ (the longest possible path through the network) are held in the matrix. If any of the elements in the diagonal

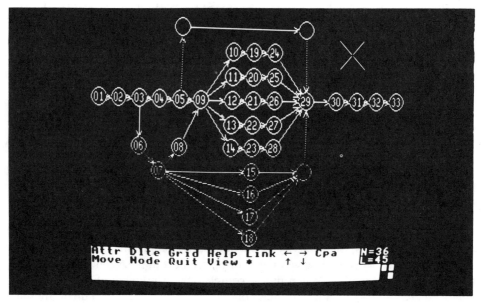

Figure 1. Network display.

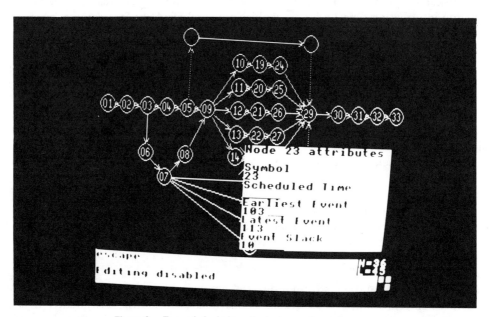

Figure 2. Expanded window displaying node attributes.

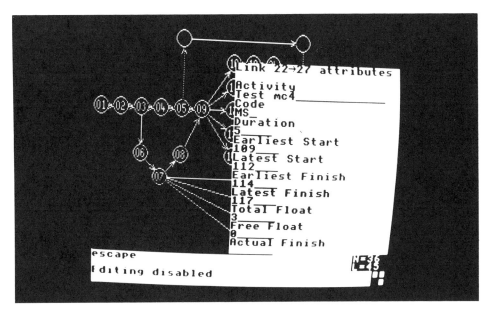

Figure 3. Expanded window displaying link attributes.

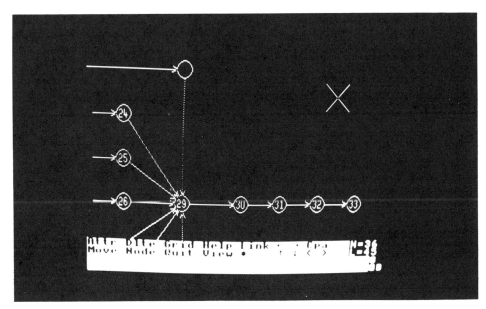

Figure 4. Magnified network.

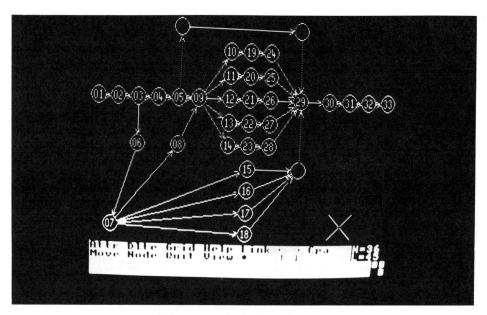

Figure 5. Rubber banding of nodes.

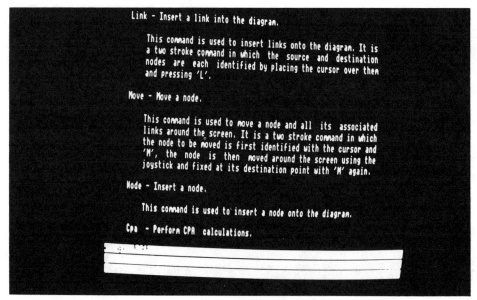

Figure 6. Help text display.

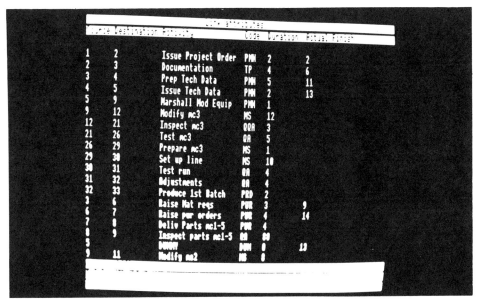

Figure 7. Tabular display of activity attributes.

are '1' then this means there must be a path from a node to itself, thereby indicating the existence of a loop. Thus, the adjacency matrix facilitates the validation of the network rules; checking start and end nodes and loops.

There is a need to traverse from all start nodes to all termination nodes to perform the forward pass (earliest event time) calculations, and vice versa for the reverse pass (latest event time) calculations.

In ICPA a recursive directed graph traversal algorithm was developed. It requires one argument, the current node number, and a global flag ('direction') which determines the direction of the traversal. On the forward traversal, outward links are those which have their tail on the current node, and inward links their head. On the reverse pass the opposite convention is adopted. For a forward traversal, once a node has had its 'earliest event time' (forward pass value) calculated all links emanating from that node may have their heads calculated; this acts as a testable flag. The algorithm is detailed in Figure 8.

4. System evaluations

4.1 *Difficulties and hazards of micro-based applications*

ICPA is written in BBC BASIC; a hybrid of BASIC ideally suited to structured, procedural-based software. As such the program was written using many modern software design techniques; structured top-down design; recursion; etc. Structured programming demands larger amounts of memory to cope with the extended variable and procedure titles given to elucidate the code.

The BBC model B microcomputer, equipped with a Z80 second processor has approximately 41 k of user memory (44 k for the 6502 second processor). There are no overlay facilities that readily exist and therefore the entire program must permanently

```
PROCEDURE traverse graph (node)
    find all inward and outward links (node, direction)
    IF NOT (all inward links have been calculated)
        traverse graph (node at the tail of one of the
        inward links not calculated)
        traverse graph (node)
    ELSE
        IF direction = forward
            earliest event time = maximum of all inward
            links
        ELSE
            latest event time = minimum of all inward
            links
        ENDIF
        IF total number of outward links < > 0
            calculate outward link values
        ENDIF
    ENDIF
ENDPROCEDURE
```

Figure 8. Recursive directed graph traversal algorithm.

reside in memory. In its source structured format the body of the ICPA program is 39·4 kbyte long and requires a further 16k for variable storage and stack. Obviously the equation is somewhat unbalanced. To overcome this inequality the program space had to be reduced. This was achieved by writing a second program which operates on the source to produce an efficient, compact, though illegible run-time version with minimum redundancy.

In the light of the development of ICPA a principle hazard of implementing such an application on a micro may be summarized: it is dangerous not to respect the constraints of a system and therefore be seduced into setting the objectives too high.

4.2 *The value of the system*

ICPA has been implemented as far as possible to a standard appropriate for use by project managers and it is currently undergoing thorough testing in a practical environment. Feedback to date can be summarized as follows.

The system is easy to use, friendly and requires no computing skills for operation. In all stages of operation the available commands are displayed in the prompt window: this together with the messages given and error detection facilities combine to make data entry for network construction a simple and error-free manœuvre. For small projects the network size catered for is perfectly adequate, as is the range of event and activity attributes. The fact that the graphical display is spread over four screens causes no anxiety since all commands can traverse the boundaries with ease. ICPA provides the ability to view the consequences of a proposed plan in a matter of seconds, thereby enabling 'What if ...' analyses. Moreover, being inexpensive enough to be offered as a personal desktop system permits responsive, local processing to be used to update and monitor the project with great ease in real time.

The main reservation about the system in operation appears to be its lack of resource-handling ability. However, the system was not designed to be all things to everyone; its original purpose was to implement CPA.

Facilitation of resource-allocation, scheduling, costing and so on is possible by modifying the database created by ICPA. Work is currently being carried out in this area with the view, in the longer term, to develop an integrated project management intelligent advisory system.

5. Knowledge engineering applications

A branch of computer artificial intelligence (AI) is that of intelligent knowledge-based systems (IKBS). These systems attempt to use knowledge about a particular problem domain to reach sensible conclusions relating to problems. The research programme from which ICPA has emerged is applying this technology to the problem domain of project management. The resultant IKBS will embody knowledge relating to:

(i) the construction of project plans for a given range of projects;
(ii) the analysis of project plans for risk areas and strategies to overcome project hazards using expedition, etc.

These systems will be able to bring the project manager's knowledge to bear on project proposals, or existing projects, to assist in the planning and control processes.

Because the knowledge required is not simply textbook material, but is largely the experience gained by project managers from years in the field, the process of eliciting knowledge so that it may be utilized by a computer is a difficult one—this process is termed knowledge engineering. A knowledge engineer needs to coax and assist the project manager in uncovering this often elusive knowledge. There are various techniques suggested for expediting this process, such as lengthy interviews, questioning decisions on-line whilst the project manager is at work, and so on. ICPA has, and will continue to have, an important part to play in this difficult process. Being a small, portable system, it is possible to transport it to any given project management site. *In situ* it provides a talking point upon which discussions can be based. A significant virtue of this interactive system is that it is easily put into action and so it is possible to simulate difficult project situations as network plans in order to provide a basis for project managers to describe the decision-making processes. The 'what if ...' analyses have proved to be invaluable to the dialogue between the knowledge engineer and project manager. Additionally, ICPA has provided the authors with an excellent tool upon which insights to network construction techniques can be based, and with which the true anatomy of projects can be appreciated. The development of decision support systems for project proposal (bid control) and project expedition, using the experience gained with ICPA acting as a knowledge engineering tool, forms the basis of a future paper.

6. Conclusions

6.1 *A new approach*

ICPA addresses an area of management much neglected by other CPA systems; the site manager and the small businessman who previously had only the use of pencil and paper to support their experience. In this area it provides a more natural environment for network creation. The ICPA package provides:

(1) rapid experimentation with different planning proposals;
(2) a means of simulating can be the consequences of projects running behind schedule (i.e. actual finish times can be entered).

6.2   *The way ahead*

The trend in most computer applications is towards personal workstations, and the proliferation of microprocessors emerging on the marketplace brings this ideal closer. As speed and capacity increases with the move towards 16- and 32-bit micros, the wealth of packages will blossom to provide engineers and managers with a wide range of planning and decision support tools with which to function.

At present the state of the art in graphic resolution on micros makes the graphical approach to network analysis described in this paper suitable only for a relatively small number of nodes and links. With the advent of new microcomputer systems having greater memory and graphics capabilities similar to those employed in some of the large CAD systems in use, and with the ability to display the resulting larger networks onto projection screens, the interactive graphics terminal will become the accepted medium for project planning communication.

References

Cooke, D. J. & Bez, H. E. 1985. *Computer Mathematics*, p. 201. Cambridge: CUP.
Harrison, F. L. 1981. *Advanced Project Management*, pp. 91–94. London: Gower.
Lockyer, K. 1964. *Critical Path Analysis and Other Project Network Techniques Solution Manual*, p. 13. London: Pitman.
Woodgate, H. S. 1977. *Planning by Network*, pp. xi, 63. Business Books.

A Microcomputer-Based Image Database Management System

B. E. PRASAD, AMAR GUPTA, SENIOR MEMBER, IEEE, HOO-MIN D. TOONG, MEMBER, IEEE, AND STUART E. MADNICK, MEMBER, IEEE

Abstract—Industrial applications frequently involve manipulation and management of pictorial information. In spite of the fact that digitized images and pictorial information are becoming more significant as parts of user databases, conventional database techniques have focused primarily on numerical and textual information. The Image Database Management (IDBM) system extends these techniques to encompass images, pictures, and graphs. Designed to run in a microcomputer environment, the design of IDBM integrates efficient database algorithms and compression techniques to permit fast retrievals as well as an unusually large number of images to be set up as a single database. The support of a synonym base is another important characteristic of the IDBM system.

I. INTRODUCTION

IN TERMS OF basic computer power, the mainframes of the early 1960's, the minicomputers of the early 1970's, and the microcomputers of the 1980's are all in the same performance bracket [1]. However, each of these three decades is characterized by emphasis on a different type of information. During the 1960's, the focus was on processing numerical information. The 1970's witnessed attention geared towards processing of textual information. During the present decade increasing efforts are being directed towards efficient representation and manipulation of pictorial information.

To illustrate the above trend, consider the maintenance manual for any major industrial equipment. The manual typically contains engineering numbers, descriptive text, and some black-and-white or full-color pictures. In the 1960's, computers were used to generate the numbers. By the late 1970's, computers began to be commonly used for processing and updating the text. Now, computers are used to create and to manipulate graphical and pictorial information [2], [3].

Even images of average complexity require large amounts of storage. A single high-resolution image, in color, typically requires about 10^6 bits of memory space. In spite of this fact, until recently little attention was paid to the management of nonalphanumeric information. The advent of powerful low-cost microcomputers has motivated use of these systems for image-oriented applications in many different areas including interactive computer-aided design (CAD), robotics, computer-aided manufacturing (CAM), and automated process control [4]-[6], [28].

At this stage, it is pertinent to distinguish between two aspects of image management. One relates to the physical storage of pictorial information, and encompasses issues such as the development of new data compression techniques and error correction algorithms to enable compact and accurate representation of images. The other relates to management of image databases, and includes investigation of strategies that enable a desired subset of images to be retrieved based on a group of selection criteria specified by the user. The latter aspect alone is examined in this paper.

II. IMAGE DATABASE SYSTEMS

An image database is a system in which a large amount of pictorial information is stored in an integrated manner. A collection of many images does not mean it is a database. To be classified as an image database, the management aspect must also be present.

One method to extend a conventional alphanumeric database is to add images as a data type. Each image can be assigned a unique picture name, and sets of images are retrieved in a manner analogous to numbers and text. This approach has been employed in several early systems including Aggregate Data Manager [32] and Spatial Data Management System. The latter project was originally conceived at the Massachusetts Institute of Technology (MIT) [33], and subsequently a commercial model was developed at the Computer Corporation of America [34].

Instead of considering the entire picture or screen as a single indivisible unit, more sophisticated image database systems allow the image to be described in greater depth. For example, in a system called IMDS, each Landsat image is defined in terms of its name, the image matrix, the spectral channel, the geographic coordinates, the scale factor, the date of creation, and a legend. In cartographic applications, maps are specified in terms of primal components such as points, line segments, and polygons. Image specification strategies adopted by different designers, and instances of new languages used to specify and to retrieve pictorial information from different image databases can be divided into four categories:

1) efforts within the framework of a relational database model [7], [9], [11], [12], [20], [21];
2) extending/modifying of relational database model to include new features for handling images [13], [17], [18];
3) special hardware for image processing [14], and
4) specific applications [4], [5], [8], [14], [15], [20], [28] such as medical images, Landsat photos, and cartography.

Manuscript received November 26, 1985; revised February 27, 1986.
The authors are with the Sloan School of Management, Massachusetts Institute of Technology, Cambridge, MA 02139.
IEEE Log Number 8612517.

Reprinted from *IEEE Trans. Indust. Electron.*, vol. IE-34, no. 1, pp. 83–88, Feb. 1987.

Whereas the preferred strategy for handling alphanumeric databases is to use the relational model, the choice is not clear in the case of image databases. In [28], McKeown points out three major disadvantages of using relational database techniques. First, the use of the basic attribute–value pairs implies that all primary key attributes must be duplicated in each relation, since there is no mechanism for allowing multiple-valued entities. Second, the relational database operators (union, join, project, etc.) are ill-suited for implementing geometric notions of proximity and intersection. Third, partitioning of large image databases is difficult using the relational model. These issues become even more significant in the context of microcomputers, which inherently possess lesser computing power and smaller storage capacity than available on mainframe computers and minicomputers.

III. Design of IDBM

The Image Database Management System (IDBM) is designed to serve as a generalized tool for storing and retrieving pictorial information in a microcomputer environment. Unlike other strategies that are geared to one discipline (e.g., medical image databases, and cartographic databases), IDBM employs techniques that are suitable in many different disciplines.

We distinguish between two forms of pictorial representation. A "slide" refers to a picture occupying the entire screen. A "pix" is a subset of a picture. The size and content of a pix is determined by the user by moving and scaling a pix rectangle on the screen and enclosing the desired section of the screen in this rectangle. The difference between slides and pixes is explained in [2] and [31]. The use of the dual structure allows full pictures, as well as parts of pictures, to be referenced individually. In IDBM each slide is assigned a unique slide name. If the slide contains more than one pix, then these pixes are numbered 1, 2, 3, and so on. By concatenating the slide name and the pix number, a unique identifier (ID) is generated for each pix.

The Create module of IDBM enables the image to be described in terms of four sets of attributes. In the present implementation of IDBM, these attributes are termed: 1) Subjects; 2) Emotion; 3) Action; 4) Physical Characteristics. In each set any desired number of elements can be specified. For example, an image may contain a computer, a table, and a man. All these three elements will be specified as subjects. The other three attributes are described in a similar manner. Further, modifiers can be used with each descriptor, i.e., personal computer, mechanical part, power supply, etc. By using multiple modifier–descriptor pairs, any image can be defined with as much precision as desired.

Images pertaining to one discipline can be organized into a library. The retrieve module of IDBM allows images to be retrieved in three different ways:

1) by specifying the library number to retrieve all images in a particular discipline;
2) by specifying the unique identifier to retrieve a particular slide or pix; and
3) by specifying conditions in an attribute list to retrieve the particular set of slides that meet all the criteria.

While 1) and 2) are easy to implement, the process of selective retrievals is more complex. Before discussing how images are selectively retrieved, it is necessary to first describe the basic structure of IDBM.

IV. Structure of IDBM

IDBM consists of four main modules: 1) the specification database which contains information about each image; 2) the syntactic database used to validate and to decompose a user query; 3) the pictorial database which contains the images; and 4) the user interface routines. These four modules are described in the following paragraphs.

A. The Specification Database

The specification database is logically organized as shown in Fig. 1. The physical structure of the specification database is shown in Fig. 2. Because a user is more likely to specify a list of attributes than of the image ID's, an inverted file structure has been used. When an image is initially specified in terms of the library number, image ID, and attributes (see top left of Figs. 1 and 2), the files containing these pieces of information are updated. At Level 1 the library file (middle top of figures) contains a pointer to the block (shown on top right) containing ID's of all images in that library. If the block space is insufficient to hold the information, overflow blocks are used.

The bottom left of Fig. 2 is shown in greater detail in Fig. 3. For each value of the attribute, there is a pointer indicating the beginning entry of the list of modifiers for that value. If Subject-1 had four different modifiers, there would be four entries in the row in Level 3 for this subject. Each entry, in turn, contains a pointer to the block (Level 4) containing ID's of all images corresponding to that particular set of descriptor and modifier. Again, overflow blocks are automatically employed, when required.

Level 5 (see Fig. 2) contains image ID's and the corresponding physical location of the respective slides and pixes. Level 3 serves as the image directory. In Fig. 2, the image ID's have been shown as SP1, SP2, etc., to denote that an image can be either a slide or a pix. Apart from the ID and the corresponding address, there is a pointer to the location containing the full description (descriptors and modifiers) for the image. Actually, the description for any image can be assembled from the information contained in Levels 2 and 3. However, the latter process is very tedious and time consuming. As such, the descriptors are duplicated and stored in Level 5 in the form of a packed description. This enables the full description for any image to be retrieved immediately without having to read all the entries in Levels 3 and 4.

It is appropriate to clarify one important aspect of Level 3. The right side of Fig. 3 shows the set of modifiers for Subject-1, Subject-2, and so on. In the parenthesis of the modifier, the first number relates to the subject, and the second to the modifier. With this convention Modifier-(1, 2) implies the second modifier relating to the first subject. The same modifier may occur under several subjects. For example, the word "electronic" can be modifying "computers" and "communications." It may appear that the duplication of

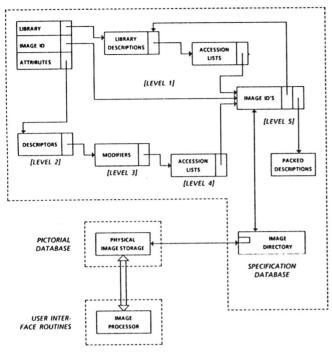

Fig. 1. Logical structure of IDBM.

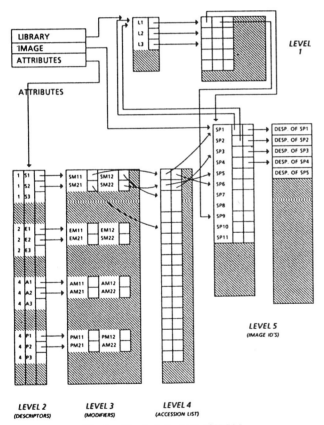

Fig. 2. Physical structure of IDBM.

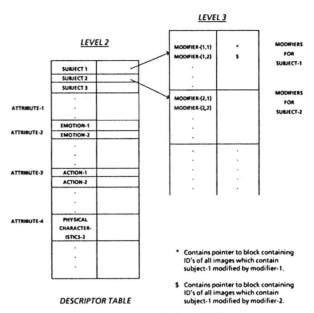

Fig. 3. Storage attributes in inverted file structure.

In our opinion, the image specification structure described above offers the best response time, given the typical memory sizes available on contemporary microcomputers.

B. The Syntactic Database

In most cases, the person retrieving images is different from the person who initially stores the images. This makes it unrealistic to contemplate that the two persons would define a particular image in an identical manner. For example, at the initial stage, the word "memory" may have been chosen as a subject. Later, another person could specify "storage" as the selection criterion. For the system to be truly effective, there must be a mechanism to know that these two words are functionally equivalent.

The above objective is one of the goals of the syntactic database. This database consists of two sets of dictionaries. The entries in each of these dictionaries are of the form:

$$(n, w, p_s)$$

where

   n the unique number assigned to the particular word,
   w the word, and
   p_s the pointer to the synonym.

The value of p_s is zero in two cases: 1) when there is no synonym for w; or 2) when w happens to be the word to which all its synonyms point. The set of words characterized by $p_s = 0$ are called basic words. The unique numbers associated with such words are used for internal coding. For all other words, the corresponding basic words are first assigned, and the unique numbers assigned to the latter words are then used.

As an example, assume "computing" and "computational" are desired to be stored as synonyms. Then the two entries in the dictionary may well appear as (150, computing, 0) and (180, computational, 150). This implies that "computing" is a basic word, and "computational" is its synonym. Also, the unique number 150 will be used when storing or retrieving an

modifiers is leading to inefficiency, but this is not so. First, each modifier occupies only 2 bytes of storage and as such the overall contribution to program size is minimal. Second, it is essential to store modifiers, in the present form, in order to directly determine the descriptor value, to obtain efficient retrieval, and to handle accession lists with speed and accuracy.

image containing either of these words. Apart from mitigating the problem of functionally equivalent words, this technique reduces the number of descriptors for each image.

Of the two dictionaries, the first dictionary contains words of universal importance. The data in this dictionary is an integral part of IDBM. The second dictionary is application dependent, and its vocabulary is created and expanded by the user. Although both dictionaries contain the same structure of entries, the size and contents of the first dictionary are invariant whereas the second dictionary gradually grows in size. When a retrieval criterion is specified, the standard dictionary is first searched and then the application-dependent one. If the word is located in either dictionary, then the corresponding basic word is identified and the query process proceeds. If the word is not currently in either dictionary, the user can add it to the application-dependent dictionary and also indicate its synonyms, if any.

C. The Pictorial Database

The image database management routines of IDBM can operate in conjunction with any pictorial database system capable of running in an IBM Personal Computer or compatible environment. Since all programming has been done in the "C" language, it is relatively easy to tailor IDBM routines to execute in many other computing environments. It can be used to store, catalog, and retrieve pictures, images, graphs, photographs, maps, and virtually anything that can be displayed on the screen.

Depending on the environment, the image may be drawn, generated by a digitizer, or created using another package. IDBM does not deal with the issues of creating the pictorial database. Our research has focused on identifying management strategies that can work in conjunction with state-of-the-art off-the-shelf graphics software. To demonstrate the viability of our strategies, VCN ExecuVision was selected as a test case since it offers the largest number (over 4,000) of prerendered images [2]. Independent reviewers have highly recommended it as "The Cadillac of presentation graphics software" [35] and, "What a word processor is to words, VCN ExecuVision is to graphics" [36]. This graphics package uses sophisticated data compression algorithms to store images in a very compact mode. We used this software to design and test various routines of IDBM.

D. Total Storage Requirements

The total storage requirements for IDBM program routines, and the four modules (including the pictorial database) for 2,000 images are as shown in Table I. Note that the total storage requirements of 8 Mbytes fall within the storage capacity of contemporary hard disks. IDBM program routines account for only 84 kbytes. The rest is comprised of data.

V. USING IDBM

When a user enters a set of selection criteria, the sequence of steps performed by IDBM is summarized in Fig. 4. The general form of a query based on attributes is as follows:

$$A_1(m_1, v_1) \& A_2(m_2, v_2) \& \cdots \& A_k(m_k, v_k)$$

TABLE I
STORAGE REQUIREMENTS FOR AN IDBM SYSTEM WITH 2,000 IMAGES

ENTITY	SIZE/ASSUMPTION	STORAGE IN BYTES
Standard Dictionary	10,000 words	300,000
User Dictionary	2,000 words	50,000
Level 1	25 libraries	9,250
Level 2	4,000 attribute values	28,000
Level 3	2 modifier/attribute values	128,000
Level 4	10 attribute values/ID	256,000
Level 5	2,000 IDs	208,000
Hash Overhead	----	100,000
	Total =	1,079,000 (i)

Average storage requirement per image = 3.5 Kbytes
Storage requirement for 2,000 images = 2,000 x 3.5 = 7,000 Kbytes (ii)
Total storage requirements = (i) + (ii)
= 1,079,000 + 7,000,000 bytes
≈ 8 Mbytes

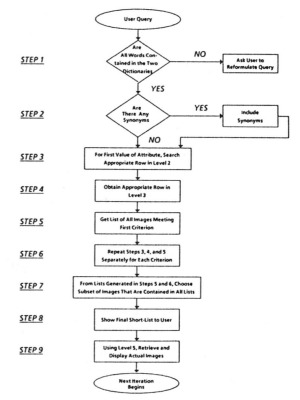

Fig. 4. Sequence of steps in response to user query.

where

A_1 one of the attributes: Subject, Action, Emotion, or Physical Characteristics,

m_i a modifier, and

v_i an attribute value also known as descriptors.

Suppose a user wanted to retrieve all images that pertained to the subject "CAD/CAM applications on personal computers." Under an IDBM environment, this requirement would be translated as "show all images containing subjects ⟨CAD; CAM; application; personal computer⟩." The word "personal" is a modifier to the descriptor "computer," while the other descriptors carry no modifiers. This user query can be written formally as:

$$A_1(@, \text{CAD}) \& A_2(@, \text{CAM}) \& A_3(@, \text{application})$$
$$\& A_4(\text{personal, computer})$$

where @ refers to null string and A_1, A_2, A_3, and A_4 are all subjects in this case.

Based on the above query, IDBM first searches for all images containing CAD and its synonyms (computerized design, automated design, etc.) and generates a first list. Similarly, three lists are generated for the other three descriptors. Finally, a short-list is compiled containing image ID's in all four lists. From a technical perspective, the process can be visualized in terms of the following four steps.

Step 1: Using the ordered pairs (m_1, v_1), (m_2, v_2), $\cdots$, (m_k, v_k), search the standard dictionary to get the corresponding numbers. Ignore any m_i which is a null string or a blank. If a word is not found in the standard dictionary, search the application-dependent dictionary. If the word is still not found, trigger an error message. If Step 1 is completed properly, assume that the number pairs obtained for the query are

$$(nm_1, nv_1), (nm_2, nv_2), \cdots, (nm_k, nv_k)$$

where

$$nm_i = 0 \text{ if } m_i = @ \text{(null string)}.$$

Step 2: Depending on attribute A_i associated with (m_i, v_i), search the corresponding attribute file for the number nv_i. Then if $nm_i = 0$, take all pointers to the accession list associated with modifiers of nv_i; and if $nm_i > 0$, take only the pointer associated with nm_i. Repeat this step for all the pairs in the query.

Step 3: Accession lists obtained by Step 2 contain pointers to slide data file. Assume that B_1, B_2, $\cdots$, B_k are the accession lists for the given query. Since each query condition is connected by an AND operation, we select those pointers which appear in all the accession lists. Denote this set by B^*. The number of values in B^* is equivalent to the total number of images (slides and pixes) that meet the criteria specified by the user.

Step 4: Using the pointers in B^*, retrieve the slide names and pix numbers which are then passed to the Image System for display.

After completing Step 3, the total number of images that meet all the selection criteria is displayed. On request, the number of images fulfilling individual criterion is also displayed. This enables the user to reframe his or her query to come up with the appropriate number of images. These images are then displayed using the pictorial database and the interface routines.

Instead of retrieving information, if the user desired to add an image to the database, a template is provided to enter the specifications for the particular image. If the user entered a descriptor that is not contained in either of the two dictionaries, the user is informed accordingly. There are two possibilities: either 1) the user specified an incorrect spelling and as such he or she can now state the correct word; or 2) the

user wishes to enter a new word in the dictionary. In the latter case, IDBM provides the facility for specifying synonyms as well.

It is clarified that the current version of IDBM supports only the logical AND between values specified in the retrieval criteria. A user desiring to specify an OR operation must use a succession of queries. For example, to get all images containing either a "car" or a truck, the user first obtains all images specifying "car" alone. Then, he or she can retrieve images containing truck. As this process can get cumbersome, we are currently enhancing the logical set to allow for operations other than a simple AND.

The retrieval speed and efficiency of IDBM is heavily influenced by: 1) the size of the syntactic database; 2) the level of specification of each image at the time of storage; and 3) the level of detail of the retrieval criteria. Using a subset of VCN ExecuVision libraries containing 400 (of the 4,000) images, and specifying each image in terms of an average of ten descriptor–modifier pairs, the observed response time has been 5 s or less using an IBM PC/XT system. The performance will be still better using a faster computer. This response time is acceptable for most applications.

VI. UNIQUE FEATURES AND NEW DIRECTIONS

As explained earlier, the subject of the IDBM system has received attention of several researchers in recent years. In our opinion, the unique features of IDBM are as follows:

1) Whereas almost all other image database management systems have been hosted only on mainframes or minicomputers, IDBM has been specifically developed to work in an IBM Personal Computer (or compatible) environment.

2) IDBM has been designed for storing and retrieving icons, symbols, and images, unlike other microcomputer-based database packages (e.g., dBase-II) which are directed towards numeric and textual information.

3) IDBM allows multiple values per attribute to be specified at the time of storage and also at the time of retrieval.

4) IDBM supports the mechanism for automatic checking for synonyms. This eliminates the need for the user to be aware of what particular descriptors have been used previously in the Create mode.

It is pertinent to mention here that IDBM can be used in conjunction with any pictorial information database. This includes the spectrum of areas from maps used in cartographic applications to graphs used in industrial applications and from spreadsheets used in the office environment to photographic information gathered by satellites. The first version of IDBM has been tested in conjunction with VCN ExecuVision [2], [31] presentation graphics software. This package was preferred because it offered immediate access to several thousand prerendered professional quality images, and because it is widely used in industrial and business applications.

The concept of IDBM was originally conceived to encapsulate the intelligence by which a user is able to selectively recall the images that pertain to a particular topic of interest. However, in most environments, information of many different types, besides images, is needed, and no distinction is made among numeric, textual, graphical, and pictorial information. IDBM has recently been enlarged to allow for storage and retrieval of numeric and textual information. At present, new input and output routines are being developed to allow IDBM to operate in conjunction with the software packages commonly used for manipulating numbers and text in a microcomputer environment.

REFERENCES

[1] H.-M. D. Toong and A. Gupta, "Personal computers," *Sci. Amer.*, vol. 247, no. 6, pp. 88–99, Dec. 1982.

[2] H.-M. D. Toong and A. Gupta, "A new direction in personal computer software," *Proc. IEEE*, vol. 72, no. 3, pp. 377–388, Mar. 1984.

[3] S. Feiner, S. Nagy, and A. Van Dam, "An experimental system for creating and presenting graphical documents," *ACM Trans. Graphics*, vol. 2, no. 1, pp. 59–77, Jan. 1982.

[4] J. C. Dorng and S. K. Chang, "Design considerations for CAD/CAM databases," in *Proc. Int. Computer Symp.* (Taipei, Taiwan), Dec. 1984.

[5] Y. C. Lee and K. S. Fu, "A CAD/CAM database management system and its query languages," in *Languages for Automation*, S. K. Chang, Ed. New York: Plenum, 1985.

[6] S. K. Chang, "Image information systems," *Proc. IEEE*, vol. 73, no. 4, pp. 754–764, Apr. 1985.

[7] R. B. Abhyankar and R. L. Kashyap, "Pictorial data description and retrieval with relational Languages," in *Proc. IEEE Picture Data Descript., Mgmt. Workshop* (Asilomar, CA), 1980, pp. 57–60.

[8] T. Ichikawa, T. Kikuno and M. Hirakawa, "A query manipulation system for image data retrieval by ARES," in *Proc. IEEE Picture Data Descript., Mgmt. Workshop* (Asilomar, CA), 1980, pp. 61–67.

[9] N. S. Chang and K. S. Fu, "A query language for relational image database systems," in *Proc. IEEE Picture Data Descript., Mgmt. Workshop* (Asilomar, CA), 1980, pp. 68–73.

[10] S. Levialdi, "Programming in PIXAL," in *Proc. IEEE Picture Data Descript., Mgmt. Workshop* (Asilomar, CA), 1980, pp. 74–82.

[11] B. S. Lin and S. K. Chang, "GRAIN—A pictorial database interface," in *Proc. IEEE Picture Data Descript., Mgmt. Workshop* (Asilomar, CA), 1980, pp. 83–88.

[12] S. Uno and H. Matsuka, "A relational database for design aids system," in *Proc. IEEE Picture Data Descript., Mgmt. Workshop* (Asilomar, CA), 1980, pp. 89–94.

[13] K. Yamaguchi *et al.*, "ELF: Extended relational model for large, flexible picture database," in *Proc. IEEE Picture Data Descript., Mgmt. Workshop* (Asilomar, CA), 1980, pp. 95–102.

[14] M. Friedell *et al.*, "The management of very large two-dimensional raster graphics env.," in *Proc. IEEE Picture Data Descript., Mgmt. Workshop* (Asilomar, CA), 1980, pp. 139–144.

[15] D. M. McKeown, Jr., "Knowledge structuring in task oriented image databases," in *Proc. IEEE Picture Data Descript., Mgmt. Work-shop* (Asilomar, CA), 1980, pp. 145–151.

[16] P. G. Selfridge, "Name-value slots and the storage of image information," in *Proc. IEEE Picture Data Descript., Mgmt. Workshop* (Asilomar, CA), 1980, pp. 152–157.

[17] G. Y. Tang, "A logical data organization for the integrated databases of pictures and alphanumerical data," in *Proc. IEEE Picture Data Descript., Mgmt. Workshop* (Asilomar, CA), 1980, pp. 158–166.

[18] G. Y. Tang, "A management system for the integrated databases of pictures and alphanumerical data," *Comput. Graphics, Image Process.*, vol. 16, pp. 270–286, 1981.

[19] K. R. Sloan, Jr. and A. Lippman, "Databases of/about/with images," in *Proc. IEEE Comput. Soc. Conf. Pattern Recognition, Image Process.*, 1982, pp. 441–446.

[20] M. Nagata, "A relational image data base system for remote sensing (LAND DBMS)," in *Proc. IEEE Comput. Soc. Conf. Pattern Recognition, Image Process.*, 1982, pp. 491–495.

[21] N. S. Chang and K. S. Fu, "Query-by-pictorial-example," *IEEE Trans. Software Eng.*, vol. SE-6, no. 6, pp. 519–524, 1980.

[22] N. S. Chang and K. S. Fu, "Picture query languages for pictorial database systems," *IEEE Trans. Comput.*, vol. C-14, no. 11, 1981.

[23] S. K. Chang and K. S. Fu, *Pictorial Data Base Systems*. Berlin, Germany: Springer, 1980.

[24] S. K. Chang and T. L. Kunii, "Pictorial database systems," *IEEE Trans. Comput.*, vol. C-14, no. 11, 1981.

[25] A. Blaser, Ed., *Data Base Techniques for Pictorial Applications*. Berlin, Germany: Springer, 1980.

[26] H. Tamura and N. Yokoya, "Image database systems: A survey," *Pattern Recognition*, vol. 17, no. 1, Jan. 1984.

[27] G. Nagy, "Image database," *Image, Vision Comput.*, vol. 3, no. 3, Aug. 1985.

[28] D. M. McKeown, Jr., "Digital cartography and photo interpretation from a data base view point," in *New Applications of Databases*. New York: Academic, 1984, pp. 19–42.

[29] M. Crehange *et al.*, "Exprim: An expert system to aid in progressive retrieval from a pictorial and descriptive data base," in *New Applications of Databases*. New York, Academic, 1984, pp. 19–42.

[30] S. K. Chang and S. H. Liu, "Picture indexing and abstraction techniques for pictorial databases," *IEEE Trans. Pattern Anal. Machine Intell.*, vol. PAM-6, no. 4, 1984.

[31] A. Gupta and H.-M. D. Toong, Ed., *Insights into Personal Computers*. New York: IEEE Press, 1985.

[32] Y. Takao, S. Itoh, and J. Iisaka, "An image-oriented database system," in *Data Base Techniques for Pictorial Applications*, A. Balser, Ed. Berlin, Germany: Springer, 1980, pp. 527–538.

[33] W. C. Donelson, "Spatial management of information," *Comput. Graphics*, vol. 12, pp. 203–209, 1978.

[34] C. F. Herot, "A prototype spatial data management system," *Comput. Graphics*, vol. 14, pp. 63–70, 1980.

[35] K. Alesandrini *et al.*, "Great and 'Not-So-Great Graphics'," *PC*, pp. 160–161, June 11, 1985.

[36] W. J. Hawkins, "Bits and bytes," *Popular Sci.*, Jan. 1984.

SOFTWARE DEVELOPMENT EFFORT AND SCHEDULE ESTIMATES USING
THE COCOMOx KNOWLEDGE SYSTEM AND INSIGHT 2+ SHELL

by

P. Chapman
Jet Propulsion Laboratory
California Institute of Technology
Pasadena, California

ABSTRACT

This paper describes an expert system that can assist engineers and managers in estimating software development efforts and schedules. The expert system shell was developed by Level Five Research. The knowledge bases were developed by the author using Barry W. Boehm's (TRW) COCOMO software cost models.[1] The assistant is referred to as COCOMOx, whose contract is to assist the user in estimating person-months and schedule over the development phases of a software project or task. The assistant actually employs four separate knowledge bases (thus, the x in COCOMOx), one of which provides a pointer to the proper knowledge base for a specific development effort. That is, the application instructions are related to the user through the expert system itself.

INTRODUCTION

Conventional computer programs require precise sequences of instructions (algorithms) carried out in a prestructured manner. Expert system programs entail symbolic processing, which results in working with ideas and knowledge rather than algorithms. This symbolic processing is purported to be analogous to the way humans reason using knowledge they possess. This type of processing has proven effective in dealing with complex problems, interpreting information, using "rules of thumb" gained by experienced people (experts), and handling uncertain or incomplete information. Expert systems (computerized consultants or assistants) are designed to simulate the reasoning processes (inferencing) of experts in a specific field or domain. This type of system requests information and opinions from the user and applies rules used by human experts to analyze the situation or problem. Then the system advises or assists the user by making recommendations or suggesting answers. It has the capability of relating its chain of reasoning to the user and can provide the user with a measurement of its confidence with respect to its recommendations or answers.

COCOMOx is such an expert system. It consists of a third-generation inference engine and control strategy developed by Level Five Research (Melbourne Beach, Florida), which provided the knowledge engineering tool for constructing a software development cost estimator assistant. The assistant will aid management in determining the person-months and time (schedule) required to develop a system of software elements or individual software modules.

The costing assistant runs on an IBM PC, XT, AT, or true IBM-compatible machine with 512 kbytes of memory and one floppy disk drive. An 80-column or 132-column printer is required if the predicted effort and schedule report forms are to be used for funding justification, audit trails, or project reports. The software is contained on one 5 1/4-in. floppy disk and consists of an integrated run-time environment including the expert system inference engine, the cost model knowledge bases, a Pascal engine coupled to a database management system, and a user friendly human-machine interface.

The COCOMOx assistant has been used to estimate the software development cost for two Federal Aviation Administration software intensive projects at the Jet Propulsion Laboratory. These projects provided the development test bed for the assistant.

JUSTIFICATION FOR AN ASSISTANT

Almost all software development costs are initially estimated inaccurately.[2, 3] To make matters worse, the annual cost of software in the United States is now well over 40 billion dollars. Compared with the cost of computer hardware, the cost of software will continue to escalate. With respect to the overall computer and information processing industry of the future, software will continue to be the dominant portion of an industry expected to grow to 13% of the Gross National Product by 1990.[4, 5]

There is good reason to expect software development cost estimations to be an inaccurate process. Software development is tied back to the developers' minds: how they think, their past software development experiences,[6] their personal lives, their working conditions, and their daily general well-being. The productivity of a coder, for example, can change from day to day depending upon "mood," i.e., personal problems, family life, workload, etc.

A software cost model provides a consistent methodology for estimating the funds and time required to develop a software product. Software development cost estimating uncertainties are a function of a lack of definition or understanding of the job to be done. In the initial planning stages, the predictions from cost models can be expected to be within perhaps a factor of two of the ultimate (actual) costs. The uncertainty of cost upon acceptance of the software product by the customer is essentially zero. The uncertainty function is exponential in between[7] and is shown in Figure 1. It is doubtful that one skilled in the use of any model can be expected to estimate better than 20% of the actual costs 60 percent of the time. This, however, is generally considered acceptable compared with historical results using no consistent method (model).

Wrapping an expert system around a software cost model should theoretically not increase the accuracy of the cost prediction over using the stand-alone model. In practice the expert system will provide a tool for more accurate development cost estimations. The expert system allows managers, software systems engineers, and designers to participate in the estimating process as well as the individual who has, no doubt, spent months understanding and using the stand-alone model. There is a significant amount of subjectivity in using most analytical software development cost models. The expert system concept provides a consensus-of-opinion (i.e., Delphi) approach to the subjectivity portion of the model. This approach will result in more meaningful predictions and provide the funding sponsor with a more comfortable audit trail and funding justification.

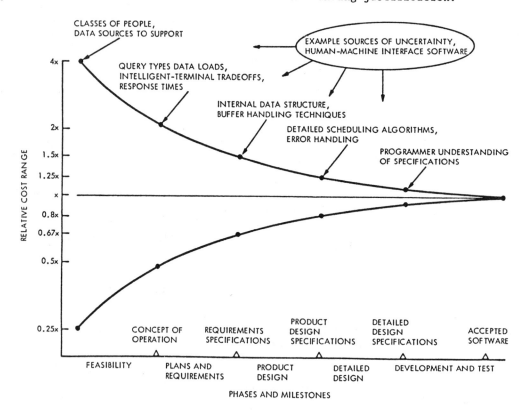

Fig. 1. Software Cost Estimation versus Development Phase

THE MODEL

The assistant uses the COCOMO (COnstructive COst MOdel), which was developed by Barry Boehm (TRW) and described in Software Engineering Economics.[1] This reference is regarded as the definitive description of COCOMOx. Specific portions of this reference that directly pertain to software development costing and scheduling were converted to production rules (IF...THEN...ELSE rules) to form the knowledge bases of COCOMOx.

The COCOMO model is actually three models: Basic, Intermediate, and Detailed. Each model can have one of three modes: Organic, Semidetached, or Embedded. Within this structure, each mode of every model can have one of five different efforts. The Intermediate and Detailed models are associated with 15 different cost drivers, making a large number of possibilities for selecting improper COCOMO elements for analyses by the occasional user, a fact that complicates the stand-alone use of COCOMO.

Currently, COCOMOx implements two of the three models (Basic and Intermediate) and is a COCOMO assistant whose mission is to infer which combination of all possible combinations implemented is the most reasonable set of elements for the user's software development case at hand. Clearly, this is an example of the utility of small expert systems (200 to 500 rules) within narrow domain fields to assist non-expert and occasional users in making decisions based upon possibly incomplete knowledge.

Besides its mission of inferencing, COCOMOx is responsible for making the analytical calculations once the proper elements have been determined, then presenting these calculations in a user-understandable format acceptable for project reports and audit trails.

THE EXPERT SYSTEM SHELL

An expert system shell is an expert system with no knowledge base. The costing assistant uses a vendor-supported expert system shell called INSIGHT 2+ and, as previously mentioned, the COCOMO knowledge as defined in Reference 1. Once populated with knowledge, the shell is no longer a shell, but this section of the paper briefly describes the INSIGHT 2+ shell to provide a baseline of understanding for the next section, which describes parts of the assistant in some detail.

Figure 2 indicates the architecture of INSIGHT 2+. The software includes a set of editors for developing both the knowledge base production rules and algorithmic programs to manipulate data to and from the inference engine, if required. The production rules are written in an English-type language called Production Rule Language (PRL) and then compiled. Any required accompanying algorithmic programs are written in an included version of Turbo Pascal (a product of Borland International, Scotts Valley, California) and compiled. The Pascal programs have the capability of linking to an included version of dBASE II (a product of Ashton-Tate, Culver City, California). The linkage between the inference engine, the Pascal engine, and the database generated by dBASE II is totally transparent to the user. Provisions are included with the shell software to allow testing of the compiled Pascal programs without normal linkage to the inference engine. A developer can use his favorite text editor, dBASE II software, or his favorite C compiler, rather than the vendor-supplied development support software. The editor supplied with the shell is an enhanced version of Borland's Turbo Pascal editor.

The fact that the production rules are compiled (actually tokenized) leads to an important result. In a fully populated memory machine, one can have knowledge bases consisting of between 1000 and 2000 rules, depending upon the complexity (the length) of the rules. Furthermore, the compilation of the rules results in extremely fast execution, with the user rarely noticing any delay after responding to a query or screen display. The production rules are compiled incrementally. If an error is detected by the compiler, the editor is envoked and the editor cursor sits at the error location, allowing the developer to correct the error and continue with the compilation.

The INSIGHT 2+ control structure provides both backward or forward chaining to make heuristic conclusions. The COCOMOx assistant uses the control structure in the backward chaining (goal-driven) inference engine mode. That is, the goals are selected first, and then supporting evidence is sought by the expert system to verify the goals.

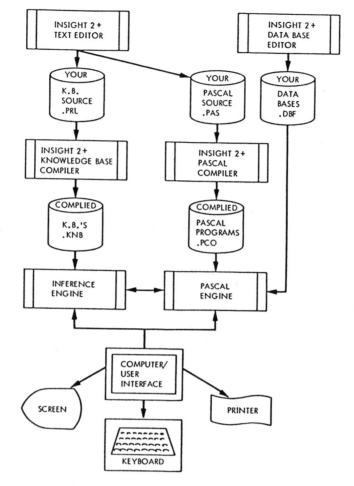

Fig. 2.   INSIGHT 2+ Architecture

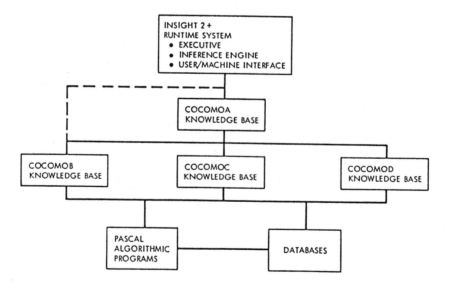

Fig. 3.   COCOMO/Expert Elements

The INSIGHT 2+ shell was selected for the COCOMOx software development costing assistant because the shell is designed as a complete tool for knowledge engineering development.

THE ASSISTANT

The COCOMOx assistant runtime software consists of INSIGHT 2+, COCOMOA, COCOMOB, COCOMOC, and COCOMOD compiled knowledge bases, multiple databases consisting of several hundred numeric items required for the COCOMO models, and compiled Pascal programs that access the numeric data to solve the analytical equations. All elements of the assistant are linked together so that once the program is invoked, the user need not exit the runtime environment until satisfied that the development effort assessment is complete. Figure 3 shows this integrated runtime architecture.

A user can use the assistant in any one or all of four different ways:

(1) To determine which knowledge base is appropriate for the costing analysis at hand (COCOMOA).

(2) To predict the effort associated with converting inherited code (if any) to the new product (COCOMOB).

(3) To predict the effort and schedule to implement a total product (COCOMOC or COCOMOD).

(4) To predict the effort and schedule to implement single modules or elements that are to make up an entire software product (COCOMOC or COCOMOD).

The user input consists of responses to queries presented on the screen. If the user does not understand a query, he can request an expansion of the query for more information, as shown by an example in Figures 4A and 4B. With regard to Figure 4A, the user would be asked if there is to be software conversion. If the user is unsure of the meaning of the question or how to respond, he can request additional information (by pushing a specific function key on the keyboard) which would be presented to him in the format of the EXPAND function of Figure 4B. That portion of the production rule "AND KDSI >0" in Figure 4A will result in a question expressed by the words associated with

```
        RULE 171 to determine software conversion
  (A)   IF      There is to be software conversion
        AND     KDSI > 0
        THEN    There is a code adaptation effort
        AND     There may be some software redesign


        !
        TEXT  KDSI
        How many THOUSANDS of source instructions are to be
        converted from existing (ie., inherited) code for this
        new software development effort?
        !
        EXPAND There is to be software conversion
  (B)          The assistant will help determine the development effort
               required to convert inherited code for use on this new
               software project or task.  The conversion effort consists
               at most of REDESIGN, CODE REWORK, and modified code
               INTEGRATION with new code.

                         Press F5 to continue...

        !
```

Fig. 4. Knowledge Base Structure Example with TEXT and EXPAND Functions (from COCOMOB)

TEXT KDSI in Figure 4B. EXPAND is a user option function, whereas TEXT customizes a query.
Non-customized queries have default formats.

Sometimes screen DISPLAYs are more appropriate for user assistance or direction and for output
reports. Figures 5A and 5B are an example of the DISPLAY function in RULE 171 of COCOMOA.

```
        !
        RULE 191 to determine the knowledge base
        IF    The COCOMOx model for this development is known
        AND   The model is INTERMEDIATE
        AND   The components of the S_W product are defined
        AND   NOT The component teams are equally capable
        AND   NOT The component teams are equally experienced
(A)     AND   NOT Each component is equally complex
        THEN  We can select a knowledge base
        AND   DISPLAY msg2
        AND   CHAIN COCOMOD
        ELSE  We can select a knowledge base
        AND   DISPLAY msg3
        AND   CHAIN COCOMOC
        !


        !
        DISPLAY msg2
                You are about to be placed in the COCOMOD knowledge base
                which is appropriate for estimating development effort
                and schedule for individual software elements that are
                known to fall in the category of the COCOMOx INTERMEDIATE
                model.

(B)                             IF YOU DO NOT WISH TO CONTINUE
                                PRESS THE F7 FUNCTION KEY...

                                IF YOU WISH TO AUTOMATICALLY BE PLACED
                                IN THE COCOMOD KNOWLEDGE BASE ENVIRONMENT
                                PRESS THE F2 FUNCTION KEY...
        !
```

Fig. 5. Knowledge Base Structure Example with DISPLAY Function (from COCOMOA)

As the user responds to the expert system queries (with help from the assistant), the INSIGHT 2+
inference engine chains through the selected knowledge base always attempting to gather supporting
goal evidence. Figure 6 lists the goals for COCOMOC and a rule that forces the inference engine and
control strategy to search for supporting evidence to substantiate the top-level goal "1." by
attempting to first find supporting evidence for the subgoals 1.1 through 1.9.1. This is discovered
immediately by the control system of INSIGHT 2+ when it evaluates RULE 1. There are many rules that
must be evaluated to substantiate each subgoal. The number of the rule is convenient for designing
the knowledge base, but has no significance in the sequence of inferencing steps, nor does the order
(position) of the rules within the knowledge base.

At times during the session, calculations are required, and results need to be displayed or
printed. A linkage example from the COCOMOD knowledge base to one of the compiled Pascal programs is
shown in Figures 7A and 7B. Figure 7A shows the production rule providing the linkage, and Figure 7B
shows a portion of the Pascal end of the linkage. The SEND variables, determined in the expert
systems environment, are required by the Pascal module to determine the RETURN variables (see
Figure 7A). In turn, the Pascal engine RECEIVEs the SEND variables and RETURNs the calculated values
to the inference engine (see Figure 7B).

```
!Goals
    1.   We can determine an estimate
        1.1   The effort is determined
        1.2   The model is determined
        1.3   The mode is determined
        1.4   We can select a worksheet
        1.5   We can calculate mainform
        1.6   We can determine plans and requirements
        1.7   We can determine product design
        1.8   We can determine programming
        1.9   We can determine integration and test
        1.9.1   We can determine maintenance

    !


    !
    RULE 1 to determine the primary goal
    IF       The effort is determined
    AND      The model is determined
    AND      The mode is determined
    AND      We can select a worksheet
    AND      We can calculate mainform
    AND      We can determine plans and requirements
    AND      We can determine product design
    AND      We can determine programming
    AND      We can determine integration and test
    AND      We can determine maintenance
    THEN     We can determine an estimate
    !
```

Fig. 6.   Concept of Goals and Primary Goal Driver (from COCOMOC)

(A)
```
RULE 160 to print the mainform
IF       We can select a worksheet
AND      CALL MFORM
SEND     RECNUM
SEND     KDSI
SEND     DEM
SEND     MEM
SEND     MOPAY
SEND     HRPAY
SEND     RATIO
RETURN   FACTOR
RETURN   PM
RETURN   EPR
RETURN   EPD
RETURN   EPROG
RETURN   DD
RETURN   CUT
RETURN   EIT
RETURN   TDEV
RETURN   SPR
RETURN   SPD
RETURN   SP
RETURN   SIT
RETURN   PROD
RETURN   WPAV
RETURN   WH
RETURN   COST
RETURN   PMAM
RETURN   MMP
RETURN   AMCOST
AND      DISPLAY mainform
THEN     We can calculate mainform
!
```

(B)
```
PROGRAM MFORM (RECEIVE  RECNUM, KDSI, DEM, MEM, MOPAY, HRPAY, RATIO
RETURN FACTOR, PM, EPR, EPD, EPROG, DD, CUT, EIT, TDEV, SPR, SPD, SP, SIT,
PROD, WPAV, WH, COST, PMAM, MMP, AMCOST);

CONST
    TWO = 2.0;
    TDEV1 = 2.5;

VAR
    F1, F2, E1, E2, EP, EPDX, EPROG1, EPROG2, DD1, DD2, CODE1, CODE2  :REAL;
    ETEST1, ETEST2, TDEV2, SP1, SP2, SPD1, SPD2, SPROG1, SPROG2  :REAL;
    STEST1, STEST2, KLUDGE  :REAL;
    Y,Y1,X,CNT,C,C1,C2  :REAL;
    RNUM  :INTEGER;
    MODEL,MODE,EFFORT       :STRING(12);
    FORM                    :STRING(6);
    MFORM:RECORD
        FORM        :STRING(6);
        MODEL       :STRING(12);
        MODE        :STRING(12);
        EFFORT      :STRING(12);
        F1          :REAL;
        F2          :REAL;
        .
        .
        .
```

Fig. 7.   Example of (A) Knowledge Base-to-PASCAL Engine Linkage and
          (B) PASCAL-to-Knowledge Base Linkage (from COCOMOD)

327

The COCOMOx output predictions and estimates are designed to fit on 8 1/2-in. by 11-in. paper for reports and audit trails. The commercial version of COCOMOx has the capability of storing session results over the life cycle of a software development project, thus archiving the estimates and predictions as the development proceeds.

ACKNOWLEDGEMENTS

The author wishes to thank the Federal Aviation Administration for the opportunity of using COCOMOx to estimate software development costs for the Central Weather Processor (CWP) and the Weather Message Switching Center Replacement (WMSCR) projects. I also wish to thank the Section Manager, Jeff Leising, of the Systems Engineering Section for his understanding in the production of this paper.

This paper was produced by the Jet Propulsion Laboratory, California Institute of Technology, through an agreement with the National Aeronautics and Space Administration.

REFERENCES

[1] B.W. Boehm, Software Engineering Economics, Prentice-Hall Inc., NJ, 1981.

[2] L.H. Putnam, A. Fitzsimmons, "Estimating Software Costs," Datamation, Technical Publishing, NY, September 1979.

[3] L.H. Putnam, Software Cost Estimating and Life-Cycle Control: Getting the Software Numbers, Computer Society Press (IEEE Catalog No. EHO 165-1), COMPSAC80, October 1980.

[4] T.A. Dolotta, et al., Data Processing in 1980-85, John Wiley & Sons, NY, 1976.

[5] T.B. Steel, Jr., "A Note on Future Trends," in P.S. Nyborg (ed), Information Processing in the United States: A Quantitative Summary, AFIPS, Montvale, NJ, 1977.

[6] B.G. Silverman, "Software Cost and Productivity Improvements: An Analogical View," Computer, Computer Society Press (IEEE), May 1985.

[7] B.W. Boehm, "Software Engineering Economics," IEEE Transactions on Software Engineering, Vol. SE-10, No. 1, January 1984.

VERIFICATION OF MEDICAL DIAGNOSES USING A MICROCOMPUTER

by

Douglas D. Dankel II, Ph.D.
University of Florida
Gainesville, FL

Giuliano Russo, M.D.
Humana Hospital
Dade City, FL

ABSTRACT

Over the past decade artificial intelligence researchers have developed numerous medical diagnostic systems, yet very few have gained acceptance in the daily delivery of medical practice. At the same time, many forces have been pushing for the development of such systems, including the decreasing cost of microcomputers and the increasing concern about containing medical care costs. Why have these current systems failed to be accepted by the medical community?

One of the problems with existing diagnostic systems is their exclusion of the physician from the diagnostic decision making process. They treat the physician as a technician who has data but no conclusions about the patient. In fact the physician, in most cases, has already formulated a correct diagnosis. He is merely looking for a confirmation. We believe that for a program to help the daily delivery of medical services, it must integrate and verify the diagnostic work of the physician rather than exempt him from such a task.

This paper discusses VERIFIER I, a microcomputer-based medical diagnostic system. This system is designed to contain sets of well classified pathological entities. In most instances VERIFIER I simply acts as a reminder to the physician displaying an algorithm detailing the correct analytical steps and treatment to follow for his working diagnosis. Only in the case of discrepancies or inconsistencies is the intelligence of the system applied to accept, reject or elaborate on the given diagnosis. It is anticipated that this approach is more likely to gain acceptance by physicians, because of its simplicity and operational characteristics which maintain the physician's autonomy and diagnostic pride.

1. INTRODUCTION

During the past two decades numerous computer-based programs have been developed to assist physicians in diagnosis. These systems fall in one of two categories. The simpler category uses a "main symptom to diagnosis" approach [INTE84]. In this approach the user is presented a sequence of menus. Each menu contains a listing of symptoms or sub-menus. The user progresses through these menus identifying the various symptoms which exist in the patient. Once all of the symptoms have been entered, the physician is presented with a prioritized list of suspected entities exhibiting all or some portion of the symptoms.

While the accuracy of these systems is high (the correct entity is normally near the top of the list of suspected entities), their drawbacks make them totally useless in a clinical setting. These drawbacks include (1) a disregard of patient categorizing data (e.g., sex, age, etc.) which could greatly aid the diagnostic process, (2) a use of preset menus which might organize the symptoms differently than the physician's cognitive model resulting in input errors, (3) the use of subjective descriptors of the symptoms which might not correspond with the patient's or physician's descriptions, and (4) the lack of any true man-machine interaction allowing the physician to question the selection of entities and their ordering. In fact, this category of systems does not present the physician with any startling new results. Any physician of merit should have already determined the major diagnoses which are returned.

The second group of systems is significantly more sophisticated [AIKI80, AIKI82, BLUM82, POPL82, SHOR82]. These systems support an intelligent man-machine interaction and perform a true differential diagnosis. Initially, these systems collect clinical data on the patient through an interactive question and answer session with the physician. The analysis of this data produces a set of possible entities, which is then pruned using a series of discriminating rules. Two major disadvantages exist for these systems. First, they ignore the possibility that the physician might already have a good idea as to the identity of the suspected entity. To obtain the system's conclusion the physician is forced to proceed through a considerable work-up. While such an approach is ideal when differentiating between very similar entities or when diagnosing some "mystery" disease, it fails to satisfy the needs of the general practitioner. Second, and no less important, is their cost. They are designed to run on large, expensive, single-user computers, making them impractical for use in anything other than a research environment.

In our community-general hospital we need a program that verifies the physician's admitting diagnosis at the time of admission. This program should also suggest the most common differential diagnoses to keep in mind, offering the standard work-up and treatment for the suspected entity. This system should be versatile enough to support a dialogue with the physician about the patient, explaining its reasoning and logic. Additionally, this system must be affordable. With these goals in mind, VERIFIER I was designed.

2. OPERATION

When a physician performs an initial anamnesis on a patient, he normally requests a few baseline tests, e.g., a blood count (CBC), urinalysis, electrocardiogram, chest X-ray. After examining the results of these tests the physician forms a tentative diagnosis, or has, at least, an idea of the organ/system needing investigation. At this point we ask the physician to spend some time at a personal computer verifying that (1) his working diagnosis fits the collected data, even if these data are grossly incomplete, and (2) the diagnostic procedures he is anticipating to undertake are required and pertinent to the working diagnosis.

The physician starts by entering background data and a working diagnosis for the patient. The diagnosis entered can either be a specific entity (i.e., streptococcal pharyngitis, gonococcal urethritis, Lennec cirrhosis) or a pathological syndrome (i.e., renal insufficiency, upper respiratory infection, liver disease). If a pathological syndrome is specified, the physician is asked to select a particular entity from a group of entities exhibiting that syndrome. Once a specific entity is identified, VERIFIER I displays the primary criteria required for confirmation of this entity. If the physician determines that the patient satisfies these criteria, he can terminate the session, obtaining a summary of his findings and a recommended treatment.

For example, suppose that an elderly patient has anxiety with a feeling of suffocation and labored breathing producing a rattling sound. After examining the patient the physician might form a working diagnosis of Cardiogenic Pulmonary Edema. For this diagnosis VERIFIER I displays the criteria shown in Figure 1. Four conditions are identified as being required for confirmation of this diagnosis. Currently, the first two of these conditions are satisfied, so the physician might order a chest X-ray to check for infiltrates in the lungs and consult with the patient to determine any historical evidence to support the fourth criteria. Should all of these criteria be satisfied, VERIFIER I presents the required treatment.

Often the physician is able to verify all of the primary criteria for the working diagnosis, but many times he will be unable to do so. If, in the above case, he was unable to obtain a chest X-ray, the physician would simply identify that all of the criteria are not satisfied. The physician is then prompted for the presence of each of the primary and secondary criteria. For each the physician is allowed to specify that the criteria is present, absent, or not observed. Figure 2 illustrates a portion of a typical sequence of prompts and responses for a suspected case of Cardiogenic Pulmonary Edema. Note that should the physician have some doubt, he can specify a numeric value, between -1 and 1, stating his confidence in the absence or presence of that criteria, respectively. For example, if he feels that there is some evidence supporting the presence of A. S. H. D., but not conclusive evidence, he could specify 0.7 to identify his strength of conviction in its presence.

Once the primary and secondary criteria have been examined, VERIFIER I determines what actions should be taken. Absolute confirmation of the working diagnosis requires the presence of all primary criteria. Should the presence of any of these be unknown, VERIFIER I specifies the necessary actions to confirm their presence. A treatment may also be specified if it is warranted, even though the presence of all of the primary criteria might not be determined. See Figure 3.

While a working diagnosis can be partially verified and treatment started in the absence of

DIAGNOSTIC CRITERIA FOR PULMONARY EDEMA INCLUDES:
1. Severe Dyspnea
2. Pulmonary Rales
3. A diagnostic chest X-ray
4. A clinical history which includes:
     A.S.H.D. with or without M.I.
     Valvular disease
     Congenital heart disease
     Atrial Myxoma, etc.

ARE ALL OF THE ABOVE CRITERIA MET (Y/N):

Figure 1. The Diagnostic Criteria for Cardiogenic Pulmonary Edema

Does John Galt have Dyspnea?
** YES

Does John Galt have Pulmonary Rales?
** YES

Does John Galt have X-ray evidence of Pulmonary Infiltrate:
** WHY

Rule PULMED004 states:
If: The patient does not have X-ray evidence of Pulmonary Infiltrate
Then:
We can conclude that the patient does not have Pulmonary Edema
We need no longer consider this working diagnosis

Does John Galt have X-ray evidence of Pulmonary Infiltrate?
** UNKNOWN

Does John Galt have A. S. H. D. (Arteriolosclerotic Heart Disease)?
** YES 0.7

Does John Galt have chest pain?
** YES

Does John Galt have evidence of right side failure (e.g., increased venous pressure, ECG signs of
right side overload)?
** NO

Does John Galt have Asthma?
** WHY

Rule PULMED024 states:
If: The patient has Asthma
Then:
We can conclude that the patient has Pulmonary Edema (CF=-.5)
We can conclude that the patient has additional or alternative diagnoses (CF=.1)

Does John Galt have Asthma?
** NO

Figure 2. Primary and Secondary Prompts and Typical Responses for Pulmonary Edema
(Physician responses are on lines starting with "**")

SEVERAL PRIMARY CRITERIA HAVE NOT YET BEEN CONFIRMED. THE FOLLOWING ADDITIONAL TEST(S) OR OBSERVATION(S) SHOULD BE MADE TO STRENGTHEN CONFIRMATION OF THE DIAGNOSIS:

Take a chest X-ray and look for evidence of pulmonary infiltrates.

EVEN THOUGH THE ABOVE TEST(S) OR OBSERVATION(S) ARE NEEDED, TREATMENT SHOULD BE STARTED.

TREATMENT FOR PULMONARY EDEMA:

1. Patient should sit upright with legs dangling.
2. Give patient high concentrations of oxygen by mask or nasal cannula.
3. Increased expiratory pressure may be helpful.
4. Administer morphine sulfate (4-6 mg IV or 10-15 IM) to:
       reduce agitation
       decrease respiratory rate
       slow heart rate and lower BP

SEVERE CASES:

Add valvodilator drugs like N.T.G., calcium blockers, etc.

Figure 3.   Treatment Specified for Pulmonary Edema

confirmation for one or more of the primary criteria, should any primary criteria be denied the working diagnosis is denied. For example, the working diagnosis of Cardiogenic Pulmonary Edema would be denied if the patient did not have dyspnea or any of the other primary criteria. At that point the physician is free to enter an alternative working diagnosis for confirmation.

Returning to the example shown in Figure 2, note that in several places the physician asked "why" when prompted about a particular symptom. VERIFIER I supports a limited dialogue with the physician allowing the physician to question why knowledge of possible symptoms is desired. This interaction creates an environment where the physician feels he is consulting an expert not just answering random questions.

3. ORGANIZATION

VERIFIER I is organized as an expert system using a Mycin-like knowledge base [BUCH84]. The knowledge of the system is organized as a context tree. See Figure 4. Each context contains knowledge about its own particular domain, so the PATIENT context contains general knowledge about patients and the PULM-EDE context contains knowledge about Pulmonary Edema.

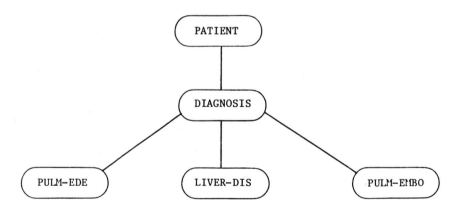

Figure 4. A portion of the Context Tree.

332

Associated with each context is a number of parameters and rules. The parameters are important pieces of knowledge needed by the context to interpret the particular case at hand. For example, the PATIENT context contains parameters for general features describing the patient such as the patient's age, temperature, blood pressure, etc., while the PULM-EDE context contains parameters for specific symptoms of Pulmonary Edema like dyspnea, chest pain, etc. The rules describe actual knowledge about the context. For example,

```
IF    (PULM-EDE-SYMP CARDIOGENIC TRUE)
      (SYMPTOM DYSPNEA FALSE)
THEN (CONCLUDE PULM-EDE FALSE)
```

states that if the patient is thought to have the Cardiogenic variety of Pulmonary Edema and the patient does not have Dyspnea then we can conclude that Pulmonary Edema is not the correct diagnosis.

Knowledge gathered about the patient is stored as a list of facts. Each fact is a 4-tuple containing the name of the parameter, the context where the parameter's value was determined, the value of the parameter, and the degree of certainty that this value is correct. For example, the following list:

```
(   (NAME PATIENT-1 (John Doe) 1.0)
    (AGE PATIENT-1 67 1.0)
    (PULM-EDE-SYMP PULM-EDEMA-1 CARDIOGENIC 1.0)
    (DYSPNEA PULM-EDEMA-1 YES 1.0)
    (XRAY-EVID PULM-EDEMA-1 UNK 0.0)
    (ASHD PULM-EDEMA-1 YES 0.7)
    (CONCLUDE PULM-EDEMA-1 PULM-EDE 0.4)
    ... )
```

contains facts stating that the name of the patient is John Doe, his age is 67, it is suspected that he has Cardiogenic Pulmonary Edema, Dyspnea is present, a chest X-ray has not been taken so evidence of pulmonary infiltrates is unknown, A. S. H. D. appears to be present, and so far we have some positive evidence supporting the conclusion that the patient has Pulmonary Edema.

When VERIFIER I executes a rule from a context, it first checks the list of facts to determine if the premises (IF clauses) of the rule are already known. If all of the premises are satisfied, the conclusion (THEN clause) is added to the list of facts. If a premise has not been previously examined, an attempt is made to first derive that premise through the application of some other rule. Should no rules exist which can derive it, the physician is queried for its presence. After gathering as much information as it can about the patient, VERIFIER I determines if any additional tests should be performed by the physician and if a treatment should be specified.

The strength of VERIFIER I's approach is the way in which the rules are structured for each diagnostic entity. It has been correctly observed that the skill of a great physician consists in formulating questions whose answers can rule out or identify entire classes or discrete groups of diseases. The skilled questioning by this system will also unmask or suggest diagnostic entities that may have been overlooked. By simply being asked certain questions, alternative diagnoses can be suggested to the physician.

4. CONCLUSION

As physicians increasingly become employees of medical corporations and lose their privilege to complete autonomy in their practice, some means of verifying and documenting their decisions is required. This need occurs from a desire on the part of these corporations as well as the government to minimize health care costs by only performing those actions absolutely necessary to confirm a diagnosis and, additionally, to document that an adequate diagnosis was performed in case of a possible malpractice suit. It is hoped that VERIFIER I provides a first step in this direction. Once adapted as a standard tool, this and other similar systems will help ensure complete and adequate health care at a minimum cost.

REFERENCES

[AIKI80] Aikins, J. S., "Prototypes and Production Rules: A Knowledge Representation for Computer Consultations", STAN-CS-80-814, Stanford University, Stanford, Ca., August 1980.

[AIKI82] Aikins, J. S., J. C. Kunz, E. H. Shortliffe, and R. J. Fallat, "Puff: An Expert System for Interpretation of Pulmonary Function Data", STAN-CS-82-931, Stanford University, Stanford, Ca., August 1982.

[BLUM82] Blum, R. L., "Discovery and Representation of Causal Relationships from a Large Time-Oriented Clinical Database: The RX Project", STAN-CS-82-900, Stanford University, Stanford, Ca., January 1982.

[BUCH84] Buchanan, B. G. and E. H. Shortliffe, Rule-Based Expert Systems, Addison-Wesley, Reading, MA, 1984.

[INTE84] THE INTERNIST: Instruction Manual, N-Squared Computing, Silverton, Oregon, 1984.

[POPL82] Pople, H. E., "Heuristic Methods for Imposing Structure on Ill-Structured Problems: The Structuring of Medical Diagnostics", in Artificial Intelligence in Medicine, Edited by P. Szolovits, Westview Press, Boulder, Co., 1982, pp. 119-189.

[SHOR82] Shortliffe, E. H. and L. W. Fagan, "Expert Systems Research: Modeling the Medical Decision Making Process", STAN-CS-82-932, Stanford University, Stanford, Ca., August 1982.

Author Index

Subject Index

(Number denotes first page of article.)

338

Editors' Biographies

Amar Gupta (SM'85) is Principal Research Associate at the Sloan School of Management, Massachusetts Institute of Technology, Cambridge. He holds a bachelor's degree in electrical engineering from the Indian Institute of Technology, Kanpur, a master's degree in management from the Massachusetts Institute of Technology, and a doctorate in computer technology from the Indian Institute of Technology, New Delhi. He conducted the research for his doctorate dissertation at three prestigious universities in India, England, and the United States.

Dr. Gupta has been involved in research, management, and publishing activities since 1974. Since joining M.I.T. in 1979, he has been active in the areas of multiprocessor architectures, performance measurement, distributed homogeneous and heterogeneous data bases, expert systems, personal computers, and transfer of information technology. He serves as a consultant to a number of corporations, government agencies, and international bodies on various aspects of computer technology, and is an active technical advisor to several international organizations and committees.

Dr. Gupta is the Chairman of the Technical Committee for Microprocessor Applications of the IEEE Industrial Electronics Society, and Assistant Chairman for several annual IECON conferences. He was also involved with the Very Large Data Base Conference (VLDB '87), held in England in 1987. He received the Rotary Fellowship for International Understanding in 1979 and the Brooks Prize (Honorable Mention) in 1980.

He has written more than 30 technical articles and papers, and produced seven books.

Dr. Gupta is a permanent resident of the United States.

Bandreddi Eswara Prasad (M'87) received his master's degree in mathematics from Andhra University, India, in 1976, and the Ph.D. in computer science from the Indian Institute of Technology, Delhi, in 1980. He worked as a lecturer at the latter institute from 1980 to 1983. Subsequently, he joined the University of Hyderabad in 1983, where he currently holds the position of associate professor. His research interests include techniques for integration of artificial intelligence and data base technologies, knowledge-based pictorial information systems, and heterogeneous data base systems. He is a member of the Institute of Electrical and Electronics Engineers, the Association for Computing Machinery, and the American Association for Artificial Intelligence.

Dr. Prasad co-edited this book during his tenure (1985–1987) as a visiting scientist at the Sloan School of Management, Massachusetts Institute of Technology, Cambridge.